ESSAYS OF TODAY

THE MACMILLAN COMPANY
NEW YORK · BOSTON · CHICAGO · DALLAS
ATLANTA · SAN FRANCISCO

MACMILLAN & CO., Limited
LONDON · BOMBAY · CALCUTTA
MELBOURNE

THE MACMILLAN COMPANY
OF CANADA, Limited
TORONTO

ESSAYS OF TODAY

Edited by

RAYMOND WOODBURY PENCE

PROFESSOR OF ENGLISH IN DEPAUW UNIVERSITY

New York

THE MACMILLAN COMPANY

1935

TO

Harry M. Shafer

THIS VOLUME IS INSCRIBED

PREFACE

THE governing purpose of this collection has been to show—as well as can be shown within the limits of one volume—expository writing of the last ten years. Consequently, the term "essay" has been stretched to embrace the familiar essay at one extreme and the formal article at the other. Only work that has appeared during the period from 1925 to 1935 has been included. There has been no attempt to fashion a collection of "best" essays; nor is this a collection of essays on "timely" subjects. Rather, it has been the aim of the editor to make a book that might prove usable in the classroom. The first test for inclusion, then, has been whether or not a given paper has genuine interest for the student. Consequently, the range of subjects has been kept deliberately wide. Further, a goodly number of articles have been chosen from writers that the editor believes are just coming into their own. For it has been his experience that students in composition are more interested in writers who are just "arriving" than they are in those who are already firmly established. Yet the work of established writers must always be included, if for no other reason than to provide certain standards of judgment by means of which the work of the younger and less experienced writers may be evaluated.

Because this volume represents the work both of writers of unquestioned literary standing and of writers who are more or less in the process of establishing their literary reputations, it is hoped that it may be regarded as a cross-section of the kind of expository writing that has made itself effective during the decade just closing. What the future standing may be of any particular essay—or of any particular writer—is not of major importance at the moment; for after all that is a matter that had better be left to the future writers of literary manuals to record.

ACKNOWLEDGMENTS

SUCH a collection as this, including as it does valuable literary property, would be utterly impossible without the co-operation of the authors and publishers represented. Proper copyright notices have been printed in connection with each selection. But I wish to make specific acknowledgment to the following, who have granted me permission to reprint material that they control in copyright.

Mr. James Truslow Adams, Professor Walter Barnes, Professor Charles A. Beard, Mr. William Beebe, Mr. Robert C. Benchley, Mr. Ralph Bergengren, Professor George Boas, Mrs. Mary Borden Speare, Mr. Ernest Boyd, Mr. Van Wyck Brooks, Mr. Earnest Elmo Calkins, Mr. Stuart Chase, Mr. Gilbert K. Chesterton, Professor Robert P. Tristram Coffin, Governor Wilbur L. Cross, Mr. Bernard De Voto, Professor Felix Frankfurter, Mr. Claude M. Fuess, Professor Edgar J. Goodspeed, Mr. George Ellery Hale, Mr. A. P. Herbert, Professor Robert Herrick, Professor Walter S. Hinchman, Mr. Aldous L. Huxley, Mr. Julian S. Huxley, Professor Howard Mumford Jones, Father Ronald A. Knox, Mr. Joseph Wood Krutch, Mr. John Langdon-Davies, Professor Harold J. Laski, Mr. "Geoffrey Layman," Mr. Stephen Leacock, Professor James Weber Linn, Mr. Edward V. Lucas, Mr. Robert Lynd, M. Andre Maurois, Professor L. Wardlaw Miles, Mr. Meredith Nicholson, Mr. Albert J. Nock, Mr. Johnson O'Connor, Professor William Lyon Phelps, Mr. J. B. Priestly, Mr. Bertrand Russell, Professor F. A. Spencer, Mr. Vincent Starrett, Professor Chauncey Brewster Tinker, Mr. Frank H. Vizetelly, Mrs. Frances Lester Warner Hersey, Mr. John P. Waters, and Mrs. Edith Wharton.

American Scholar, D. Appleton-Century Company, the *Atlantic Monthly*, Bobbs-Merrill Company, John Day Company, Dodd, Mead and Company, Doubleday, Doran and Company, E. P. Dutton Company, the *Forum*, Harper & Brothers, *Harper's Magazine*, Henry Holt and Company, Houghton Mifflin Company, J. P. Lippincott Company, The Macmillan Company, the *Nation*, the *Saturday Evening Post*, *Saturday Review of Literature*, *Scribner's Magazine*, University of Chicago Press, *Yale Review*, and Yale University Press.

I am grateful to my colleagues on the English Faculty of DePauw University, who have aided me with their advice and suggestions.

Finally, I wish to express my indebtedness to my students, who with their frank—and sometimes devastating—criticism—have helped shape my judgment as to what to include and exclude in connection with such a collection as this.

R. W. PENCE

GREENCASTLE, INDIANA
July, 1935

TABLE OF CONTENTS

xi

ESSAYS OF TODAY

ESSAYS OF TODAY

DIMINISHING RETURNS IN MODERN LIFE

A WORD TO THE APOSTLES OF PROGRESS

By *James Truslow Adams*

THROUGH increasing knowledge of natural laws man
has enormously increased his control over his environment. This is so obvious as to make any amplifi-
cation of the simple statement unnecessary. Our type of
culture today is based solely on power, the power hidden in
coal, steam, electricity, or the chemical combination of atoms,
and is due to our having discovered and utilized natural laws.
Because of the enormous increase in our control over the
environment due to such knowledge, we have come instinctively to think of the discovery of each additional law as en-
larging the possible scope of human life and activities. We
never think of them as indicating limits. The changes realized
have been so overwhelming that the possibilities have come
to appear illimitable, and scant attention is paid to those laws
which put definite limits to our advance in any desired direction. They are brushed aside, and any discussion of them is as
unpopular as was conservative economic reasoning at the top
of the recent bull market. Unfortunately, the unpopular laws
as well as the popular ones are ceaselessly at work, as the
enthusiastic speculators found, and disregard of them is bound
to end in trouble. Laws are merely formulations of the ways
in which things invariably and inevitably happen or act; and
to get in the way of a law of nature which does not work the
way we should like, and to insist on having our own way is

about as futile as for a cow on the track to dispute the right
of way with the Chicago Flyer at sixty miles an hour. The
laws of nature do not work for us. All we can do is to find out
how they work, to make use of some of those going in our
direction, and to get out of the way of others as fast as we
can.

So far, most of the laws discovered belong to the physical
sciences. Psychology, economics, politics, sociology, and the
others are grievously behind. Any astronomer can predict
with absolute accuracy just where every star in the heavens
will be at half-past eleven tonight. He can make no such
prediction about his young daughter. From this fact—that
one group of sciences has got entirely out of step with another
—our civilization is becoming warped out of shape. For a
good many centuries, in spite of defects, the social and political
life of peoples fitted on the material base almost as neatly as
the top layer of a chocolate cake fits on the bottom. Today
the top layer has altered little, but the bottom one, the material base of our life, has gone spinning, with grave danger of
ruining the cake and losing the chocolate. The cake is, in
fact, acting like a thing bewitched, and if we are to make it
stick together again we have got to do something with the
upper layer, for the under one has clearly gone too far to get
it back in its old place if we would.

It is clear that we have got to know a great deal more about
psychology and sociology than we do now, keeping them
"ologies" and not making them "isms." Our chemists and
engineers will look after our T.N.T.'s and dynamos, but we
must learn how to use them, and come to some new terms
with our ethics, politics, and social life in the largest sense.
A chemist who tried to make T.N.T. according to his emotions
and not his science might bring it off but, a million to one,
would more likely be brought off himself. It is the same with
our social and institutional life. If, on the scale of modern
nations, we try to adjust them only to our vague emotions
and callow aspirations, something very violent and unpleasant

can be rather certainly predicted. We must hunt for laws to guide us—Nature's not lobbyists'. It is also essential to find the unpopular as well as the popular ones, those which tell us what we cannot do as well as those which tell us what we can. The Garden of Eden and the flaming sword were myths— excellent ones, by the way; but a definite limit here and there to self-expression and undirected aspirations is not. I do not pretend to be a scientist, but when one observes the cow on the track and the Chicago Flyer coming one does not have to be one to predict that something is going to happen immediately to the cow. I wish, in a word, to call attention to what is an apparent law, and about as unpopular a one as could exist.

II

Economists, observing the way things happen, have established what they call "the Law of Diminishing Returns." I shall not try to give it in scientific terms or bother with graphs. Briefly it is that working in a given direction there is a point up to which profit increases and beyond which it inevitably declines. Let us illustrate this with a few examples comprehensible to every practical man. I once lived in a farming community. The farmers would figure very carefully how much to spend per acre on fertilizer. Twenty-five dollars per acre would increase the value of the crop so much, less cost of fertilizer. Fifty dollars would do so to a greater extent, as would a hundred dollars; but two hundred would not. There was a point at which the cost of fertilizing, profitable up to then, overtook the increased value of the crop, and became unprofitable. The wise farmer, who knew his land, his fertilizer, and his crop, knew just how far to go and where to stop to get the last dollar out of all three—perhaps I should say cent.

Let us turn to another great industry, mining. Gold is found in rock, a very small amount of gold to a fearsome amount of rock. To extract it requires costly machinery and labor. Up to a certain point an increase in outlay on the best machinery will pay, but beyond that it will not. There is a relation between the percentage of gold in the rock and the cost of getting at it, as I once found out.

Let us consider our pet toy, the skyscraper. I used to have an office at 2 Wall Street. Across the street there was a lot with a four-story building on it, forty feet square. It has been called the most valuable piece of real estate in the world. Indeed, I was told as a boy many years ago that the then owner was asked what he would take for it, and answered that his price was the sixteen hundred square feet covered with gold dollars. This was figured out, and the offer made, whereupon he smiled and answered, "I meant, stood on edge." However that may be, it did change hands, and a high building was put on it which became known as "the chimney." I have forgotten how high it was, but here is the point: its height was limited by the fact that it could have only one elevator; and architects tell us that although up to a certain point every floor you add to a building increases the rental, there is a point, given a certain ground space, at which the space required for elevators to carry people to the added floors will offset the increased rental space gained by adding such floors, which sounds reasonable. Of course, you can buy the adjoining lots, tear down the old buildings, and build a higher, but the limit is the city block, and there is a point at which the increased rental space will be offset by the increased lost elevator space.

Let us take one more illustration. Everyone who builds a house for himself has the same problems I had. There was the question, for example, of the cost of the copper sheathing I was to put around my windows and the copper gutters under my piazza floor. Knowing I wished to cut cost as much as might be, the architect suggested copper of a certain thickness and cost. The builder suggested that it would last only so many years, whereas the shingling and piazza floors would last longer. If I spent more on the copper I should save in the long run. I, therefore, added to the weight, but it was quite obvious that there was a point beyond which to add to the weight and cost would cease to be profitable and prove merely loss. It was our job to determine that point.

Perhaps these illustrations have made my basic point clear. Let us now work toward somewhat broader problems.

I suppose it will make me seem antediluvian to the young generation but I well remember when taxis were introduced into New York. As a matter of fact, it was not so long ago in spite of the fact that most young people today cannot imagine Peter Stuyvesant getting about in any other way. At first they were a great help in saving time. When one was in a great hurry one took a taxi and swept along Fifth Avenue at what seemed a terrific rate. But taxis multiplied like rabbits in Australia with the result that today when I am really in a hurry I now have to walk to get from Thirty-Third Street to Forty-Second. It once took me twenty-five minutes in a taxi. In other words, as a time-saver, when there were few taxis and few of us used them, they served their purpose admirably. Now that there are, apparently, millions of them and the million use them, they are of no use, for that purpose, to anybody. It is not that the mob has got what a few used to have, but that nobody has got anything, in this particular aspect.

In 1913 I built a house at the east end of Long Island. Cars, of course, were coming into use by then but there were still comparatively few of them. Ten years before that the only way to get to that beautiful bit of wild scenery, Montauk Point, had been to take a train to Amagansett, and then get a "rig" to drive one across the mosquito-infested Napeague Beach and about ten miles or more on to Montauk, a slow nag plowing through heavy sand. The road was improved, and I had my modest little car. It was delightful to make Montauk in an hour, without mosquitoes, and enjoy the beauty and solitude without all the old discomfort. But what has happened? The last holiday I was at home before I sold my place there were said to be two thousand cars at the Point. I admit that according to the Declaration of Independence and the New Testament there was no reason why only a privileged few

should enjoy the solitude and beauty of the Point. Theoretically there is no reason why the whole million cars of New York
State should not have been there instead of the half dozen of
the earlier days.

Theory, however, has nothing to do with it. The plain fact
is that those eight thousand people, allowing only four to a
car, were not sharing what I had enjoyed before. There were
no longer the empty spaces, the moorland hanging over-cliff
to the sea. Instead of solitude, there were eight thousand
people; instead of bare rolling downs, there was a landscape
littered with lunch boxes, papers, and ginger ale bottles by
the thousand. I have not the slightest objection to people
enjoying themselves as they will. *De gustibus non est dispu-
tandum.* The point is that by the mere fact that eight thousand
people tried to enjoy the solitude and beauty of Montauk at
once, the solitude and beauty evaporated. They did not get
what I had had. It was simply that none of us got it. I am
not discussing whether it is better for eight thousand people
to have what our English cousins call "ginger-pop" and sand-
wiches in a mob and the fresh air than that a few should enjoy
the stillness of what used to be one of the few unspoiled spots
in New York, or not. The point is that "the many" did not
get what "the few" had had. Up to a certain number they
might have done so. Beyond that the law began to work;
and to turn eight thousand people loose on a quiet beauty spot
of nature and expect returns was as absurd as for a farmer to
put a thousand dollars' worth of fertilizer on every acre, or
for the owner of 1 Wall Street to have built fifty stories on
forty square feet only to find that all his floor space was taken
up with elevator shafts instead of offices to rent. What the
many got was something entirely different from what the few
had got. Which of these, for the whole human race for generations to come, might be the better would baffle the mathematics of even an Einstein to figure out.

Let us take the old English inn, one of the most delightful
places, when it is good, in which a wayfarer can find rest and

simple comfort at a reasonable cost. It is clear that an increasing number of guests, up to a certain point, adds to the value of the inn for the guests themselves. One which had only a stray guest every few weeks, and did not pay, could not offer the facilities and ready service of one that was daily prepared for the few guests who could be relied upon to turn up from somewhere. If, however, there are too many, the place ceases to be one of comfort. If we succeed in getting a room only once in a dozen times; if every chair in the lounge is occupied; if we have to wait an hour for a meal until the mob ahead of us has eaten, not only is our comfort destroyed but that of everyone else. If, as would inevitably happen in America, the owner should add to the building, and then again, until, as I have seen so often in the last thirty years, a comfortable inn has grown into a huge caravansary housing hundreds of guests, the inn has really ceased to exist. The old Mitre at Oxford, for example, could conceivably have added a couple of hundred rooms and changed the small coffee room with its dozen chairs by the fire into a lounge that would seat a hundred. But by doing so it would have subtly ceased to exist, and the three hundred tourists who would put up at it to get the flavor of the old Mitre would seek in vain for something which their own numbers had destroyed. They would get shelter and meals but they would not get the Mitre.

In the rise of a city there is a point up to which the gain in comfort and interest is steady. We get paved streets, sewers, lights, better schools and shops, a few good theaters, perhaps, as in most European cities, an opera, a museum, and so on. Traffic is easy, people are not too crowded in their housing, can live comparatively near their work, and the advantages have not been counterweighted with serious disadvantages. But as the city growth continues, as in the greatest of modern cities, the disadvantages begin to weigh more and more heavily. It becomes more and more difficult to secure decent living space at any price that most can pay. Land becomes so valuable that houses give way to apartments, and large apartments are subdivided into small ones, in the process we have come to know so well. People have to live farther and farther from their work, while, owing to traffic congestion, it becomes harder and harder to reach office or home. Owing to increasing costs of all sorts, the expense of doing business mounts. For many, the point has been reached at which the law has worked and the return for living in a city has begun to diminish. Individuals move into the suburbs. Factories, in many cases, move to smaller towns.

III

Let us look at labor-saving devices in the home. In order to avoid complicating the case with any question as to man's and woman's work, let us suppose a woman is earning her own income and running her home herself. The labor-saving devices she can install are already innumerable, and almost every month brings a new one. She can put in an electric washing machine, a dish-washer, vacuum cleaners, electric refrigerator, and so on indefinitely. Every one of these things is admirable in itself and undeniably saves her trouble in connection with its specific function. But there is another point. A vacuum cleaner is infinitely preferable to a broom, but it costs about sixty times as much; old fashioned dishwashing was boring and hard on the hands but cost nothing, whereas a dishwasher is expensive; the new refrigerators are much handier than the old type, but whereas they used to cost, say, about thirty dollars, the new cost about three hundred. Garbage incinerators and various delightful and tricky contrivances in the newer apartments save trouble but mean higher rents to be paid. Now somewhere along the line there is a point up to which it will save this woman labor to work so that she can pay for all these labor-saving devices; but somewhere the law we are discussing will begin to work, and she will begin to expend so much energy and anxiety in trying to make the extra money needed to save labor in one department of her life that she is expending more than her nature permits in another. The devices, although still saving labor in one sphere, have so added to it in another that, taking life as a whole, they have ceased to function profitably.

The law works in the same way with a lot of our modern contrivances to give pleasure. Up to a certain point the possession of our modern toys, radios, cars, and so on adds to our pleasure, as do increasing numbers of bathrooms, increased luxury in hotels for those who like it, more gorgeous theaters, more costly scenery, and magnificent offices and shops; but there comes a point at which the increasing and in many cases intolerable burden of cost necessitated by these advances in number and quality of things used becomes so great as to destroy the pleasure or offset it by a still greater anxiety. In some cases the result will be to deprive the person of the pleasure entirely. For example, the opera of today in New York is far better than that of fifty years ago. For the ordinary music lover, who is apt not to be a hard-headed successful maker of money, there was a point somewhere where the increase in quality was not neutralized by the increase in cost; but there was also the fatal point at which the law began to work and at which the cost became so great that for him the opera, as a regularly recurring pleasure in his life, ceased to exist as completely as though there had been none at all.

Let us consider another type of case, that of the birth and up-bringing of children. The medical care surrounding childbirth is infinitely better than a generation ago, and about fifteen times as costly. The opportunities for the child in school, summer camp, mental and physical activities of all sorts are also far greater and more costly. Somewhere along the line there was a point up to which these new advantages were clear gain, like the fertilizing by the farmer, but a point was reached at which the added cost has resulted not in better and happier children but in many a family not being able to afford one. By trying to make the child, like the opera, too fine and luxurious, it has in all too many cases ceased to exist at all.

Take the involved problem of woman in business. For a while it seemed all clear gain that the unmarried woman not financially independent, the widow who had to support children and herself—all, in a word, who had to earn money—should have the whole business field open to them. But it was impossible to draw a line at which money-making ceased to be necessary and was merely desirable. As business opportunity for those who needed it became wider, more and more flocked to offices. The competition for jobs with men became keener, and as married women added their earnings to those of their husbands, the standard of living in such households was raised. The burden on the man who was trying to support a home single-handed in competition with the "two-worker" homes became greater. It may be asked, for the women themselves, whether the point is not being reached at which the law is beginning to work. On the one hand, the lower type that used to do household work is not only competing with the cheaper-paid type of man in factory or office but has thrown the manual labor of the household, which she used to do, on the higher-type woman who is capable, given time and strength, of doing something more worth while for social life as a whole than cooking and cleaning. On the other hand, the steadily increasing strain to maintain the single-worker home is forcing more and more women who would much rather be in the home than out of it to go to work; and the vicious tendencies are strengthened while the competition becomes fiercer and fiercer. There would seem to be already clearly indicated the working of the law and the fact that there is a point somewhere at which the gain to woman of having business open to her will be offset by the loss.

IV

Let us finally consider briefly the problem of democratic government, simplifying it as much as possible. If we have government solely by an oligarchy, an aristocracy, or an upper class, there will be evils. With the best intentions, it will be to some extent a class government. It is obvious that there will be gain if other classes or interests have representation. In all modern democratic countries this representation has been given and steadily increased until we have practically universal suffrage, tempered by influences wielded by certain groups, influences losing power as democracy increases. With universal suffrage, however, the control of votes lies with the laboring class, which is the most numerous. As this class comes to realize and exert its power, the legislation becomes again class legislation, of which we have a glaring example in the steadily widening and increasing dole in England. What we do is to substitute one class for another, the so-called lower for the so-called upper. Both classes when in power will unconsciously think in terms of their own class, but the upper class is bound to have a better understanding of the extreme complexity of modern civilization, and the exercise of their power has limits in the very numbers of the lower class. A socialist government, for example, might well lay a capital levy of fifty per cent regardless of the fact that it would mean ruin for the whole country, poor as well as rich, whereas the upper class would never think of making a "labor-levy," taking fifty per cent of the labor of the country free. Somewhere along the line increased representation was an all-round gain, but we reach the point where the law begins to work, and increased representation, instead of doing away with the evils of a class government, begins to substitute the evils of government by another, and on the whole, for governing purposes, a less able class.

The possible existence of this law in all social life is not a mere theory to be toyed with. It is of just as much practical importance to us in considering our institutions as it is to the farmer in considering his fertilizing. Consider, for example, the situation in English education at this very moment. I take England rather than America because we have ignored the possibility of such a law entirely, as well as a certain range of human values, whereas in England those values, if not the law, are recognized by many. There seems to be a general impression at home that English education for the masses is a very poor affair, so far as it may be existent at all. Of course, this is not the case. There is a good system of public education, and every child has to attend school up to the age of fourteen, soon to be made sixteen. There are also the great and rapidly growing "provincial" universities, access to which is practically as easy as to our own, State and other. There is no difficulty in England for a poor boy, if he has a mind, to get an education including a university course.

But obviously, a boy from a meager home background, who has to count on his education (and his degree) getting him a remunerative job in as many days after graduation as may be possible, requires and will insist upon a different sort of education from one whose home background is rich in the best sense, that is one who has opportunities for good social and mental contacts, travel and other sorts of informal education outside his school and university, and who, while expecting to make a career later, does not have to look upon his education as narrowly heading toward some very special remunerative job but can regard it as a general broadening and developing of his mind and all his nature. That, in the past, has been the ideal of the great endowed schools like Eton and Harrow, and the universities of Oxford and, to a lesser extent, Cambridge. Such a group of students and such an ideal have created a certain type of teaching and a certain atmosphere, alien to that in most American institutions and to the public "job-training" institutions in England. To any-one who wishes to understand the situation and problem better than it can be touched upon briefly here, I commend a small volume just out called *Isis, or the Future of Oxford*, in the excellent "Today and Tomorrow" series, which should be read by American educators as well as English Labor politicians.

There is at present a good deal of agitation in England on

this subject, the agitators claiming that the special atmosphere and opportunities of Eton, Harrow, Oxford, Cambridge, and such places, should not be confined only to the few but should be enjoyed by the many and that, in some way, the State should make it possible by financial acts of some sort for large numbers of the poorer classes to attend these institutions. A few do now, but it is quite clear, if the Laborites have their way, that the law we have been discussing will also have *its* way, and that instead of the masses enjoying Eton and Oxford, Eton and Oxford will merely evaporate. Swamped with students of the same type as those who now attend the State schools and universities, they will become like them; and instead of the many enjoying the privileges of the few, those privileges will have disappeared for everyone.

In some of the above instances I have, perhaps, stretched the strict letter of the Law of Diminishing Returns but I have, I think, indicated that there is some general law at work that is worth our studying and recognizing. It appears to be a very unfortunate one for idealists, but we did not make the universe. Such as it is we have to accept it and work with it, not against it. It is to be regretted that, having found a profitable lead, we cannot follow that lead forever but instead find that it invariably turns back on itself at some stage and gets us into trouble. It is also to be regretted that everyone cannot have everything, that eight thousand people, for example, cannot enjoy the same solitude at the same spot at once, but there seems to be something in the foundation of the universe that prohibits it, and there is no use in our insisting that the contrary is true and that the thing is possible. The cow can insist that it has as much right to follow the track in its direction as the Chicago Flyer has in its, but that does not prevent the catastrophe to the cow.

In the last century and a half we have heard a great deal about rights—"natural rights," the rights of man, woman's rights. The word is an unfortunate one for it carries an implication that somehow the universe is back of the human wishes and desires embodied in the word "right." There are, of course, no "natural rights." Nature knows nothing of rights. She knows only laws. Man, on the other hand, has ideals and aspirations. These, however, can be fulfilled only when they run with, not counter to, nature's laws, and there is no use blinking that fact.

Because a hundred dollars an acre in fertilizer will double the crop, it does not follow that five hundred dollars will quintuple it. Because a thirty-story building on a given lot is more profitable than a ten, and sixty is more profitable than thirty, it does not follow that a hundred is more profitable than sixty. Because a hundred motor cars on a given road will give people pleasure, it does not follow that a thousand will give ten times the number pleasure. Because twenty people can enjoy a beauty spot, it does not follow that two thousand can. Because going into business may benefit some women, it does not follow that it will benefit all. Because government becomes juster if the laboring class has some votes, it does not follow that it will become still juster if we give them still more. Unfortunately the reverse seems true. There seems to be a law also that although up to a certain point we can increase the number of people who can have, see, and enjoy, if we go beyond a certain point, instead of giving everybody everything, nobody has anything. A Labor Government could destroy Eton and Oxford. They could not, with all the power in the world, give Eton and Oxford to the mob. The universe would say "you are paying no attention to my laws," and the real Eton and Oxford would disappear under the very eyes of the mob which had gone to look for them.

Is it not time that we recognized more clearly the law, or perhaps two laws, hinted at in this article? They are laws that are unfortunately hostile to many of man's aspirations and especially to much of the democratic doctrine, but that has nothing to do with their existence and power. If they are there we have got to recognize them or suffer the consequences. We have refused so far to recognize them for the simple and childish reason that we do not like their implications. We do so to some extent in our economic life but not in our social and political. May not we account in some part, at least, for the rise and fall of civilizations in the past by the working of these laws that man has declined to recognize, the law, if we separate them, that returns increase up to a certain point and then decline, and the law that if too many people strive to enjoy the same good, that good disappears? The farmer, the miner, or the business man studies to find the exact point at which, according to the law of Diminishing Returns, advantage begins to turn into disadvantage. If there is any chance of regulating society scientifically and saving it from the recurring cycle of the rise and fall, have we not got to seek the same point for our political and social tendencies as our "practical" men do for our economic? If the farmer, the miner, and the manufacturer pay no attention to this law, they go bankrupt and are sold up. If society pays no more attention to it in the future than in the past, it will do likewise, as it has a thousand times before, and no amount of declaiming about "rights" will save it for a moment longer than the law will take to work out its own inevitable end. The rights of man, the rights of labor, the rights of woman as expressions of ideals to be worked out in harmony with nature's laws are beneficent concepts. When, however, they are proclaimed as superior to her laws they are of no more avail than the twittering of sparrows on the roof when Ætna breaks loose and the lava flows over the house.

THE THINNESS–FATNESS OF
ENGLISH TEACHERS

Being a Review of

The Thinness (and Fatness) of English Teachers and Their
Theme Corrections

By Mathew Prymme, Ph.D.

By *Walter Barnes*

WE are describing below one of the most recent and admirable publications of Almostany University. As is usual, the review will concern itself chiefly with the technique of the study, the conclusions and their significance being relatively unimportant. We make no apology for the simple, untechnical nature of the language, inasmuch as we are addressing laymen rather than technical scholars in the field.

This is an investigation of the correlation between the weight of teachers of composition and the amount of their theme corrections. The investigator was led, through casual observation, to set up the following hypothesis: that the heavier the English teacher the fewer the number of marks he made on pupils' compositions, or, to state it more significantly, the smaller the teacher the greater number of marks. But preliminary and tentative investigation sharpened the inquiry. It was determined (the data are not presented herewith, but are preserved in the archives of the Bureau of Research of Almostany University) that it was not the gross weight of the teachers that had most relevancy and validity, but rather the ratio between height (in inches) and weight (in pounds avoirdupois). (This is the well-known "Spearmint" formula $\frac{H}{W}$. In popular terms, it is the degree of fatness or thinness of the teacher.)   The working hypothesis then becomes: the leaner the teachers the more marks they place upon the learners' compositions.

It goes without saying that, of course, the investigator had not really made up his mind about this; he merely set it up as an assumption.   No capable scholar ever tries to prove anything or "make a case" by a scientific study; he is devoted to the greater task of discovering the proof.   It is probably better (judging by good contemporary practices) for the research worker not to form any considered judgments on any subject until all the facts have been weighed.   Many reputable scholars do not form judgments even then.

A word might be said as to how the investigator discovered the working hypothesis.   This is not revealed in the study, but the reviewer is of the opinion that *possibly* (one ought never to be too dogmatic about such matters) the investigator formed empirically the assumption that fat people are good-natured, hence would not be so critical.   We do not criticize such empirical assumptions so long as they are recognized as mere assumptions.

The problem, then, was to determine the correlation between the degree of fatness of the teacher and the amount of his theme correcting.   (Note: this study did not concern itself with the value of theme corrections.   That would have been difficult to compute statistically, and, moreover, there is fairly conclusive evidence that there is no value attached thereto.)

At the beginning, a careless investigator might easily have fallen into a blunder which would have vitiated [1] his findings. It would seem that if the investigator secured the $\frac{H}{W}$ of a sufficient number of representative English teachers, and then secured representative samplings of themes they had corrected,

---

[1] The word "vitiate" is not in the Thorn-like word list, but is used in 93.01 + % of the reviews of scientific studies.

the correlations (individual and for the average) could have been determined. But, of course, the fault in this procedure is that it is too direct and obvious. The trained investigator always suspects that the simplest and most practical technique will vitiate his findings. In this instance, if this obvious method had been utilized, the investigation would have taken up only about twenty pages; it would have involved only two difficult formulæ, and would have had only eight tables and three graphs. Certainly, no findings derived from such meager statistical treatment would be acceptable.

The investigator, therefore, looking around for factors to make his problem more intricate, almost immediately made the following (tentative) discovery (Note: all discoveries are tentative until they have been corroborated by statistical procedures. This is the reason why the discoveries of Admiral Byrd and Christopher Columbus have always been suspect): that the degree of $\frac{H}{W}$ varies with the temperature. Normally, this variation might be expected to conform to the Boreas-Hell Law: "The higher the temperature the more one perspires; the more one perspires, the smaller the $\frac{H}{W}$." But no observer would reasonably expect English teachers to conform to a normal curve of distribution (see Hudelover's Study, *The Ten Thousand Grades English Teachers Give to One Composition—Ancient Language Notes*, Volume CCCMIXCIV, Number 2). Besides, there was the question of whether (and if so, to what extent) English teachers perspired while they were correcting themes, and whether as their perspiring decreased their weight (if it *did* decrease his (or should one say her?) weight), they placed more marks on the theme. (Note: there is some acceptable (*very* acceptable) evidence that English teachers place fewer marks on the themes after the first four hours of daily theme correction.) The investigator, therefore, worked out the heat wave quotient, and corrected for consequent *attenuation*, arriving at the following (probably new) formula:

$\dfrac{\sqrt[3]{P}}{\dfrac{T}{H}}$, which he proposes to call, descriptively, the Weather-

Vane or Whether-Vain formula. Then by taking the individual $\dfrac{I}{Q}$ (if any) of the teachers, and dividing by the individual vari-

ation, $\dfrac{V}{I}$, he reached the following formula: $\dfrac{\dfrac{I}{Q}}{\dfrac{V}{I}}$, which, by can-

cellation, gives $\dfrac{V}{Q}$ or variation quotient. Dividing the weather-vane formula by the variation quotient (probably as accurate results would have been obtained by multiplying by the va-

riation quotient) the result is the following formula: $\dfrac{\dfrac{\sqrt[3]{P}}{\dfrac{T}{H}}}{\dfrac{W}{L}}$. Since

P precedes Q in the alphabet, P and Q cancel one another by the Law of Alphabetical Probabilities, giving the simpler

formula $\dfrac{\dfrac{T}{H}}{\dfrac{W}{I}}$, which can be further reduced to $\dfrac{TW}{HI}$. The prob-

able error is here, only .01 of .1 degree Fahrenheit. This con-stitutes the major part of the $\dfrac{H}{W}$ aspect of the problem.

Space will not permit us to give the details of that part of the study devoted to the teachers' markings of themes. The investigator first found, by consensus of authority, "that all teachers are English teachers," and that "anyone can teach English"—hence included all teachers in his study. Further preliminary investigation revealed the fact that teachers always mark themes with red ink or red pencil (there are definite laws on the statute books of several states on this point). By computing the number of red pencils and bottles of red ink used during the period of investigation, and allowing for pencil points broken and ink spilled, because of increased temperature during the time of theme correcting, the investigator was able to employ very elaborate and complicated instruments and techniques. One interesting, though incidental finding, was that women teachers (who were divided equally between fat and not-so-fat, though not on their own statements) did not spill as much ink as the men teachers (Query: and, therefore, succeeded in getting more on the themes?) except when they were wearing red dresses or (occasionally) kimonas. It is not known at present what bearing this has on the main problem, but the investigator is to be commended for introducing this additional complication.

To abbreviate—the investigator found that 623,712 red pencils (mostly Arm and Hammer brand) and 3,167,802 bottles of ink were used up in making marks on the themes (including ink spilled en route). This allowed for 20+ marks on each page of manuscript, which accords with the findings of other studies, and with common observation, and would indicate that this is probably probable within limits and during the winter months.

Adding the 3,167,802 bottles of ink to the 623,712 red pencils, and subtracting twice the square root, once removed, of $\dfrac{TW}{HI}$, the investigator reaches this conclusion: (surely the only one possible under the terms of this study): that, while there is a closer correlation between thinness and the amount of theme correcting than between either fatness and thinness (probably because it is easier to secure *close* correlation with thinness); between fatness and the mean temperature (care should be taken to discriminate between mean temperature and mean temper); or between (or among) the fatness and the perspiration and the color of the dress or (occasionally) kimonas worn during the exercise of theme correcting. There is a second conclusion: that more red ink and red pencils are employed than are, in the judgment of the pupils, desirable; but this conclusion is vitiated because of the failure to limit two variables, human nature and common sense, neither of which, of course, has any place in a genuine, scientific investigation.

All in all, a competent study, ranking in usefulness with other studies fostered by Almostany University. In our judgment, the procedures and findings will add materially to the confusion and complexity of contemporary education.

THE MYTH OF RUGGED
AMERICAN INDIVIDUALISM

By *Charles A. Beard*

"THE House of Bishops would be as much at sea in Minneapolis as at Atlantic City." This bit of delicious humor, all too rare in America's solemn assemblies, sparkled at a tense moment in the late conference of the Episcopalian magnates at Denver when the respective merits of the two cities as future meeting places were under debate. But the real cause of the caustic comment seems to have been a heated discussion, led by the Honorable George W. Wickersham, over a dangerous proposal to modify, not the Volstead act, but the sacred creed of rugged American individualism.

That contest had been precipitated by the report of a special commission in which occurred these highly inflammatory words: "It is becoming increasingly evident that the conception of society as made up of autonomous, independent individuals is as faulty from the point of view of economic realism as it is from the standpoint of Christian idealism. Our fundamental philosophy of rugged individualism must be modified to meet the needs of a co-operative age." This frightful conclusion flowed from a fact statement which the commission summarized in the following language: "Side by side with such misery and idleness, there are warehouses bursting with goods which cannot be bought; elevators full of wheat while bread lines haunt our cities; carefully protected machinery lying idle, while jobless men throng our streets; money in the banks available at low rates."

These shocking passages Mr. Wickersham read to the assembled delegates with considerable indignation, and denied their truth. Then he added an illuminating exposition all his own: "I think this is an expression of a social philosophy that is expressed by the Soviet Government of Russia. It is a negation of the whole concept of American civilization. I think it would be a sad day when the American people abandon the principles on which they have grown to greatness." Coming to specifications, he particularly attacked a point in the report, that "compulsory unemployment insurance is feasible." Realizing that Mr. Wickersham was a specialist in individualism, since he was the chief author of a collective report from which each individual signer apparently dissented, the congregated deputies at Denver voted down the proposal that the commission's statement should be taken as "representing the mind of the Church," and substituted a mere pious recommendation that it should be given "careful consideration" by members of the Church. Such, at least, is the story reported in the press.

This is only one of many straws in the wind indicating a movement to exalt rugged individualism into a national taboo beyond the reach of inquiring minds. From day to day it becomes increasingly evident that some of our economic leaders (by no means all of them) are using the phrase as an excuse for avoiding responsibility, for laying the present depression on "Government interference," and for seeking to escape from certain forms of taxation and regulation which they do not find to their interest. If a smoke screen big enough can be laid on the land, our commercial prestidigitators may work wonders—for themselves.

Still more direct evidence confirms this view. For example, in the autumn of 1930, a New York bank published, as a kind of revelation from on high, a slashing attack on "Government interference with business," written by that stanch English Whig, Macaulay, a hundred years ago; and a few weeks later one of the leading advertising firms took a whole page in the *New York Times* to blazon forth the creed anew under the captivating head: "Cheer Up! Our Best Times Are Still Ahead of Us!" And the whole gospel was summed up in these words from Macaulay: "Our rulers will best promote the improvement of the people by strictly confining themselves to their own legitimate duties—by leaving capital to find its most lucrative course, commodities their fair price, industry and intelligence their natural reward, idleness and folly their natural punishment—by maintaining peace, by defending property, by diminishing the price of law, and by observing strict economy in every department of the State. Let the Government do this—the people will assuredly do the rest." In other words, here was put forth in the name of American business, with all the pontifical assurance that characterized Macaulay's shallowest sophistry, the pure creed of historic individualism, and here was served on the Government and people of the United States a warning revelation of confident expectations.

A year later, in a release to the press, Mr. Otto Kahn discussed the subject of planning and intimated that the fortunate position of France today is to be ascribed to the fact that the French Government interferes less with business than does the Government of Germany or Great Britain, with the implication that the United States might profit from this experience. About the same time the Honorable Newton D. Baker made a long address at Williamstown which was evidently designed to show that nothing important could be done in the present crisis by the Federal Government, except perhaps in the way of tariff reduction by international agreement. And now comes from Chicago the announcement that a number of rugged business men are forming a national association to combat Government in business, to break up this unholy alliance. There is not a professional lunching-and-dining fellowship in America that is not now applauding to the echo such ringing cries as "Let Us Alone," "Take Government Out of Business," "Hands Off," "Unburden Capital." With an eye on such straws in the wind, President Hoover publicly states that all notions about planned economy come out of Russia, thus placing such distinguished men as Gerard Swope and Owen D.

Young under the horrible Red ban. As one of the high-powered utility propagandists recently explained, the best way to discredit an opponent is to pin a Red tag on him—without reference to his deserts, of course.

II

Hence it is important to ask, calmly and without reference to election heats, just what all this means. In what way is the Government "in business" and how did it get there? Here we climb down out of the muggy atmosphere of controversy and face a few stubborn facts. They are entered in the indubitable records of the Government of the United States and are as evident as the hills to them that have eyes to see. Let us catalogue a few of them *seriatim* for the first time in the history of this adventure in logomachy.

1. Government Regulation of Railways, from 1887 to the last Act of Congress. How did the Government get into this business? The general cause was the conduct of railway corporations under the rule of rugged individualism—rebates, pools, stock watering, bankruptcy-juggling, all the traffic will bear, savage rate slashing, merciless competition, and the rest of it. If anyone wants to know the facts, let him read the history of railroading in the sixties, seventies, and early eighties, or, if time is limited, the charming illustrations presented in Charles Francis Adams' *A Chapter of Erie*. And what was the immediate cause of the Government's intervention? The insistence of business men, that is, shippers, who were harassed and sometimes ruined by railway tactics, and of farmers, the most rugged of all the rugged individualists the broad land of America has produced. And the result? Let the gentle reader compare the disastrous railway bankruptcies that flowed from the panic of 1873, including bloodshed and arson, with the plight of railways now bad as it is. Government regulation is not a utopian success, but it is doubtful whether any of our great business men would like to get the Government entirely out of this business and return to the magnificent anarchy

of Jay Gould's age. President Hoover has not even suggested it.

2. Waterways. Since its foundation the Government has poured hundreds of millions into rivers, harbors, canals, and other internal improvements. It is still pouring in millions. Some of our best economists have denounced it as wasteful and have demonstrated that most of it does not pay in any sense of the word. But President Hoover, instead of leaving this work to private enterprise, insists on projecting and executing the most elaborate undertakings, in spite of the fact that some of them are unfair if not ruinous to railways. Who is back of all this? Business men and farmers who want lower freight rates. There is not a chamber of commerce on any Buck Creek in America that will not cheer until tonsils are cracked any proposal to make the said creek navigable. Dredging companies want the good work to go on, and so do the concerns that make dredging machinery. Farmers are for it also and they are, as already said, the ruggedest of rugged individuals—so rugged in fact that the vigorous efforts of the Farm Board to instill cooperative reason into them have been almost as water on a duck's back.

3. The United States Barge Corporation. Who got the Government into the job of running barges on some of its improved waterways? Certainly not the Socialists, but good Republicans and Democrats speaking for the gentlemen listed under 2 above.

4. The Shipping Business. The World War was the occasion, but not the cause of this departure. For more than half a century the politicians of America fought ship subsidies against business men engaged in the ship-building and allied industries. At last, under the cover of war necessities, the Government went into the shipping business, with cheers from business. Who is back of the huge expenditures for the merchant marine? Business men. Who supports huge subsidies under the guise of "lucrative mail contracts," making a deficit in postal finances to be used as proof that the Government cannot run

any business? Business men clamor for these mail subsidies and receive them. Who put the Government into the business of providing cheap money for ship building? Business men did it. Those who are curious to know how these things were done may profitably read the sworn testimony presented during the investigation of W. B. Shearer's patriotic labors on behalf of the ship-building interests, especially the exhibits showing how money was spent like water "educating" politicians. Who wants navy officers on half pay to serve on privately owned ships? Business men. Who wants the Government to keep on operating ships on "pioneer" lines that do not pay? Business men. And when the United States Senate gets around to investigating this branch of business, it will find more entertainment than the Trade Commission has found in the utility inquest.

5. Aviation. The Government is "in" this business. It provides costly airway services free of charge and subsidizes air mail. Who is behind this form of Government enterprise? Gentlemen engaged in aviation and the manufacture of planes and dirigibles. Then the Government helps by buying planes for national defense. Who is opposed to air mail subsidies? A few despised "politicians."

6. Canals. Who zealously supported the construction of the Panama Canal? Shippers on the Pacific Coast who did not like the railway rates. Also certain important shipping interests on both coasts—all controlled by business men. Who insisted that the Government should buy the Cape Cod Canal? The business men who put their money into the enterprise and found that it did not pay. Then they rejoiced to see the burden placed on the broad back of our dear Uncle Sam.

7. Highway Building. Who has supported Federal highway aid—the expenditures of hundreds of millions on roads, involving the taxation of railways to pay for ruinous competition? Everybody apparently, but specifically business men engaged in the manufacture and sale of automobiles and trucks. Who proposes to cut off every cent of that outlay? Echoes do not answer.

8. The Department of Commerce, its magnificent mansion near the Treasury Department, and its army of hustlers scouting for business at the uttermost ends of the earth. Who is responsible for loading on the Government the job of big drummer at large for business? Why shouldn't these rugged individualists do their own drumming instead of asking the taxpayers to do it for them? Business men have been behind this enormous expansion, and Mr. Hoover, as Secretary of Commerce, outdid every predecessor in the range of his activities and the expenditure of public money. Who proposes to take the Government out of the business of hunting business for men who ought to know their own business?

9. The Big Pork Barrel—appropriations for public buildings, navy yards, and army posts. An interesting enterprise for the United States Chamber of Commerce would be to discover a single piece of pork in a hundred years that has not been approved by local business men as beneficiaries. When Ben Tillman shouted in the Senate that he intended to steal a hog every time a Yankee got a ham, he knew for whom the speaking was done.

10. The Bureau of Standards. Besides its general services, it renders valuable aid to business undertakings. Why shouldn't they do their own investigating at their own expense, instead of turning to the Government?

11. The Federal Trade Commission. Who runs there for rulings on "fair practices"? Weary consumers? Not often. Principally, business men who do not like to be outwitted or cheated by their competitors. If we are rugged individualists, why not let every individualist do as he pleases, without invoking Government intervention at public expense?

12. The Anti-Trust Acts. Business men are complaining against these laws on the ground that they cannot do any large-scale planning without incurring the risk of prosecution. The contention is sound, but who put these laws on the books and on what theory were they based? They were the product of a clamor on the part of farmers and business men against the

practices of great corporations. Farmers wanted lower prices. Business men of the smaller variety objected to being undersold, beaten by clever tricks, or crushed to the wall by competitors with immense capital. And what was the philosophy behind the Sherman Act and the Clayton Act? Individualism, pure and undefiled. "The New Freedom" as President Wilson phrased it in literary language. "Break up the trusts and let each tub stand on its own bottom." That was the cry among little business men. As lawyers put it in their somber way, "the natural person's liberty should not be destroyed by artificial persons known as corporations created under the auspices of the State." Whether any particular business man is for or against the anti-trust laws depends upon his particular business and the state of its earnings.

13. The Tariff. On this tender subject it is scarcely possible to speak soberly. It seems safe to say, however, that if all the business men who demand this kind of "interference"—with the right of capital to find its most lucrative course, industry and intelligence their natural reward, commodities their fair price, and idleness and folly their natural punishment—were to withdraw their support for protection, cease their insistence on it, then the politicians would probably reduce the levy or go over to free trade; with what effect on business no one can correctly predict. At all events there are thousands of business men who want to keep the Government in the business of protecting their business against foreign competition. If competition is good, why not stand up and take it?

14. The Federal Farm Board. This collectivist institution is the product of agrarian agitation, on the part of our most stalwart individualists, the free and independent farmers; but President Hoover sponsored it and signed the bill that created it. Now what is its avowed purpose as demonstrated by the language of the statute, the publications of the Farm Board, and the activities carried out under its auspices? It is primarily and fundamentally intended to stabilize prices and production through co-operative methods. And what has the Board done?

It has encouraged the development of co-operation as distinguished from individualism among farmers; it has financed co-operative associations; it has denounced individualistic farmers who insist on growing as much as they please, and has tried to get them to increase their earnings by a common limitation of production. If the Agricultural Marketing Act means anything, if the procedure of the Farm Board is not a delusion, then co-operation is to be substituted for individualism in agricultural production and marketing. If there is ever to be a rational adjustment of supply to demand in this field, the spirit and letter of President Hoover's measure must be realized through organized action by millions of farmers under Federal auspices. The other alternative is simon-pure individualism: let each farmer produce what he likes, as much of it as he likes, and sell it at any price he can get. But under the happy title "Grow Less—Get More," the Farm Board has given instructions to farmers: "One thing the successful manufacturers learned long ago was that they could not make money when they produced more than they could sell at a profit." The obvious moral is for farmers to get together under Government leadership or hang separately.

15. The Moratorium and Frozen Assets. The latest form of Government interferences with "the natural course" of economy is the suspension of payments due the United States from foreign powers on account of lawful debts and the proposal to give public support to "frozen assets." What was the source of inspiration here? American investment bankers having got themselves into a jam in their efforts to make easy money now demand Government assistance. In 1927 one of the most distinguished German economists told the writer of this article that the great game in this country, as in other parts of Europe, was to borrow billions from private bankers in the United States, so that it would ultimately be impossible to pay reparations, the debts due the Federal Government, *and* then the debts owed to private parties. The expected result? American bankers would then force their Government to forego its claims

for the benefit of private operators who wanted to make bankers' commissions and eight or ten per cent on their money. Well, the game worked. American taxpayers are to be soaked and American bankers are to collect—perhaps.

And what is a "frozen asset"? It is a gaudy name for a piece of paper representing a transaction in which the holder expected to get a larger return than was possible on a prudent, rock-bottom investment. A Hartford, Connecticut, municipal four is not frozen; a holder can get better than par in the present dark hour of Wall Street's sorrows. A seven per cent Western farm mortgage is frozen tight—and ought to be, and the holder frozen with it. So is a Bolivian seven. Why should there be Federal interference to save investors from reaping the fruits of their folly and greed? No reason, except that the latter want the Government to bring home their cake so that they can eat it. The trouble is that American capital, in finding "its most lucrative course," has fallen into a slough, and if it gets out with its gains intact the Government must bring a derrick to hoist it.

III

In this survey of a few leading economic activities of the Federal Government the emphasis is not critical; so far as the present argument is concerned, any or all of these functions may be justified with respect to national interest. Indeed it is difficult to find any undertaking of the Government which is not supported by some business men on the ground of national defense. In the early days of our history even those statesmen who generally espoused free trade or low tariffs were willing to concede the importance of making the nation independent in the manufacture of munitions of war. And in the latest hour, subsidies to the merchant marine, to aviation, and to waterways development are stoutly defended in the name of preparedness. Transforming a creek into a river navigable by outboard motor boats can be supported by military engineers on the theory that it gives them practice in their art. No; the emphasis here is not critical. The point is that the Federal Government does not operate in a vacuum, but under impulsion from without; and all of the measures which put the Government into business have been supported by rugged individualists—business men or farmers or both. The current tendency to describe the Government as a meddling busybody, prying around and regulating for the mere pleasure of taking the joy out of somebody's life, betrays an ignorance of the facts in the case. The Government of the United States operates continually in the midst of the most powerful assembly of lobbyists the world has ever seen—the representatives of every business interest that has risen above the level of a corner grocery; and there is not a single form of Government interference with business that does not have the approval of one or more of these interests—except perhaps the taxation of incomes for the purpose, among other things, of paying the expenses of subsidizing and regulating business.

For forty years or more there has not been a President, Republican or Democratic, who has not talked against Government interference and then supported measures adding more interference to the huge collection already accumulated. Take, for instance, President Wilson. He made his campaign in 1912 on the classical doctrine of individualism; he blew mighty blasts in the name of his new freedom against the control of the Government by corporate wealth and promised to separate business and Government, thus setting little fellows free to make money out of little business. The heir of the Jeffersonian tradition, he decried paternalism of every kind. Yet look at the statutes enacted under his benign administration: the trainmen's law virtually fixing wages on interstate railways for certain classes of employees; the shipping board law; the Farm Loan Act; Federal aid for highway construction; the Alaskan railway; the Federal Reserve Act; the Water Power Act; and all the rest of the bills passed during his régime. Only the Clayton anti-trust law can be called individualistic. No wonder Mr. E. L. Doheny exclaimed to Mr. C. W.

Barron that President Wilson was a college professor gone Bolshevist! And why did Democrats who had been saying "the less government the better" operate on the theory that the more government the better? Simply because their mouths were worked by ancient memories and their actions were shaped by inexorable realities.

Then the Republicans came along in 1921 and informed the country that they were going back to normalcy, were determined to take the Government out of business. Well, did they repeal a single one of the important measures enacted during the eight years of President Wilson's rule? It would be entertaining to see the sanhedrim of the United States Chamber of Commerce trying to make out a list of laws repealed in the name of normalcy and still more entertaining to watch that august body compiling a list of additional laws interfering with "the natural course of business" enacted since 1921. Heirs of the Hamiltonian tradition, the Republicans were not entitled to talk about separating the Government from business. Their great spirtual teacher, Daniel Webster, a pupil of Hamilton, had spoken truly when he said that one of the great reasons for framing the Constitution was the creation of a government that could regulate commerce. They came honestly by subsidies, bounties, internal improvements, tariffs, and other aids to business. What was the trouble with them in the age of normalcy? Nothing; they just wanted their kind of Government intervention in the "natural course of industry." Evidently, then, there is some confusion on this subject of individualism, and it ought to be examined dispassionately in the light of its history with a view to discovering its significance and its limitations; for there is moral danger in saying one thing and doing another—at all events too long.

IV

Historically speaking, there are two schools of individualism: one American, associated with the name of Jefferson, and the other English, associated with the name of Cobden. The former was agrarian in interest, the latter capitalistic. Jefferson wanted America to be a land of free, upstanding farmers with just enough government to keep order among them; his creed was an agrarian creed nicely fitted to a civilization of sailing ships, ox carts, stagecoaches, wooden plows, tallow dips, and home-made bacon and sausages; and since most of the people in the United States, during the first century of their independence, were engaged in agriculture, they thought highly of Jefferson's praise of agriculture and his doctrine of anarchy plus the police constable. Cobden's individualism was adapted to capitalist England at the middle of the nineteenth century— early industrial England. At that moment his country was the workshop of the world, was mistress of the world market in manufactured commodities, and feared no competition from any foreign country. English capitalists thus needed no protective tariffs and subsidies and, therefore, wanted none. Hence they exalted free trade to the level of a Mosaic law, fixed and eternal. They wanted to employ labor on their own terms and turn working people out to starve when no profitable business was at hand; so they quite naturally believed that any Government interference with their right to do as they pleased was "bad." Their literary apologist, Macaulay, clothed their articles of faith in such magnificent rhetoric that even the tiredest business man could keep awake reading it at night.

Closely examined, what is this creed of individualism? Macaulay defines it beautifully in the passage which the New York bank and our happy advertising agency quoted so joyously. Let the Government maintain peace, defend property, reduce the cost of litigation, and observe economy in expenditure—that is all. Do American business men want peace all the time, in Nicaragua, for instance, when their undertakings are disturbed? Or in Haiti or Santo Domingo? Property must be defended, of course. But whose property? And what about the cost of litigation and economy in expenditures? If they would tell their hired men in law offices to cut the costs of law, something might happen. As for expenditures, do they really mean to abolish subsidies, bounties, and appropriations-in-aid from which they benefit? Speaking brutally, they do not. That is not the kind of economy in expenditures which they demand; they prefer to cut off a few dollars from the Children's Bureau.

Then comes Macaulay's system of private economy: let capital find its most lucrative course alone, unaided: Government tariffs, subsidies, bounties, and special privileges. That is the first item. Do American business men who shout for individualism believe in that? Certainly not. So that much is blown out of the water. Macaulay's next item is: let commodities find their fair price. Do the gentlemen who consolidate, merge, and make price understandings want to allow prices to take their "natural course"? By no means; they are trying to effect combinations that will hold prices up to the point of the largest possible profit. Macaulay's third item is: let industry and intelligence receive their natural reward. Whose industry and intelligence and what industry and intelligence? When these questions are asked all that was clear and simple dissolves in mist.

Then there is Macaulay's last item: let idleness and folly reap their natural punishment. That was a fundamental specification in the bill of Manchesterism. Malthus made it a law for the economists: the poor are poor because they have so many babies and are improvident; nothing can be done about it, at least by any Government, even though it enforces drastic measures against the spread of information on birth control. Darwin made a natural science of it: biology sanctified the tooth and claw struggle of business by proclaiming the eternal tooth and claw struggle of the jungle. If the Government will do nothing whatever, all people will rise or sink to the level which their industry or idleness, their intelligence or folly commands. No distinction was made between those who were idle because they could find no work and those who just loved idleness for its own sake—either in slums or mansions. Those who hit bottom and starved simply deserved it.

That is the good, sound, logical creed of simon-pure individualism which Herbert Spencer embedded in fifty pounds of
printed matter. To him and all his devotees, even public
schools and public libraries were anathema: let the poor
educate themselves at their own expense; to educate them
at public expense is robbery of the taxpayer—that industrious, intelligent, provident person who is entitled to keep
his "natural reward."

Do any stalwart individualists believe that simple creed
now? Not in England, where Liberals, professing to carry
on the Cobden-Bright tradition, vote doles for unemployed
working people. Why not let idleness and folly get their
natural punishment? Why not, indeed? There must be a
reason. Either the individualists betray their own faith, or,
as some wag has suggested, they are afraid that they might
find themselves hanging to a lantern if they let the idle and
the foolish starve, that is, reap the natural punishment pre-
scribed by Macaulay. Nor do American individualists propose to let nature take her course in this country. There is
no danger of revolution here; as Mr. Coolidge has said, "we
have had our revolution"; yet business men agree with the
politicians on feeding the hungry. It is true that they seem
to be trying to obscure the issues and the facts by talking
about the beneficence of private charity while getting most
of the dole from public treasuries; but that is a detail.
Although our rugged individualists advertise Macaulay's
creed, their faith in it appears to be shaky or their courage is
not equal to their hopes. Then why should they try to delude
themselves and the public?

There is another side to this stalwart individualism that
also deserves consideration. Great things have been done in
its name, no doubt, and it will always have its place in any
reasoned scheme of thinking. Individual initiative and energy
are absolutely indispensable to the successful conduct of any
enterprise, and there is ample ground for fearing the tyranny
and ineptitude of Governments. In the days of pioneering

industry in England, in our pioneering days when forests were to be cut and mountain fastnesses explored, individualism was the great dynamic which drove enterprise forward. But on other pages of the doom book other entries must be made. In the minds of most people who shout for individualism vociferously, the creed, stripped of all flashy rhetoric, means getting money, simply that and nothing more. And to this creed may be laid most of the shame that has cursed our cities and most of the scandals that have smirched our Federal Government.

That prince of bosses, Croker, put the individualist creed in its bare logical form when he said that he was working for his own pocket all the time, just as "every man in New York is working for his pocket." Fall, Doheny, and Sinclair were all splendid individualists; they explained that they hoped to make money out of their transactions, even while they covered their operations with the mantle of patriotism— national defense. Tammany judges, Connolly and his iron pipe, Doyle with his split fees, and policemen growing rich on vice are all individualists of the purest brand. W. B. Shearer collecting money from ship-building concerns to make a naval scare so that they might increase their profits belongs to the same school. Britten, bringing a fleet to Montauk Point to boom real estate in which he is interested, does nothing reprehensible under the Manchester creed; his capital is finding "its most lucrative course." Wilder and Bardo, representing shipping interests, when they spend money in Washington "educating" members of Congress, are following the law of the game. They are perfect individualists. The ruinous chaos in coal and oil is to be attributed to the same Darwinian morality. Finally, Al Capone, with his private enterprise in racketeering, is a supreme individualist: he wants no Government interference with his business, not even the collection of income taxes; if he is "let alone" he will take care of himself and give some money to soup kitchens besides.

The cold truth is that the individualist creed of everybody

for himself and the devil take the hindmost is principally responsible for the distress in which Western civilization finds itself—with investment racketeering at one end and labor racketeering at the other. Whatever merits the creed may have had in days of primitive agriculture and industry, it is not applicable in an age of technology, science, and rationalized economy. Once useful, it has become a danger to society. Every thoughtful business man who is engaged in management as distinguished from stock speculation knows that stabilization, planning, orderly procedure, prudence, and the adjustment of production to demand are necessary to keep the economic machine running steadily and efficiently. Some of our most distinguished citizens—Owen D. Young, Gerard Swope, Nicholas Murray Butler, and Otto Kahn, for example—have, in effect, warned the country that only by planning can industry avoid the kind of disaster from which we are now suffering; on all sides are signs of its coming— perhaps soon, perhaps late, but inevitably.

And all of them know that this means severe restraints on the anarchy celebrated in the name of individualism. The task before us, then, is not to furbish up an old slogan, but to get rid of it, to discover how much planning is necessary, by whom it can best be done, and what limitations must be imposed on the historic doctrine of Manchesterism. And to paraphrase Milton, methinks puissant America, mewing her mighty youth, will yet kindle her undazzled eyes at the full midday beam, purge and unscale her long abused sight, while timorous and flocking birds, with those that love the twilight, flutter about, amazed at what she means, and in their envious gabble would prognosticate a year of sects and schisms.

THE SHARKS OF NARBOROUGH

By *William Beebe*

I

I ANCHORED the glass-bottomed diving-boat as close to the cliffs of northern Narborough as I dared, in a cove where the water was so deep that the swells remained unbroken until shattered against the lava itself. The rocks at this point showed very clearly their division into successive lava-flows, some like frozen, black molasses-candy six feet thick, alternating with thinner strata in the shape of huge bricks. The topmost layer was the same old ploughed field of cinder crags and snags with which we were so familiar on Albemarle. This is probably the eruption of one hundred years ago of which Morell wrote so vividly.

This, my seventieth descent, took me into a submarine world as strange as and as unlike that of Tagus Cove—which we could still see in the distance from the ship—as that differed from Tower. If they were jungles and deserts, this was a wheat-field. Swallowing as I went, I climbed down and down, and stood at last on a gigantic rounded boulder, thirty feet below the surface.

This roundness itself spelled a distinct difference between this and other shores of the Galapagos. The surf had pounded and rolled the rocks on this unprotected coast until they had become huge pebbles. This explained the absence of tide-pools along the shore—the water simply filtering away as soon as the tide-level went down.

The dominant note of the underwater scene in this marvelous island-eddy was the seaweed. Great fields of it extended to the limit of vision, with bare or sponge-covered boulders between. Sargassum, with small berries, grew on long, slender fronds, two or three feet in length, which gave completely to every surge, more so than any land growth to the wind. While I have dived where steady currents hold strong day and night, yet by the very force of circumstances my puny efforts are usually confined to the surge-affected shore. Like a tide which changes every twelve seconds instead of every twelve hours, the whole underworld swayed outward and then, with infinite grace, inward again. All the innumerable strands of greenish-olive bent and flattened away from me, and then, with the slow movement attained only rarely by such growths as weeping willows, rolled toward and wrapped around me, reaching out toward the steep ascent marking the beginning of that upper world which seemed so little a part of my life at a moment like this.

As the grass shifted and vibrated, many weird little inhabitants were disclosed for a moment, and then scuttled back to shelter—wrasse never seen before or since, twisting worms, crabs, and snails, all identical in color with the weed. The numbers and size of the fish were remarkable, almost every species being represented by larger individuals than elsewhere, perhaps due to the unusual abundance of food on these current-bounded shores. My old friends, Xesurus, the yellow-tailed cows, were grazing in schools of two to three hundred, shadowing slowly about the corners of boulders.

I was halfway up a steep slope, and by twisting the boat around with me I succeeded in reaching the summit, where I could look down upon a sinister valley, narrow and dark and deep, with the opposite ridge covered with long, waving weed. As I stretched full-length upon a mat of the sargassum, a gang—they were too ugly and dangerous looking to be called a school—of giant groupers parted the fronds and drifted through towards me, all dark in tone with the olives and browns. They mouched along, their ugly jaws chewing eternally on the cud of life, when suddenly, without the slightest warning, there came a distinct glow, and next to the last grouper came one of the golden ones. In their evident opinion there was no difference. He impatiently nudged a neighbor and in turn was pushed aside by the fish following him. The most careful dissection shows absolutely no physical difference, and yet, instead of being clad in mottled olive-green of the dullest, darkest shade, he is solid gold from mouth to tail. The weed was appreciably illumined when he passed through it. One strange thing has been that, rare as the golden groupers are, both two years ago and during the present trip it has been only these gorgeously colored individuals that have attacked the propeller of our little outboard motors. Whether the color of the glistening brass attracts this shining caste more than the other duller grouper persons I have no idea.

A few minutes later a shadowy school, a second lot, of even larger groupers swept past in the blue distance with another golden brother in their number. He is all the more wonderful because there are no intermediates—one either has regal golden blood, or is of mottled-brown polloi caste. Here is materialized the mental effect which creates in fairy tales the one most beautiful creature or prince or lady among a host of dull or ugly ones.

Once again a huge sea-lion gave me a start. As I stood watching a mist of grazing Xesurus, I felt a sudden water-pressure against my back and legs, and turned in time to see a monstrous black shape bank and veer away, having rushed in a lightning sweep within a foot of me. His eyes were no longer the dull, soft, deerlike, half-seeing organs with which he gazed at me on land, but bright and clear and keen; the long whiskers stood out white and bristling, the mouth partly opened as he turned, and the dog teeth gleamed wickedly. As my eye caught the form I leaped involuntarily toward the ladder, forgetting that I was in a land where mighty acro-batics could be achieved with a push. I landed on a boulder at a height of about four rungs up, and some eight feet beyond the ladder—a standing high jump which broke the world's record in the upper air by feet. The strangest thing was that whenever I did such a thing as this I accomplished it slowly. I took off with deliberation in spite of my strongest effort, I went through the water with conscious elapse of time, and I landed as in a slow-motion picture.

The instant I leaped I realized my mistake and watched the wonderful form as it swung up from me. It turned just below the surface and again shot down. I think a considerable percentage of these manœuvres was pure side, executed for the benefit of a smaller, probably a lady, sea-lion who hung between earth and air a short distance away and watched. The big male—he was certainly over seven feet long—began his second rush at an acute angle, heading for the bottom some distance away. Turning like a meteor the moment his head touched the waving seaweed, he again cleared me by inches. I could not help flinching, not so much from a fear of being bitten, as from a disbelief that such a great body could possibly stop its impetus and avoid smashing into me. As he passed, I stretched out a hand and felt the smooth, hard body brush against my fingers. This was apparently a surprise to the animal, who in alarm inserted an extra curve into his simple parabola, and in the effort gasped out a mouthful of bubbles. This time he shot to the surface and half out, followed by his admirer, while the string of bubbles ascended slowly—coalescing, as it went, into larger and fewer spheres, like the puff of smoke from an aeroplane engine, or the blossoming of white shrapnel against a blue sky. In each bubble I could see a distorted reflection of myself, my helmet, and all my surroundings.

A glance around showed that every fish had vanished, and not until two or three minutes had passed did they begin slowly to come into view. The sea-lions are the masters of these waters, and I was surprised to see even a great turtle slide hastily out of the way when one came too near. Sharks always disappeared with the fish.

Even if the fish had not returned I could have watched the

movement of the seaweed for hours, it was so unlike the movement of wheat or grass. The whole mass seemed alive,—a field of Medusa growth,—each stem writhing and curling and twisting of its own volition, in its own particular way, and yet the whole ebbing and flowing as one frond in obedience to the rhythmic breeze. It was the old story over again of the single corpuscle tumbling and rolling individually, while yet helpless in the general current of the blood; and of the colonial organism, each individual ant doing his own work and bound irrevocably to the will of the whole; and—who knows?—it is perhaps no whit different from the apparent freewill personalities of our separate selves, compared with the destiny of the human race.

I sat me down on a couch of golden, blowing weed, with beautiful green-armed starfish sprawled here and there, and, leaning back, watched the bubbles of my life's breath tumble out from beneath my arms and shoulders. From invisibility, from the colorless, formless stream of gas flowing down the length of black hose, they became definite spheres, painted and splashed with all the colors in sight. Once, when I was making my first flight in a plane, I had for a short space of time the soul-devastating sensation of being suspended motionless in the ether while the earth dropped away from me. That has never been repeated; but here on the bottom of the sea, looking upward, I can as often as I wish conjure up the belief that I am actually looking at a constellation, a galaxy of worlds and stars, rolling majestically through the invisible ether. The background is as mysteriously colorless and formless as space itself must be, and as I peer out through my little rectangular windows I seem to be actually living an experience which only the genius of a Verne or a Wells can imagine into words. It suddenly flashes over me that in giving over my moon and stellar longings for the depths of the sea I have in a manner achieved both.

I have even the sensations of a god, for in each of the spheres I have created I see very distinctly my own image. But I also see many more interesting things, and my moonings in the present instance are brought to an abrupt end by a glint of gold which appears on each globule of air—a fiery pin-point which becomes an oval, and soon a great spot as if a sun were rising behind me. If I were looking at a real planet such a thing might be a tremendous volcanic eruption on the surface. Twisting slightly and peering obliquely through my little periscope, I saw what after all is the most joyous thing in life, an old friend in a new guise—another great golden grouper was just behind me, revealed to me by his reflected image on my ascending breath.

II

To my left the rope from the anchor-weight led up in a grace-ful curve to the distant, dark silhouette of the boat. Now and then a window opened in the ruffled ceiling and framed the anxious face of my faithful assistant peering down, on the lookout for approaching danger. The face vanished, the win-dow slammed shut as the water glass was withdrawn—and I am again visually lost to the upper world.

Two small, black forms approach from the offshore side of my aquatic sky, looking from below like the keels of funny, diminutive tugboats, but driven by a pair of most efficient propellers. These were rather turbines of sorts, furling and unfurling in a curling, spiral manner, which offered the most and the least resistance respectively to the water. Long rudder tails, two slender, sharp beaks, and sinuous snaky necks came into view, and a swirl sent both birds into my world—meaning complete submersion for them. There followed a chase which no man's eyes have ever seen before—a pair of flightless cormorants pursuing a scarlet sea-bass, viewed from below. The fish saw them coming and fled at full speed, not in a straight line, but in a series of zigzags, perhaps, like a chased hen, seeing the pursuers first out of one eye, on one side, then out of the other, apparently on that side. The cormorants separated, one diving deeply while the other followed its prey directly. Soon the confused fish dived at right angles, and before it had time to turn again was in the beak of the second bird. The moment he was captured, both birds relaxed every muscle, and with dangling wings and feet let themselves be drawn up to the surface. There, even from my depth, I watched a second race begin, and surmised the details of what I had seen enacted twice the day before from the boat—a cormorant coming up with a fish and instantly chased by another, both traveling at such high speed that, with wings spattering and feet going, their entire bodies were almost out of water. At the first opportunity there was a quick upward toss, reversing the fish, and a gulp, and down it went head-first. On this occasion I saw only the frantic disturbance of the surface, rapid dodging, and then cessation of motion, after which the leading bird immersed and shook its beak in the water several times, and I knew that if I so chose I could write in my journal that *Nannopterum harrisii* includes *Paranthias furcifer* as an article of diet.

The surface ripples had hardly ceased when a cloud drifted across my sky. And at this place may I digress parenthetically long enough to make a certain point clear. As I ramble on of the adventures and sights which came to me in my underworld, there would seem to occur there almost a rhythmic succession of happenings, one after the other, as with circus performers who wait in the wings for their turn to come. This works a hopeless injustice to this water world. Please remember that the exigencies of my place in that world and the physical make-up of my helmet enabled me to see only the merest fraction of occurrences even in an acute-angled single direction. A horse with blinders is a reasonable simile; or, better still, a half-blind old man, crippled with rheumatism and palsy, dropped suddenly into the busiest of a city's streets and requested to narrate the happenings about him, and give to them some sort of explanation!

Now, again, the ripples of the surface above me had scarcely died away to the usual heaving, opaque, moonstone appearance of my water sky, when a cloud came drifting past. If I had been looking behind me some time before, and had eyes which could penetrate the wall of blueness in the distance, this cloud might at first have seemed no bigger than a man's hand. Overhead, however, it was large enough to darken the whole bottom, and, except along the rim, formed a solid mass. At least twenty thousand slender little Galapagos snappers floated over and around me. They were only two to three inches in length, slender and sinuous, grayish-black above, silvery below, with seven or more narrow dark stripes running parallel down the head and body. This was the clear-cut vision I had as the host drifted slowly, almost without individual movement, toward and over me. Some danger, unknown to me, wrought a whirlwind in this living cloud, and instantly every fish vanished, the whole becoming a mass of blurred lines—a great gray something out of focus. As quickly, fear passed, and every fish again became clear-etched in its place among its thousands of fellows. Slowly all passed from view, a few hundreds along the lower edge sifting through the uppermost fringe of weeds. It occurred to me then that their man-given name was a singularly appropriate one—*Xenocys*, strange swift! It should have been *Xenocys xenocys;* they were too delicate, too immaterial, for any noun.

My sea-lion returned for a last look, but slewed off, and then a turtle, almost as long as myself, swam into my ken. He was much more satisfactory a constellation than those in the heavens, of most of which I have never been able to make head or tail. But he was also a turtle at its best. Until one has looked up and seen eight hundred pounds of sea turtle floating lightly as thistledown overhead, balanced so exactly between bottom and surface that the slightest half-inch of flipper motion is sufficient to turn the great mass partly over and send it ahead a yard—until then one has never really seen a turtle. Two years ago when I visited these islands, I watched the little penguins waddling about with their Charlie Chaplin gait; I saw the cormorants awkwardly climbing over land, even hauling themselves along by means of a crook in their necks; the sea lions unlovelily caterpillaring along the ground; and great hulks of turtles ploughing their way as much through as over the sand of the beaches. It was now my privilege to see these same creatures in their chosen element, graceful, glorified reincarnations of their terrestrial activities. In all this I had no false illusions concerning my own relative functioning. While I have never heard any rumor as to my possessing any grace even at my best, yet on these same islands and beaches I can at least correlate my activity, and I can easily run down any of the creatures that I am discussing. Whereas here at the sea bottom I sprawl awkwardly, clutching at waving weeds to keep from being washed away by the gentle swell, peering out of a metal case infinitely more ugly than the turtle's skull, and superior to them only in my hearty admiration of their perfect coördination in an exquisitely adapted environment.

My nice turtle friend still floated motionless when suddenly he was the means of my making a delightful discovery in Einstein relativity—making clear the fact that he was motionless and yet not motionless. I was resting lightly on a bed of weeds with a generous tuft of them in each hand. I was aware that with every surge there was a very decided movement of the whole mass, but as everything in sight was equally shifted my mind registered no definite motion. Of one thing only was I certain: that, however we plants and organisms at the bottom were blowing and vibrating back and forth, the turtle at least, isolated in mid-water, was as still as the distant rocks themselves. Becoming cramped, I decided to stand upright for a while, and gently lowered my feet until I felt them fit into convenient crevices of the concealed rocks beneath me. This gave me safe anchorage, and in a minute more all my surroundings, my whole world, went trailing off as far as it could; then, with equal unanimity, all faithfully returned. I glanced upward and was as astonished as if, when on land, I should suddenly see the moon or sun begin to bob back and forth in the sky, for my turtle was behaving like everything else and was being swayed back and forth, suspended in the invisible medium, exactly as we at the bottom.

To look back upon it, no more silly lack of reasoning could be imagined on my part; but when you leave the world for which God made you, and willfully enter other strange ones, it is reasonable to suppose that your senses and brain have to become readjusted as well as your more physical being. For five minutes I derived infinite delight from alternately swaying with the weed and holding to the rock, and thereby at will giving to my turtle absolute stability or rhythmical swaying through space. He seemed quite unaffected by the theory, but appeared fascinated by the sight of this strange copper-headed, white-skinned, wormlike being, with an enormously long, curving tentacle from the tip of its nose, forever pouring forth a mass of white, bubbly gas—a being that idiotically kept standing up and sitting down. Never for an instant did the great chelonian take its eyes from me. If I could put down what it actually thought of me, no halting words of mine would be necessary in this essay.

And still the turtle hung in the sky when two penguins arrived. For a time they swam around in little intersecting circles, constantly plunging their heads beneath the water to stare at me. Finally curiosity overcame them, they could stand it no longer, and down they came, clad in mantles of silvery bubble-sheen. They encircled me once and started on another round, but then became fascinated by the black hose and, after an examination, half paddled, half drifted, to the surface and were gone.

Two mighty schools of Xesurus passed me, grazing slowly. When within six feet they left off their eternal feeding and formed up into more or less orderly ranks which flowed like some enormously long sea-serpent around the identical corners of rocks where had passed the leaders yards and yards in advance. Invariably the formation of an irregular line led very close to me, the closing-up of ranks evidently being connected with the presence of danger or at least something suspicious or strange. It was an amusing sensation to have these hundreds of fish file past, all rolling their eyes at me as they went. I felt almost embarrassed at times, as perhaps "the remains" must occasionally feel as the viewing crowds stream past. With these yellow-tailed cows were widely scattered single individuals of a species of fish which we never caught or identified. In shape and in the general grayish-blue color of body they bore a considerable resemblance to the Xesurus, their characteristic marks being two white spots above the eyes; but they were not grazers, nor even, I believe herbivorous. I never saw them graze even when the school of their associates remained in one spot, doing nothing else for a half-hour but scrape the algæ from the rocks. Once, too, I saw one of these white-spotted chaps pursue a small fish, and though he did not capture it, yet I could not mistake his intent—there was nothing of play or yet of sudden anger in the attempt, but a very evident desire for food. They were much more timorous than the yellow-tailed surgeon fish, and at any hint of danger would dart into the thick of the school. All this makes me think that they are very likely examples of real mimicry, gaining a good percentage of immunity by the resemblance to and close association with fish which by their great numbers and poisonous spines are well able to fight off ordinary dangers.

III

When I rolled over and looked about, there came to me a vision of the abundance of life in the sea. The cloud of little fishes had gone, even the ubiquitous yellow-tailed surgeons were out of sight for once, and yet from where I sat I could see not fewer than seven or eight hundred fish, not counting the wrasse and gobies that played around my fingers as thickly as grasshoppers in a hayfield. Out of the blue-green distance or up from frond-draped depths good-sized gray sharks appeared now and then. Two came slowly toward me, closer with the in-surge, and then floating farther off with the out-swing. They turned first one, then the other, yellow, catlike eye toward me, and after a good look veered off. Near them were playing round-headed pigfish; a few Xesurus swam still closer; and even small scarlet snappers, the prey of almost every hungry fish or aquatic bird, even these went by without any show of nervousness. The pair of sharks passed on, almost unnoticed, and all the mass of life of this wonder world seemed going smoothly and undisturbed. Far away in the dim distance one of the sharks appeared again, or it may have been another—when, looking around me, I saw every fish vanishing. While I have mentioned what must seem an identical occurrence before, yet this was as different as a great battle is from a street accident. Through copper and glass and air I sensed some peril very unlike the former reaction to the sea-lion, and I rapidly climbed a half-dozen rungs, swallowing hard as I went to adjust to the new altitude. Clinging close to the ladder, I looked everywhere, but saw nothing but waving seaweed. The distant shark had vanished, together with all the hosts of fish, even the bullying, fearless groupers. I was the only living thing except the starfish and the tiny waving heads of the hydroids which grew in clusters among the thinner growths of weed, as violets appear amid high grass. Whether the distant shark was of some different, very dreaded kind, or whether some still more inimical thing had appeared, fearful even to the strange shark, I shall never know. Five minutes later, fear had again passed, and life, not death, was dominant.

I climbed to the surface at last, my teeth chattering from the prolonged immersion. This water, although in no sense the Humboldt current, is much cooler than that at Cocos, and I became numb and chilled without knowing it. Excitement and concentrated interest keep me keyed up, and the constant need of balance requires that every muscle be taut; then, when I reach the surface and relax, the chill seems to enter my very bones. Fortunately there is always either rowing or pumping to do, and this soon warms me.

During my last dive I had noticed five or six new species of fish and, hoping to hook some of the smaller ones, I decided to get some bait. I had the boat backed near the shore, and at a propitious moment, on the crest of one of the lesser swells, I leaped off. The scarlet crabs here are remarkably tame, far more so than on any of the other islands—a fact for which I can in no way account. The casual visits of man may be, of course, ruled out, as having nothing to do with it, and yet here birds and fish, the crabs' most deadly enemies, are unusually abundant.

With two big scarlet crabs, I vaulted back on the crest of another convenient little swell, fortunately just avoiding the succeeding three, any one of which would have tossed our cockleshell high up on the jagged lava. I found to my disappointment that we had between us only one hook, and that a large one. However, I anchored again near the spot where I had last dived and threw over the hook. I immediately caught one of the round-headed pigfish. As I was pulling a second one in, a six-foot shark swung toward him, and this gave me a hint upon which I acted at once. I pulled in the fish quickly and studied the situation through the water glass. Two sharks were swimming slowly about the very rock where I had been sitting a few minutes before, probably the same individuals who had then been so curious about me. A small group of the pigfish swam around, over, and below the sharks, as they had also done when I was submerged, sometimes passing within a foot of the sharks' mouths without the slightest show of emotion, of fear or otherwise. An angel fish and two yellow-tailed cows passed; a golden grouper and two deep-green giants of the same species milled around beneath the boat, now and then cocking their eyes up at us.

I baited the hook with a toothsome bit of crab and lowered it. All the pigfish rushed it at once, and as it descended the sharks and groupers followed with mild interest, almost brushing against it, but wary of the line. Failing to elicit any more practical attention from the golden grouper, I allowed one of the pigfish to take the bait and hook. Then, watching very carefully, I checked his downward rush, and swung him upward. He struggled fiercely, and like an electric shock every shark and grouper turned toward him. Without being able to itemize any definite series of altered swimming actions, I knew that something radical had happened. The remainder of the school of pigfish, while they stayed in the neighborhood, yet gathered together in a group and milled slowly in a small circle. There was no question that, from being a quiet, slowly swimming, casually interested lot of fish, the three groups—pigfish, groupers, and sharks—had become surcharged with interest focused on the fish in trouble. I drew the hooked fish close to the boat, and could plainly see that the hook had passed only around the horny maxillary. There was not a drop of blood in the water, and the disability of the fish consisted only in its attachment to the line. Yet the very instant the struggle to free itself began, the groupers and sharks, from being at least in appearance friendly, or certainly wholly disregarding the pigfish, became concertedly inimical, focused upon it with the most hostile feeling of an enemy and its prey.

For half an hour I played upon this reaction and learned more than I had ever seen or read of the attacking and feeding habits of groupers and sharks. When the struggling began, the sharks all turned toward the hooked fish. Not only the one nearest, who must easily have seen it for himself, but two far off turned at the same instant, and within a few seconds two more from quite invisible distances and different directions. What I saw seemed to prove conclusively that sharks, like vultures, watch one another and know at once when prey has been sighted by one of their fellows. The numerous sharks thus call one another all unintentionally; as happened when one of our party caught a shark at Cocos, and in an incredibly short time there were seventeen close by. On the other hand, it must be admitted that sharks differ from vultures as widely as the poles in the matter of scent. Vultures probably all but lack this sense, while we know that fish have it well developed. But, even in the case of blood in the water, it seems to me that diffusion cannot be nearly rapid enough to account for the instantaneous reaction on sharks near and far. The phenomenon is as remarkable in general aspects as the apparent materialization from the air of a host of vultures where a few minutes before none were visible.

Even more than this problem did the method of feeding of sharks and groupers hold my attention. After making sure of the first phase of interest, I allowed a six-foot shark to approach the hooked pigfish. It came rather slowly, then with increased speed, and finally made an ineffectual snap at the fish. The third time it seized it by the tail and, with a strong sideways twist of the whole body, tore the piece off. The second fish attacked was pulled off the hook, and two sharks then made a simultaneous rush at it. So awkward were they that one caught his jaw in the other's teeth and for a moment both swished about in a vortex of foam at the side of the boat.

I noted carefully about thirty distinct efforts or attacks on the hooked fish, and only three times was I able by manœuvring the fish to get the shark to turn even sideways—never once on its back, as the books so glibly relate. I sacrificed seven pigfish, and then tried to get the golden grouper, but it was too wary. A giant five-foot green grouper, larger than any we had taken thus far, was becoming more and more excited, however, and when I had tolled him close to the surface I let my fish lure drift loosely. One swift snap and the entire fish disappeared; then a single slight nod of the head, and the line parted cleanly. The general effect was of much greater force and power exerted in a short space of time than in the case of the sharks. When it comes to lasting power. however, the groupers fight for only a short time after being landed, while the sharks smash and thrash until they are actually cut to pieces.

After this exhibition I would, without hesitation, have dived in the helmet again in the very spot. I had had these sharks close to me a little while before; and, although my efforts under water seem to me no less awkward and helpless than those of a hooked pigfish, yet to these so-called man-eaters there is apparently all the difference in the world, and I am certain I should be absolutely safe from attack. The pig-fish which entered into the experiment with no enthusiasm or volition were *Orthopristis forbesi*, the groupers were *Mycteroperca olfax*, and the sharks were *Carcharias galapagensis*.

"I AM IN THE BOOK"

By *Robert Benchley*

THERE are several natural phenomena which I shall have to have explained to me before I can consent to keep on going as a resident member of the human race. One is the metamorphosis which hats and suits undergo exactly one week after their purchase, whereby they are changed from smart, intensely becoming articles of apparel into something children use when they want to "dress up like daddy." Another is the almost identical change undergone by people whom you have known under one set of conditions when they are transferred to another locale.

Perhaps the first phenomenon, in my case, may be explained by the fact that I need a valet. Not a valet to come in two or three times a week and sneak my clothes away, but a valet to follow me about, everywhere I go, with a whiskbroom in one hand and an electric iron in the other, brushing off a bit of lint here, giving an occasional *coup de fer* there, and whispering in my ear every once in a while, for God's sake not to turn my hat brim down that way. Then perhaps my hats and suits would remain the hats and suits they were when I bought them.

But the second mysterious transformation—that of people of one sort into people of another sort, simply by moving them from one place to another in different clothes—here is a problem for the scientists; that is, if they are at all interested.

Perhaps I do not make myself clear. (I have had quite a bit of trouble that way lately.) I will give an example if you can get ten other people to give, too. Let us say that you went to Europe this summer. You were that rosy-faced man

in a straw hat who went to Europe this summer. Or you went
to the seashore. My God, man, you must have gone *somewhere!*

Wherever you were, you made new acquaintances, unless
you had whooping cough all the time. On the voyage home,
let us say, you sat next to some awfully nice people from Grand
Rapids, or were ill at practically the same time as a very
congenial man from Philadelphia. These chance acquaintances
ripened into friendships, and perhaps into something even
more beautiful (although I often think that *nothing* is really
more beautiful than friendship), and before long you were
talking over all kinds of things and perhaps exchanging bits of
fruit from your steamer baskets. By the day before you
landed you were practically brother and sister—or, what is
worse, brother and brother.

"Now we must get together in the fall," you say. "I am in
the book. The first time you come to town give me a ring and
we'll go places and see things." And you promise to do the
same thing whenever you happen to be in Grand Rapids or
Philadelphia. You even think that you might make a trip to
Grand Rapids or Philadelphia especially to stage a get-
together.

The first inkling you have that maybe you won't quite
take a trip to Grand Rapids or Philadelphia is on the day when
you land in New York. That morning everyone appears on
deck dressed in traveling clothes which they haven't worn
since they got on board. They may be very nice clothes and
you may all look very smart, but something is different. A
strange tenseness has sprung up and everyone walks around
the deck trying to act natural, without any more success than
seeming singularly unattractive. Some of your bosom friends,
with whom you have practically been on the floor of the bar
all the way over, you don't even recognize in their civilian
clothes.

"Why, look who's here!" you say. "It's Eddie! I didn't
know you, Eddie, with that great, big, beautiful collar on."

And Eddie asks you where you got that hat, accompanying the question with a playful jab in the ribs which doesn't quite come off. A rift has already appeared in the lute and you haven't even been examined yet by the doctors for trachoma.

By the time you get on the dock and are standing around among the trunks and dogs, you may catch sight of those darling people, the Dibbles, standing in the next section under "C," and you wave weakly and call out, "Don't forget, I'm in the book!" but you know in your heart that you could be in a book of French drawings and the Dibbles wouldn't look you up—which is O. K. with you.

Sometimes, however, they do look you up. Perhaps you have parted at the beach on a bright morning in September before you went up to get dressed for the trip to the city. The Durkinses (dear old Durkinses!) were lying around in their bathing suits and you were just out from your last swim preparatory to getting into the blue suit.

"Well, you old sons-of-guns," you say, smiling through your tears, "the minute you hit town give us a ring and we'll begin right where we left off. I know a good place. We can't swim there, but, boy, we can get wet!"

At which Mr. and Mrs. Durkins scream with laughter and report to Mr. and Mrs. Weffer, who are sitting next, that you have said that you know a place in town where you can't swim but, boy, you can get wet. This pleases the Weffers, too, and they are included in the invitation.

"We'll have a regular Throg's Point reunion," Mrs. Weffer says. Mrs. Weffer isn't so hot at making wisecracks, but she has a good heart. Sure, bring her along!

Along about October you come into the office and find that a Mr. Durkins has called and wants you to call him at his hotel. "Durkins? Durkins? Oh, *Durkins!* Sure thing! Get me Mr. Durkins, please." And a big party is arranged for that night.

At six o'clock you call for the Durkinses at their hotel. (The Weffers have lost interest long before this and dropped out.

The Durkinses don't even know where they are—in Montclair, New Jersey, they think.) The Durkinses are dressed in their traveling clothes and you are in your business suit, such as it is (such as *business* is). You are not quite sure that it *is* Mrs. Durkins at first without that yellow sweater she used to wear all the time at the beach. And Mr. Durkins looks like a house-detective in that collar and tie. They both look ten years older and not very well. You have a feeling that you look pretty seedy, too.

"Well, well, here we are again! How are you all?"

"Fine and dandy. How are you—and the missus?"

"Couldn't be better. She's awfully sorry she couldn't get in town tonight. (You haven't even told her that the Durkinses were here.) What's the news at dear old Throg's Point?"

"Oh, nothing much. Very dead after you left."

"Well, well— (A pause.) How have you *been* anyway, you old son of a gun?"

"Oh, fine; fine and dandy! You all been well?"

"Couldn't be better. What was going on at the old dump when you left? Any news? Any scandal?"

"Not a thing."

"Well, well— Not a thing, eh?— Well, that's the way it goes, you know; that's the way it goes."

"Yes, sir, I guess you're right— You look fine."

"Feel fine—I could use a little swim right now though."

"Oh, boy, couldn't I though!" (The weather being very cold for October, this is recognized by both sides as an entirely false enthusiasm, as neither of you ever really cared for swimming even in summer.)

"How would you like to take a walk up to Sammy's for a lobster sandwich, eh?"

"Say, what I couldn't do to one right now! *Boy!* Or one of those hot dogs!"

"One of Sammy's hot dogs *wouldn't* go bad right now, you're right."

"Well, well— You've lost all your tan, haven't you?"

"Lost it when I took my first hot-water bath."

This gets a big laugh, the first, and last, of the evening. You are talking to a couple of strangers and the conversation has to be given adrenalin every three minutes to keep it alive. The general atmosphere is that of a meeting in a doctor's office.

It all ends up by your remembering that, after dinner, you have to go to a committee meeting which may be over at nine o'clock or may last until midnight and they had better not wait for you. You will meet them after the theater if you can. And you know that you can't, and *they* know that you can't, and, what is more, they don't care.

So there you are! The example that I gave has been rather long; so there isn't much room left for a real discussion of the problem. But the fact remains that people are one thing in one place and another thing in another place, just as a hat that you buy in the store for a natty gray sport model turns out to be a Confederate general's fatigue-cap when you get it home. And if you know of any explanation, I don't care to hear about it. I'm sick of the subject by now anyway.

SOMETHING MUST BE DONE

By *Ralph Bergengren*

IT will now and again happen to almost any man in moderate circumstances to be reminded by his wife that something must be done in or about the house. And there are some, no doubt, who leap to the occasion—and do something at once. The bathtub faucet, for example, is almost suddenly provided with a new washer; a trap is set for the mouse that has got into the cellar and will soon be running all over the house, the mouse murdered, and the corpus delicti unostentatiously disposed of; a stepladder is carried upstairs, mounted, balanced upon, the spare-room window shade taken off, its roller shrewdly examined, the spring tightened, the stepladder descended and again hidden away.

The condition, however, is often one that a philosopher would put up with, content to sit in meditation under his Bo Tree and reflect, when reminded, that no Bo Tree is perfect. The faucet (he will subconsciously argue) drips into the tub; mice come and mice go; it will be time enough to do something about the window shade when a guest is expected. Such a man will agree pleasantly that something must be done—but without getting up. Or again, in the case of an active and willing man whose intention to do something is indisputable, unless he does it at once he will do something else first. So performance lags behind intention. So many other affairs, tasks, duties, concerns, and so forth, seemingly of more immediate insistence, intervene that he forgets the reminder. The faucet will continue to drip; the mouse will presently be running all over the house; the unexpected guest will be embarrassed by having to turn off the light and undress in the dark.

For some time past there had been no question but that
something must be done about the lock on my kitchen door.
A lock, if anything, should be obedient to its key; but none
could any longer say whether this lock would respond with
alacrity or would have to be coaxed. Then one gently jiggled
the key, violently shook the door, thinking regretfully of
Acadia, where

> Neither locks had they to their doors, nor bars to their windows;
> But their dwellings were open as day and the hearts of the owners.

Usually the lock coyly responded in a few minutes; but once
it had had to be coaxed, off and on, for several days. The door
being unlocked, I had then contrived what is called a "button,"
fastening it securely from the inside and practically answering
all purposes, for the house could still be locked up externally
with the front-door key. But one had to remember to use the
button, and sooner or later something must undoubtedly be
done about the kitchen-door lock.

Wherever situated, a lock is symbolic of the evolution of man
from his early home in a cave to his present home in a suburb.
It became, in some form, a necessity as soon as he gave up
living in a tree, and—except briefly in Acadia—has so continued, constantly urging and encouraging his ingenuity both
to make it and to break it.

"To primitive man, living in a favorable climate," wrote
Professor Julius Lippert in his *Evolution of Culture*, "the chief
desideratum of his abode must have been protection from
dangerous animals. This was easily provided by blocking up
the entrance of a cave." Professor Lippert, I think, should
have tried blocking up the entrance of a cave himself. With a
good-sized entrance this must have been a regular sunset job
for the whole family, the primitive man, his primitive wife
(if one may so call her), and his primitive little ones. Every
morning they would have had to unblock the entrance; and
sometimes, during the day, whoever happened to be at home
or had returned in haste would have had to block it up in a

hurry. The will to live, so important in evolution, would have kept them at it; but the will to live with the least possible labor, equally important, would have kept them dissatisfied. *They would not have agreed with Professor Lippert.* The feeling that something must be done about the entrance of the cave, working from one millennium to another, would at last have resulted in something being done.

Thus we see the dawn of domestic architecture, for the patiently budding architect must have made some sort of house before he could make some sort of door, and some sort of door before he could fasten it against dangerous animals with some sort of button. The family took their lives with them when they went out, and, except for the dangerous animal, it was all quite simple and Acadian. But, as possessions multiplied, the desirability—much as one hates to admit it—of locking up the house when away from home became more and more exigent. Something must be done about the button; and so at last was invented the lock. The key, no doubt, was cumbersome, but it was a great improvement, as I think Professor Lippert would have admitted, over blocking up the entrance of a cave.

But these thoughts about the past do nothing about the present.

As anybody knows who has ever looked, the lock on a kitchen door is cleverly concealed in the woodwork and there held in place by two screws. Nothing is easier, after a man has found his screwdriver, than to remove such a lock, thus leaving to be admired a neat cavity of exactly corresponding proportions. Keyholes in the door coincide so nicely with keyholes in the lock that anybody who will stoop to this method can look through the door. But the inner anatomy of the lock, its physiology and psychology, is still further concealed and protected by a metal body held together by yet another screw. *And sometimes a screw sticks.* One must unscrew this screw, pressing the screwdriver inexorably against the screw and at the same time twisting it irresistibly in a direction opposite to that followed by the hands of his watch; and until that screw is unscrewed it will remain impossible for one to examine the anatomy of that lock. When I held it up to the light and tried to look in through the keyhole, I saw the house across the street and my neighbor sweeping down her front steps, a pretty spectacle that did nothing whatever but sweep down the front steps. One can, of course, put the lock back in the door; but this, too, really does nothing about it. One merely wastes time trying to find the screws. I laid the lock down on the kitchen table, and threw the screwdriver in the coal hod.

"The thing to do about this lock," I said to my wife, "is to scrap it. Now that I have got it out, I will run down to the hardware store—"

My wife looked alarmed.

"Do you think," she said, "that you will have time to run down to the hardware store before lunch?"

I looked at my watch and about the kitchen. The grocery-man had that morning left a half peck of potatoes in a paper bag. I expeditiously dumped out the potatoes, put the lock in the bag, and the bag in my pocket. I reassured my wife.

"Allowing ten minutes to go," I said, "five minutes in the store to exchange this interesting specimen of junk for a new lock, ten minutes to come back, and five minutes to put the new lock in the door, there will be just enough time."

"I hope so," said my wife. "You're not forgetting the key?"

"No," I said. "I am not forgetting the key."

I found the key and put it in the paper bag with the lock.

It was the noon hour in our village, and only one clerk—an intellectual-looking young man, as such clerks are apt to be— was in the hardware store. He adjusted his spectacles, looked at the exterior of the lock and at me through the keyholes. He tried the key, and for once I was glad that it stuck.

"I guess we'll have to open her up," he said. "I haven't got another lock of this make in stock, so I'd have to send for it. Maybe all she needs is a drop of oil."

"I tried that through the keyhole," I said. "It didn't seem to do any good."

"It wouldn't," he said. "Not through the keyhole. Wait a minute till I get a screwdriver."

In a hardware store it ought not to take very long to find a screwdriver. Yet I presently began to wonder whether he was not out of screwdrivers and having to send for one. I looked at my watch, and was surprised to see that he had been gone less than two minutes. He came back with a screwdriver, whistling a little tune as he came, and nonchalantly tackled the screw. Then he stopped whistling and tackled the screw seriously. The screw passively resisted, and I found myself betting on it. Finally he put the lock on the floor, stood on it with both feet, grasped the screwdriver with both hands, bent over at the waist, and again tackled the screw. Watching him anxiously, I could not but think that here at last was the man who never neglects his morning exercises. This time the screw yielded reluctantly.

"Wait a minute," he said, wiping his forehead and the palms of his hands with his pocket handkerchief, "till I get some oil."

A lock, as I have since read in my encyclopædia, is "an arrangement or contrivance for fastening doors, lids, boards, plates, etc., by means of an enclosed bolt which is shot back and forth by means of a key or other device to engage with some form of staple, plate, or box. The enclosed bolt is usually guarded by an obstacle which must be overcome by the action of the key." While he was gone for the oil I examined, but without touching, these now exposed mysteries of the lock. But this soon palled; and I began pacing back and forth—six steps one way and six steps another, like a dangerous animal in front of a primitive dwelling—as a man will when he is waiting for somebody to keep an appointment. He came back with an oil can, skillfully applied a drop here and a drop there, closed her up, tightened the screw, inserted the key, shot the enclosed bolt out, was unable to shoot it in, removed the key, and opened her up.

"It's funny," he said, "how interested you get in a job of this kind. Wait a minute till I get a rag."

So he got a rag and began cleaning all the inner parts of the lock.

When one man is doing his best to help another is no time for the other to exhibit impatience. He must govern himself. He must neither pace back and forth like a dangerous animal nor keep tabs on the time like a harmless lad who has but just been given his first watch. As Burton long ago wrote in his *Anatomy of Melancholy*, "Hope and patience are the sovereign remedies for all, the surest reposals." Oh, repose on them! Content yourself with teetering gracefully from one foot to the other like a person in no particular hurry. He cleaned all the parts and examined them carefully with eye and forefinger.

"Wait a minute," he said, "till I get a file."

By this time life had resumed in the hardware store. Wellfed clerks had returned from lunch. Customers came and went. Automobiles passed in the street. Somebody had turned on the radio, and somewhere the Better Biscuit String Ensemble was playing a Brahms Hungarian dance. He came back, dancing (it seemed to me) like a young Hungarian, and began to file the parts of the lock. When he had filed one part he put that part aside and filed another part. It was not astonishing, if the lock needed so much filing, that it had ceased to work properly. As he had said, it was funny, in the colloquial sense, how interested a man could get in that kind of job. So, I thought, patient prisoners file away by night at the bars of their prisons while guards pace ramparts. I remembered Acadia, where

Neither locks had they to their doors, nor bars to their windows;
But their dwellings were open as day and the hearts of the owners.

The Better Biscuits seemed to be playing it in Hungarian. He filed while I paced. *But at last he escaped!* He wiped his face with the oily rag, put it in his pocket, reassembled the parts of the lock, closed her up, tightened the screw as if tightening it forever, and inserted the key.

"If she won't work *now*," he said, "it is my opinion that she never will."

He turned the key easily back and forth, but the enclosed bolt never budged. I suspect now, after consulting the encyclopædia, that he had filed away the obstacle that must be overcome by the key or other device.

Since then he has sent me the new lock, and I should have already put it in the kitchen door except that something must be done about the door. The new lock fits nicely into the cavity, but the keyholes do not coincide with those in the door.

IN DEFENSE OF MACHINES

By *George Boas*

SO much has been written about machines and the Machine Age that the very words are taboo in polite conversation. The Machine Age, like Freudianism and War Guilt and Flaming Youth, is a topic of which everyone is sick and tired. But so much that has been said on the subject is muddled or beside the point or both, that one who is interested in the analysis of ideas may be pardoned perhaps for continuing the conversation, even though the audience gets up and leaves when he begins.

It is in a way absurd to discuss any great social movement in logical terms. Social movements are made by psychology, not logic. Yet it is barely possible that if everyone caught in the current would stop and think he might find a way of crawling out on dry land. But as a matter of fact no one to speak of is going to stop and think. Some people stop and scream, like the poor English weavers when the Industrial Revolution began concentrating production in factories or the conscientious objectors during the War. But such screaming is rarely effective because it is bad form. All the more difficult is it for people to stop and think. For thinking is not only bad form but hard. There is, moreover, the possibility that society as a whole, or even its major sub-divisions, gets what it wants, and when large sections of society find that what they want is illegal—as is happening in American cities in regard to alcohol—they simply devise their own ways of nullifying laws or resisting change. Note the electoral status of the Negro in the South, the success of the Russian Revolution, the survival of Anglo-Saxon culture in England and, for that matter, the absorption of pagan divinities by institutionalized Christianity.

Thinking, therefore, may do no actual good in changing anything but men's minds, but it is at least harmless, which one cannot say of screaming.

To turn, then, to machines. We are first told that though man invented them to be his servants he has become theirs. The Frankenstein motif, as Mr. Stuart Chase pointed out in *Harper's* in March, 1929, seems to be the most prominent theme of the screamers. As Mr. Chase clearly indicated in that article, this argument is a gross exaggeration. Man is no more a slave of his machines now than he has ever been, or than he is to his body, of which they are—as I think Samuel Butler first suggested—an extension. A farmer is certainly as much of a slave to his primitive plow or sickle as a factory hand to his power loom or engine. Anyone who has ever lived on an old-fashioned farm knows how the farmer and his family get up at four in the morning to sharpen their instruments, filing, cutting, nailing, repairing, lest the machines on which their lives depend fall to pieces. I have lived closely enough to French peasants to observe them sweating and groaning over their tools. When they have no automatic binders and reapers they cut their wheat with sickles and bind it idyllically by hand. Are they who spend endless brutalizing hours in the fields because of the laziness and general inefficiency of their machines more free than our Western ranchmen with their tractors? I have seen milk become diseased and filthy because there was no ice or ice-machine and eggs wasted because there were no incubators and grain rotting because there were no reapers. The machines of primitive men, the handlooms, the sickles, the wooden plows, the animals—which modern machines have often replaced—tyrannize over their owners not by their power but by their very weakness. Primitive men, with the possible exception of the Bushman who strangles his prey and eats it raw and goes naked and sleeps in the open and has no family life—if there be such a creature—are like the dutiful husbands of professional invalids.

In the second place, so far as I know, no clear definition of a machine has ever been given. A steamboat is a machine, according to Silas Bent—and in his opinion indeed the beginning of the steam age is the beginning of the machine age. But what makes a steamboat a machine and a sailboat a non-machine? The fact that condensed vapor instead of the wind makes it go? The fact that human beings had to freeze and half starve to catch the wind? But after all they roast and suffocate at least to boil the water to make that steam, if it is manpower one is thinking of. Steam undoubtedly produces much of the ugliness and dirt of our cities, but we are not for the moment discussing the æsthetic aspects of the question. Why steam is more mechanical than wind or falling water or muscle-driven hammers is somewhat obscure. A sailboat, a rowboat, an inflated goatskin, a log are all equally machines. A linotype, a handpress, a pen, a reed, a charred stick are all machines. They are all mechanical supplements to man's corporeal inadequacies. They differ in quantity of output, in excellence of production, in speed, *i.e.*, in what is usually called efficiency. A stone hurled from a sling at an insolent neighbor is as mechanical as shrapnel hurled from a cannon. It does not kill so many men; it is a worse machine. But man has always relied in part on mechanical devices, although he has dreamed of a time in the distant past when they were unnecessary because of the fertility of the earth, the simplicity of human desires, the general health of humanity, and its blissfully divine ignorance. No one would call the time of Nero a machine age; but read Seneca's Ninetieth Epistle. Machines are precisely what differentiate us from the brutes. Some people of course would prefer that the differentiation be less marked.

When I have pointed this out in conversation with primitivistic friends I have been invariably charged with sophistry. They have always insisted that my definition of "machine" was too broad. My answer is that the only alternative they offer arbitrarily identifies a machine with a bad machine. But any student of "Logic I" knows that either all machines are bad because they are machines or because of something else. And if only some and not all machines are bad, then their badness is not the fact that they are machines. Take the case of the woman who calls a player-piano a machine but refuses to call a piano a machine. Yet a piano is a harp whose strings are plucked not by fingers but by little pieces of crow-quill or hard leather. The harpsichord does not do much more than could be done by hand. Does that put it in the class of player-pianos? The answer to this question does not lie in any principle of construction. It lies in what you want to get out of the instrument. People who call player-pianos machines feel that it is better to play a piece of music inaccurately so long as one has maximum responsibility for what is played than to reproduce even the good playing of someone else. People who call all three instruments machines want above all an accurately rendered piece of music. One group thinks of the producing, the other of the product.

But that is not a question of machines *vs.* non-machines. It is a question of whether producing or consuming is better. Romanticists tend to think that activity, doing, originality are the greatest goods, regardless of what one does. Anti-romanticists are likely to think in terms of ends. The ungracious answer is that there is plenty of room in the world for both producers and consumers, and that no one can be exclusively one or the other. As a matter of fact, the present age furnishes amazing possibilities for the producers. There has probably never been a time when artists and scientists were freer to satisfy their desires for creation. Think of the universities and learned foundations which support men not to teach others, not to think of utilitarian ends, but simply to pursue research. The most absurd investigations are sanctified by the superstition that pure research is noble and deserves free maintenance. It is taken for granted nowadays that artists "be true to themselves," and few would dream of minutely prescribing what a painter or poet should produce.

II

In fact the real clash in opinion is probably ethical. We are—a great many of us—unhappy today and, following a long tradition, we attribute our unhappiness to the economic structure of our civilization. But one can find such outcries of woe as early as eight hundred years before Christ in the works of Hesiod. The crop of cynicism and despair which we uncritically think of as modern is simply human. There has often in the past been as profound and as general despair among the articulate members of society. We read more books and essays of our own time than we do of other times. But those of us who know anything about the history of ideas can find the most striking analogues to our contemporary attitude from Hesiod—if not from Homer—down: yearning for the past, which was of course better than the present; yearning for a society without arts, sciences, or crafts, where the earth bears spontaneously and there is neither money, trade, nor private property; yearning for happy islands beyond the seas, praise of noble savages. The Golden Age took the place of the Age of Handicraft, the Scythians and the Hyperboreans of American Indians, pre-Conquest Mexicans, or South Sea Islanders. This unhappiness of ours, which in its literary form expresses itself in tirades against steam, electricity, urban life, manufactures, cannot, therefore, be attributed to machines.

Machines are not the cause either of happiness or unhappiness. They may be present or absent at the time when a man is miserable or blissful. They are irrelevant to what is called our spiritual welfare. Just because a man has a radio is no reason why a man should feel that he has been transported either to Heaven or Hell, unless a man wants to have or to brag of having what his fellows have. The same thing is true of our other possessions. Some of us snooty members of society feel a certain self-esteem in not having many of the right things to have. As for mechanized industry, it is simply not true that the farmer on his isolated farm in the old days in New England, without radio, telephone, automobile, tractor, reaper, and so on was any happier than the factory hand in Lowell or Lawrence—when there actually was industry in those cities. Some of them were probably happy; others were living a mean, stinted, swinish life, crabbed and thwarted, sickly in mind and body, full of the lowest motives that ever disgraced the human soul. If rustic life was so delightful, why did the rustic fly to the city as soon as he could find a city to fly to and the railroad fare? The pastoralist is usually either a genuine lover of rural things or a city dweller to whom the country means the spring gardens, the old swimming hole, barn dances, and corn husking, rather than winter, weeding and "cultivating," hauling water, the wood pile, drought, and insect pests.

To be sure factory hands can play a good second to farm hands so far as a dreary life goes. They are as a mass an unlovely lot. In my boyhood in Providence I used to see men, women, and children trudging to the mills at six-thirty in the morning, tin dinner pails in hand—and not so full at that, in spite of Mark Hanna—to return at six-thirty at night. They were pale and rickety, God knows, and nothing for the mill owners to look in the eyes. But that does not mean that their contemporaries on the farms were red-cheeked and stocky, effervescing with vitamines, sleeping late in the morning and going to bed early, delighting in robust rural pleasures.

Who has yet found the key to human happiness? Who knows whether there is a key to be found? We do know that it is not always produced by possessions—though it sometimes is. And, furthermore, we know that a man who has health is more likely to be capable of happiness than a man who is sickly. Can we attribute modern hygiene to anything other than our various 'scopes and 'graphs? Instruments of precision have been all important in producing modern longevity and health. For it was not unaided brains. The brains have always been there. But the brains could not see without lenses. I am no worshipper of mere hygiene nor am I extolling two-fistedness and red-bloodedness and he-manship. But it simply does not make sense to say that the millennium would set in if we could all relapse into dirt and disease. It would make no difference to some of us, I admit, and doubtless the human race would get used to it in time. But the fact that Occidentals have spent such effort to eliminate the combination is some evidence of its lack of charm. Unless it was done for self-mortification.

This point needs no emphasis, although many of the opponents of the machine seem to think that Oriental squalor is a help to the inner life. There are, to be sure, greater opportunities for a would-be saint in filth than in cleanliness, but that is precisely because human beings dislike it so. But the inner life is not entirely an affair of corporeal asceticism. I venture to suggest that the inner life of a Noguchi or an Einstein is as fine as that of a St. Simeon Stylites. I admit that I cannot prove it. Still one could point to dozens of men and women today whose works show as noble a perception of human values as those of their ancestors in a supposed machineless age. We still have mystics, devoted scientists, great artists. Religion, love, creative power, intelligence seem to be no less in evidence today than they ever were, and the lack of them no less bewailed in literature. A period which has produced a new religion (Christian Science), seen the increasing hold of an old one (Roman Catholicism), the rise of pacifism and internationalism, a new physical science, an artistic style in painting, sculpture, architecture, music, and literature has not been deprived of its inner life.

Machines are as indifferent to the inner life as they are to happiness. The inner life—if the term indicates the ability to think and to dream and all that is entailed in thinking and dreaming—is independent of the presence or absence of machines. Introverts have been and still are able to crawl into themselves in spite of factory whistles and automobile horns, and extroverts had no difficulty in finding trees to chop down and men to fight when they could not swat flies or pilot airplanes. One of the best proofs of the irrelevancy of machinery to the spirit is the flood of anti-machine literature. How in the world do these writers find the time to compose their essays and sermons in a breath-taking age dominated by a soul-gobbling Moloch? It is true that many of their productions seem to have required a minimum of reflection. But the Twentieth Century has no corner on unintelligence. If people would only read past as well as present literature, they would understand why President Eliot was able to house what was worth salvaging of three thousand years of writing on a five-foot shelf. But when we think of the past we forget the fools and remember the sages. We reverse the process for our own time.

III

One of the points especially emphasized by the enemies of machines is that they substitute something lifeless for something vital and human. Concretely, this means that a farmer cannot love a tractor or an incubator as he could a horse or a hen. This is very probable, particularly if the farmer started farming with horses and hens. But it is not absolutely certain otherwise. Machines can be as lovable as animals. Who has not known engineers who literally love their locomotives, or boys who care for their radios, speed boats, and automobiles as if they were alive? People are constantly personifying their machines as they do boats. They brag about their accomplishments as if the machines were able to accomplish things independently of their operators. One can always love that with which one can identify oneself, and a man can identify himself with a power loom or a turbine as well as with a football team, his family, or his wife. Think of a musician and his beloved violin or flute about which so many romantic stories are invented. Some machines are lovable and some aren't. As a boy I used to hate the old coal furnace which I was delegated to feed and water and clean, and it required all the attention that a voracious and diarrhœic infant might demand. Today I worship my gas furnace with its exquisite little thermostat and its complete autonomy. It costs as much as a steam yacht, but love is blind. It can go the limit as far as this doting old fool is concerned. Another man might hate it and love the now abandoned coal furnace. The lovableness and hatefulness of these things is not entirely a function of their mechanical nature. It is in large measure a function of the person who owns or tends them. The old debate on the relative merits of cats and dogs as pets is very much like this—and no more sensible. For emotional qualities are in popular speech attributed to the things that arouse them and not to us in whom they are aroused. So we say that a chair is comfortable, meaning that we are comfortable in the chair. And until human beings all react emotionally in the same way on all occasions to the same things—until women cease to ask, "What in the world could he see in her?"—there is no laying down the law about the inherent lovableness or hatefulness of anything.

Nor is it true that modern machines absorb us and make us part of them more than primitive machines did. A day laborer is as much part of his pick and shovel as the operator of a steam shovel is part of it. If a man is assumed to be his own boss, to be living on a small farm near the Equator, where we shall imagine that he can work or not without either starving or freezing, where there are no malevolent micro-organisms, and food drops from the skies like manna, then of course he can lay down his tools at any time and pick them up at any time, as a woman can lay down and pick up a piece of embroidery. But such an earthly paradise has not existed since Adam ate the apple, and there is no sense in arguing as if it had or could. The Gloucester fisherman out for cod off the Grand Banks is probably living as non-mechanical and primitive a life as is possible for modern Americans. Is he less a part of his boat, sails, and tackle than the factory hand is of his levers and belts and spindles and presses? He makes more

different motions and he may find them more interesting—
though it is questionable whether the factory hand would—
but he is no less absorbed into his tools.

It will be said that the old machines, actuated by human
muscles rather than by steam or electricity, at least helped a
man's creative power. Friends of the machine are constantly
being told that hand-weaving is creative whereas machine-
weaving is not. The old French artisan, we are told, lived a
life of creativity; he stamped things with his own individuality;
he projected his personality into his products. The modern
American factory hand is passive; he makes nothing; his
product is standardized. This, within limits, is true of the
factory hand. But it was also true of the artisan. He had
certain styles and patterns which he reproduced endlessly, as
our great-grandmothers reproduced world without end the
same old quilting patterns. That man's products have always
been standardized is proved by archæology and the history of
taste. If there had not been standardization, how could
archæologists date works of art by their style, material, and
subject matter? There is no more individuality in the cave
drawings at Les Eyzies—which are the most primitive works
of art we have—than in the photographs of today. Yet
drawing and painting are practically free of mechanical fetters.
Peruvian pre-Columbian weaving is hardly the product of the
machine age, yet we see running through it the same standardized weaves, the same colors, the same designs. Artists up
to modern times almost always were working on commission;
they executed orders; and it is a sheer falsification of history to
think of their carrying out in matter the fancies of their
dream-life. We have so much evidence of this that there is an
embarrassment of choice.

One who knows history knows that the love of the individual,
the different, the original is modern, wherever it exists at all.
Where we find standardization of taste today we find not a
product of the machine age but the survival of a long tradition.
People in general have always wanted to be like everyone else

in their social group—have we not books of etiquette running back to the fourteenth century at least? There are undeniably a great many people today—perhaps even the majority for all I know—who still want to be indistinguishable from their fellows. At the same time it is possible, if not always easy, for people even to think differently, whereas a century or so ago it was literally impossible if one wished to save one's skin.

As one digs into this discussion one finds the instinctive hatred that many people have always had for innovation. We do not hate machines, we hate new machines. A woman will object to buying a dress cut out by machine, but will not object to buying one sewn by machine. The very person who objected to the player-piano had no objections to a phonograph; she grew up with one and learned all the music she knows from it. I find myself fuming at automobiles and yearning for the old bicycles. I can remember old folks shaking their heads over telephones as their juniors now curse out the dial phones. I have heard a gardener in France inveighing against chemical fertilizers which *violent la terre*, as if horse manure were non-chemical. Sailors in the windjammers railed against the steamboat, and steamboat crews think none too kindly of the johnnies who sail oil-burners. Greek and Roman literature is full of invective against any kind of navigation, for it takes the pine tree off its mountain top and sends men wandering.

Obviously a new machine, like an old one, must be judged on its merits, not on its novelty. But the fact that it is novel should not condemn it. Here are two stalwart platitudes. But think of the fools who objected to anæsthesia, to aeronautics, even to cooked foods, because they were not "natural." The question cannot be settled by the wild use of question-begging epithets. We must each establish a system of values for ourselves or absorb that of our social group, and judge machines by it as we do everything else. There is no other way of evaluating anything.

As we all know—we have certainly heard it frequently

enough—the real question is what to do with our leisure. There is no doubt that we can have more of it now than we ever could in the past—if we want it. If it be true that movie palaces, dance halls, and speakeasies are crowded, that radios are going night and day, and automobiles are whizzing about like whirling atoms, it would seem as if most people had found the answer. It is an answer which displeases the magazine writers. That is because writers are by nature people who enjoy and need quiet and solitude and cannot understand other people's enjoying and needing noise and society. But can they point to a time when the leisure class as a mass was less ignobly amused? We happen to have a very large leisure class. It acts as idle human beings have always acted: the theater, the gaming table, the divan. Did anyone seriously think that it would take to improving its mind or sit cross-legged in rapt contemplation of its collective navel? Leisure is man's one opportunity to satisfy whatever appetites he happens to have. And no one can say that he is forced by lack of libraries, educational institutions, museums, and the like to spend it staring at films or boozing and petting. The fact is that most people are what their cultured fellows would call sots and always have been. And the probability is that in modern times— whether because or in spite of machines—they have more chance to rise from the sty than they have ever had. The machine has neither given them wings nor cloven hooves. In the very nature of the case it could do neither.

MANNERS

AMERICAN AND ENGLISH

By *Mary Borden*

WHAT are good manners? Do they make the man or do they, as some who admire rough diamonds think, only make him less of a man? Sometimes one is half persuaded by the old people who remember wearing furbelows, feather boas, and bustles that manners have sadly deteriorated since their day; but I fancy that they have merely changed, and that the pattern of good manners is a simpler thing than it used to be, just as our frocks are simpler, and for the same reason.

There is a close connection between manners and clothes. You can't curtsy in a tight skirt. But the connection is not only with frocks. Manners must adapt themselves to the paraphernalia and tempo of life. There is no time nowadays for elaborate bows and the sweeping flourishes of top hats. If an admiring male tried on Fifth Avenue or Piccadilly the sort of greeting suitable to ladies in sedan chairs or in open carriages, he'd be run over or run in for holding up the traffic. The most he can do is wave a hand toward the hand that is waved to him. Hurry and noise fix the style of our behavior. Good style, good form, good manners, these are not good unless they fit their surroundings. And so the elaborate decorative standards of the leisured nineteenth century have been replaced by a simplicity, a severity, and a brevity befitting a hurried world of dust and crowds and snorting machines. Motors and aeroplanes, undergrounds, elevators, and telephones have designed our clothes for us and our manners. And whether we like the

From *Harper's Magazine*, December 1929; copyright, 1929, by Harper & Brothers Used by special permission.

new style or the old is of no consequence. We are helpless. We are not consulted. The great machine rushes on, whirling us up and down, sucking us in and blowing us out of the funnel of life, like some enormous vacuum cleaner; and the problem of decent, becoming, agreeable behavior becomes a problem more serious than that of the curve of a bow or the pattern of a greeting. Indeed, the question presents itself, will good manners survive at all in this frenzied modern world? Is it possible to remain serene in the hustle and lend to life by one's gestures, words, and expression of countenance something of the charm that depends upon gentleness?

Again, another question, and the young world of today seems to be asking it: do manners really matter any more? Is courtesy important? Elegance of demeanor, charm of gesture, grace of phrase, aren't these worn out hypocrisies, unsuitable and worthless relics of an elaborate insincerity that we are glad to be rid of? And the answer of youth seems to be, "No more nonsense of that sort. No more humbug." And the young women say, "We don't want chivalry; we want equality." And the young men say, "We've no time and no use for fine clothes, fine manners, fine phrases. If you want to be treated as men, so much the better. It'll save us time." And as most of what they say to one another is said on the telephone or to the accompaniment of a jazz band, what they do say and the way they say it do not really seem to matter at all.

They understand one another, and that, presumably, is the main thing. They've evolved a sort of shorthand conversation, a telegraphic social style; a technic that, compared with the soft subtleties of the French salon and the French boudoir, resembles the rattling of typewriters and the syncopated beat of drums and cymbals. Young America laughs with derision at the foppish elegance of nineteenth-century France. Young America condemns affectation. It is in search of reality. It exalts sincerity, truth, naturalness. It is enamored of life, real life, life in the raw, life lived at the highest pitch of excitement. It is vigorous, greedy, gallant, ruthless, and militant.

And in its pursuit of these things, inevitably, good manners are not considered as of very much value. The tendency is not to bother about them. And this is true of English youth too, to a certain extent. The young people of today are all social Bolsheviks of various shades of red. It is not a bad thing. I am one of the middle-aged who suspect that the young people of today are more interesting than we were at their age.

But all this deals merely with a superficial aspect of our topic, with what one may call the mannerisms of our period. The question of what constitutes good manners in the truest sense goes deeper. In the last analysis, the good or bad manners of a nation depend upon character, and are an evidence of the most secret hidden springs in that character.

I take it that the essence of good manners is the gift of putting people at their ease, not the chosen few people whom one likes, but all people. Yes, ease is the word that describes good manners. The great lady is at her ease with the gardener, the housemaid, the ragamuffin, the outcast, and she makes them all feel comfortable in her presence. And bad manners is the faculty of making everyone uncomfortable, whether by being abruptly rude, or overwhelmingly gushing, too cordial or too lacking in cordiality, too contemptuous or too flattering. Too much of anything is bad manners. It destroys ease and makes people fidget. A manner that makes other people nervous is a bad manner, whether it be frankly unpleasant or too pleasant by far.

It is very dangerous to generalize, and in comparing the manners of English and Americans, I know that I am heading straight for trouble. Nevertheless, I believe that a certain kind of comparison is possible and is interesting. Quickly then, at once, to throw off without allowing oneself time to hesitate, a few of these dangerous generalizations. Americans have on the whole too much manner when they have good manners, and the English have too little. The courtesy of an American is apt to be excessive. He overdoes it when he wants to be nice. The Englishman very often so underdoes it that one doesn't know he is trying to be nice at all. It took me ten years to find this out, and I am only now beginning to appreciate the good intentions of some of my taciturn, awkward, glowering English acquaintances. But now that I've grown accustomed to their sort of understatement and am used to the mild mutterings of such friendliness, I find myself bewildered by the voluble cordiality of my own compatriots. They sometimes, I confess, make me feel quite jumpy, and sometimes I quite unfairly suspect their honesty.

In America it is the young ones that are rude, and the old people who are polite. In England it is the other way round. Young people and children are still severely sat on in England. They are brought up to show a decent indiscriminating respect for their elders. A man doesn't really begin to indulge his taste for being disagreeable until after he is thirty. Or, if one divides a nation in a different way, in France it is the common people and the middle classes who have the best manners; it is the great aristocrats who are insolent. In England the middle class has no special title to good manners because it lacks polish and imagination and is essentially less artistic than the French bourgeoisie. Indeed, I think the French middle class the most cultivated, the best read, the most critical of almost any class of people in the world. America has not yet evolved fixed types or classes. Perhaps it never will, so that such a division has no point. Nor would it be to the point to talk of the American farmer as one of nature's gentlemen. When I say that the common people of France have the best manners, I don't mean in the least that they are nature's gentlemen; I mean that they have the exquisite polished manners of men of the world, and a way of expressing themselves that would put many an English squire or Wall Street magnate to shame.

In England people care less about good manners than good form. The two are not at all synonymous. Good form may, and often does, allow one to be very rude. Good form is a question of style, of the way one does the ordinary things of life, like dressing, eating, and walking. It involves taste and a rigid standard of taste. It is the stupid man's refuge, a kind of class egotism. Its temple is the smart club whose shining lights may be the most disagreeable, crotchety old bores on the face of the earth. The English people are in general too insensitive and too lacking in curiosity to have really good manners; for the lack of curiosity means lack of sympathy and a wide indifference to what others feel or think. Being very modest people or, what is the same thing, excessively proud but not vain, and with an intense positive dislike for showing off, their manners on the whole are better than one might expect; for, though they don't care a rap about pleasing, they don't care either about showing their displeasure, and so probably they show little or no sign of any kind. Indifference is their prime social quality; that it does not make for the gaiety of nations goes without saying. But everyone knows that the English are dull dogs among strangers. What all of us don't realize is that their dullness is not blank stupidity, but is probably a decent veil drawn over an insufferable boredom or an intense contempt. Among themselves, the members of an English set are of course charming. Once they are your friends, no friends wear so well; but we are talking of manners, and I take it that the supreme test of good manners is your way of behavior in the presence of people whom you do not know well and do not love dearly. And—well—let us be frank, on such a test, the Englishman can be the rudest man in the world.

Why is he rude? What does his rudeness spring from? Shyness? Sometimes. But not always by any means. Very often it is the opposite of shyness, an intolerable sense of superiority. Sometimes a sudden instinct for cruelty does it. He wants savagely to see the other fellow wince. Often it is sheer callous indifference. I repeat again, the Englishman doesn't care what strangers think of him. He assumes that he is better than they are, and in any case he knows that he is self-sufficing. His blank classic stare means that he wouldn't care a rap if the whole of Europe and the Americas sank under the sea, so long as the British Isles and, incidentally, the British Dominions, survived the cataclysm.

England is a land that has produced amazing contrasts and types of extraordinary interest. The manner of the great English lady, if she is gifted with human kindliness, is the perfection of gentleness and ease, of measured friendliness and suitability. She has been trained in a very thorough school. She knows how to handle crowds and individuals, how to receive royalty and beggars. She is equally at home in Buckingham Palace or a collier's cottage, and everywhere, being totally unself-conscious, she acts rightly, without effort, and makes everyone comfortable. There is no fuss where she is and no flurry. She is quiet, she makes few gestures, she doesn't talk much. She is neither languid nor aggressive. She appears to be quite unaffected. Why, one wonders, is she so natural and so easy? How is it that she is able to adapt herself to so many people without apparent effort? The secret lies, I believe, very deep. Beneath her admirable training is a motive and a motive force that carry her unruffled and serene through a mass of social duties which would crush any other woman in the world. The truth is that she is behaving well from no desire to please, but from a sense of responsibility. She doesn't expect to get anything out of it all, and she doesn't expect appreciation. She is discharging a duty and doing her job, just as the cook, the head gardener, and the cowman are doing theirs, and she preserves through it all an admirable detachment. I mean by her sense of responsibility something very definite. The well-bred Englishwoman feels under a perfectly definite obligation to her village, with its villagers, her tenants, her servants and, if her position is a great one, to half the county with its hospitals and its schools, its political organizations, its girl guides, its boy scouts, its farmers, colliers, tradesmen, milkmen, parsons, bishops, publicans, and village idiots. All these are her intimates, and have in her eyes a claim on her; and in moving among them on easy terms of a very special intimate friendliness she knows that she is merely doing her duty, and so she doesn't lay herself out to charm, dazzle, or impose on anyone. She remains perfectly natural and, quite naturally, has the right sure touch with them all.

But take her out of her county and out of her set, put her down in a railway carriage, or a hotel, or a house in Palm Beach, behold her among people who have no claim on her, should they presume to lay any claim, presto! she may quite suddenly become, our great lady, a very rude woman indeed. For, remember, she doesn't care about people who are not in her own world, and her vanity, if she has vanity, is not of the kind that can be flattered by the attentions of strangers. The main difference between her and her American sister is that she has no worlds to conquer. Her world is her own, and she is satisfied to rule it; and her instinct with a newcomer is always to draw back where an American will lean forward.

The American woman wants to please. She is naturally sociable. She craves stimulus, amusement, admiration, and distraction. She would find the life of our great English lady very dull, with its lone winter evenings in the country. It would surprise her to learn how many evenings the English-woman spends alone, and how many days in the society of her tenants and villagers. She doesn't understand the contentment of such a woman, or suspect the truth that what the English-woman enjoys most is a solitary walk through the beechwoods with her dogs. The American woman, city bred, member of a society that is constantly in a state of flux, is restless, insecure and, if she is alone, ill at ease. It seems so very unnatural to be alone in such crowds. If she is left alone for an evening she feels something is wrong. And so she surrounds herself with people. Her life is an affair of gathering in and sifting out people. Popularity, that is her fetish. But to be popular, one must lay oneself out to please—and sometimes the effort shows.

It is this sense of effort, of a straining for effect, of exag-gerated cordiality that strikes the Englishwoman as so strange in the American. Very probably the Englishwoman discounts unfairly the genuine good will and friendliness underneath. She doesn't understand anyone who really feels like making friends with everybody. She can't believe that the American woman is rushing about like this because she enjoys it. She merely thinks that she is an incomprehensible idiot so to waste her time. It doesn't occur to her when she goes from London to New York that all these hospitable people are genuinely worried about her having a good or bad time. Sympathy? Pity for a lonely stranger? A charitable impulse to be kind to the passer-by? None of these things occurs to our English-woman or her husband when they visit America. They are amazed by the hospitality. And not understanding it, they don't of course appreciate it. The English can't understand American manners because they are themselves neither generous, extravagant, warm-hearted, nor impulsive. They are cool, cautious, reluctant people, shy and reserved, intolerant and incurious; and so American generosity and kindliness strike them very often as very odd indeed.

It is their loss. If any harm is done by such ebullitions of Yankee spirits, the harm is not to the slapdash, innocent, generous, kind-hearted souls who spend themselves being unnecessarily agreeable to the stranger within their gates.

I suppose the truth is that Americans are really more kindly and more sensitive and more vulnerable than English people, with the result that their manners are more unreliable. Social life in America is not smooth. It is jerky, turbulent, changeable. The social climate is an April climate. Clouds rush up, storms break, the skies clear again, all in the course of an evening party. As I have said elsewhere, one is reminded of children. Observe a children's party. The youngsters to begin with are on their best behavior, but presently they grow excited, boisterous, rows begin, tears are shed, and so on. Self-control, an iron self-discipline, an invincible quiet under provocation are not striking characteristics of the American. If he is annoyed he loses his temper. If he is amused he shouts with laughter. If she is jealous she shows it. Indeed, Americans almost always show their feelings too much for perfect manners. Good manners demand that one should ignore one's personal feelings and, if they are disagreeable, that one should hide them.

But this involves us in just what the American despises, hypocrisy. And so we find ourselves back again where we started. America does not, I believe, set very much store by good manners. It suspects its own society leaders. It loathes snobbery and affectation. It becomes impatient, dressed up in its best clothes. It rebels against the multiple conventions of social life. Especially masculine America. Masculine America protests against the elaborate social technic of its women. It digs its toes in and talks through clenched teeth. It goes out of its way to be outspoken. Quite recently it has started a crusade against the foreigner and foreign ways. Nevertheless, were I a waif, a castaway, a stranger, I would rather knock on the door of a hundred per cent American than on any other door in the world, for I know that having no claim on him would be my greatest claim; having no letter of introduction my surest introduction; having no gift to give, my most certain assurance of a kind reception.

What it all comes to is that the American is a kinder and more sociably disposed being than an Englishman, and that he would seldom tread on anyone's toes deliberately. If you care more for genuine friendliness than you do for easy and accomplished technic, plump for the American, but if you prefer the artistry of social intercourse, don't; for the Englishman is a more finished artist in social matters; and the Frenchman, in spite of what our young Americans may say, is the most perfect artist of all. Like the Englishman he has been trained in a very careful school, but he adds to his knowledge as to how things should be done, a real delight in doing them. The Englishman or Englishwoman knows very well how to be agreeable, and for the most part doesn't bother to be so. The American wants to be, but very often doesn't quite know how it is done. The Frenchman both knows how to do it and delights in doing the graceful, pleasant thing. Perfect manners in the last analysis require a sociable heart, a quick, intuitive flair, and a knowledge of the ways of the world. The Englishman has the last, the American the first two, and the Frenchman all three.

IN DEFENSE OF CYNICISM

By *Ernest Boyd*

IT is commonly assumed that cynicism is the mark of embitterment and that a cynic, in consequence, is a man who cannot enjoy life. Women, for some reason, are never credited with being cynical, but it would be rash to assume that they get more enjoyment out of life on that account. On those rare occasions when the mere male gets a momentary glimpse of a woman's real conception of life, when he is shown the world about him as it appears to the feminine eye, he usually thanks God that the struggle for existence does not seem to him quite so fierce as that—that is, if he is a cynic. If he is not he probably spends the evening at his club in the company of unhappy sentimentalists like himself. Women, apparently can take refuge neither in cynicism nor drink; they are pure realists.

Thus, at the very outset, one is confronted by the first tangible evidence of the advantages of cynicism: it is the secret of true masculine happiness, of that happiness which women once imagined they could attain by voting, wielding a latchkey, and refusing to call themselves by their husband's name. A man—cynically—would be perfectly willing to call himself by his wife's name in the circumstances, since he would derive a sardonic pleasure from the thought that, in so doing, he was supposed to be imperiling his personality (if any). The true cynic, so far from resenting, welcomes all opportunities of cheerfully sacrificing the shadow for the substance. He is probably the one person in the world who really enjoys and appreciates the society of the other sex. The cynicism of men is the only moral equivalent of the realism of women.

No man is born cynical, nor—contrary to the popular belief —can cynicism be thrust upon one: it must be achieved by experience. Yet at the same time it is not a conscious aim; one cannot speak of the pursuit of cynicism as one speaks (so ingenuously) of the pursuit of happiness. A cynic if asked to account for himself would have to reply, like Topsy, "I just growed." To the right kind of temperament it is a benign, painless, and almost insensible process whereby the corrupting influences of idealism are lost, the fierce intolerance of youthful optimism is softened, the unprincipled arrogance of constructive thinking makes way for a sweet and natural disbelief in human nature. A beautiful serenity is the skeptic's reward as he views without indignation the ever-charming spectacle of human folly, while on his happily deaf ears fall the appeals which have immemorially stirred hapless men to futile action. Not for him the facile tears, the wasted emotion, the puerile hopes, and the childish despairs which are the sum of that vicious circle known as the story of mankind. It is unnecessary to address to him that warning which Diderot uttered against Rousseau, "Beware of that man, he believes every word he says."

That is the instinctive attitude of the cynic who has realized the deadly perils of sincerity. On the whole, society knows how to deal with the patent charlatan: we throw him to the mob for its solemn delectation or put him out of the way if his charlatanism appears to be inopportune. But it requires all the highest resources of cynicism to deal with that subtlest of menaces to life, liberty, and happiness—the absolutely sincere man. It is he who has a constructive program, or is the frenzied supporter of one. It is he who will selflessly labor for the good of his fellow-men, while they groan in helpless resentment, and the immortal gods laugh sardonically. He is the male counterpart of the good woman, whose devastating righteousness is more obvious, but less fatal, because it is practiced in the more restricted field of domestic and personal conduct. Where the good woman may wreck a family or two, the sincere man will cause rioting, civil war, and the desolation of continents.

The cynic knows well the monstrous egotism of selfless devotion and the ruthless cruelty of pure idealism. He has looked with clear eyes on the victims of the hallucination which prompts these phenomena, and prefers the product of a generous and tolerant skepticism. He applies in the realms of ideas, morals, and conduct a code which is almost universally accepted as a matter of superficial social routine so long as it is restricted to matters of passing convenience. The humblest purchaser of the book of etiquette knows that social life would be impossible if everyone were perfectly honest and truthful, and that one must be prepared not to take certain conventions too seriously, or to seek behind them for eternal verities. But people who are willing to make a garden-party a success on those terms will make existence unendurable by ignoring them, as if it were more important and more intelligent to put up with the conversation of a bore at dinner, or to refrain from asking indiscreet questions, than to be as detachedly polite in the presence of the facts of life itself.

Cynicism teaches that it is as naïve and ill-bred to expect a solution to most human problems as to query the white lies with which we ease the machinery of social life. The fanatical truth-seeker, bent upon reform, believing that progress is anything more than an improvement in plumbing, presents to the cynical mind a picture as distressing as that of a guest insisting that the hostess's hair is false, or insisting that her husband state the exact amount of his income, or where he actually was the last time he telephoned that he was detained at a board meeting. The cynic feels, with Judge Brack, that "people don't do these things," but the contemplation of many metaphorical and actual Hedda Gablers has convinced him that they alarmingly do, thereby providing the *raison d'être* of cynicism, which is the recognition of precisely that fact.

At bottom it is a species of intellectual tact, a feeling that it is slightly indecent, and certainly dreadfully bad manners, to believe too earnestly the usually unbelievable things which engage the attention of the credulous sentimentalist. History and one's own experience show that more tangible good has come of smiling tolerance than from fanatical zeal. If Pontius Pilate had had his way the history of the Western world would have been changed. Horace and Montaigne and Voltaire and Anatole France are nearer to the civilized man's heart than Savonarola, Cotton Mather, or Dwight L. Moody. At their worst they did no positive harm but were charming companions; at their best they did more to make life endurable for others than the solemn altruists. They accepted the fantastic rules of human existence because they were not tortured by that fundamental pessimism, that profound discontent, which can alone explain the actions of those who set out to reform the world.

II

It is always a peculiarity of professional optimists that their own lives are miserable. They can never seize the day, enjoy the hour, accept unreservedly the exquisitely fleeting moments of pleasure which come to one as irrationally and as unexpectedly as everything else in nature's far from divine plan. Nor do they experience that Nirvana-like condition when, in the absence of positive enjoyment, there is a general sense of well-being as each day dawns and finds the human race as ridiculous and as amusing as ever. Oh! that daily reassurance as one unfolds the newspaper and discovers that one wasn't wrong, that the circus is going on as it has from the beginning of time, with perhaps an extra ring or two added each century. No wonder the serious thinker, whatever his professions, is depressed by the evident futility of his hopes, even though his retort is to plunge still deeper into the labyrinth of progress and reform!

It is obviously impossible to hurl oneself during a lifetime against the jagged rocks of reality and feel happy about it save on the same principle as ascetics flagellate themselves, sadists inflict pain, and masochists beg to be hurt and humiliated. While the pleasure of these perversions is admitted, we know the pleasure to be pathological and do not take it as a normal index of enjoyment. Similarly, while martyrs invariably—their admirers tell us—rejoice in the torture inflicted upon them, their doing so is merely a reflection upon their inability for normal rejoicing, their unhealthy satisfaction in substitutes for the pleasures and satisfactions of this world. As well argue that a girl would not prefer to know that she was pretty than to hear herself acclaimed the foremost authority on cuneiform inscriptions in South Dakota. The wish to be both would, of course, be sheer idealism at its worst.

Every cynic knows that his optimism dates from the moment when he began to lose his youthful belief in human perfectibility and his youthful conviction that he was born to help to improve it. In the anguished years of one's nonage, armed with a highly plausible and unscrupulously optimistic theory of the universe, one's own personal feelings were pessimistic. If it takes the ingenuousness of youth to be a theoretical optimist, it takes the cynicism of later years not to be a practical pessimist. Nature, with characteristic malignity, saddles one at that age with the crushing burden of an optimistic philosophy of life in general, without supplying the fortitude requisite to reconcile it with the brutal facts of which one is all too conscious. Hence the deep-seated melancholy of a young man with a scheme for peopling the earth with supermen or establishing a reign of justice and freedom amongst men.

It is a curious fact that, while convention pretends that youth and happiness are more or less synonymous, we have embodied in the proverbial phrase "if youth but knew" our profound conviction of the contrary. What are the implications of the proverb? Obviously, that knowledge and experience are essential to a proper understanding and enjoyment of life, and that the average man usually acquires these too late to enable him to profit by them. In the circumstances his existence falls into two periods of frustration—when he is too

young to know any better and too old to do any better. It is
the cynic's good fortune to have avoided that fate; he knows in
time to take the fullest advantage of his knowledge. Hence the
resentment of the sentimentalists and Utopians, expressed in
the current superstition that cynicism is a manifestation of
bitter rage, and in Bernard Shaw's statement that every man
over forty is a scoundrel—which, being interpreted, means
that he is then best equipped to resist the persuasion of the
soothsayers.

When we are young we are unhappy because we believe too
many things which are either untrue or unprovable. In disillusionment lies true happiness if one has the good luck to become disillusioned gracefully, that is, cynically. Indignation
and cynicism do not properly belong together; in fact, the latter
excludes the former, and the reason why cynicism is so widely
misunderstood and mistrusted is that so many people either
refuse to grow up intellectually or are unable to stand successfully the shock of disillusionment. A person troubled
by morbid fears and terrorized by superstitions is seen at
once to be a pitiable object by people not similarly affected. One man's beliefs are another man's superstitions,
yet only the cynic is capable of drawing the obvious conclusion that the fewer one's beliefs the greater one's peace of
mind.

Here and there occasional exceptional individuals are found
who can be trusted with an idea, a belief, but it is evident that
these things were never intended for general consumption.
They are bad for the average human being, both individually
and collectively. Personally he is miserable when the weight
of an idea affects his consciousness; in the mass he is dangerous
when he rallies his fellows to action on behalf of it. What is
history, after all, but the record of the periodical crusades for
or against some bogey which believing men have evolved out
of their credulity and fear? Sometimes it is an idea, sometimes
a person, sometimes a nation, sometimes a race, but at all times
it is a phantom, usually inexplicable to posterity, and often to

the crusaders themselves, once they have recovered from the stampede.

A cynic can be trusted neither to make his own life nor the lives of others miserable on principle. His social agnosticism is his salvation. He does not and cannot prevent others from bemusing themselves and bedevilling their existence, but he is temperamentally unable to join in. He can be trusted with even the most explosive ideas, for his attitude towards them is comparable to that of a book-collecting connoisseur who handles the most priceless volumes without damaging them, whereas the earnest student returns his dog-eared volume to the library in even a worse condition than before. Like many an honest bibliophile, he may not even open them. Cynicism is, therefore, conducive to peace, to urbanity, to all the virtues which spring from a skeptical feeling of neutrality in the thousand and one matters over which the mass of men groan, exult, and—fight. It will hardly be denied that Copenhagen and Barcelona were more agreeable places of residence in 1915 than Rheims or Cologne. Cynicism is a species of benevolent intellectual neutrality. Neutrals, of course, are always scoundrels in the eyes of the combatants.

However, as a matter of realistic fact rather than sentimental fiction, there is no doubt that a soldier on leave who could have gone to a good hotel in Barcelona, instead of London or Paris, would have enjoyed his leave much more, and have taken a somewhat different view of the question of Spanish neutrality than the eminent statesmen who so bitterly resented the existence of any unviolated spot in Europe. On the same principle, one would instinctively turn to a cynic for understanding and guidance in time of trouble, for his help would be forthcoming without tracts and sermons. It was not the cynical but the pious father who drove his erring daughter into the streets, when a little common sense and knowledge of the world might have saved her from a life of shame and playgoers from many a heart-rending scene.

A vast amount of trouble in the world could be avoided if we were only blessed with the gift of cynicism. If it were the business of a cynic to make converts and outline a program with which to lure customers one might dwell on some of the manifold advantages which would automatically follow conversion. Death would lose its terrors because it would be accepted without the faintest thought or hope of reward, punishment, or survival. Life would lose some of its horrors, for no army could be enlisted from recruits cynically convinced that militarism and pacifism were equally absurd and a hero's grave the most undignified imaginable; no politician could orate, because cynical laughter would greet his preposterous rodomontade; no government could be elected along popular lines because cynicism and adult suffrage are incompatible terms.

Minor amenities resulting from a world inhabited by convinced cynics are too numerous to mention. The marriage problem would be solved without the aid of Judge Lindsey, because jealousy and domestic sentimentality are emotions unknown to the disillusioned affection of cynicism. Follow-up letters, sales talks, fraternal orders, Mother's Day, publicity agents, radio programs, law enforcement, non-refillable bottles —but why enumerate all the varied and variegated strains upon human credulity which are so profitably used to beguile the tedium of the average life between one slaughter and another, between the unwanted cradle and the unremembered grave? Seek ye first the serenity of cynicism and all these will be added unto you.

III

One unconsciously adopts the evangelical manner and steps out of character in thus preaching the cynic's gospel. Of course, he has none. All he can say, speaking for himself, is that he is unmoved by most of the things that seem to disturb his fellow-men, and he concludes that if there were no demand for buncombe there would be no supply. That is why he has no remedies to suggest, no discipline to enforce, no great moral truth to vindicate. He has never discovered that life has any particular meaning, and he strongly suspects the meanings read into it by ingenuous people who are patently incapable of drawing a sound conclusion from the obvious facts before them. He has noticed that the kind of person whose lips move when spelling out a tabloid newspaper has no difficulty in settling the profoundest questions which have engaged the best minds of history.

If he had a gospel and were uncynical enough to imagine he could get converts, his cynicism would restrain him, for how could a cynic be cynical if there were no material for his cynicism to feed upon? If the infinitesimal minority of civilized and, therefore, skeptical minds became a majority, the cynic would have a rude awakening; something would have to be done to restore his disbelief in humanity. He knows, however, that his fears are groundless. Nature began her work well, but we have improved upon it. Whatever illusion may have been possible when the masses were inarticulate, it is now humanly impossible for any but the professional optimists to believe that civilization is the aim of mankind. Save in its plumbing implications, the word grows more and more meaningless, and in due process of time, when every bedroom is equipped with a radio and inspirational talks in Moscow can be heard every night in Pittsburgh, when go-getting salesmen can telephone to Tokyo and see one another's intellectual countenances through television, when airplanes leave for Paris every hour on the hour, when every theater is a movie and every basement in New York a speakeasy—when the triumphs of progress are even more manifest than now, the very memory of what was once and for so long understood as civilized will be a vague memory.

In the approaching synthetic civilization new values will be substituted for old, and people will no more understand what the term really connotated than a post-Prohibition flapper can realize what was once meant by drinking. Graduates in How to Build Up a Mail Order Business courses will doubtless assume that such were the preoccupations of the scholars of

Oxford or the Sorbonne, and a hip-flask culture will be the logical sequel to the hip-flask alcoholic initiation of the rising generation.   In such a world of live wires and exponents of Service there is little danger of too much cynicism.   It may be hard-boiled and corrupt, but it will be sentimental, not cynical. The decline of cynicism corresponds roughly with the rise of industrialism, and the eighteenth century saw its last and finest flowering in literature.   It is an ornament, perhaps the chief ornament, of a civilization that is on the wane.

There will be, presumably, unless they have been lynched, a remnant of the old order, and in that dwindling number the cynics of the future will be found.   By that time the pleasures of cynicism will have become so acute and exquisite that these survivors will be to the cynic of today what a thoroughbred is to a Clydesdale, both fine animals, but one of a more refined quality.   That is as it should be, for the most delicate instrument will be required to measure the complacent and barbarous ignominy of the absurd spectacle.   One sighs cynically for the privilege of being present and of seeing one's worst suspicions confirmed.   The show will be on the grandest scale, and that ridiculous biped, man, will have surpassed himself.   The mountain of industrial and scientific progress will bring forth its mouse, and it will be a little tame, white mouse, running around in its cage, not even the sturdy household variety which still adventures in search of cheese, at the risk of encountering the feline enemy.   It will eat out of its master's hand.

It is not easy in advance to measure the density of cynicism nor the volume which will be provoked in that surviving remnant, but a cynical guess may be made by estimating the effect of modern civilization upon Swift or Voltaire, upon Horace or Juvenal.   Swift at the signing of the Treaty of Versailles, Voltaire in the League of Nations Council, Horace in conference with an efficiency expert, Juvenal writing the Sixth Satire in terms of Hollywood—of such stuff the dreams of cynicism are made.   With the relatively meager material at their disposal, they have left us records that are imperishable, while the vast wealth of our accumulated imbecility lies unexploited. The reason probably is that the cynic of today has no longer even the illusion that his cynicism can help. He keeps it to himself, a refuge in his daily hours of need, and the last stronghold of masculine privilege which has not been invaded by women. When that invasion takes place, the cynic's occupation will be truly gone, for the end will be in sight. Life will not go on.

But, the cynical mind reflects, that would mean progress in the best sense of the word. A truce to such pretty, sentimental daydreams.

LONELY AMERICANS

By *Van Wyck Brooks*

ONE cannot have wandered far from America, either in the flesh or in fancy, without coming to feel that the destiny of the American is a lonely destiny. Loneliness is stamped on the American face; it rises like an exhalation from the American landscape. We are the most inarticulate of peoples, and the most essentially unsocial. We go through life, nine-tenths of us, without establishing a true communication with any other human soul.

To the casual eye, no doubt, the contrary is the truth. If we are lonely, we are also gregarious; ours is preeminently, for example, an urban civilization. In our actions we follow the laws of the herd as no European people follows them. And consider the mutual-benefit societies that gather in their vast nets such multitudes of the plain folk. We are inarticulate, but surely we are also talkative. All day long, in offices, in hotels, at conventions, our chatter goes up among the sky-scrapers. But is it not a perpetual attempt, this very gregariousness, to establish communications that we have never been able to establish in our private persons? In what measure do they really meet one another, these frequenters of conventions, these brothers of the badge, these loquacious men of business? They meet in the field of superficial interests, on the plane, not of the highest common factor, but of the lowest common denominator. There is no more solitary spectacle in the world than that of a burly drummer sitting by himself after the convention is over.

Certainly real friendships are always rare. History itself records very few the memory of which may truly be called immortal. And in times of transition like ours—and America is always in transition, in societies that have no settled order, friendship seems all but impossible. Our life, as the war revealed it, is devoured by suspicion. We are of such different races and traditions, we are so constantly passing one another in our pursuit of such incompatible ideals, we have experienced so few things in the same way and at the same moment in our development we undergo and we believe so little in common, that we are able to meet one another in confidence only at intervals and then only on one or two sides of our natures. How many of the facts of our social, our economic, our artistic life are to be explained by this! And what a formidable prospect it suggests of the day when the social revolution that has invaded every other land invades this land of ours where already "ignorant armies clash by night"! In such conditions, to close one's eyes for the moment to these ghastly inferences, the most singular aptitude for friendship is continually baffled.

It has always been so: it was so even in New England in a day when many men, bred under the same conditions, pursued similar ends. "I have felt sure of him, in his neighbourhood, and in his necessities of sympathy and intelligence," wrote Emerson in his journal in the day of Hawthorne's burial, "that I could well wait his time—his unwillingness and caprice— and might one day conquer a friendship. . . . Now it appears that I waited too long." And of Thoreau he said, that he would as soon think of taking Henry's arm as the arm of an apple-tree. This morbid reticence in the American character springs in part from the deep distrust of human nature that belongs to our Calvinistic heritage. "Good fences make good neighbours," says Robert Frost's poem, and the old Yankee believed it, afraid, perhaps, to let down the bars, for the devils that might enter into him. Aside from Bronson Alcott, Emerson's greatest friendship was that with Carlyle; and it is characteristic of American friendships that one end of the rainbow is apt to drop on the other side of the ocean. This explains a part of the singular cordiality that European travelers have noted in us. Americans have always found it easier to make friends of foreigners. There is much to reassure us in the space between the hemispheres.

Undoubtedly, too, this cultivation of reticence has its practical aspect. To foster our distrust of human nature is to sharpen the competitive instinct: when we understand one another, we find it difficult to cut one another's throats. There is something symbolic of the unity of Puritanism and commercialism in the story of John Muir, whose life was divided, one might say, between two activities, that of adoring God in the wilderness and that of cornering the fruit-market in Los Angeles. Solitude has its compensations, and like silence they are sometimes golden.

This loneliness of American life is responsible for certain anomalous types of character we have produced, characters like monstrous growths or fungi that sprout and spread only in shadowy places. Since the days of Mohammed the world had scarcely produced a figure like Brigham Young; and these fabulous and sinister shapes are by no means rare in our history. The Leatherwood God of whom Howells wrote was a familiar phenomenon in the old West, and in our own time we have witnessed, among the founders of strange religions, more than one portent equally disquieting; for we really know so little about one another, and we are at the same time so willing to be deceived and so unfamiliar with any rational standard in human relations, that we are easy victims of imposture. A priest of Mumbo Jumbo is a miracle of sunny candor beside the popes of our American sects.

But it is the gifted ones who are the loneliest in this dark continent where everyone, after the bustle of the day, retires not into the castle of his household but into the dungeon of his confused and anxious ego. Never was the sensitive man so exiled. It is not the artists, perhaps, who feel this; who have struck water from the rock and to whom even the wilderness affords its manna. But those who lack this power surely feel it, and theirs are the voices one hears, in countless stories and poems, endeavoring to establish a network of communications. For there are two kinds of solitude, as there are two kinds of poverty, the voluntary and the involuntary. In one we find ourselves, in the other we lose ourselves, and often it is by escaping from the one that we become eligible for the other.

THE LOST ART OF PLAY

By *Earnest Elmo Calkins*

I

THIS country is destined to cope with the problems of leisure on a scale never before experienced. No matter what we think of technocracy and its alarming conclusions, it is obvious that the necessary work of the world can now be done in comparatively few working hours. This conclusion is inescapable, although the figures of the technocrats have now been scaled down to something like scientific accuracy and show no such crisis as its propounders would have us believe. But, even in a time of prosperity, production was increasing faster than jobs for displaced workers. After the exaggerated figures and the melancholy interpretations are discounted, it is still evident that technological unemployment has been a bigger factor in the depression than was at first suspected; so, even when we settle the major problem of a job (or at least an income) for every breadwinner, the problem of greatly increased leisure will remain with us.

The increase of leisure is not a new thing. It began fifty years ago when working hours and waking hours were almost identical, and no one had yet heard of technological unemployment. Stores were open from seven in the morning until nine at night, and later on Saturdays. Professional men got to their offices at seven-thirty and remained until six. As a young advertising man I was rebuked by the president of one of the large manufacturing companies of the Middle West because I did not reach my office until eight o'clock. He had been waiting half an hour. He was at his office, he said, every morning at seven, summer and winter. Each successive generation has snipped off an hour or so.

My first job, in 1885, was from six-thirty to six-thirty (with one hour off at noon for dinner) on week days, and one hour less on Saturdays—65 hours a week. I was the "devil," and came earlier and worked later than the journeyman printers, but even they put in 59 hours, as did I as soon as I graduated to a "case." In some occupations the hours were longer. After I had walked home, washed up, and eaten my supper, it was time to go to bed, especially in view of the early rising which this schedule imposed. Not much thought was given to leisure then, but, in the fifty years since, the average working time has steadily decreased. Not only the machine, but more efficient methods, contributed, and behind this was the steady, insistent demand for shorter hours. The eight-hour workday, the Saturday-afternoon holiday, the two weeks' vacation, and daylight saving brought daytime leisure to millions. The motor car, moving pictures, radio, and athletic sports took up the slack. Machines that created the leisure produced the apparatus for enjoying it.

The depression has added a larger number of people with more leisure than they know how to occupy. The effect has been apparent in every field that supplies entertainment or recreation. Libraries have been thronged; playgrounds and community centers are crowded; correspondence courses, adult schools, and other methods of self-improvement available at little or no cost are patronized as never before. The proprietors of amusement parks in convention assembled the last month of the old year heard their president predict a bigger and better year for merry-go-rounds, scenic railways, and Ferris wheels. The report of the Westchester Park Association contained the gratifying information that the work is self-supporting, the income from concessions and recreations for which a fee is charged, such as public golf links and bathhouses, showing a net profit over the costs of operation. The National Recreation Association, the body that guides the movement toward community centers and playgrounds, finds the public turning to these amusements in greater numbers.

Already, before the economic problem is solved, the demand for recreation has reached impressive proportions, and is steadily increasing.

Just how much of our time will be needed to do the work of supplying every consumer with what he needs has not been and cannot be worked out until we have first solved that delicate problem of balance between machine production and human consumption, but the disproportion between them is bound to increase. Speaking to the toy manufacturers recently, Paul T. Cherington said:—

"With labor leaders threatening to use force to get a 30-hour work week, you have something real to think about. There are 112 waking hours in a week of 7 days of 16 hours each. Subtracting these 30 hours spent in gainful labor would leave 82 hours. Allow 21 hours for meals, and there are left 61 hours of waking time with which 45,000,000 working people are to do as they please. They will sorely need a technique for utilizing leisure. That will be more play time than we had in our childhood. You as toy manufacturers will find your best abilities called on to provide the equipment by which the play technique can be developed and exercised. It will take something more absorbing than ordinary games to keep 45,000,000 adults happy for 3172 hours a year each. They will need toys to teach them how to play, and playing equipment to enable them to do it as adults."

The grown-up who takes his pleasures and himself seriously may be affronted to hear his apparatus of sport and recreation characterized as toys. There is an anecdote which may give him another point of view. A maid putting a room to rights came upon the chessboard still set up for an unfinished game, and asked her mistress, "Shall I put the master's little playthings away, or will he be using them?"

II

Millions of people, presumably, are going to have in the near future, whether they want it or not, more time off than they ever dreamed of. An entire nation which has never learned to play has been presented with the great gift of leisure. Our playing is, for the most part, done by proxy. We make paid entertainers rich by our inexperience in amusing ourselves. "Since the war," says Professor Cherington, "American expenditure on the various forms of recreation has more than doubled. The *Business Week* estimated that expenditures for recreation in 1919 were $1,700,000,000. In 1927 they were over $4,000,000,000, and in 1929 they were $5,200,000,000, and even in 1930 they were still over $4,000,000,000."

But vicarious amusements are not going to suffice to fill the spare hours which the future will bring. We must do better than that. At the rate that labor-saving machinery is being developed, even Mr. Green's 30-hour week may be outmoded. True, his firm demand in the interest of organized labor was more concerned with distributing what employment still exists than in increasing the leisure of workers, but the outcome will be the same in any case. We must consider, therefore, what we are going to do with so much spare time. We have not been trained for it, and all our traditions are against it. We do not, as a people, care for those quieter and simpler amusements which are easily and cheaply available, which do so much for the spirit—walking, observing, studying, learning, gardening, practicing a craft, engaging in community activities, making the most of human companionship. It is an encouraging sign that many of the unemployed have turned to self-improvement, but these are a small fraction of the army, and their studies are mainly devoted to improving their earning capacity rather than to developing their qualities as well-rounded human beings.

Play for grown-ups is just beginning to figure in the scheme of things. Before the days of leisure it was a small problem for adults. The craving for amusement and recreation was checked by the fact that it was a full-time job to earn a living. The century-old houses which we modernize for our summer homes had no porches, no outdoor sitting rooms. Their occupants had no time to sit down and admire the scenery. Play was then the heritage only of children, who, when they grew up, put away childish things for the serious business of life. But now we have to consider what use might profitably be made of leisure by some fifty million adults with at least nineteen solid weeks a year free from all duties, who will finish their short workday with abundant energy, and must find a safe, sane, satisfying outlet for that energy if their new-found leisure is not to become a menace.

These people now turn naturally to popular organized amusements which are destitute of the spirit of play. They must acquire a new conception of play, one that demands active participation instead of passive acceptance. Radio, movies, athletic spectacles, will all have a large place, but they will no longer suffice for a grown-up, healthy population. There must be something to make demands upon them physically and mentally, to develop and express them, and to give exercise to invention and imagination. Since play begins in childhood and is the natural expression of the young, when not stifled by too many predigested toys, it is well to look at the playthings of children today to see what they promise for a future that will offer so many opportunities.

III

Possibly the art of play is lost in childhood. I wonder if children play today as they did when I was a boy. A glance at contemporary toys convinces me that little is left for a child to do. Just the other day I saw a marvelous miniature railroad train—indeed, the complete rolling stock of a system, with engines both electric and steam, cars both passenger and freight, day coaches, Pullmans, baggage cars, freight cars, gondolas, and tanks, faithful in detail and accurately reproduced to scale—designed for boys whose parents are able to pay five hundred dollars for a toy. When a modern boy is confronted with a plaything so complete and so realistic, I wonder what he does with it. Does he get a tithe of the fun out of it that I did sixty years ago from a string of cars of oblong paste-board box covers mounted on empty spools?

The gap between my primitive train and the real thing was the measure of my amusement; I had to fill the gap with imagination. Modern toys seem to overshoot the mark they aim at. They leave nothing for the child to do. Child psychology is peculiar in these matters; it goes unerringly to the heart of the thing. The child is honest in his preferences; he cares nothing for cost, and he knows what he likes; he selects the toys that still have some play left in them. Who hasn't seen a little girl pass up dolls with real hair, eyes that open and shut, and a wardrobe like a movie star, for some forlorn, shapeless rag baby?

On the last Christmas of the pre-slump era, I spent the day with a brother at a family gathering where there were many of the third generation, including three grandsons. The child who was host brought out his toys for his cousins to play with—a great box of corrugated packing board filled with realistic models of motor cars, trucks, railroad trains, and airplanes, of the sort that fascinates grown-ups more than children. The boys examined the toys with interest, but soon I noticed that they were all piled in the corner of the room, and the boys were playing with the pasteboard box. They played with it all the afternoon, and the toys never got another look. They were too complete, too finished. There are a lot of things you can do with a big pasteboard box and a little imagination.

Why has no one thought of asking children what toys they prefer? That is the approved method in other fields. Research is used to test out and improve all sorts of products, from vegetable shortenings to free wheeling in motor cars, but so far as I know no toy maker has made a study of child play habits to learn what toys have the most play in them. This should be a research directed at the ultimate consumer, not the grown-up intermediary. Presents for children are selected by parents and other adult relatives, and represent what they think children like. Those toys presumably bought for chil-

dren but monopolized by the grown-ups have become a
standing joke. Perhaps it is something more than a joke.

IV

Some worthy folks gathered together at the New York
Museum, the week before Christmas, an exhibition of toys
of other days. Most of these dated from the sixties, about the
time of my own childhood, but they did not represent to any
great degree the toys I knew best. The very fact of their preservation showed that they were not played with, that they were
far too fine and good for childhood nature's daily food. They
were, in fact, antiques of considerable virtuosity, examples of
skilled craftsmanship, preserved rather than used. Toys which
stimulate the qualities of real play are not likely to survive.

I missed among this collection the simpler and more inspiring playthings of my childhood. Here were paper dolls,
but they were a special hand-painted set—the work, no doubt,
of some gifted mother, brought out to show the minister or
Aunt Marion and then put away on the whatnot in the parlor,
but not played with. I should have liked to see a sheet of
paper soldiers, a toy drum, a monkey on a stick, a cat's cradle,
a buzzer. This last was a round disk of tin with holes in the
center, through which a string was passed; when made to revolve rapidly by the twisting and untwisting of the string, it
emitted a faint hum, the pitch of which could be changed by
cutting notches in the disk. There was but one small bag of
marbles, which properly should have been represented by a
complete set—commies, clay of all colors (ten for a cent),
chinas (two for a cent), potteries, glassies, agates (one cent),
and carnelians, usually reserved for taws by affluent sportsmen
(five and ten cents).

It was significant that toys for girls showed greater powers
of survival. There were many dolls of the more elegant class,
with complete wardrobes in contemporary styles, even to
gloves, shoes, and stays; there were beds that were fully
equipped, sets of furniture, trunks, and a miniature practicable

cookstove. But I missed the dolls we knew as "one-cent dolls," "five-cent dolls," and "ten-cent dolls." The one-cent dolls, about $1\frac{1}{2}$ inches tall, had stiff bodies of china, but the five-and-ten variety had flexible cloth bodies with china heads, hands, and feet. I should have liked to see a specimen of that lethal weapon, the rubber gun (a crotch with two rubber bands and a leather tab for the missile), and a whistle made from a willow wand. There should have been quantities of building blocks in various geometrical shapes, one of the most satisfying toys ever devised.

The supreme advantage of the toys of the past was their limitations. Even this selection at the New York Museum lacked the almost ferocious realism and efficiency and completeness of the playthings which fill the windows of modern toy emporiums. Ours were largely homemade, by grown-ups sometimes, but often by the child. They were crude, primitive, and quaint, lacking the slickness and technological completeness of modern machine-made toys. Ingenuity, invention, resourcefulness, and imagination were required, not only to make them, but to play with them. Toys are not a means to an end; they are not tools. Efficiency, therefore, is a drawback rather than an advantage.

Bought toys were mostly of European origin, largely handmade products of German and Swiss craftsmen, and they reflected, of course, the life of the country of origin. The dolls were European types in European dress; the animals those common to European barnyards—asses and oxen, so familiar to the Bavarian peasant, but rarely seen by prairie-bred children. The houses were made of their stone instead of our wood. The building blocks were adapted to the construction of German or Swiss buildings. From them emanated an atmosphere which we, as children, thought to be the peculiar mark of toys, though it was, of course, simply the reflection of their European origin. Today toys are replicas of the life the child sees around him. Ninety per cent are now made in this country. There may be some educational value in this, though there is a loss of charm and picturesqueness; but the question is: Has not something of the spirit of play been sacrificed in making toys so sophisticated?

V

Let me use my own childhood as a temporary laboratory. Most of our playthings were handmade. When Mother's tired fingers dropped a plate, the fragments became a set of dishes on which we partook of Barmecide repasts. When the local dry-goods store delivered a drayload of packing cases to be later chopped up into kindling, we made houses of several rooms, each room a box, and built a small village which lasted until the hatchet fell. With a piece of chalk and a handful of beans, grains, and nuts, we laid out a farm on the attic floor, drawing the ground plan with chalk—here the house, there the barn, cowsheds, and fields—and stocking the place with beans for horses and cattle. There was a black-and-white bean that made admirable Holsteins. Or we set up circuses, with hazelnuts for deer, peanuts for camels, "niggertoes" for rhinoceri, and butternuts with the bark on for elephants. There was a set of chessmen, never used for its ancient and honorable purpose, out of which we created ceremonies and pageants, the unlikeness of the pieces to what we pretended they were giving the games their charm.

The most useful "boughten" toy appears to have been building blocks, originally those oblongs and cubes with "A a," "B b" on them. They rapidly became more complex and versatile, until they culminated in the "erector" outfits of today. Even in their primitive form they were a source of unending amusement. Their combinations were infinite, and developed our ingenuity amazingly. There was a variety known as Anchor, made of clay, their weight adding to the stability of the structures built of them, with arches and keyed shapes and rounded pillars, the possibilities of which seemed inexhaustible. Do the complete and expensive toys of today offer as much?

Shrewd parents got home tasks done by disguising them as games. I did a lot of weeding when I was a boy by pretending I was George Washington and the weeds were Hessians. I pinned up my straw broad-brim into a cocked hat and wore a belt with a wooden sword. The big burdock in the onion bed was General Burgoyne. It was useless for him to surrender. He died with his cohorts.

There is more play in riding a stick than in a lifelike mechanical horse. Children are able to evolve complete games with only a few anomalous objects as counters, to which they assign names and functions of their own. This creative faculty is precious, and should be encouraged. Toys and playthings too complete and realistic stifle it, besides adding to cost without corresponding advantages.

VI

The child is father of the man; as the twig is bent the tree is inclined—so runs a whole chapter of proverbial philosophy. Only after one has lived a considerable portion of his life does the truth of such sayings come home with full force. I realize that much of my ability to get the most out of life in the way of amusement, occupation, entertainment, is the direct product of learning to play as a boy. My present interests are largely the lengthened shadow of my boyhood hobbies. Having been deaf most of my life, I have been driven, more than most normal persons, to find my amusements within myself. Even so, I am merely a little more complete example of the resources of intelligent intellectual and physical amusement which are stored up in most human beings.

I find in myself the same curiosities and satisfactions which I remember experiencing as a boy,—the pleasure of making, of doing things with my hands, with tools, with pen and pencil and brush,—and in them I find my primary escape. I realize now how deep were the impressions made in childhood, and wonder whether this is sufficiently considered by those who design toys and playthings. No one seems to ask whether they are of the sort which will create that proper spirit of play which is going to be so necessary for adults in the greater leisure that impends. Children are in danger of losing all that knack of using their faculties for amusement, that handiness, adaptability, resourcefulness. These are the qualities which lend color to life, the qualities which once made *Robinson Crusoe* a best seller.

There is some contemporary realization of this. There are play schools where children are taught along the lines of their interest, where no great divide exists between play and work; but such institutions are few and small, available only to the well-to-do. Such methods have not penetrated the public schools, though the latter have advanced greatly since my day, when the processes of education were painful and any effort to make school interesting was looked upon with suspicion. Today we are just beginning to realize what an ideal approach to a child's mind is afforded by the painless method of teaching by play.

The Boy Scout movement is intended to teach and encourage proficiency in various crafts and skills that are in danger of disappearing in our present-day civilization. There are groups of boys interested in miniature-yacht racing and model-airplane flying, though the yachts and planes are too frequently bought rather than made. An important contribution toward the development of craftsmanship among boys has been made in the last two years by the Fisher Body Corporation, which deserves for its efforts more commendation than it has obtained. This is the offer of valuable prizes to boys from thirteen to nineteen who complete miniature models of Napoleon's coach. I had supposed that this was a publicity stunt pure and simple, but the company has actually made little capital out of it, preferring, perhaps wisely, to let it advertise itself.

Briefly, the awards, which total $30,000, are led by four grand prizes of full courses in any technical school the winner selects, with smaller state prizes and awards for excellence in

particular phases of the work. The contestants are supplied
with complete working plans to scale, and the problem is one
that would tax the patience, skill, and taste of an experienced
model maker. It requires exactness to fractions of an inch,
intelligence in reading plans and setting off measurements,
exceptional skill in handling wood, metal, cloth, leather, glass,
and paint. Over 400,000 boys have entered the two contests,
and over 2000 completed coaches were submitted to the judges
last year. Herr Walther Leuschner, the German craftsman
who made the pattern coach and drew the plans, admits that
at least one of these youngsters equaled his own master model.

To complete such a coach involves wood carving and
turning, joinery, pattern making, metal casting, gluing,
soldering, and brazing, the use of taps and dies, needlework
and upholstery, leather working, painting, and decorating.
No boy can undertake the task without learning much, and no
boy can finish among the winners without having acquired
skills that will be useful all his life—not the least of which are
patience and thoroughness, and, particularly, the satisfaction
that comes from doing something extremely well.

VII

Play is active. All the connotations of the word suggest the
idea of movement. The word "amuse" might be analyzed
etymologically as signifying "away from musing," coming out
of one's self. Even stronger in this sense is the word "dis-
tract," to draw away, or "divert," to turn away. Play is an
alternative for those lazy entertainments which find us idle and
leave us passive, since it gives us something we can do or make
to exercise our faculties and cause us to experience that glorious sense of achievement.

Play may be either mental or physical, but the best form is
that which is both, which exercises mind and body, a game
that demands brain and brawn, a walk heightened by understanding interest in the surroundings, scenery, bird life, or
growing things, in topography or geology. Walking is a stim-

ulus to the mind, and the mind should have something to work on. Play divides also into social and solitary kinds. I am more proficient in the solitary kinds because my deafness is a bar to social intercourse. But the advantages of self-starting amusements should not be ignored by even the keenest-eared and most socially disposed. They make one independent and perhaps bring the most satisfying reward. They divide roughly into study, craft, and collecting, though each borrows something from the other two. Social amusements range all the way from games to intelligent participation in community activities.

High on the list of activities which may be pursued as private hobbies but which shower their benefits on the public is the ancient art of gardening. Like Portia's famous quality of mercy, it blesses both gardener and beholder. A love of gardens and a bit of ground upon which to lavish that affection are a fortunate equipment. For not only is gardening full of rewards and surprises for the gardener, but, since a community is only a number of plots, each under the control of a different individual, the collective result of numerous gardens is a beautiful community, and ultimately a beautiful country. No one can care for a home place, and endeavor to make it æsthetically pleasing, and remain indifferent to the condition of his neighbors' yards. Thus community spirit is developed by emulation.

Gardening is a combination of physical and mental effort, that combination of mind and muscle which gives to any effort its interest. There is the joy of digging in the earth with the sun on one's back, which is so satisfying, and the study of flowers, which can be carried as far and made as special as one pleases. Its inevitable progress is to landscape next, developing an interest in the country which belongs to all, streets, parks, and public buildings. If we loved gardening as universally as the Swiss or the English, the country would be transformed, for there would be developed a public opinion to influence public projects, highways, reservations, the great heritage of scenery, and save them from the vulgarization and destruction that now threaten them. Professionally our gardens are unsurpassed. An English visitor recently bore testimony to that fact. But it is like our golf or tennis. A few play well enough to beat the best English, but the average is much lower here than there. Nearly every country cottage yard in England is ablaze with color of homely old-fashioned flowers, and gardening fills a large place in the lives of many people.

It is inevitable that many in this new era of daylight playtime will turn to gardening, but there is need of a popularizer, something that will make the interest as keen as it now is in contract bridge.

The wise use of leisure may easily be an important, perhaps the most important influence on the future course of our civilization. People express themselves more frankly in their play than in their work. When they are free they turn naturally to that which they most want to do. If these diversions are of the kind that develops the complete man, mentally, socially, and physically, they will profoundly influence the course of human events, and have economic reverberations as well. Already amusement is a big business, though unfortunately it has developed thus far more largely along the "escape" side than the auto-creative. It offers forgetfulness of dreary tasks rather than the inspiration of self-expression.

But all forms of recreation, even those followed by devotees at least cost, when sufficiently popular and widespread, create demands that must be supplied—not merely what Professor Cherington calls "adult toys," but paths for pedestrians, community playgrounds, and other public works. It is easily possible that the millions freed by short working hours will create entirely new consumption of goods, products, and services to supply the needs of diversion. It is a new version of writing a nation's songs rather than making its laws.

Professor Cherington was talking to toy makers when he advised the creation of more grown-up playthings, and these will surely come. Trust American enterprise to see to that. But what are most sorely needed and should be given the most earnest thought are less artificial occupations, those things which develop the spirit, satisfy the whole being, call forth one's powers, capacity for study or research, skill, proficiency— a new language, a musical instrument, interpretative dancing, not in a showy sense, as accomplishments, but for one's own satisfaction.

Few people can do common everyday things well. How many are there who can tie a knot? Most still use the granny knot, when what sailors call a square knot is easy to tie, is unslippable, and can be untied as easily as tied. The other day I noticed a tennis net at a small hotel held by guy ropes the loops of which had been neatly spliced. I suspected a sailor and found him in the handy man of the place, formerly able seaman on a Danish bark. Why should not more of us know how to make a splice, or a hitch, or a tackle? Why do we not learn the simple laws of mechanics that apply to the things around us, which we use daily? It would reduce the friction of living if we were all handier, and there is a certain indefinable satisfaction in using one's hands and wits aptly.

It would be futile to catalogue all the ways in which the human spirit expresses itself in those hours which are gloriously its own. A glance at the windows of any sporting-goods store suggests that there are at least a thousand games and sports played with apparatus, and this is but one and not perhaps the highest department of human diversion. While it does take skill and brains to play many games (though it denotes something, I am not sure what, that so many games are conditioned by the element of chance), games and sports do not as a rule develop the creative instinct which is the divinest impulse in our natures. But it will be a real advance if any large number of people can be taught or persuaded to play in any capacity. That is the first step.

Perhaps this is the opportunity of the National Recreation Association. It is organized around the idea of affording facilities for community amusement. It is a non-profit body, privately supported, which acts as leader and guide to local groups desiring to create community houses, public playgrounds, and other nuclei of recreation. It is significant of the spirit in which it takes its work that this Association inspired and sponsored the visit to this country of Dr. L. P. Jacks, whose lectures on recreation through education or vice versa set up an admirable program for the Association that backed him.

THE FUTURE OF THE GREAT CITY

By *Stuart Chase*

A DISTINGUISHED savant has perfected a mechanical contrivance which measures the intensity of noise. To my knowledge nobody has yet invented a device to register quantitatively likes and dislikes. During most of one's Conscious hours spent in a great city—or anywhere else for that matter—one is so intent upon his job, his food, his sweetheart, or his transit connections that no reactions, in the sense of liking or disliking the impending environment, are registered at all. Here it is, world without end: nothing can be done about it; why bother to appraise it?

Suppose, however, we begin this inquiry into the future of the great city by halting for a moment the remorseless pursuit of the next sixty minutes and deliberately allowing both the pleasurable and painful sensations of city living to filter through to consciousness.

Fifteen years ago I enjoyed residing in Boston—pleasure slightly outweighed pain. Ten years ago I enjoyed living in Washington, with a higher pleasure margin. In the interim I took up residence in Chicago and suffered a large debit balance. This was not due to human intercourse but only to the physical impact of the town. The people of Chicago are the pleasantest I have ever met. For the past decade I have lived in New York, with an adverse reaction only less than that experienced in the headquarters of the racketeers.

Coming into Manhattan, I begin to feel a strange uneasiness like a slight attack of seasickness; leaving it, I suddenly grow more cheerful. Why? I am no confirmed bucolic; no city-hater in cheese-cloth and sandals. The thoughts which men

generate in cities are as important to me as bread. For the
past few weeks I have been noting specific impressions in an
attempt to come to closer terms with this mysterious total
feeling. The record is voluminous, running to hundreds of
cases. Here is space for only a few of the more typical, together
with certain generalizations into which many of the cases fall.
You realize, of course, that we are here dealing more with the
testimony of the five senses than with economics, or philosophy, or divination. You realize, too, that lacking a machine like that of Dr. Free, the intensity of the reaction cannot
be given, only the bare fact.

Positive Reactions—pleasurable
    The city from the East River at sunset
    Brooklyn Bridge
    Cube masses against blue sky
    Corrugated ridges of step-backs—say at 34th Street
    Fifth Avenue below 14th Street—where fine old houses and a
        Ghost of dignity remain
    The interior of the Graybar Building—many of the newer build-
        ing interiors
    Inside block gardens—say Mark Van Doren's
    The view of the city from a high roof garden, particularly at
        night; towers indirectly illuminated
    Bars of sunlight under the elevated railroad
    The interior of the Grand Central Station
    The Bronx River Parkway
    Girls on Fifth Avenue above 42nd Street (one out of six is lovely)
    Building excavations with a nuzzling steam shovel
    The inside of power houses
    Morningside Heights and Riverside Drive, looking across to the
        Palisades
    The American Wing in the Metropolitan Museum
    The new Hudson River Bridge
    Here and there a shop window with extraordinary modern
        decorations
    The oaths of taxicab drivers
    A Stadium concert on a summer night

Negative Reactions—painful
    Jammed traffic
    Fire-engine sirens, motor-car horns, the cacophony of riveting,

loud speakers, steamboat whistles (at night), most people's voices, the rasp of elevator doors, the roar of traffic in general, and that of the elevated in particular

All trucks (probably because I saw a woman killed by one on Seventh Avenue)

The insignificance of the sun and moon

A feeling akin to being at the bottom of a well

Central Park (it reminds me of a warmed-over meal)

The lower East Side with its dreadful old-law tenements

Park Avenue and its apartment houses like so many packing cases

The expression on the faces of most people

The smell of incompletely burned gasoline, of barber-shops, of Grand Street, of the garbage mountain with the locomotives on the top of it in Queens, of Chinatown, of the subway, of soda fountains

Movie palaces—with one or two exceptions

Delicatessen stores

Signboards and car signs

All travel by subway, tunnel or street car

The noon-hour crowd in front of establishments manufacturing garments

Suburbs—with a few exceptions

The outside of power houses

The gentlemen with no immediate purpose in life around Times Square

The ripping open of streets—like a public operation

Filling stations

Trees—probably because I love trees

Dust, dirt, and cinders

Most restaurants, particularly cafeterias (In Paris the reaction is mainly pleasurable. Why the difference?)

The huddle of skyscrapers around the Grand Central—the big bullies

City refuse on Long Beach—even on Fire Island, forty miles away

These lists give, I fear, a shattering insight into the short-comings of the compiler's character, but they are at least honest. There is not a "wisecrack" in either category. These are the sorts of things which alternately elevate and depress that unique system of electrons which comprises my earthly temple. You, gentle reader, will disagree in detail, but will you disagree in general? Our electronic systems may diverge but all follow a basic pattern known as *homo sapiens*. What the lists say, in essence, is this:

There are more painful than pleasurable sensations in one's contact with a huge American city of the the present day.

Pleasure is found in sudden glimpses, in certain lights on architectural masses, in occasional arresting and amusing adventures, in the arts which the great city has to display.

Pain is found in noise, dust, smell, crowding, the pressure of the clock, in negotiating traffic, in great stretches of bleak and dour ugliness, in looking always up instead of out, in a continually battering sense of human inferiority.

These mile-high walls are everything, man is nothing. In Boston and Washington the walls were negotiable; one could respect oneself. That was years ago. Now the traffic roars on Boylston Street and Pennsylvania Avenue as it does at Herald Square. Internal-combustion engines are not so dwarfing as mile-high walls but in such boiling steel masses they overawe the pedestrian, force him below the plane of human dignity. Why should we scamper like rats rather than walk like men?

II

Megalopolis is not a pleasant home for many of its citizens, awake or asleep. Even for those—and they may be the majority—whose pleasure quotient exceeds the pain, the gross volume of the latter, however unconscious, does much to retard a gracious and civilized life. Look at the faces in the street. The machine has gathered us up and dumped us by the millions into these roaring canyons. Year by year more millions are harvested, the canyon shadows deepen, the roar grows louder. No man, no group of men, knows where this conglomeration of steel and glass and stone, with the most highly complicated nervous system ever heard of—a giant with a weak digestion—is headed. So, with an open field, I make bold to present three main alternatives.

First—Megalopolis can continue its present course of becoming increasingly congested, hectic, and biologically alien to an ordered human life; its vast transportation systems pumping us back and forth from "places where we would rather not live to places where we would rather not work"— until a saturation point is reached. This may take the form either of a sudden and disastrous technical breakdown or a less dramatic surfeit of citizens with their environment, resulting in steady emigration and an ultimate collapse of land values. In the case of New York, with its twenty billions on the assessors' rolls, such a collapse would rock the financial structure of the nation. A mechanical breakdown is not as probable for horizontal cities, such as Washington; but Clarence Stein, the distinguished architect, regards it as very probable for vertical cities such as New York.

Second—By virtue of an aroused public opinion or of a benevolent dictatorship—of which there are few signs to date—it is conceivable that in the case of those cities which had not entangled and enmeshed themselves beyond all human aid, drastic measures of coördination and preplanning might be introduced, fundamental enough really to adapt Megalopolis to civilized existence. We have the technical knowledge to do it, machines are always ready to help as well as to hinder; we have the engineering ability, and even for some areas the specific blueprints. But nobody has yet found a practical way to reckon with the land speculator and his colossal pyramid of values, duly capitalized on congestion. As Mr. Lewis Mumford acutely points out, the trouble with American cities is not that they have not been planned, but that the plan—in the configuration of a gridiron—has had no other purpose than to provide the most advantageous method for selling and reselling real estate. Cities have been laid out for profitable speculation, not for human use, and in the defense of that plan the most powerful forces in the Republic have fought, now fight, and will fight so long as they can stand and see. It is for this cogent reason that no fundamentally constructive program can be anything more than "impractical." In such a city as Washington, laid out a century ago with an eye to living rather than to rent collecting, the chances of introducing the necessary adjustments are, of course, somewhat brighter than in Chicago or Philadelphia or New York.

Third—Whether we save our cities by functional planning or continue somehow to exist in their ever grimmer canyons, there is always the possibility that on some fine morning a swarm of bombing planes will appear above the skyscraper tops, laugh heartily at the impotent clamor of anti-aircraft guns and, by means of a few judicious tons of radium atomite, poison gases, and, shall we say, typhus-fever cultures, dropped at strategic points, put an end to our hopes or to our miseries, as the case may be, and that quite finally. In the next war it is the great city which is to come in for the most intensive extermination. Upon this point all military experts of any intelligence seem singularly unanimous.

I shall not examine this last alternative in any detail. It deserves mention and is now mentioned. Perhaps there will be no more wars. Perhaps by virtue of the League of Nations and Mr. Kellogg and Messrs. Hoover and MacDonald arm in arm, the institution of war now stands officially liquidated. Your smile answers mine. And as you smile you accept unreservedly the probability of another major conflict. There is always the chance, of course, that it will not be your city which the enemy selects for scientific experimentation. But it will be some hefty member of *genus megalopolis*, and probably more than one.

Turning now to the more immediate enemy within. What are the chances of technical breakdown? Is a saturation point approaching? What is the evidence, beyond the likes and dislikes of one insignificant citizen, that Megalopolis provides physically and spiritually an alien home? First let us sketch briefly its nervous system.

Below its streets you will normally find:

1. Water mains—from six inches to six feet in diameter. If the latter burst, they "cause more havoc than dynamite"
2. Gas mains—spreading wholesale death if punctured

3. Steam mains—carrying heat from central plants to office buildings, and also temperamental
4. Sewers—some of them big enough to drive a truck through, and not particular where they end
5. Subways—140 miles of them in New York. In some places there are four tubes one below the other. They carry the equivalent of the total population of the United States every two weeks. The whole system is now being doubled at the cost of $700,-000,000. It will only make congestion worse. Blasting must be carried on close to four-foot water mains, while many men die from silica dust. ("Fifty-seven per cent of all rock drillers, blasters, and excavators examined were suffering from a probably fatal pulmonary disease resulting from the inhalation of rock dust")
6. Electric light and power cables
7. Telephone cables—up to 2400 wires on a single cable
8. Telegraph cables
9. Pneumatic mail tubes
10. Sidewalk vaults—always good hosts to sewer gas, as we shall see

Here are ten subterranean nerves—that is, theoretically subterranean. As a matter of fact, it is a dull day on any block when gentlemen in goggles and dun-colored overalls, armed with prodigious flares and ripping mechanisms, are not hauling one or another of the arteries towards the surface, to pound and batter them unmercifully. In a hundred yards of street, I counted eleven separate assaults in a week. Four of them cost me a good many hours' sleep. But Dante would have enjoyed the midnight spectacle.

On and above the surface is another great series of nerves, equally important if less mysterious. It comprises:

1. Bridges and causeways which admit traffic, particularly foodstuffs, to the city
2. Trolley lines
3. Elevated railways
4. Railroad terminals and switch yards
5. Milk and ice supply, the truck delivery service generally
6. Traffic control
7. Fire-fighting apparatus
8. Ambulance, hospital, and burial services

9. Garbage and waste collection—an obstreperous nerve
10. Street cleaning and snow disposal
11. Building and safety inspection
12. Elevator service—without which hardly more than ten per cent of normal business could be carried on
13. Radio wave-length control. And soon
14. The maintenance of landing fields, and the control of transportation by air

There is hardly an item in either the subterranean or the surface systems which is not cardinal to the continued functioning of Megalopolis. If one prime nerve is cut for any length of time, the urban environment starts rapidly to disintegrate, leaving the wayfaring man—who has not the faintest notion of the technic which provisions him—as helpless as an airplane in a tail spin. For him the water supply runs no farther back than the faucet; the food supply than the delicatessen store. Furthermore, so interlocked is the whole structure that the failing of one nerve is almost sure to result in the rupture of others.

That these arteries are not functioning altogether smoothly some recent occurrences demonstrate. Last December a mile of London streets was suddenly ripped open by gas explosions—"thrown into the air like confetti." Many citizens were hurt, while the surrounding population was frightened as it had not been since the Zeppelin raids. The property damage was immense. The Surveyors Institution proceeded to investigate this and other mysterious gas explosions and has recently handed down its report. It finds that automobiles and trucks are now putting a strain on road surfaces and the terrain thereunder which they were never designed to meet. Pipes, conduits, and mains continually increase their diameters; the load from above grows heavier, and the vitally essential cushion of earth between the two grows scantier. Steel, like flesh and blood, is subject to fatigue. Iron and steel mains suffer an accelerating deterioration due to vibration and the sudden temperature changes which the scantier earth promotes. Proper inspection is utterly impossible under modern traffic conditions. Meanwhile the steady removal of trees and the open spaces of loose earth about them takes away the natural outlets through which gases may harmlessly escape. Increasingly, gases are compressed beneath a solid roof of stone, brick, and asphalt. "The closing of these outlets," says the Institution, "results in either the accumulation of gaseous mixtures in abandoned sewers and subsoil cavities, or gas may penetrate laterally into adjoining vaults and basements. Actual ignition may occur through the use of a naked light or from a spark produced by the short circuiting of an electric fitting." As the vault and its inhabitants take their skyward way, it is often difficult to determine which method of ignition furnished the inciting cause.

A great surgeon has given his life to mitigating human suffering. He established a clinic in the city of Cleveland. Suddenly he found himself working desperately to save the lives not only of his patients but of his colleagues and hospital staff. For forty-eight uninterrupted hours he labored, but at the end more than a hundred persons were dead. An unknown gas had exploded in the X-ray film room, to kill every human being whose lungs it touched. Thus a place of healing had turned into a shambles—no man quite knowing why.

A few weeks later a coroner's jury of pathologists and chemists in Chicago were trying to determine how methyl chloride was liberated in artificial ice machines and why it had just killed fifteen people.

Among those who testified at the inquest was Dr. Robert Jacobson. He told the jury that he had attended the family of Mr. and Mrs. Irving Markowski of 4856 Milwaukee Avenue, when three young children became ill and died mysteriously. The physician said the same slight odor that was present in the Clark apartment was also in the Markowski home and that he had become convinced that all had died of methyl chloride. . . . Several representatives of the ice machine company also testified, and said that 1500 of their refrigerators were in use in Chicago.

Not long ago the Muggerberg Company of Hamburg, Germany, allowed phosgene gas to escape through its stacks at night. It formed a blanket over the city and, before it could be dissipated, eleven persons had been suffocated to death.

On one page of one newspaper we read the headlines:

Sixteen Killed and Seven Injured in Factory Blast.
One Burned to Death, Twenty-five Overcome in Gas Explosion.
Man Rescues Four in Ammonia Blast.

In New York, the ninth car of a subway express jumped the track at Times Square, crashed through a concrete wall and was cut in two. All safety devices were working, but the switchman's normal reflexes were momentarily in abeyance. This "man failure" cost 17 killed and 101 wounded. The situation in the tunnel at the rush hour was indescribable. Can we expect ever to eliminate man failure in the gigantic pressure of the rush hour? Cars with seats for 44, straps for 56, a total of 100, now carry 252 persons at the morning and evening peaks. The close-up as the last sardines are kicked and battered into their cans, strong-armed guards assisting, is likewise indescribable. Indeed, subways have been shrewdly designated by Mr. E. K. Lindley as "feedpipes for sky-scrapers," constituting the perfect vicious circle. The higher the skyscrapers, the more subways are dug to fill them. The greater the subway capacity, the more skyscrapers are reared to absorb it. Thus the new Eighth Avenue line in New York produces automatically a new one hundred and ten story building on Eighth Avenue.

A short circuit in a power house at Fiftieth Street started a tiny fire, but a smoky one. Almost instantly all power left the Grand Central Station. Throughout the night no train could move in or out. In the tunnels powerful electric engines came helplessly to rest, and the frightened passengers climbed ladders through manholes to the street. The great haughty continental expresses stopped at the city limits. Suburbanites milled and jostled in the terminal, ultimately to decide that it was a long walk home, and to begin searching for a bed.

Two thousand truck drivers recently threatened to strike

in one great city. Immediately the entire perishable food supply was imperiled. If they could have held their ranks, a mortgage on the City Hall would not have been too great a price
to buy them off. Nor would two thousand have been necessary. An engineer once explained to me how one hundred key
technicians in power houses, flood-gate stations, and signal
towers could bring the entire life of Megalopolis to an abrupt
conclusion. A tiny piece of carelessness in a Springfield gen-
erating station shut off all light and power from the city for
many hours. Business was brought to a standstill, traffic
ceased, one factory alone lost 3,500 man hours.

An epidemic may secure a start in an hour's time from an
unnoticed flow of polluted water into the municipal supply.
It is physically impossible for chemists to analyze water continuously in order to determine how much chlorine is needed
to purify it. And here at last is a ray of sunshine. A Swiss
has invented an "automatic chemist," which keeps the
chlorinating process on duty twenty-four hours in the day.
It was exhibited recently but has yet to be adopted and installed by any American city. It induces speculation as to how
many other vital services are in need of similar automatic
controls.

III

So much for the factor of technological tenuousness. The
nerves of Megalopolis are jumpy, and under the going custom
of hit-and-miss nobody makes it his business to find out how
jumpy, or to plan any rational system for lessening the pressure. The drift is toward an even worse confusion, and so, inevitably, toward the possibility of an ever more serious technical collapse.

Let us turn now to human nerves. The wayfaring man remains sublimely unaware of a chlorine deficiency in his water
until an epidemic overwhelms him, but motor cars and their
collateral smells and noises pursue him every moment of the
day and night. In the first eight months of 1929, 821 persons

were killed by automobiles in the streets of New York, against 666 during a similar period in 1928. Deaths in all American cities from this cause have increased nine per cent in the current year. In less than two years motor cars have killed as many people in the United States as there were American soldiers killed in the War and wounded seven times as many as there were soldiers wounded. One in three of the fatalities is a child under fifteen. City-driving speeds have doubled in twenty years.

As I go about American cities, and particularly as I drive about them in taxicabs, I notice how the margin of safety continually declines. Where I allow, let us say, a five-foot tolerance when driving myself, the taxicab chauffeur will cut it to two feet, one foot, aye, to nothing at all. Indeed, I have been forced to give up back-seat driving altogether. I cannot bear to forecast the probabilities of such narrow margins. At the present time motor traffic is operating on inches where it used to operate on yards. Probably the only thing which saves us from ten times the death toll is that when we are not cutting corners on one wheel, we are hopelessly stalled in a frozen traffic jam. Recently, on foot in New York, I started with a bus at Washington Square, and proceeded north along Fifth Avenue. At Fifty-ninth Street I halted and, taking out my watch, counted out fifteen minutes before that particular bus appeared. The trouble is that the nervous strain of waiting makes for an embittered recklessness when the lanes are opened up—and no better evidence of that strain can be found than in the insane tooting of every horn in the whole congealed mass. The Queensboro Bridge has been christened by a New York editor, The Bridge of Nervous Breakdowns. "Given a reasonable expectancy of life, steady nerves, infinite patience, and a Christian resignation to fate, a man will no doubt get from one end of it to the other. But how many of us can boast these qualities at 6 P.M.?" He calls for double-decking— which, when the news is abroad, would, one fears, simply mean doubling the nervous breakdowns.

The evening of Labor Day, 1929, was unbearably hot and sultry. It was—according to the sublime processes of the New York holiday custom—the evening selected by some three million people to return to town. Two million had spent the day at Coney Island (and there is one of Megalopolis' most incredible sights: lucky the man who can fight his way into the water on such a day) or at Long Beach or Rockaway Beach or Altantic City; the other million comprised the returning vacationists. Twenty-two persons were killed on the streets. Eighteen sections of extra trains arrived simultaneously at the Grand Central Station. The subways were choked beyond all endurance; trains ran ninety minutes late; buses, five hours late; the jam of the Holland Tunnel under the Hudson River was so prodigious that incoming motorists left their cars in every New Jersey gutter and fought for standing room on the ferries or in the tubes. Bumper to bumper, the steel files ran thirty, forty miles into the country over the Albany Post Road, the Boston Post Road, the Merrick Road, the Jericho Turnpike; with bed long after sun-up for those at the remoter ends of the file. Thus Megalopolis enjoys its holiday.

Citizen A: "Are you going to the country for the week-end?"

Citizen B: "How could I get back?"

It would be a great mistake to suppose that such conditions are found only in New York. Manhattan is a sublime exhibit, but one to which every other American city aspires with the utmost enthusiasm. Look at the skyscrapers shooting out of the Texas plain—congestion deliberately created amid unending square miles of open space. I sometimes wonder if the erection of lofty buildings does not often transcend the economic basis altogether. How many are built for the sheer satisfaction of registering the highest altitude yet reached; how many to expand the ego of the promoter?

British scientists predict the coming of the deaf age owing to metropolitan noises and, justly enough, select New Yorkers as the first who are to lose their hearing. Herald Square, according to Doctor Free's instrument, is fifty-five sensation units above quiet. To talk to a person in front of Macy's one must shout as loudly as to a person more than half deaf. Ordinary street noises produce a result comparable to that of one-third deafness, with certain locations doubling this rate. A badly serviced truck will make five times as much clamor as one of the same make in good repair. But where is space for the repair shops? Typists require nineteen per cent more energy to work in a noisy room than in a quiet one. Twenty per cent of all office workers' energy is wasted combating sound. The Wright Whirlwind motor and the New York subway both register seventy-five units on Doctor Free's machine, five units higher than a riveting machine in full cry.

The Health Commissioner of New York tells us that people are taking to drugs and sedatives to make them sleep. In the laboratories of Colgate University white rats, continuously exposed to normal city sounds, grow less, eat less, are less active and playful than their brothers exposed only to quiet. School children, it has been found, are very seriously handicapped in their work by street noises. To make matters worse, it has been determined that short skirts increase the racket. Legs bounce the sounds back, where millions of yards of textiles on city streets used to absorb a measurable fraction! Professor Spooner of Oxford, overwhelmed by such facts, calls despairingly upon the League of Nations to attack the problem. "Never," he says, "has civilization been confronted with such a malignant plague."

Not to be outdone by Doctor Free, Mr. Howard C. Murphy, a heating and ventilating engineer, has invented a machine for measuring dust, and so deluged us with another shower of gloomy statistics. The dirtiest city in America is St. Louis, fighting its way through 17,600 dust particles per cubic foot—with Cincinnati, Pittsburgh, and Detroit, in that order, following close behind. New York for once loses its crown, having only 9,700 particles per cubic foot; but this is about four times as much as in country air. Winter death rates in cities have now passed summer death rates "due to one outstanding factor—smoke, dust and contaminated air." Meanwhile, though the sun may occasionally shine, all health-giving ultra-violet rays are completely excluded by the dome of dust and smoke which forever hangs above the skyscraper tops.

In brief, Megalopolis, for all its gaudy show, its towering architecture, its many refinements and cloistered comforts, is not physically fit for ordinary people to live in. And as the noise, dust, accident, explosion, and traffic congestion figures show, it grows continually worse. The technological limits of the machine have been repeatedly outraged until now the tangle of vital nerves is so complicated and involved that it is safe to say no one understands them or realizes in the faintest measure the probability and extent of some major lesion.

This, the first of the three alternatives submitted earlier, is my favorite for the future of great cities. They will drift blindly into breakdown. The final collapse may be very sudden and very terrible, due, let us say, to unendurable pressures of underground gases. Or, and more probably, Megalopolis will become so alien to normal living that even Jews, with two thousand years of urban adaptation in their inheritance, will leave it. Nor will the irate citizen return until guaranteed space in which to breathe, move, and function adequately. This will demolish the whole structure of land values, and in the end demand the complete rearrangement of metropolitan anatomy.

IV

Can we reverse the process, and rearrange before the breakdown? Logically we can, psychologically we probably shall not. No one in his senses would advocate that Megalopolis should abandon its mechanical arteries, and go back to the London of Doctor Johnson. But it is difficult to see why anyone in his senses should not demand that technological tenuousness be adequately appraised and squarely met. If we are to live in mechanical cities—and that is the path we have chosen—we ought to respect the mechanism. If the structure of real estate values—the subway-skyscraper complex, for instance—insists on choking the mechanism, then we ought either to abolish the structure and run the city on sound engineering principles or abolish the city as a complicated mechanical phenomenon altogether. Nor can the choice be indefinitely delayed.

If we want a city to use and enjoy we must give up great sections of the real estate racket. It must be planned for function, its nervous channels protected with space, open areas, "balanced loads," adequate and incessant supervisions. Dynamite as a clearing agent must be freely employed, a whole new orientation of work areas, play areas, home areas, established. If the landlord refuses to budge, then dynamite the landlord—by vigorous condemnation proceedings if you prefer. Technically the thing is complicated, but certainly negotiable. One can nominate a dozen engineers and architects who, given a free hand, could make even New York genuinely habitable and reasonably safe within a decade—and at a cost not so much greater than that of the new subway program. Dynamite is relatively cheap.

But the job would have to be done with the same high-handedness and vigor which characterized the War Industries Board when, overriding a thousand encrusted traditions and petty rights, it put the nation on a war footing. A perfectly ruthless civic will must operate. Tear down a square mile here, a square mile there. Obliterate this reeking slum. Double the width of this street; abandon and build on that one. Construct great causeways to by-pass through traffic. A year in Sing Sing for any loud speaker audible after ten o'clock. No private motor cars at certain hours below Fifty-ninth Street, New York, and only 15,000 taxicabs. Two years in Atlanta for an unserviced truck making five times the noise it should. Fifty thousand trees to be set out immediately. Sidewalk cafés to be widely encouraged. Half of all subways to be permanently sealed, with a two-day festival and free beer. Three years in the Andaman Islands for a reeking chimney. Garbage to be completely carbonized and by-producted. Four years on Nova Zembla for polluting river or harbor waters with oil refuse. Forty per cent of all industry to move outside the city limits to designated areas. (Suburbanites can thus commute *outward* as well as inward to their work.) The death penalty for all the officers and employees of companies caught broadcasting advertising matter from airplanes (as recently recommended by a hospital doctor in a letter to the *World*). And so on.

You are smiling again. But I am not. When I think of the city fit for the high gods to live in which modern engineering might build . . . when I think of what Megalopolis might be . . .

ON ESSAYS

By *G. K. Chesterton*

THERE are dark and morbid moods in which I am tempted to feel that Evil reëntered the world in the form of Essays. The Essay is like the Serpent, smooth and graceful and easy of movement, also wavering or wandering. Besides, I suppose that the very word Essay had the original meaning of "trying it on." The serpent was in every sense of the word tentative. The Tempter is always feeling his way, and finding out how much other people will stand. That misleading air of irresponsibility about the Essay is very disarming through appearing to be disarmed. But the serpent can strike without claws, as it can run without legs. It is the emblem of all those arts which are elusive, evasive, impressionistic, and shading away from tint to tint. I suppose that the Essay, so far as England at least is concerned, was almost invented by Francis Bacon. I can well believe it. I always thought he was the villain of English history.

It may be well to explain that I do not really regard all Essayists as wicked men. I have myself been an essayist or tried to be an essayist; or pretended to be an essayist. Nor do I in the least dislike essays. I take perhaps my greatest literary pleasure in reading them; after such really serious necessities of the intellect as detective stories and tracts written by madmen. There is no better reading in the world than some contemporary essays, like those of Mr. E. V. Lucas or Mr. Robert Lynd. And though, unlike Mr. Lucas and Mr. Lynd, I am quite incapable of writing a really good essay, the motive of my dark suggestion is not a diabolic jealousy or envy. It is merely a natural taste for exaggeration, when dealing with a point too subtle to permit of exactitude. If I may myself imitate the timid and tentative tone of the true essayist, I will confine myself to saying that there is something in what I say. There is really an element in modern letters which is at once indefinite and dangerous.

What I mean is this. The distinction between certain old forms and certain relatively recent forms of literature is that the old were limited by a logical purpose. The Drama and the Sonnet were of the old kind; the Essay and the Novel are of the new. If a sonnet breaks out of the sonnet form, it ceases to be a sonnet. It may become a wild and inspiring specimen of free verse; but you do not have to call it a sonnet because you have nothing else to call it. But in the case of the new sort of novel, you do very often have to call it a novel because you have nothing else to call it. It is sometimes called a novel when it is hardly even a narrative. There is nothing to test or define it, except that it is not spaced like an epic poem, and often has even less of a story. The same applies to the apparently attractive leisure and liberty of the essay. By its very nature it does not exactly explain what it is trying to do and thus escapes a decisive judgment about whether it has really done it. But in the case of the essay there is a practical peril; precisely because it deals so often with theoretical matters. It is always dealing with theoretical matters without the responsibility of being theoretical or of propounding a theory.

For instance, there is any amount of sense and nonsense talked both for and against what is called mediævalism. There is also any amount of sense and nonsense talked for and against what is called modernism. I have occasionally tried to talk a little of the sense, with the result that I have been generally credited with all the nonsense. But if a man wanted one real and rational test, which really does distinguish the mediæval from the modern mood, it might be stated thus. The mediæval man thought in terms of the Thesis, where the modern man thinks in terms of the Essay. It would be unfair, perhaps, to say that the modern man only essays to think—or, in other words, makes a desperate attempt to think, but it would be true to say that the modern man often only essays, or attempts, to come to a conclusion. Whereas the mediæval man hardly thought it worth while to think at all, unless he could come to a conclusion. That is why he took a definite thing called a Thesis and proceeded to prove it. That is why Martin Luther, a very mediæval man in most ways, nailed up on the door the theses he proposed to prove. Many people supposed that he was doing something revolutionary, and even modernist, in doing this. In fact, he was doing exactly what all the other mediæval students and doctors had done ever since the twilight of the Dark Ages. If the really modern Modernist attempted to do it, he would probably find that he had never arranged his thoughts in the forms of theses at all. Well, it is quite an error to suppose, so far as I am concerned, that it is any question of restoring the rigid apparatus of the mediæval system. But I do think that the Essay has wandered too far away from the Thesis.

There is a sort of irrational and indefensible quality in many of the most brilliant phrases of the most beautiful essays. There is no essayist I enjoy more than Stevenson; there is probably no man now alive who admires Stevenson more than I. But if we take some favorite and frequently quoted sentence, such as, "To travel hopefully is better than to arrive," we shall see that it gives a loophole for every sort of sophistry and unreason. If it could be stated as a thesis, it could not be defended as a thought. A man would not travel hopefully at all, if he thought that the goal would be disappointing as compared with the travels. It is tenable that travel is the more enjoyable; but in that case it cannot be called hopeful. For the traveler is here presumed to hope for the end of travel, not merely for its continuance.

Now, of course, I do not mean that pleasant paradoxes of this sort have not a place in literature; and because of them the essay has a place in literature. There is room for the merely idle and wandering essayist, as for the merely idle and wandering traveler. The trouble is that the essayists have become the only ethical philosophers. The wandering thinkers have become the wandering preachers and our only substitute for preaching friars. And whether our system is to be materialist or moralist, or sceptical or transcendental, we need more of a system than that. After a certain amount of wandering our mind wants either to get there or to go home. It is one thing to travel hopefully and say half in jest that it is better than to arrive. It is another thing to travel hopelessly, because you know you will never arrive.

I was struck by the same tendency in re-reading some of the best essays ever written, which were especially enjoyed by Stevenson—the essays of Hazlitt. "You can live like a gentleman on Hazlitt's ideas," as Mr. Augustine Birrell truly remarked; but even in these we see the beginning of this inconsistent and irresponsible temper. For instance, Hazlitt was a Radical and constantly railed at Tories for not trusting men or mobs. I think it was he who lectured Walter Scott for so small a matter as making the mediæval mob in *Ivanhoe* jeer ungenerously at the retreat of the Templars. Anyhow, from any number of passages, one would infer that Hazlitt offered himself as a friend of the people. But he offered himself most furiously as an enemy of the Public. When he began to write about the Public he described exactly the same many-headed monster of ignorance and cowardice and cruelty which the worst Tories called the Mob. Now, if Hazlitt had been obliged to set forth his thoughts on Democracy in the theses of a mediæval schoolman, he would have had to think much more clearly and make up his mind much more decisively. I will leave the last word with the essayist; and admit that I am not sure whether he would have written such good essays.

FIRST THINGS

By *Robert P. Tristram Coffin*

FIRST things first.

For rainy days it is good to have a litany of shining names to say over to yourself. I have mine. It runs like this: *a cockcrow, a mist of dandelions, a thrush in the deep woods, moving pines, a song that reaches before and after, and water high up through the trees.* These are the words which always send out a ripple in my mind, circles on circles until the world seems like the nest of crystal boxes, concentric and shining, that it ought to be. For these are the first memories I have of all that moves and sings and shines in this wonder that has turned out to be life. And the things I remember as first are the things I shall want to have with me last in the valley of the evening.

A cock that crew. . . . Somewhere, out of the dark which had been for æons came the matin of the bird that calls up the day. Darkness lifted from me for that holy night and for all the nights to come. A protoplasm turned into a child who could go about in the halls of his mind, lay hold on his thoughts when he needed them, and know himself for himself on all the darkest and the highest stairs. There had been only gropings before. There had been a house that was too high and narrow, a room full of fear with a precipice of steps going into a room lower down; there had been the antlered head of a stag just bursting with distended nostrils through the wall. But now all the half-things and the unformed things would tyrannize over me no more. I would be sure that I could stay in the high house even when the others were all gone; I would know that the room below the precipice would always be there, when I climbed down towards it, and I would never think that the stag's head had a body behind the wall again. A tall and friendly stranger had come up beside me with straight, clear eyes. I would never cry out again when things new and strange brushed my skin. I would even go to Sabbath School with that horror of angora fur about my wrists and chin and be tearless and brave. And for all that I had the cock to praise.

A field of dandelions. . . . Sometime after the cock crew, I sat at an open window and saw the world for the first time. I had been down there; but I had not seen it really until now. It was yellow with dandelions, and a mist that you could see was coming up out of it like steam. It was all alive. You could hear things moving in a mysterious way. Suddenly the dandelions trembled ever so slightly and bent, and somebody whom no one ever sees but everyone knows about when he talks and sings at the same time had gone past that way perhaps. Somebody who makes you think of church bells behind hills and who will always be at hand. In the dark and in the shine. Hereafter you would feel at times as if you were standing on a tower so high that you could see the earth turn and men rush about and yet have silence and peace up there with you, because the person no one ever sees was beside you till the end. And I have the dandelions to thank for that.

A thrush singing in the woods. . . . It was the first bird I had ever really heard sing. It was the last marvel in a long chain of marvels. The first violets, like pieces of the sky, the first anemones, like drops of snow left over into April. I had had my first trip out past all houses, out of sight of all windows and doors. I was too tired to take in anything more. Then, when the shadow of the earth was climbing up the eastern sky, the bird sang among the distant trees. Three broken little songs rising higher and higher until they faltered and failed. All at once I knew what it was to be alone and among things so lovely that they made your heart ache. For you could never tell how beautiful they were even though you were to live a thousand years and have all the best words on the end of your tongue. My father thought it was weariness that made me burst suddenly into tears. But it was the thrush I have to thank for that.

Pines that moved. . . . Again I was riding with my father into the country. I grew tired of watching the sand flow back into the paths our wheels made. I looked up from the turning wheels, and I saw with great surprise that everything around me but the sky was turning and turning. The pines by the side of the road rushed backwards, but the pines far off from the road were stealthily coming along with us as we rode. On both sides the trees were marching in great circles. The near trees ran back, the far trees ran forward. The farthest traveled ahead as quickly as we. I saw that we should never be clear of them. I felt like singing to know that those tall wonders could move, after all. I believe I did sing, too. Those things you believed to be one sort of things would probably surprise you some day and turn out matters to wonder about and quite different, if you looked at them long enough and crept up on them unawares. They would turn out to be companions too close to talk with people about. I did not tell my father what I had seen. He only knew that I sat up suddenly very straight for some reason he would never understand and smiled to myself. It is the moving pines I have to praise for that.

A song that reaches into all the past and all the future. . . . I cannot remember just where it was I heard the song. But it was somewhere in a dim place like a church. There was a new kind of music to me, not voices but bigger things and sounds that went overhead like wings. It might have been an organ. I could not tell where the sound was coming from, and that made it more mysterious. It seemed to be all through the air and high up especially. It shook you through and through, as if you were sitting under the arch of a bridge and many feet were passing over the bridge and things greater than feet. It shook you until it became a part of you, a part

of your heartbeat and the singing in your ears when you hold
your hands over them. And somehow at last you seemed to
know that the song you were hearing had never had a beginning but had been there forever and would go on forever after
you were out of this place and out of all the places you would
ever visit on earth. So steady and solemn it would never be
done. Deep and everlasting and no break or stop. Feet
marching on and on and on. Years afterwards I heard
words written two thousand years ago that sound like that
song:

> *Corde natus ex parentis*
> *Ante mundi exordium,*
> *A et Ω cognominatus,*
> *Ipse fons et clausula*
> *Omnium, quæ sunt, fuerunt,*
> *Quæque post futura sunt.*

And music, of an organ perhaps, opened such a door for me.

The sight of water through the trees. . . . Once again I rode
with my father. We went downhill, and the trees were thick
ahead. But I began to see patches of light between them.
Patches of luminous mystery and islands of light. I asked my
father what they were. He told me it was the sea. I wondered
about his answer until I suddenly saw a hill that reached above
all the trees I had been gazing through to the very sky everywhere and everywhere straight as a bowstring. Over everything in the world rose that tremendous mountain, and boats
with sails were climbing up it out of sight. Islands clung to the
sides of it, but the mountain that was all blue and calm minded
them not at all; it went up and was still. It would always be
behind things when you thought about them and looked at
them long enough. It would be there when I and the trees
and my father were far away. Great birds would be trying
to go over it, but it would never allow them. For on the other
side was something too holy for any bird or ship or island
to know about. Something that people would never soil
with their hands. Something to snow all the years with

wings. And it was the sea above the trees I can praise for that.

First things are bright things. *A cockcrow, a mist of dande-lions, a thrush in the deep woods, moving pines, a song that reaches before and after, and water high up through the trees.* . . . If one can only remember to say them over in the evening!

YOUNG MEN IN POLITICS

By *Wilbur Cross*
Governor of Connecticut

I

WHEREVER I go I find young college graduates intensely interested in the social and political affairs of Soviet Russia. If the subject comes up, as it generally does, in the talk at an informal gathering, the discussion at once becomes animated. Their remarks show that they are reading newspaper reports, magazine articles, and books dealing with Russian issues eagerly and thoughtfully. But when the conversation turns to American politics, the tone, until very recently, has at once changed. The life has gone out of it. Evidently they have not followed the speeches of our public leaders as they have followed those of Stalin. They have been inclined to treat the latest scandals in our municipal governments with boredom or cynicism. "Lousy" has been their word for the whole business.

Why is this so? Why is it that every summer increasing numbers of intelligent, alert young Americans take the fairly arduous and expensive trip to Moscow to see what is going on there and yet show so little desire to learn at first hand what is going on in Washington? I do not for a moment think that it is because they are all converts to Communism—or ever really expect to become converts. The answer is not so simple as that.

I believe that behind the enthusiasm among recent college graduates for visiting Russia is, first of all, the fact that they have been assured a warm welcome. Young people have always been peculiarly sensitive about going where they are not wanted, and the youth of our day, for all their confident air and loud talk, are no exceptions to this rule. By extensive and clever propaganda and by special facilities provided for sight-seeing, the Soviet Government makes young foreign tourists feel that they are wanted in Moscow today. And it assumes, apparently quite rightly, that they wish to learn something of the social and political life of the country as well as of its museums and picture galleries.

Again, the young are naturally empiricists, and their school and college training in the scientific laboratories, in the courses in history or economics or sociology, if it has meant anything at all to them, has deepened their interest in experimentation. Now, whatever one may think of it, the fact is that a tremendous political-social experiment is being conducted at this moment in Russia. The whole country is obviously a vast laboratory. Its present rulers lose no opportunity to advertise the novelty and boldness of their effort. The fundamental premise of the entire structure is that this is a changing world and that they are the first to give effect and direction to the new movement of post-war life.

It is easy to see why, from this point of view, Russia exerts a fascination over young Americans fresh from their studies of civilization or science as a process of evolution. Nothing is further from my intention here than to present a brief for the Soviet Government. It may well be that experiments, social or economic, if not political, are now afoot in this country that will have a greater influence on history than anything that is happening in Russia. My point merely is that, if this is the case, they have not been effectively presented to the younger generation as vital or novel issues either in the speeches of our public men or in our conventional party platforms.

And this brings me to another reason for the vividness of the young American's interest in Russia. There is no question that, all superficial signs to the contrary in this year of grace, youth is still a period of crusading. The early twenties are a time of no compromise, of ardent loyalties and equally ardent prejudices. One does not have to be a professional psychologist to detect in the casual indifference or cynicism of many of the remarks one hears or overhears from young Americans the working of a defense mechanism resorted to in order to conceal positive interest or emotion. The attempt at casualness is too pointed. Even the bored and skeptical "Yeah? " which Miss Ferber has pronounced the keyword in the speech of young America may hide a genuine spark of inquiry.

However this may be, the Russian Communists are engaged in a crusade for a program stated in no negative or uncertain terms, for which their leaders are fighting with every ounce of their energy. No one can get the impression that all groups or parties there have much the same middle-of-the-road principles at bottom or that Communist leaders fail to lead. And it is this aspect of Soviet Russia, I think, which most attracts young visitors today. They are made to feel in Moscow that the business of government is alive and serious, and that it is also the business of youth.

II

How is it with us? Let us picture the candidates who, having completed their courses in economics, history, and social science, come up for degrees each June at our colleges and universities. I have listened with thousands of them to Commencement addresses. The speaker emphasizes the duty of each graduate to take an active and enlightened part in public life. Perhaps he quotes the words of Cicero that the completion of all knowledge lies in its application to the affairs of state. If he does not, he generally expresses the same idea.

What happens as a result of all this? Usually nothing. When the college graduate returns to his home, he finds that the older men whose intelligence and integrity he most admires are "not in politics." They speak of politics as a "hopeless" or "dirty" game. They discourage any incipient desire the young citizen may have to take an active part in municipal affairs, where he would naturally expect to make a beginning. The newspapers bear out their comment. Unless he has a great deal of money which may be tapped for party funds, or some exceptional personal connection with a man in office, no party leader makes any overtures to him, much less seeks him out. And so he goes his way. During a recent state campaign, a number of young college men came to me and said that they would like to do something, but they did not want to "butt in." Rightly or wrongly, they had got the fixed impression that their services might not be welcome. They had no information at hand about the proper way of offering them.

Suppose the young college man is unusually aggressive and tries to push his way into the public life of the community. In that case, he is confronted by political organizations more closely knit than formerly for their own purposes. This is particularly true of state governments. Ordinarily the chairman himself holds no public office; but his control of his party's organization is absolute and undisputed, and sometimes relentless. He must be shrewd and astute; but beyond that he need not be overintelligent. His job is to win elections, not so much in the interest of the public welfare as in the interest of his organization, which is held together by patronage, large and small, extending downward into towns and boroughs, wherever his arm can reach. Members of legislatures may engage in hot debate over the business that is permitted to come before them. But they really initiate nothing of importance on their own motion. At the proper moment comes a crack of a whip and all talk ceases. The bill under consideration passes or the bill fails, as determined by the organization that has a majority in the legislature.

An omnipotent oligarchy, wearing perhaps the face of benevolence, may thus get into the saddle and popular government be reduced to a gesture. The young college man is not obtuse. He has a quick eye and sees exactly what the situation is. He is too independent to submerge his will in the will of a party leader. If he has succeeded in getting into the legislature, one term is enough for him. Again he steps aside and finds his occupation elsewhere.

I have said that young people are by nature and education empiricists. It is well that this is so, for without experimentation there is no possibility of intelligent advance, and the life goes out of any enterprise. Now, we are all constantly repeating the phrase that the world is changing before our eyes. The generation that has been growing up since the war has seen tremendous changes take place in the map, in government, and in social and economic organization. Naturally it looks to find some of these changes reflected in the political language of the day.

Too often what it actually finds is a restatement of time-worn ideas in slightly altered phrasings. Every four years the tariff planks and the other stocks in trade of the political orator are brought out again with little attempt to adjust them to current facts. Real issues are obscured by ambiguous terms. Prohibition is, of course, one of the great social issues now before the country. It has been rightly described by President Hoover as an "experiment," and, if one may judge by the discussion and the polls on the subject in our colleges, the younger generation takes a keen interest in this experiment. Yet the campaign speaker naturally treats it in such a way that his friends among the drys can prove that he is dry, and the wets can claim him equally well for their own faction. How can we expect to awaken young people to activity in American politics while such a state of things persists?

If a natural tendency is blocked in one direction, it will turn in another. Denied or discouraged on the political and social side, the desire of American youth to experiment and reform has lately found an outlet in the arts. I am told that in centers such as Hull House, once devoted to social crusading, the crusading is now being done more in music or painting or literature. In Yale's iconoclastic journal, the best-written article so far published dealt with the subject of architecture. It is heartening to see new blood being injected into the arts.

Yet our democracy cannot but feel seriously the loss to the public business of the best minds among its rising citizens. And on their side, these same minds are losing the chance of enrichment offered by participation in social and political causes.

III

I have remarked that youth is the time of strong loyalties. These tend to center around personalities even more than around causes. Yet this country has had since the days of Roosevelt and Wilson no preëminent political figures that appealed especially to the imagination of the young. Today no party leader commands from them the esteem and admiration in which they hold, for example, Mr. Justice Holmes. American college students read with no little enthusiasm about the unbroken line in England of fine and able men who have gone from the great universities into high positions in the state, each generation training its successor in the art of government. But they do not see ahead of them any such line of men who have gone to Washington from their own campuses.

Lately we have not only had an unfortunate lack of men in the highest public offices with the gift of arousing the respect and support of the young, but we have had worse than that. The record of the Harding administration with its pitiful slogan "Back to Normalcy" after all the terrific sacrifice of the war, and the recent disclosures of abuses in such cities as New York and Chicago, have tended to shake all faith in the integrity and intelligence of public officers. These are unpleasant matters, but they cannot be avoided if we are to understand the political psychology of the Americans who are growing up with the present century. In the circumstances, there can be small wonder that most of them have preferred to look on at the spectacle of government from the side lines.

There was a time when it was otherwise. Once it was the ambition of young college graduates to bear a hand in building up the nation. They were given a fighting chance. Jefferson, a graduate of William and Mary's college, was elected to the

Virginia House of Burgesses at the age of twenty-six. He was but thirty-three when he wrote the Declaration of Independence. Madison, a Princeton man, was only twenty-five when he was elected a delegate to the Revolutionary Convention of Virginia in 1776. In the next decade, he and Hamilton, a Columbia man six years his junior, were writing the Federalist Papers and laying the political and economic foundations of the new Republic. Washington, who at the age of twenty-three had been placed in command of the military forces at Virginia, made Jefferson his Secretary of State and Hamilton his Secretary of the Treasury, while Madison was reserved as an unofficial adviser, later to be elected President. Our government was then a young man's business.

Although I do not see any young Hamiltons or Jeffersons on the political horizon today, there are some hopeful signs. A number of gifted young college men, following the distinguished lead of Walter Lippmann, are exerting social and political pressure through editorial work in our dailies or weeklies. There is a sprinkling of them in our state legislatures and even in Congress. One of my colleagues among the state governors is just thirty-four. The organization known as the Crusaders has a good representation of men in their twenties and thirties among its members.

How can more of them be brought actively into our public life? This might happen at any moment in either of two ways. It might come about through the rise to political eminence in one of the great parties of some leader with the force of personality, mind, and speech that draws youth like a magnet. Failing the appearance of such a leader, it might still come about through the adoption by one of the parties of a bold, unequivocal, and progressive platform on the major issues of the day, and a serious effort by its organizers to recruit them into its ranks. If neither of these things happens within a reasonable time, we must be prepared for the possibility that intelligent young voters now aroused will cut loose from the old parties and form a new party, and make it one to be reckoned with, as has been the case with the Labor party in England.

There can be no doubt that among the more recent college graduates, who are feeling it sharply, the present depression is acting as a spur upon interest in public affairs and their conduct. For the first time in many years, young people are beginning to recognize that national policies directly affect them. Lacking other jobs, they may now do well to go further and look around for any jobs in municipal or state offices that may be open to them. Badly paid as these usually are, they now contrast favorably with many business positions, and the experience to be had in them cannot but prove rewarding.

This brings up the classic objection to politics as a career in this country—that men or women of integrity without private means cannot afford to embark on it. For the majority, certainly, I can see no way around that objection from the purely financial point of view. The number of positions is small indeed, even including the foreign services, in which there is today any reasonable certainty of tenure or any reasonable chance of promotion. Still there are a few such positions. Those in the consular service especially have attractions for adventurous minds beyond the salary, and many others offer training for short periods in the handling of men and affairs that may be turned to valuable account in business.

Those who have jobs but because of the slow pace of business now have also an extra amount of leisure on their hands, and those who because of financial independence need not seek for paid positions at this crisis, I advise to give politics a trial as an avocation. Party organizations do not always prove to be as tight as they look when they are approached by resourceful persons. The thing to do is to crawl in through some loophole, and then, if you find that you are in the wrong crowd, crawl out again and find or form your own crowd. One is no longer born, as in Gilbert's day, either a little Liberal or a little Conservative. Once an educated man who knows how to deal with his fellow beings is inside the right fence, he may exert influence, and with skill, patience, and zeal may win his way to some position of leadership. In any case, active-minded, observant young people should find the experience worth-while in itself as an opportunity to put to the test theories that they have studied inside college walls.

Usually a long road must be traversed by the young man who enters upon a political career before he can reach a conspicuous post in the national government. He may never arrive at the goal of his aspirations; but there is a field for him in local and state governments, where the problems, though much simpler, are equally economic. Consider, for instance, the question of taxation as it affects the welfare of a town or a municipality. In that one question is involved the organization of the local government, the prosperity of business from the manufacturer down to the small storekeeper, the maintenance and extension of roads and streets, adequate support of public libraries, public schools, and humane institutions, along with a multiplicity of other details necessary for the material and spiritual prosperity of a community. Nowhere else do the people receive so little for what they pay. With some notable exceptions, town and municipal governments are run primarily in the interest of the party in power. Offices are created to the fullest extent possible for political heelers. When the citizens threaten to revolt, then an attempt is made to appease them by shifting the burden of taxation to the next generation through bond issues, which are mounting higher and higher every year. This process has been going on for a long time until now scores of municipalities in the United States are on the verge of bankruptcy. Some have already gone over the precipice. Here at his door the young college man has a rare chance to perform a service which his fellow citizens are not likely to forget. It is one that should challenge both his intellectual powers and his public spirit.

IV

I believe that never before have American college graduates had so good a preliminary equipment for public office as they have today. I am aware that the newspapers, with lurid reports of their dissipations and cocktail parties in a land of prohibition and steady habits, sometimes give the impression that college students haven't the stamina for politics or anything else that means getting down to hardpan. It is, of course, true that there are too many wasters and drifters among them. Yet the great majority, as one who has long lived with them well knows, are really interested in a good deal of their work, including history and social science.

They have immense advantages today over former generations. Comparatively speaking, the college training of Hamilton and Jefferson was very meager. It consisted of hardly more than elementary mathematics and some Latin and Greek, with a smattering of ancient history. The great universities now provide, under the ablest scholars in the world, studies in political science, economics, sociology, government, and public law, and the political, social, and economic history of the United States and other countries. It is a wide sweep of knowledge, which embraces, beyond literature, the natural and physical sciences and the new psychology developed within the present century, all of which have important bearings upon the problems of government.

In my undergraduate days, college students as a rule were but little interested in public questions. We rarely discussed them. Not until my senior year at Yale, when William Graham Sumner spread before us the great issues in political and social science, did we come to know much about the complicated economic problems of the modern world. Then it was too late to specialize in them. Go now anywhere you please among groups of students and you will find them debating the financial crisis here and in Great Britain or Franco-German relations. They talk about war debts, reparations, and the Far Eastern situation. Some of them understand the political and economic ideas lying behind Italian Fascism, and most of them know the latest news from Russia. Partly through the exigencies of our national depression and partly through this interest in foreign affairs, in which it is clear that we are daily becoming more entangled, the attention of students and young graduates is being turned toward American political and economic questions. The next step should be to translate intention into action. This is the moment to make the experiment—with the most exciting election since the war nearly with us.

Such a deadlock as now exists between the older and the younger generations in the field of politics always looks hopeless until some able man or able group rises to break it. The present situation is in the nature of a direct challenge to the older generation. If the seasoned leaders are wise, they will take account of the political and social awakening which the current crisis is producing among the young, and they will turn it to constructive use by speedily placing before them candidates and issues that will rouse them further from lethargy.

The present situation is a still stronger challenge to robust American youth. I should emphasize the word *robust*, for the political scene is no place for the anæmic dilettante, who is unwilling and unable to learn how to meet hard blows and stubborn opposition. But the opportunity is already in the hands of our muscular young citizens to take the initiative, to make up their minds what our democracy needs, and to use all their educational equipment and organizing powers to get it. From my brief experience in state government, I have learned one thing that our democracy needs today above all others. It is the energy of intelligent, aggressive, and well-trained young men and women in practical efforts for the public welfare. For their own full and vigorous development as much as for that of the country, I have no hesitation in saying to those who can stand a cold plunge: Come on in—the water's fine!

HOW NOT TO WRITE HISTORY

A NOTE ON THE WORKINGS OF THE LITERARY MIND

By *Bernard De Voto*

D
URING the War vaudeville managers were accustomed
to save a weak act by appealing to the dominant sentiments of the time. A team of ham acrobats or a
group of badly trained seals was coached to come into their
finale brandishing the Stars and Stripes. When a mind-reader,
a hoofer, or a whisky tenor seemed unlikely to make his own
way the orchestra was cued to play the "Star Spangled Banner" at curtainfall. Universally effective during wartime, the
practice has by no means lost its value now, and it may be
supposed that the practice of theater managers represents a
sound principle of psychology. It does. The flag is irrelevant
to acrobatic skill and the "Star Spangled Banner" has no relation to a hoofer's art, but relevancy and relationship are
supplied by the logic of sentiment. Because the flag and the
anthem symbolize to the audience certain sentiments which
they possess, they promptly identify those sentiments with the
performers, and so break into applause. Thus stated, the principle is seen to be one of the most useful in the literary world.

The first chapter of a book which has been widely recommended to college freshmen is called "The Origins of the
American Mind." Halfway down the first page the author
states his intention of finding those origins. In the course of
the book he finds them, describes the American mind in detail,
and on the basis of his description proves many interesting
theses about the history and civilization of the United States.
But the title of the first chapter states a fallacy that vitiates
the whole book, "The Origins of the American Mind." It

seems not to have occurred to the author that his book was dedicated to a description of something which does not exist, or that his analysis of the non-existent can have no meaning. For, of course, there is no such thing as the American mind. The phrase represents to any given person merely a group of his private sentiments, and though it may be used to symbolize those sentiments for people who share them, it is barren of meaning to people who do not. Its meaning, that is, does not derive from any objective thing but depends on the logic of sentiment, precisely like the applause that greets a ham actor waving a flag.

The fallacy is elementary but, because it has been so wide-spread in contemporary thinking, it may be examined at some length. If we set out to demonstrate the existence of the American mind we may, of course, establish it by definition, a procedure to which no objection may be made. We may say, for example, that we shall consider Benjamin Franklin a representative American, and that we shall call minds which are like his American minds, those unlike his being necessarily non-American. We may now make generalizations about the American mind and they will be unexceptionable so long as we hold rigidly to our definition—we must say nothing about the American mind that is not true of Franklin's mind. But now we think of one of Franklin's contemporaries, Jonathan Edwards, who was quite as characteristic an American as he. It, therefore, seems desirable to enlarge our definition to include Edwards; but since two minds could not readily be more different than his and Franklin's, our definition becomes untrustworthy. It can justify few generalizations, and any statement we may make on the basis of it is likely to be challenged on the ground that, though true of Edwards or of Franklin, it is not true of the other one, and is, therefore, untrue of the American mind. But J. Hector St. John Crèvecœur, a contemporary of Franklin and Edwards, was a characteristic American, and so was Samuel Adams, and it is clear that their minds cannot be called similar to each other or to those already included in our definition, or to either of them. If the definition is expanded to anatomize these four as the American mind it has already become almost meaningless, since what must be disregarded is much greater than what they can be shown to have in common. What can be said about the American mind on the basis of these irreconcilables? Nothing with certainty and very little with sense. Add now such characteristic American contemporaries as Count Rumford, Lorenzo Dow, Thomas Jefferson, Daniel Boone, Benjamin Rush, Thomas Paine, Alexander Hamilton, John Sevier, Robert Morris, Hugh Henry Brackenridge, William Findley, James McGready, John Hancock, Mother Ann Lee, John Singleton Copley, Aaron Burr, and Manuel Lisa. All generalization has ceased to be possible; the common characteristics of these persons, from which the American mind is to be derived, are so purely formal that nothing can be said except that they were all bipeds and spoke more or less similar dialects of English. To select a few characteristics of some of them and to ignore the opposite characteristics of others would be farcical. Yet analysts of the American mind ask their fiction to harmonize such disparate Americans as these, and then extend it backward to cover the colonies for a century and a half, and require people who quarreled endlessly with one another to agree for the sake of sweet hypothesis. Thereupon, this essence having been distilled, they find it capable of reducing to a unity of indigenous American characteristics such intelligences as Emerson and Henry Ford, Brigham Young and Abraham Lincoln, Kit Carson and the late Gamaliel Bradford, Willard Gibbs and Frances E. Willard, Francis Grierson and Thomas A. Edison, Henry James and Mary Baker Eddy, Ulysses S. Grant and Henry Adams, Bronson Alcott and Jesse James, Andrew Mellon and Eugene V. Debs, John Noyes and Commodore Vanderbilt, Charles A. Lindbergh and Julia Ward Howe, Jefferson Davis and Babe Ruth and the Fox sisters and Henry George and Edgar Allan Poe and John D. Rockefeller and William Lloyd Garrison and Jim

Bridger and Emily Dickinson and Theodore Roosevelt and Mae West.

What any two of these minds have in common for the distillation of a national mind is enormously diluted when any third one is added, till a generalization about any six of them is worthless. The American mind thus comes down to the human mind; but it was in an effort to distinguish from the latter what was unique in the former that the original effort was made. Here the logic of sentiment begins to operate. Since the heterogeneity of the American cannot be reduced, the phrase "the American mind" corresponds to nothing real; but it is given a subjective meaning by a very simple mechanism.

The person who goes in search of the American mind has certain sentiments about it and, usually, wants to say certain things about it. The phrase represents those sentiments, and he selects from America or the Americans whatever corresponds to them and dismisses the rest. That selection and dismissal make the phrase a symbol, and to personify it requires but a short step beyond. Personification having occurred, the phrase has a life of its own and one may reason about it as if it were an entity, as if it really existed. Although there is no such thing as the American mind, the searcher may think beautifully about it. The abstraction is in accord with his sentiments: when he says something about the American mind he is really saying "Certain aspects of America or of certain American minds, which I prefer to consider, excluding those which differ from or contradict them, fulfill my ideas of what the American mind should be." The assertion is disarming but would serve as a warning that what he alleges about America is subjective—which is why it is never made. It shows that appeal is being made not to objective fact, to history, sociology, or psychology, to the United States and its inhabitants—but only to similar sentiments. Whoever has such sentiments about those selected aspects will probably applaud as the curtain comes down. But a person who does not share them, together with one who is thinking objectively about America or the Americans, will find himself trying to find meaning where no meaning is possible. To such a person the search for the American mind, whether accompanied by the "Star Spangled Banner" or the "Internationale," will be only an annoying kind of nonsense.

II

For many years the search for the American mind—and such similar personifications as "the American point of view," "the soul of America," and "the American experience"—was a prerogative of politicians, clerical spellbinders, and foreigners, especially Englishmen, on tour. About 1914, however, a number of literary critics, feeling confident that an acquaintance with a number of American novels and essays gave them authority about the past, undertook to rewrite American history in accordance with their sentiments. Their apprenticeship, observe, had been served in literary criticism, a profession in which impreciseness of idea is a virtue and a generalized sentiment is much better than a fact. It followed that the history they wrote was an "interpretation," a search for symbols that could be personified.

It would be unsafe to generalize about the literary mind, but the books of these critics are tangible data and subject to analysis. They reveal a group of curiously disparate sentiments which, nevertheless, have in common a desire to project their prejudices on the past in the shape of general ideas. In addition, they have in common an invincible ignorance of the history they are endeavoring to rewrite. Ignorance is not a satisfactory equipment for a historian, and it is not helped much by disdain of the methods and material of history. The literary historian practices intuition as a method of research. He has frequently announced his superiority to facts and customarily dismisses as a pedant the historian who insists on saying nothing that facts do not justify. He prefers truths— poetic perceptions, guesses, and beautiful notions.

He prefers, that is, the literary idea. His criteria are those of literary criticism, of fantasy and poetic necessity, not those of the objective world. The symbol is the final authority. When Mr. Mumford, for instance, symbolizes his sentiments about the Middle Ages by remarking that their world went to hell when people began to hang clocks in steeples, he is within the privileges of a poet. The idea has much sentimental force and suggests a great many pleasing and persuasive if somewhat indefinite emotions: in literary criticism, therefore, it has absolute validity. But when a writer forsakes literary criticism in order to make statements of fact about the past he must meet other criteria than those of pleasure and persuasiveness. For the past is a fact of experience. The events that happened during it actually happened and, within varying limits, are recoverable. A statement about it is worth nothing, is worth less than nothing, if it does not correspond to the recoverable facts. When you set out to write history, no poetry however beautiful and no sentiments however commendable can be substituted for statements of fact.

Such literary ideas about America may be illustrated, on a simple level, by Mrs. Mary Austin's doctrine of occupational rhythms. Mrs. Austin feels deeply that the rhythms of our daily lives must have a formative effect on our minds and so on our speech and writing. It is a pleasing idea, and so in the domain of literary criticism it is valid. But the logic of sentiment projects it into the area of fact. The "must be" of poetry becomes the "has been" of history. Lincoln at the dedication of the Gettysburg cemetery, Mrs. Austin says, "fell unconsciously into the stride of one walking a woodland path with an ax on his shoulder." To illustrate the rhythm of that stride forming the rhythm of speech, she quotes from the peroration of the Gettysburg address, setting it off as follows:

It is rather for us
Here to be dedicated to the great task
Remaining before us;
That from these honored dead we take

Renewed devotion to that cause
For which they gave the last full measure of devotion.
That we here highly resolve
That these dead shall not have died in vain;
That this nation under God
Shall have a new birth of freedom.

It is probably pedantic to wonder why the rhythm of one of Lincoln's occupations should form this speech to the exclusion of his experiences as a storekeeper, flatboatman, lawyer, and politician, and to inquire just how the ax on the shoulder is discernible or how the path is shown to be in the woodland. It is not pedantic, however, to point out that in her quotation Mrs. Austin twice departs from the text of the speech [1] and that one departure alters the rhythm, nor is it pedantic to bring what she says to the test of fact. If the passage means anything outside of poetry, it means that the quoted words have the same rhythm as a man walking. It means that his steps mark the accents of the lines. Well, anyone who cares to make the experiment will find out that they cannot be walked.

Mrs. Austin goes on: "Thus the rail splitter arrives at his goal with the up-swing and the down-stroke:

That government of the people
For the people
By the people
Shall not perish from the earth!

And the ax comes to rest on the chopping log while a new length is measured." Mrs. Austin here achieves the triumph of misquoting the best-known line ever written by an American.[2] If this means anything it means that logs can be chopped or rails split to the quoted lines. But they cannot be—either

[1] The accepted text of the Gettysburg address, the one which is usually reprinted today and the one which Mrs. Austin appears to be quoting, is Lincoln's sixth manuscript copy—sent to the Sanitary Fair at Baltimore. It reads "for us to be here dedicated," and "we take increased devotion." The quoted words are unchanged in all the other manuscript copies that still exist and in the only accepted transcript of the speech actually made by a listener at the time of its delivery.

[2] Quoted from *The American Rhythm*, 1923. In 1930 a second, enlarged edition was published: the quoted passages are unchanged.

by an amateur or by a woodsman. And if they cannot be, what happens to Mrs. Austin's beautiful idea? This I think: it retains its power of evocation as poetry, but in the domain of fact, into which she projects it by discovering the rhythms of woodchopping in the Gettysburg address, it is utter nonsense.

That is a comparatively simple projection of a literary idea into history but it shows the process clearly. Because it is beautiful (*i.e.*, because it accords with certain sentiments) it must be true, and because it must be true, therefore it is true. The same process appears in, for instance, Mr. Lewis Mumford's discovery of the Golden Day in American life. This is an effort to find a place and time in American history which please the discoverer (accord with his sentiments), so that by describing them he will be able to express his dislike of other portions of that history. It is a selective *a priori* undertaking. By ignoring all parts of the past, all sections of the country, and all Americans that contradict his thesis, Mr. Mumford easily satisfies the requirements of his Golden Day. But it is the Golden Day of Mr. Mumford, not of America, for his analysis disregards all that cannot be harmonized with the thesis. So far as it is history at all, it is a history of Mr. Mumford's sentiments—which are interesting but should not be mistaken for the United States. Mr. Willian Aylott Orton, on a similar subjective quest, has recently identified another Golden Day in American history. The most interesting aspect of his discovery is the fact that his Golden Day ends just before Mr. Mumford's begins. The Regionalists of the South have also produced a Golden Day—in a time and a society antipathetic to both Mr. Orton and Mr. Mumford. . . . It is a characteristic of objective fact that when people refer to it they can, whatever their sentiments, agree on a description of it. No one can object to a critic's writing his emotional autobiography in terms of the United States. It is not autobiography that is objectionable, but the attempt to pass off autobiography as history.

All these literary efforts display a hunger for unity. They are efforts to impose order and simplicity upon an obstinate multiplicity, and their authors are incorrigible monists. The realities of the American past refuse to form coherent sequences, being full of contradictions, disparate elements, eccentric and disruptive forces that war on one another, events and tendencies and personalities that cannot be reduced to formula. Against this multiplicity the monist makes headway by sheer violence of personification. He has his words, his symbols, the embodiment of his sentiments, and by treating the words as things, he is able to perceive a subjective order in the data that refuse to arrange themselves. Mr. V. F. Calverton's effort to force American history into a Marxist commentary on American literature is at once regrettable and absurd. Regrettable because history has not yet adequately studied the inter-class and intra-class struggles in America and their amazing shifts, and it could use more analysis from even the simple Marxian formula than it has yet received— and Mr. Calverton thus disregarded a promising opportunity. Absurd because, though engaged in a work of history, he decided to remain within the area of his preconceptions. He was content, that is, to write his history by *a priori* deduction from a half-dozen phrases. Simplification enabled him to reduce the complex and inharmonious class and sectional interests of three centuries to a simple article of faith, the Marxian Class Struggle. Personification enabled him to make such phrases as "bourgeois ideology," "bourgeois philosophy," "bourgeois conception of life" crush the disorderly into order. They are subjective phrases; they symbolize Mr. Calverton's sentiments but are barren of meaning. What is "bourgeois"? What is it, especially, when applied to the expansion of a nation across a continent through three centuries? Mr. Calverton asks us to assume that the "ideology" of a Salem shipowner of 1800 is reconcilable, even identical, with that of a Charleston factory of 1700 and that of a San Francisco stockbroker of 1900. This monster of contradiction, even, is not enough, and we are re-

quired to believe that frontiersmen of all sections and all
periods, although mystically opposed to this ideology, also
share and condition it. Well, by convention or agreement, we
might permit the phrase to stand for one of them and so avoid
fallacy, but a statement made about America in terms of them
all can only be preposterous. In three centuries America has
contained not one but fifty bourgeoisies, and their interests,
on which their "ideologies" primarily depend, have mostly
been in violent conflict with one another. To identify one with
another, to detect a fundamental agreement among them, is to
make an irreparable blunder. It is to be struck blind to the
realities of history, and to lose the objective world in the de-
lusions of faith or fanaticism.

Mr. Calverton's survey, chasing bourgeois ideology through
American history by means of American literature, appeared
only a few months after Mr. Ludwig Lewisohn had hunted another personification through the same covert. Mr. Lewisohn's
quarry was the Puritan, and the Puritan turned out to be a
person whose sexual behavior and philosophy Mr. Lewisohn
could not bring himself to admire. The two books may well
signify a change in critical fashions. A good many literary
critics before Mr. Lewisohn had denounced America in the
name of the Puritan, but it was difficult to get them to agree
about the nature of their prey. The Puritan was alleged to be
so many incompatible things that he had identity only in the
logic of sentiment: he was whatever, at the moment, you happened to dislike in American history. Very possibly, that
burden of symbolical cliché may have permanently shifted
to the bourgeois ideology. The literary lynching of the Puritan, and especially of his sexual timorousness, Mr. Calverton
decides, dealt chiefly with myth. . . . Yes. And the bourgeois ideology?

III

Another of Mr. Calverton's phrases is "frontier individualism," which brings us to the favorite personification of the

literary historians. Discovering the frontier something more than a generation after legitimate historians had exhaustively surveyed the facts about it, they have given it a fundamental place in their systems. It has proved possible for historians to arrive at a few generalizations about the frontier. But it has proved possible only by means of a long study of an almost infinite number of facts. When a historian speaks of the frontier he refers to those facts, whereas in the mouth of a literary historian the word means only another projection of his sentiments precisely like "the American mind." It means, that is, another simplicity, another unity—which is to say one more distortion of history.

Let us examine "frontier individualism," a cliché which Mr. Calverton received from a long line of critics. Such a word as "individualism" is dangerously vague; it cannot possibly be qualitative but only at best, and doubtfully, quantitative. Yet the literary historian uses it as if it designated a thing as precisely as the "oxygen" or "acid" of chemistry. There were many frontiers and they differed considerably, and to lump them all together as individualistic is to avoid meaning anything. Are we to think of the individualistic enterprise of bear-hunting, or the coöperative enterprise of roof-raising or tariff-fighting? A man may be one hundred per cent individualistic on land-tenure and zero per cent individualistic on water-rights: is he an individualist or an advocate of community coöperation? The frontier which expropriated Spanish land-grants, riparian rights, and the grazing privilege would seem to be notably less individualistic than the one which enforced the right of preëmption. If piratical laissez-faire was characteristic of some frontiers, coöperative enterprise, and even communism, were quite as characteristic of other frontiers. What does the phrase mean? Clearly, whatever sentiments it symbolizes.

The method is to annihilate by a personification whatever contradicts the literary historian or diminishes the effectiveness of his thesis. Thus the birth of a demiurge: the "pioneer," a person who went West and created the frontier. To the critic he was one kind of person, a quite simple kind. It is a kind, however, that changes with the nature of the critic's aversions; so that the pioneer who for one analysis is a Rousseauian conducting "an experimental investigation of Nature, Solitude, the Primitive Life," is for the purpose of another a Puritan (a Calvinist, a believer in a completely antagonistic set of ideas) who is in search of the only good that religious people recognize, financial gain. He goes West because he is "unadjusted" or "maladjusted," because he is an economic misfit, because he resents authority or cannot stand discipline, because he is driven to escape reality, because he is under a compulsion to "revert." It turns out, too, with the happiest results, that he is coarse, hard, extraverted, unintelligent, devoid of imagination and culture, resentful and contemptuous of everything he does not understand. He is a pretty accurate summary of the critic's phobias. And he wears well, for throughout history he does not change.

It would be a mistake to expect complexity in the society which so simple a person creates. The life of the frontier, we are told, "is life at a rudimentary animal level, a life that does not rise above the latitude of the spinal column." Frontier society was "an infantile society, infantile in its homicidal impulses, infantile in its mental development, infantile in its humor . . . infantile, in fact, in most of its tastes and interests and preferences." Observe with what assured ease the critic reduces to unity the greatest confusion of cultures, nationalities, and races in modern history, diffused over one of the largest national areas and most diversified geographies in the world, subject to change and circumstance through three centuries. This is literary intuition, and it asks us to suppose that on the frontier climate, geography, wealth, commerce, and occupation produced no differentiation. All races, all degrees of intelligence, all individual variation, that is, and all the differences of religion and private interest and group effort and civil war were overcome by some process of mystical disintegration. If you remember that, elsewhere in the literary scheme, the frontier is inhabited by a race of obstinate individualists, you are to submerge the recollection in the realization that the logic of sentiment recognizes no contradictions.

One might inquire whether infantile is not an apt adjective to describe a mind which finds chaos so singularly unified. From any point of view such a description of the frontier is naïve; from the historian's point of view it is incomprehensible. A historian does not speak of the frontier's "tastes and interests and preferences." He sees the frontier as many different places in many stages of development, inhabited by many different people with many different kinds and degrees of culture, intelligence, racial tradition, family training, and individual capacity. He cannot speak of the life of the frontier, for he knows many kinds of frontier and many kinds of people living many kinds of lives. He cannot call any of them infantile, for he does not assume that people lapse to an infantile level when they move to a place which a literary critic happens to dislike. He sees many kinds of civilization, many kinds of education, many interests, many institutions, many forces. He deals, that is, with a complexity, with a constantly changing, extremely intricate set of relationships. When he thinks of Timothy Flint, publishing Byron and Shelley and reviewing French politics in his magazine, while the swamps of frontier Cincinnati were still undrained, he does not lump him with a *mangeur du lard* on Black's Fork and say that their mental development was infantile. It is beyond the reach of his integrity to assert that both the squatters of Bayou Tensas and the Chouteau family of frontier St. Louis lived at a rudimentary animal level. In most of the frontier explorers, many of the frontier politicians, many of the frontier teachers and inventors and parsons and organizers—in Ashley and Jedediah Smith, in Benton and Lincoln, in Judah and Sutter and Brigham Young—he fails to find evidence of the infantile mind. He does not ignore such a frontiersman as

Francis Grierson, or the biography of his neighbors which Grierson wrote, when he considers the spiritual squalor of the frontier. He does not ignore the commonwealths and social institutions which the frontier built when he considers its failure to rise above the level of the spinal column. . . . The frontier is not a person to him; it is a relationship among many variables, and his analysis of it must be complex. To select any one or any group of those variables and to ignore the rest is as ignorant, or as dishonest, as to describe the soil of the frontier as clay or its rock as sandstone. Clay and sandstone, rudimentary animal life and infantile mental development were there—as elsewhere in the known world. But a report which confines itself to either is unusable as fact and childish as judgment.

Ignorance or dishonesty—it is an unpleasant dilemma. Happily, we need not impale the critic on either of its horns, for there is another explanation. His ignorance of history, of course, tends toward maximum, but his profession is the better key to him. He comes to history from the criticism of literature, an activity in which success is attainable by means of sustained thinking. If you sit down and think about a literary problem it will eventually yield. It is because he tries to apply this combination of intuition and introspection as a historical method that he produces his grotesque results. His frontier is just one more unity, another personification, a cliché like "the American mind," significant only as an embodiment of his sentiments.

Method and results are summed up in a passage which one of these critics devotes to the coarsening effects of the frontier on the pioneer, in which he quotes an English traveler's reflections. After looking at the frontier, this traveler decides that man is more virtuous when subjected to culture. He supports his declaration by mentioning the wild strawberry, which is insipid in flavor, wild peaches which are tasteless as a turnip, and wild roses which have little or no scent. No historian, I imagine, believes that an analogy from botany is worth much as historical judgment. But such an analogy as this one is a splendid literary idea and so it is irresistible to the literary historian. It is striking and picturesque—it must be true. But even so, it would have been wiser to investigate. For, whatever tasted like turnips on the frontier, wild peaches did not. Peaches are not indigenous to America: there is no such thing as a wild American peach. And the traveler could not even have tasted an "escape"; for if it was frontier, there had not been time for trees to escape from cultivation, and if there had been, the escaped peach does not ripen. Also, some varieties of wild roses have a strong, distinctive perfume. And finally, the wild strawberry has more flavor than the domesticated varieties—which have achieved size, color, texture, and stability at the expense of flavor.

These are facts, the inconvenient data to which the literary historian is superior. The first of them is available in all histories of American horticulture, in all botanies, in most general histories, and even in the encyclopedias. The other two are more accessible still, facts of experience open to everyone. But the English traveler's literary ideas, exactly opposite to the facts, were persuasive—and they served the critic's purpose. Why, then, should they be verified? His sentiments, in this instance, require wild strawberries to be tasteless, and that ends the matter. He has found a symbol, he has projected his resentments and dislikes. He has written a portion of his autobiography, and the facts of history, an objective pursuit, seem to him trivial and pedantic. They are irrelevant to his higher truth, and, besides, they provide him with no mirror in which to find himself.

IV

These historians divide into sharply differing schools of thought. Each of them has identified and isolated these various phantasms—the American mind, the Puritan, the frontier, the bourgeois ideology, and a good many more. Each one can identify them to the last watermark, and invariably they turn out to be a summary of the sentiments and prejudices for which the school stands. They are never, by any chance, the same for two different groups, and so there is much warfare in the name of heresy. With that term the somewhat puzzled onlooker at last gets on familiar ground; it gives him a key to the controversy and he knows what to expect. He recalls another, earlier argument equally endless and fundamentally the same. Substance, essence; generation, creation; emanation, incarnation; *homoousion, homoiousion*— over these words other generations fought the same battles. Our historians of the intangible are the Fathers, the Schoolmen, Eusebius, Athanasius, Peter Abelard, William of Champeaux. It is only an accident of time that has them searching for the American mind—they are metaphysicians, they are theologians, and they pursue the *nous* through material that differs only in appearance from that which their predecessors treated. They work on a plane altogether separated from the desire of the earthbound for ideas that correspond to something in the real world. With the history that is the past of men, ideas, and events they have only a formal relationship: it is the springboard from which they dive into dogma and systemmaking. Their significance is primarily that of the unconscious mind or, if you like, of the soul, not of logic. And Miss Gertrude Stein, who is the Sibyl of this age, supplies a description of it. Miss Stein found occasion to tell Bertrand Russell that a knowledge of the classics was not essential in the United States. She has Miss Alice B. Toklas thus report her: "She grew very eloquent on the disembodied abstract quality of the American character and cited examples mingling automobiles with Emerson and all proving that they did not need Greek." That is the method of literary history in America. It is very eloquent. It deals with disembodied abstract qualities and with such spectral shapes as the American character. It mingles automobiles with Emerson. And it proves a lot.

It is an attractive and no doubt entertaining pursuit, but it belongs somewhere within the wide, elastic boundaries of literature. Nearly everyone enjoys metaphysical debate, many of us derive great profit from it, and for many people it is the most important thing in the world. Only, metaphysics is not experience, and the philosophy of history is not history. It is nice to be told how imaginative people wish the past had arranged itself or how they can arrange it on their own behalf; but that information differs in important ways from the past. It would, therefore, seem desirable to hold our literary historians to a responsibility at least as strict as that which we try to exact from manufacturers. No code of fair practices in thinking beautifully about America seems practicable; there is no way of insisting that the vendor shall beware. But he is constantly misbranding his product and selling it as something different from what it is, to the possible damage of the consumer. For fraud of that sort neither generous emotion nor sheer ignorance would excuse a manufacturer of canned ham. Why should it excuse the manufacturer of history?

There is an eternal, fundamental, and irreconcilable difference between fantasy, any kind of fantasy, and fact. The fantasies of the literary historian are frequently beautiful and nearly always praiseworthy, but they are a form of protective or of wishful thinking, a form of illusion and even of delusion, and they must be constantly denounced as such. The past of America is immensely complex and immensely at war with itself. No unity exists in it. Its discords and contradictions cannot be harmonized. It cannot be made simple. No one can form it into a system, and any formula that explains it is an hallucination. The person who wants to understand it must enter upon a tedious, rigorous, and almost endless labor. Without that labor, and without a mind both able and willing to distinguish between the thing that is and the thing that is desired, nothing profitable can be said about our history. With them, nothing whatever can be said that implies simplicity, unity, or beautiful ideas. For that reason, or some other, literary historians have unanimously declined the labor, preferring the *must be* and the *ought to be* to the cold fact. Theirs is the easier method—to think it out. Doubtless that results in comfort of a kind, and in certainty. But also it is a fantasy. No one can object to it as such, but it should be labeled.

DEMOCRACY AND THE EXPERT

By *Felix Frankfurter*

I

EPITAPHS for democracy are the fashion of the day. Both Left and Right acclaim the failure of democracy. Those who chafe at governmental intervention are as distrustful of popular institutions as are the romantics who expect from government heaven upon earth. Dictatorships are dramatic and *coups d'état* feed the imagination, while democratic régimes have about them the humdrum qualities of John Bull, who, first in the modern world, devised talk as the chief instrument of government. Sensational and violent rule in Russia and Italy throws out of perspective more plodding popular institutions. But it is simply not true that the area of democratic government has contracted. Barring Italy, no country has abandoned democratic institutions, whereas democratic government has extensively replaced oligarchy, and the democratic idea is steadily corroding ancient autocratic traditions. The replacement of Romanoffs by Bolsheviks was certainly not a democratic loss. Nor did the short-lived Spanish dictatorship supplant a virile democracy. For the democrat, only Fascist Italy is a retrogression. But, on the other hand, a stable German Republic has displaced the Germany of the Kaiser. In succession to the feudalism of the Hapsburgs, Hungary and Jugoslavia have reigns at least not more autocratic than they were in pre-war days, while Czechoslovakia has the heartening rule of President Masaryk, and Austria is a stout though poverty-stricken little republic. The ferment of democracy is active in modern Turkey, and is leavening the ancient fabrics of India and China with hope and danger. Nor should the most summary account of recent democratic trends omit the steady invigoration of the mentality as well as the processes of democracy in Latin-American countries, particularly Mexico.

The ultimate justification for democracy still remains the lack, in the long run, of a decent and workable substitute. The case for democracy has just been vindicated by General Smuts, the philosopher-statesman, in the full perspective of recent history and his great experience in war and peace:—

> The end of government is not merely good government, but the education of the people in good government, its self-education in running its own affairs. . . . The short cuts do not really bring us much farther, except to the next turn of the wheel of revolution. Liberty as a form of political government is a difficult experiment, and it is not without its dangers. . . . But it is at any rate less dangerous than its alternatives, and under modern conditions it is probably the only political system that promises to endure. . . . Bolshevism and Fascism, which are the current alternatives to democratic liberty, may be defended as a way out of intolerable situations, but they are temporary expedients, often tried and discarded before, and they will be discarded again after the present trials. . . . No enduring system can be established on the negation of liberty, even if it comes with the temporary gift of good government.

This is a firm expression of allegiance to democracy, but one misses the lyric note which characterized the democratic faith a hundred years ago. The tasks and conditions that confront democracy leave no true friend without concern. Oversimplification is a great deceiver of reason, and nineteenth-century democracy suffered from the illusions of simplicity.

This early democratic faith was sustained by a gracious and civilized conception of society. But the difficulties in the way of its attainment were grossly undervalued. The tenacity of old habits, the fragility of human material, the conflicting forces within the individual no less than the clash of interests within society—all these and more were much too lightly weighed. The appeal of a generous society subordinated the question of means by which it was to be attained. Vast hopes were founded on simple devices. Popular rule was expected to work miracles almost automatically. Abolish autocratic rule; remove tyranny, and the innate goodness of mankind will prevail! It was indeed largely a negative faith.

The day of such comfortable thoughts is over. We now know that democracy is dependent on knowledge and wisdom beyond all other forms of government. The grandeur of its aims is matched by the difficulties of their achievement. For democracy is the reign of reason on the most extensive scale. It seeks to prevail when the complexities of life make a demand upon knowledge and understanding never made before, and when the forces inimical to the play of reason have power and subtlety unknown in the past. We have seen the intricate range of problems thrown up by our industrial civilization; the vast body of technical knowledge, more and more beyond the comprehension even of the cultivated, which is required for an analysis of the issues underlying these problems and an exploration of possible remedies. We have also noted the opportunities for arousing passions, confusing judgment, and regimenting opinion that are furnished by chain newspapers, cheap magazines, the movies, and radio. And we now know how slender a reed is reason—how recent its emergence in man, how deep the countervailing instincts and passions, how treacherous the whole rational process. Moreover, the whole tempo of our society is hurried; its atmosphere and appurtenances hostile to reflection. Thus reason is asked to flourish when the conditions for it are least favorable.

Little wonder that, for many, democracy seems ripe for the museum of political institutions. They assess its results as bankruptcy and find its inherent difficulties fatal. The naïve champions of democracy at least built on hope; these latter-day assailants are moved by fear. Both present foes and early friends disregard time and history. The apostles of democracy expected quick results. Those who despair of democracy also lack patience. The former thought they were writing on a clean slate; they forgot the obduracy of the past. Those who concentrate on the defects of democracy are blind to what history discloses of the weaknesses of alternative forms of government.

The answer to the defects of democracy is not denial of the democratic idea. Judged by the most pragmatic tests, democracy has weathered the cataclysm of the World War and extended its rule. It is the worse for wear, but at least it wears. We need not fly from one romantic absolute to another. If we focus attention on the human origin of all government, we shall have a more scientific temper for dealing with its frailties. We shall equally avoid blind attachment and romantic impatience only if we recognize the essentially provisional nature of all political arrangements. Such an attitude will treat government not only as a mechanism for day-to-day adjustments, but also as an hypothesis in action, to be modified by the experience which it adduces.

II

Democracy has now been submitted to tests of time and stress that call for a reconsideration of its processes and assumptions. Such an examination must build on the new gains of knowledge since modern forms of democracy were evolved, and more especially upon the insight into the dark recesses of man's nature, which pioneers like Freud and Jung are slowly making possible. Acceptance of the democratic idea by no means implies the exhaustion of the forms in which the idea has been clothed. Indeed, we may be sure that the implements and inventions of government have not sufficiently responded to the overwhelming transformation of the external arrangements of society.

If the continuance of our civilization is to be based upon democracy, obviously knowledge and the capacity for judgment must permeate the whole community. But about education, and how to attain it, we are also far less naïve and hopeful than we used to be. The aims and methods of education are today as much under fire as are those of government. For its underpinnings, too, have been shaken by new knowledge, and we are far more humble in assuming that wisdom and a conception of the public weal attend learning. Though we are doubtful as to the true nature of education and uncertain how to pursue it, there is no paradox in assuming that effective democracy presupposes a continuous process of adult education. "We must educate our masters," said a British statesman after the Second Reform Bill gave workingmen the vote. Time has only reënforced the deep wisdom of Robert Lowe's dictum. But he overlooked the complementary truth that the people must educate their rulers. At least they must see to it that rulers are educated for the tasks of government.

I am the last person to undervalue the extent to which devotion, intelligence, and technical equipment are enlisted in government. Not political philosophy, not farsighted planning, but the same pressure of circumstances which has made government penetrate into such a wide range of affairs has compelled resort to skill and training in its work. The all too common depreciation of men in public service is at once shallow and cruel. It mocks where it should praise; it debilitates where it should encourage. Publicity headlines the occasional egregious blunder, but the detailed day-by-day achievement is unchronicled. The clash of politics, the friction between executive and legislature, the scrutiny of the press and taste for scandal, tend to make us know when things go wrong in government. It is right that it should be so. The critics of government cannot be too Argus-eyed. But no such conjunction of forces educates the public to a knowledge of the good in government. Virtue is proverbially not news, and an appreciation of achievement in government, except when attained on the colossal scale of a Panama Canal or in the dramatized conflict of foreign relations, is dependent on dull, technical details. The public is therefore surprisingly ignorant of the extent to which its servants contribute to the public good.

A very acute student of affairs thus characterizes the quiet work of public administration:—

> Most tax payers, including many who ought to be better informed, have a wholly inadequate idea of what they are getting for their money. The tendency is to regard taxes as a debit without any offsetting credit. They know what they pay out, but they fail to realize what they receive in return. The direct contact, so far as the Federal Government is concerned, is apt to be with the tax collector or the prohibition agent, men performing tasks which are extraordinarily difficult, but which, it may be, are not popular in all quarters. Now my observation of the public service . . . is that with all the defects of that service, and there are many of them and some scandals just as there are in private business, the true story of its accomplishments would disclose an astonishing and magnificent net balance on the credit side.

These are the observations of Mr. Joseph B. Eastman, who has watched government closely all his life, and now is himself one of the ornaments of the public service. He furnishes striking proof of the extraordinary gifts which government does attract. That Mr. Eastman's reappointment as member of the Interstate Commerce Commission should have been strongly urged by railroads whose views on vital issues he has rejected also proves that, so far as the public opinion which asserts itself is sufficiently informed regarding the quality of public work, disinterested capacity in government will find support.

III

That talent should find its way into public administration is the more striking since our public service enjoys so little public esteem. The rewards neither of money nor of prestige go with it. It is right that government should not even pretend to compete with the enormous salaries by which private enterprise tempts. The satisfactions of government service lie on a different level. But it is wholly wrong to expect civilized standards of public service from officials whose salaries are too low to enable them to meet the minimum standards of cultivated life. The public cannot expect the professional training, the detached judgment and moral courage, necessary for the conduct of such intricate public affairs as, for instance, the administration of public-service laws, from officials who are under financial pressure to meet the cost of decent education for their children. It is grotesque to put the solution of public-utility problems in the hands of commissioners who are paid $1600 a year. The average for all commissioners in the country is about $5000—an average which includes exceptionally high salaries in two states. Public officials should set an example of simplicity, but they ought not to be subjected to penury. Economy in public service means a wise expenditure of money. It does not mean salaries so low that only the unfit and the transient are attracted.

But that the public service, except in the highest offices, is so largely without prestige is even more disastrous than that its material rewards are unduly meager. The whole tide of opinion is against public administration as a career for talent. The enormous rewards which industry offers to able young lawyers, engineers, economists, serve as a powerful attraction to ambitious youth. As against that, there are some, and more than we suspect, who find real satisfaction in work whose aim is the public good. But they have to contend against the whole mental and moral climate of our times—the impalpable but terrific pressure of current standards of achievement. These are overwhelmingly on the side of private gain.

In Great Britain the traditions of public service are as yet powerful enough to enlist the best brains of the country. In its Civil Service is found probably the largest concentration of distinguished talent. Nor is it conceivable that Great Britain would have come through its storms and stresses since the Crimean War without the very high quality of its public administration. The accession of the Labor Party to power in 1924 marked a political revolution in British history. Yet the break with the past involved in a government committed to the principles of socialism was accomplished with a shift in personnel of less than one hundred persons. In large matters of foreign policy one can hardly conceive of more contrasting types than Lord Curzon and Mr. Ramsay MacDonald. Yet, when Mr. MacDonald succeeded Lord Curzon at the Foreign Office, the official who had served Lord Curzon continued as Mr. MacDonald's private secretary. Perhaps nothing could more pithily reveal how ingrained is the Civil Service in the stuff of English life. Yet the transition from the days when public office was bartered as though it were the private property of politicians to the present system of professional public administration is a surprisingly recent development. It was introduced within the memory of men still living.

Experience in India had made it abundantly clear that the government of a great empire required special training, and disinterested selection. Therefore, as early as 1833, the government bill introduced by Macaulay for the renewal of the charter of the East India Company provided that "East India cadetships should be thrown open to competition." This radical change as to Indian administration did not become effective until 1855.

In the meantime, however, Sir Charles Trevelyan, a former Indian Civil Servant and Macaulay's brother-in-law, began to occupy his mind with problems of Civil Service reform at home. "The revolutionary period of 1848," he explained years later, "gave us a shake, and created a disposition to put our house in order, and one of the consequences was a remarkable series of investigations into Public Offices which lasted for five years and culminated in the Organization Report." Of that report, issued in 1854, Sir Charles Trevelyan himself, in collaboration with Sir Stafford Northcote, was the author. "It was based throughout upon the positive idea of Government, upon the idea that Government must be carried on by men who think as to what ought to be done, instead of merely doing that which must be done. The idea frightened some of the ablest of the existing heads of departments." Even the famous Undersecretary for the Colonies, Sir James Stephen, father of James Fitzjames and Leslie Stephen and grandfather of Virginia Woolf, found the innovation too drastic. "The world we live in is not, I think, half moralized enough for the acceptance of such a scheme of stern morality as this."

Sir James underestimated, as the worldly-wise often do, the tough fiber of the world he lived in. Or perhaps it is more accurate to say that the painful experience of the Crimean War helped immensely to educate British opinion to an acceptance of Trevelyan's proposal. The conduct of that war exposed the terrible mischief of an administrative system based on patronage. So hard-headed a politician as Lord Palmerston, by an order in council, carried into effect the recommendations of the Trevelyan-Northcote report. "In consequence, in 1855, the first Civil Service Commissioners were appointed, with the duty of carrying on an independent examination of the nominees of Members of Parliament. They had their difficulties: the idea was new that the nominees of Members of Parliament should be subject to criticism by a commission, and on one occasion Lord Palmerston sent to Somerset House, where the Civil Service Commissioners used to sit, ordering them to come to him and bring the answers of a certain candidate and the papers which they had set, in order that they might be carpeted by the Prime Minister." The Civil Service Commissioners, writes Graham Wallas with pride, "replied that unfortunately their regulations prevented them from doing anything of the kind, the papers could not go out of their possession, but if the Prime Minister would come to their office they would be only too happy to show them. Lord Palmerston saw the writing and arithmetic of his nominee and ceased to interfere." By 1870 the system had so thoroughly proved itself that Gladstone established open competition throughout the English Civil Service, by an order in council, "which was practically uncriticized and unopposed."

Students of public opinion will find it illuminating to explore the influences which made possible such a profound change in political institutions. Here, as elsewhere, working-class en-franchisement introduced powerful solvents into politics and government. But Mr. Wallas finds a deeper cause of change than the mere transference of voting power. "The fifteen years from the Crimean War to 1870 were in England a period of wide mental activity, during which the conclusions of a few penetrating thinkers like Darwin or Newman were discussed and popularized by a crowd of magazine writers and preachers and poets. The conception was gaining ground that it was upon serious and continued thought and not upon opinion that the power to carry out our purposes, whether in politics or elsewhere, must ultimately depend." "Serious and con-tinued thought" requires systematic training. And the founda-tion of the British Civil Service is laid upon the British univer-sities—until latterly the two ancient universities. The system is based upon the conviction of John Stuart Mill that "medio-crity ought not to be engaged in managing the affairs of State."

I do not mean to claim perfection for the British Civil Service, nor even the attainment of its own ideals. In the current stocktaking of English institutions, the Civil Service has not escaped. It is urged that the system has become too wooden, is not attuned to modern needs, and in some instances, particularly in the Colonial Office, defeats national policies in administrative action.

New educational developments, profound social changes, the new share of women in politics, call for a reconsideration of the assumptions and performances of the British Civil Service. With these vexing problems of statecraft and education a Royal Commission is now engaged. But the basis of political thinking by all the parties is the pervasive responsibility of a highly trained and disinterested permanent service, charged with the task of administering the broad policies formulated by Parliament and of putting at the disposal of government that ascertainable body of knowledge on which the choice of policies must be based.

The revolutionary movements of 1848 touched the United

States only by bringing to our shores liberty-loving rebels from
the Continent. While, in England, 1848 led to a searching inquiry into the defects of her government, it renewed America's
assurance of the virtues of our system. Moreover, America
had no Crimean War, and perhaps no Charles Trevelyan.
Besides, we were young and had an abundance of resources.
Standards come late, and where there is plenty the temptations
to waste are usually not resisted. The key to our history of
public administration, as to much else in history, is found in
Emerson's quiet observation, "Mankind is as lazy as it dares
to be."

IV

In any event, while England was making the beginnings of a
change from patronage to public service, the United States was
justifying patronage by a political philosophy and establishing
it as a public policy. The naked defense of the spoils system
was expressed in the classic remarks of Senator Marcy in the
debate on Jackson's nomination of Martin Van Buren to be
Minister to England:—

> It may be, sir, that the politicians of the United States are not
> so fastidious as some gentlemen are as to disclosing the principles
> on which they act. They boldly preach what they practice. When
> they are contending for victory they avow their intention of
> enjoying the fruits of it. If they are defeated, they expect to re-
> tire from office. If they are successful, they claim, as a matter of
> right, the advantages of success. They see nothing wrong in the
> rule that to the victor belong the spoils of the enemy.

A hundred years have elapsed since Marcy's engaging candor. But his sentiments are still acted upon and occasionally
they survive even in avowal. Woodrow Wilson is the only
political scientist who ever occupied the Presidency. Yet it was
his Secretary of State who naïvely thought that technical posts
requiring high skill and training should be filled by "deserving
Democrats." No President has had better reason to know than
Mr. Hoover the irrelevance of purely party politics in the dis-

charge of professional duties. And yet in the appointment of judges to the lower Federal courts he has apparently, in some instances, for political reasons departed from the professional standards set by his Attorney General.

Behind the spoils system and all its survivals there is a crude logic of democracy and the versatile energy of the pioneer. Both combined to indoctrinate Americans with a distorted belief in the simplicity of government. Someone has called the British Civil Service the skill department of government. But if public administration can be improvised, if it requires no particular skill, there is no need of special training, no need of the permanence of professionalism, no need of a skill department. That is precisely what Andrew Jackson thought. He practiced rotation in office because he thought permanence makes for "corruption in some and in others a perversion of correct feelings and principles." "The duties of all public officers," Jackson wrote in his first message to Congress, "are, or at least admit of being made, so plain and simple that men of intelligence may readily qualify themselves for their performance; and I cannot but believe that more is lost by the long continuance of men in office than is generally to be gained by their experience. I submit, therefore, to your consideration whether the efficiency of the Government would not be promoted and official industry and integrity better secured by a general extension of the law which limits appointments to four years."

There is this much to be said for Jackson's rustic view. Government then was operating within a relatively limited scope. In large measure, it was forbidding conduct; it was not itself an extensive participant in devising complicated arrangements of society and composing the conflict of its manifold interests. But Harding, nearly a hundred years after Jackson, had not even Jackson's excuse. The growing complexity of social organization had compelled a steady extension of legal control over economic and social interests. At first this intervention was largely through specific legislative directions, depending for enforcement generally upon the cumbersome and ineffective machinery of the criminal law. By the pressure of experience, legislative regulation of economic and social activities turned to administrative instruments. The extent and range of governmental participation in affairs, the complexity of its administrative devices, and the intricacy of the technical problems with which they were dealing had never been greater than when Harding came to the Presidency. There never was a more pathetic misapprehension of responsibility than Harding's touching statement, "Government after all is a very simple thing."

I recall the sentence, and it deserves to be remembered, because Harding expressed the traditional American conception of government still deeply inured in American opinion. Until these notions of deluding simplicity are completely rooted out, we shall never truly face our problems of government.

The theoretical defense of the spoils system could hardly withstand its practical results. It was with the moral aspects of political jobbery that the promoters of early civil-service reform, Carl Schurz, George W. Curtis, E. L. Godkin, were mostly concerned. Corruption, not only of individuals, but of the whole democratic process, was involved. "The allurements of an immense number of offices and places exhibited to the voters of the land," wrote Cleveland, "and the promise of their bestowal in recognition of partisan activity, debauched the suffrage and robbed political action of its thoughtful and deliberative character."

But the problem, as we now see, is much more complicated. No doubt democracy is peculiarly dependent on clean and disinterested government. By the very fact of numbers, a corrupt and jaundiced democracy can be most blind and oppressive. But in the modern world the simple virtues of honesty and public devotion are not enough. Indeed, honesty and public zeal without training and a sophisticated judgment may very readily become the unwitting tool of half-truths and misrepresentation. Compelled to grapple with a world more and more dominated by technological forces, government must have at its disposal the resources of training and capacity equipped to understand and to deal with the complicated issues to which these technological forces give rise.

There is a good deal of loose talk about science in politics. If by "science in politics" is meant the availability of an irrefragable fund of knowledge in the possession of a few wise people who could, out of hand, solve the conundrums of government, it is merely another romantic delusion. But if by science we mean an intellectual procedure and a temper of mind, there must be science in government, because science dominates society. It then becomes a question of how much science government employs and how good it is.

The great political issues of the nineteenth century thrived, in the main, on the levels of feeling and rhetoric. The extension of the franchise, popular elections, the abolition of slavery (apart from its economic aspect), are not matters that yield to statistics or economic learning. But feeling and rhetoric are blind guides for the understanding of contemporary political issues. For the staples of contemporary politics—the organization of industry, the control of public utilities, the well-being of agriculture, the mastery of crime and disease—are deeply enmeshed in intricate and technical facts, and must be extricated from presupposition and partisanship. Such matters require systematic effort to contract the area of conflict and passion and to widen the area of accredited knowledge as the basis of action.

The history of reparations since the Versailles Treaty illustrates the extremely technical basis of political controversies which affect the economic balance of a good part of the world, and the social standards of millions of people. It would not be true to say that reparations presented questions merely for economists. But certainly the political judgments which were involved could only be taken blindly and in passion without an appreciation of those intricate economic factors which Maynard Keynes was the first to elucidate courageously at the bar of public opinion. Similarly, any solid judgment upon public-utility controversies presupposes the capacity to see the meaning of complicated technical data. In both these fields of politics, agitation and advocacy have their place. They are instruments of education, means for making effective the findings of knowledge and the lessons of experience. But the quiet, detached, laborious task of disentangling facts from fiction, of extracting reliable information from interested parties, of agreeing on what is proof and what surmise, must precede, if agitation is to feed on knowledge and reality, and be equipped to reach the mind rather than to exploit feeling.

"It is difficult to realize"—I quote from Graham Wallas— "how short a time it is since questions for which we now rely entirely on official statistics were discussed by the ordinary political methods of agitation and advocacy." But in the United States many of these questions are still anybody's guess—are still the football of political debate. In 1830, the House of Commons wrangled as to the existence of economic distress and its extent. In England these facts—the condition of trade and the state of unemployment—are now as dependably revealed as the barometer registers atmospheric pressure. Debate continues to be anxious and even bitter about modes for relieving unemployment. But at all events search for remedies is not confused and diverted by doubt and denial that anything needs to be remedied. We are still where England was in 1830. Congress still debates whether unemployment really exists, and, if so, where and how much. And we have the extraordinary spectacle of the Secretary of Labor of the United States issuing unemployment estimates which the Commissioner of Labor of the State of New York denies.

V

Let me take another illustration of the limited application of scientific standards in public administration. Just as in eighteenth-century England it was matter for political controversy whether the population was rising or falling, so in twentieth-century America the homicide or burglary rate in our great cities is a recurring subject for political debate. And this is a very fair index of our whole attitude toward problems of crime. That the level of professionalism, of trained capacity, in our administration of criminal justice is very low, compared with that prevailing in Great Britain and on the Continent, is one of the most patent facts about our system. In saying this I hope I can avoid the appearance of being too simple about crime. I share the conviction of all who have been long immersed in these problems that crime is a true measure of the standards of our civilization. One cannot worry much about these questions without realizing that they touch the motives and purposes and directions of contemporary society. But that our lack of professionalism affects the whole situation hardly admits of doubt. Crime is age-old and ubiquitous, but by common consent it assails in greatest measure the most prosperous country in the world.

No one will deny that problems of crime are at least as difficult as problems of public health and hydraulic engineering. But public health and hydraulic engineering are now as a matter of course made the concern of specialists who give to their problems the devotion of a lifetime. That is the essence of professionalism—men adapted by nature for inquiries for which they are elaborately trained and which they pursue as a permanent career. In regard to crime, this condition on the whole does not obtain. Knowledge of the causes of crime, the ways for its prevention and detection, the modes of its treatment, are widely deemed the common possession of the man in the street. Even where professional training is exacted, namely, from lawyers and judges who at present play such an undue rôle in the administration of criminal justice, merely a general and not a specialized training is required. But even these professionally educated functionaries play their parts for only short terms or discontinuously. In the United States there is no body of highly trained, capable men who are drawn to the enigmas of crime as problems to be solved, who are adequately disciplined for their exploration, and who give the preoccupation of a lifetime to their solution. Broadly speaking, the directing officials are not technically trained for their work before they attain office, and the want of permanent careers through office deprives the community of capitalizing office itself as a school of training. There is thus no professionalism in administration. Partly cause and partly effect, there is equally no professionalism (always broadly speaking) of research into crime, as there is research in medicine and research in the natural sciences. The two indispensable interacting forces in the promotion of knowledge and the control of natural phenomena—to wit, professionalism in inquiry and professionalism in control—are thus lacking as to crime.

There can hardly be room for difference of opinion that indispensable to any effective or candid dealing with crime is the continuous, disinterested, scientific study of its problems. Just as disease has been withdrawn from the realm of quackery and magic, so crime must be subjected to that systematic, disciplined, continuous attack of reason which we call scientific procedure. Neither crime commissions nor presidential pronouncements will make a lasting dent upon crime unless we can secure acceptance of the standards of professionalism as a postulate of our government, similar to the acceptance by the British of the ideas which underlie their Civil Service.

I am far from suggesting that the conquest of science calls for a new type of oligarchy—namely, government by experts. I mean no such thing. To call the administrative régime of the British Civil Service "the new despotism," as does Lord Hewart, is to use the language of lurid journalism. But the power which must more and more be lodged in administrative experts, like all power, is prone to abuse unless its exercise is properly circumscribed and zealously scrutinized. For we have greatly widened the field of administrative discretion and thus opened the door to arbitrariness. The dangers and difficulties have been acutely analyzed by General Smuts:—

Beneficent if kept under proper control, it [the power of the Civil Service] becomes an unmitigated bureaucracy if it assumes control itself, as it tends to do under weak and rapidly changing governments. . . . An ideal public service would go far to supply the deficiencies of democratic government, with its vacillation and inexpertness. But in the complicated organism of the state, any organ which becomes independent of the rest becomes a danger, and nothing is so dangerous to the state as a public service which does not march with the people, and becomes a drag on well-ordered progress; it may even have to be dynamited out of its fixed position.

Undoubtedly ultimate protection is to be found in ourselves, our zeal for liberty, our respect for one another and for the common good—a truth so obviously accepted that its demands in practice are usually overlooked. But safeguards must also be institutionalized through machinery and processes. These safeguards largely depend on very high standards of professional service, an effective procedure (always remembering that "in the development of our liberty insistence upon procedural regularity has been a large factor"), easy access to public scrutiny, and a constant play of alert public criticism, especially by an informed and spirited bar. Moreover, while expert administrators may sift out issues, elucidate them, bring the light of fact and experience to bear upon them, the final determinations of large policy must be made by the direct representatives of the public and not by the experts. Whether, for instance, the government should itself operate Muscle Shoals or lease its water power raises questions beyond the authority of engineer or economist. In the final analysis, we are in the realm of judgment regarding values as to which there is as yet no voice of science. The very notion of democracy implies the right of the public to decide these matters on its own choice.

VI

Government is itself an art, one of the subtlest of arts. It is neither business nor technology, nor applied science. It is the art of making men live together in peace and with reasonable happiness. Among the instruments for governing are organization, technological skill, and scientific methods. But they are all instruments, not ends. And that is why the art of governing has been achieved best by men to whom governing is itself a profession. One of the shallowest disdains is the sneer against the professional politician. The invidious implication of the phrase is, of course, against those who pursue self-interest through politics. But too prevalently the baby is thrown out with the bath. We forget that the most successful statesmen have been professionals. Walpole, Pitt, Gladstone, Disraeli, and Asquith were professional politicians. Beveridge's recent life of Lincoln serves as a reminder that Lincoln was a professional politician. Politics was Roosevelt's profession, Wilson was, all his life, at least preoccupied with politics, and Calvin Coolidge, though nominally a lawyer, has had no profession except politics. Canada emphasizes the professionalism of politics by making the Leader of the Opposition a paid officer of state.

In a democracy, politics is a process of popular education— the task of adjusting the conflicting interests of diverse groups in the community, and bending the hostility and suspicion and ignorance engendered by group interests toward a comprehension of mutual understanding. For these ends, *expertise* is indispensable. But politicians must enlist popular support for the technical means by which alone social policies can be realized. Æ summed it all up when he said, "The expert should be on tap, but not on top." In this country we have been so anxious to avoid the dangers of having the expert on top that we suffer from a strong reluctance to have him on tap.

We must also develop much more than we have another device for attaining knowledge for the guidance of public judgment. The permanent process of public administration must be reënforced from time to time by special commissions of inquiry. The history of British democracy might in considerable measure be written in terms of the history of successive Royal Commissions. We too have had notable commissions of inquiry, but, in the by and large, the experience and tradition of the British Royal Commissions are lacking in the United States. We have no standards to guide the technique of inquiry, the mode of procedure, the relations to public and executive. Yet such commissions of investigation ought more and more to be called into use to deflate feeling, define issues, sift evidence, formulate alternative remedies. If guided with imagination and courage, such commissions are admirable means for taking the nation to school. They should aim to ascertain facts, pose problems, and seek to enlighten the public mind. To be effective, such inquiries into political problems must be pursued in a scientific temper. Therefore ample time for thorough study is essential. There must be a total lack of the urgencies of the immediate, indifference to the compromises that may become pertinent after the problems are duly analyzed and alternative proposals for action suggested. Like all scientific work, this must be pursued with complete indifference to politics. It must be dedicated to the search for fact and be as free from dependence on the actual or supposed wishes or needs even of the President as is the Supreme Court of the United States.

The difficulties of our social-economic problems will not abate with time. One may be confident that they will become more complicated. They will make increasing demands upon trained intelligence. If government is to be equal to its responsibilities, it must draw more and more on men of skill and wisdom for public administration. As Oxford and Cambridge of old, our institutions of higher learning must be training schools for public service, not through utilitarian courses, but by the whole sweep of their culture and discipline. Above all, the universities must be reservoirs of disinterestedness. For the more contentious issues of politics lie not in the domain of the natural sciences. They depend on the wisdom of the social sciences. But in our generation at least, the social sciences still rest ultimately not upon verifiable and controlled experiments, but, in large measure, upon tentative conclusions and judgments. It is therefore absolutely vital that judgment be as disinterested as possible, that it be not exposed to the undertow of unconscious influences other than those which inhere in our present limited understanding of the workings of the mind. Thinking and reflection in the universities ought not to be guided along the smooth path of material interest or any of its derivatives, in all their subtle forms.

THE BIOGRAPHER AND HIS VICTIMS

By *Claude M. Fuess*

I

MY title may not seem inappropriate if we remember that the subject of any biography, except, perhaps, those written for campaign or advertising purposes, is helpless—as helpless as a criminal being led to his execution, and even more so, for a condemned murderer, though his fate is unavoidable, can at least kick and shout, while most heroes of biographies are already dead. The Great Lexicographer had been lying inanimate in Westminster Abbey for over six years before Boswell's immortal work appeared. He could not protest when Boswell revealed his absurd mannerisms and pictured him as abstractedly withdrawing a slipper from a young lady's foot. For once Dr. Johnson was silent. If the dead could rise, I suspect that the Sesquipedalian Pachyderm would have burst his cerements in 1791 and stalked forth to haunt and blast the Scotch attorney. But Boswell was safe—safe until, after his own demise, a new group of biographers pounced upon him as their victim, portrayed him as an egotistic and amorous "boozer," and exposed his indiscretions to a smiling posterity.

Some farsighted persons, like Benjamin Franklin and George Frisbie Hoar, not to mention Colonel Roosevelt and Mr. Coolidge, have attempted to forestall attack by preparing their recollections, or confessions; but even this precaution has not insured them against the future. Even after a statesman, with a disarming candor, has revealed all the blunders which he wishes the world to know, some literary scavenger is likely to prowl through those papers in the attic and expose the one shameless indiscretion which the hero was most anxious to hide. Says one of Oscar Wilde's inveterate "wise-crackers," "Every great man nowadays has his disciples, and it is always Judas who writes the biography." This is particularly true of the twentieth century, during which the good old Latin maxim, *De mortuis nil nisi bonum,* has been relegated to the rubbish pile of outworn phrases. "We are overrun," continues Wilde's Gilbert, "by a set of people who, when poet or painter passes away, arrive at the house along with an undertaker, and forget that their one duty is to behave as mutes."

The advent of the professional "debunker" has considerably changed the fashion in biography and, by popularizing it, has enormously increased its sales. It is astounding that, in an era when Maurois and Ludwig receive almost as much in royalty checks as Mr. Fletcher or Mr. Oppenheim, no one has opened a School of Biography, like the excellent institutions of Mr. Gallishaw and Dr. Esenwein, which have emitted such an army of short-story writers. More money can usually be made by telling others how to do a thing than by doing it one's self. Bond salesmen seldom get rich by investing in the securities which they so warmly recommend; and I have never heard of a croupier's finding diversion during his vacation by trying his luck at roulette. But perhaps there are two major difficulties: biography may be so simple that anybody can practice it, even without instruction; or it may be so exacting that nobody can teach it. I suspect that it is both. It is easy to do it badly, as scores of amateurs are demonstrating every year; and it is correspondingly hard to do it well, as the paucity of really first-class biographies indicates. Under the circumstances only a supremely audacious man would undertake to prescribe how biography should be written, and even he would be rushing in where more than one angel has feared to tread.

II

The preliminary question, "Is biography really a fine art?" must be answered in the affirmative. It does not, of course, require the originality, the creative power, and the inspiration—to employ a much-abused word—which distinguish the lyric poet, the composer of a symphony, or the painter of a landscape. The biographer rides on shanks' mare rather than on Pegasus. Neither James Boswell nor Emil Ludwig will be placed by the side of Keats, of Beethoven, or of Corot. There is no biographer in our American Hall of Fame. But biography does, when properly carried on, demand certain qualities which belong, in a less or greater degree, to all the arts—the wise selection of material, its arrangement in accordance with the principles of proportion and climax, and its vivid and attractive presentation. Nor can the biographer function without imagination. It is his business to become acquainted with his hero and the influences which formed his consciousness; to study his physical and mental peculiarities, his habits, his secret dreams and ambitions; to penetrate as far as possible into the recesses of his soul. To accomplish this successfully, the biographer needs discernment and sympathy, but he needs even more the gift to put himself in the place of the man about whom he is writing.

These basic attributes will always be essential to any good biographer. They belonged to Plutarch and Izaak Walton just as much as they do to Mr. Gamaliel Bradford. But the technique and aim of biography have in some respects changed very rapidly in the last thirty years. Biography used to be concerned very largely with a man's public and official acts, when he was, so to speak, decorated and on exhibition. Then someone rediscovered the disconcerting truth that the ordinary man—and the extraordinary one as well—is, in one respect at least, like an iceberg. Only about one fifth of him is actually visible. The remainder is concealed beneath the surface. So, with modern psychology to aid them, biographers have been trying to find out what flesh and clothes really cover. They are interested still in the Webster of the Seventh of March Speech; but they are fully as much concerned with what happened when the show was over and the orator, tired after the ordeal, took off his blue coat with the brass buttons, untied his thick, heavily starched stock, and settled down in his carpet slippers with his glass of whiskey toddy by his side. Complexes and inhibitions and frustrations have assumed a new significance. The quest of abnormality has been overdone, but in the process George Washington, John Marshall, and Abraham Lincoln are beginning to emerge as genuine human beings, instead of mythical demigods.

George Washington is a typical illustration of this humanization. During his lifetime, he was the center of bitter controversy. He was denounced scathingly as a President who wanted a crown, as a "snob," a "dictator," and a "traitor." To Knox and Hamilton he seemed very real. Yet after his death, when he was consecrated as the "Father of His Country," his personality was almost deified. A series of conventional biographies evolved the stately and desiccated figure of tradition, beautifully perpetuated in Greenough's statue of him in a Roman toga—a statue which was said to have maintained the "dignity of history," but which is somewhat unlike George Washington, the Virginia planter.

Like most American children in the 1890's, I was brought up on the cherry-tree episode, and I can distinctly recall being shocked by reading in Henry Cabot Lodge's delightful *Early Memories* an anecdote told to him by William Wetmore Story of a gloomy evening after the Battle of the Brandywine when the American Commander in Chief called a council of his officers. In the midst of the discussion, Washington directed one of his staff to cross the river and examine the location of the British forces. Hours passed, while they waited for the important report. Finally the aide stumbled into the tent and, in faltering tones, confessed that the storm had prevented his reaching the opposite shore. Glaring ferociously at him for a moment, Washington seized the heavy leaden inkstand on his desk and hurled it at his subordinate's head, exclaiming, "God damn your soul to Hell, be off with you and send me a man!" The tale does not make it clear whether or not Washington missed his aim. But there is something Homeric, berserker, about the episode, revealing the tremendous passions veiled by his customary self-control. Nothing, however, in the imposing biographies of Sparks and Marshall and Washington Irving and Everett indicates that the Commander in Chief was capable of such an outburst.

III

It is natural for anyone planning to perpetrate a biography to face the problem, "What should I wish posterity to say about *me?*" If Mr. Bradford were, in some whimsical mood, to turn his analytic gaze in my direction, what should I like him to notice: that golden Phi Beta Kappa key or that unpaid laundry bill; that ten-dollar check sent to an indigent cousin or that towel pilfered from the Pullman Company; that unprinted ode to spring or that kick furtively bestowed upon a stray cat? Ought not the biographer to obey the Golden Rule? Is not his responsibility grave, dealing, as he does, with another's reputation, free from the danger of a possible libel suit? Was not Iago right?

> Who steals my purse steals trash; 't is something, nothing;
> 'T was mine, 't is his, and has been slave to thousands;
> But he that filches from me my good name
> Robs me of that which not enriches him,
> And makes me poor indeed.

But it is precisely these trivialities and peccadillos which, according to modern theories, we should know if we are to reproduce the whole man. The eager credulity with which William Lloyd Garrison swallowed every newly advertised patent nostrum throws light on his mental and moral characteristics. There is much significance in President Roosevelt's remark to Owen Wister, when, after the latter had been questioning him about immortality, "T. R." replied sententiously, "One world at a time." Dr. Johnson's casual observation that "a second marriage is the triumph of hope over experience" is a sufficient comment on his marital felicity. Benvenuto

Cellini in his memoirs tells a succession of prodigious "whoppers," interspersed, however, with so much gossipy detail that we close the book feeling acquainted with the author; Mr. Coolidge, in his autobiography, deals entirely with the truth, but in such generalities that we are given no clue to the mystery of his personality.

Mr. Franklin MacVeagh related recently a story of William Jennings Bryan, who, at a Fourth of July dinner in London, after speaking with witty extemporization for five minutes, pulled out of his pocket a typewritten manuscript, and, to the disgust of his audience, read a solemn paper on European problems. The guests, expecting entertainment, soon grew resentful. The speech was obviously a failure. Afterward, Mr. MacVeagh saw the "Commoner" all by himself in the hotel corridor, looking vainly for his hat and overcoat. As the two met, Mr. Bryan said plaintively, "Mrs. Bryan told me I ought not to do that." The anecdote is slight enough; yet the picture of the great orator, neglected and disconsolate, is unforgettable.

IV

What is legitimate material for the biographer? There are, of course, the printed documents, the speeches included in the *Congressional Record*, the published essays or poems, and often the imposing edition of "collected works." In these are the hero's writings as he desired to have them, preserved, corrected, and polished for all time. Here is the man in full dress, hair neatly trimmed, shoes shined, and cravat adjusted. Lincoln is entitled to be judged as a statesman by his debates with Douglas, his Inaugural Addresses, his messages and proclamations. These are his official utterances, as much his as *Hamlet* is Shakespeare's or the "David" Michelangelo's. Contemporary newspapers, also, are of the highest importance, as showing the immediate popular reaction to significant occurrences. No one can deal fairly with any phase of United States history during the period between Grant and Roosevelt without consulting *Harper's Weekly* and the *Nation*.

Then there are the letters, many of them conventional, others expressing informal opinions representing a transitory caprice. Are we entitled to judge a man by a hastily scribbled note, mailed without any idea that it would be preserved? Perhaps not! And yet it is in these intimate communications that a man is most likely to disclose his true self. The letters of Carl Schurz to his wife during the heat of the Lincoln campaign of 1860 show an orator strong in his own conceit. "I have had a succession of triumphs," he writes, "and my exertions have been almost superhuman. . . . All my meetings are crowded, and I drive everything before me." This reveals a Carl Schurz quite different from the modest reformer of the 1880's.

Next come those impetuous acts performed without deliberation, frequently under the stress of jealousy or irritation, but only too often recorded inexorably by some unnoticed chronicler. It would be a boon to biographers if each hero's wife kept a secret journal, to be deposited in the government archives and published a century after his death. We might then know by 1952 how Webster behaved when the breakfast coffee was brought in cold or what he muttered as he glanced through the monthly bills. Perhaps the reticence of wives on these unromantic topics is the surest demonstration of connubial loyalty. As it is, we have a sufficient store of gossip, of scandalous anecdotes which have traveled in whispers from lip to lip until the original tale has been distorted beyond recognition. Every student of our history becomes familiar with books like Ben: Perley Poore's *Reminiscences*, full of fascinating stories but generally untrustworthy. Even the memories of the closest relatives and friends cannot be relied on, but must be ruthlessly checked on dates and details. The experienced biographer soon learns the necessity of authenticating every "fact" which reaches him by word of mouth. From a crowd of witnesses, one contradicting another, he must extract the essential truth, that which testifies to what the man himself was like.

The extant material regarding Henry Cabot Lodge, who

was in the public eye for nearly half a century, is enormous in bulk and amazing in variety. Here is folder after folder of letters, many of them in indecipherable longhand, any one of which may hold some memorable phrase or important opinion. Here are huge scrapbooks of clippings from newspapers, each relating to Lodge's career. Here are invitations and magazine articles and photographs and telegrams and badges, as well as packages of receipted bills. One portfolio contains over a thousand telegrams of congratulation sent to him following a fisticuff encounter with a pacifist in the lobby of the Capitol. One great box holds nothing but correspondence between Lodge and Henry White; another, the long series of letters between Lodge and Roosevelt. All this must be sorted out, read, and, if necessary, copied. There is far more material on Senator Lodge than there is about Julius Cæsar, Charlemagne, William the Conqueror, and Queen Elizabeth put together.

Do we need it all? Obviously not. In it is much useless stuff, which will eventually be discarded. But Lodge's biographer cannot ignore even the smallest scrap of paper. Somewhere in a bundle of unprepossessing documents may repose a page which will change permanently the accepted version of an important event. I once found, tucked away in a pile of worthless circulars, a list of Daniel Webster's debts in his own handwriting, showing the extent of his obligation to the Bank of the United States. The conscientious biographer must survey all the material, for any acceptable biography must be founded securely on facts.

The building of a book like Beveridge's *Lincoln* or Professor Nevins's *Henry White* involves long hours of sheer drudgery, occasionally relieved by a thrill at a notable find. Mr. George F. Milton, in preparing his forthcoming life of Stephen A. Douglas, is plodding through thousands of letters which nobody but their recipients has ever read. Before what we call an "interpretative" account of Lincoln, like that by Carl Schurz or Lord Charnwood, could be written, Nicolay and Hay and others had to assemble and evaluate the evidence.

Maurois's diverting *Disraeli* could not have been done if the preliminary research had not been carried through by Monypenny and Buckle.

As an illustration of the wrong method, I should like to cite Theodore Roosevelt's life of Thomas H. Benton, included in the American Statesmen Series. On February 7, 1886, Roosevelt, then in New York City, wrote to Lodge, "I feel a little appalled over the Benton. I have not the least idea whether I shall make a flat failure of it or not. However, I will do my best and trust to luck for the result." On March 27, at his Elkhorn Ranch in Dakota, far from libraries or files of newspapers, he reported, "I have written the first chapter of the Benton." On May 20, he boasted, "I have got the Benton half through." Finally, on June 7, he wrote, "I have pretty nearly finished Benton, mainly evolving him from my inner consciousness; but when he leaves the Senate in 1850 I have nothing to go by."

He then appealed to Lodge to hire someone to look up Benton's career in his declining days. Here are some of the questions: "He was elected to Congress; who beat him when he ran the second time? What was the issue? Who beat him, and why, when he ran for Governor of Missouri? And the date of his death? . . . As soon as I can get these dates I can send Morse the manuscript." Lodge, himself a laborious and scrupulous scholar, cautioned his friend not to be too hasty, but the latter mailed his copy to the general editor, John T. Morse, Jr., on August 9. Roosevelt had written the *Benton* in rather less than six months, without, apparently, looking up any of the sources. It would be a rash biographer indeed who would dare to adopt a similar procedure in these days when so many Doctors of Philosophy are ready to pounce upon a slip in date or name.

V

All this leads up to a pertinent query—what do we really want to hear about other men and women? We want to know, obviously, what they did, what contribution they made to culture and civilization, what achievements of theirs will be remembered. It is important to the world that Tennyson wrote "Ulysses," that Grant fought the battle of Shiloh, that Whistler painted the Old Battersea Bridge, that Wagner composed *Lohengrin*, and that Roosevelt "took" the Panama Canal. All these are matters of record. It is relatively easy for the biographer to portray the artist, the musician, the statesman, in the light of his actual production. Granite and canvas, melody and printed page, do for a time endure, and may be consulted and criticized. To measure Stevenson or Hardy it is essential, first of all, to acquire their novels and study them. Here is what these authors deliberately left behind them as their own.

Leslie Stephen has declared that "no person deserves a biography unless he be, in the literal sense, distinguished." Personally, however, I am inclined to agree with Carlyle, who, in his *Life of John Sterling*, said, "I have remarked that a true delineation of the smallest man, and his pilgrimage through life, is capable of interesting the greatest man." Some of the most entertaining biographies of recent years have been written about such quaint sensationalists as Phineas T. Barnum, John L. Sullivan, Anthony Comstock, and Lydia Pinkham—names which are not likely to shine in any galaxy of immortals. The new *Dictionary of American Biography* includes not only Anson, the professional baseball player, but also Jesse James, the notorious outlaw. An attractive sinner is better material for biography than a dull saint. But the life of even the most obscure and insignificant wastrel may be made to seem significant by a biographer who understands the convulsive drama of the human soul.

In its higher manifestations, biography is indubitably the revelation of a personality, the effort to do for somebody else what Pepys and Rousseau did unblushingly for themselves. Entrusted with this responsibility, the biographer is no longer a drudge, but a psychoanalyst, a diagnostician, a seer, and a judge. After all, we are made of star dust and grimy earth soil in varying proportions. We can rarely ourselves explain the wild desires, the illogical ambitions, the impossible day-dreams and low perversities which sometimes torment us. How, then, could it ever be possible for anyone else to put into words what we really are? For this part of his duty, the biographer must have sensitiveness and discernment and discrimination, the shrewdness to disentangle what a man says from what he thinks, the ability to pierce beneath the protective crust of pride and reserve.

Philip Guedalla has said, "The essential thing in biography is to tell the whole truth about your man. That is your only job." But again we must ask, with Pilate, "What is truth?" What if a specified act be susceptible of two different interpretations, depending on whether you view the perpetrator as a selfish cynic or as a guileless altruist? Often a man's motives are not clear, even to himself. It is a delicate matter to weigh the good and evil in the career of Charles James Fox or Lord Byron, to say nothing of certain more notorious figures, such as Aaron Burr or "Ben" Butler, who, though far from immaculate to their contemporaries, seem to have had no disturbing sense of sin.

Richard Croker, better known as "Boss" Croker, was generally regarded as a not too scrupulous politician who was for years the evil genius of New York City. But when his widow was in the witness box in Dublin, Ireland, after his death, she took oath as follows: "In addition to all the beautiful things that have been testified to about my husband by the previous witness, I have to add this, that my husband was a saint."

This possibly prejudiced estimate is not that which history will perpetuate; yet it is unquestionably part of the truth, and cannot be altogether ignored.

VI

Perhaps the most contemptible of biographers is he who, from a sense of family pride or an unwillingness to be too severe on his victim, withholds some of the facts. An incident in W. Somerset Maugham's *The Moon and Sixpence* satirizes this vice. Charles Strickland, the hero—or villain—of that striking novel, abruptly deserted his wife and, fleeing to Paris, became there the painter that he had always longed to be. Later his son William, writing the artist's biography, said, "My father really loved my mother. He once called her an excellent woman." Not long after, a pertinacious "debunker" of the German pedant type wrote a thesis on Charles Strickland and caustically reprinted in facsimile the passage from which William Strickland had quoted. Read in its entirety, the paragraph was as follows: "God damn my wife. She is an excellent woman. I wish she were in Hell."

We are harassed, on the other hand, by small-minded purveyors of backstairs gossip, who win a temporary place in the limelight by exposing the foibles and irregularities of the great and the near-great. The muckraker and the "debunker" have both gone to extremes in the twentieth century. Too much attention focused on Webster's convivial habits leaves one blind to the Reply to Hayne. The story should be told with some sense of proportion. No harm can come, however, from the knowledge that the usually staid Benjamin Franklin did not always obey the aphorisms of Poor Richard, that Abraham Lincoln had his domestic disharmonies, and that Woodrow Wilson's physical ailments had their effect on American history. Often a trivial anecdote or a casual phrase in a conversation will offer us a glimpse of the real man.

Probably the longest biography of any American is Edward L. Pierce's life of Charles Sumner, in four huge volumes—an important work, packed with information. It tells us much about the abolitionist statesman. But a great deal also may be deduced from Sumner's confession that he never assumed in his own library a posture which he would not have taken in the Senate of the United States. General Grant was ordinarily a reticent, uncommunicative person. But one evening, during his quarrel with Sumner over Santo Domingo, he strolled with George F. Hoar past Sumner's house in Lafayette Square, in Washington, and, looking up at the library windows, clenched his fist and burst out, "The man who lives up there has abused me in a way which I have never suffered from any man living." Much light is thrown on the character of Blaine by the story of how, in 1876, when he wanted the Republican nomination for President, he once exercised his seductive arts on Carl Schurz and, at the close of an evening walk with him, threw his arm around Schurz's neck, looked him appealingly in the face, and said, "Carl, you won't *oppose* me, will you?" Senator Lodge's dislike of England and the English, imprinted on his mind in his impressionable early years, undoubtedly had a determining effect upon his political policies. Details of this kind are easily stored in the memory, like Matthew Arnold's characterization of Thomas Gray in the sentence, "He never spoke out," or his description of Shelley as a "beautiful and ineffectual angel beating in the void his luminous wings in vain."

The biographer is often tempted, in an endeavor to make his hero a completely consistent character, to pervert or disguise the truth. The writer of prose fiction can, of course, achieve this through his unifying imagination. Dickens's Mr. Micawber, Hardy's Bathsheba Everdene, Mrs. Wharton's Ethan Frome, and Mr. Lewis's Babbitt are perfectly rounded conceptions, at the mercy of their creator, who can mold them to his will, transporting them here and here to elucidate or amplify his preconceived theory of their personalities. Real life, however, is less simple. The biographer cannot, if he has a conscience, start with any fixed conception of what his victim is like. If he does form such an hypothesis, the hero, through some waywardness, is sure sooner or later to knock it into a cocked hat. Then comes the test as to whether the biographer is sincerely trying to present a true picture, or whether he is attempting to invade the province of fiction.

Few manifestations of the so-called "modern spirit" are more obnoxious than the "fictionized biographies" with which the book market has recently been inundated. The historical novel at its best, as in *Henry Esmond* or *The Refugees*, has entirely justified itself. But the fictionized biography is neither soup nor roast nor pudding, neither fiction nor biography. Except in rare and special instances, like Gertrude Atherton's *The Conqueror*, it fails to produce a fair impression of its subject. The author is trying to paint a literary portrait in accordance with his own theories—nicely balanced, smoothly consistent, and entirely harmonious. He insists on pushing his hero along a logical path from the cradle to the grave, without halts or divagations. Life is not like that. The influence of prose fiction on biography has been good in so far as it has taught biographers how to mass material effectively, how to secure dramatic effect, and how to arrange details in accordance with the laws of evolution and climax. But it has done harm by encouraging sensationalism and by fostering the idea that consistency of character must be established where it does not exist.

VII

Biography, then, is an interpretative, selective, and analytic, not a creative art. The biographer's business is to tell the truth as he sees it, regardless of its implications. It is a mistake for him to interpose his own personality. It may be, as someone has intimated, that every biography of importance is one half at least made up of the biographer, but he must always subordinate himself. His job is done when he has accumulated and assimilated the available facts, arranged them so that they will have coherence, proportion, and symmetry, and allowed the victim to be his own revelator.

Part of a biographer's equipment is a wise tolerance and impartiality, together with a genuine, although not necessarily a blind, sympathy with his victim. If Woodrow Wilson had written an interpretation of Henry Cabot Lodge, it would probably have had its faults. Although the result might have been entertaining, it is probably just as well that John Tyler did not leave a character sketch of Henry Clay. The ideal biographer should doubtless maintain an attitude of judicial aloofness. But the best biographies, as a matter of fact, have been produced by authors who have been rather enthusiastic about their heroes—books like Boswell's *Johnson*, Trevelyan's *Macaulay*, Paine's *Mark Twain*, and Amy Lowell's *Keats*. Masters's *Lincoln*, so provocative to sane historians, is an example of how poor a book can be written by an able but wildly prejudiced poet in a field other than his own.

The biographer, no matter how hopeful, will seldom win a unanimity of approval. There are always two points of view, if not more. The Calvin Coolidge of Gamaliel Bradford is plainly not that of Bruce Barton. The picture of Colonel Roosevelt in his *Autobiography* is quite different from that in Millis's ironic study of the Spanish War, called *The Martial Spirit;* indeed the two are almost as far apart as Saint Paul and Mephistopheles. Or consider the attitudes of various schools of political thought toward Thomas Jefferson, whom Roosevelt thought to be a feeble and futile politician.

The weaknesses of contemporary biography are apparent to anyone who does much reading. The recent "bull market" in biographical literature resulted in a natural operation of the economic law of supply and demand, and many books were prepared rapidly for the satisfaction of a greedy public. A score of enterprising journalists with a certain facility in absorbing information and skimming the surface of history were—and are—ready to dash off in a few weeks lives of Horace Greeley or John Randolph or Aaron Burr. Such impatient work is bound to be spotted with errors. Senator Beveridge spent years of research on his monumental *Abraham Lincoln*, one of the classics of American biography; Emil Ludwig, after a few weeks of travel in the United States, produced a volume under the same title. The difference between the two is not unapparent to those who know anything about the subject.

The influence of such brilliant writers as Lytton Strachey and Philip Guedalla, not to mention André Maurois and

E. Barrington, has led their imitators to seek for themes which will grip the attention of the public. The impulse to produce a startling book is not, however, in itself a sufficient motive for competing with Mr. Strachey in a field where he is likely to remain supreme. A law-abiding career like that of the late President Eliot of Harvard does, of course, seem a trifle lukewarm after one has spent a few hours in hot water with Jesse James or Old King Brady. No doubt, too, a generation jaded by the "movies" is not to be lured by the outward tameness of the American Statesmen Series and must be stimulated by gorgeous green or yellow bindings, by extravagant "blurbs," and by the promise of a series of amorous misadventures now revealed for the first time in our annals. Approximately every month the "greatest biography of the century" is launched, only to sink into oblivion before the season closes. Time has its revenge on this ephemeral literature. After all, it was Henry James's *Eliot* which was awarded the Pulitzer Prize in biography for 1931. Cheap biography is like cheap poetry or cheap furniture—it is soon worn-out and consigned to the ash barrel.

It was inevitable that books prepared so hurriedly should be careless and slipshod in their writing. In their defense, it is maintained that their style is breezy and informal. But biography, more than most forms of literature, should be equipped for permanency. If it is not true, it should never be printed; and if it is true, it should be expressed in a style which will endure. Lockhart's *Scott*, Morley's *Voltaire*, and Professor Palmer's *Alice Freeman Palmer* owe their success to the painstaking care which their authors used. How many "masterpieces" of our prolific contemporary biographers will be in circulation twenty years from now? Hastily composed, hastily set up in type, hastily bound, and hastily dumped into the bookstores, they must be sold in a few weeks if they are to be sold at all. The fact that only a few of them have indexes shows that they are intended to be merely the pastime of an idle hour.

VIII

So much for one phase of the picture. On the other hand, modern biography is not without its triumphs. Competent biographers were probably never more numerous than they are in 1931; and they have often in a quiet way rehabilitated personages who, in their own time, were much misunderstood. Take, for illustration, the case of Andrew Johnson, Lincoln's successor as President of the United States. For nearly fifty years he was depicted by prejudiced Northern historians as a drunkard and a vulgarian, an obstructionist and a traitor. And then, within a very brief period, at least five books on Johnson were published, each one prompted by sympathy and a sincere desire to show what the "Tailor President" was really like. As a result of this extensive research by Judge Winston, Claude G. Bowers, George F. Milton, and others, we now conceive of "Andy" Johnson as a rugged, industrious, well-intentioned statesman, crude in his manners, perhaps, but trying earnestly to ascertain and do the right thing, and undertaking, in defiance of a bold and unscrupulous Congressional clique, to carry out Lincoln's policies on Reconstruction. Once thought to be the villain of the post-war era, he now emerges as the hero, encompassed by the sinister forms of Thaddeus Stevens, "Ben" Butler, and "Ben" Wade. Because of this new and correct interpretation, history has had to be rewritten.

In another respect also strides have been made. The old authorized or subsidized biography, frequently entitled "The Life and Times of George F. Blank," is now looked upon with distrust. We all know what it was like. Usually written by a relative, it adhered to the spirit of a sentence in a recent book, reading as follows: "The writer of this memorial has not thought it necessary to call attention to defects in the character she has sought to portray." A conspicuous example is Hallam Tennyson's life of his father, in which the Victorian Bard stands out like his own King Arthur—flawless and uninteresting. After reading it, I turned with delight to the remark of the iconoclastic Swinburne: "Mr. Tennyson, we understand, of course, that Queen Victoria is Guinevere and that the Prince Consort is King Arthur; but would you mind telling me who is Lancelot?" In the field of American political biography, there are many such undiluted eulogies, and they are all untrustworthy.

The best of the modern biographies are less solemn, less rhetorical, less packed with platitudes and didacticism, than similar books would have been half a century ago. The work of Mr. Lytton Strachey struck a new note in biographical literature. Fortunately for his method, earlier scholars had smoothed his way by gathering facts regarding certain picturesque and rather vulnerable people. With this material before him, he applied to it an appreciation of the significance of details and an instinct for dramatic values, tinting it always with the hues of a consummate irony—an irony sometimes too vividly colored, but more often so subtly employed that it escapes dull eyes. The gift of irony is, of course, a constant temptation to its possessor to wander from the truth in the quest of some miracle of wit. For my part, however, I would far rather have Strachey's caustic sketch of Thomas Arnold than Stanley's reverential two-volume panegyric of the Headmaster of Rugby—and Strachey is probably nearer the truth.

The same intellectual distinction attaches to Philip Guedalla, although one occasionally wearies of his ostentatiously brilliant phrasing in which a *mot juste*, like "vague," is repeated too often. His manner, the glitter of which may be tinsel as well as gold, is admirably fitted in his book, *The Second Empire*, to a subject like Napoleon III, but is less successful with Lord Palmerston, a more substantial and less scintillating figure. Mr. Hilaire Belloc is another of the modernists who worship at the shrine of Cleverness. These three men have transformed biography by making it less cumbersome, less dully formidable, and thus emphasizing its possibilities for entertainment as well as instruction.

IX

Our own period has been notably rich in biography and autobiography. The pedagogically-minded still hark back to the classics—to Plutarch and Boswell and Lockhart. It is still difficult to surpass such "purple patches" as Boswell's introduction to the Great Lexicographer in the shop of the bookseller, Davies, or the description of the meeting at dinner of Johnson, the Tory, and John Wilkes, the Radical. But there are books in our day which are not sufficiently praised. Among the autobiographies, Gosse's *Father and Son* and Hudson's *Far Away and Long Ago* must be placed with the masterpieces of the past. As for biographies, such works as Croly's *Hanna,*— an amazingly fair estimate of a Conservative by a Liberal,— Beer's *Stephen Crane*, Paine's *Mark Twain*, Beveridge's *Lincoln*, and Strachey's *Queen Victoria*, are, if we can forget their suspicious recentness, far better than, let us say, Southey's *Nelson.*

We have a group of authors in the United States today, including M. A. DeWolfe Howe, Allan Nevins, Gamaliel Bradford, Albert Bigelow Paine, George F. Milton, Claude G. Bowers, Samuel E. Morison, Ray Stannard Baker, and several others, any one of whom can be counted upon to produce a distinguished biography. James Ford Rhodes was in no sense a romantic personage, but a sedentary historian, who spent most of his waking hours among his books. Yet Mr. Howe has skillfully made him the protagonist of a not unexciting drama. Mr. Nevins's *Henry White* moves along so gracefully that we forget how difficult to write such easy reading is. Mr. Bowers, by his extensive use of newspaper files, has shown their high value as source material. All these men have breadth of knowledge, devotion to research, fair-mindedness, and a passion for truth. Their literary and historical consciences have not atrophied.

The question is often asked by youngsters, "Where can I find a subject for biography? All the claims seem to be staked out." The answer is that there is always room for a new good book. Although there are long lives of John C. Calhoun and Ulysses S. Grant, no one has yet said the final word on these men. Nobody has yet explained how a person so unmagnetic as Benjamin Harrison could be elected President of the United States. The raw stuff of biography is all around us. Think of the opportunity for a Strachey-like treatment of the pompous Roscoe Conkling; or for an account of Theodore Roosevelt in the manner of Philip Guedalla!

There is no danger that biography will become unfashionable. So long as humanity is dominated by forcefulness or led by charm, so long as Mussolinis and Lenins fascinate us by their personalities, so long will there be a demand for the stories of their lives. Biography, furthermore, will continue to be one of the leisurely arts, requiring investigation, meditation, and revision. In prose fiction, enthusiasm and intensity may conceal many crudities, but biography cannot be scribbled off in a few hours, like an account of a professional hockey match. Finally, it is well to remember that there will always be charlatans and sensationalists in every branch of literature. When we are troubled by them, as we occasionally must be,—especially if we have to review their books,—it is consoling to know that we still have honest craftsmen, who uphold their ideals and are not likely to abandon them.

THE ART OF BEING OUTSHONE

By *Edgar J. Goodspeed*

I

SOMEBODY is forever sending me literature about how to shine at dinners and in the social circle generally. It seems there are books full of anecdotes, repartees, and bright remarks, which, if memorized and opportunely remembered, are supposed to enliven these occasions. The master of these books dazzles and entertains every circle he enters. He holds the spotlight and the center of the stage. Murmurs of admiration attend his brilliant sallies. He is, in short, the life of the party.

Others, it appears, just as good as he, go home depressed and disheartened. They have not shone. The spotlight has not rested well-pleased upon them. They have been obscure. Sound cause for gloom! Their minds, destitute of the thousand epigrams of the master spirits of the ages, have contributed nothing brilliant to the conversation.

It is evident from the amount and tone of this literature that one must shine to be happy. Without shining, life is not worth while. One is a failure, and might as well give up. It is the obviousness of this truth that provides a public for the literature. People have, indeed, often felt the sense of discouragement these circulars describe, and are glad to find a promise of relief, even though at the fateful moment they fumble in memory for the bright saying of Marcus Aurelius or Mark Twain which the occasion so pressingly demands. Perhaps, after all, it may be more practical to go to a dinner with just one bright but borrowed remark stored up for the occasion, and, watching narrowly your opportunity, to hurl that, like Bruce's heart, into the fray, than to carry in such a sackful of anecdotes gathered at random from five hundred minds.

There is of course nothing new about this yearning for notice and conspicuousness. It is an inheritance from childhood and even from antiquity. Epictetus discussed it. It is hard, he admits, to hear another man discoursing brightly on a subject beyond your depth, and on which you have nothing to say. But courage! Another time the talk will be of grammar, and it will be your turn to shine.

The illuminating thing about this is that the fine old Stoic himself was not above the common desire to shine, only he had sense enough to see that no sensible person expects or wishes to do all the shining. Every dog is entitled to his day— that is, of course, if he can get it. I do not say he would have ordered the books advertised above; he knew he needed no such meretricious aids to luminosity, being convinced that, taking the season together, he and every other well-disciplined philosopher were sure in due time to get their conversational innings. But he was evidently strongly disposed to have those innings soon or late.

It is odd that it did not occur to the ancient Stoic or the modern Epicurean that the true solution of the problem, which is evidently so vital to them, is the cultivation of the art of transition. To the master of transition, it matters not whether the talk be of the Taj Mahal or of the composition of rubber. Give him but the suspicion of a lull in the conversation and he will with a mere phrase bring it round to port.

Only last night on the way into the dining room I heard an accomplished converser lamenting the general lack of interest in Africa—one of his best themes. What weakness! Let him but contrive a set of good transitions, and I'll warrant he can bring the talk back to Africa though it have strayed as far afield as the nebula of Andromeda or the Great Hereafter. As thus: "How different that is from Africa, now!" or "You don't say so! Well, I remember once in Africa . . ."

Of course we all know the conversational superman; he has been with us since boyhood, to which period of development he properly belongs. He is always capping your modest contributions with something bigger. If you have slain your thousands, he has slain his tens of thousands. You timidly intimate that your assessed valuation is two thousand dollars; he cries that his is four. You say that you are to speak in Freeport; he says that they had previously asked him. You tell how long it took to drive a certain route; his time was better by hours. It does not matter that you happen later to detect much exaggeration in these quick rejoinders—as that his assessment is only about half yours. The mischief is done, or, rather, the success achieved. For evidently the skill of the thing lay in thinking quickly of the better story and putting it over convincingly. It is not a matter of fact, but of art.

Such men are not liars. They are great hearty boys who have never learned the art of being outshone. Their fish are always bigger, their scores lower, their losses greater, their winnings larger, their operations dreadfuler than yours. They have no need of the thousand best epigrams of the world's five hundred brightest minds, nor need they, like Epictetus, wait for another day when the talk is of grammar in order to shine. Their simple art is to snatch a reflected glory from every other's remark and multiply it thirty, sixty, a hundred fold.

What a good thing it is that there are no such women! Yet this may seem to have an ungracious ring; which reminds us: Let us now praise gracious women, the noble army of hostesses and dinner partners who listen patiently and with interest marvelously sustained—or simulated—to your interminable anecdotes and expositions, which are often no better than the thousand best efforts of the world's master minds, to say the least. Surely if there be pretense in this, the Recording Angel, if he must jot it down, will never be better occupied than in dropping some of his tears upon the page.

II

I have just had a delightful interview with a charming old gentleman. I enjoyed it exceedingly, but as I look back upon it two or three things emerge like islands from a sea. He was, it appeared, the best student and the best speaker his ancient college had ever produced, and to this day his record has not been surpassed. He next formed the laudable ambition of making himself the best preacher in the country, and, from all I can gather, he made decided progress in that direction. But I am fearful that he has never progressed far in the gentler art of being outshone.

A distinguished editor, on being asked on what principle he chose the articles that he printed, said that if a thing was so absorbing that a man would stop eating his roast beef to listen to it, he thought it worth publishing. No fairer description of prandial achievement can well be framed. And yet, with hundreds of thousands of copies of the select epigrams of the master minds flying about and equipping the most ordinary people overnight to hold dinner tables spellbound, even the roast-beef test may fail. To have the art, literature, history, politics, and business of the world on the tip of your tongue (What a tongue, to have such a tip!) may deceive even the elect into supposing that you know something about them. Better not make any pauses,—except for the inevitable murmurs of admiration, which, it seems, are guaranteed,—else some dull, malicious fellow may ask a disconcerting question. Still, not if he is spellbound; the thing is unthinkable. But for safety's sake a good dashing transition should always be taken along, as a kind of conversational parachute, in case your gas fails.

I have long been thinking that our artists should be painting scenes in real life, such as an automobile salesman and his prey. But whose pencil could portray the dinner table at which two accomplished possessors of the thousand epigrams of the master spirits should meet? The imagination reels at the

picture.   Gastronomically, the dinner would of course be a
failure, for no one would have a moment's attention to give
the food.   One would inevitably get the jump upon the other
at the start, and then, pausing presently for the inevitable
murmur of admiration, would be dismayed to hear the other
strike in with some apposite observation of Josh Billings or
Hippocrates, and feel the spotlight fading from his brow. Can
he regain it? His adversary is forewarned by now, and, if he
knows his stuff, will give him no further chance, but rather a
much-needed lesson in the Art of Being Outshone.

This "hyperlampophobia," or dread of being outshone, has
begun to affect literature. Where is the so-called hero of yore?
In many a modern tale the hero is really the simplest, fondest,
most blundering being in the whole cast. Is it not clear that
the old-style smart individual who easily gets his own way in
all circumstances—an obvious aristocratic type—is out of
date? The modern hero does not command your homage; he
appeals to your compassion. You perceive that the poor fellow
needs help, and how you long to be at his side and warn and
cheer him, as, helpless with horror, you behold him blindly
plunging deeper and deeper into difficulties. Only when his
situation has become absolutely irremediable does the author
let up on him. All this, of course, is for your good, so that you
may not feel yourself too palpably outshone.

Take the old detective story. All was hopelessly obscure
until the great detective entered. It presented no particular
difficulties to him. A few blood drops, cigarette stubs, or bits
of tweed, and the thing was done, all by himself. But nowadays
there is a whole school of detective literature from which the
detective hero has actually disappeared! He has simply
vanished, leaving no trace. The truth is, we have grown tired
of the omniscient detective who finds everything so easy, and
prefer to see difficulties more democratically unraveled by a
number of people, each contributing his bit and making the
solution a social process.

Modern publicity methods have long since accustomed us

to having our failings of every kind familiarly assumed and played upon, and we do not so much mind this unless our moral characters are impugned. Thus the frank challenge, "Why let Blunders in speech and writing put you at a Disadvantage? Beware of shabby English! Errors in Pronunciation can ruin the whole Effect of what you say!" while perhaps unconventional, does not offend us. Our English may be blundersome, shabby, and mispronounced, as the advertiser so calmly assumes, but if it is a bit informal at times, it is our own business, no doubt. But to approach us on the cool supposition that we go home from a party unhappy if we have not done all the talking is a different matter, and seems to assume that we are all indeed but children of a larger growth, if even that. To monopolize conversation is a thing no civilized man should ever want to do.

Psychologists suggest that it is really better for our mental health to do a good deal of listening, claiming that in this way we may get some of the stimulus and intellectual pabulum that our spirits require. Experienced diners-out, with a large and quick turnover, will certainly confirm this, telling tonight the best things they heard last night, but keeping silent long enough to pick up a few new trifles for tomorrow, when they sincerely hope to encounter a new circle of guests to try them on.

Such is, we believe, the democratic way of life, but it is not that of the conversational crammers, on the one hand, or of Epictetus on the other. They both aim at a larger but slower business; at least, Epictetus did. This was his professorial bent: unhappy except when lecturing; an evident stranger to the joyful activity of the intercreative mind. But how much better, really, to match wits with some capable table companion, until some new phase of common experience or interpretation emerges, to the general joy! A far better thing this than lecturing each other alternate evenings, you tonight, I tomorrow night! Little genius in such division of labor.

For what we are here concerned with is of course nothing less than the art of conversation. How many a man who thinks he is talking well, if lengthily, has really been launched and steered upon his course by the unobtrusive skill of his neighbor at table, who listens with apparent delight as he details the exploits of his lifelong hero:—

"I said, 'Stand up; tell your story.' He did. I said, 'Sit down. Now tell yours.' She did. I said, 'You were right; he was wrong,'" and so on.

Such people are doomed to starvation, psychologists declare. They merely recite their little Odyssey until they are exhausted, and when rested up recite it over again, never giving themselves any chance to take in new ideas. It is perhaps comforting to reflect upon this righteous law of conversational compensations; and yet it is too often we rather than they who suffer the direct effects of their famine.

III

I am not exactly a hermit. To me the most interesting thing about this world through which I am passing is the people who live in it. They are also the most amusing thing in it. This is the heart of humanism—the world of personality over against the material world. The latter sometimes seems to engross us, and it is heresy to depreciate it. But, vast as it is, I sometimes wonder if it is any more stupendous than a great man's idea of it. Wonderful as it is, is it any more wonderful than that he can form and carry in his mind an image, however imperfect, of it? Yet he is but one of millions, every one of whom forms and carries such an image, material, social, moral, economic. Every person carries a world about with him of his own creation or, at least, discovery. None of these images is wholly true, yet every one of them possesses some truth. No two of them are alike; perhaps no two of them should be alike. They are of an inexhaustible variety, of attitude, opinion, information. It is a mistake to suppose that only the intelligent have definite opinions; the most definite opinions are held by the unintelligent, and they also hold them most strongly.

It is this that literature seeks to mirror, catching perhaps a hundred-millionth part, the best or worst, and "reducing it to writing," as we rightly say—for how much it is reduced! Which is what gives to literature such interest and glory as it possesses. But the thing itself is vastly greater than any record or even experience—not to say fancy—of it.

You see a man coming up the street, a person perhaps of little social, political, or financial standing. None the less, he carries about with him a private individual universe, as definite as your own, and in some parts, at least, sounder than yours. In it he alone is judge; his estimates and opinions prevail. You yourself are to him but a part of it, and subject to his verdicts and appraisals. If he is informed, capable, and wise, his ideas will be sounder; but many an ignorant and prejudiced person, if he be reflective and kind, carries about a universe well worth knowing.

Everybody is, in short, a kind of peripatetic Atlas bearing a world upon his shoulders. More than a world—a universe. It is no great flight of fancy to imagine the city streets filled with people so occupied. Yet most of them give no sign of finding the task burdensome. They are more like people carrying balloons. This is certainly a better figure, for if some are weighed down with the weight of their universe, others are plainly buoyed up by theirs. These balloons are of very different sizes, so that while one is hardly visible, another fills the whole sky. But, you will say, this means endless collisions between rival universes. And of course that is precisely what is constantly taking place, unless one knows how to handle his private universe with good taste and good manners. It is like the conflict of umbrellas on a crowded street on a rainy day, only on a much grander and more serious scale. The balloons are also of very different densities, and of different colors—black, blue, gray, brown, rose, yellow, purple, and orange. Everyone is very sensitive about his own particular one; nobody likes to have any liberties taken with his universe. And how fortunate it is that they are really or nearly invisible! Otherwise we should all be too often and too palpably outshone.

DEEPER INTO SPACE

THE NEW TELESCOPE AND OUR UNIVERSE

By *George Ellery Hale*

I

FIVE years ago the Rockefeller Trustees, with the approval and support of John D. Rockefeller, Jr., made provision for two far-reaching explorations. One of these, organized by my old friend Breasted, involves the most comprehensive study ever undertaken of the origin and rise of civilization in the Near East. This combines the excavation, recording, and interpretation of ancient remains and inscriptions at numerous carefully chosen stations in Egypt and the Near East with a geological survey of the Nile Valley, linking the partially known historic period to the remote prehistoric era. Thus Breasted is creating a unified picture of human progress in the most strategic region of the world, with a sweeping vision reaching back over hundreds of thousands of years into the dim and distant epoch of the past.

The other grant made by the Rockefeller Trustees was for an investigation complementary to that of Breasted and his associates. Sixty centuries ago, on the banks of the Nile, the pioneer astronomers of Egypt watched the meridian passage of the stars and mapped the principal constellations. Hundreds of Babylonian tablets also preserve astronomical records, which were continued for centuries and led to the capital discovery of the precession of the equinoxes. In those early days the great distance of the stars was unknown, but, as the centuries rolled by, the heavens seemed to recede from the earth. Increased precision of observation showed the stars to be very

From the *Atlantic Monthly*, April 1934; copyright, 1934, by The Atlantic Monthly Company. Used by special permission.

remote, and enhanced the desire for greater knowledge. The speculations and observations of the early Greeks and the persistent work of the Alexandrian School added largely to the already vast literature of astronomy. Even the decline of Alexandria and the ignorance of the Dark Ages did not long hamper progress, as the books of the Greeks were preserved and their observations continued in all parts of the Arabian empire. Astronomy thus spread through Moorish Spain to other parts of Europe, and in the century of Copernicus the most elaborate observatory of the period was established by Tycho Brahe on a Danish island. Here were obtained the positions of the planets from which Kepler derived their laws of motion, which finally led to the great generalization of Newton. At the end of the seventeenth century the only known stars were the small number visible to the naked eye. Then came Galileo's telescope. Suddenly tens of thousands of hitherto unseen stars burst into view, and with them the mountains on the Moon, the satellites of Jupiter, and the phases of Venus. Thus the reasoning of Copernicus, who had placed the sun instead of the earth at the center of the solar system, was finally confirmed. The telescope continued to grow, recently attaining a diameter of one hundred inches and revealing thousands of millions of stars. During the last century its efficiency has been greatly enhanced by combining with it such chemical and physical devices as the photographic plate, the spectroscope, and the photoelectric amplifier.

My own experience, covering a period of fifty years, has led me to realize the importance of a broad and constantly developing research policy. I do not believe in hastily casting aside the methods and experience of the past, but rather in utilizing and improving them in harmony with the steady advance of science. As a boy I made the most of my own apparatus, and experimented in chemistry and physics before I entered astronomy. My first spectroscope was in use before I built my first telescope, and a small camera preceded them both. Thus it was natural to combine all three, as Huggins and others had done, and to give sufficient space in my first observatory to a laboratory and workshop. Such a policy, continued at the Yerkes and Mount Wilson Observatories, is also the fundamental principle of the new project described in these pages.

Another prime element in this policy is that of coöperation in research. Research laboratories and observatories should not be organized as competing institutions, largely intent on their own glory. On the other hand, a group of observatories should not be conducted as unthinking machines, operated by a single head. Whenever possible, plans of coöperation should be devised, in which all of the originality of each individual investigator is stimulated and encouraged without sacrifice of the great advantages of joint operation and control. I could give numerous examples of local, national, and international coöperation in research which have proved extremely fruitful.

The most richly endowed research agencies in the United States are those directed by the Rockefeller and the Carnegie Trustees. While these bodies differ in certain respects in organization and procedure, their purposes have much in common. Thus in 1903 the Carnegie Institution of Washington established a large observatory on Mount Wilson and in Pasadena, and later it greatly aided in the development of the California Institute of Technology, also in Pasadena. The Rockefeller Boards showed a special interest in the California Institute, to which, with their assistance, such outstanding leaders of research as Arthur A. Noyes, Robert A. Millikan, and Thomas Hunt Morgan were drawn.

In 1928 the Rockefeller Trustees offered to the California Institute a sum sufficient to build a 200-inch reflecting telescope, together with such instrument shops, laboratories, and other facilities as would be required to establish a well-rounded Astrophysical Observatory. This Observatory was designed to be complementary to the Mount Wilson Observatory, and in no sense a rival institution. A necessary condition of the gift was therefore that the Carnegie Institution of Washington should coöperate in the most complete way with the California Institute. Such coöperation was cordially promised by the President and the Executive Committee of the Carnegie Institution. Reciprocally, the California Institute offered the use of its facilities to members of the staff of the Mount Wilson Observatory. The Institute's Physical and Chemical Laboratories, not to speak of the possibilities of its new astrophysical equipment, will thus be available for researches in which they may be needed by the Mount Wilson observers.

II

The reader may inquire why, when so many stars are known, we need an instrument large enough to add hundreds of millions more. The answer is easy to give. The discovery of stars previously unknown because of their faintness is important only in so far as they may contribute to our knowledge of the structure of the universe and the nature of its constituents. Until recently all of the heavenly bodies have generally been looked upon as parts of a single Galaxy, a flattened aggregation with its greatest extension in the plane of the Milky Way. The first nebula recognized to have a spiral form was detected by Lord Rosse's great reflecting telescope in 1845, but a few years ago strong arguments were advanced for the belief that the hundreds of thousands of spiral nebulæ then known were members of our own Galaxy.

Other astronomers, however, already held opposite views. Indeed, the conception of "island universes," scattered through the depths of space, goes back more than a century. But speculation is a very different thing from proof. Gradually, by the aid of powerful telescopes equipped with photographic and spectroscopic appliances, the distance of the spiral nebulæ has been measured, and they are now generally regarded to be outside our galactic system, most of them at enormous distances. We have also learned that the Galaxy, with its hundreds of millions of stars, is probably itself a spiral nebula, whirling with the astonishing velocity that characterizes these objects. Long-exposure photographs of the nearest spirals have partially resolved them into extremely faint stars, and afforded means of comparing them with similar stars in our own system and thus of measuring their distance. Finally, the millions of "island universes" (many of them spiral nebulæ) scattered through space appear to be separating at velocities which are almost comparable with the velocity of light. But there are some apparent contradictions in this picture, which can be investigated only by the aid of a telescope capable of reaching farther into space.

This, however, is only one side of the problem of modern astrophysics. We have learned that the earth is one of the smallest members of a group of planets revolving about the sun, and that the sun, far removed from the center of the Galaxy, is one of the smallest stars. The study of the structure and evolution of the stars began about the time of Darwin's publication of *The Origin of Species*. Indeed, the first chemical analysis of the sun was made by Kirchhoff and Bunsen in that same memorable year—1859. Similar analyses of the brighter stars, conducted within a decade by Huggins and Secchi, showed the presence of the same elements found in the earth and sun. They also revealed a distinct sequence among the stars, pointing toward a definite law of evolution. As time went on, it also appeared that we must look to the stars for the solution of some of the most fundamental questions of chemistry and physics.

Thus the true rôle of astrophysics is a very broad one. It shows us a vast universe, aglow with near and distant objects which appeal to us in a double sense. To the celestial problem, which the work of many centuries has shown to be one of the earliest and most persistent interests of mankind, is added a great terrestrial asset. For we now realize that the heavens contain innumerable stellar laboratories, where problems of physics and chemistry, far beyond the capacity of our laboratories on earth, are open to solution.

When Einstein conceived his theory, and stimulated its test

by means of the sun and stars, no physicist could have shown in the laboratory that the passage of light rays near a mass of matter would result in the bending of their path. Nor, without the aid of a huge gaseous body like the sun, could the physicist have proved that the radiation of luminous atoms is altered by the neighborhood of such a mass. Scores of illustrations might be given to indicate the value of "cosmic crucibles" in solving laboratory problems. As astronomy is dependent, in still greater degree, upon the fundamental sciences of physics and chemistry, it is perfectly clear that all three should be cultivated together, with the indispensable aid of mathematics.

In this extensive unified work a telescope much more powerful than any yet available is urgently needed. It is not a question, as is so commonly supposed, of great magnifying power. What we must have is more light, focused in a sharply defined image. To get more light it is necessary to enlarge the curved optical surface used to concentrate all the rays falling upon it. The problems involved in constructing and operating a greater telescope are easy to name but difficult to solve.

The first necessity is to make disks of glass or some other suitable material of sufficient size, stiffness, homogeneity, and freedom from marked distortion by change of temperature.

The next is to give such a disk a practically perfect optical surface and to coat its curved face uniformly with a highly reflecting film of silver or other suitable metal.

While this process, involving many years of work, is under way, a telescope mounting must be designed and built. This must be capable of supporting the massive optical disk so perfectly that it will be undistorted in any position. It must also automatically follow the stars with great precision throughout the night.

At the same time a careful comparative study must be made of promising sites for the telescope, in a region where much clear weather and other favorable conditions prevail. The long construction period will also give opportunity for other work of equal importance, including the erection of shops and laboratories and the design and construction of auxiliary apparatus capable of multiplying many fold the efficiency of the telescope.

Throughout the centuries separating Galileo from the earliest astronomers, the only collector of starlight available was the unaided eye. The huge astronomical instruments erected in Cairo, India, Denmark, and elsewhere revealed no stars beyond the range of ordinary vision; they served merely to determine the positions and motions of the visible stars and planets. Although lenses had been used earlier as aids to vision, Galileo was the first to apply them to the heavens. His telescope, with its simple convex lens about two and one-quarter inches in diameter, collected about eighty times as much light as the pupil of the eye. This gain was sufficient to add hundreds of thousands of stars to the two or three thousand previously seen. Now it is a question, not so much of multiplying the hundreds of millions of stars already known, as of brightening their images and of making possible a satisfactory exploration of the vast world of distant galaxies lying beyond the limits of the Milky Way.

III

After years of ingenious experimentation by the General Electric Company with fused quartz, which offers hitherto insuperable difficulties in very large masses because of its extremely high melting point, we turned to Pyrex glass, so widely known because of its superiority to ordinary glass for cooking purposes. Its high quartz content greatly reduces its expansion by heat, and explains why Pyrex utensils withstand without cracking the sudden changes of temperature to which they are often exposed. The casting and annealing of large Pyrex disks demanded, however, extensive studies by experienced physicists, and we were very fortunate to be able to call upon the knowledge and experience of Dr. Arthur L. Day, Director of the Geophysical Laboratory of the Carnegie

Institution of Washington, and the able research staff of the Corning Glass Works.

After a 60-inch Pyrex disk had been successfully made, a glass much superior for our purposes to ordinary Pyrex was developed for us, and used to make the 72-inch disk for the telescope of the new Toronto Observatory. A 120-inch disk (needed for testing the 200-inch mirror) was then cast for us last June. It was carefully annealed by a special process, and when taken from the annealing furnace in December it was shown by preliminary tests to be of the highest quality. On the last day of the year, an 80-inch disk, for the new observatory of the University of Texas, was cast at Corning from the same kind of glass. Thus the Rockefeller gift to the California Institute, as will be shown more fully later, is accomplishing the purpose of developing new methods and materials needed by many institutions, instead of being solely devoted to the establishment of a single new observatory.

A 120-inch disk having been cast, with an area half again as great as that of the largest telescope mirror previously made, we may look forward with confidence to the success of the 200-inch disk. This will be cast within a few weeks (shortly after the casting of a 60-inch disk for the Harvard College Observatory), and its annealing should be completed by the end of 1934. Then follows the long and delicate process of grinding, polishing, and figuring the disk after its arrival in Pasadena.

At this point a word should be said regarding the preparations already made at the California Institute. The first need was a suitable machine shop, equipped with the tools required to build the special instruments, of many new types, called for in this enterprise. Here, too, a large grinding and polishing machine has been designed and built. This machine is nearly ready for work on the 120-inch disk in our new optical shop, completed a few months ago. No such building is available elsewhere, because of the large scale and the special requirements of the task. It must not only permit the 120-inch and 200-inch disks to be ground, polished, and figured to the highest perfection, but also to be tested optically in combination with each other. These operations demand a room 54 feet wide, 162 feet long, and 39 feet high, in which the dust-free air can be maintained for many months at nearly constant temperature and humidity. Overhead an electric crane, tested for loads of fifty tons, spans the room and travels its entire length. By this means the heavy disks can be lifted on or off the polishing machines and moved about at will. Small optical shops adjoin the main room and afford space for all the minor work. When finally completed, the 200-inch mirror will have a polished concave face, not differing from a true paraboloidal form by more than two millionths of an inch.

The ordinary method of coating such a telescope mirror is to deposit on it chemically a very thin layer of pure silver. Four years ago, however, John Strong developed at the University of Michigan a process of vaporizing various metals, and depositing the vapor on glass or any other substance in a high vacuum. Now a member of the research staff of the California Institute, Strong has recently coated with aluminum mirrors up to thirty-six inches in diameter (the Crossley Reflector of the Lick Observatory), besides many smaller mirrors and gratings used on Mount Wilson and in Pasadena. The remarkable permanence of such aluminum surfaces and their great superiority to silver, especially in the violet and ultra-violet, lead us to hope that this process can be used for coating the 200-inch mirror.

Photographic exposures of faint celestial objects often last for hours, or even for several successive nights. During this time the stars must be kept accurately in position on the plate, in spite of their apparent westward motion caused by the rotation of the earth. The 200-inch mirror, weighing nearly twenty-five tons, must therefore lie on a special support system (to prevent distortion) at the bottom of a steel skeleton tube hung on trunnions between the arms of a huge polar axis, kept in steady rotation by a driving clock and worm gear.

The skeleton tube, about twenty-five feet in diameter and sixty feet long, will be so rigid that the observer can be carried at its upper end, within a small cartridge-shaped house at the center of the tube. The parallel rays of light from the stars, entering the open end of the tube unimpeded except by the central observer's house and its four narrow supporting steel webs, will fall on the concave mirror at the lower end of the tube and be reflected back to form images which can be observed visually, photographed, analyzed with a spectroscope, or measured with such an instrument as a photoelectric amplifier. The loss of the light obstructed by the observer's house is unimportant, because it is so small a fraction of the whole light received and also because the central part of the mirror must be covered in any reflecting telescope.

IV

An exceptional feature of the 200-inch telescope will be its great angular aperture. In most reflectors the focal length is five or six times the diameter of the large mirror. The focal length of the 200-inch will be only 3.3 times its aperture. Thus the photographic intensity of a given star at its focus will not be merely four times that of the same star at the focus of the 100-inch telescope, but more nearly ten times as great. This means that the 200-inch telescope should penetrate fully three times as far into space, and thus open for investigation an unexplored sphere of about thirty times the volume of that hitherto sounded.

The observations mentioned above are to be made at the primary focus of the 200-inch mirror. In other classes of work different arrangements are called for. A convex mirror about forty inches in diameter, mounted at the center of the tube below the observer's house, can be instantly turned into position by an electric motor. This will cause the light rays to converge less rapidly, and form an image of a field of stars on a photographic plate about seventeen inches square just below the 200-inch mirror, which will be pierced with a central hole to transmit the beam. Or the photographic plate holder can be swung aside and replaced by a spectrograph. Because of the varying refraction of the atmosphere, the star images cannot be held precisely in place by the driving clock of the telescope. An observer, carried by the massive tube, must watch a star under considerable magnification and, with the aid of suitable mechanism, make the small corrections necessary to keep it in position at the intersection of two cross hairs or on the slit of the spectrograph.

When longer spectrographs or other auxiliary instruments are needed to analyze the light of stars or nebulæ or to measure their radiation, one or more plane mirrors can be swung into position, displacing the focus to apparatus on either side of the telescope tube or in a fixed constant temperature chamber due south of the polar axis. In this way it will be possible to photograph the spectra of the brighter stars on a scale as great as that ordinarily used in the study of the sun.

The selection of a suitable site for the 200-inch telescope is not an easy problem. Should it be north or south of the equator, and at what latitude? For instruments up to one hundred inches aperture this might prove to be a difficult question, as the southern stars have been explored much less completely than those of the northern sky. But for a 200-inch telescope, which must be devoted exclusively to work beyond the range of smaller instruments, there can be no manner of doubt. The selection of celestial objects for special study cannot be made intelligently without the aid of all the knowledge available. As this is far more abundant for the northern heavens, a site north of the equator is evidently needed. As for its latitude, it is obviously desirable to include as much of the sky as possible, without depressing the north celestial pole too far. A latitude between 30 degrees and 35 degrees, where three fourths of the entire heavens are visible, is thus indicated.

Much clear weather is wanted, and this means a site far removed from the paths of the principal storms, which cross the United States from west to east near the Canadian border and from south to north along the Atlantic coast. Great distance from storm centers is also favorable to sharp definition of star images, a prime requirement. As the unsteadiness of these images is naturally greater in the denser and more disturbed air of low altitudes, a high altitude is required, where the loss of light by atmospheric absorption is also low. But the site must not be too high, because of the extremely low temperatures and the consequent distortion of the telescope mirror when it is exposed to the sky at night (it is tightly enclosed in a nearly constant temperature case throughout the day). Local causes of disturbance, such as winds, electric lights, and so forth, must also be borne in mind.

Finally, the easy accessibility of coöperating laboratories and observatories is of vital importance. After previous study of these questions in selecting the site of the Mount Wilson Observatory thirty years ago, combined with the work accomplished since that time with many telescopes up to one hundred inches in diameter, it is clear that a site should be chosen not far distant from the many observatories, laboratories, and instrument shops in and near Pasadena. Although comparative telescopic tests of several neighboring mountain summits have been made during the past five years, a final decision has not yet been reached.

V

The question of auxiliary apparatus and facilities, both for attachment to the telescope and for the interpretation of the observations obtained, is one of the most important problems before us. The Observatory Council, placed in full charge of the entire project by the Trustees of the California Institute, comprises Robert A. Millikan, Director of the Norman Bridge Laboratory of Physics; Arthur A. Noyes, Director of the Gates Laboratory of Chemistry; Henry M. Robinson, long experienced in national and international economic affairs; Walter S. Adams, Director of the Mount Wilson Observatory of the Carnegie Institution of Washington; and the writer, Honorary

Director of the Mount Wilson Observatory of the Carnegie Institution of Washington (chairman). John A. Anderson, the executive officer of the Council, has had long experience as a physicist and astronomer at Johns Hopkins University and the Mount Wilson Observatory. We are also aided by a large group of mathematicians, astronomers, physicists, chemists, and engineers, selected from the research staffs of the Mount Wilson Observatory and the California Institute and from universities and other institutions in this country and abroad. A few specific illustrations will make clear our procedure.

While it was recognized that an exceptionally short focus for the 200-inch mirror was desirable in order to concentrate the feeble light of the most remote celestial objects, we were faced by the fact that the sharply defined field of such a mirror is very small. Ross of the Yerkes Observatory was accordingly asked to devise a new type of correcting lens, to mount before the plate and enlarge the field of good definition. He has had remarkable success in this work, as tests of his lenses with the large reflecting telescopes on Mount Wilson abundantly prove. We also wished to multiply the efficiency of the new telescope for the photography of the very faint spectra of distant objects, especially for measuring the velocity of the remote spiral nebulæ. For this purpose an extremely short-focus lens was needed, far faster than the most rapid movie lenses, the best of which had been tried on Mount Wilson. Rayton, of the Bausch and Lomb Optical Company, succeeded in devising an incredibly fast lens, on the principle of a microscope objective, with an aperture of two inches and a focal length of but little more than one inch.

It is with this lens, attached to the spectrograph of the 100-inch reflector, and extending earlier work to more distant objects, that the law of the "expansion of the universe" has been found by Hubble and Humason. At present, through the coöperation of Jackson, Moore, and Bracey of London, a still more rapid lens of similar type is being developed for us by the British Scientific Instrument Research Association.

Other methods of increasing the efficiency of large telescopes include the improvement of photographic plates and of other sensitive detectors of faint radiation, such as thermocouples, photoelectric cells, and radiometers. We have therefore sought to stimulate such work, and have found great satisfaction in the splendid results obtained by Mees and his associates in photography, Pettit and Nicholson with the thermocouple, Abbot and Sinclair Smith in radiometry, and Stebbins, Dunham, and Whitford in the development of the photoelectric amplifier. With the new Eastman plates it is now possible to record solar, stellar, and planetary spectra in the extreme infra-red, while the photoelectric amplifier used on Mount Wilson with the 100-inch telescope has recently shown the Great Nebula in Andromeda to be twice as wide as it was formerly supposed to be. Without mentioning other similar advances, it is easy to imagine the great gain in space-penetrating power, only partially foreseen at the initiation of this enterprise, now promised by the 200-inch telescope.

In his most recent book, *The Dawn of Conscience*, Breasted gives a striking historical picture of human experience and personal character gradually and slowly arising out of the developing universe. His reasoning is based on observation reaching far behind the dawn of written Egyptian history. Though we can find no convincing evidence of man's presence on bodies other than the earth, it would be strange if life did not exist, in lower or possibly higher forms, on some of the planets and probably revolve about many distant stars. Breasted and those who look back through geological time to the earliest ages of the earth are exploring the past. Astronomers are doing likewise, in a vastly extended region. They have no expectation of detecting signs of life, but they can study the evolution of the universe in which the earth plays a part. Although light travels through space at the rate of 186,000 miles per second, we see the sun as it was eight minutes ago, Arcturus as it looked when the light now entering our eyes left it forty years ago, the distant stars of the Milky

Way as they were thousands of years ago, the nearer spiral nebulæ as they were a million years ago, the remote nebulæ as they were thousands of millions of years ago. In other words, the heavens as we see them do not appear as they existed at any one time, but rather in the form of a composite picture, covering a period of countless years.

Is it surprising that we still push our observations outward, urged by the same desire for knowledge that has persisted through so many centuries? Or that Poincaré, recognizing what astronomy has done to stimulate all forms of research, once queried, in *La Valeur de la Science:* "What would our modern civilization have been if the earth, like Jupiter, had always been surrounded by clouds?"

GOOD WOMEN AND TRUE

By *A. P. Herbert*

TRIX DARLING my *heart's* apologies. I've not written
to you for an *epoch*, and no wonder, my dear when I tell
you, well for *five* days I've been *incarcerated* in the courts
and my dear I *rather* think I've *rather* inserted my fascinating
little *foot* and it's *quite* possible my *next* letter will come from
Holloway *Jail* or somewhere, well my dear some time ago I
ran into *poor* old Rosemary Dune and my dear she was an utter
blanc-mange of emotion because after *thirty-five* years of *patient*
endeavor she'd at *last* got blighted in matrimony or rather
she's *just* about to but of course on the *same* day she had a
summons to serve on a *foul* jury, my dear *so* like men *no* tact
or *humane* feelings anywhere, well of course I did the *Christian*
thing and said *Let* me do it for you, because my dear *nobody*
ought to function on a *British* jury who's thinking the *whole*
time *what* undies shall I buy and *where*, which my dear from
what I can make out is the *sole* thing these brides on the brink
do think don't you agree darling?

Well my dear of course the poor bat merely *liquified* with
gratitude, so I put on my oldest and left the nose *quite* luminous
and I *answered* winningly to the name of Rosemary *Dune*, well
the old man *ogled* me somewhat but he didn't say anything and
after *centuries* of *sitting* about *in* I walked to the jury-box and
there I sat for *five* days, my dear the *agony*, the *hardest* wood,
like sitting in the *Strand*, well there was only one other doe, and
she sat next to me, my dear with the *possible* exception of the
widow Wockley the *most* emetical creation since the *jelly-fish*,
my dear a *crustacean*, I christened her the *Whelk*, my dear I
can't tell you, *coated* with *jet* and *black* velvet *tickle-me's*, my

From *Topsy;* published, 1930, by Doubleday, Doran and Company. Used by special
permission.

dear definitely *unmagnetic*, and of course the moment our *hips* touched there was a sort of *mutual* spasm of *utter* repugnance, my dear I'm *positive* she writes *righteous* postcards to the B.B.C., *that* kind of ullage, well I'm sorry to say that it was a conjested *Divorce* case and *rather* unsuitable, my dear *too* French, but my dear I must say I do think that lawyers can be *rather* atmospheric, because my dear the judge was *divine* and not the least bit *gagga*, and of course, the *husband's* barrister my dear I surrendered at *sight*, with the *most* morocco *skin*, for a man, and the *most* insinuating *dove-like* voice, and of course those *wigs* are *indecently* becoming, well *whatever* he said you felt was *too* equitable, and they all have darling snow-white *bibs* and my dear they *all* look as if they washed *thrice* daily, before *and* after meals, which is more than I can say for the wife, well *rather* hairy at the hocks darling, you know the type, well she said he beat her and as I said to the Whelk Who *wouldn't*, but my dear she *quivered* at me, *too* antagonous.

Well my dear on the *second* day I *rather* lost control and powdered the old nose in the middle of one of the judge's *longest* interruptions, because my dear what with the *intense* tribulating of *sitting* on mahogany I *had* to do something or scream like a woman, well my dear the *judge* gave me the *most* ecclesiastical *look* so I smiled *radiantly* at him till the *Whelk* inflicted on me the *cruelest* prod with her totally unupholstered *elbow*, my dear returned *cum* dividend, so the *next* day I thought better be hung for a *sheep* et cetera so I put on everything pearls and all and the *new* cami-*underloons*, my dear *have* you seen them, well *after* that I may have been wrong but it *seemed* to me that the case was attracting more and more interest because my dear absolute *troops* of *seraphic* young barristers merely *thronged* into the court, my dear *standing* for hours and I should have said *staring*, of course Mr. *Haddock* says, who *by* the way my dear was once *called* to the bar but it seems *failed* to turn up, *too* characteristic darling, well he says that the handsome lads must have merely come to study law points, but I don't know darling I *rather* fancied they were *rather* attracted, anyhow my dear the *more* expensive and virginal I looked the more embarrassed were the *K.C's.* because my dear whenever they had to be *at all* French they *kept* apologizing with their *lovely* eyes, my dear like *dogs*, and they tried so hard to express everything *too* nicely for me, only the judge kept *chipping* in and said he would *not* have a *spade* called an *implement* of a *certain nature*, however the most of it was about his beating her and whether it was *cruelty* to read in *bed*, and so it went on, well my dear the *husband's* K.C. made an *infatuating* speech and I was utterly convinced that *he* was *too* right, only the wife's K.C. *rather* persuaded me too, and of course after the *judge* I was a *mere* muddle of conflicting hypothetics anyhow at last we *retired*, my dear the *dingiest* sort of *third-class* waiting-room with nothing in it but a *jug* of tooth-water, my dear *too* masculine, however I thought one can at least have a *smoke* and attend to the old face, but my dear you should have *seen* the Whelk's expression especially as some of the men heaved *sighs* of thanksgiving and produced their pipes, well my dear the foreman was the *merest* blotting-pad and the Whelk took charge of the *entire* proceedings, of course she was *utterly* for the *injured* wife and my dear by the end of my *first* gasper they'd *all* decided to divorce the *husband*, and my dear I've often wondered *how* it is that you can always get *twelve* people to agree about a law-case when I've never met *three* bipeds who could agree about *anything*, and the *reason* is I suppose that *every* jury has its particular *Whelk*, only fortunately it *doesn't* have its particular *Topsy*, because my dear none of them seemed to be exactly *absorbed* in my opinions, so when the foreman said We're *all* agreed then, I said no we weren't because I said if the man was floppy enough to want to adhere to *that* woman, then let him *adhere*, sensation darling!

Well my dear the Whelk *detonated* and she said Perhaps you're not a married woman so I said No perhaps you never had a father, my dear *too* crude, well then she said she had a luncheon appointment, and I said I wasn't interested in her meals, and she said I couldn't possibly understand a case like this so I said if she meant I had a *nice* mind she was *too* right but weren't they allowed on juries, and I said anyhow I understand the wife *quite* lucidly because I know the type, well then we got down to it, talon and tooth darling, some of the men became *too* courageous and began to argue with the Whelk, and my dear we were there for *five* inflammatory hours, *no* lunch, *fainting* for tea and I *rather* think the Whelk was one of those *orange-juice* breakfasters, so *what* she was feeling, however I was *quite* remorseless and my dear *one* by *one* those *gelatinous men* came round to my side, because my dear some of the younger jurors I *rather* fancy were *rather* attracted and the others were yearning for Surbiton Home and Beauty, and my dear *last* of all the Whelk yielded *also*, my dear *rather* poignant because she was *so* shattered with nerves and famine she could only *hiss* at me but at *four* o'clock I said O gosh teatime and my dear *at* that she suddenly became *too* unanimous, well we trooped out into the court and during the verdict and everything the Whelk hissed at me *Chits* like you ought not to *be* empanelled at *all*, so I said *Too* right, I wasn't, I'm doing it for a *friend*, well then she asked questions and I was *girlishly* candid and my dear she *rose* in her place like *Joan* of Arc or one of those flapping *infallible* females and told the *whole* story to the judge, *can* you believe it, sensation *again*, and my dear it seems the *whole* trial may have to be *re*-done because the *Whelk* said I'd *corrupted* the jury by *brazenly* exploiting my personality, and Mr. Haddock tells me it's a *miss*-demeanor at *Common* Law punishable with imprisonment for *simply* ever, so pray for me darling though of course the really *black* feature is that *when* I think of the *Whelk* I long to do it *again*, so farewell Trix your felonious little Topsy.

LET US TALK ABOUT UNPLEASANT THINGS

By *Robert Herrick*

AMONG those blessings of adversity that we are, slowly, discovering these calamitous days is that an unpleasant truth does not hurt as badly as one politely ignored or denied. At long last we are turning from the ideal of "normalcy," "ninety days to Prosperity," from the theory that our economic muddle is "largely psychological," and from the many other varieties of anodyne with which as a people Americans have been fond of doping themselves. We are accustoming ourselves to look unpleasant facts in the face without squinting. Dr. Julius Klein's radio patter leaves us cold; the latest billion-dollar panacea from Washington does not even flutter the stock market; platform bunk is merely cause for mirth in the silly season—and when not sufficiently hilarious, the broadcasting companies kindly turn it off. In time we may even come to realize that we are not the richest, luckiest, happiest, most generous people that ever lived on this earth; that all our financiers are not Wizards; our bankers, Pillars of Society; our million-dollar executives, Supermen; our petty politicians, Astute Statesmen. We Americans are somehow mortal like the rest of the world, and a little searching of the heart will do us good. We are deflating more than commodity and security prices: we are deflating some of our national conceits. No longer will one be considered a tiresome pessimist or a "red" if he happens to blurt out an obvious if unpalatable truth that his neighbors are trying to forget. The habit of closing our senses to the ordures on our path, of singing ourselves to sleep with headline lullabies, may be unsafe.

What we have needed the past ten years is a Voltaire, a Swift, not a Coué nor a Pollyana. A little cleansing acid on the greasy windshield of public consciousness will clear the vision.

This habit of seeing only silver linings in the clouds is deeply rooted in the American temperament. We are proud of it. Upon the principle of self-delusion we have created the only religion that appeals vitally to the American people. The cult which ineptly calls itself Christian Science because it is neither scientific nor Christian, and its many imitators, designed to teach their votaries how to cheat their intelligence, are immensely popular. As a people we like to fool ourselves. This tendency has made our literature feeble, our politics infantile, and our daily life monotonous. A prolonged period of adversity when distressing truth could not be evaded by the most robust was needed to make us adult.

One of the more irritating forms of criticism that, as a young novelist, I used to hear from dear friends who wished me well was that I should write about "nice" people like themselves (people one would like "to receive into the home" as it was sometimes put), and treat only "pleasant" subjects, the list of unpleasant subjects being then longer than at present. How the pages of Balzac, of Dostoievsky, of Thackeray would shrink under such a test! Even Shakespeare might become insipid. When somewhat later I was writing of the roaring background of Chicago, my boosting fellow-citizens deplored the fact that I chose deliberately to depict the squalor of Cottage Grove Avenue (then one of the world's dreariest thoroughfares) and the miles of shambling dingy flat buildings on the scrawny wastes of prairie "subdivisions" rather than the elegancies of the Gold Coast and the neo-classic beauty of the Art Institute of Chicago as seen in the vision of the "Chicago Plan" at Commercial Club banquets. A similar instinct to deny the unpleasant condemned Barbusse's powerful picture of men at war, which the soldiers at the front were eagerly reading, glad that at last some of the horrors they had to endure had found their way into print instead of sweetly romantic tales of heroism and the distortions of war correspondents. When I praised *Le Feu* in a review as the one authentic presentation of war then published, I was solemnly warned by a member of our Military Intelligence Bureau that Barbusse was considered "defeatist" and, therefore, seditious by the high command. Reading his book might make American mothers and fathers uncomfortable about the fate of their sons. The angel of Mons and German rapings were safer literature!

So it was with Russia when that great country refused to fight any longer in a war that was in no sense hers. The facts were unpalatable and, therefore, must be denied as long as possible. The foremost American newspapers chronicled every few days the immediate collapse of the new régime—as they still do at longer intervals—which has somehow survived to a quite respectable age as governments go these years. Some day Americans may regret that they allowed themselves to be deceived about what has been happening to that huge slice of the world's population, and wish that they had accepted the facts pragmatically instead of denying them "idealistically."

The same mental attitude has asserted itself from the start of the recent unpleasantness in business and finance. Millions were without work and starving long before our government, the press, or the public would admit the facts and recognize the situation. Washington, of course, set the lullaby to words and tried heroically to Coué the nation back to prosperity. The President and members of his cabinet bombarded us with optimistic prophecies. Great industrialists marshaled their billions to double an already swollen capacity of production. The people were exhorted to buy, buy, buy more goods. Meanwhile great financial institutions were tottering or crumbled into dust, savings and "investments in American equities" were disappearing into air like soap bubbles—but why speak about it? These were but necessary incidents of "readjustment," from which, phœnixlike, we should emerge ere long richer and merrier than ever in this world of rugged individualism. The rôle of the strong was to sit silent and listen to the drip-drip of their fortunes ebbing away like blood from an open artery, grimly resolved to "carry on" (in the melodramatic lingo of the war) or hold on while our world was taking a flop and shriveling into nothing.

"Don't talk about such unpleasant things!" my charming hostess exclaims reprovingly when someone carelessly mentions the impending disasters to be read between the lines of carefully censored dispatches from Asia or Europe or America. "I don't want to hear it! You may be wrong. . . . I know everything will come out right some day, some fine day!"

It is amazing how many good women of native intelligence are convinced that human society as they have become accustomed to think of it will endure forever, a divinely conceived instrument. No historical instances of former recessions of civilization can swerve their faith in the continuance of the world they were born into. "All that was somehow different." They *know* that the familiar sun will shine upon them tomorrow morning or at the latest the day after,—same sun, same world, same self as always hitherto. This is what is popularly known as having "faith" and greatly praised. Every true woman is both a capitalist and an optimist from birth. This may be from biologic necessity or from an invincible ignorance, but I bow before it whatever its cause and am convinced that as long as American women are what they are there is no need to worry about communism or socialism or even a little national planning. Fascism, yes: they understand fascism and have a weakness for Mussolinis. They (like Mussolini) know how God made this world and why: he made it for them, with its ups and downs (but chiefly ups), with motor cars and country places and rich husbands for the lucky ones; cosy apartments and movies for the less lucky; decent homes and plenty of dull work for the great uninteresting mass of humanity; and charity for the poor whom we have always with us . . . Life without end, Amen!

So being duly warned I take another drink and tactfully ask my neighbor how her garden is thriving during this dry season, and whether she has reduced the cook's wages ten or twenty per cent?

II

Something not unlike this ostrich act the political High Hats of Europe have been doing ever since the War was officially declared off, on the whole disastrously for the peace and comfort of the world. Anything to avoid admitting publicly what they knew to be the truth! Conference after conference has been held in charming resorts, resulting inevitably in more or less meaningless formulas prepared by the "experts," who are skilled in "agreeing in principle" while scuttling all the essential facts. Ever since an American president announced to a shocked world that the lamentable treaty embodied his Fourteen Points, statesmen the world over have been playing harder than ever the great game of bluff—up to this very hour when, after vainly trying to decide how more armament can be made to appear disarmament, the Geneva conference has adjourned for six months in the hope that another year will be more opportune for the telling of unpleasant truths. If at any time during the past twelve hectic years those in high command politically—who should know all the tragic facts—had said in public what they have all been saying to one another confidentially over luncheon, tea, and dinner tables, we should be nearer that healthy understanding of what ails the world, which must precede any real amelioration of conditions. Instead of delusive generalities (stalling with Dawes and Young plans) they might have blurted out what has been in the back of their minds; they might have said something like this:

"Men and women of this troubled world, it is useless to pretend any longer—and too dangerous. The old formulas won't work. Germany can't be made to pay the entire cost of the international spree or any considerable part of it. We can't go armed to the teeth and prate of our longings for peace. We can't get rich again by simply refusing to buy one another's goods. We can't sit forever on the lid of potential revolution while our peoples grow hungrier and more desperate each year. One awful mistake was made at Versailles and a thousand since. We propose now to tear up that cursed treaty and begin over, sincerely. And from now on we propose to tell the world what we know as fast as we know it."

What would happen? Would the French invade Germany again to gather their rainbow gold? Would the people of these United States send three million more bonus-begging legion-naires back to Europe to collect our loans? Never! Just nothing at all would happen, except that everybody everywhere would sigh and say, "Well, we knew it was all make-believe. Now let us forget it and go to work." The hush-hushers and the bitter-enders alike would be stilled forever, once what every informed person has realized for years was out in the open, told in screaming headlines until it no longer hurt.

There are other, more personal, unpleasant truths nearer home that we might well let escape into the open. First, that whether we like it or not we are not and never can be sufficient unto ourselves. It may be humiliating to American pride to admit that we need the goods—and the good will—of other peoples even as they need ours. The air of aloof superiority which we have assumed toward the rest of humanity since the conclusion of the War we shall have to exchange for something nearer humility as each day piles up proofs that the rest of the world can get along without us quite as well as we can without them. Next we must recognize without rancor that Europe will pay us practically nothing of what remains of their debts to us on the war account, because it is desirable neither for them nor for us to have these debts paid. No matter who owes whom or what or however sanctified by right, this debt-and-reparation account (practically one in fact if not in political theory) was all a nightmare of revengeful, fearful, cowardly statesmen and metaphysical financiers, with their endless bargains and rats'-nests of paper obligations. Wars are fought in present time, and the attempt to foist the burdens for their payment upon succeeding generations is both futile and dangerous. Next, we can't hope to trade, which is the one thing we most care to do, unless we are willing to swap. Even a child can perceive that! Again, not all of us, one hundred and twenty millions of us, can expect to live entirely at the expense of the government—which is only a figure of speech for all of us. Nor is it safe to truckle to "veterans," thus raising a prætorian guard to bully weaklings in Congress: it might easily become a more serious menace to democracy than all of the reds that ever peopled the imaginations of heretic hunting congressional committees! Again, we can't for long make even paper profits out of selling worthless securities to people more foolish than we are ourselves.

Still more wholesome if unpalatable truths: Americans are fast losing that reputation for common business honesty which they once shared with the Chinese. We have lied so much to ourselves that we are becoming hazy about certain basic moral axioms. Our corporations, of course the largest and best in the world, with their million-dollar executives and fat bonuses, have been extravagantly and, in many instances, dishonestly managed for the profit of directors and other speculators rather than for their stockholders. Our investment bankers are sometimes criminally stupid (the reader can supply the proper specification from his personal experience) and sometimes mere rascals, too rarely "trustworthy" (an old-fashioned word!), which explains incidentally why so many of us who are timid now prefer the mattress or the safety deposit box to the bank or investment banker. A government campaign with customary ballyhoo urging these timid souls not to hoard as "unpatriotic" would be more effective if the authorities had taken a little pains to enforce common honesty in our banks. "Whispering campaigns against the integrity of our financial institutions engineered by communists" is the latest farcical explanation of runs upon banks. All the talk by all the communists between Washington and Moscow could not affect the solidity of any American bank if the bankers themselves had not given ample cause for distrust of their methods and their principles.

One need not resort to the hackneyed bogies of communism and socialism—or even fascism—to explain the unrest of this troubled day. It is indeed marvelous that with the accumulating evidences of bungling, dishonesty, and insincerity written large before the eyes of all, incidents that cannot be concealed (and how many others covered up but dimly suspected?), the common man should remain as trusting and patient as he is with the lords and masters of his destiny! Our leading citizens and members of the government need not look so far as Russia for the cause were they to awake one morning to a lively and disastrous revolution. They need merely recall the record of their management of society for the past ten years. If the irresponsible rule of *laissez-faire*, so agreeable to its beneficiaries, has come to an end, as many shrewd observers fear, those who have benefited most largely from its license have themselves to thank for the ensuing chaos. Even today, at the end of the eleventh hour, they might by striving disinterestedly to put their house in order instead of trusting to blind chance and "the working of economic law," preserve for a while their special privileges and possibly regain some of their prestige. But they must show a different comprehension of the situation that has overtaken them from that of their great advocate in Washington: they must realize how narrow the margin of their safety has become and mend their ways before it is too late. Will they? Humanity is long-suffering. A poor system can be worked indefinitely if it inspires confidence, security; that is, if the majority trusts the minority which runs it. Few human beings like violent changes and the risks of chaos. But with water in a boiler over a hot fire there comes a point beyond which it is unsafe to sit on the safety valve. Human society obeys natural laws as well as chemical elements.

III

Finally, how about ourselves, each one of us, little Everyman and Everywoman? We too have believed that we could live handsomely without much hard work, could become rich overnight Aladdinlike, get by with dishonest shoddy substitutes for thinking. We couldn't. It never can be done for long. Are we quite ready to deflate ourselves, to admit that all of us along with our richer neighbors have been on a prolonged, delirious, and vulgar spree, during which we have talked a lot of drunken nonsense and committed more follies than we now like to remember? Our values somehow got all askew. We babbled about individual fulfillment, individual freedom, "the right to live our own lives," lives which were fast becoming meaningless. We were so deafened by the roar of what was going on around us that we never looked within to see if all was well there. The Litany is a fine piece of human psychology as well as of literature. It is time to repeat once more its great refrain: "Have mercy upon us, miserable sinners!"

How different from our attitude was that of the old Greeks in the presence of disaster! The evil that befalls man, the Greeks felt, must be caused by some offense against the gods, some neglect or unwitting wrong committed, which must be discovered and set right, ample amends having been made, repentance and due sacrifice, before the deadly plague or other calamity would vanish. Purification was essential—self-purification and social purification. Compare such a direct method with our pretentious "reconstruction" measures (feeding more poison in the shape of "credit" to the sufferer from delirium tremens!) or with passages from the *Congressional Record*, denouncing and excoriating somebody else, or with either the Republican or the Democratic platform, promising the impossible! In ultimate analysis every economic phenomenon is a manifestation of human conduct; and economic problems cannot be resolved until the human factors underlying them are properly adjusted, disagreeable as the process may be.

Our depression may be "mainly psychological"—hysterical
—if you like. Most things that affect human beings individually or in mass are "psychological." We are so made. But
this fact does not imply that all we have to do to become comfortable and happy is to change our psychology from depression to boom. We must first correct the wrong thinking that
caused both boom and depression, which is not easy. Hard
times are but one unpleasant symptom of internal maladjust-
ments. No doubt man is what he thinks and—more important
—becomes what he thinks. So the sooner we put off the Polly-
anna habit of mind and cease hunting panaceas, searching our
hearts instead for the secret of our misfortunes, the sooner
shall we be prepared for the new—and let us hope—saner
world.

So I say let us talk only about unpleasant things until we
understand them and their cause, which is ourselves. Let us
examine one by one all the bugaboos and the hollow pretenses
and the ugly facts in due order. Let us eat and sleep with misfortune until we have lost all fear of it! By so doing, for one
thing, we shall discount our own personal losses. For any
situation calmly faced and accepted becomes automatically
less intolerable. I am filled with admiration for the many
families in my acquaintance that are already quietly accepting
a cut of fifty or more per cent in their incomes, which means in
modern terms a drastic transfer of class. They have forgotten
their illusions about what they never really possessed. Therefore, they are already far on the way to the future with little
encumbering baggage. Indeed the courage and the good
humor, the decency and the generosity displayed by all sorts of
people in the face of a disaster which has cut savagely into
their private ambitions suggests that humanity may not be so
inextricably tied to the profit motive as we have been led to
believe; that more modest returns for individual efforts would
be cheerfully accepted provided there were greater equality
and sense of security, of the ground being solid beneath. The
majority of reasonable human beings neither expect nor desire

to ascend once more into cuckoocloudland as our politicians so fondly promise. Gamblers and other deluded optimists may endeavor to stage a premature "recovery" in the security markets, buying back at rising prices what they frantically threw away a few months before. But a too swift return to prosperity (of the 1929 variety) would be in fact a disaster even were it likely to happen. Instead of a program of "reflation," what we need is to consolidate the gains we have made in the bitter school of adversity so that we may prepare the way for a society in which there is neither boom nor depression. Let us grip this unpleasant and unstable present into which we have dreamed ourselves, until we have squeezed from it all its venom, knowing that the unpleasantness comes mostly from our own inharmonious egos. Our secret hopes and fears and prejudices and lusts and weaknesses are hurt by an open recognition of the truth. Not life itself, which remains enjoyable and adventurous.

THE PEDESTRIAN MIND

By *Walter S. Hinchman*

PEOPLE generally walk because they cannot afford to ride. For my part, I have long cherished the notion that few of us can really afford to ride; and like most cherished notions, it has grown into a conviction with me. Of course a great deal may be said for walking, in a purely physical sense; it is not a mere accident of some passing civilization, like chariots and sedan-chairs, but is one of the few things, like loving and eating, which have been common to all generations of men.

But I am thinking rather of the advantages of *mental* pedestrianism. It is with some alarm, I confess, that I observe the increase in vehicular traffic of this mental sort. The pedestrian mind doesn't get very far in one day, to be sure, but it has ample opportunity to see where it is going. It proceeds slowly enough to observe and record. It can stop altogether when it gets tired—a great virtue truly, for it is not likely to mistake motion and sound for progress.

Then, too, your mind afoot is not confined to the highroad; it may follow by-paths; it may even explore unbroken wilds; it is not bound to the automotive "wheel of things." I don't make much of the fact that it can climb a tree, for Fords, they say, can do that too, though I do say for it that it still looks like a mind after its arboreal excursion.

But the great advantage of the pedestrian mind, to my thinking, is that, while it makes retirement possible, it is not "retired leisure." It has to work to get on; it moves often with the great procession of mankind. It knows, on the one hand, the starry solitude, the high mountain where one may pray,

From the *Forum*, January 1925; copyright, 1925, by The Forum Publishing Company. Used by special permission.

and, on the other, the crowded highroad where the race is to be run "not without dust and heat."

Are you a both—ander?

"Which side are you going to take, Liberal or Conservative?" said a friend to me not long ago, as we approached a house of controversy.

"Why should I take either side?" I answered—"especially when I am not sure what either means."

"That's No Man's Land," he said; "you'll get shot if you don't take sides."

Like most of us, my friend was an *either—or* person, brought up on the foolish proverb that you can't have your cake and eat it too. Why not a *both—and* state of mind for a change? It might be diverting to be both liberal and conservative; and in point of intelligibility, it would be emphatically lucid compared to the *either—or* position of most people who call themselves one or the other. For the great alternatives, opposites though they may once have been, seem to be fairly interchangeable nowadays. Liberty, for instance, would seem to get on about as well when it assumes the engaging rôle of Tyranny as it did when it paraded with Equality and Fraternity or when it "inhered," among our forefathers, "in some sensible object." What a slogan, Liberty and Tyranny, one and inseparable! Perish the thought! Very well, let the thought perish, but, Mr. Voter, meet the fact.

All a man has to do, it would seem, is to pronounce his notions good and loud, and we follow like sheep or attack like wolves. A senator comes out with the astonishing discovery that the next political issue will be between progressives and reactionaries. Some papers, it is refreshing to note, are serious enough to treat this *pronunciamiento* with the persiflage it deserves, but a great many editors, and their readers with them, are foolish enough to imagine that he has said something and so get themselves into a hopelessly *either—or* state of passion over it. Incidentally, even his hostile critics give him the sort of free advertising that Barnum loved. Men and women evidently must be forever taking sides and biting their thumbs across the street at one another, sometimes when there is no issue at all, at other times when the issue is "highly unimportant to Gods and men."

For instance, this altercation about Fundamentalism. I should have supposed that anything *fundamental* in religion had primarily to do with truth and its rock-bottom basis, but very likely that's just an odd fancy of mine; at all events, the disputants, unquestionably audible, have revealed that the fundamental thing is to decide whether your wife is descended from a monkey or from one of Adam's ribs. Most of the American people find it easy to take sides on this question. I don't. I'll admit it's disquieting to reflect that your wife's ancestry may be Simian—it's rather disillusioning when you thought you had married a goddess; awkward, too, to break it to the children; but I confess to as much discomfiture when I reflect that I may be wedded to a spare rib. Also there's an unpleasant suggestion of the charnel house; to this favor we knew we should come at the last, but to think of happy living men everywhere wedded to bones—pah! "mine ache to think on 't!" But that's a digression. The point is that the disputants are *either—or* people. How they bite their thumbs!

Now of course there's no objection to taking sides when you know what you mean and the cause is worth fighting for. Professor Root's article on "The Virtue of Intolerance" a few years ago was a fine rebuke to those vacillating creatures who fancied that because their brains were shallow they must be broad. They are still at large among us, but they are not *both—and* people just because they fail to be *either—or* people. In fact, they are really *either—ors* thinly disguised: they are so committed to the process of selecting alternatives that, after persuading themselves that they are not *either—or* bigots, they leap to the conclusion that they must be *both—and* prophets. Better to be frankly *either—or* than that, even if it does commit you to Simian frolic or to the conjugal felicity of a sarcophagus.

But in many matters, when you stop to think about it, a *both—and* attitude is salutary. For instance, why not believe in Capital *and* Labor? Why not believe in Science *and* the Classics? Why not revive the spirit as well as the letter of that fine old phrase, Business *and* Pleasure? Why not, even, believe in the Bible *and* Evolution? It's quite possible, too, that a *both—and* attitude, even in the closed shop of marriage, might enable us to endure the worse as well as the better, the sickness as well as the health. There's a good deal to be said for walking down the middle of the street. Flying vehicles look dangerous, but they really have a tender regard for pedestrians; they are not half so dangerous as the snares of the sidewalk. Clear calls may come, when one or the other side is the only place; but, till then, let us not rush to the wall merely for the sake of being on a sidewalk.

Perhaps we may take counsel from the perennial boy, who replies, when asked whether he will have pie or ice cream, "I'll take both, please." That boy sees life steadily and sees it whole.

VULGARITY IN LITERATURE

By *Aldous Huxley*

WAS Edgar Allan Poe a major poet? It would surely never occur to any English-speaking critic to say so. And yet, in France from 1850 till the present time, the best poets of each generation—yes, and the best critics, too—for, like most excellent poets, Baudelaire, Mallarmé, Paul Valéry are also admirable critics—have gone out of their way to praise him. Only a year or two ago M. Valéry repeated the now traditional French encomium of Poe and added at the same time a protest against the faintness of our English praise. We who are speakers of English and not English scholars, who were born into the language and from childhood have been pickled in its literature—we can only say with all due respect, that Baudelaire, Mallarmé, and Valéry are wrong and that Poe is not one of our major poets. A taint of vulgarity spoils, for the English reader, all but two or three of his poems—the marvelous "City in the Sea" and "To Helen," for example, whose beauty and crystal perfection make us realize, as we read them, what a very great artist perished on most of the occasions when Poe wrote verse. It is to this perished artist that the French poets pay their tribute. Not being English they are incapable of appreciating those finer shades of vulgarity that ruin Poe for us, just as we, not being French, are incapable of appreciating those finer shades of lyrical beauty which are, for them, the making of La Fontaine.

The substance of Poe is refined; it is his form that is vulgar. He is, as it were, one of Nature's gentlemen, unhappily cursed with incorrigible bad taste. To the most sensitive and high-souled man in the world, we should find it hard to forgive, shall we say, the wearing of a diamond ring on every finger. Poe does the equivalent of this in his poetry; we notice the solecism and shudder. Foreign observers do not notice it; they detect only the native gentlemanliness in the poetical intention, not the vulgarity in the details of execution. To them, we seem perversely and quite incomprehensibly unjust.

It is when Poe tries to make it too poetical that his poetry takes on its peculiar tinge of badness. Protesting too much that he is a gentleman, and opulent into the bargain, he falls into vulgarity. Diamond rings on every finger proclaim the parvenu.

Consider, for example, the first stanza of "Ulalume."

> The skies they were ashen and sober;
>   The leaves they were crisped and sere—
>   The leaves they were withering and sere;
> It was night in the lonesome October
>   Of my most immemorial year;
> It was hard by the dim lake of Auber,
>   In the misty mid region of Weir—
> It was down by the dank tarn of Auber
>   In the ghoul-haunted woodlands of Weir.

These lines protest too much (and with what a variety of voices!) that they are poetical, and, protesting, are therefore vulgar. To start with, the walloping dactylic meter is all too musical. Poetry ought to be musical, but musical with tact, subtly and variously. Meters whose rhythms, as in this case, are strong, insistent, and practically invariable offer the poet a kind of short cut to musicality. They provide him (my subject calls for a mixture of metaphors) with a ready-made, reach-me-down music. He does not have to create a music appropriately modulated to his meaning; all he has to do is to shovel the meaning into the moving stream of the meter and allow the current to carry it along on waves, that, like those of the best hairdressers, are guaranteed permanent. Many

nineteenth century poets used those metrical short cuts to
music, with artistically fatal results.

> Then when nature around me is smiling
> The last smile which answers to mine,
> I do not believe it beguiling
> Because it reminds me of thine.

How can one take even Byron seriously, when he protests
his musicalness in such loud and vulgar accents? It is only by
luck or an almost superhuman poetical skill that these all too
musical meters can be made to sound, through their insistent
barrel-organ rhythms, the intricate, personal music of the
poet's own meaning. Byron occasionally, for a line or two,
takes the hard kink out of those dactylic permanent waves and
appears, so to speak, in his own musical hair; and Hood, by an
unparalleled prodigy of technique, turns even the reach-me-
down music of "The Bridge of Sighs" into a personal music,
made to the measure of the subject and his own emotion.
Moore, on the contrary, is always perfectly content with the
permanent wave; and Swinburne, that super-Moore of a later
generation, was also content to be a permanent waver—the
most accomplished, perhaps, in all the history of literature.
The complexity of his ready-made musics and his technical
skill in varying the number, shape, and contour of his permanent waves are simply astonishing. But, like Poe and the
others, he protested too much, he tried to be too poetical.
However elaborately devious his short cuts to music may be,
they are still short cuts—and short cuts (this is the irony)
to poetical vulgarity.

A quotation and a parody will illustrate the difference
between ready-made music and music made to measure. I
remember (I trust correctly) a simile of Milton's:—

> Like that fair field
> Of Enna, where Proserpine gathering flowers,
> Herself a fairer flower, by gloomy Dis
> Was gathered, which cost Ceres all that pain
> To seek her through the world.

Rearranged according to their musical phrasing, these lines
would have to be written thus:—

> Like that fair field of Enna,
>   where Proserpine gathering flowers,
> Herself a fairer flower,
>   by gloomy Dis was gathered,
> Which cost Ceres all that pain
> To seek her through the world.

The contrast between the lyrical swiftness of the first four
phrases with that row of limping spondees which tells of Ceres's
pain, is thrillingly appropriate. Bespoke, the music fits the
sense like a glove.

How would Poe have written on the same theme? I have
ventured to invent his opening stanza.

> It was noon in the fair field of Enna,
>   When Proserpina gathering flowers—
>   Herself the most fragrant of flowers,
> Was gathered away to Gehenna
>   By the Prince of Plutonian powers;
> Was born down the windings of Brenner
>   To the gloom of his amorous bowers—
> Down the tortuous highway of Brenner
>   To the god's agapemonous bowers.

Of the versification of "The Raven" Poe says, in his "Philosophy of Composition": "My first object (as usual) was
originality. The extent to which this has been neglected in
versification is one of the most unaccountable things in the
world. Admitting that there is little possibility of variety in
mere *rhythm*, it is still clear that the possible varieties of meter
and stanza are absolutely infinite—and yet, *for centuries, no
man, in verse, has ever done or ever seemed to think of doing an
original thing.*" This fact, which Poe hardly exaggerates,
speaks volumes for the good sense of the poets. Feeling that
almost all strikingly original meters and stanzas were only
illegitimate short cuts to a musicalness which, when reached,
turned out to be but a poor and vulgar substitute for individual

music, they wisely stuck to the less blatantly musical meters of tradition. The ordinary iambic decasyllable, for example, is intrinsically musical enough to be just able, when required, to stand up by itself. But its musical stiffness can easily be taken out of it. It can be now a chasuble, a golden carapace of sound, now, if the poet so desires, a pliant, soft and, musically speaking, almost neutral material, out of which he can fashion a special music of his own to fit his thoughts and feelings in all their incessant transformations. Good landscape painters seldom choose a "picturesque" subject; they want to paint their own picture, not have it imposed on them by nature. In the thoroughly paintable little places of this world you will generally find only bad painters. (It's so easy to paint the thoroughly paintable.) The good ones prefer the unspectacular neutralities of the Home Counties to those Cornish coves and Ligurian fishing villages, whose picturesqueness is the delight of all those who have no pictures of their own to project on to the canvas. It is the same with poetry: good poets avoid what I may call, by analogy, "musicesque" meters, preferring to create their own music out of raw materials as nearly as possible neutral. Only bad poets, or good poets against their better judgment, and by mistake, go to the Musicesque for their material. "For centuries no man, in verse, has ever done or ever seemed to think of doing an original thing." It remained for Poe and the other nineteenth century metrists to do it; Procrustes-like they tortured and amputated significance into fitting the ready-made music of their highly original meters and stanzas. The result was, in most cases, as vulgar as a Royal Academy Sunrise on Ben Nevis (with Highland Cattle) or a genuine hand-painted sketch of Porto-fino.

How could a judge so fastidious as Baudelaire listen to Poe's music and remain unaware of its vulgarity? A happy ignorance of English versification preserved him, I fancy, from this realization. His own imitations of medieval hymns prove how far he was from understanding the first principles of versification in a language where the stresses are not, as in

French, equal, but essentially and insistently uneven. In his Latin poems Baudelaire makes the ghost of Bernard of Cluny write as though he had learned his art from Racine. The principles of English versification are much the same as those of medieval Latin. If Baudelaire could discover lines composed of equally stressed syllables in Bernard, he must also have discovered them in Poe. Interpreted according to Racinian principles, such verses as

> It was down by the dank tarn of Auber
> In the ghoul-haunted woodland of Weir

must have taken on, for Baudelaire, heaven knows what exotic subtlety of rhythm. We can never hope to guess what those ghoul-haunted woodlands mean to a Frenchman possessing only a distant and theoretical knowledge of our language.

Returning now to "Ulalume," we find that its too poetical meter has the effect of vulgarizing by contagion what would be otherwise perfectly harmless and refined technical devices. Thus, even the very mild alliterations in "the ghoul-haunted woodlands of Weir" seem to protest too much. And yet an iambic verse beginning "Woodland of Weir, ghoul-haunted," would not sound in the least over-poetical. It is only in the dactylic environment that those two w's strike one as protesting too much.

And then there are the proper names. Well used, proper names can be relied on to produce the most thrilling musical-magical effects. But use them without discretion, and the magic evaporates into abracadabrical absurdity, or becomes its own mocking parody; the over-emphatic music shrills first into vulgarity and finally into ridiculousness. Poe tends to place his proper names in the most conspicuous position in the line (he uses them constantly as rhyme words), showing them off—these magical-musical jewels—as the *rastacouaire* might display the twin cabochon emeralds at his shirt cuffs and the platinum wrist watch, with his monogram in diamonds. These proper-name rhyme-jewels are particularly flashy in

Poe's case because they are mostly dissyllabic. Now, the dissyllabic rhyme in English is poetically so precious and so conspicuous by its richness that, if it is not perfect in itself and perfectly used, it emphatically ruins what it was meant emphatically to adorn. Thus, sound and association make of "Thule" a musical-magical proper name of exceptional power. But when Poe writes,

> I have reached these lands but newly
> From an ultimate dim Thule,

he spoils the effect which the word ought to produce by insisting too much, and incompetently, on its musicality. He shows off his jewel as conspicuously as he can, but only reveals thereby the badness of its setting and his own Levantine love of display. For "newly" does not rhyme with "Thule"—or only rhymes on condition that you pronounce the adverb as though you were a Bengali, or the name as though you came from Whitechapel. The paramour of Goethe's king rhymed perfectly with the name of his kingdom; and when Laforgue wrote of that "*roi de Thulé, Immaculé*" his *rime riche* was entirely above suspicion. Poe's rich rhymes, on the contrary, are seldom above suspicion. That dank tarn of Auber is only very dubiously a fit poetical companion for the tenth month; and though Mount Yaanek is, *ex hypothesi*, a volcano, the rhyme with volcanic is, frankly, impossible. On other occasions Poe's proper names rhyme not only well enough, but actually, in the particular context, much too well. Dead D'Elormie, in "The Bridal Ballad," is prosodically in order, because Poe had brought his ancestors over with the Conqueror (as he also imported the ancestors of that Guy de Vere who wept his tear over Lenore) for the express purpose of providing a richly musical-magical rhyme to "bore me" and "before me." Dead D'Elormie is first cousin to Edward Lear's aged Uncle Arley sitting on a heap of Barley—ludicrous; but also (unlike dear Uncle Arley) horribly vulgar, because of the too musical lusciousness of his invented name and his display, in all tragical seriousness, of an obviously faked Norman pedigree. Dead D'Elormie is a poetical disaster.

It is vulgar, in literature, to make a display of emotions which you do not naturally have, but think you ought to have, because all the best people do have them. It is also vulgar (and this is the more common case) to have emotions, but to express them so badly, with so much too many protestings, that you seem to have no natural feelings, but to be merely fabricating emotions by a process of literary forgery. Sincerity in art, as I have pointed out elsewhere, is mainly a matter of talent. Keats's love letters ring true, because he had great literary gifts. Most men and women are capable of feeling passion, but not of expressing it; their love letters (as we learn from the specimens read aloud at inquests and murder trials, in the divorce court, during breach of promise cases) are either tritely flat or tritely bombastic. In either case manifestly insincere, and in the second case also vulgar—for to protest too much is always vulgar, when the protestations are so incompetent as not to carry conviction. And perhaps such excessive protestations can never be convincing, however accomplished the protester. D'Annunzio, for example—nobody could do a job of writing better than d'Annunzio. But when, as is too often the case, he makes much ado about nothing, we find it hard to be convinced either of the importance of the nothing, or of the sincerity of the author's emotion about it—and this in spite of the incomparable splendor of d'Annunzio's much ado. True, excessive protestings may convince a certain public at a certain time. But when the circumstances, which rendered the public sensitive to the force and blind to the vulgarity of the too much protesting, have changed, the protests cease to convince. Mackenzie's *Man of Feeling*, for example, protests its author's sensibility with an extravagance that seems now, not merely vulgar, but positively ludicrous. At the time of its publication sentimentality was, for various reasons, extremely fashionable. Circumstances changed and *The Man of Feeling* revealed itself as vulgar to the point of ridiculousness; and vulgar and ridiculous it has remained ever since and doubtless will remain.

The case of Dickens is a strange one. The really monstrous emotional vulgarity, of which he is guilty now and then in all his books and almost continuously in *The Old Curiosity Shop*, is not the emotional vulgarity of one who simulates feelings which he does not have. It is evident, on the contrary, that Dickens felt most poignantly for and with his Little Nell; that he wept over her sufferings, piously revered her goodness, and exulted in her joys. He had an overflowing heart; but the trouble was that it overflowed with such curious, and even rather repellent, secretions. The creator of the later Pickwick and the Cheeryble Brothers, of Tim Linkwater and the Bachelor and Mr. Garland and so many other gruesome old Peter Pans was obviously a little abnormal in his emotional reactions. There was something rather wrong with a man who could take this lachrymose and tremulous pleasure in adult infantility. He would doubtless have justified his rather frightful emotional taste by a reference to the New Testament. But the childlike qualities of character commended by Jesus are certainly not the same as those which distinguish the old infants in Dickens's novels. There is all the difference in the world between infants and children. Infants are stupid and unaware and subhuman. Children are remarkable for their intelligence and ardor, for their curiosity, their intolerance of shams, the clarity and ruthlessness of their vision. From all accounts Jesus must have been childlike, not at all infantile. A childlike man is not a man whose development has been arrested; on the contrary, he is a man who has given himself a chance of continuing to develop long after most adults have muffled themselves in the cocoon of middle-aged habit and convention. An infantile man is one who has not developed at all, or who has regressed towards the womb, into a comfortable unawareness. So far from being attractive and commendable, an infantile man is really a most repulsive, because a truly monstrous and misshapen being. A writer who can tearfully adore those stout or cadaverous old babies, snugly ensconced in their mental and economic womb-substitutes and sucking, between false teeth, their thumbs, must have something seriously amiss with his emotional constitution.

One of Dickens's most striking peculiarities is that, whenever in his writing he becomes emotional, he ceases instantly to use his intelligence. The overflowing of his heart drowns his head and even dims his eyes; for, whenever he is in the melting mood, Dickens ceases to be able, and probably ceases even to wish, to see reality. His one and only desire on these occasions is just to overflow, nothing else. Which he does, with a vengeance and in an atrocious blank verse that is meant to be poetical prose and succeeds only in being the worst kind of fustian. "When Death strikes down the innocent and young, from every fragile form from which he lets the panting spirit free, a hundred virtues rise, in shapes of mercy, charity, and love, to walk the world and bless it. Of every tear that sorrowing mortals shed on such green graves, some good is born, some gentler nature comes. In the Destroyer's steps there spring up bright creations that defy his power, and his dark path becomes a way of light to Heaven." And so on, a stanchless flux.

Mentally drowned and blinded by the sticky overflowings of his heart, Dickens was incapable, when moved, of recreating, in terms of art, the reality which had moved him, was even, it would seem, unable to perceive that reality. Little Nell's sufferings and death distressed him as, in real life, they would distress any normally constituted man; for the suffering and death of children raise the problem of evil in its most unanswerable form. It was Dickens's business as a writer to recreate in terms of his art this distressing reality. He failed. The history of Little Nell is distressing indeed, but not as Dickens presumably meant it to be distressing; it is distressing in its ineptitude and vulgar sentimentality.

A child, Ilusha, suffers and dies in Dostoievsky's *Brothers Karamazov*. Why is this history so agonizingly moving, when the tale of Little Nell leaves us not merely cold, but derisive? Comparing the two stories, we are instantly struck by the incomparably greater richness in factual detail of Dostoievsky's creation. Feeling did not prevent him from seeing and recording, or rather recreating. All that happened round Ilusha's death bed he saw, unerringly. The emotion-blinded Dickens noticed practically nothing of what went on in Little Nell's neighborhood during the child's last days. We are almost forced, indeed, to believe that he didn't want to see anything. He wanted to be unaware himself, and he wanted his readers to be unaware, of everything except Little Nell's sufferings on the one hand and her goodness and innocence on the other. But goodness and innocence and the undeservedness of suffering and even, to some extent, suffering itself are only significant in relation to the actual realities of human life. Isolated, they cease to mean anything, perhaps to exist. Even the classical writers surrounded their abstract and algebraical personages with at least the abstract and algebraical implication of the human realities, in relation to which virtues and vices are significant. Thanks to Dickens's pathologically deliberate unawareness, Nell's virtues are marooned, as it were, in the midst of a boundless waste of unreality; isolated, they fade and die. Even her sufferings and death lack significance because of this isolation. Dickens's unawareness was the death of death itself. Unawareness, according to the ethics of Buddhism, is one of the deadly sins. The stupid are wicked. (Incidentally, the cleverest men can sometimes and in certain circumstances reveal themselves as profoundly—criminally—stupid. You can be an acute logician and at the same time an emotional cretin.) Damned in the realm of conduct, the unaware are also damned esthetically. Their art is bad; instead of creating, they murder.

Art, as I have said, is also philosophy, is also science. Other things being equal, the work of art which, in its own way,

"says" more about the universe will be better than the work
of art which says less. (The "other things" which have to be
equal are the forms of beauty, in terms of which the artist
must express his philosophic and scientific truths.)   Why
is *The Rosary* a less admirable novel than *The Brothers
Karamazov?* Because the amount of experience of all kinds
understood, "felt into," as the Germans would say, and
artistically recreated by Mrs. Barclay is small in comparison
with that which Dostoievsky feelingly comprehended and
knew so consummately well how to recreate in terms of the
novelist's art. Dostoievsky covers all Mrs. Barclay's ground
and a vast area beside. The pathetic parts of *The Old
Curiosity Shop* are as poor in understood and artistically
recreated experience as *The Rosary*—indeed, I think they
are even poorer. At the same time they are vulgar (which
The Rosary, that genuine masterpiece of the servants' hall,
is not). They are vulgar, because their poverty is a pretentious poverty, because their disease (for the quality of
Dickens's sentimentality is truly pathological) professes to be
the most radiant health; because they protest their intelligence,
their lack of understanding with a vehemence of florid utterance that is not only shocking, but ludicrous.

CLIMATE AND HUMAN HISTORY

By *Julian S. Huxley*

I

O F late years a determined attempt has been made to rewrite history in economic terms. But this does not go deep enough. Man's thought and social life are built on his economic life; but this, in its turn, rests on biological foundations. Climate and geology between them decide where the raw materials of human industry are to be found, where manufactures can be established; and climate decides where the main springs of human energy shall be released. Changes of climate cause migrations, and migrations bring about not only wars, but the fertilizing intermingling of ideas necessary for rapid advance in civilization.

Disease and hygiene play as important a part; half the population of the world is permanently below par on account of animal parasites such as the hookworm and the microscopic malaria germ; and disease may bring about the rise or fall of empires. Nor has selection ever ceased its rigorous activity. To pass from one mode of life to another is not a simple affair for a people; a settled agricultural life demands a very different temperament from hunting, and the hereditary make-up of the race must be altered if a people is to pass successfully from one to the other. Most migrations, too, are selective; to take but one example, the Puritans who first colonized Massachusetts did not bring with them a random sample of the genes responsible for the qualities of the English people. But selection is altered and reduced. The better care of the young and the elaboration of social life allow all sorts of variations, which otherwise would be snuffed out, to survive and often to play an important part in progress. Knowledge for knowledge's sake is out of place in a primitive hunting tribe.

When the world's climatic belts are sharply marked (as they are today, in contrast to epochs like the late Eocene, when climate was much more uniform), the temperate zones, flanked poleward by the subarctic and the arctic, are separated from the tropics by two dry belts, along which all the world's great deserts are strung. The only zones where vegetation is abundant and man can easily flourish are the temperate and the tropical. But the temperate has another advantage. It contains the belt of cyclonic storms—in other words, of rapid and frequent changes of weather. And this type of climate, as Ellsworth Huntington has shown, is the one most stimulating to human energy and achievement.

We are still so ignorant of the earliest steps in the evolution of man from his simian ancestors that ideas as to the influence of climate on this phase of his history are highly speculative. It can scarcely be doubted, however, that the progressive desiccation of the world that took place in the late Tertiary Era helped to drive our ancestors down from the trees and out into the plains. We know that the Himalayas were elevated at this time; and it has been plausibly suggested that man originated to the north of them. For, as the land here grew drier, the forests shrank southward, where they were met by the impassable mountain barrier, and disappeared from Central Asia. Their anthropoid inhabitants were therefore forced either to disappear too or to become adapted to the new conditions, growing more terrestrial and more carnivorous. However this may be, men of a sort were undoubtedly in existence before the beginning of the Ice Age, half a million years ago. But until we shall have found new traces of Eolithic and Lower Paleolithic man in other parts of the world than Europe (which was doubtless a mere outlier of human development) we shall not be able to piece together the fascinating story of the influence of the different advances and retreats of the ice, or the slow progress of Old Stone Age man. We must content ourselves with the last chapter only.

When the ice of the Glacial Period was still in the early stages of its last retreat, the storm belt must have lain over North Africa, making what is now the Sahara green and fertile. It was through Africa and perhaps eventually from Southern Asia that Europe received its modern men, perhaps about 20,000 B.C. (Until about 4000 B.C. our dating must be regarded as provisional only; for the most part the chronology of Peake and Fleure, in their series, *The Corridors of Time*, is here followed.)

Gradually, as the ice withdrew northward, the belts of climate followed it up. The Sahara began to come within the limits of the dry belt. Today, in certain parts of the Sahara, crocodiles and certain fresh-water fish exist in scattered oases. But these oases are isolated, without possible connections with other bodies of water. The water beasts that inhabit them are living in the sparse remnants of the well-watered, and indeed probably swampy, expanse of verdure that once spread over the Great Desert. This drying of the Sahara must have sent wave after wave of migrating men out of it, both northward and southward.

II

Meanwhile the zone of greatest fertility and greatest human vigor came all along the Mediterranean, through Mesopotamia and across to Turkestan. This again set great movements afoot. The Magdalenians, last of the Old Stone Age men, pushed northward with the forests in the wake of the retreating game of the treeless plains; till eventually, hemmed in between forest and sea, they were forced to lead a wretched existence as gatherers of shellfish and berries on the Baltic coast. The descendants of the other Stone Age peoples, who had remained behind in North Africa and Spain, evolved what is called the Caspian culture; later they too trekked northward and eventually fetched up in Western Asia.

As the open plains shrank before the advance of the forests, big game grew scarce, and men turned to other sources of food. They became food gatherers as well as hunters, eating nuts and berries and wild grain. This must have seemed a misfortune to those early hunters. But it was the spur to progress, for from food gathering to food growing, to real agriculture, was a natural step. It seems to have been somewhere before 5000 B.C., in the Near East, that the art of agriculture was discovered. Legend has it that Isis, the great goddess, found corn on Mount Hermon in Syria, and gave it to her sacred son. The legend may well contain two kernels of truth. It is probable that women rather than men first hit on the idea of planting grain, for the men's work would still be afield, hunting; and it is probable that it was discovered somewhere in Syria or its near neighborhood. By 5000 B.C. grain growing had spread round from Palestine to Mesopotamia, and permanent settlements had come into being. The polish gained by stone implements used for hoeing probably gave men the idea of deliberately polishing their tools; if so, agriculture was the cause of the change to the Neolithic Culture. In any case, agriculture and polished neolithic stone implements appear at about the same time.

The arts of pottery and weaving were in all probability discovered about the same time as that of grain growing, and the first permanent houses were built. Domestic animals followed soon after; domestication seems first to have been learned by hunters, but the art spread rapidly and was extended and improved by the settled agriculturists. Metal working was not long behind, though for centuries only copper and gold were employed—copper for use and gold solely for ornament.

The Glacial Period did not die steadily away; it left the earth in a series of spasms or oscillations, a time of rapid retreat being followed by a standstill or even an advance of the ice, brought about, it would seem, by an elevation of the land. For a century or so about 4500 B.C., there was such an elevation. This seems to have had two interesting consequences.

For one thing, the increased snowfall round the Mesopotamian basin gave rise to such violent spring floods, year after year, that some towns were abandoned, and the memory of the disastrous time has been preserved, it seems, in the story of Noah's flood and the corresponding Mesopotamian legends. But more important was its effect on Egypt. In the centuries before this time, the Nile Valley seems to have been marshy and largely uninhabitable; the elevation must have drained it. And the long ribbon of marvelously fertile land thus provided for the use of man tempted in the agriculturists of neighboring countries. This, it appears, was the real beginning of the civilization of Egypt; but, once started on its career, its geographical position was such that it soon outstripped its rivals.

Thus, largely as a result of the pressure of changing climate on early man, hunting gave place to agriculture. Well before 4000 B.C. what we may call the Archaic Civilization, based on corn and a settled life,—with houses and pottery, woven fabrics and metal work, in addition,—was fully established, from Egypt round by Syria to the Tigris and Euphrates. This corner of the globe was predestined to be the cradle of the modern world—by its climate, by its great rivers, by the fact of its being the original home of wheat, by its being a natural meeting place for different streams of culture brought by different migrations of men, east and west as well as north and south.

Before 4000 B.C. there had been added to the achievements of settled man the art of writing, the framing of a calendar, irrigation, the wheel, and the making of fermented liquor. Through the whole of the next millennium this remarkable civilization was free to develop its own potentialities. It was a time of depression of land, a moist time over the steppes and the Arabian peninsula, and so a time when the nomad inhabitants of these regions could thrive and multiply in their own homes, not driven by drought to irrupt into the lands of their richer neighbors. To what height the Mesopotamian civilization reached is attested by the marvelous workmanship of the objects from Ur of the Chaldees, which date from about 3500 B.C. The organization of the State under a priest-king, even the welding of empires a million strong, stone architecture, the arch, written codes of law, seagoing ships—these were some of the achievements of this millennium.

But the available land in this corner of the world was being filled up by the natural increase of population; and this filling up coincided with a new elevation of the land and a new period of drought. Between them, the two caused such a movement in the world of man that the Archaic Culture, though made to totter in its original home, was forced to spread its influence far and wide over Europe, Africa, and Asia.

III

The new millennium dawned favorably enough. Egyptian civilization, borne along on its own momentum, reached new successes. Beautiful temples of stone, and the Pyramids, with their astounding exactitude and colossal size, date from its earliest centuries. Mathematics and astronomy take their rise; the State is run by a regular bureaucracy. A little later, in Mesopotamia, King Sargon comes on the scene, the first of the great conquerors to build an empire with armies.

For armies were another new invention. The primitive hunters had doubtless fought, but it had probably never been organized fighting; and the early food gatherers and cultivators seem to have been peaceable on the whole. There was assuredly never any Golden Age of Peace, as Perry and other enthusiasts imagine, but the early ages of human life were probably on the whole peaceful, because deliberate and organized warfare was not necessary and did not pay. War began as settled man quarreled over his property and his privileges. The idea of war soon spread to the less civilized peoples who fringed the settled lands; and it became possible for these peoples to practice war efficiently because they had passed from the state of hunters to that of nomads, disciplined herdsmen, and horsemen. The horse must have been domesticated on the steppes somewhere before 3000 B.C. A little later, drought began, and the nomads, lacking food at home, poured down on the settled lands with their horses. These were as terrible an innovation in warfare then as were the tanks in the wars of our own day some 4500 years later; and both Egypt and Mesopotamia were overrun and their civilization put in peril.

Meanwhile the pressure of population, of climatic changes, of invasions in the rear, forced the grain growers out in all directions. Not till about 3000 B.C. did any settle on the continent of Europe; but well before the close of the succeeding millennium they had spread over its greater part, to Thrace, to Germany, to Belgium, to France. And the push was felt by sea as well as by land. The whole Mediterranean became a great trade-lake, and the Ægean sailors had reached the Atlantic at latest by 2200 B.C. At the same time a great wave of migration spread eastward, and a new culture reached Northern India and right across to China, which thus seems to have received the first rude germs of her culture. It is possible that the American continent also received its first dose of civilization during this period, by a migration over the landbridge where now are the Behring Straits.

The maritime expansion continued into the next millennium, and so did the dry climate, which was especially marked in Northwestern Europe. Sea trade reached Ireland and Scandinavia. Ireland attained a very high level of culture, which was probably only made possible by this dry and bracing climate, before the excessive moisture of later centuries damped the energies of her inhabitants.

About 1800 B.C. there was again a change. The climate became gradually moister and cooler. From about 1200 B.C. to 200 A.D. there was a new cycle of wet and cold, reaching its maximum about 400 B.C. and then gradually falling off, to pass over to drought about 500 A.D. The belt of storm tracks again passed through the Mediterranean, giving opportunity for the rise of Babylonia and Assyria, Canaan and Phœnicia, of latter-day Crete and Egypt, of Mycenæ and Troy, Greece,

Carthage, and Rome. North Africa was then the granary of the world. The Mediterranean was the focus of human energy, and, since the nomads could live comfortably on their steppes while the wet time continued, could pursue its destiny little troubled by barbarian invasions.

But the change of climate was disastrous to the northern lands. On them, cold and wet descended; the peat bogs spread; the forests died off as the swampy moors extended. There was a marked falling off of culture in Ireland and Scandinavia; and the worst cold spell, in the fifth and fourth centuries B.C., has apparently left its permanent trace in the northern legend of the Twilight of the Gods, which pictures a disastrous world bound in the grip of snow and ice.

After this, the classical Mediterranean civilization began to fail. Jones, some twenty-five years ago, suggested in a remarkable book that the downfall of Greece was due to malaria imported from Africa. Now that we know that a progressive desiccation was in progress at the time, the idea gains in probability. The rivers, drying up to a series of pools in summer, would afford countless new breeding places for the larvæ of the malaria-carrying mosquitoes. Malaria probably contributed to the downfall of Rome as well; but since Italy has more rainfall than Greece, the malaria-spreading change would have struck her later. But in addition the yield of agriculture in the Mediterranean began to grow less; and about the same time the first of a new series of barbarian invasions poured in.

For the period from 500 to 1000 A.D. was definitely a dry one. This it seems to have been which in the South drove the Huns and Goths to the limits of Europe, and stimulated the expansion of Islam from drought-stricken Arabia. But it brought new life to the swampy North. The culture of Ireland revived. In Scandinavia this was the great age of the Vikings, the Norsemen. As toward its close it grew less dry, the wet began to rob the Vikings of their livelihood and their lands as surely as the drought had robbed the steppe dwellers of theirs; and they poured forth in a burst of migration which took them across the Atlantic, and eventually, in the guise of Normans, as far as Sicily.

IV

In the New World too the climatic changes were similar and had the same general effects, notably upon the story of the remarkable Maya civilization of Yucatan. The huge monuments of the Mayas are now buried in dense tropical jungle, which no primitive people could hope to keep at bay. After the first flourishing period of the Mayas, civilization retreated for centuries from Yucatan, but recolonized its northern part for a short time about 1000 A.D. The two flourishing periods of Maya history correspond with what we have called cold, wet periods. But these were wet only in regions at a certain distance from the poles. During these times, the storm tracks shifted farther toward the equator; and accordingly the dry belts between temperate and tropical were shifted equatorward too. Today, Yucatan lies just south of where the northern dry zone passes over into the tropical. When the temperate rainy zone shifted south, the margin of the dry zone also was forced southward over Yucatan, the forest melted, and the Mayas could build an empire there.

In the temperate zones, after the short wet period of the eleventh century, there followed a series of minor and drier fluctuations. There was one cold spell in the thirteenth century. There was another in the first half of the seventeenth, in which the tradition of the "old-fashioned" severe winter probably takes its origin (though doubtless perpetuated by the common failing of age to decry the present in favor of the past). Since then there has not been any great change. True, there have been shiftings of sea currents, such as that which brought the herrings to the Baltic, or that which sent the cod away from the coast of Brittany; but there have been no marked movements of the storm belt.

This long string of conclusions is drawn from the most diverse sources—from the deposits in northern peat bogs, from the old shore lines of the Caspian, from the salt lakes of Central Asia, from the now waterless cities, such as Palmyra, that once lay on great trade routes, from legend and historical record. But they find a wonderful corroboration within the trunks of the big trees of the western United States. Rain is the limiting factor of the tree's summer growth, and so the size of the growth ring in its wood preserves for us the record of the season. By measuring the growth rings of over two thousand big trees, Douglass has given us a curve of climate which corresponds with remarkable accuracy with what we have deduced from other sources. Some of these trees date back four thousand years. In their trunks we can read of the dry periods which spread civilization over the world but spelled the ruin of the first Archaic Culture; of the "classical" rainfall maximum, as Brooks calls it, which allowed Greece and Rome and Yucatan to achieve their destiny; of the new drought which brought the barbarians into the Holy City and raised the Norsemen to their first height of activity. And they record for us the final settling of the fertilizing, energy-giving belt of cyclonic weather in its present place, a thousand miles and more northward of its old position.

Thus climatic belts have not shifted seriously for almost a thousand years. What will happen to civilization when they move again we can hardly foresee; but we cannot suppose that shifting climate will respect our modern balance of power, any more than it spared the civilizations of Mesopotamia. Climate is inexorable.

V

The question of the effects of climate and other natural phenomena on human history is not all speculative. We can see some of its very practical ramifications in the problems of cattle, soil, and grasslands. Here the chemistry of soils enters in as well as climate, but the two are not without relation.

From time to time, in different parts of the world, cattle

exhibit perverted appetites. They take to chewing bones, and will sometimes even devour the carcasses of other cattle that have died. These abnormal instincts are invariably the prelude to grave disorders. In typical cases the bones grow soft, the joints become swollen, the animals get thin and feeble and move stiffly and awkwardly; their hoofs grow abnormally long; sterility and abortion are common. Milch cows and young growing beasts are invariably the most seriously affected; and imported modern breeds suffer worse than the poorer native types. Sheep may be affected in the same sort of way; and horses too, though more rarely.

These outbreaks, which may inflict severe losses, may only recur every few years; or they may continue unabated for long periods. In every case they are confined to particular regions. In such a region, even in years when there is no actual disease, the animals are generally below par. Their fertility is very low; there is much infant mortality among the calves; growth is slow and stunted; milk yield is subnormal.

Much search has been made for the causes of this state of affairs. Bacteria have been blamed, and other parasites, and poisonous plants. But all these were gradually eliminated. It became more and more evident that the cause was some deficiency in the beasts' food; and since the food they eat draws all its supplies (save carbon and oxygen from the inexhaustible air) from the soil, the deficiency must ultimately lie in the soil.

Chemical analysis has confirmed this verdict. The cause of this poor performance and actual loss, specially grave in dry countries like Africa and Australia, is a deficiency of one or more of the elements supplied to plants from the mineral salts of the soil. The commonest deficiency is that of phosphorus or of calcium—or of both at once. Since both are necessary ingredients of bone, a shortage of either will prevent proper bone growth. Both are also necessary for the universal processes of metabolism in the body; and if the supply falls short of the vital minimum needed for tissue life, the tissues draw on the reserves held in the skeleton. The mineral framework of the bones is redissolved to be used up by the living cells, hungry for the missing elements, and the skeleton grows weak and soft. The milk too grows poor in calcium and phosphorus, the calf has to go short of them, and, as he is a rapidly growing organism, feels the lack even more acutely than his parents.

The depraved appetite for carcasses and bones is a last resort for getting back some of the missing elements into the system. It is, however, often disastrous, for many animals thus eat disease-producing bacteria in the decaying bones, and develop serious illness from this cause; and even if they avoid poisoning, the mineral shortage eventually becomes so acute that the animal sickens and dies. In other cases, mere stunting is the chief result. In the Falkland Islands, for example, whose pastures are very short of calcium, an ox will hardly reach five hundred pounds in weight, and the offspring of good breeds of horses grow up no bigger than ponies.

The symptoms vary a good deal from place to place, largely according as the defect is a defect mainly of phosphorus,— perhaps the commonest condition,—or of calcium, or of both. But they all agree in taking origin in a lack of necessary bone-building elements.

Here and there, though much more rarely, the cattle farmer attempts to ply his trade on areas where there is a shortage of other mineral constituents. When the missing element is iron, as in parts of Kenya and New Zealand, the animals suffer from a progressive anæmia; they grow thinner and thinner, and finally lose control of their limbs. In certain parts of the plain region of the United States and Canada, on the other hand, iodine is the defaulter, and farm animals (like the human population) suffer from the swelling of the thyroid known as goiter, with all the attendant symptoms of low chemical activity and stunted growth. In some areas, the lack of iodine is so pronounced that the young pigs lose all their hair and hardly any of them survive.

VI

The shortages, as we have said, are primarily due to a deficiency native to the soil. It is surprising but true that there are great stretches of country which from the outset are unsuitable (without special treatment) for stock raising on any large scale, because the ground simply does not have enough of one or another chemical element. Countries composed of igneous rock often have a shortage of calcium. In much of the west of Scotland, where the soil is poor in calcium and phosphorus and the pastures have long been depleted by grazing without any return in the shape of artificial manure, the sheep are frequently afflicted with disease, there is a high rate of mortality among growing lambs, and the carrying capacity of the land is falling. Iodine is generally low in limestone districts, or where, as in parts of North America, the great meltings that followed the Ice Age have leached it out of the soil.

Phosphorus is the trickiest of all these elements. It is the one which usually is nearest to the border line, and there are very big tracts of phosphorus-poor soil. In addition, drought apparently makes it harder for plants to get phosphorus out of the ground, so that an arid climate will turn a soil that elsewhere would be adequate into a phosphorus-deficient one.

Why, then, are these regions of the earth's surface not bare of wild animals? And how is it that man can generally thrive where his cattle sicken? The answer is that the demands are a matter of degree. No region is entirely without any of the essential elements. In nature, a balance is soon struck. The country supports what it can support. If animals fall sick, they are speedily eliminated; as soon as overmultiplication of any grazing animal brings down the supply of any element per individual to the danger point, migration relieves the pressure. Man, on the other hand, attempts more intensive operations. He wants the land to carry the maximum amount of stock, and to carry it all the time. Furthermore, different animals make very different demands on the mineral resources of the soil. It is the quick-growing beast which suffers, because it has to lay by a large quantity of calcium and phosphorus in its skeleton, of iron in its blood, of iodine in its thyroid, all in a short time; while the slower-growing kinds escape—just as in man a degree of shortage of vitamins which is almost without effect on grown men and women may produce serious rickets in growing children.

Now cattle are in any case quick-growing animals. A human infant takes six months to double his weight after birth; a calf, in spite of his much greater size, takes only about a month and a half. And in domestic breeds of cattle man has intensified this quick growth, since his prime aim is the biggest possible return of meat in the shortest possible time. Besides, he breeds for milk-yielding capacities so enlarged as to be almost unnatural. Whereas, for instance, in the natural state cows at one lactation produce two or three hundred gallons of milk, we ask the best modern breeds to give us up to a thousand gallons. The native cattle of Nigeria have their first calf at about six years; a well-fed cow of a modern breed has hers at three. In beef breeds, the rate of putting on flesh has been doubled. In all these ways, domesticated cattle have been deliberately bred to make more demands upon the soil than other beasts, and the better they are as cattle, the more demands they must make. Accordingly, when good European bulls have been used to grade up native cattle in India or Africa, the result has frequently been merely that the sickness and mortality due to mineral deficiencies have leaped up.

Man the stock breeder has thus been putting new and unprecedented demands upon the mineral resources of the world's soil. But that is not all. He has also been depleting those resources without making any return. As Dr. Orr says in his recent book, *Minerals in Pastures:* "Accompanying the visible movement of milk and beef, there is a slow invisible flow of fertility. Every cargo of beef or milk products, every ship ton of bones, leaves the exporting country so much the poorer."

For, in nature, animals die where they live, and the constituents of their bodies are returned to their native soil. But man changes all that. He ships off the bodies of his animals or the products of those bodies to distant countries, and in every exported pound of meat or cheese or bone meal so much phosphorus and so much calcium and iron and magnesium have been extracted from the soil and removed from the country's shores. Richardson calculates that since 1870 the export of animals from Victoria alone has taken out of its soil the equivalent of two million tons of superphosphates.

As we are now beginning to see, man's difficulties about grassland and the products of grassland are not merely due to local and natural deficiencies. They are due too to deficiencies of his own making, and these artificial deficiencies are cumulative and world-wide. In old days, the cattle of mineral-deficient areas would make periodic journeys to salt licks, where the instinctive cravings for the elements they lacked would save them from disease and death. It is interesting to find the same instinctive cravings in man. In some parts of Africa, where mineral deficiency is serious, the black children spend their pennies, not on sweets, but on lumps of unpurified salt, imported from distant salt pans and full of all the elements for which their systems are crying out. Today, fencing has often made the cattle's annual "cure" impossible. In one part of Kenya, for instance, the settling of the country happened to put an important salt lick on to land allocated to whites, to the great detriment of the native cattle, which either could not get at their necessary supply of minerals, or strayed and trespassed in search of it, and were lost to their owners. Economic restrictions may have the same effect. In the old days of the heavy French tax on salt, you could tell without a map when you crossed the boundary in the Jura from France to Switzerland by looking at the cattle. The French cows looked poorly, the Swiss beasts fine and healthy.

The next step was the discovery that the amount of mineral which would prevent disease in a pasture was not enough to give the best results. By adding more, up to a definitely ascertainable point, sheep and cattle could be made to grow faster, to yield more milk, and especially to be more fertile.

Thus what began as a study of local cattle diseases has turned into a problem of the soil chemistry of grasslands. The problem is one of first-rate importance. Cereals may be the staff of life; but the products of grass are more varied. Grass gives us not only meat, but also wool, leather, milk, butter, cheese, and various valuable by-products from bones and hides and horns. The value of the products of grass consumed annually in Britain alone is over £400,000,000, and the quantity of this which is imported makes nearly a quarter of the country's total imports. And some countries, like New Zealand, live almost wholly by grass.

VII

The question at issue becomes the question of the future of the world's grass. We have spent an enormous amount of energy on improving wheat and maize, and have hardly given a thought to grass; but there is little doubt that by proper attention to the ecology and genetics of grasses we could double the output of the world's pastures.

For one thing, proper dosing with mineral salts helps the growth of plants which make greater demands on the soil, and so takes the ecological succession a stage further to a richer herbage. In dry areas it often helps also by conserving more moisture in the soil. Then there are strange and subtle interrelations between grass and the beasts that eat it. Their trampling and their browsing alter conditions for the herbage. Too little grazing may allow scrub or moor to invade the pasture; too much may impoverish the sward. Such problems are especially prominent in new countries—in New Zealand, for instance, there seem to have been no indigenous grazing creatures, save possibly the giant flightless bird, the moa; yet today 94 per cent of the country's exports are the products of grass-eating animals. Here, to clear scrubland for sheep, not only must the scrub be cut and rooted up and burned, but cattle must be introduced to keep the bracken and brush from winning back the land they have lost. As Dr. Stapledon says, "Cattle, no matter how prices rule, are essential to the reclamation and maintenance of scrublands. They are implements as necessary to the wool grower on hilly, scrubby country as the plough to the producer of wheat on the plains." Trampling, too, prevents the grass from getting coarse and rough. The amount of grazing a pasture will stand depends a good deal on climate. If grassland (as in so much of Europe and New Zealand) is not the natural climax of plant life, but is only a "sub-climax," which would go on to a richer type of vegetation, such as forest, if left to itself, then it will stand very heavy grazing. If, however, the climate is so dry that grass of sorts is the natural climax, it has fewer reserves, so to speak, and heavy grazing may seriously damage it.

But the amount of grazing will also depend on the kinds of grasses there are to be grazed. In New Zealand the native vegetation, unused to being nibbled down to the ground, succumbs to this new treatment. A judicious mixture of the right grasses and clovers from all over the world (only we must remember that what is right for one place may be very wrong for another!) is rapidly raising the productive power of grass. This will soon get to a limit; but then the geneticist can step in and continue the process by deliberately breeding richer and more resistant pasture plants. A beginning has been made with this at places like the Grass Research Station at Aberystwyth, and the results already obtained, together with the comfortable knowledge of what has been actually achieved with wheat, warrant great hopes for the future.

We could easily double the productive power of the world's grasslands by deliberately working for types of beast that make greater demands on the grass, and types of grass that make greater demands on the soil. We have only got to make sure that we can continue to provide the soil with the necessary chemical ingredients. But to achieve this result we need the services, not only of the farmer and the scientific agriculturist, but of the plant and animal geneticist, the soil chemist, the systematic botanist, and the ecologist; nature cannot be improved upon without the amassing of a deal of knowledge and the expenditure of a deal of pains.

THOSE EMINENT VICTORIANS

By *Howard Mumford Jones*

They didn't invent "Victorianism" but rebelled against it. Under conditions similar to those now facing us, they give us lessons in tolerance and wit.

OUR present economic chaos has been given its full measure of discussion, but I have been moved to wonder, in following such of it as I could, why we write and talk about unemployment and the problems of the machine age as if these particular questions were entirely novel and strange, and why, in view of the ineffectual way we handle them, we continue to patronize the nineteenth century, the central problems of which were similar. Indeed, I go even farther. I think it high time to re-examine that whole maligned period, not only for what it may teach us in new adjustments, but for what it offers in tolerance and wit as well.

I

We are all too familiar with the attacks on the Victorians. They conjure up the hair-cloth sofa, the Sunday-school tract, the antimacassar, the what-not, the bustle, and the unhygienic skirt. Victorianism is the elder generation. Victorianism is the pretense that if you do not name a thing, it isn't there. Those who dislike to discuss sex merely in terms of biology are apt to be classified with the lady who noted sadly the difference between the home life of Cleopatra and that of our dear Queen. Those who admire Gladstone (if anybody does) are Victorians, albeit those who admire Disraeli (and the Victorians admired him enough to make him premier) are not. To talk of duty, honor, the obligations of being a gentleman, the responsibilities of matrimony, or the sacredness of religious belief is to be Victorian. The Victorians were so bent on being moral that they ignored the unpleasant aspects of life. They had no use for art which was not ethical; they displayed, it is alleged, an embarrassing familiarity with the purposes of the Almighty. Did not one of them proclaim that God's in his heaven and all's right with the world, though the world was palpably maladjusted; did not another sing aloud that he was going to be Queen of the May? Victorian stuffiness, Victorian decorum, Victorian prudery, Victorian solemnity!

Well, in one sense they had a right to be solemn. The first half of the century, like our own, was a period of recurrent crises, but whereas we confine our discussions to "serious weeklies" and long-faced conferences and ineffectual newspaper editorials, the Victorians were of the opinion that the national conscience was concerned, and sought in their writings to arouse thinking on the subject. Our own fiction is monotonously compounded of sex and psychology; we pooh-pooh the purpose novel; and (except for Upton Sinclair) almost no contemporary author of importance is concerned in fiction to arouse public interest in public questions. The Victorians thought otherwise. From the day when Bulwer Lytton in his first novel converted Pelham to utilitarian thought, to the day when George Gissing laid down his pen, a consciousness of the importance of man to society and of society to man is a constant theme in nineteenth-century fiction. Mrs. Gaskell and Charles Kingsley cry out against social injustice. Thackeray studies the adjustment of the parvenus and the upper classes. Disraeli outlines a political philosophy in the Young England novels, a genre in which Trollope followed him. George Eliot bases her books on a social philosophy, and to George Meredith a reading of life is a reading of earth. Similarly the poets— Tennyson, Mrs. Browning, Swinburne, Meredith—are aware of political issues and turn them into beautiful and enduring verse.

Now I am far from thinking that literature is any better for being sociological, but most of us will agree that literature tends to be better when it is written with a "large discourse," and I confess that the relative thinness of American fiction since our own Victorian age ended seems to me to arise from the fact that it is based on a very narrow reading of life—the reading which sees the be-all and the end-all of the novelist's business as sex and psychology. And I wonder, in view of the relative brittleness of most contemporary fiction, whether we are quite entitled to patronize the Victorian novelist? Have we mastered the art of the novel so completely that we can afford to dismiss as naïve a Dickens who, more than any other single figure, in the opinion of his contemporaries, made readers aware of social chaos in England? Our solitary exhibit in the way of broad canvases and social satire is Sinclair Lewis (perhaps some would add Dreiser), a humorist of great power, but is it not odd that whereas we produce only one of this kind, the Victorians produced a score?

I have said that the problems of that period and our own were similar. On the one hand, there was, for example, the inherited system of the universe. There was God, whose wondrous hand the nightly stars hymned as of old. There was an intricate and reasonably formed universe which He had invented, and everywhere traces of His handiwork could be found. There was the Anglican Church as by law established. There was man, who certainly had a body, and who was presumed, as even Shelley admitted, to have a spirit and probably a soul. There were the Queen, God bless her, and England's wooden walls, and the Duke of Wellington. In fact, there was a noble world inhabited by noble beings. And then there came crashing down on the Victorians a bewildering variety of changes, discoveries, and revolutions.

Startling theories of geology ruined the comfortable chronology of the King James Bible and reduced the life of man to an inconsiderable second in infinite time. Astronomical investigations extended the regions of heaven until earth was lost in infinite space. More and more it appeared that man was a great deal lower than the angels, and about the middle of the century he appeared to be a good deal closer to the animals. A succession of brilliant investigations in science smashed the good old comfortable mathematical universe of the eighteenth century into bits. In the heavens there was only anarchy, and on earth nature was red in tooth and claw. The Anglican faith was split by a schism which sent some of its most brilliant minds into the Roman Catholic fold, and Arnold later pleaded in vain with the Puritans to return to the Established Church. Could it be that the old system was wrong? The system that seemed as certain as the Duke of Wellington and as invincible as the Life Guards at Waterloo? Amidst the wreck of matter and the crash of worlds the Victorians clung to one essential belief—they were not under any circumstances going to admit that human life was any less interesting or important or dignified or noble, even though the heavens fell and hell blew up—in fact, one of them, Frederick Denison Maurice, helped in the explosion. They did their best to reconcile the smashing impact of the new science, which threatened to reduce everything to anarchic materialism, with their inherited belief in the dignity of human life. If we are today anything more than certain worms writhing in midnight, we owe our sanity to the Victorians. They conserved the human tradition, and without the human tradition, we should be stark, raving mad.

While the physical universe was crashing around them, the political and social world, too, seemed to be going to pieces, as Carlyle and others gloomily observed. The fixed and immutable laws of political economy, traced logically to their tragic conclusion by Ricardo, McCulloch, and the Manchester School, seemed to indicate that modern life would have to be one of increasing misery. They saw poverty in the streets and heard revolutions across the water. From 1820 to 1870 the Victorians struggled with depressions at home and counted a succession of crashes abroad; yet the streets of London, unlike the streets of Paris, Berlin, Vienna, or Richmond, never ran red with blood or echoed to the tread of a conquering army.

The Victorians went into the nineteenth century with an England that was in many ways the little old England of Walpole's time, and they emerged with an empire that, with all its defects, was the most remarkable the world had seen since Rome. Theirs is one of the most extraordinary examples of national continuity and astonishing readjustments in the history of mankind.

How did they manage it? I suspect we have overstressed Victorian prejudice; for they managed it by a tolerance for unexpected developments which far surpasses ours. They were capable of absorbing strange food. They made a Jewish novelist prime minister of England, despite his curls and his waistcoats; and I need not comment on the chances of either a Jew or a novelist, much less both, being elected President of this enlightened republic. They elected an atheist to parliament, and when parliament threw him out, they continued to elect him until not atheism, but parliament, gave way; and I hardly need mention the possibility of electing a Charles Bradlaugh to the Senate of the United States. They suffered a group of aliens to tie up the business of the House of Commons night after night under the leadership of O'Connell and his followers; and I cannot imagine delegates from the Philippine Islands and Porto Rico enjoying the same liberty in the House of Representatives. Huxley told a bishop to his face in a public meeting that in his opinion the bishop was a fool and hinted that he was a liar; yet Huxley served on more public commissions (or so his biographer states) than any other British scientist. Would an American professor in a State university be similarly honored? I think we have talked too much about Victorian moral conformity.

II

You cannot, said Burke, indict a whole people; and it is difficult to indict a whole century. That the Victorians (to confine ourselves to them) had their characteristic weaknesses is evident; but one grows weary by and by of so monotonous and one-sided an argument and longs for a little more attention to a few obvious facts.

For example, one is confronted by the charge of moral prudery. It is evident one can retort that the Victorians were often refreshingly immoral, and if this form of argument is hilariously absurd, it will at least awake the jaded attention of modern critics. Against the charge that the Victorians insisted upon the standards of middle-class respectability for all forms of conduct, let us set some bits of biography. The period opens in 1837, with the arrest of Thomas Griffiths Wainewright, artist and designer (the friend of Charles Lamb), who poisoned various harmless persons, partly for cash and partly for pleasure, and closes with Oscar Wilde, who wrote charmingly of Wainewright, and whose particular form of vice even our advanced generation has not brought itself to condone. The philosophical thought of the age was largely shaped by John Stuart Mill, who ran off with another man's wife, and its most characteristic novelist is George Eliot, who lived for over twenty years quite openly with a man she was not married to, for the sufficient reason that he was another woman's husband. The most amusing essay of Thomas De Quincey, who did not die until 1859, is a whimsical defense of murder considered as one of the fine arts, and his best-known work is an æsthetic description of the dreams of an opium-eater. Rossetti took chloral; James Thompson drank himself to death; and from Ford Madox Hueffer's absorbing *Memories and Impressions* I cull the following pleasing anecdote concerning a visit paid by William Sharp to the house of Philip Marston, the blind poet:

"He found the poor blind man in the clutches of the poet I have just omitted to name, crushed beneath him and, I think, severely bitten. The poet had had an attack of delirium tremens and imagined himself a Bengal tiger. Leaving Marston, he sprang on all fours toward Sharp, but he burst a blood-vessel and collapsed on the floor. Sharp lifted him onto the sofa, took Marston into another room, and then rushed hatless through the streets to the hospital that was around the corner. The surgeon in charge, himself drunk, seeing Sharp covered with blood, insisted on giving him in charge for murder; Sharp, always a delicate man, fainted. The poet was dead of hemorrhage before assistance reached him."

And in the same book I am reminded that Madox Brown, "whose laudable desire it was at many stages of his career to redeem poets and others from dipsomania, was in the habit of providing several of them with labels upon which were inscribed his own name and address." The poets, when too drunk to get about, were then brought by cabmen or others to Fitzroy Square, where the maid and the cabman promptly put them into a bath and made them drink strong coffee, the bath being selected because the poet would "not be able to roll out and injure himself." But let us continue.

Charles Dickens, in the minds of many the chief purveyor of Victorian sentimentality, separated from his wife and quarrelled incessantly with his publishers. George Meredith left his first wife, the daughter of Thomas Love Peacock, and celebrated in *Modern Love*, published in 1862, not a triangle situation, but a quadrilateral one. M. Lafourcade, the French student of Swinburne, points out that Richard Monckton Milnes owned a library of erotica, introduced the poet to the works of the Marquis de Sade, and encouraged him to write poems celebrating various sexual perversities, that are unpublished and unpublishable. Among Swinburne's friends was Sir Richard Burton, whose chief masterpiece cannot for obvious reasons go through the mails. Swinburne himself got drunk ("and how drunk he used to get!" writes Julian Field, an Oxford student who knew him); indulged in the most outrageous language; and was frequently referred to by the erudite Furnivall, the Shakespeare editor, as "Pigsbrook." As for the literary groups with which the Victorian period closes, their "morality," as any reader of Holbrook Jackson's *The Eighteen Nineties* knows, was a little to seek—Francis Thompson took opium, John Davidson killed himself, Aubrey

Beardsley is remembered for decadent drawings, and Ernest Dowson's brief career was scarcely memorable for ethical balance.

Now of course these tergiversations do not prove anything except as they raise doubts about careless judgments on the Victorians. As it is sometimes argued, however, that facts like these are exceptional and that the true tone of Victorianism is to be sought in the work of Tennyson, Browning, Thackeray, and Dickens, let us look at some of it. There is no doubt that Dickens invented Little Nell and Paul Dombey; that George Eliot wrote a Sunday-school story in *The Mill on the Floss;* that Tennyson was often sentimental; and that Browning was an irritating optimist. But is this all the story? Is there anywhere a more vigorous denunciation of cant and hypocrisy than in the novels of Dickens, the creator of Mr. Pecksniff and Mr. Chadband and Mr. Podsnap? Thackeray certainly complained that he could not write with the openness of Fielding, but if the author of Becky Sharp and Major Pendennis was really hampered in depicting them, the fact is not patent; if there is a more appalling picture in brief compass of human greed and depravity than in the story (too little read) of the Honorable Mr. Deuceace as set forth by Mr. Yellowplush, his footman; if there is anywhere a more succinct statement of the lack of connection between worldly success and the official principles of that success than *Pendennis,* I do not know where it is. George Eliot undoubtedly wrote *Silas Marner;* but exactly what moral lesson is to be drawn from the loss of Mr. Tulliver's fortune, and what is the precise application of the seventh commandment to the life of Dorothea Brooke? Has anybody surpassed the sharpness with which Trollope pictured worldly clergymen in the Barchester series, or worldly aristocrats and parvenus in the parliamentary novels? Is any reader of Disraeli still of the opinion that cynicism was unknown in the nineteenth century? Did or did not the Victorians produce those great eccentrics, George Borrow and Edward Fitzgerald, the author of *Hajji*

Babba, and the author of *The Way of All Flesh?* The Victorian novel begins, if you please, with Peacock the satirist and closes with Meredith volleying arrows of silvery laughter; it includes the great apology for the natural man to be found in *Lavengro* and *The Romany Rye;* and it numbers among its principal exhibits (a fact frequently forgotten) the serried titles of one Thomas Hardy, who was emphatically of the opinion that God is not in his heaven and that all is not right with the world.

As for poetry, let us look at Tennyson, that arch example of all the Victorian qualities. Arthur, it must be admitted, is not much of a man, but what about Ulysses? "Enoch Arden" is rather bad, but what about the poem which reads:

Raving politics, never at rest—as this poor earth's pale history runs,—
What is it all but a trouble of ants in the gleam of a million million suns?

I cheerfully surrender Galahad to anybody who wants him, but this same Tennyson wrote "The Revenge"; and if the true test of poetical worth is pessimism (for so our modern argument seems to run) I submit in evidence this product of Tennyson's last years:

Act first, this Earth, a stage so gloom'd with woe
You all but sicken at the shifting scenes.
And yet be patient. Our Playwright may show
In some fifth Act what this wild Drama means.

And then there is Browning. On the literary exchange Browning stock has at present sunk to its lowest level since the organization of Browning clubs, and there are almost no takers. I do not count myself among the Browning enthusiasts, but even the author of "Pippa Passes" is entitled to fair play; and I would merely observe that the famous phrase about the exact whereabouts of God with respect to the rightness of earth is not spoken by Browning *in propria persona,* but by Pippa herself as part of the dramatic action of the story, which has for its end to show the unconscious effect that the words of one human being may have in the lives of others—a theme not unknown to our stream-of-consciousness novelists. And this same Browning, so cheery, so irritatingly glad, had a fine eye for a scoundrel, as witness "Mr. Sludge the Medium" and "Prince Hohenstiel-Schwangau" and "The Bishop Orders His Tomb at St. Praxed's Church"; argued on occasion that it was better to be vitally immoral than passively moral; stole an invalid woman from her father; and (unless I am much mistaken) set a fashion for writing dramatic monologues which the admirable E. A. Robinson and other modern poets are still following without surpassing.

III

The truth is that, instead of inventing "Victorianism," the Victorians engaged in incessant warfare against the cant and hypocrisy they inherited from the maudlin sentimentality of the eighteenth century. At the opening of that epoch Shaftesbury taught that there was inherent in the human heart a something which his disciple, Hutcheson, was to label the "moral Sense." In the innumerable volumes of Daniel Defoe England read that nothing succeeds like success; that when you have money you ought to invest it prudently; that a bad woman can be made good by putting her funds out at six per cent; and that a wicked pirate becomes respectable when he retires to trade and to overreaching his fellow man in a bargain. The fashionable pens of Steele and Addison were presently at work refining female manners in the direction of modesty, good sense, and prudery; admonishing noblemen not to duel, drink, or gamble, but to follow the example of Sir Roger de Coverley and look after their tenants benevolently and morally. Soon on the stage you learned that female delicacy is always to be protected—read the *Conscious Lovers* for an example; and if you attended the *London Merchant*, which moved the acid Mr. Pope to tears, you learned a good sound moral lesson as to the fate of the idle boys—for the apprentice takes up with a prostitute, embezzles money, shoots his good old uncle, is caught, repents, and is

hanged, to the accompaniment of such a salvo of moral platitudes as no Victorian novelist ever dreamed of.

And the doctrine was continually preached throughout the
eighteenth century. What are the novels of Richardson but
involved Sunday-school lessons in a low and prudential order of morality? What is Fielding's *Amelia* but an object
lesson in the domestic virtues? What are the poems of Edward
Young except lessons in religiosity? What is *The Vicar of
Wakefield* (in this connection at least) but a lesson in impossible goodness, and what is Samuel Johnson, among other
things, but a dispenser of ethical commonplaces? No, it is
not in the Victorian age that heroines begin to faint on the
slightest provocation; it is in the novels and plays that preceded the nineteenth century. Nineteenth-century writers,
with all their faults, never preached so ostentatious a morality
as did Richardson, nor taught, like Defoe, that money is the
test of virtue. No religious poetry of the Victorian era is as
lugubrious as Young's "Night Thoughts" or Hervey's prose
"Meditations among the Tombs." The moral story for the
young was really founded by the heavily virtuous female
writers of the eighteenth century, and the moral tale flowed
from the pens of Samuel Johnson, Mrs. Barbauld, Hannah
More, and John Gay long before Little Nell died and Colonel
Newcomb was called away and Tito ruined Romola's life.

Of course this is not the whole truth about the eighteenth
century, but it is a truth critics of Victorianism ignore when
they declare that the Victorians, forgetting the glorious freedom of Byron and Shelley, invented a pall of morality and
snuffily turned from art to the sermon. Their leaders did
nothing of the kind. They took what had been given them
and made the best of it. They were a race of rebels. They
had little use for the ethical codes which had cramped average
human conduct for a hundred years and which, reinforced by
the eighteenth-century reasoning of the utilitarians and the
laissez-faire economists, threatened to cramp human conduct
still. Indeed, we read them ill if we continue to forget that

they were struggling with the great burden of "morality" which they inherited from the century before them.

IV

There still remain, however, the undeniable Victorian Sunday, the black clothing, and the sober faces in the faded daguerreotypes; the solemn discourses of John Ruskin and Matthew Arnold; Herbert Spencer and Bishop Wilberforce, Mrs. Hemans and Mrs. Humphry Ward. But even granting them, there is yet another aspect of the Victorians which we all too often neglect. We fail to remember that this gloomy age is likewise the age of British humor and that the nineteenth century has actually given more first-rate humorists to English literature than any other century in the long roll of English letters.

The wit of the century which invented *Punch* is perhaps its most enviable possession. The Victorians did not take themselves half so seriously as we take them now. Anecdote after anecdote exists to prove that the period was a time of exuberance and gaiety. William Morris, for example, stepped to the head of the stairs in that amazing household which contained the pre-Raphaelites (when they were not joyously quarrelling) and called down to the cook: "Mary, those six eggs you served me for breakfast were bad. I ate them, but don't let it happen again." There is Edmund Yates's biting comment on Thackeray's first lecture, when, asked his opinion of the performance, he meditated solemnly and remarked with becoming laconicism: "Very good. Wants a piano." Swinburne on one celebrated occasion met Tennyson at the house of a friend and said, "We understand, of course, that Arthur is Prince Albert and Guinevere is Queen Victoria, but, Tennyson, who is Launcelot?" There is W. S. Gilbert's famous comment on Beerbohm Tree in *Hamlet:* "Funny, without being vulgar." There is, in short, an endless stream of anecdote and persiflage which makes Victorian letters and memoirs an infinite delight.

In fact, when drollery is almost a major theme in the Victorian period, it is wonderful to see how critics forget to account for it. The age begins with Sydney Smith, who once dryly remarked: "Benevolence is a natural instinct of the human mind; when A sees B in grievous distress, his conscience always urges him to entreat C to help him"—and from that witty punster goes its scintillating way to Oscar Wilde, the epigrammatist. Was there ever such a feast of humor as Victorian fiction alone presents—the brilliant pages of Disraeli, the inimitable Dickens; Thackeray, over whose "Victorian" novels there plays a constant stream of satire and fun; George Eliot with her great comic peasant creations; George Borrow with his joy in life and humor; Trollope and the vagaries of cathedral life; the wit and wisdom of George Meredith? And as if this were not enough, there are the great eccentric novelists from Peacock, the irresistible, to Mallock's *The New Republic* and John Davidson's half-mad concoctions. There is Browning, a master of grotesque satire; Tom Hood—and when next it is argued that the Victorians could not call a woman's "limb" by its right name, let the cynic read *Miss Kilmansegg and Her Precious Leg;* there is the long succession of verse humorists from Father Prout to Charles Stuart Calverley. How in the name of common sense can a period be writ down as unmitigatedly solemn which produced Edward Lear and the *Ingoldsby Legends*, Lewis Carroll, and W. S. Gilbert? Has any one arisen in this earnest age to create another Pooh-Bah or a new *Pirates of Penzance?* Had anybody until *Of Thee I Sing* was written laughed at the Senate as Gilbert laughed at the House of Lords, and do we dare treat our bishops as airily as that great man depicted the Bishop of Rum-Ti-Foo? It would appear from all this that the Victorians were not all such grave deacons as the world imagines. In fact, I believe that the absurd seriousness with which we read novels based on the fairy-tales of Freud, and ponderous works of fiction based upon the insubstantial fabric of disordered syntax and stream-of-consciousness anarchy must awaken mirth among the Victorians. And I think we might profit from the Gargantuan gales of laughter which come to us across the what-nots and set the patent rocking-chairs a-rocking, and which, blowing more softly, sigh through the woods where Alice and the White Knight walk forever to the delectation of mankind.

ON HUMOUR AND SATIRE

By *Ronald Knox*

WHOEVER shall turn up in a modern encyclopædia the article on humming-birds—whether from a disinterested curiosity about these brightly-coloured creatures, or from the more commonplace motive of identifying a clue in a crossword—will find a curious surprise awaiting him at the end of it. He will find that the succeeding paragraph deals with the geological formation known as a *humus;* or if his encyclopædia be somewhat more exhaustive, with the quaintly-named genius of Humperdinck. What will excite his speculation is, of course, the fact that no attempt is made by his author to deal with humour. Humour, for the encyclopædist, is non-existent; and that means that no book has ever been written on the subject of humour; else the ingenious Caledonian who retails culture to us at the rate of five guineas a column would inevitably have boiled it down for us ere this. The great history of Humour in three volumes, dedicated by permission to the Bishop of Much Wenlock, still remains to be written. And that fact, in its turn, is doubly significant. It means, in the first place, that humour, in our sense of the word is a relatively modern phenomenon; the idea of submitting it to exhaustive analysis did not, for example, present itself to the patient genius of John Stuart Mill. And at the same time it is an uncommonly awkward and elusive subject to tackle, or why have we no up-to-date guide to it from the hand of Mr. Arnold Bennett?

Assuredly this neglect is not due to any want of intrinsic importance. For humour, frown upon it as you will, is nothing less than a fresh window of the soul. Through that window we see, not indeed a different world, but the familiar world of our experience distorted as if by the magic of some tricksy sprite. It is a plate-glass window, which turns all our earnest, toiling fellow-mortals into figures of fun. If a man awoke to it of a sudden, it would be an enlightenment of his vision no less real than if a man who had hitherto seen life only in black and grey should be suddenly gifted with the experience of colour. More, even, than this; the sense of humour is a man's inseparable playmate, allowing him, for better or worse, no solitude anywhere. In crowded railway-carriages, in the lonely watches of a sleepless night, even in the dentist's chair, the sense of humour is at your side, full of elfin suggestions. Do you go to Church? He will patter up the aisle along-side of you, never more at home, never more alert, than when the spacious silences of worship and the solemn purple of prelates enjoins reverence. I could become lyrical, if I had time, over the sense of humour, what it does for men and how it undoes them, what comfort lies in its companionship, and what menace. Enough to say that if I had the writing of an encyclopædia the humming-birds should be made to look foolish.

Humour has been treated, perhaps, twice in literature; once in the preface to Meredith's *Egoist*, and once in Mr. Chesterton's book, *The Napoleon of Notting Hill*. What it is still remains a mystery. Easy enough to distinguish it from its neighbours in the scale of values: with wit, for example, it has nothing to do. For wit is first and last a matter of expression. Latin, of all languages, is the best vehicle of wit, the worst of humour. You cannot think a witty thought, even, without thinking in words. But humour can be wordless; there are thoughts that lie too deep for laughter itself. In this essay I mean to treat humour as it compares with and contrasts with satire, a more delicate distinction. But first let us make an attempt, Aristotle-wise, to pin down the thing itself with some random stab of definition. Let us say that the sphere of humour is, predominantly, Man and his activities, considered in circumstances so incongruous, so unexpectedly incongruous, as to detract from their human dignity. This, the prime source of humour is a madman or a drunkard; either of these wears the semblance of a man without enjoying the full use of that rational faculty which is man's definition. A foreigner, too, is always funny: he dresses, but does not dress right; makes sounds, but not the right sounds. A man falling down on a frosty day is funny, because he has unexpectedly abandoned that upright walk which is man's glory as a biped. All these things are funny, of course, only from a certain angle; not, for example, from the angle of ninety degrees, which is described by the man who falls down. But amusement is habitually derived from such situations; and in each case it is a human victim that is demanded for the sacrifice. It is possible, in the mythological manner, to substitute an animal victim, but only if the animal be falsely invested with the attributes of humanity. There is nothing at all funny about a horse falling down. A monkey making faces, a cat at play, amuse us only because we feign to ourselves that the brute is rational; to that fiction we are accustomed from childhood. Only Man has dignity; only man, therefore, can be funny. Whether there could have been humour even in human fortunes but for the Fall of Adam is a problem which might profitably have been discussed by St. Thomas in his *Summa Theologiæ*, but was omitted for lack of space.

The question is raised (as the same author would say) whether humour is in its origins indecent. And at first sight it would appear yes. For the philosopher says that the ludicrous is a division of the disgraceful. And the gods in Homer laugh at the predicament of Ares and Aphrodite in the recital of the bard Demodocus. But on second thought it is to be reflected that the song of Demodocus is, by common consent of the critics, a late interpolation in Homer; and the first mention of laughter in the classics is rather the occasion on which the gods laughed to see the lame Hephæstus panting as he limped up and down the hall. Once more, a lame man is funny because he enjoys, like the rest of us, powers of locomotion, but employs them wrong. His gait is incongruous—not unexpectedly so, indeed, for the gods had witnessed this farce daily for centuries; but the gods were children, and the simplest farces always have the best run. No doubt the psychoanalysts will want us to believe that all humour has its origin in indecency, and, for aught I know, that whenever we laugh we are unconsciously thinking of something obscene. But, in fact, the obscene, as its name implies, is an illegitimate effect of humour. There is nothing incongruous in the *existence* of sex and the other animal functions; the incongruity lies merely in the fact of mentioning them. It is not human dignity that is infringed in such cases, but a human convention of secrecy. The Stock Exchange joke, like most operations on the Stock Exchange, is essentially artificial; it does not touch the real values of things at all. In all the generalizations which follow it must be understood that the humour of indecency is being left out of account.

Yet there is truth in the philosopher's assertion that the ludicrous is a division of the disgraceful, in this sense, that in the long run every joke makes a fool of somebody; it must have, as I say, a human victim. This fact is obscured by the frequency with which jokes, especially modern jokes, are directed against their own authors. The man who makes faces to amuse a child is, objectively, making a fool of himself; and the whole *genre* of literary humour of which *Happy Thoughts*, the *Diary of a Nobody*, and the Eliza books are the best-known examples, depends entirely on the fact that the author is making a fool of himself. In all humour there is loss of dignity somewhere, virtue has gone out of somebody. For there is no inherent humour in things; wherever there is a joke it is Man, the half-angel, the half-beast, who is somehow at the bottom of it. I am insisting upon this point because, on a careless analysis, one might be disposed to imagine that the essence of satire is to be a joke against somebody. That definition, clearly, will be inadequate, if our present analysis of humour in general be accepted.

I have said that humour is, for the most part, a modern
phenomenon. It would involve a very long argument, and
some very far-reaching considerations, if we attempted to
prove this thesis of humour as a fact in life. Let us be more
modest, and be content for the present to say that the humorous in literature is for the most part a modern phenomenon.
Let us go back to our starting-point, and imagine one pursuing
his researches about humming-birds into the *Encyclopædia
Britannica* of 1797. He skims through a long article on
Mr. David Hume, faced by an attractive but wholly unreliable
portrait of the hippopotamus. Under "Humming-bird" he
will only read the words "See Trochilus." But immediately
following, he will find the greater part of a column under the
title "Humour." Most of it deals with the jargon of a psychology now obsolete, and perhaps fanciful, though not more
fanciful, I think, than the psychological jargon of our own
day. But at the end he will find some valuable words on
humour as it is contrasted with wit. "Wit expresses something that is more designed, concerted, regular, and artificial;
humour, something that is more wild, loose, extravagant, and
fantastical; something which comes upon a man by fits, which
he can neither command nor restrain, and which is not perfectly consistent with true politeness. Humour, it has been
said, is often more diverting than wit; yet a man of wit is as
much above a man of humour, as a gentleman is above a
buffoon; a buffoon, however, will often divert more than a
gentleman. The Duke of Buckingham, however, makes humour to be all in all," and so on. "Not perfectly consistent
with true politeness"—oh, admirable faith of the eighteenth
century, even in its decline! "The Duke of Buckingham, however"—a significant exception. It seems possible that the
reign of the Merry Monarch saw a false dawn of the sense of
humour. If so, it was smothered for a full century afterwards
by an overpowering incubus of whiggery. The French Revolution had come and gone, and yet humour was for the age of
Burke "not perfectly consistent with true politeness."

One is tempted, as I say, to maintain that the passing of the eighteenth century is an era in human history altogether, since with the nineteenth century humour, as an attitude towards life, begins. The tone of Disraeli about politics, the tone of Richard Hurrell Frouds about all the external part of religion, seems to me quite inconceivable in any earlier age. But let us confine ourselves to literature, and say that humour as a force *in literature* is struggling towards its birth in Jane Austen, and hardly achieves its full stature till Calverley. I know that there are obvious exceptions. There is humour in Aristophanes and in Petronius; there is humour in Shakespeare, though not as much of it as one would expect; humour in Sterne, too, and in Sheridan. But if you set out to mention the great names of antiquity which are naturally connected with humorous writing, you will find that they are all the names of satirists. Aristophanes in part, Lucian, Juvenal, Martial, Blessed Thomas More, Cervantes, Rabelais, Butler, Molière, La Fontaine, Swift—humour and satire are, before the nineteenth century, almost interchangeable terms. Humour in art had begun in the eighteenth century, but it had begun with Hogarth! Put a volume by Barrie or Milne into the hands of Edmund Burke—could he have begun to understand it?

You can corroborate the fact of this growth in humour by a complementary fact about our modern age, the decline of *naïveté*. If you come to think of it, the best laughs you will get out of the old classics are laughs which the author never meant to put there. Of all the ancients, none can be so amusing as Herodotus, but none, surely, had less sense of humour. It is a rare grace, like all the *gratiæ gratis datæ*, this humour of the *naïf*. Yet it reaches its climax on the very threshold of the nineteenth century; next to Herodotus, surely, comes James Boswell. Since the dawn of nineteenth century humour, you will find unconscious humour only in bad writers, Ella Wheeler Wilcox, and the rest. Humour kills the *naïf*, nor could any great writer of today recapture, if he would, Boswell's splendid unselfconsciousness.

Under correction, then, I am maintaining that literature before the nineteenth century has no conscious humour apart from satire. I must now pass on to an impression which all of us have, but an impression so presumptuous that we seldom have the courage to put into words. It is this, that humour, apart from satire, belongs to the English-speaking peoples alone. I say, the English-speaking peoples, a cumbrous and an unreal division of mankind. But, thank God, you cannot bring any preposterous ethnographical fictions in here. Not even Houston Stewart Chamberlain ever ventured to congratulate the Germans on their sense of humour; not even the Dean of St. Paul's will dare to tell us that the sense of humour is Nordic. The facts speak for themselves. Satire still flourishes on the Continent; Anatole France was no unworthy citizen of the country of Voltaire. There is satire, too, among the Northern peoples; I believe that if I expressed my private opinion as to who was the world's greatest satirist I should reply, Hans Anderson. Only in spots, of course; but the man who wrote the *Ugly Duckling* and the *Darning Needle* and the *Story of the Emperor's New Clothes* seems to me to have a finer sense of the intrinsic ludicrousness of mankind than Swift himself. Satire is international, as it is of all ages; but where shall humour be found, apart from satire, on the Continent of Europe? Who, unless he were a laugher at the malicious or the obscene, ever picked up the translation of a foreign book in search of a good laugh? Who ever found a good joke in a Continental illustrated paper? Cleverness of drawing abounds, but the captions beneath the drawings are infantile. I have seen a Swedish illustrated supplement, and I do not believe there was a single item in it which would have been accepted by *Comic Cuts*. I am told that the humorous drama of modern France forms a complete exception to this statement of the facts. I am content to believe it; there must, of course, be exceptions. I put forward the rule as a rule.

Some, no doubt, on a hasty analysis, would limit the field still further by saying that humour is purely English. And it would be easy to defend this contention by pointing to the fact that the English enjoy their joke very largely at the expense of their neighbours. Nothing belongs more decisively to the English-speaking world than the anecdote. We are for ever telling stories, and how many of those stories are about a Scot (we call it a Scotchman), an Irishman, a Jew, or an American? But this, if our definition of humour was a sound one, is in the nature of the case. A foreigner is funny, because he is like ourselves only different. A Scot or an Irishman is funny to the Englishman because he is almost exactly like himself, only slightly different. He talks English as his native tongue, only with an incorrect accent; what could possibly be funnier? A Scot is more funny than a Frenchman just as a monkey is more amusing than a dog; he is nearer the real thing.

But, in fact, all such judgments have been distorted beyond recognition by national hypocrisy. It is the English tradition that the Irish are a nation brimming over with humour, quite incapable of taking anything seriously. Irish people are in the habit of saying things which English people think funny. Irish people do not think them funny in the least. It follows, from the English point of view, that Ireland is a nation of incorrigible humorists, all quite incapable of governing themselves. The Scot, on the other hand, has an unfortunate habit of governing the English, and the English, out of revenge, have invented the theory that the Scot has no sense of humour. The Scot cannot have any sense of humour, because he is very careful about money, and drinks whisky where ordinary people drink beer. All the stories told against the Scottish nation are, I am told, invented in Aberdeen, and I partly believe it. There is (if a denationalized Ulsterman like myself may make the criticism) a pawkiness about all the stories against Scotland which betrays their Caledonian origin. The fact is that the Scottish sense of humour differs slightly from the English sense of humour, but I am afraid I have no time to indicate the difference. There is humour in the country of Stevenson and Barrie; and if the joke is often against Scotland, what better proof could there be that it is humour, and not satire?

Whatever may be said of Americans in real life, it is certain that their literature has humour. Personally I do not think that Americans are nearly as proud as they ought to be of this fact; Mark Twain ought to be to the American what Burns is to the Scot, and rather more. The hall-mark of American humour is its pose of illiteracy. All the American humorists spend their time making jokes against themselves. Artemus Ward pretended that he was unable even to spell. Mark Twain pretended that he had received no education beyond spelling, and most of his best remarks are based on this affectation of ignorance. "What is my which?" "He spelt it Vinci, but pronounced it Vinchy; foreigners always spell better than they pronounce"—that is perhaps one of the greatest jokes of literature, but the whole point of it lies in a man pretending to be worse educated than he really is. Mr. Leacock, as a rule, amuses by laughing at himself. America, on the other hand, has very little to show in the way of satire. Lowell was satirical occasionally, in a way that seems to me purely English. I want to allude to that later on; for the present let it be enough to note that the Americans, like the English and the Scots, do possess a literary tradition of non-satirical humour.

Thus far, we have concluded that the humorous in literature is the preserve of that period which succeeds the French Revolution, and of those peoples which speak the English language under its several denominations; unless by the word humour you understand "satire." It is high time, obviously, that we attempted some definition of what satire is, or at least of the marks by which it can be distinguished from non-satirical humour. It is clear from the outset that the author who laughs at himself, unless the self is a deliberately assumed one, is not writing satire. *Happy Thoughts* and the *Diary of a Nobody* may be what you will; they are not satire. *The Tramp Abroad* is not satire; *My Lady Nicotine* is not satire. For in all these instances the author, with a charity worthy of the Saints

—and indeed, St. Philip Neri's life is full of this kind of charity —makes a present of himself to his reader as a laughingstock. In satire, on the contrary, the writer always leaves it to be assumed that he himself is immune from all the follies and the foibles which he pillories. To take an obvious instance, Dickens is no satirist when he introduces you to Mr. Winkle, because there is not the smallest reason to suppose that Dickens would have handled a gun better than Mr. Winkle. But when Dickens introduces you to Mr. Bumble he is a satirist at once, for it is perfectly obvious that Dickens would have handled a porridge-ladle better than Mr. Bumble did. The humorist runs with the hare; the satirist hunts with the hounds.

There is, indeed, less contempt in satire than in irony. Irony is content to describe men exactly as they are, to accept them professedly, at their own valuation, and then to laugh up its sleeve. It falls outside the limits of humorous literature altogether; there is irony in Plato, there is irony in the Gospels; Mr. Galsworthy is an ironist, but few people have ever laughed over Mr. Galsworthy. Satire, on the contrary, borrows its weapons from the humorist; the satirized figure must be made to leap through the hoops of improbable adventure and farcical situation. It is all the difference between *The Egoist* and *Don Quixote*. Yet the laughter which satire provokes has malice in it always; we want to dissociate ourselves from the victim; to let the lash that curls round him leave our withers unwrung. It is not so with humour: not so (for instance) with the work of an author who should have been mentioned earlier, Mr. P. G. Wodehouse. To read the adventures of Bertie Wooster as if they were a satire on Bertie Wooster, or even on the class to which Bertie Wooster may be supposed to belong, is to misread them in a degree hardly possible to a German critic. The reader must make himself into Bertie Wooster in order to enjoy his Jeeves, just as he must make himself into Eliza's husband in order to enjoy his Eliza. Nobody can appreciate the crackers of humour unless he is content to put on his fool's cap with the rest of the party.

What, then, is the relation between humour and satire? Which is the parent, and which the child? Which is the normal organ, and which the morbid growth? I said just now that satire borrows its weapons from the humorist, and that is certainly the account most of us would be prepared to give of the matter off-hand. Most things in life, we reflect, have their comic side as well as their serious side; and the goodhumoured man is he who is content to see the humorous side of things even when the joke is against himself. The comic author, by persistently abstracting from the serious side of things, contrives to build up a world of his own, whose figures are all grotesques, whose adventures are the happy adventures of farce. Men fight, but only with foils; men suffer, but only suffer indignities; it is all a pleasant nursery tale, a relief to be able to turn to it when your mind is jaded with the sour facts of real life. Such, we fancy, is the true province of the Comic Muse; and satire is an abuse of the function. The satirist is like one who should steal his little boy's water-pistol and load it with vitriol, and so walk abroad flourishing it in men's faces. A treacherous fellow, your satirist. He will beguile the leisure of an Athenian audience, needing some rest, Heaven knows, from the myriad problems of a relentless war with powerful neighbours, by putting on a little play called *The Birds*. Capital; we shall enjoy that. Two citizens of Athens, so the plot runs, take wings to themselves and set out to build a bird city, remote from the daily instance of this subnubilar world. Excellent! That is just what we wanted, a relief for tired brains! And then, the fellow has tricked us, it proves, after all! His city in the clouds is, after all, only a parody of an Athenian colony, and the ceremonies which attend its inauguration are a burlesque, in the worse possible taste, of Athenian colonial policy. We came here for a holiday, and we are being treated to a sermon instead! No wonder the Athenian audiences often refused the first prize to Aristophanes. Skip twenty-one centuries, and find yourself in the times of the early Georges. There has been a great vogue, of late, for descriptions of travel in strange countries; and now (they are saying in the coffee-houses) the Dean of St. Patrick's, Dublin, has written a burlesque of these travel narratives, about countries that never existed at all—the ingenious dog! And then, as we read, it dawns upon us suddenly that Lilliput and Brobdingnag are not, after all, so distant, so imaginary; in fact, we have never really got away from the England of the Georges at all. The spirit of satire has overlooked us, like a wicked fairy, and turned the milk of human kindess sour as we churned it.

My present thesis, not dogmatically asserted but rather thrown out as if for discussion, is that this way of viewing the relations between humour and satire is a perversion of history. To think of satire as a particular direction which humour may happen to take, a particular channel into which humour may be diverted, is to neglect, surely, the broad facts as we have stated them above. Humour is of an age, satire of all ages; humour is of one particular civilization, satire of all countries. Is it not, then, more reasonable to suppose that satire is a normal function of the human genius, and humour that has no satire in it a perversion of the function, a growth away from the normal? That our sense of the ridiculous is not, in its original application, a child's toy at all, but a weapon, deadly in its efficacy, entrusted to us for exposing the shams and hypocrisies of the world? The tyrant may arm himself in triple mail, may surround himself with bodyguards, may sow his kingdom with a hedge of spies, so that free speech is crushed and criticism muzzled. Nay, worse, he may so debauch the consciences of his subjects with false history and with sophistical argument that they come to believe him the thing he gives himself out for, a creature half-divine, a heaven-sent deliverer. One thing there is that he still fears; one anxiety still bids him turn this way and that to scan the faces of his slaves. He is afraid of laughter. The satirist stands there, like the little child in the procession when the Emperor walked through the capital in his famous new clothes; his is the tiny voice that interprets the consciousness of a thousand onlookers: "But, Mother, he has no clothes on at all!"

Satire has a wider scope, too. It is born to scourge the persistent and ever-recurrent follies of the human creature as such. And, for anybody who has the humility to realize that it is aimed at him, and not merely at his neighbours, satire has an intensely remedial effect; it purifies the spiritual system of man as nothing else that is human can possibly do. Thus, every young man who is in love should certainly read *The Egoist* (there would be far less unhappiness in marriage if they all did), and no schoolmaster should ever begin the scholastic year without re-reading Mr. Bradby's *Lanchester Tradition*, to remind him that he is but dust. Satire is thus an excellent discipline for the satirized: whether it is a good thing for the satirist is more open to question. *Facit indignatio versum;* it is seldom that the impetus to write satire comes to a man except as the result of a disappointment. Since disappointment so often springs from love, it is not to be wondered at that satirists have ever dealt unkindly with woman, from the days of Simonides of Amorgos, who compared woman with more than thirty different kinds of animals, in every case to her disadvantage. A pinched, warped fellow, as a rule, your satirist. It is misery that drives men to laughter. It is bad humour that encourages men first to be humorous. And it is, I think, when good-humoured men pick up this weapon of laughter, and, having no vendettas to work off with it, begin tossing it idly at a mark, that humour without satire takes its origin.

In a word, humour without satire is, strictly speaking, a perversion, the misuse of a sense. Laughter is a deadly explosive which was meant to be wrapped up in the cartridge of satire, and so, aimed unerringly at its appointed target, deal its salutary wound; humour without satire is a flash in the pan; it may be pretty to look at, but it is, in truth, a waste of ammunition. Or, if you will, humour is satire that has run to seed; trained no longer by an artificial process, it has lost the virility of its stock. It is port from the wood without the depth and mystery of its vintage rivals. It is a burning-glass that has lost its focus; a passenger, pulling no weight in the up-stream journey of life; meat that has had the vitamins boiled out of it; a clock without hands. The humorist, in short, is a satirist out of a job; he does not fit into the scheme of things; the world passes him by.

The pure humorist is a man without a message. He can preach no gospel, unless it be the gospel that nothing matters; and that in itself is a foolish theme, for if nothing matters, what does it matter whether it matters or not? Mr. Wodehouse is an instance in point, Mr. Leacock nearly so, though there is a story in *Arcadian Adventures with the Idle Rich* about the amalgamation of two religious bodies on strictly commercial lines, which comes very close to pure satire. Barry Pain is a humorist who is seldom at his best when he attempts satire; the same fate dogged Mark Twain, though I think he would have liked to be a satirist. Mr. A. A. Milne is in a similar case, and so indeed are all the modern Punch writers by the terms (you might say) of their contract. No contrast is more surprising than the contrast in atmosphere between the letterpress of *Punch* before 1890 and its letterpress since. The old *Punches* are full of very bad satire; there is hardly anything else in them; it is all on the same sort of level as *John Bull* in its Bottomley days—anti-aristocratic, anti-foreign, anti-clerical, very much like some rag of the Boulevards. Today, it is the home of superbly finished humour—humour cultivated as a fine art. But satire is absent.

Some of the greatest humorists have halted between two destinies, and as a rule have been lost to satire. Sir W. S. Gilbert, a rather unsuccessful satirist in his early days, inherited the dilemma from his master, Aristophanes. Patience is supreme satire, and there is satire in all the operas; but in their general effect they do not tell: the author has given up to mankind what was meant for a party. Mr. Chesterton is in the same difficulty; he is like Johnson's friend who tried to be a philosopher, but cheerfulness would keep on coming in. The net effect of his works is serious, as it is meant to be, but his fairy-like imagination is for ever defeating its own object in matter of detail. But indeed, Mr. Chesterton is beyond our present scope; for he is rash enough to combine humour not merely with satire but with serious writing; and that, it is well known, is a thing the public will not stand. A few modern authors have succeeded, in spite of our latter-day demand for pure humour, in being satirists first and last: Samuel Butler of *Erewhon*, and W. H. Mallock, and Mr. Belloc, I think, in his political novels. The very poor reception given to these last by the public proves that there is more vinegar in them than oil.

Humour, if we may adopt for a moment the loathsome phraseology of journalism, has "come to stay." It is, if our analysis be true, a by-product and in a sense a waste-product; that does not mean that it has no significance. A pearl is a by-product, and from the fishmonger's point of view a waste-product; but it has value so long as people want it. And there is at present a public demand for humour which implies that humour should take its place among the arts, an art for the art's sake, not depending on any fruits of practical utility for its estimation. There is art in O. Henry, though he does not scourge our vices like Juvenal; there is art in Heath Robinson, though he does not purge our consciences like Hogarth. What rank humour is to take as compared with serious writing is, perhaps, an unanswerable problem; our histories of nineteenth century literature have not yet been bold enough to tackle it. It is probable, I think, that humour is relatively ephemeral; by force of words humour means caprice, and the caprice of yesterday is apt to leave us cold. There is a generation not yet quite dead which says that nothing was ever so funny as the *Bongaultier Ballads*. The popularity of the *Ingoldsby Legends* is now, to say the least, precarious; and I doubt if the modern youth smacks its lips as we did over the *Bab Ballads* themselves. Read a book of A. A. Milne's, and then turn to an old volume of *Voces Populi*, and you will realize that even in our memory humour has progressed and become rarefied. What

reputations will be left unassailable when the tide has re-
ceded, it would be rash to prophesy. For myself, I like to believe that one name will be immortal at least, that of Mr. Max
Beerbohm. Incomparably equipped for satire, as his cartoons
and his parodies show, he has yet preferred in most of his work
to give rein to a gloriously fantastic imagination, a humorist in
satirist's clothing. One is tempted to say with the prophet:
May I die the death of the righteous, and may my last end be
like his!

Meanwhile, a pertinent question may be raised, What will
be the effect of all this modern vogue for pure humour upon the
prospects of satiric writing? We are in danger, it seems to me,
of debauching our sense of the ridiculous to such an extent as
to leave no room for the disciplinary effect of satire. I remember seeing Mr. Shaw's *Press Cuttings* first produced in Manchester. I remember a remark, in answer to the objection that
women ought not to vote because they do not fight, that a
woman risks her life every time a man is born, being received
(in Manchester!) with shouts of happy laughter. In that
laughter I read the tragedy of Mr. Bernard Shaw. He lashes us
with virulent abuse, and we find it exquisitely amusing. Other
ages have stoned the prophets; ours pelts them instead with the
cauliflower bouquets of the heavy comedian. No country, I
suppose, has greater need of a satirist today than the United
States of America; no country has a greater output of humour,
good and bad, which is wholly devoid of any satirical quality.
If a great American satirist should arise, would his voice be
heard among the hearty guffaws which are dismally and
eternally provoked by Mutt, Jeff, Felix, and other kindred
abominations? And have we, on this side of the Atlantic, any
organ in which pure satire could find a natural home? I believe
the danger which I am indicating to be a perfectly real one,
however fantastic it may sound—the danger, I mean, that we
have lost, or are losing, the power to take ridicule seriously.
That our habituation to humorous reading has inoculated our
systems against the beneficent poison of satire. Unhappy the

Juvenal whom Rome greets with amusement; unhappier still the Rome, that can be amused by a Juvenal!

I am not sure, in reading through this essay again, that there is any truth in its suggestions. But I do not see that there can be any harm in having said what I thought, even if I am no longer certain that I think it.

CIVILIZATION AND THE POET

By *Joseph Wood Krutch*

" THE world," said Emerson, "seems to be always awaiting its poet," and though the saying is a true one we are,
perhaps, not wrong in supposing that the need of our
particular world for "its poet" is more than usually acute.
Emerson certainly intended the term to be taken in its widest
significance to mean the possessor of one of those articulate
imaginations which can communicate a sense that the world of
our experience has a unity and meaning, and it is certainly just
from the absence of any such sense that we suffer. Our best
writers of verse themselves define rather than triumph over the
prevailing mood produced by the feeling that we are lost in a
meaningless chaos. But the phenomenon is not merely literary
and we lack a satisfactory life for the same reasons that we
lack our comprehensive poet. Poems and civilization are alike
the result of affirmations sweeping enough to make form out
of what seems confusion.

Nor is this analogy between the kind of affirmation which
makes poems and the kind which makes civilizations merely an
analogy. The poem and the civilization are parallel phenomena—one occurring in the realm of thought and the other in the
realm of action, but each the result of some passionate faith
inclusive enough to give form either to living or to contemplation. Each implies an imagination powerful enough to interpret in humanly usable terms the data present in the consciousness, but each implies also that these data shall be capable of
such interpretation; and the first question which inevitably
arises in connection with contemporary conditions is the
question whether or not the data of the contemporary con-

sciousness is susceptible of such a humanly usable interpretation.

It has long been suspected—justly or not—that an *Iliad* was easier to write in the year 1000 B.C. than it would be today. The anthropomorphic religion and the naïve patriotism of the primitive Greeks were in themselves so simply human, so in harmony with instinctive human thought and behavior, that they made easily possible the attempt to see human life as ample, significant, and harmonious. But this religion and this patriotism were themselves possible only because these primitive Greeks knew so little of nature that they could construct a universe made almost exclusively from the materials which they found in themselves and could people it with gods made in their own image. Since their time, knowledge has been constantly busy with the criticism of every structure erected by the human mind. It has been posing ever more difficult problems to the imagination which would arrange that knowledge into a humanly satisfactory pattern, until men have begun at last to wonder whether or not any imagination is equal to the task, whether we have not been overwhelmed by knowledge (or what seems like knowledge) and compelled to witness a triumph of Nature over Art.

Many of the data which the imagination has found it so difficult to find a place for in any humanly useful conception of the universe as a whole are, of course, scientific. The pattern into which we have arranged what we know of nature is obviously incompatible with those conceptions of man's place in it which underlie some of the noblest poems as well as some of the noblest civilizations. Science has also encouraged certain tendencies of thought which increase the difficulty since it has promoted, for example, a general distrust of the validity of spontaneous conviction and a tendency to seek out the prejudice behind what seems to us at first sight our most inevitable affirmations. But it would be a mistake to suppose that all knowledge of the sort which makes epic poetry or epic culture difficult has been the result of scientific thought.

The artist himself, hardly less than the scientist, has peered into many dark and unlovely corners. He too has the passion, perhaps ultimately fatal, for knowing; and that passion has led him on, horribly fascinated, from discovery to discovery. Hence the satirist and the realist, no less than the astronomer and the biologist, stand between us and any Homeric conception of the world amidst which we live. Zola, Baudelaire, and Ibsen; Gissing, Hardy, and Dostoevski—these men, hardly less than Darwin and Freud, have disillusioned mankind with the universe and with itself. Though perhaps none of them actually discovered anything, all called our attention to much and made it an inescapable part of our consciousness. Doubtless there are, in all their works, few ugly facts which Shakespeare did not in some sense know. But there was a meanness in human nature and a sordidness in human fate which he could somehow disregard, which he could blithely ignore in a fashion no longer so easy. This meanness and this sordidness have been examined with a care and described with a force which rendered them no longer negligible. Art has acknowledged them; and for that reason they have become, not merely facts, but facts which have taken their place solidly in the human consciousness.

For this reason, also, they must be dealt with, and any imagination which proposes itself as competent to make art out of the modern world must find a place for them, whether the work which it is endeavoring to create be literary or social. There is no golden age of faith, of simplicity, or of ignorance to which we can return—unless, indeed, society as we know it should suffer some overwhelming catastrophe which would break the whole continuity of its development and return the few straggling survivors to savagery. Those eccentric converts to fifth-century paganism, thirteenth-century Catholicism, and seventeenth-century Anglicanism, who proposed to live and write as though they were in the heyday of the culture which they have chosen, are mere refugees whom few will follow.

Few would seek to deny that modern life has its compensations, or that many of the experiences peculiar to it are delight-ful. The very sense of freedom associated with it, even the sense of having escaped the restrictions and the burdens which convictions impose, seem sometimes more than enough to compensate for any losses entailed. But few would refuse also to admit the curiously disjointed or fragmentary character of this life. Whole sections of our experience, both pleasurable and the reverse, seem not only unconnected with one another, but positively incompatible. Some—like those which arise out of the cultivation of romantic love, of honor, and of our personal integrity—are apparently survivals from a world already dying; others—like those connected with power and speed and freedom, with our plunge into the material richness of the modern world—seem to give us hints of a way of life still imperfectly organized and imperfectly understood; but these two classes of goods are mingled without being combined.

The very cynics whose documented relativism mocks any attempt to spell Duty or Justice or Right with a capital letter find themselves passionately devoted to defending Communist victims of police clubs or denouncing the Society for Suppres-sion of Vice with bursts of oratory whose appeal is wholly moral. Lovers who rediscover the value of those illusions which are very old nevertheless change mistresses or wives with a facility which is very new and seem determined to live several lives for the very reason that they are incapable of leading one. Even humanitarianism, perhaps the most characteristic of our attempts to live nobly, does not dare to examine the founda-tions upon which it rests for it is devoted to the task of saving human lives without being really sure that human lives are worth saving.

What appears to be lacking is any logical or even any emo-tional connection between our various motives, various beliefs, and various impulses; any sense that they are a part of one whole or that they could be put together in any fashion which we enable them to reinforce one another. We are overwhelmed, not only by the diversity of knowledge, but also by the diversity of possible deeds, of possible values, and of possible judgments. Such artists as we have offer us constructions whose essential deficiencies arise out of the fact, not that they are artificial or partial, but that this artificiality or this partiality is so glaringly, so unforgettably evident. And if we babble of the necessity of seeing life steadily and seeing it whole we babble without conviction because we are struck by the fear that the more steadily we see it the less will it appear to be any whole which we can comprehend.

We may realize that the wholeness which seemed to characterize certain previous philosophies or civilizations was illusory, and that the connections between the parts of any previous peoples' experience were purely imaginary connections whose existence was merely assumed. But that realization does not help us very much because it is the inability to imagine or assume any such connections for ourselves which constitutes the difficulty and we do not know even where or how we ought to begin.

But let us grant that art, in the broad sense in which it has here been defined, is still possible; that the apparent triumph of diverse and alien nature is only temporary. Let us assume, that is to say, that a modern world, complete and unified, will emerge. Is that world close enough for us to imagine, even vaguely, what it would be like?

Certainly the prophets who proclaim its coming differ widely enough among themselves, but probably the most polite and respectable among them are those who assure us that civilization is not to be remade but only salvaged and that the new world will be more like the world of the past than the world of this present. Some of them, like Mr. Chesterton, are sure that if only beer flowed as freely as it once did in Merrie England we should all very happily put our trust in the Pope and all would be well again. Others, like Professor Millikan, have faith in telescopes and confidently expect that we shall some day construct one which will discover the ten commandments written in letters of fire a hundred thousand light years away. But they agree in the essential, which is that we need only to recover a few principles which we have lost in order to get along very nicely in the world we now know. But polite and reasonable as these prophets seem, there is, nevertheless, something singularly tame about their gospels, something plaintive and elegiac about their pleading, something which seems hardly adequate to influence very effectively a world which may not know where it is going but which is certainly going somewhere under the force of impulsions not to be controlled by the pious suggestions of frightened respectability. The men who speak most earnestly of the claims of authority are the very ones whose voices most conspicuously lack its ring and it is, paradoxically, those who tell everyone to do as he likes who have achieved the largest following. If leadership is to be recognized by the confidence with which it asserts itself, if art is to be known by the power and the persuasiveness we feel before we can analyze, then the beginnings of the new world which may be forming are to be sought among those who are concerned with nothing less than with mere conversation.

Wherever this world of ours competes directly with the past, it loses. Its religions are anæmic and foolish; its poems and its pictures often seem to be trivial and feeble; just in so far as their aims and methods are identical with those of the past. But in certain other activities it exhibits a competence which seems, in comparison with previous efforts in the same field, as nearly superhuman as the competence of Shakespeare seems superhuman in comparison with the efforts of our contemporaries to write tragedy in blank verse. Its instruments for measuring the stars, its machines for hurtling through space, are successful beyond the wildest dreams of previous ages; and the most significant thing about them is not that badly articulated or rationalized faith in their importance which is sometimes expressed by philosophers or humanitarians, but that passionate and implicit faith in the immediate, unassailable value in the thing itself which made them possible.

Whatever else we may say of it, we know that the ecstasy of

the pilot is authentic and that it is communicated unreasonably to society. Crowds carry transatlantic fliers in triumph from the field just as crowds are said to have carried Cimabue's Virgin in triumph through the streets of Florence; and each crowd acts for the same reason—because it has recognized a kind of achievement which it can understand. The world is not interested in machines because they save labor or because they increase production. These are the excuses it makes to itself. It is interested because the affirmation was made spontaneously and does not need to be defended. In that case the will to believe did not explain its rights; it believed.

Even those of us who are, by temperament and education, most attached to values of another sort and, for that reason, least capable of feeling what many of our contemporaries feel, catch at moments some hint of it. We drive in their cars, fly in their airplanes, and live in their cities. We are caught up by this world, gasp with its excitements, and, by moments, we feel that we belong. But we cannot completely identify ourselves with the representatives of the present. The very inarticulateness of their philosophy, of their poetry, if you will, baffles us. The world of speed and power and exactitude in which they live is a world which still exists only upon the periphery of the consciousness. It is known chiefly through a world not yet given form by art, a world which has been directly experienced but never successfully thought out. Since no symbols have been found for its aims or its joys it cannot be substituted for—it cannot even take its place beside—those worlds which have a different kind of existence in the consciousness because they have been symbolized and interpreted in terms appropriate to that consciousness. Yet the materials may possibly be there. Art has, in the past, many times revealed to mankind perceptions, emotions, and valuations of which it had not known itself capable.

No one can say beforehand whether or not the new interests and the new ecstasies are capable of being thus humanized. Certainly it is difficult to conceive any connection between them and those which a Shakespeare celebrated. Certainly they seem less outgrowths of previous interests than something radically different, and it may be that they are entirely inexpressible in terms similar to those which literature uses. Perhaps the tendency of the plastic arts to abandon the imitation of nature for pure geometry is merely one relatively comprehensible sign of a break with tradition which is destined to be more complete than even the most extravagant of the "post-," "neo-," or "sur-" schools can imagine. Perhaps the wildest eccentricities of the "modern" poets may be taken as evidence either that poetry is beginning to grapple with the problem or that it is disintegrating under the realization that the problem is not capable of being grappled with.

But in any event there is no escaping the fact that much of the old world has grown dim. The academicians who plead for standards in art, the versifiers who talk of taste in poetry, the moralists who plead that we still *can* believe what our fathers did—there is not one of them whose voice has more than a spectral quality. Even those who believe them righter than their opponents must confess that the conservators are, at least, no match for those who do not bother even to answer. Vitality is all on the other side and those of us who confess our inability to accept the modern world without reservation or to say what can ultimately be made of it, do feel sure, nevertheless, that vitality of some sort is as indispensable to art as it is to life; and we shall take courage again when we find somewhere some evidence that the values which are dearest to us can be affirmed with a passion equal to that with which scientists, technicians, and mere sportsmen daily make the affirmations by which they live.

It is only in the sense which has been here implied that there can be any meaning to the statement that life is art and that esthetics can take the place left vacant by religion and morality. To say that is to say only that one work of art may be replaced by another; but the other must still be found. Some unified aim, some hierarchy of values, some sense that something is supremely worth-while, must impose itself upon us with a self-justifying inevitability.

What we seem to have is an embarrassing profusion of almost equally unsatisfactory possibilities. What we lack among the advocates of each is an imagination strong enough to make that possibility seem inevitable. Nor is it, so long as this is true, worth-while to affirm any abstract faith in art. If love and honor and duty can be salvaged then someone must write about them in a fashion which carries conviction. If we are to get along without them, then someone must describe a world from which they are absent in a fashion which makes that world seem still worth the having. And it is just its failure to do either of these things quite adequately which reveals the weakness of contemporary literature.

This latter has enjoyed, at moments, its triumphs of honesty and accuracy. It has even, at moments also, transcended these virtues in order to achieve beauty—that quality which we attribute to anything when it makes reality seem identical with desire and convinces us that what ought to be is the same as what is. But contemporary literature is too fragmentary and too varied to rank among the supremely great literatures, much less to assume unaided a task which the literatures of other times could perform only with the help of philosophy and religion. It is—like ourselves—doubtful, divided, eclectic, and experimental. It has never succeeded in making us believe anything wholeheartedly or for long. It has given us no self-justifying image because its creators have achieved no self-justifying vision.

We know that this world of ours is interesting. The very vividness of its never-failing stimuli and the very richness of the possibilities which it is continually suggesting, make us unwilling to sacrifice any of them. Even its distresses are so exciting that we are not convinced by those who long for a return to the good old days and none of the unities which have been proposed seem to include enough. What we long for is the ability to function in this complicated world as easily and as freely as others seem to have functioned in a simpler one; to find life, not merely exciting, but satisfactory and meaningful as well. We want to see it whole but we want also to see it all; to find a name for every one of its sensations, an explanation for every one of its phenomena, and a justification for every one of its values. We want a philosophy which is more than merely cold and reasonable, a philosophy whose ultimate expression is one of those works of art which seem not only to sum up but also to justify a civilization.

Perhaps some of these desires are incompatible with others. Perhaps all satisfactory affirmations are partial, and perhaps they seem satisfactory only because they make us forget what they are not able to include. But if this is so, the very fact that we are not able to forget anything about the world in which we live is proof that such an affirmation has not been made. And, at least until it has, we shall continue to long for some attitude which would unify the modern consciousness without depriving us of any of those fragmentary goods which it affords. Only one thing is certain. We shall know what artist we ought to accept when we find ourselves accepting him and we shall know what authority ought to be obeyed when we find ourselves obeying it. Life may be an art—but only when it is characterized by art's spontaneous inevitability.

ENGLISH AMATEURS AND AMERICAN PROFESSIONALS

By *John Langdon-Davies*

IN 1929 an innocent Englishman abroad in America was apt to pain his American friends with a pessimism, which, they felt, should have been left on the other side of the Atlantic. In 1932 Englishman and American contemplate hand in hand the ruins of their ways of living and wonder what can be done about them. Sometimes in this new communion of spirit we may even go so far as to agree that our countries are making such a mess of things that only because we are trapped animals do we persist in them instead of migrating to countries like Spain and Mexico. For there at least, though comforts may not be omnipresent, we should be spared the consciousness that a growing proportion of our fellows are a prey to gnawing uncertainty. We should exchange our baths and telephones for freedom from bread lines and bank smashes.

But when an American says to me, "Oh, let's escape from the machine age into Spain or Mexico," I suspect that he is merely talking. For there is no real peace for the distracted American soul in that direction, although I believe that there is peace for the English soul. When Americans begin to emigrate they will go to Russia and leave us to go to Spain alone; that is inevitable, because of a fundamental difference in our national passions—a difference which can be traced throughout all the phases of our daily lives and which lies at the bottom of our several failures in the face of modern scientific civilization.

In a sentence this difference is that the Englishman worships the cult of amateurism, he wants to like doing things; but the American worships the cult of professionalism, he wants to get things done. Even in habits of drinking you see the difference: the Englishman drinks slowly because he likes his liquor; the American gulps because he wants the effect. And whenever England has failed in modern life it can be shown to be because of amateurism in the wrong place, while in the case of America it can equally be shown to be because of professionalism in the wrong place. A very brief survey will prove the truth of this sweeping generalization.

In the first place the cult of the amateur has forced the Englishman to live in the maximum of discomfort and inconvenience. Amateurishness in England begins at home. The stately homes of England are monuments to it. To the tourist they are picturesque; but we should never forget that the picturesque is better to look at than to occupy, and of the English home it may be said that, as with the orthodox heaven, "*one* day in thy courts is better than a thousand."

A little while ago a progressive school in England was building new boarding accommodations. The dietitian—American-trained, since we English, in our amateurish way, still eat food rather than vitamins and calories—looked over the plans. She knew that for x children it would take y cubic feet for equipment to raise the necessary bath water to an appropriate temperature. She told the architect that although his Gothic features were sufficient, there was not enough room in the kitchen for essential heating apparatus. "If you want more hot water," he replied, "all you have to do is to get the servants up an hour earlier." No single sentence could have given contemporary England away more completely. In the old days the English home was an exquisite hybrid; the cult of the amateur pervaded the boudoir, the library, and the rose garden; the slaves were in the kitchen. You could live and be happy then. But conditions have changed, and the growing discomfort of the English home today is due to our having clung to the cult of the amateur after we have lost our slaves. We continue to build, to furnish, to cater with that thoughtlessness which is all very well when you can pay professionals to make the best of it and to gloss over our faults with their hard work, but this is apt to pall when it becomes a question of doing the work ourselves. We scorn to train our daughters to do the jobs they will have to do if they are to be homemakers; we neglect to learn about the slaves of the new world such as electricity, and we are so used to assuming that the bell will be answered that long after the race of servants has disappeared we keep on ringing for them metaphorically.

The age-long symbol of the home, the family hearth, is a symbol also of our national differences. In England the hearth is open and inefficient; there are very few architects who can build a fireplace which does not smoke. The orthodox procedure is to build your house and suffer a few weeks of asphyxia and then you call in an expert on smoky chimneys to remodel at great expense the aperture, the flue, and the chimney pot. Then you are at liberty to burn wood and coal in the most extravagant way known to man, to be an English gentleman, and to remain cold all the rest of your days. A by-product of the system is the notorious English complexion, due not so much to health as to frost bite. In America, on the other hand, professional heating has insured that no room shall be fit for anything but hothouse plants and a fauna used to dry desert air and wearing practically no underclothing to speak of. Again we have the by-product of the American complexion and an obsession with what seems according to the advertisements to be the American botanical study, the vagaries of the "intestinal flora."

The pity is that thanks to the cult of the amateur and the cult of the professional there is no third choice; you cannot be just comfortably warm unless you abandon civilization altogether and choose climate rather than companionship.

II

The cult of the amateur begins at home, but it does not stay there. It is to be found in the wrong places throughout English life. Take for example the English woman. At home she can-

not make herself or her man comfortable because she scorns to
be professional in anything.   Instead of investigating labor-
saving devices, she sighs for servants and leaves it at that.
As to her own person, for the most part she regards the use of
cosmetics, the proper care of the hair, the proper wearing of
clothes as turning a woman into a professional in the most
deplorable sense of the word.   She runs her house and herself
on the assumption that she must be an unsullied amateur
first, last, and all the time.   In consequence one often feels
that, whereas in France even the plainest women never give
up, in England even the most potentially beautiful are as like
as not never to begin.

Now it is quite possible that American women are too
professional in their pursuit of the art of being and looking
charming and that this accounts for the twelve-in-a-box
feeling one sometimes has on the sidewalks of Fifth Avenue.
It is certain that a lady hiker in rough tweed breeches, silk
hose, thick walking shoes, and lipstick has an amphibious air,
as she takes the train for an outing up the Hudson.   It is also
certain that the English woman knows better how to dress for
certain practical purposes such as getting wet in the rain.   But
it is a thousand pities that her cult of misguided amateurism
prevents her from taking the little trouble that would make
her natural charms irresistible.   Though she may not be as
inveterate a gardener as Miss Ruth Draper would have us
believe, she certainly knows better than to pretend that the
prettiest flowers grow in a state of nature.   Yet she is afraid,
owing to her traditions, to be thought too professional if she
cultivates the garden in her face where cherries and white
lilies should grow.

But she has even less excuse for worshipping the amateur
when she becomes a business woman.   It is there that her
cousin in America out-distances her completely.   Compare
the serving of a meal in any public restaurant in New York
with the same thing at our popular London human filling
stations.   It is not only the absence of iced water and grape-

fruit that makes the American at breakfast in London a symbol of human despair; it is also the air of the typical English waitress. If you must be served with bad coffee and unwanted foods, at least they should not be conferred on you as a favor.

If the impartial observer may take an English waitress as a symbol of amateurishness in the wrong place, it is not difficult to find for America a companion symbol of professionalism in the wrong place. It is those middle-aged ladies, looking like past vice-presidents of the W.C.T.U. called, I believe, floor clerks, who beam at you as you make for your burrow in certain large American hotels. These ladies have the obviously unattractive job of superintending the keys for men who are seeking a night's lodging during the distressing circumstance of a business trip. Yet they act as beaming hostesses to willing guests and hold up your progress to and from your rest by sententious remarks intended to create the atmosphere of that unpalatable fiction, a home away from home. Here we have the American woman learning bad habits from her brother; for one of the worst features of professionalism in the wrong place is the "keep smiling" attitude in situations where neither smiles nor tears are required but mere stolid vacuity of expression. But though this is bad enough, it is not worse than the English waitress who never stops reminding you that she is really the merest amateur without any professional pride. "They also serve who only stand and wait" should be the motto of their trades union.

An Englishman is always impressed by the fervent loyalty of the American business woman to her employers. I have quarreled violently with a friend who worked in a big department store simply because I claimed to have bought an article cheaper elsewhere. This is the thing which does not exist at all in England, a loyalty to one's business like the loyalty of one's grandmother to her church. To the Englishman it seems to lead to a complete distortion of values, and he finds it hard to adjust himself to a community where everybody not only is a

salesman, but is proud of being one; where a man sells baths
in the same reverent spirit towards the bath as a missioner
has towards the gospel he preaches to the heathen. It seems to
lead directly towards the worship of things, the true idolatry
which is the deadly sin.

III

We pass on to an example of how the cult of amateurishness
deprives the Englishman not merely of his comfort but of his
health. No one can be familiar with the two countries without
marveling at American teeth and English toothlessness. It is
not a matter of calcium and diet, but of social attitudes.
Because the Englishman must have the amateur in the wrong
place and thereby sometimes excludes essential professionalism,
he resembles a gift-horse in one important particular at least.
I know of nothing more likely to astonish the American than
the contrasted English attitudes to the dentist and the doctor.

The English doctor is an amateur of the very finest type; he
occupies a position in society with the Anglican clergyman and
the country squire. It is true he has a profession, but it is one
which by its very nature he can profess *con amore*. His work,
in the first place, is with people; and to the English that is
most essential if you are to retain amateur status. Work with
things such as stocks—if stocks are still to be called anything
so tangible as a thing—or money, or goods, or even art products, tends to degrade anyone below the level of him who
works with personalities. It is worthwhile repeating perhaps
that the English doctor knows people as well as their diseases;
for one is told that elsewhere over-professionalism has changed
this, as in the case of the lawyer. The Englishman's doctor
and lawyer concern themselves as much with his complete
ego as if they were both his father confessors. And so the
doctor can enjoy his work, and indeed he had better, since
much of it has to be done for love—he gets as many "God-
bless-yous" as paying patients. Since he enjoys his work, he is
an amateur, a gentleman, respectable; his wife will be a leader

of society in any country town; his children, could he afford to send them, would be admitted to the best schools.

Now look at the dentist. He does not deal with people but only with people's mouths, and unless he is abnormal he cannot possibly enjoy his work. And so his wife is not called on and he has some difficulty in getting into the best club. He is more or less on the same level from which the surgeon graduated when he ceased to be the barber. He takes it out on the barber. He takes it out on the doctor as best he can by earning more money and by insisting on his bills being paid; for whereas you pay your doctor last, your dentist is paid along with the grocer. Can we wonder that on the whole dentistry in England is on a lower level than any other branch of medicine, and teeth the most neglected of English tissues.

I know of a cultured American dentist married to an English woman, who wanted to send his children to a good English school. Fortunately it was not until later that the authorities discovered that his doctorate was of dentistry rather than of medicine, for otherwise they would not have admitted the daughters to a school designed for the daughters of gentlemen.

And for all this we English have to pay heavily through the teeth, while our health suffers that amateurishness may live. We are not merely uncomfortable, but ailing, in the cause of our cult.

I understand that a great deal can be said about the effect on health in America of professionalism in the wrong place; but this is not the person or the place to dwell upon that subject, except by way of contrast. The Englishman, we may say in passing, can never reconcile himself to the fact that in America the last generation was the last to be born in homes, since all children who can afford it are born in hospitals today. He feels that there was something respectably amateur about the older habit, while it never seems to smack too much of mass production and hyperprofessionalism. This is probably mere prejudice—although the value of the new way has not yet been shown in mortality statistics—and in any case even

England in this matter is becoming slowly Americanized. I know of a cultured English lady who succeeded in bringing forth a child alive with the help of two obstetricians, an anæsthetist, the family physician, with, in case of complications, a psycho-analyst in waiting in the next room; but even she preserved the home atmosphere.

Although the cult of the amateur in England has such deplorable results we must be willing to give it honor where honor is due. It is certainly of importance to human welfare that those whose business is with persons should retain as much as possible of the spirit of the amateur, for without it much that is essential will be lost. Thus the doctor, the lawyer, and the teacher enter into human relationships with their clients just as much as do husbands and wives, fathers and sons, brothers and sisters with one another. The basis of their contact is, or should be, emotional; they should feel affection, or their labors, whatever their technical qualifications, will be in vain. Substitute the clinic for the family physician, or the mechanical law firm for the family solicitor, and you are doing for those professions what intelligence tests and all the paraphernalia of grading and measurement have done to education: you are degrading a profession which has to do with people to the level of those which have to do with things. It is the reverse process that is needed, the exaltation of the dentist, not the mechanization of the doctor.

In England the family doctor, to whom a lifetime of sympathy has given a true insight into ailing humanity, will tell you modestly that he is a bit of an amateur psychologist. America seems full of professional psychologists whose statistical study of behavior patterns, motivations, and the rest have not left them time to notice that persons exist. I have known several amateur psychologists stop people from suicide, often for poor reasons no doubt, but your professional psychologist tends to confine himself to explaining why people commit suicide when they have done so. If I am right in believing that there is more of the latter than of the former in America, is it not because of the fetish that such knowledge comes from "taking a course" rather than from living? Do we not need the love of a friend, of a beloved amateur physician, even more than the "transference" a psychological doctor can give us, just as another doctor can give us a counterirritant or blister?

IV

The cult of the amateur in the wrong place can be studied in another aspect by considering the English attitude towards games, and especially towards that national emanation, which is so English as to seem as pointless to an American as *Punch* itself, cricket. We have seen that the amateur is always regarded as socially, even morally, superior to the professional, with strange results; but in cricket you see it most clearly enunciated that a professional cannot possibly be a gentleman.

Cricket is played by mixed teams of amateurs and professionals, unlike football where the two types seldom meet on the same side or even in the same competitions. You might think that the little fact that one player makes sufficient money elsewhere in another business so that he does not have to demand payment for his share in the game, while another gives all his time to the game and must, therefore, get his subsistence from it, should make no difference if both are admitted to the same team. But you would be wrong. It makes very nearly all the difference.

To begin with, if an amateur and a professional chance to begin the innings together—in cricket there are two "batsmen" instead of one as in baseball—they will start their journey to the playing field from different doors of the players' pavilion. The professional must not use the fact that he is playing on the same team with the amateur to impose himself on his company when off the field of play; he must occupy separate quarters like a colored man on a Southern street car.

When next day the *Times* or *Morning Post* gives an account of the game with the full score, the distinction is rubbed well in. If you are an amateur your name will appear as Mr. W. Smith, but if a professional you will be Smith (W). The man who is so good at the game that he can make money by it is obviously not entitled to a prefix, while the bank clerk who plays "for the love of the game" is singled out by the mark which stands, in this particular, for a gentleman. At the end of the season a team captained by Mr. W. Smith meets another captained by Smith (W)—his only chance for leadership—and it will be called "Gentlemen versus Players."

There is in all this a suggestion that in some way or other it is not good form to be *too* good at anything, or at least that nothing should be taken very seriously. It is in keeping with the fact that cricket, which after all involves a considerable amount of running, was until two generations ago played in top hats and is still played in long trousers, as if to prevent perfection by handcuffing the free movement of the performer. Moreover, the Englishman in America when he is honest must confess that the clothing of a football player is quite repulsive to him, savoring as it does of a professional efficiency more suitable for diving as a business or for the battlefield. It is probably the same national trait that laughs at the ponderousness of German scholarship. It is constantly cropping up in unexpected places; for instance we English are great gardeners, but nowhere in England could you find anyone capable of transplanting a large tree, as is done daily in America. Perhaps the amateur gardener would feel too much like a professional quarryman. In the same way the gentleman farmer refuses to have anything to do with the sort of co-operative methods which have made a success of the California citrus industry. It is as if he wants to know his cabbages personally and is afraid of having them mixed, as babies are said to be mixed in large lying-in hospitals. In this feeling for the individuality of products of industry we have indeed but another instance of this fundamental trait which distinguishes the English from the Americans. The English attitude to industrial products is that of William Morris, just as the American is that of Henry Ford, although so far neither nation follows its leader in practice except spasmodically and as often as not in the wrong context.

To return for a moment to sport. We can discern yet another of the obscure characteristics of this cult of the amateur in certain religious attitudes. The only games which may be played widely and without protest in England on Sunday are those which are least associated with professionalism, notably golf and tennis. There are various reasons suggested for this, among them the most hypocritical is that professional games would force people to work on Sundays. Again we have the curious assumption that the amateur playing cricket for the love of it enjoys his afternoon though he fails to score, while the professional on the same side, who scores a century, must be miserable since he is paid to do it.

We cannot go deeply into the question of how the cult of the amateur affects religion. It is clear that the country parson of the Church of England is regarded as an amateur and a gentleman, whereas the minister of a non-conformist chapel, Methodist, Baptist, Congregationalist, is hardly a gentleman at all. It is possible that this is because the parson does not take his business of cure of souls very seriously, while the other often goes methodically to work to save his congregation. The two are really like Mr. W. Smith and Smith (W); they belong to the same team, but they go from different doors, and for the same reason.

I am told that the attitude towards sport in America is different, and one reads frequently that professionalism is a curse in colleges and elsewhere. The cult of the professional in the wrong place may very well do for American sport what the opposite cult does in England. But the danger to sport in America seems to me not so much that some people may be paid for their services to a team, but that inevitably hypocrisy will find a way round any defense that can be put to safeguard the amateur status. Surely the only safety for sport in the modern world is to abolish therein the very idea of amateurism. To retain it is to court the same hypocrisy that comes from having the nations sign agreements not to use the most efficient weapons in wartime, but only to kill one another with out-of-date firing pieces and to maim with laughing gas rather than lethal. It is the cult of the amateur that makes sport crooked.

v

The cult of the amateur in the wrong place forces the Englishman to be uncomfortable, unhealthy, and even absurd in his sport and religion; because of it he takes not only his pleasures but his wife and home and God a little sadly. Farther than this, it affects his education, his business, and his political life.

In the last century the cult of the amateur was advantageous in all three activities: in education it preserved the timelessness of the Middle Ages amid the rapid change of the industrial revolution. Oxford and Cambridge, until the bombshell of August, 1914, were perfect places in which to let the hours go by. It is not surprising that post-war Americans, nauseated by the cult of professionalism, dream of transplanting Oxford to New England or Lake Michigan.

The amateur in business produced the Forsyte saga, a rigid combination of love of your work with business methods. The amateur in politics, with its happy warrior imperialists, its House of Commons as the best men's club in the world, its proconsuls and its philanthropist reformers, was in its way a very noble thing. It is perhaps regrettable that changing times have cast a gloom upon all three.

Take first of all the politician. Until the War, at least, England had nicely balanced the need for the amateur and the professional; statesmen and parliamentarians, who expected to gain nothing at all financially from their labors were backed by professional but incorruptible civil servants, who worked just as well under a socialist as under a conservative government. The spirit of the disinterested amateur inspired legislation and the spirit of proud professionalism loyally administered it, whatever the private opinion of the administrator upon party political issues. Behind it all was the theory that if a man had been educated at the right school, Eton, Harrow, Winchester, and had gone to the right college at Oxford or Cambridge he was by that reason fitted for politics. Moreover "right" in this context was defined by a scale of social values and involved no technical training of any sort.

Strangely enough, the theory worked even in the most unlikely cases. You sent a young man out to Africa and gave him fifty thousand square miles of territory to administer with no other white man near him, and he did it admirably. The natives recognized his amateur status and trusted him as a bulwark against the unscrupulous trader. There in the midst of swamps and fevers he would remain obsessed by only two emotions, desire to do his job perfectly and homesickness. Kipling was his Homer.

But now all that is gone. At home socialist members of Parliament have come to Westminster seeking not a club but a judgment seat. In the opinion of Dean Inge—who represents in our time the England which Dr. Johnson represented in the eighteenth century—it is a change for the worse. Abroad the natives seem to want to take upon their own shoulders the burden once accepted by the English amateur. Meanwhile, instead of problems taking a generation to mature and permitting men to be stupid about them for years without destroying civilization, vital matters come up needing to be solved overnight and requiring expert professional knowledge if they are to be solved aright. The amateur is distinctly out of place in the new politics; he can never get over the effect of his last great achievement, the Treaty of Versailles. Everybody agrees that the great political question of the day is the rival merits of a dictatorship of experts and a democracy of amateurs.

When we think that the cult of the amateur in politics has as its larger achievements the British Empire, the Balance of Power, the Entente Cordiale, and the Treaty of Versailles we are likely to be somewhat impatient of it. We shall do well, however, to remember that the cult of the professional in the wrong place in politics has done a good deal of harm in America and elsewhere.

I have been several times told by wealthy Americans that the reason why politics is corrupt in America is that "we are a young country and our men have been so busy building up the wealth of the country that they have not had time yet to turn to politics." There is in this, among other absurdities, the idea that politics is a job like selling bonds, only less lucrative and, therefore, to be left to less gifted men. That you should feel your politics much as you feel your being in love is not expected by the average American. Politicians are not supposed to be in politics for their health, and yet it might be better if everyone were in politics for his spiritual health. One feels sometimes, looking on from the outside, that at election time the electorate feel themselves voting for rival business firms which are expected to make money out of their job. Instead of voting for an attitude towards life, votes are cast as a contract might be given for delivering a million bathroom fittings.

It may seem curious that the cult of the amateur should have been allowed to play havoc with English business, and yet it has certainly had its effect even here. We have seen that the English waitress insists upon defending her amateur status by rationing her civility, but we may be inclined to regard this as a phenomenon of feminism rather than of national business methods. British business was built up in the first instance on a foundation of amateurism; the foreign trader's strong card was his being a gentleman. Jones built up his family "house" on his character and handed it on to his son. Now the amateur is of course an individualist, since personal taste is his chief guide, and Jones and Son regarded their individuality as the most important thing about them. Jones and Son as a business was worthwhile chiefly because it was not Robinson and Son which dealt in precisely the same market and in precisely the same way. All the mutual interests of the two businesses were as nothing to the really important fact that Jones could not possibly be Robinson and vice versa. And then there came an age where changing conditions meant that if the two gentlemen and their two sons were to survive economically they must lose their separate identities; they must amalgamate; they must become Jones and Robinson or even, worse still, Smith and Co. But by doing this the mainspring, the spirit of the amateur, would be thrown on the scrap heap; the Forsyte tradition discarded; and what would it profit the participants if they gained all the business in the world and lost their own private souls? Thus the cult of the amateur has prevented the adoption of new methods of business organization and aggravated the harm done by other adverse factors which England has had to face.

Abroad we see the same thing: two generations ago the "you can take it or leave it" attitude of the amateur in business was successful because there were few competitors and the things were good. Today nobody wants such good things and the competitors are implacably professional. Take, for example, the German in Spain and the Englishman in Spain. Hardly had I settled into my little mountain village to be an amateur undisturbed, when there came to my door a Spanish workman sent from a factory fifteen miles away to consult me. They had bought some expensive and, I expect, excellent machinery from England, but they could not use it, as all the instructions for setting it up were in English. Knowing as I did, that the typical Englishman's idea of how to translate his language into a foreign language is to shout it louder, I was not surprised; but I could not but compare the amateurism with the German efficiency. A German wishing to trade in Spain settles down, learns the language, and imitates the habits of the natives. Rather than segregate himself with his fellow-expatriates in a club, he will as like as not marry a Spanish wife. How can England hope to compete against such thoroughness? She can merely revenge herself with the contempt of an amateur for a professional.

VI

The cult of the amateur in the wrong place in England and the cult of the professional in the wrong place in America have brought the two countries to a precarious position, and it is not surprising that quite a number of their inhabitants long for escape from the tedium which they have caused. Taking a long view, we can see in them the starting point of a new period of nomadism, for I doubt whether either England or America, as communities, will ever rid themselves of such fundamental characteristics. The only way for the discontented individual to save himself is to migrate. And English and American will migrate in different directions. The Englishman wants to get back into the past where England was more amateur than she is now, the American to migrate into the future where professionalism, set on its legs again, will achieve even greater triumphs. And so the Englishman's escape from the machine age is to a country like Spain, which he will come to regard as simply a more amateur England; the American on the other hand will migrate to Russia where today one hundred per cent Americanism really flourishes. In Spain the Englishman will not have to do anything except what he likes doing; in Russia the American will find that nothing matters so long as you get it done.

At the moment we are suffering all the unpleasantness of a transition period wherein masses of people have reached a stage of discontent, but have not yet felt the intolerable urge to push on somewhere else. We try to stabilize ourselves at present by learning from the other; England murmurs gently about Ford and rationalization, America about Oxford and leisure and Mexico versus Middletown. But soon we shall come to ourselves, the rebel English will raise the standard of the amateur and push off into the past by way of Spain and such countries; the rebel Americans will return to the life of the frontier and the pioneer and recross the Atlantic to their new geographical abode in the Union of Socialist Soviet

Republics. When the rebels have gone, England and America will settle down in earnest to their curious pastime of imitating one another's vices and ignoring one another's virtues. The American will take from the amateur his polo and tall hats, his nonchalance and snobbery, and will retain his own professional politics and justice and his worship of work for work's sake. England will retain what America takes and take what America retains, and the result will be true hands across the sea and English-speaking unity.

It would, of course, be better for each country to accept the fact that it does certain things well and other things badly and to solve the problem by continuing to do what it does well and getting the other country to do the rest. Then we should have both the cult of the amateur and the cult of the professional, back in the right place; but the chance of this happening is remote. We are more likely to wake up suddenly and find that while we have been thinking of all this, millions of our fellow-men through our inefficiency are starving and insisting upon being fed. And out of the turmoil will come a community fit neither for amateurs nor professionals but only for machines.

THE DANGER OF BEING A
GENTLEMAN

REFLECTIONS ON THE RULING CLASS OF ENGLAND

By *Harold J. Laski*

IT is the boast of England that the idea of being a gentleman is peculiar to her people, and I think there is solid substance in the boast. As an ideal, it has at least the supreme merit of simplicity. The gentleman is, rather than does; he maintains towards life an attitude of indifferent receptivity. He is interested in nothing in a professional way. He is allowed to cultivate hobbies, even eccentricities, but he must not practice a vocation. He must not concern himself with the sordid business of earning his living; and he must be able to show that, at least back to his grandfather, none of his near relations has ever been engaged in trade. It is desirable that he should have attended one of a limited number of schools, preferably Eton or Harrow; and it is practically essential that he should have been to Oxford or Cambridge. He must know how to ride and shoot and cast a fly. He should have relatives in the army and navy, and at least one connection in the diplomatic service. It is vital that he should belong to a club, urgent that he be a member of the Conservative Party, and desirable that his ideas should coincide with those of the *Morning Post*. An ability to endure the Riviera in the winter, and to make the round of English country houses from August to November is a valuable, though not an integral, part of his equipment.

These may be termed the foundations upon which the ultimate superstructure is raised. But there are certain emotional

From *Harper's Magazine*, August 1931; copyright, 1931, by Harper & Brothers. Used by special permission.

and intellectual penumbræ which should not go unemphasized. His favorite authors should be Surtees and Kipling. He should deprecate the moral elasticity of modern fiction. He should feel the fine sanity of Gilbert and Sullivan while he is alien to any profound concern about Beethoven or Mozart. He should know how to arrive late at the opera, and his feeling about the theater should be that a man wants to be amused there. A visit to Paris should leave him with a sense of pleasant proximity to sin, and he should be quite unable to speak intelligible French or German. He should play most games in some fashion and feel that their cultivation is the secret of national greatness; but he should play none so well that he is thereby distinguished from his fellows and he should be convinced that professionalism ruins the true spirit of sport. Under no circumstances can he be a teetotaler except upon medical grounds.

Certain other qualities are important. He should know nothing of political economy and less about how foreign countries are governed. He should equate bolshevism with original sin. While he should never be a freethinker, he should not be enthusiastic about religion; to be so is to run the risk of obtrusiveness. He should be properly conscious of the merits of Empire and feel that only the strong hand can maintain our prestige in the East. When he dines out he must be able either not to talk at all or to confine his conversation to that plane which indicates a full knowledge of the right gossip without being an index to a dangerous profundity in any special theme. He must feel that America is passionately materialist; but if he marries an American he must take care to ally himself only with those properly endowed families who are received into the best London houses. He may be good at gardening. He may become a director of a company, provided he is not too well informed about its business. He must find speech difficult, and eloquence impossible. He must feel intensely the moral beauty of good form; and he must recognize that to wear, for instance, a black tie with a tail coat in the evening is proof (unless one is a head waiter) of a debased origin which cannot be outgrown. If, finally, he travels he must return without having suffered the deformation of a broader mind.

There are great qualities in the English gentleman which must not be overlooked. He believes with ardor in playing the game with those of his own status. He has the habit of graceful command. Save to Indians, Socialists, trade union organizers and poachers, he is almost uniformly tolerant. He is invariably courageous and, to women of his own class, chivalrous and deferential. He rarely parades his vices and he has a horror of ostentatious virtue. If he forgets to pay his tailor, he is always punctual with gambling debts. He profoundly respects the Royal Family (of whose failings he breathes no word in public), and bishops, and those Ministers of the Crown who belong to his own party. He rarely pushes a claim too far and he is too intellectually humble to take long-term views. If he grumbles much, at least he can laugh at himself; and no one is so apt to extricate himself skilfully from a dangerous situation. He enjoys the exercise of power; and since he rarely knows how to make money, it is still more rare for him to be corrupted by it. Having, in general, received a classical education, he has, like Shakespeare, as a rule, small Latin and less Greek.

He is the type by whom, with the aid of the lawyer, England has been governed until the last half-dozen years; it is only since the War that his supremacy has been seriously threatened. For the greatest event in English history was the fact that we have had no revolution in the modern time. Our social structure has remained largely unchanged since at least the middle of the eighteenth century; and a people with a genius for deference has preserved almost entirely the allotted privileges of leisure and of station. Your average Englishman still admires the class which does not have to earn its living; he feels safe and respectable in its hands. He may have doubted Lord Rosebery when he published a book; but he admitted his title to the Premiership when he won the Derby. Between a self-made Welshman like Mr. Lloyd George and a squire whose mind, like that of Mr. Henry Chaplin, is unstained by thought, the Englishman has seldom hesitated to choose the latter type. The workingman rarely respects his master; it is rare for him not to respect the peer who lives by owning. The employer may like the individual worker but, in the mass, he is convinced of his unfitness to govern; free trade apart, therefore, all his natural aspirations tempt him to look upwards to the class which represents past tradition and the glamour of high estate. Since the gentleman has always realized how much his power depends on the prosperity of business, the alliance between them has been mutual; and intermarriage with the more eminent of the business community has always persuaded the latter that the preservation of the gentleman is his own best safeguard. And the gentleman's tenacious hold of power has given him something like an instinctive knowledge of when compromise and concession are desirable. However much he may have opposed the wants of other classes, he has never so far challenged them as to threaten his own security. His genius for compromise and his capacity for absorption have given him control for two hundred years of English destiny.

II

The condition upon which he maintained his supremacy was simple enough. For a century after the Industrial Revolution, England's commercial leadership was unchallenged. The state was largely a negative state, and there were neither grave economic nor grave international problems to solve. The prosperity of the upper and middle classes was solid and ample and, save for the brief moment of the Chartist Movement, the rights of private property were never in serious question. England was in a position to afford government by gentlemen. No one had, in politics at least, to take long views; and the main questions in issue did not seem to require any complicated or technical *expertise*. Just enough national education to produce the foreman who could read and write; just a high enough level of national health to prevent the recurrence of

cholera and typhus; a well-advertised charity to meet the
wants of the really deserving unemployed—upon these foundations Englishmen might well feel that their lines were fallen in
pleasant places. Political economists proved to demonstration that the more exuberant hopes of the working class were
impossible of fulfilment; and the capitalist had the satisfaction
of knowing that his abstinence made him the effective author
of the prosperity which was the wonder of the world.

In that epoch, indeed, the gentleman imposed himself upon
civilization. No one in England seriously challenged his right
to leadership; and English domination of foreign markets
made his habits the example upon which the leisured class of
every other state sought to model itself. All the best people
used English materials; and their solidity and workmanship
gave them an unquestioned title to pre-eminence. The gentleman's conquests were unending. He made it the right thing to
go to the Riviera, to Switzerland, to Egypt. His picture
galleries formed the basis of future American triumphs. He
made the world mad on golf and tennis; he invented the week-
end; he showed how to polish the rough edges of business enterprise by casting the kindly eye of patronage upon the more
expensive fine arts. To the theory that a little learning is a
dangerous thing, he invented the reply (which England, at
least, accepted) that much learning is ungainly, and in any
case drives men mad. He made Wimbledon and St. Andrew's
into international cathedrals; while fashionable women of all
countries went to St. James's and Ascot as a Mahometan might
go to Mecca. Until, at any rate, the outbreak of the War, the
gentleman had persuaded the world to believe that he was the
final term of human evolution.

Men, of course, there always have been who doubted the
hypothesis; but they have been too few in number to affect
the argument. One has only to read the letters of Ambassador
Page to see how a distinguished American could fall, even in
middle age, beneath the gentleman's spell. One had only to
meet Lord Balfour to appreciate the exquisite artistry of the

type. One might resent Lord Curzon's superb insolence; at least it was impossible to deny that so imperial a manner was obviously born to rule. And those who doubted were, after all, for the most part unsuccessful men—exiled scholars like Marx, dyspeptic prophets like Carlyle, thin-lipped and poverty-stricken agitators like Philip Snowden, poetic craftsmen like William Morris. Who listened in America to Debs or Henry Demarest Lloyd while the gilded age was coming to maturity?

There is, in fact, little evidence that before the War Englishmen, at least, questioned the title of the gentleman to lead them. There were passing waves of unrest; but, in general, the sense of security was sufficiently widespread for so careful an observer as President Lowell to report that the British Labor Party was destined to remain a mere wing of Liberalism. The gentlemen of England had made her what she was; not merely Waterloo was won upon the playing fields of Eton. The traditions they embodied saved England from the materialism of America. They prevented her from seeming, like the new industrial Germany, a nation of *nouveaux riches*. Her tolerance permitted wide dissidence of opinion. Her social experiments showed the amazing adaptability of her ideas. The War proved not only that her gentlemen knew how to die; the solidity of her credit in crisis showed that she had absorbed the best lessons of bourgeois economy. Matthew Arnold's plea that England needed to temper her gentlemanly tradition by a dose of social equality seemed largely falsified, at least to the gentlemen themselves, by the victory of 1918.

III

Yet it may be predicted with some certainty that the historian of England in the last century will be largely occupied in explaining the dangers of being a gentleman. For no small part of the present difficulties of England are the outcome of his leadership. He has been the model to imitate, the example to follow. His habits, his tastes, his way of life have determined the conduct of all save a small handful of insurgent Englishmen. Broadly speaking, his philosophy has been a refusal to think in terms of principle. Do not be forehanded. Meet the day's problems as they arise. Make your ideal of life one in which there is neither excessive effort of intelligence nor undue ardor of emotion. Follow your own bent and assume that the world will adjust itself to your requirements. Be suspicious of the thinker and skeptical of the man who dwells upon the heights. Be so certain of yourself that your code of behavior is imposed as a universal. Never doubt your superiority over other people. Never show yourself so ardent in pursuit of an object as to convince the foreigner that you may be pained by failure to attain it. Take life as a game in which excessive seriousness is fatal to the spirit of play. Never be driven by a purpose so as to be its slave; thereby, like Robert Owen and Bentham, Clarkson and Plimsoll, you may become a bore to other people. Remember that manners and tradition give to life that dignified emollience without which it loses half its savor. Be sure that in every sort of conflict the rules (which you must take care to make) are more important than the victory. Never allow the unpleasant to obtrude. Do not discuss inconvenient truths if there is danger that they may give offense.

The roots of this attitude are historically clear. They result from the mingling of the aristocratic ideal of chivalry with the Puritan notions of the successful middle class. In it all, the predominance of the aristocracy is obvious, for the main objective of the successful middle class in England has always been alliance with the aristocracy. And let it be said that the attitude, as it has worked, has always possessed a certain mature graciousness. It has imposed itself without conveying an undue sense of domination. It has won allegiance from its inferiors without excessive strain. It has been kindly, it has had a sense of obligation, there has been about it a certain shrewd worldly wisdom which it is impossible not to admire. With something like the grand manner, the English gentleman keeps his word. He can administer with less bureaucratic irritation than any other type I have known. He can arbitrate commercial or international differences with the same fine equity that he umpires a cricket match. Once he has won, it is difficult for him (as the General Strike and the War made clear) to bear a grudge. He does not like to see the weak and the helpless go unnecessarily to the wall.

But the problem is not the virtues of the type so much as its adequacy for its function; and it is here that grave difficulties begin to arise. For there is no field of activity in the modern world in which the amateur, however benevolent, can retain his function as leader without risking the survival of those who depend upon him. The gentleman's characteristics are a public danger in all matters where quantitative knowledge, unremitting effort, vivid imagination, organized planning are concerned. How can the English gentleman govern India when he starts from the assumption that the Indian is permanently his inferior? How can he measure the strength of Russia in 1914 when Sir George Buchanan, his Ambassador there, does not even think it necessary to learn the language of the people to which he is accredited? How can he prevent the rise of the Labor Party when England is divided, as Disraeli said, into those two nations of rich and poor neither of which has effective acquaintance with the other's life? How can his aristocracy breed great soldiers when a large part of the officer's life in a crack regiment is passed not in professional study, but in the fulfilment of traditional social obligations?

The general theme admits of innumerable illustrations. Here, as I think, its implications can best be shown by tracing its results in three entirely disparate realms. Of these, perhaps industry is the most important, as also the most obvious. It is significant that foreign challenge to English industrial supremacy became effective at the moment when the alliance between the aristocracy and the middle class became an essential feature of English life. The main defects of British enterprise have been exactly those most characteristic of the gentleman. A refusal to consider adequately the wants of the customer; he must buy not the thing he desires but the thing you have to sell. An inadequate attention to technological development; the scientist in industry ought not to have the weight of the practical man. A disbelief in the necessity of large-scale production in the modern world; just as the gentleman would rather lose his income than his uniqueness. A passionate devotion to excessive secrecy both in finance and method of production; so the gentleman must live his own life in his own way without counsel or interference from outside. An incurable and widespread nepotism in appointment; so the gentleman has always been loyal to his relatives without undue regard for their fitness for the posts to which he has called them. This enables you, further, to discount ability and to rely upon a mystic entity called "character," which means, in a gentleman's mouth, the qualities he traditionally possesses himself. A refusal to be absorbed by one's business activities; so Saturday afternoon becomes gradually a holiday which extends from Friday until Monday, with golf on weekdays, a fortnight at Christmas in Nice, and a conspicuous expenditure which satisfies the craving for social prestige; so the business man comes to think that by adopting the *mores* of the gentleman he may be regarded as free from the taint of trade. If his business becomes a limited company he may invite a couple of needy aristocrats on to the Board of Directors and thus find a side door into society. As he grows more wealthy he may send his son to a public school, there, in all probability, to acquire the habits of mind which the born gentleman possesses by inheritance.

Or, in the second place, we may examine the history of the two traditional political parties in England. From the nineties of last century they were increasingly unable either to devise a program which should attract the working classes to their ranks, or to select from among proletarian leaders men who should represent them either in the House of Commons or the Cabinet. From the enfranchisement of the urban worker in 1867 until the close of the War, Liberals and Tories between them had never had a score of working-class supporters in the House; today neither has one. Mr. John Burns is the only workingman who has ever sat in a Cabinet not distinctively Labor in complexion. The reason of this inelasticity is simply absence of imagination; for many of the older leaders of the Labor Party today began as members of the traditional parties, and left them through the experience that there was no effective place in their counsels for men of a working-class origin and outlook. The gentleman, in fact, is prepared to broaden the basis of power; but he is willing to share the entrance to its inner citadel only with his friends. Neither Liberal nor Tory has known how satisfactorily to define the place of trade-unionism in the state. They have not, as Lord Haldane sorrowfully confessed, appreciated the real importance of a system of national education. They have never really sought to democratize either the army or the navy; the officer class in each has been carefully preserved for those who were fortunate in the choice of their parents. Right down to the close of the War, the diplomatic service was preserved also as what John Bright called the "outdoor relief department" of the British aristocracy. So, too, the legal and episcopal Benches have been rigidly confined to members of the upper middle class and the aristocracy. Even a Labor government finds it difficult to appoint working men and women to the unpaid magistracy.

The political failure of the gentleman, in a word, is that he had not the imagination to perceive that the inevitable accompaniment of political democracy would be the demand for social equality. In any case, he did not believe in it; and even the weak Labor government of 1924 seemed to him something like a convulsion of nature. Just as he could never bring himself to believe that brown men or yellow men might resent white control, so he could not convince himself that poverty might give rise to claims. The rich and the well-born had always governed and they were strongly allied. To him it was intolerable pretension that people like Ramsay MacDonald or

Arthur Henderson should claim an equal share in the disposition of the state. Like Mr. Churchill, they could not believe in Labor's fitness to govern. They were the victors in the battle of life; and it was part of the rules of the game that to the victors should belong the spoils.

The result on English politics is decisive. The gentleman's lack of imagination, the narrowness of his social loyalties, has ranged against him one of the fundamental estates of the realm. Even today he does not know why. For him the workers have been misled by wicked agitators whose ideas are probably inspired by Russia. He, the leisured and secure, thinks that the workingman has been pampered into disobedience against his masters by reckless social legislation. He believes that there is too much education abroad, and that the natural loyalty of his inferiors has been unsettled by training above their station. He is incapable of that imaginative realism which admits that this is a new world to which he must adjust himself and his institutions, that every privilege he formerly took as of right he can now attain only by offering proof that it is directly relevant to social welfare. He has no sense that the urge of the common people to expansion is one with which he must come to terms. His heart is in the old world; and because he is utterly unconversant with life as it exists for the vast majority, he cannot adjust himself to the new. The gentleman in the presence of modern democracy is as bewildered as Pilate before the spectacle of Christianity.

Another consequence of his influence has peculiar significance in England. As a people, said Bagehot, the English have a genius for deference; by which, I take it, he meant that they know their betters when they see them. One of the results, certainly, of governance by gentlemen has been a curious humility in the average Englishman which has the most complex ramifications. It affects even the Labor Party, many of whose members assume that the battle of social justice has been won because they dine at the great houses. For them the appearance of a man like Sir Oswald Mosley in the ranks

of Labor has a significance of distinction which far outweighs
the socialism of Mr. Shaw or Mr. Wells. They assume that a
gentleman who throws in his lot with them is entitled to the
reward of office. They are anxious themselves to show that
they can act and think as gentlemen do. They maintain all
the panoply of a court; they appoint only aristocrats to the
posts which aristocrats traditionally occupy. A people, in
brief, which has been ruled by gentlemen is more timid in
affirming its own essence than one which has been accustomed
to the self-exercise of power. That is why there is so much less
servility in France and America than in England. That is
why the eminent English man of letters is proud to be selected
as poet laureate and to accept social recognition from the
great families. That is why the *Times* will print a letter, however absurd, from a duke in large type, and one, however important, from the secretary of the Trade Union Congress, in
small. That is why, also, the births, marriages, and deaths of
even the remotest members of the Royal Family cast light and
shadow upon every home in England, why the coming of age
of a great gentleman like the Duke of Norfolk, of whose character and intelligence nothing is known, is almost a national
event, and the fit subject of leading articles in the press.

Foreign observers, Dibelius, for example, have severely
criticized this English snobbery and argued that it shows how
complete is the lack in England of a democratic spirit. But
this is to take too superficial a view. English snobbery is a
collective inferiority complex. It is the result of two hundred
years and more of instruction in the thesis that only the gentleman is fit to govern. The distance between the workers and
their governors in wealth and refinement and access to distinction has been so vast as to seem to the majority an un-
bridgeable gulf. And most of the things in which, accordingly,
they have sought refuge—their grim Nonconformity, their
coarse pleasures, their narrow and confined homes—have done
little to develop elasticity of mind or that graceful skepticism
which enables man to question where he does not understand.

They have been limited in outlook because they have been limited in opportunity. Like most prisoners, they have grown accustomed to their chains; when they are struck off they are bewildered and act as though they were still bound.

The gentleman, in fact, has become a public danger to England because he is now merely a costly, if decorative, appendage to a civilization in which he has no longer a useful function to perform. He has never encouraged himself to use his imagination; and for our problems imaginative leadership is above all essential. He has never disciplined his intellect to organized analysis; and it is only from that scientific approach that authority can be maintained. His distractions have been so many, his luxuries so great, that he has become concerned rather to enjoy life than to master it. He has been too individualist to welcome organization and too self-confident to welcome ideas. Having been born to power, he does not know how to share it; having inherited unquestioned leadership, he does not know how to act so as to justify its retention. He has been so long unchallenged in his preëminence that rivalry tends, by its surprise, to embitter him. He has had so much certitude of temper that he is paralyzed by the new uncertainties. He has been so much accustomed to command that he feels it unnatural to be called upon to obey. His familiar landmarks are disappearing, and he thinks and acts like a sailor upon an uncharted sea. The prestige of his superiority has gone because the ideal of life he embodied no longer commands universal respect even among those of whom he was once the spoiled favorite. He has lost the basis of his self-esteem because he has no longer either a purpose to maintain or that conviction of its necessity which might give it life.

IV

Yet no one, I believe, will see the passing of the gentleman without a brief annotation of regret. In the period of his apogee, he was a better ruler than any of his possible rivals. I, at least, would rather have been governed by Lord Shaftesbury than Mr. Cobden, by the gentlemen of England than by the Gradgrinds and Bounderbys of Coketown. There was something picturesque about his thickheadedness, something monumental about his complacency. Compare him with the elegant trifler who was the gentleman of the *ancien régime*, or the rigid disciplinarian whom the German aristocracy provided, and he shines in the comparison. He was often capable of the generous gesture, he was frequently tolerant, there could be about him a fine quixotism it was difficult not to admire. He threw up odd men of genius like Byron and Henry Cavendish, statesmen of public spirit like Lord John Russell and Hartington; he would found great public galleries and establish the British Museum. He was very costly, and, in the mass, depressing and dull. Yet, through it all, he always had the saving grace of a sense of humor.

Nor is it certain that we shall replace him by a more admirable type. The new Renaissance bravo like Mussolini, the new Jesuit writ large like Stalin, those new plutocrats of whom Mr. Barron's *Diary* has been giving us so striking, because so innocent, a picture; are we certain that these represent a change for the better? The leader of the future seems not unlikely to be the remorseless one-idea'd man, who governs us by hewing his way to his goal. He has no time for the open mind. He takes clemency for weakness and difference of opinion for crime. He has a horror of a various civilization and he means by freedom only a stronger kind of chain. Where we would be peaceful, he calls us to the affirmation of power. For the music of idle dreams he offers us the relentless hum of giant machines. The majesty of the forest is, for him, the volume of a timber supply, the rush of waters in the river, the source of electric power. The gentleman scourged us with whips. We must beware lest our new masters drive us to our toil with scorpions.

AN ENGLISH VIEW OF PERSONAL RIGHTS

By *Geoffrey Layman*

Fining a butcher 40s. at Tottenham for keeping his shop open after the hour of 8 p.m. [he served five customers between 8.08 and 8.15], Mr. Lewin, the magistrate, remarked: "You cannot do as you like these days. No one can. As long as Dora is in existence you will have to comply with the order."—London Evening Standard, *June 27, 1929.*

AS I write, a General Election in Great Britain has just swept from power, by a quite unmistakable expression of the popular will, a Conservative Government which, with the exception of the short period of a few months of minority Labor Government in 1923, had been in power, either alone or in coalition, since 1916, and during the last five years had enjoyed one of the greatest Parliamentary majorities in our history. Many and various explanations have been put forward for this surprising and largely unexpected reversal of fortune; but it is almost universally agreed that among the causes of it was the fact that the Conservative Government, traditionally in favor of the freedom of the individual from governmental control, had failed to repeal the last remnants of the wartime restrictions on personal liberty. It is, I think, a fair statement that the coming into power of the Macdonald Government, with all the profound effects which that event may have on international relations, and especially on the relations between Great Britain and America, is due at least as much to the resentment of the average Englishman at being prevented from buying a packet of cigarettes after eight o'clock P.M. as to any widespread discontent with the foreign policy of the late Government.

Yet the reader who would deduce from this statement that

the English, as a nation, are naturally intolerant of the restraint of law would be surprisingly wide of the mark. On the contrary no nation, not even the German, is more law-abiding than the English. Not only does the individual obey the law, but he supports the authorities in enforcing obedience on his neighbor. The ratio of crimes to population is amazingly low, and the ratio of convictions to crimes amazingly high. Not only is the criminal class in England small, and, to judge by the latest criminal statistics, diminishing, but the criminal himself shares with his more respectable neighbors the law-abiding instincts of the race. The safe-breaker, surprised in the midst of his nefarious operations by the solitary policeman on his beat, may in nine cases out of ten be expected to "go quietly." He is himself unarmed, and he knows that the policeman is unarmed, except for a "truncheon," or club, so carefully concealed that I, the average citizen, have never even seen one in the hands or anywhere about the person of a policeman, although I know that it is there. There is a recognized etiquette in these matters. If the safe-breaker or burglar can finish his job and get away unseen, the trick is his; but if he is so clumsy as to allow the policeman to come upon him unawares, he murmurs "it's a fair cop, gov'ner" and submits. No English policeman, unless he is on plain-clothes escort duty, or on some very rare occasion when there is strong probability that he will be met, almost certainly by aliens, with violent and murderous resistance, is ever armed with any weapon more lethal than a truncheon; and it is very rarely, and usually only in street rows, that he has occasion to use even that. He has no need for anything more. Very occasionally, after some sensational shooting case in which a policeman has been injured or killed, there is a demand from the public, or rather from the press, that the police should be armed; and the first to resist the proposal are the chief officers of police themselves, who fear that if the police carry arms, the criminal may begin to do so also—that the criminal, in fact, may cease to be as law-abiding as he is at present.

But if even our criminals are law-abiding, how does it happen that we are so intolerant of restraint that even such a mild restriction on liberty as the prohibition of the sale of cigarettes after eight o'clock P.M. should produce, or at least contribute to, so great an electoral revolution as that which has just taken place? How can we reconcile in the same people, on the one hand, an extreme respect for the law and, on the other, an extreme impatience at even the mildest encroachment by the law on what we regard as the right of the individual citizen to personal liberty of action? Are not law and authority almost synonymous, and how can one and the same man be so patient of the law and so impatient of authority? What is the fundamental difference in outlook between the German and the Englishman—both highly law-abiding peoples—which makes the one placidly content under a multiplicity of *verbotens* which would drive the other to almost instant rebellion?

II

The explanation of this apparent inconsistency is, I think, to be found in the English conception of the rights of the individual against the State, on the one hand, and of his duties towards the State, on the other, which has grown up through many generations of comparatively ordered government, and has long ago changed from a personal and conscious belief common to a number of individuals to an unconscious and communal instinct inborn in the nation.

The idea of democracy in the true sense of the word—government of the people by the people for the people—came to birth from the marriage of the Saxon and Norman stocks after the Conquest of 1066; and no other race save the new English race which emerged from that marriage in the twelfth and thirteenth centuries, and which four hundred years later began to people the great new Continent of the West, has ever really understood what democracy means—what privileges it offers and what services it demands. The so-called democratic governments of the Greek States and of Rome were in reality narrow oligarchies in which all power and all privilege rested with the free, who were as a rule outnumbered by those of their own race and blood who were not free; and they tended constantly to degenerate into tyrannies as oppressive as any in history. The Latin republics—even the French—are neither stable nor in any true sense of the word democracies. But the original ungoverned and ungovernable passion for freedom which split Saxon England into petty kingships was never wholly crushed by the Norman domination; and in the new race it was tempered by the Norman love of order, of duty, and of efficiency. Magna Carta was not solely a charter of liberties; it was also an avowal of duties; but it was above all a recognition that the one depended on the other. That recognition survived the Angevin and Plantagenet and Tudor and Stuart autocracies; it was carried across the Atlantic in 1620 and by every shipload of emigrants since then; it gave to the rebellions of 1642 and 1688 their keynote of ordered liberty; it fashioned the Constitution of the United States of America just as it shaped the Constitutional Monarchy in Great Britain, and has given birth to free governments in the British Dominions; and now in this generation we can recognize its force in the cheerfulness with which we submitted to unheard of restrictions and deprivations in time of war, and in the impatience with which we endeavor to throw them off in time of peace. But is there in that impatience a note of petulance? Are there not signs, both in Great Britain and in America, that the insistence on personal freedom has obscured the dependence of freedom on duty, and that the demand for "liberty" is beginning to mean a demand that everyone shall be allowed to do as he pleases regardless of the rights of others? And if, on the one hand, freedom is degenerating into license, is there not room for fear that, on the other hand, in the growing complexity of our social and national life, both here and in the States, the machinery of government is beginning to overwhelm the people for whom and by whom it should be operated?

III

America I know only in books. England I live in; as a citizen I am governed, as a voter I help to govern, and as a civil servant I am part of the machinery of government. How much of true democracy, of that sense of the interdependence of freedom and obligation to which I have referred, survives in England today?

I have already alluded at the beginning of this paper to one manifestation of the strength of that real democracy which prevails, I think, as strongly in England today as it has ever done. The English are fundamentally law-abiding; and they are law-abiding not because they fear the law and the power which lies behind the law, not because, as seems to be the case with the Germans, they are naturally submissive and have a genuine liking for being ordered about, but precisely because the passion for personal liberty is still strong and it is instinctively recognized that liberty can be made secure only in a society in which the reign of law is as nearly absolute as is possible. Law, it is true, manifests itself in a series of prohibitions, that is to say, in a series of restrictions on the power of the individual to do as he pleases. But if every individual is allowed to do as he pleases, it is quite certain that his wishes and desires will come into frequent and violent conflict with the wishes and desires of his neighbors, and that, while perhaps a certain number of the strongest will enjoy complete license, the great bulk of the population will suffer grievous infringements of their personal liberty.

All this, of course, is the most obvious and elementary of truisms; but there are many truisms to which lip-service only is paid, and that law preserves freedom is one of them. It is a peculiarity of the English stock and of its derivatives throughout the world—a peculiarity derived from the coalescence in one race of the Anglo-Saxon passion for freedom with the Norman passion for order—that they not only pay lip-service to this truism but that they instinctively react to it in their daily life. England is the only country in Europe, except Scotland, in which the jury system works at all tolerably well. Any English jury of twelve men and women picked, as it were, out of a hatful represents with extraordinary fidelity the average Englishman, and that is why it is very rare for either the defense or the prosecution to challenge a juryman; nothing is to be gained by securing the removal of one man or woman from the panel to have him or her at once replaced by another who, so far as his conception of the duty which he is called upon to perform is concerned, is as like his predecessor as one pea to another. And such a jury, quickly formed, may be counted on with absolute certainty to return a verdict based on the facts and on the law and on nothing else. The practice of making sentimental appeals to the sympathies of the jury, of reminding them of the prisoner's mother and of his wife and little children, still prevalent for example in Ireland, has long ago wholly died out in England because it is wholly ineffective. If the jury believe that the prisoner has done what he is accused of having done, and if the act which he has done is contrary to the law as explained to them by the judge, they will convict him however extenuating the circumstances and however numerous and hungry his family. It is not that the average Englishman is, in this respect at any rate, particularly self-righteous or vindictive or fearful; it is simply that he instinctively recognizes that theft or murder are infringements upon that measure of personal right—security of property and security of person—that the State is bound to secure for him and for all his fellow-citizens, and that the fact that the thief or murderer was hungry or jealous does not make his act any the less an infringement upon the personal rights of his victim. We are, contrary to one of our most cherished beliefs, a highly sentimental race; but in this matter no appeal to our sentiment or our sympathy is able to detach us from our determination to secure as far as possible that no individual, however strong his temptation, shall be allowed to infringe upon the personal rights of his neighbors.

IV

So far then as the actual administration of the law is concerned, I see no signs that the post-war England of today is losing any of its traditional determination that the personal rights of the individual citizen shall be secured against any infringement by other individuals—its instinctive recognition that the law-breaker is not merely attacking an abstraction called the State, but is a menace to each of the individuals who constitute the State. That instinctive recognition is well illustrated in the position which the policeman occupies in our social organization, and in the respect, affection, and support which he enjoys.

The position of the policeman in England—I do not know whether it is different in America—is fundamentally distinct from that of the soldier. The soldier is a servant of the Crown, and as such is at the disposal of the central executive authority; the policeman is a representative of the people, and as such is at the disposal of the local authority—the Borough Council or the County Council, as the case may be. It is true that the Crown has now become an expression of the people's will, so that a servant of the Crown is as such a servant of the people; but, nevertheless, the distinction between the soldier and the policeman remains a real distinction. The policeman, in our theory, is an ordinary citizen, one of ourselves, with very few powers other than those which every citizen possesses. It is the natural duty of every citizen to prevent wrong-doing when he sees it, and to join with his fellow-citizens in the maintenance of public order. But as, in the modern State, it is more convenient that a certain number of the citizens should be primarily charged with this duty as the representatives of the whole body of citizens, and should for this purpose be relieved from the necessity of doing other work for their living, we pay some of our neighbors to keep the wrong-doer in check and to help us by controlling the traffic and assisting in the prevention of fires and other accidents. But we do not regard this as relieving the rest of us of the obligation to assist in securing these objects. That obligation devolves on the policeman first, but not on the policeman alone, and in the absence of the police or in the event of the police being overpowered, the obligation rests as fully upon the ordinary citizen as upon the police. The citizen who fails to come to the assistance of the police when called upon to do so commits an offense, and convictions and penalties for that offense regularly occur. On the other hand, we never allow the policeman to forget that he does not represent any authority external to ourselves, but is merely our own representative. The powers which he possesses other than those possessed by the ordinary citizen are very limited. The policeman in England who killed a man otherwise than strictly in self-defense—who killed for example a prisoner who was attempting to escape—would certainly be convicted of murder and would quite probably be hanged, just as would the citizen who shot at and killed a burglar whom he found escaping out of the window. And on the rare occasions when it has been necessary to call in troops to assist the police, the soldier likewise acts not as a soldier but as a citizen—a citizen who conveniently happens to be armed and organized and is, therefore, better able than his unarmed and unorganized fellow-citizens to carry out the citizen's duty of preserving public order. The soldier, in such circumstances, acts only at the request of the civil magistrate conveyed to him through his officer, and he is in no way absolved from the citizen's obligation to obey the law. He may fire, at his officer's command, if it is clear that firing is necessary to preserve life or to prevent riot and destruction; but if the firing is held to have had no such justification, the fact that it was done at the command of his superior officer will be no answer, although it may be a palliation, to a charge of murder brought against the private soldier.

The policeman, then, in carrying out on behalf of the whole body of citizens the citizen's duty of preserving order in the community is regarded as the representative, not of any external authority, but of his fellow-citizens, and as such he is entitled to expect the support and respect of those whom he represents. And he still gets that support and respect to a very great—even to a surprising—extent. Surprising, because in the days, not so very long ago, when the State was an infinitely less complicated organism than it is today, when the laws were comparatively few and the reasons for them correspondingly obvious, it was easy enough for the ordinary citizen to recognize that the policeman was a friend rather than an enemy, and it was not difficult for the policeman to appreciate that his authority was derived not from "the Government" —some abstract power superior to the mass of individuals constituting the State—but from those individuals themselves. Now that the State has become a vast and growing machine, the intricacies of which the average citizen does not attempt to comprehend, the recognition by the citizen that the policeman is his friend, and the appreciation by the policeman that his employer is the citizen, have become less easy. There is in this growing complexity of the State machine a real danger that the State itself may cease to be regarded as consisting merely of the aggregate of its citizens, bound together for mutual protection and assistance and, therefore, an institution entitled to their support and respect, and may come to be looked upon, and to regard itself, as a power deriving its authority from some source other than the combined will of its individual citizens and entitled, in the interests of its own perfection, to encroach upon their liberties. If and when that happens in England, the Englishman will cease to be a law-abiding person.

V

It was, I think, the fear that this was happening, that the State, or the Government, was beginning to impose regulations for the sake of imposing them (for to retain a regulation is the same as to impose it) and thereby to encroach upon the Englishman's traditional right to conduct his own life in his own way provided that he pays due regard to his neighbor's right to do likewise, that led, or at any rate contributed, to the revolt against the late Government in the recent General Election which I have already mentioned at the beginning of this article. It so happened that that Government was a Conservative Government, and in its traditional regard for the rights of the individual, if in no other respect, the Conservative Party, more nearly than any other, represents the average Englishman: its fault on this occasion was not that it was Conservative but that it was the Government.

The Act under which, during the War, the Government was empowered to impose various regulations and restrictions upon the liberty of the individual, on his right to buy and sell what he likes when he likes, to eat and drink what he can afford, to drive his car as far and as often as he pleases, to regard his home as his castle, and to be tried, if he offends, by a jury of his peers, was called the Defense of the Realm Act. It was not long before the Man in the Street christened it, from its initials, Dora, and the cartoonists gave to Dora a personality befitting her name, that of an elderly spinster with a prying nose and gleaming spectacles, looking through keyholes to see what the plain citizen was doing and telling him not to. Under Dora the Government (which, in wartime, is equivalent to the Army and the Civil Service) could make pretty well any regulations they pleased without the tiresome necessity of having to obtain the approval of Parliament; and the regulations they made were very numerous, and their bearing on the great object of winning the War not always very clear. But we recognized that we were living at a crisis of our history. The more we were harried by prohibitions and restrictions the more we felt that we were contributing to the great cause of Victory. We hugged our chains to our breasts, but with a mental reservation that the moment the War was over we would demand our freedom again or know the reason why.

Then came the Armistice, and we were told that, having won the War, we had now to win the Peace. For a time our burdens were even increased, but we recognized that the age was out of joint and were patient. By degrees the more obvious encroachments on our liberty were withdrawn; but we still felt and resented the supervision of Dora. Many of the wartime regulations which had proved in practice to be beneficial and unoppressive were converted into laws and made permanent. No one any longer may disturb the peace of a whole street by whistling shrilly for a taxi at any hour of the day or night, but then no one feels any the worse for not being allowed to do so. (The bearing of a regulation prohibiting whistling for cabs on the winning of the War is not perhaps very obvious; but it was made in the interests of the wounded who lay in innumerable makeshift hospitals in London and other big cities, where they could obtain the services of the best surgeons until they were fit to be sent to the country to convalesce, and thence back, in those evil days, to fight once more.) No one may carry or possess a firearm without a permit from the police, but no one wants to.

But in addition to the many regulations thus made permanent which everyone regarded as reasonable were others the reasonableness of which was not so obvious; and of these the most prominent, and those which impinged most on the daily life of the average citizen, were those relating to the sale of goods after eight o'clock. The universal early closing of shops during the War, when enemy aircraft were liable to visit us at any time during the night and the energies of every man and woman were required during the day for the national business, was reasonable enough; but, why the devil, said the plain citizen to his neighbor, now that peace is here, shouldn't I be allowed to buy a packet of cigarettes after eight o'clock if I want to buy it and the other fellow wants to sell it to me? The justification for the law, no doubt, lay in the interests of the whole class of shop assistants, for whom it has secured a reasonable day's work in place of the fourteen- or even sixteen-hour day which was often demanded of them before the War; and if shops which have assistants are compelled to close, then in fairness those which have none and are run by the proprietor himself must also close. But this argument for making the little shop round the corner close at eight, when its proprietor asked for nothing better than to be left in peace to sit in his shirt-sleeves behind his counter and chat to his customers till midnight, was too indirect for the plain citizen. The proprietor was deprived of the society of his neighbors, and the plain citizen who ran out of cigarettes after hours had to spend his evening without tobacco. Both of them regarded the law as a direct attack upon their liberties; and who shall say that they were wrong? Dora must go, they cried; and because they didn't know how to get rid of Dora, they got rid of the Government. It was a plain warning that the Englishman doesn't like *verbotens* the reason for which he can't see. It will be interesting —and not unamusing to the detached observer—to see what the Labor Government is going to do about it.

VI

The truth of the matter is that the Englishman demands of a law not only that it shall be a good law in itself, but that it shall command general assent. If you tell him that abstention from alcohol, except for medicinal and sacramental purposes, is a good thing, he will probably agree with you; but if you propose to make a law prohibiting the consumption and sale of alcoholic liquor, he will certainly vote against you, because he knows that even if he himself were prepared to obey the law, a very large number of his neighbors would seek to evade it, and he regards a law which is at all generally evaded as being for that reason alone a bad law. The Englishman believes in law, but he believes in it not as so many words printed on paper but as a code of conduct which, when he is called upon to assist the police or to serve on a jury, he is prepared to enforce upon his fellow-citizens by his own hands, if necessary, or by his own voice. If you go to a law library, you will find that the entire body of English Statutes in force, from the year 1235, when the Statutes of Merton. some of which are still operative, became law, down to the year 1929, occupies no more than seven feet or so of shelf-space; and of that perhaps a tenth has been repealed since 1900 when the last revision took place. Of the rest at least ninety per cent is not only the law, *but is enforced*, today. Public opinion in England instinctively recoils from the danger that, if laws are passed which do not truly represent the feeling of the man in the street for what is just and reasonable, and which, therefore, the man in the street will not assist in enforcing, either they will not be enforced, in which case the law as a whole will fall into disrespect, or, if they are enforced, a chasm will begin to open between the State and the people, between the police and the public, such as can be seen today in almost every country in Europe.

In two directions, fortunately comparatively unimportant, we can already see signs of the appearance of such a chasm—or perhaps we need only call it a crack—namely in relation to the laws on the subject of street betting and the motor speed limit. The fact that these laws are hopelessly out of touch with modern popular opinion is due not to the fact that they were freak laws when they were introduced—for they were not—but to the fact that circumstances have greatly changed since their introduction, and that they have not been repealed because no one is agreed what to put in their place. They are on the Statute Book and, therefore, they are enforced in so far as it is possible to enforce them. But the public, anxious and ready to assist the police, will not assist them in this. Every motorist, and even the pedestrian, will warn other motorists, if he can, of a speed trap, and every passerby will tell the street bookie's tout that "the Cop's coming round the corner." The evils of this state of affairs are two-fold: not only does it set the police and the public, who, in our view, always should, and as a rule do, work together, working against each other, but it lays the police, normally entirely free from corruption of any kind, open to a very strong temptation to take money for neglecting to enforce laws which they know the public will not blame them for failing to enforce.

VII

So far we have concerned ourselves solely with the enforcement of the actual law. There are, however, other rules of conduct—conventional, moral, religious—by which the behavior of the average man is affected, and which, though enforced by sanctions other than those of the law, command, or at least used to command, a respect and obedience not less universal than that which was given to the law. To what extent do the principles which still, it seems, hold good in the Englishman's reactions to the law hold good also in his reactions to these other rules of conduct?

In his conception of law the Englishman demands of it two things, which are really the same thing seen from different sides, that it shall respect as far as possible what he regards as the inalienable rights of the individual, and that it shall restrain the individual, himself included, from encroaching, in pursuit of the fulfilment of his own desires, on the rights of others: in short, that it shall secure to each individual as full a measure of personal freedom as is consistent with the securing of an equally full measure of personal freedom to every other individual. And as circumstances and conditions, the machinery of living and the structure of society, change, he adapts his laws to conform to those changes. But the adaptation of the laws tends to lag behind the changes which they are intended to meet, for the Englishman never likes to destroy anything unless he can see pretty clearly what he means to put in its place: which is one reason why the Communists and Bolshevists find him such poor material to work on.

We should expect to find these tendencies visible in the sphere of conventional conduct as they are visible in the sphere of legal conduct; and we should not, I think, be disappointed. In the ordering of so much of his life as does not affect his neighbors, the Englishman demands a fairly complete measure of freedom; he is not, on the whole, in any such matter a slave to convention. If it pleases him to have supper instead of dinner, he has supper. If he keeps a motor car, it is because it amuses him to do so and because he can afford it, and not because his neighbor has one. If he would rather read his paper in the train going to his work every morning than talk to his fellow-passengers, no one for that reason writes him down as stand-offish. In the Universities every variety of outlook, from Dadaism to the most complete snobbery, is tolerated and even respected. Above all, the Englishman claims to be entitled to his own political creed. He suffers singularly little, in this respect, from the tyranny of local public opinion; nevertheless, if you ask him how he voted at the last election he is as likely as not to tell you that the ballot, he believes, is supposed to be secret, and that if you'll mind your business, he'll mind his—a trait which makes the path of the political canvasser a hard one.

But in the matters in which his private life touches at all upon the life of the community, the case is different. English public opinion on the subject of marriage is a case in point. I gather from the American reviews that the revolt against marriage has gone to pretty considerable lengths in the States. In England not one per cent of the population has any idea that the excellence and value of the institution has ever been seriously questioned. It is not, I think, that the proportion of happy and successful marriages in the past has been any higher in England than in America, nor that we are any more subject to religious or moral or conventional taboos than you are— on the contrary I should venture to say that we are less subject to them. But the life of the community as at present organized is based on the institution of marriage, and not marriage alone, but a stable and permanent marriage in which divorce is, comparatively speaking, rare. And for that reason, until some other obvious and equally secure foundation for the social structure is found, the sense of the community, that civic instinct which is still very strong in England, repels almost unconsciously any idea of change in the status of marriage. I do not mean to suggest that the individual sufferer from an unhappy marriage who would like to get a divorce, or the undergraduate boy who would like to make an experiment in free love with an undergraduate girl, consciously says to himself that divorce, or free love, as the case may be, if widely practiced, would undermine the present structure of society, and that, therefore, he must abstain. Nothing so conscious as that, indeed nothing conscious at all, actuates him—the idea simply never enters his head. The individual citizen shares unconsciously the civic instinct.

VIII

In his article on "The Dangers of Obedience" in the June issue of *Harper's* Professor Laski spoke of the tendency in our modern civilization for the judgment of the individual to be swamped by the opinion of the mass. It was a timely warning, but a warning, I venture humbly to think, more needed in the States than in England. I have suggested in the earlier part of this paper the danger to liberty inherent in the rapid growth of the State machine; and in the State machine I should perhaps include the Press, even where, as in England and America, the Press is totally free from governmental influence or control. The influence exercised by the Press is comparable with that curious phenomenon of mob psychology whereby the passion or emotion of a crowd as a whole greatly exceeds the mere sum of the passions and emotions of the separate individuals who compose the crowd.

But, if it is possible for one who has never been in the States to judge from what he reads, the Englishman is less amenable than the American to this kind of influence. I find it impossible to imagine, for example, an English University swayed by the same kind of emotion as that which, I gather, takes possession of the souls and bodies of the members—students and faculty, undergraduates and alumni—of an American University on the eve of a great game or on certain solemn anniversaries. The Englishman, with very rare exceptions, is not capable of surrendering himself wholly to an idea. It is a negative quality which has its advantages as well as its defects: if we have produced very few great saints, we have produced a large number of admirable practical administrators. And just as the English are not easily swayed by communal passions or emotions, so also they are not particularly susceptible to the influence of the Press. A comparison of the circulation of the morning and evening papers (all of them with strongly expressed political convictions) and of the voting strength of the various parties which they support shows curious results. All the papers with the biggest circulation, one or other of which is read by at least ninety per cent of those who read a newspaper at all, are conservative. The Liberals have three or four papers of respectable circulation and great literary and cultural influence. Labor has one paper with a comparatively infinitesimal circulation. Yet at the recent election, at which over eighty-five per cent of the adult population voted, Labor cast the biggest vote.

The Englishman, in effect, regards his right to judge of everything for himself as one of the rights which he will in no circumstances surrender; and yet, oddly enough, his judgment, more often than not, is not a conscious but a subconscious process. He does not really judge for himself; his inherited instincts do it for him. We are not an intellectual race; we are not, I think, even a very intelligent race; but we have an unusually strong racial memory. Intellect and intelligence are qualities which can be dealt with: they can be convinced by logic or crushed into submission by tyranny. But logic has no effect on the unconscious cerebration which proceeds from generations of Saxon and Norman and English forbears, and tyranny merely drives it into revolt—the tyranny of kings into the revolts of 1642 and 1688, and the tyranny of a bureaucracy into the revolt of 1929.

It is because the Englishman's insistence on his personal rights is so largely instinctive that I doubt whether he is in any danger of being tricked or bludgeoned into foregoing it.

I have been reading over this article before sending it off, and have been a good deal struck with the note of rather smug self-satisfaction which pervades it. I am afraid that we English are very self-satisfied. I say "I am afraid," but I am not sure that I ought not to substitute "fortunately." For, infuriating as our self-satisfaction must be to others, it is undoubtedly advantageous to ourselves!

I have just had an opportunity of reading a letter from a distinguished Judge of the State of New York to an acquaintance of his, a New Zealander, who had written to him from England, where he was paying a visit. "What you say," says the Judge, "of the English lack of sociability, or rather aloofness, is most amusing. That however is not, if I have them right, what has tended to make them unpopular with the rest of the world outside of England. Shyness we all have in some measure, and we learn to see through it in others. The unpopularity of some Englishmen, regarded as typical though very likely not so at all, and not extended to Colonials, is due, as I size it up, to the material success of the Victorian era accompanied by a supposed feeling of superiority towards the rest of the world and a supposed hypocrisy involving the same thing. Thus if you analyze it, you will find the same elements, though accompanied by different phenomena, which seem to make Americans unpopular today. We are now, as the English were then, the greatest of creditors; we have, or some of us have no doubt, the bad manners of the rich, with the difference that our riches were more suddenly acquired, so perhaps some of the manifestations are more flagrant and objectionable. We too are accused of giving virtuous reasons for selfish designs. The interesting thing about human nature, as has been better said by many others, is that it is so much the same."

Whether there is any truth in what the Judge says of America I don't know. But it is certainly true that the English have the appearance, to foreigners, of being both unsociable and hypocritical; and as their apparent possession of these undesirable qualities has, I think, a bearing on the questions discussed in this paper, I venture to add this postscript.

The apparent unsociability of the Englishman arises, I believe, not from shyness nor (at any rate so far as his unsociability towards his own fellow-countrymen is concerned) from any sense of superiority. It is simply that he is an individualist, and that he regards himself, his personality, as a possession which he is not prepared to share with anyone except his family and his intimate friends. A conversational opening by a stranger in a railway carriage, and still more the somewhat intimate questions which he is liable to be asked by the New York reporter, embarrass him not because he is shy, but because he regards them as an intrusion upon his privacy and, therefore, almost, as it were, as an indecency. Consider the high walls and thickset hedges which we build round our gardens, and compare them with the wall-less and hedge-less gardens of the New York suburbs—there you have a good symbol of the difference which has grown up between our two peoples.

This insistence upon the security of his personal privacy is of a piece with the Englishman's insistence upon the security of his personal rights. He draws a sharp distinction between his public and his private life. His private life belongs to himself and to his family and intimate friends; and he deeply resents any intrusion upon it either by the State, in the person of the police or the bureaucrat, or by his fellow-men. In his public life, on the other hand, when he is acting in his capacity as a citizen as opposed to his capacity as an individual, he is prepared to recognize that the claims of the community must, if necessary, override his personal emotions and predilections— and that is why he makes such a good juryman, and turns out eighty-five per cent strong to vote at a general election.

As for the Englishman's alleged hypocrisy, this, I think, is an illustration of the large part which, as I have already suggested, the subconscious or instinctive plays in his mental make-up. Hypocrisy, as I understand the word, means *con-*

sciously making yourself out to be a better man than you are. Now the Englishman doesn't do that. He really and truly believes himself to be a much better man than anyone else! That belief is not based on any rational evidence—indeed there is much evidence to the contrary—but then in such matters as this he has no use for evidence; logic is not one of his strong suits. Indeed, his belief in his own superiority is hardly a belief at all, in as much as it is not a conscious but a subconscious element in all his thoughts and actions. It is clearly not due, as the Judge suggests, to the material success of the Victorian era, for it dates from long before that—the Elizabethan English certainly had it. And if it is true, as the Judge says, that the American also has this sense of superiority, he no doubt inherited it from us.

If, then, this paper has a smear of self-satisfaction all over it, I can't help it. Being an Englishman I was born that way.

AMERICANS ARE QUEER

By *Stephen Leacock*

AMERICANS are queer people: they can't rest. They have more time, more leisure, shorter hours, more holidays, and more vacations than any other people in the world. But they can't rest. They rush up and down across their continent as tourists; they move about in great herds to conventions; they invade the wilderness, they flood the mountains, they keep the hotels full. But they can't rest. The scenery rushes past them. They learn it, but they don't see it. Battles and monuments are announced to them in a rubberneck bus. They hear them, but they don't get them. They never stop moving; they rush up and down as Shriners, Masons, Old Graduates, Bankers—they are a new thing each day, always rushing to a reunion or something.

So they go on rushing about till eventually the undertaker gathers them to a last convention.

Americans are queer people: they can't read. They have more schools, and better schools, and spend more money on schools and colleges than all Europe. But they can't read. They print more books in a year than the French print in ten. But they can't read. They cover their country with one hundred thousand tons of Sunday newspapers every week. But they don't read them. They're too busy. They use them for fires and to make more paper with. They buy eagerly thousands of new novels at two dollars each. But they read only page one. Their streets are full of huge signs. They won't look at them. Their street cars are filled with advertising; they turn their eyes away. Transparent colors, cart wheels, and mechanical flares whirl and flicker in the crowded streets at night. No one sees them. Tons of circulars pour through the mails, through the houses, and down the garbage chute. The last American who sat down to read died in the days of Henry Clay.

Americans are queer people: they can't drink. All of the American nation is haunted. They have a fierce wish to be sober; and they can't. They pass fierce laws against themselves, shut themselves up, chase themselves, shoot themselves; and they can't stay sober and they can't drink. They have a furious idea that if they can ever get sober, they can do big things. But they can't hold it. They got this mentality straight out of home life in Ohio, copied from the wild spree and the furious repentance of the pioneer farmer. The nation keeps it yet. It lives among red specters, rum devils, broken bottles, weeping children, penitentiary cells, barrooms, poison hooch, and broken oaths.

Americans are queer people: they can't play. Americans rush to work as soon as they grow up. They want their work as soon as they wake. It is a stimulant—the only one they're not afraid of. They used to open their offices at ten o'clock; then at nine; then at eight; then at seven. Now they never shut them. Every business in America is turning into an open-all-day-and-night business. They eat all night, dance all night, build buildings all night, make a noise all night. They can't play. They try to, but they can't. They turn football into a fight, baseball into a lawsuit, and yachting into machinery. They can't play. The little children can't play; they use mechanical toys instead—toy cranes hoisting toy loads, toy machinery spreading a toy industrial depression of infantile dullness. The grown-up people can't play; they use a mechanical gymnasium and a clockwork horse. They can't swim: they use a float. They can't run: they use a car. They can't laugh: they hire a comedian and watch him laugh.

Americans are queer people: they don't give a damn. All the world criticizes them and they don't give a damn. All the world writes squibs like this about them and they don't give a damn. Foreign visitors come and write them up; they don't give a damn. Lecturers lecture at them; they don't care. They are told they have no art, no literature, and no soul. They never budge. Moralists cry over them, criminologists dissect them, writers shoot epigrams at them, prophets foretell the end of them; and they never move. Seventeen brilliant books analyze them every month; they don't read them. The Europeans threaten to unite against them; they don't mind. Equatorial Africa is dead sour on them; they don't even know it. The Chinese look on them as full of Oriental cunning; the English accuse them of British stupidity; the Scotch call them close-fisted; the Italians say they are liars; the French think their morals loose; the Bolsheviks accuse them of Communism.

But that's all right. The Americans don't give a damn; don't need to—never did need to. That is their salvation.

PRACTICE WHAT YOU TEACH

By *James Weber Linn*

TWO men sat and chatted in a Pullman, on a crack train speeding over the flat lands of the Middle West. They seemed to be of an age somewhere between forty and fifty-five, that indeterminable period in the lives of the alert and successful during which the appearance remains unaltered almost for decades. They were well, if quietly, dressed; they might have been business men on the way to a convention. That, in fact, is what they were; only their business was education, and the convention was a meeting of the Modern Language Association of America, where one was to read a paper on Balzac, and the other was to listen, to observe, and possibly to select a new assistant professor. They were old acquaintances, classmates in a large Eastern college, and colleagues in a still larger Western university, in which one was a dean and the other a professor in the department of Romance languages.

MANUFACTURING EDUCATION

The dean was by way of being an authority on Pope; the professor was indubitably an authority on nineteenth-century French literature. Both had published books on their subjects. The dean's book on Pope had brought him, in royalties, something more than two hundred dollars; the professor's textbook on the history of French literature twice as many thousands. The professor smoked cigarettes by habit and preference, the dean a large cigar. They were, of course, talking shop, but the talk had taken a direction unusual among scholars, even though the scholars were teachers also.

"I hear," remarked the professor cheerfully, "that the new

system of undergraduate teaching at the University of Chicago is not going very well."

"It's too soon to say," replied the dean. "It isn't new, exactly. Wisconsin tried it on a smaller scale, and has just given it up. And what is more, it isn't teaching, as you call it; it is just a process of educational manufacturing without book-keeping. And finally, it can't fail. It is a blessed thought in our business, Bob, that no system of education, if persisted in, can in the long run fail to educate."

"That was John Manly's wise crack," commented the professor. "And I must say I don't agree with him. I think our whole system of undergraduate education in the American college has failed, and will continue to fail as long as we persist in it. And just for that reason I welcomed the Chicago plan, and hope they make something out of it."

"Well," said the dean, "so do I. But it doesn't seem to me that even Chicago has gone to the root of the matter. Of course, I don't agree with you that our undergraduate education is a failure. I do go so far as to admit that it has one very grave defect. And I don't think the Chicago plan touches this defect."

"Lack of standards?"

THE NEED FOR INTELLECTUAL DISCIPLINE

"Not exactly. Confusion of standards. We don't know what we want, and we don't care what the boys and girls want."

"What they want," remarked the professor with a grin, "if by 'want' you mean 'wish,' as I suppose you do, is a good time. What they need is discipline and more discipline. I don't mean moral discipline. I see no advantage, and innumerable disadvantages, in concern with their conduct. I mean intellectual discipline. We try to make them think, but we don't force them into thinking straight. Therefore they leave us intellectually as immature as they come to us, except as four more years of age have given them a bit more judgment perhaps."

"Rot," replied the dean, knocking the ash from his cigar.

"The fault, dear Bob, is in ourselves and not in lack of discipline that our undergraduates remain underlings. We are manufacturers who have neither any clear idea of what we can use in the way of raw materials, nor any definite conception of what we want to produce. No business man would put up a factory without first deciding whether he wished to make surgical instruments, locomotives, or golf clubs. But we do just that. We do not even, as Edward Lear said, 'churn salt water violently in the hope that it will turn into butter, which it seldom or never does.' No, we churn we know not what, in the hope that it will turn into something of value to our contemporary civilization. And what a tribute to American youth is the fact that it frequently does!"

"American youth!" said the professor. "I am sick of American youth. In my observation, about one-tenth of it has the brains and ambition to think at all. The women are more 'conscientious,' as the phrase goes, than the men, and so they get slightly higher marks; but they are stupider than the men, if anything. Eighty per cent of my students don't really know enough to pound sand down a rat hole, and don't want to."

"A French rat hole, you mean," commented the dean. "Why should they want to, Bob?" He looked out of the window. The train was sweeping through a little city in Ohio. There were vistas of business streets, smeared with dirty snow —for this was in the Christmas holidays—and cinematographic films of warmly clothed men, women, and children going about their affairs beside buildings not ugly perhaps, but certainly not distinguished for architectural beauty or for repose of spirit. "I don't know the name of this place, but I have no question that half of its inhabitants under twenty are either in some college somewhere or planning to go to one. Some of them will undoubtedly sit in your classroom one of these days. Ask yourself, my dear boy, why anybody brought up in Main Street should take a passionate interest in French poetry, even including the 'Chanson de Roland'—which is, by the way, rather dull reading."

"As dull," inquired the professor caustically, "as Pope?"

"I think so," replied the dean. "And certainly I do not expect one-tenth of our undergraduates to take an interest in Pope. Not a real interest; not the sort of interest that rouses them to thought. Remember your Emerson. 'What is the hardest task in the world? To think. From thinking we blench and withdraw on this side and on that.' Yes, even you and I, even when our own subjects are involved, often blench and withdraw from thinking; and yet you expect these young Main Streeters to indulge in it eagerly, upon matters which not only have never concerned them in the past but cannot possibly concern them in the future. The wonder is that a tenth of them do, not that 90 per cent refuse to do so."

MAKING COLLEGE ENTRANCE EASY

"They ought not to be in college at all," commented the professor.

"Ought not? Then why are they there? Why, my dear fellow, we go out into the highways and hedges and compel them to come in. We even offer them scholarships."

"To the one-tenth," cut in the professor.

"Did you never hear of scholarships for all-around accomplishment? Did you never hear of athletic scholarships? Did you never hear of college employment associations, which are organized for providing boys and girls not book-learned enough to win prizes with jobs that will enable them to stay in college? I say we compel, or seek to compel, and seek to encourage the compulsion by public opinion, half of these young Main Streeters to attend our colleges, and especially our state universities. That is exactly what I mean when I say that as educational manufacturers we do not know what we want in the way of raw material. At our own university we admit every boy or girl who can present a certificate of graduation from any high school. Harvard admits without examination only boys from the top seventh of the graduating classes from the public schools—and then only under special circumstances. And yet we and Harvard seek to develop exactly the same product in four years—an educated young man. And what is more, we know so little of the relation of high marks in the school class-rooms to ambition, and even to brains, that I venture to suspect if you were teaching at Harvard instead of where you are, you would still be complaining that not more than one-tenth of your students had the brains and ambition to pound sand down a French rat hole. One-tenth of the top seventh!"

PITY THE POOR STUDENTS

"I admit," said the professor, "that our own undergraduates, outside the classroom, impress me quite as favorably as do undergraduates at Harvard; at least those I have known."

"Maybe," said the dean with a smile as he took a fresh cigar, "that belief proceeds merely from your loyalty, which is, Bob, one of your most admirable characteristics, even when it leads you to the insistence that Tom, Dick, and Harry could profit by reading the ' Chanson de Roland.'"

"Or Pope," remarked the professor.

"Or Pope, as you say. But heaven forbid I should make comparisons among our college youth. They are the American mine-run, and we must certainly love them, for we have made so many of them."

"Heaven forbid, as you say," interjected the professor, "that I should love them."

"Ah, Bob, but you do, outside the classroom. Haven't you just been standing up for them to me, when you thought I was comparing our own unfavorably with those elsewhere? Yes, you love them, and that is why I can't understand why you treat them so abominably."

"I treat them abominably?"

"Yes, you, and all the rest of us. We underestimate them; we misunderstand them; we herd them here and there for our own convenience; outside the classroom we treat them as if they were all children, and inside the classroom we treat them as if they were all candidates for the doctorate. We take pay for teaching them, and spend most of our time on the study of subjects in which they are not only not interested but in which they are incompetent to take an interest."

"What do you mean?"

"I mean research. You are about to read a paper which everybody will admire and a few will even enjoy. It will enhance your reputation among your colleagues; by enhancing your reputation it will even increase your market value, and may result in the raising of your salary. No detail of your work on that paper will ever directly affect your teaching in French 102, will it?"

THE TRUE END OF EDUCATION

"No," said the professor honestly, though he saw the trend of the cross-examination.

"Then may I ask," said the dean, "how much time and particularly how much intellectual effort you have put in, during the past three months, on French 102, compared to what you have put in on that paper?"

"We-ell——" began the professor.

"Yes," objected the dean, "but in the end it is not well. Your students, dumb as 80 per cent of them may be, know that you are more interested in Balzac than you are in them. Do you expect them to share your interest in Balzac, and particularly in the narrow and technical aspects of that voluble gentleman that you have been concerning yourself with? If you do, you are a vain dreamer, and unjust into the bargain. Theoretically, you are paid a salary——"

"If you can call it that; a plumber wouldn't."

"You are paid a salary to teach, as a plumber is paid to plumb. What would you say of a plumber who spent five hours of the eight he was supposed to be working in your bathroom on an intensive study of the system of drains installed by Tutenkhamun in ancient Akhetaton?"

"Did he, really?" demanded the professor with more interest than he had hitherto shown in any of the dean's remarks.

"Bob," said the dean deliberately, "you are hopeless. You are worse; you are typical. Almost I begin to believe you have no human curiosity at all, only a restless, deep-seated, passionate intellectual curiosity. Do you really imagine that 80 per cent of our young Main Streeters are like you in that, or that they ought to be like you? I think you do. I think in that you are typical of most of our colleagues. You think the primary purpose of our undergraduate colleges is to develop scholarship. You perceive that almost all your pupils disagree with you. And therefore, as you remarked a while ago, you think our whole system of undergraduate education in the American college has failed. At times I go along with you in thinking that college education is a failure. But I do not agree with you on the reason for thinking so."

"What," asked the professor, "is your idea of the purpose of our colleges?"

"I think our main difficulty is our failure to recognize that we have two sorts of young men and women to deal with, and that the vast majority of these young men and women—you put it at 80 per cent a moment ago—are not interested in scholarship, and cannot be made to take an interest in it."

"What are they interested in?"

"When they come to college? In themselves only—which is the natural, if not the normal, interest."

"And when they leave college?" asked the professor.

"Many of them leave with their interest unchanged. In that lies our failure."

"But you say that they cannot be made to take an interest in scholarship."

"Not only so," replied the dean, "but I am glad of it. An interest in scholarship is ennobling, but it is also narrowing. An interest in scholarship is like an interest in making money —a bad thing if unaccompanied by other interests. For the 80 per cent our hope should be to provide a finer culture, to give an increased knowledge of 'the best that has been said and thought in the world,' to make more and more of our young

Barbarians and our young Philistines into 'children of light,' as Matthew Arnold phrased it. Parenthetically, what do you know about Arnold?"

"I know," said the professor, "that he was a side-whiskered, old-fashioned Victorian poet, who spent most of his life reading the papers of school children and writing essays on French essayists in which he praised all the wrong things."

"And I know," countered the dean, "that he was the most intelligent critic of society among the Victorians, and that if we made his theory of education—which was also the theory of Newman, the priest, and Huxley, the scientist—the theory of our own college education for the 80 per cent, we should soon cease to hear so much talk of our failure as educators."

"Do you mean to imply," demanded the professor, "that Arnold and Huxley agreed on what should constitute a liberal education?"

THE REWARD OF INCOMPETENCE

"They differed widely," said the dean, "in their estimates of what studies a liberal education should include. But their differences are purely incidental. We are all agreed today that philosophy—which includes religion—literature, classic and contemporary, the fine arts and science are all elements of culture. But we are not all agreed that our primary purpose so far as the 80 per cent are concerned is not to interest them in scholarship but to provide them with a finer culture. Perhaps I exaggerate our timidity when I say that we do not dare to agree on this."

"Why not?"

"Because if we once agreed on it, we should have to change, not our methods of instruction but our instructors; we should have to devise new ways of getting instructors; in our state universities we should have to offend many a taxpayer, and in our privately endowed colleges many a noble benefactor; and that would be a wrench. I think we college administrators do not wish to have to decide on the primary purpose of our institutions of higher learning. I think we prefer to muddle along. Although the colleges are complained of, they continue to flourish and to provide a sufficiently agreeable existence for many thousands of men and women who could hardly earn as much, in as pleasant company, in any other way as by teaching, and why should these teachers risk having to go to work? What other profession is so noncompetitive? In what other profession is incompetence for and inattention to the job rewarded by permanence of tenure achieved by attention to recreation?"

"Come now, Pete," objected the professor, slightly annoyed. "Do you call my research recreation?"

"For you, certainly," declared the dean. "You know I was not speaking of you when I was speaking of teachers generally, for in spite of your research you are a good teacher, or would be if you permitted yourself to be. But I do call your research recreation; as recreational for you as your golf, and no more related to your teaching than your golf is to giving me tips on the game. Still, if we agreed on the real duty of the colleges to the 80 per cent of the undergraduates, we should not have to get rid of you. We should have to get rid of perhaps 80 per cent of our present staff of teachers; or at least, transfer them to training schools for the candidates for the doctoral degrees. We should have, in other words, to pull them off the bodies of the undergraduates, whom they have got down at present and are sitting on with placidity varied by an occasional fit of sadistic pinchings and worryings."

QUALIFICATIONS OF A PEDAGOGUE

"I should say that most of our colleagues were very fair scholars," commented the professor.

"And very fair teachers?" asked the dean.

"I don't know anything about them as teachers, but——"

"Exactly," interrupted the dean, with more bitterness in his voice than he had shown hitherto. "You don't know anything about them as teachers, and you don't care; and they

don't care, and why should they? In the first place, they know
that however well or however poorly they may teach, it will
make little difference in their careers; and in the second place,
they couldn't teach well if they wanted to, most of them, because they know too much."

"You mean too little?"

"Too much about too little. Bob, where do we in the colleges get our teachers from? Out of what group? I'm going
down now, as you know, to look over a couple of men that are
highly recommended to us. Both of them were Phi Beta Kappa;
both of them took their doctors' degrees *cum laude*, one
at Columbia and one at Chicago; both of them have had years
of experience in teaching; both of them are going to read papers
day after tomorrow. If I find that one of them knows how to
mix a cocktail and drink it like a gentleman, and not like a
hungry orphan in a candy shop, and the other does not, I shall
certainly pick the one that does. He will be the nearer to what
I want, that I can get; but even he will not be very near."

"How do you know?" asked the professor.

"Because he was a Phi Beta Kappa, and took his doctor's
degree *cum laude*," answered the dean, "and because, like you,
he has presumably spent five out of the eight hours a day he
might have been giving to his teaching in the past three months
in preparing the paper he is to read the day after tomorrow.
Because, in other words, he will be strictly representative of the
10 per cent of undergraduates who, according to you, 'have the
brains and ambition to think at all,' and strictly unrepresenta-
tive of the 80 per cent of young Main Streeters who will be his
pupils. He will not understand them, and they, in consequence,
will not understand him. He will not like them, and they, in
consequence, will not like him. He will, in the classroom, de-
spise them, and they, in consequence, outside the classroom,
will not reflect for two minutes a day on what he has been saying to them. He will be able, he will be zealous, but he will be
narrow in the range of his own interests and cheerfully contemptuous of interests not his own. His world will have been

the world of the library, as, if he were in another department, it would have been the world of the laboratory; and he will quite honestly deny the truth of Robert Louis Stevenson's dictum that 'books are a mighty bloodless substitute for life.'"

"Then why take him at all?" suggested the professor.

"Because, as things are," replied the dean, "he will be the best I can get. For the 10 per cent of potential scholars in his classes, he will be highly fit. He will be, I hope, the kind of man to whom young people who find scholarship, research, really attractive will turn as naturally as sunflowers to the sun. He will, I believe, indirectly and influentially, as well as directly and personally, 'widen the circle of truth,' as we all love to say in our commencement speeches. But what can he do for the great mass of our undergraduates today, who not only have no interest in real scholarship but are quite incapable of it?

"Men of his group and type are actually uneasy in the presence of the 80 per cent of undergraduates you speak of. They look upon the facile, wide-ranging, perfectly normal emotionalism of young people as insincere; some of them even regard it as abnormal and dangerous. Having themselves been concentratedly industrious almost to the breaking point, they are inclined to sneer at the activities of youth as not only misdirected but vapid. You think not? Well, let me ask you. Haven't you a boy in French 102 this semester named Zimmerman?"

"Zimmerman? Wait a minute. W. Zimmerman. A big ox? The sort that every now and then goes to sleep in the classroom?"

"Yes, that's Bill. I gather you don't think much of him?"

"He comes and he recites. He might scrape through with a C. What about him?"

"Has he any business in college?"

MISFITS OF THE CLASSROOM

"Hardly, I should say. He is lazy, not particularly interested, and, if I remember, was reported to me as having written only four thousand words for a term paper when I asked for five."

"Bill worked all summer with a construction gang. He is getting up at 5:30 now every morning to deliver papers. He is also trying to get together a group of small boys for instruction in games next spring and summer, if he is lucky. He played a pretty fair game of football until his shoulder was hurt. No, I shouldn't call Bill lazy or uninterested—at least in life. But I agree that he has no place in your classroom. Or, to put it the other way round, even you, Bob, have no place, with your present ideas, as teacher of such a boy. And yet Bill is quite surely representative of 80 per cent of our undergraduates."

"If I am not fit," began the professor, "to teach human oxen, male or female——"

"Not, as I say, because you do not know enough, but because you know too much. Not because you are unsympathethic, but because you are too narrowly sympathetic. Scholarship, Bob, is a jealous mistress. She demands pure passion in her worship. Once she attaches a courtier, she will not let him go. He must live and die in her service alone. The rewards of that service are great in peace and content with the employment, but the limitations are strict. It decreases sympathy with society; it compels irritation with Bill Zimmerman; it makes the teaching of Bill a bore. Yet we asked Bill to come to college; in his freshman year he even had a scholarship. We shall give him a degree some day; and when he is an alumnus, and making money, we shall ask him to give some of it to us, for the salaries of whoever are to teach his sons and daughters when they come in their turn. Don't you think, Bob, that Bill is entitled to teaching by somebody who is glad to have him about? Don't you think he is entitled to teaching by somebody who is primarily interested in Zimmerman and not in research?"

"I think," said the professor a little angrily, "that you are trying to classify me among the fish. I may be cold-blooded, but I swim to the surface of life occasionally."

TEACHING JOBS FOR SCHOLARS ONLY

"I said ten minutes ago," insisted the dean, "that I did not mean you when I spoke of the general run of college teachers. It was only because you insisted on making the matter personal that I illustrated with Bill Zimmerman. We'll pass Bill; and I hope you will, too, because if you don't, he will be ineligible for basket ball, and that would be more of a college calamity than if either of us here should break a leg. Among the students, I mean. Bill was the captain of his high-school basket-ball team when we awarded him a freshman scholarship. I don't say that his captaincy had anything to do with the scholarship, but I suspect that Bill thought at the time that we expected him to play in college, and that we hoped he would be eligible."

"Bah!" said the professor. "Never mind Zimmerman. What I should like to ask is, if we are to have college teachers primarily interested in the masses and in their general culture, how are we to get them?"

"I can't imagine," said the dean. "At present, we are moving in the other direction. In many colleges, only men and women badged with the symbol of primary interest in research are permitted to teach at all; and everywhere the men and women not so badged are whispered down by the formal educationalists."

MATCHING THE STUDENTS' INTERESTS

"Look here, Pete," interrupted the professor triumphantly. "Whom do you remember of our teachers back in Willherst? Hoppy, and Phillips, and Winchester, and Suddard, eh? Well, weren't they great scholars? At least Hoppy was, and Winchester."

"And Phillips wasn't, nor Suddard," laughed the dean. "Great men if you like, but not scholars. Remember the nights in Suddard's rooms when he read us Almayer's Folly, and how Phillips used to go over and adjust the curtain just so, and then tell his classes the ghost story, just about the same time every year? And even Winchester—did you know, even when you were a senior, that Winchester was a great scholar? Not a bit of it. You knew that he could read the ballad of Sir Patrick Spens so that you could see the Scotch ladies combing their hair and waiting, waiting, but you didn't know that old Winny had dug up two entirely new versions of Barbara Allen among the Tennessee mountaineers, and you wouldn't have given a damn if you had known, except as a human-interest story—now, would you?"

"I don't suppose I should," admitted the professor. "But he was a great teacher because he was a great scholar."

"Nonsense," declared the dean. "Any really great mind transcends the limits of its instinctive interests. Socrates as a teacher would have been at home in the mind even of a born salesman, even of a baby vamp. I don't suppose Mark Hopkins cared much what sort of student sat at the other end of his log; he could match that student's interests whatever they might be. But there are few minds with any such quality of universality. And what I am trying to talk, Bob, is college business, not idealism."

"Well, then, if you aren't going to do anything about it, what are you going to do about it?"

"I wish," admitted the dean, "I knew. What we want are not brilliant students but independent thinkers; men who are genuinely interested in the best that has been said and thought in the world, not exclusively interested in little bits of it here and there; men who are all the more interested in the normal undergraduate because they know themselves to be far from unusual; men who understand the 80 per cent as the 80 per cent understand one another, but who have more to give to the young than the young have to give one another, and are better trained in communication. I think perhaps that once we made such men and women welcome as teachers in our colleges, we should find more of them turning to the profession. Good teachers are not born; they are made; but they are not made,

except in rare instances, out of the raw material of which scholars are made. In every college there are scores and scores of
undergraduates who are planning to go into the law, into newspaper work, into advertising, into manufacturing, into sales-
manship, who would be of more social value as teachers of
undergraduates. As things are, they never think of becoming
teachers—though a few of them become coaches in sports—
because they do not dream that success in college teaching is
open to them. As of course, at present, it isn't."

A NEW STANDARD FOR TEACHERS

"If I should say to Bill Zimmerman now, 'Why don't you
teach?' he would pop his eyes open, and say, 'Dean, I never
got but one A in my life,' or 'Wouldn't I have to get a Ph.D.
or something like that?' And of course I'd have to answer,
'That is so.' But I don't know that it has to stay so. I don't
know any real reason why we should not begin to realize that
scholars are fit only to inspire potential scholarship, and that
for by far the larger number of our undergraduates, no matter
what our educational system is, teachers must be recruited and
trained and rewarded who are not scholarly but merely intelligent and humane. And I do know that we are selling the
greater number of our undergraduates gold bricks today. Fortunately, the boys and girls have such a pleasant time outside
the classroom that they don't much care what goes on in it,
and, fortunately, their parents are blinded to the situation by
their memories of the Hoppys, and Phillipses, and Winchesters,
and Suddards they once knew. Heaven is my witness that they
never see any of those who teach their children in the colleges
today, except occasionally at banquets, and then they don't talk
to us; we talk to them, and there is great safety in loquacity."

"If that is so," replied the professor, yawning, "I should feel
never safer in my life. . . . What shall we have for dinner,
Pete?"

"Duck soup," replied the dean amiably. "We live on it,
Bob."

A SYMPHONY IN GREEN

By *E. V. Lucas*

HAVING found my first snowdrop of the year, I did what I always do with that flower of promise: I held it above my head to look within at its green lines, and again to marvel at the beauty of it—a beauty so often ignored, for the snowdrop usually is at our feet with only its drooping whiteness visible. But in particular was I struck once more by the quality of the green of these lines, which is like no other variety of that colour; but then, thinking about as many of those other varieties as I could, I realized that each of them has its individual character and is like no other, and that green is inexhaustible. There must be shades of it by the million.

Green is indeed the dominating colour of the world, for there is more vegetation than desert or blue sky, and the sea is often green enough to sway the balance. No sooner does one leave the town than green controls the landscape, and even in London there are no streets where, in the leafy months, green is not visible, not even in what is called "the city" itself. Left to herself, Nature imposes a touch of green everywhere, even if it is only green mould or verdigris.

> Annihilating all things made
> To a green thought in a green shade.

I have seen the theory stated that the world is mostly green because that is the best colour for our eyes; but it could never be proved, and there is nothing about it in Genesis. The only way of testing it would be to dye the grass different colours in different localities and engage an oculist to watch the

From *Lemon Verbena;* published, 1932, by J. B. Lippincott Company. Used by special permission.

children brought up there. There are rebels who want the grass to be red; but I have the feeling that green is right. When the *Westminster Gazette*, which, of an evening, I still continually miss, was started, it was printed on green paper entirely for the sake of the readers' sight. Now and then a book with green pages has been published to the same end; but whether we are in danger of blindness or impaired vision because most paper is white, I have never heard. Yet green is not universally accepted as a soothing hue, for I remember that when, many years ago, a new pavement was laid beside the lawns at Hove and people complained of being dazzled by it—in fact, it became known as Ophthalmia Walk—a pink wash was applied. Not green.

That everything should be called green—the range extending from the green of cooked spinach to the lines in the heart of a snowdrop—is another proof of the poverty of our language or the laziness of man. Long since, the artists in words, the Paters and Wildes and Stevensons and Vernon Lees, should have subdivided green into a thousand new terms. In default of this analysis, we are driven back on such weak compromises as light green, dark green, sea green, pea green, emerald green. But what does "light green" mean, when there are so many shades, including the infant shamrock and unripe apple and the sheaths from which the lily-of-the-valley miraculously and intoxicatingly emerges; or dark green, when there are maritime pines and Scotch firs and hollies? As for emerald green, there is no such hue. The green of the emerald is not colour, it is lambency, and never again, outside that radiant stone, will it be found. Nor is the green of dogs' eyes and cats' eyes and rabbits' eyes as reflected from a motorist's headlamps at night a colour. That, too, is lambency, fierce and sudden. No painter could translate either into pigment.

It was always an excitement in the early days when we were all artists—before some of us gave up the attempt in despair, leaving only the elect in—to find that our water-colour boxes omitted green altogether, so that we had to make

it for ourselves. And since most of our pictures had grass as
well as sky, green was as important as blue. Blue, however,
no mixture of colours could make. There were occasionally
green cakes of a very unsatisfactory hue which became dull
directly it was transferred to paper; but usually we had to
combine gamboge and ultra-marine or chrome yellow and
indigo, according as we wished for a light or dark variety. I
rather think that whenever a green cake did happen to be
supplied, it was called either verdant green, emerald green,
or green bice, and we were warned against putting the brush
in our mouths when we were using it, as it was a deadly poison.
I forget the taste; but I have the liveliest recollections of the
sweetness, and general attractiveness to the palate, of either
madder brown or crimson lake, or both.

There may have been a sound reason for omitting green
from the paint-boxes of those times, for I find Millais (who
rejoiced in the colour, and in his picture of the nuns in the
garden makes it intensely sombre, and in his "Ophelia" employs myriad shades of it) stating in a letter: "There are
many nowadays will not have a picture with green in it, and
even buyers who, when giving a commission to an artist, will
stipulate that the canvas shall contain none of it. But God
Almighty gave us green, and, depend upon it, it's a fine
colour."

What are the most beautiful shades of green? Each, I suppose. There is the green of the shallow sea over patches of
sand as seen from a height: such as you have from the garden
of the Eden Hotel at Cap d'Ail, for instance; or, crossing the
Channel in an aëroplane, as you approach the French coast
towards Le Touquet. This is a sparkling translucent green,
as different as can be from the green of malachite, which is
sullen and opaque. There is the green of the young beech-
leaves, so tender and limpid, and the green of old ivy, dark
and austere. There is the green of the railings and shutters
at Zaandam in Holland, and the green of aquarium tanks.
There is the Lincoln green of Robin Hood's jerkin and the

green of the yew. There is the gossamer green of the olives among the rocks and the opaque green of seaweed. There is the shimmering green of the alder and the mature and satisfying green of an old shagreen case. There is the silver green of the white-beam in a wind and the sinister green of a cypress guarding the tombs. There is the green of the treefrog and the green of Culpeper Houses; there is the green of the bud of Daphne emerging amid the pink of the blossoms and the green of the Brazilian flag. There is the wistful green of a Corot and the inflexible green of a Cézanne. There is the green of the early larch and the green of the new Tennyson volumes as I remember them in my youth. There is the green of *crème de menthe* and the green of the billiard-table; there is the green of Famille Verte porcelain and the green of the front door of No. 6 Cheyne Walk.

OBJECTIONS TO LAUGHTER

By *Robert Lynd*

I

"LAUGHTER" is a word, we are told by the philologists, that is a distant cousin of the Greek κλώσσειν, "to cluck like a hen," and also of κράζειν, " to croak." But we need not go any further than our everyday speech to have it brought home to us that when we laugh we do something that puts us on a level with the lower animals. Half the words we ordinarily use to describe anybody laughing are words borrowed from a vocabulary descriptive of the various inarticulate sounds that must have made the chief music of life in Noah's ark. We say of a laughing human being that he "bellows" or "roars" or "cackles" or "crows" or "whinnies." Some people even speak of "barks of laughter" and of "hoots of joy." We say of one man that he "laughs like a hyena" and of another that he has a "horse laugh." And, even if a man is guilty of nothing worse than that noiseless form of laughter known as a smile, we often describe him as "grinning like an ape" or "like a Cheshire cat." It is true that, in describing weeping, we also occasionally use words that suggest a comparison with the lower animals. A child, like a dog, is said to "whine," and its sobs as well as its laughter are often spoken of as "bellowing," "roaring," and "howling." Still, the vocabulary of the forest and the farmyard seems to be much more freely applied to our expression of mirth than to our expression of woe.

We have often been told that the ability to laugh is one of the chief things that distinguish man from the other animals. The report that "the little dog laughed to see such sport" when the cow jumped over the moon is generally discredited as a legend. I am confident, however, that the people who say that animals never laugh are wrong. Animals undoubtedly make slightly different sounds from ourselves in their expressions of pleasure, and possibly they are pleased with different things, but when they are pleased they have a way, like ourselves, of making inarticulate sounds, and I see no reason to doubt that pigs, geese, starlings, dogs, parrots, and green woodpeckers at times makes these sounds in a mood of what we call hilarity.

Certainly there seems nothing in the ordinary dictionary definition of the word "laugh" to suggest that laughter is something of which other animals than man are incapable. The first dictionary I consulted on the matter defined "laugh" as an intransitive verb meaning "to express mirth or joy by an explosive inarticulate sound of the voice and peculiar facial distortion." A dog undoubtedly is capable of that. The next dictionary said: "Laugh . . . to express feeling by a series of inarticulate explosive sounds due to the characteristic vibrations into which the vocal cords are thrown by the jerky, spasmodic character of the expirations." That is no better a description of a human laugh than of a donkey's bray. I doubt, indeed, whether anyone has ever succeeded in defining or describing laughter in terms inapplicable to the facial contortions and explosive sounds made by animals. All the descriptions of the act of laughter that I have met with have seemed to me equally applicable to the snarling of wild beasts and to the merriment of human beings at a dinner party.

Take, for instance, Professor Sully in that excellent book, *An Essay on Laughter*. Near the beginning of the book, he has a description of a smile—which, as he tells us, viewed as a psychological event, is rightly regarded as a laugh, though as an incomplete laugh. "Smiling," he declares, "involves a complex group of facial movements. It may suffice to remind the reader of such characteristic changes as the drawing back and slight lifting of the corners of the mouth, the raising of the upper lip, which partially uncovers the teeth, and the curving of the furrows betwixt the corners of the mouth and the nostrils (the nasolabial furrows) which these movements involve. To these must be added the formation of wrinkles under the eyes—the most characteristic part of the expression—which is a further result of the first movements. The increased brightness of the eyes is probably the effect of their tenseness, due to the contraction of the adjacent muscles and the pressure of the raised cheek, though an acceleration of the circulation within the eyeball may have something to do with it."

I confess that I do not find a smile, so dissected, particularly human. To read of it is to conjure up a picture of the expression on the face of Red Riding Hood's wolf rather than the expression on the face of La Gioconda. And, when we pass from the smile to the laugh proper, Professor Sully's description is equally humbling to those who have taken pride in the thought that when they laugh they give convincing evidence of their difference from, and their superiority to, the other animals. Laughing, says Professor Sully, "is an interruption of the natural rhythm of the respiratory process, in which inspiration and expiration follow one another at regular intervals. The obvious feature of its interruption . . . is the series of short, spasmodic, expiratory movements by which the sounds are produced. These are, however, preceded by a less noticed inspiration of exceptional energy and depth. These interruptions of the ordinary respiratory movements involve also an unusually energetic action of the large muscles by which the chest is expanded, *viz.*, those which secure the contraction and so the descent of the dome-shaped diaphragm and those by the action of which the ribs are elevated. The production of the sounds by the spasmodic expiratory movements shows that the passage from the trachea into the pharynx, *viz.*, the glottis or chink between the vocal cords, is partially closed. The quality of the sounds is explained by the particular arrangements, at the moment of the cachinnation, of the vocal apparatus, and more particularly the shape of the resonance chamber of the mouth."

Let those who are given to boasting of their sense of humor as though it were one of the highest achievements of which humanity is capable look on this "slow-motion" picture of a laugh and realize that all their sense of humor can do for them is to enable them, like any other animal, to make spasmodic expiratory movements through a partially closed passage from the trachea to the pharynx.

II

Perhaps it was their realization of the essentially animal nature of laughter that led so many philosophers, saints, and authorities on behavior to condemn it. Plato, in the *Republic*, censures Homer for having degraded the gods by making them laugh in the sentence: "Inextinguishable laughter arose among the blessed gods, when they saw Hephæstus bustling about the mansion." And he expresses his dislike of laughter still more strongly in the same book when he makes Socrates declare that the guardians of the State ought not to be given to laughter, and that persons of worth must never be represented as being overcome by laughter. Pythagoras, again, is a philosopher of whom we are told that "he would avoid laughter and all pandering to tastes such as insulting jests and vulgar tales."

It is true that there have been philosophers of a less unbending disposition, such as Spinoza, of whom it is said that "after protracted studies" he "would mix with the family party where he lodged, and join in the most trivial conversations, or unbend his mind by setting spiders to fight each other; he observed their combats with so much interest that he was often seized with immoderate fits of laughter." But it is a significant fact that among philosophers there is only one who is known as the Laughing Philosopher, and the learned assure us that Democritus was not really a laughing philosopher at all.

I do not know whether we are any longer permitted to be-

lieve the story that Democritus used to walk down to the
harbor of Abdera in his lighter moments and "laugh heartily
at such variety of ridiculous objects, which there he saw."
Even Burton, who repeats the story, describes Democritus
as "a little wearish old man, very melancholy by nature," and
an older authority declares that he used to train himself "by a
variety of means to test his sense-impressions by going at times
into solitude and frequenting tombs." Yet this man is apparently the nearest thing to a laughing philosopher that the world
has seen.

As for the saints, though many of them have been cheerful
men, few of them have been conspicuous for their hilarity.
Some of them have even thought it was a sin to laugh. Saint
John the dwarf, for example, on seeing a monk laughing un-
controllably at dinner one day was "so horrified that he at
once began to cry," and Saint Basil wrote against the wicked-
ness of laughing, declaring that it was the one bodily affection
that the Founder of the Christian religion "does not seem to
have known."

I fancy the saints of all the religions and all the churches
have been the same in this respect. One does not imagine
John Knox as a patron saint of laughter, and I am sure that
the Presbyterian elder who rebuked someone for whistling on
Sunday in the sentence, "Mon, this is no day for whustlin',"
would have equally rebuked anyone whom he had heard laughing on the sacred day.

And when we leave the saints and come to more worldly
authorities on behavior we find the same thing. The greatest
English gentleman who ever left detailed instructions as to
how to behave like a gentleman was Lord Chesterfield, and
in his *Letters to His Son* he declares emphatically in more than
one passage that a man who wishes to be regarded as a gentleman must avoid laughter above all things. Everyone knows
the passage in which he warns his son: "Loud laughter is the
mirth of the mob, who are only pleased with silly things; for
true wit or good sense never excited a laugh, since the creation

of the world. A man of parts and fashion is, therefore, only seen to smile, but never heard to laugh."

In a further letter, Lord Chesterfield returns to and reiterates his warning. He writes:—

Having mentioned laughing, I must particularly warn you against it: and I could heartily wish that you may often be seen to smile, but never heard to laugh while you live. Frequent and loud laughter is the characteristic of folly and ill manners; it is the manner in which the mob express their silly joy at silly things; and they call it being merry. In my mind, there is nothing so illiberal, and so ill bred, as audible laughter. True wit, or sense, never yet made any body laugh; they are above it. They please the mind, and give a cheerfulness to the countenance. But it is low buffoonery, or silly accidents, that always excite laughter; and that is what people of sense and breeding should show themselves above. A man's going to sit down, in the supposition that he has a chair behind him, and falling down upon his breech for want of one, sets a whole company a laughing, when all the wit in the world would not do it; a plain proof, in my mind, how low and unbecoming a thing laughing is. *Not to mention the disagreeable noise that it makes, and the shocking distortion of the face that it occasions.* Laughter is easily restrained, by a very little reflection; but as it is generally connected with the idea of gaiety, people do not enough attend to its absurdity. I am neither of a melancholy nor a cynical disposition; and am as willing and as apt to be pleased as any body; but I am sure that, since I have had the full use of my reason, nobody has ever heard me laugh.

Chesterfield then goes on to denounce the "very disagreeable and silly trick of laughing," and to speak contemptuously of "a man of very good parts, Mr. Waller, who cannot say the commonest thing without laughing; which makes those who do not know him take him at first for a natural fool." And indeed Lord Chesterfield, in his assertion that nobody had ever heard him laughing, had noble predecessors through the ages. Johnson declares that nobody had ever heard either Swift or Pope laughing. And was it not said of the grandfather of the great Crœsus that "he never laughed but once in his life, and that was at an ass eating thistles"? One feels that he might have chosen a more exciting occasion.

But it is not only the philosophers, the saints, and the authorities on manners who have belittled laughter. One of the most fastidious spirits of modern times, the poetess Alice Meynell, devoted a carefully reasoned essay to an appeal to her fellow countrymen to laugh a little less loudly and a little less frequently than they do. The English, she observed, though they speak less loudly than the Continental nations, are given to laughing more loudly in the theaters, and, disliking noise, she held up to them for imitation "the Oriental estimation of laughter as a thing fitter for women, fittest for children, and unfitted for a beard." Mrs. Meynell was mistaken, it seems to me, if she thought that in her objection to laughter she was singular. The ordinary man may occasionally laugh, but he does not think much of laughter. He has as poor an opinion of it, indeed, as Plato or Mrs. Meynell herself. That the ordinary man cares little for laughter can, I think, be easily proved.

Consider, for one thing, what has been the most widely read literature of the past two generations. Is it not a conspicuous fact that among the most popular novels four or five are by writers who never try to make us laugh, or, at least, who never succeed? Twenty years ago the "best-selling" English novelists were Miss Marie Corelli and Mr. (now Sir) Hall Caine. Today three out of four of our best-sellers are writers who depend for their effect scarcely at all upon humor of situation or character. I do not forget that Dickens, the permanent best-seller of English literature, was a humorist as well as a tragic sentimentalist. But, taking a general view of popular literature, we shall be safe in affirming that it is easier to become a best-seller with a book that does not contain a single laugh than with a book that, in the language of the reviewers, contains a "laugh on every page." A novelist may leave out the laughter of life, indeed, and appeal to the public, not only for his own time, but for all time, as Defoe does in *Robinson Crusoe* and Richardson does in *Clarissa*, but no novelist has ever succeeded in becoming immortal through laughter alone.

Sterne has his sentimental interludes. As regards Cervantes, again, we are constantly reproached by some of his most enthusiastic admirers if we do not share his sorrows with Don Quixote, instead of laughing at his misfortunes. It is the same with nearly all the masterpieces of comedy. They are most ardently appreciated, not for comic, but for serious reasons. If you take up a book on Aristophanes or Rabelais or Molière, you will almost certainly find that it sets out to explain his serious purpose rather than to echo his hilarity.

III

All this—the consensus of saints, philosophers, men of fashion, and ordinary human beings—seems to constitute a very strong case against laughter. And, indeed, laughter is open to the objection that it is not only offensive to others, but tiresome in itself. It is one of the abnormal, rather than one of the normal, activities of a human being. I notice that, even by a famous physiologist, it is included in a list of "certain abnormal forms of respiration," along with coughing, sneezing, clearing the throat, snoring, crying, sighing, yawning, and hiccoughing. All these things are good in their way, but none of them would be good all the time as a constant and normal part of our lives. Sneezing is a cure recommended by many modern doctors, for instance, for certain forms of catarrh. Useful as sneezing may be, however, no doctor has yet proposed it to us as an ideal that we should sneeze twenty-four—or even twelve—hours a day.

And the same thing is obviously true of laughter. The ordinary human being, if he went on laughing continuously for even three hours, would become totally exhausted. If you could imagine a farce so funny that every sentence sent the audience into fits of uncontrollable laughter, many people would be unable to sit out more than the first act; others would retire at the end of the second act; and the few who had enough staying power to last till the fall of the curtain would not have strength left to call the actors before it for a final round of applause. You will often notice at a farce that, however much laughter there is in the course of the performance, there is far less applause at the end of it than at the end of a tragedy or a melodrama. Even the comedies of Mr. Shaw, which have many other qualities besides laughableness, used to have an exhausting effect of this kind on the dramatic critics. Mr. Shaw once declared bitterly that during the performance of one of his plays he could see the critics rocking in their seats with laughter and that in the next morning's papers they would all solemnly denounce his play as tedious and boring. The explanation is simple. He had worn them down physically with laughter, just as he would have worn them down if he had made them sneeze or cough violently for three hours on end.

Laughter, like sneezing and coughing, is, as I have said, abnormal, and Rabelais himself would not be tolerable if it were not that he discreetly intermingles with his comedy long passages of boredom. A comic writer must be either tragic in parts or sentimental in parts—he must be a critic of society or have the saving grace of dullness—in order to take his place among the world's great writers.

Thus we arrive at the theory that laughter, being something abnormal like an accident or an electric shock, can play only a very small part in an ordinary man's life. Its very essence is surprise and a break in the monotonous continuity of our thoughts or our experience. It is a physical appreciation of the surprising things of life, such as—to take some elementary instances—the spectacle of a man falling suddenly on ice, or sitting down on the floor instead of on a chair, or being shot in the leg by someone who was aiming at a pheasant.

Such things make us laugh, of course,—as we read about them in *Pickwick Papers*, for example,—only if the results are not too serious. If a man died as the result of any of these accidents, nobody but a savage would think it funny, however surprised he might be. What makes us laugh is a mixture of the shock at an accident that looks as if it might be serious and the realization that it is not after all a hundredth part as serious as it might have been. The shock is obviously one of the things that make us laugh in such cases, but among civilized people the surprise of finding that the shock was superfluous is equally necessary.

You will see an excellent example of this in motoring accidents. At present, motoring accidents are not as a rule funny, because we are apprehensive that the results may be fatal. Recently, however, someone has invented a kind of cowcatcher for motor cars which tosses the astonished pedestrian into the air and deposits him safely in a net; and it is certain that if this comes into general use motor accidents in the future will become more generally funny. As you walk down Piccadilly on a spring afternoon, you will see whole clutches of messenger boys, policemen, clubmen in top hats, and all sorts of people, tossed by motor cars as by bulls and left sprawling, alive and kicking, in a tangle of network—a scene that, I am sure, will make most people laugh even more heartily than Democritus laughed at the sights he saw in the harbor of Abdera. Saints, philosophers, and perfect gentlemen may not laugh; but ordinary human beings will, and in this, I think, they will show their humanity. For to laugh at an accident that ends happily proves not so much that one enjoyed the accident as that one enjoyed the happy ending. We should find the accidents that happen to Don Quixote intolerable if any of them ended fatally. We enjoy them only on the understanding that the Don is a cork who sinks under the sea for a few moments to rise again and bob as buoyantly as ever on the surface. We laugh at the accident, indeed, on the assumption that the victim will speedily recover from it. The escape as well as the disaster contributes to our mirth. It is cruelty suddenly merging into kindness. Hence we find that, at its best, it is the characteristic of humane men—of Shakespeare and Cervantes, of Fielding and Dickens.

Even so we can see why, on this assumption, saints and Utopian philosophers are on the whole hostile or indifferent to laughter. The saint and the Utopian philosopher have a vision of a perfect world in which accidents do not happen. The saint realizes that, if Adam and Eve had never sinned, we should all have been as the angels, and angels never have their hats blown off or slip on the ice or sit down on the floor instead of a chair or get chased in their dressing gowns through the streets, like Mr. Winkle, by needlessly suspicious husbands. Laughter is a confession of the sins and silliness of the world, but it is also a kind of genial acquiescence in these sins and sillinesses. To the saint, the stumblings of man are tragic, proving that he is not yet an angel. To men and women with a sense of humor, the stumblings of man—even on his way to perfection—are largely comic, proving that he is only a human being after all. We may deplore, if we like, the saint's lack of humor, but in this I think we may be wrong. He has a vision that we have not. Our sense of humor is only a compensation for our lack of his vision. We should never have possessed it if we had remained in Eden. It is the grace of our disgrace— a consolation prize given to a race excluded from Paradise.

IV

Hence it is natural enough that laughter should play a comparatively small part in the great literature and records of the human race. No doubt the characters named in the Old Testament often laughed, but there is not a single laugh described in all its pages that infects us with mirth as we read of it today. The tears of David over the dead Absalom still touch the heart, but the merriment of the days before the Flood no longer moves us to sympathetic mirth. The laughter referred to in the Bible is for the most part the laughter of scorn. The more cheerful kind of laughter—the laughter of the fool, as it is called—is even compared to its detriment by the Wise Man to "the crackling of thorns under a pot." Homer, again, though he made the gods themselves laugh, has given us no supreme comic scene as a companion picture to that supreme tragic scene in which Hector parts from

Andromache. There may have been Greek writers who were as comic as Mr. P. G. Wodehouse, but their fun died with them, and even Aristophanes, the greatest comic writer of antiquity, and some say of all time, is not, I am sure, as funny as he used to be.

Tragedy can live as long as a mummy—as long, one might almost say, as one of the immortal gods. It affects us as profoundly three thousand years afterward as it affected men in the year in which it was born. Laughter, on the other hand, is as a rule as volatile as eau de cologne sprinkled on a handkerchief. A few great writers have been able to imprison this essence and give it, if not immortality, at least a life thirty times as long as that of the oldest brandy. A jest unfortunately does not improve with age as brandy does, and many even of Shakespeare's jokes have to be explained to modern readers in footnotes. At the same time, if we may change the metaphor, a small handful of men of genius have been able to make the best of their jokes permanently explosive, like Mr. Wells's radioactive bomb. This is, undoubtedly, one of the most difficult miracles in literature.

As to what the nature of the first laugh was after man had descended from the trees, the authorities on the subject differ. Father Ronald Knox has lately put himself on the side of those who hold that satire preceded humor in the history of our race, and that therefore man laughed first out of derision at the pain and humiliation of his fellow creatures. For this view there is something to be said, for primitive savages who could see nothing amusing in *Pride and Prejudice* are said to roar with laughter at the spectacle of a man getting a bad fall or writhing in pain with fever. On the other hand, the baby is the most primitive type of human being that we know, and the baby in the cradle begins to laugh long before it knows that there are such things as pain and humiliation in the world, or can appreciate the humor of an accident. You will see a baby lying on its back in a perambulator and, as it looks up at the leaves of a tree dancing and twinkling on a windy, sunny day, laughing with an exuberance equal to that of any grown-up man or woman at a disaster to a fellow creature. You can make it laugh by peeping out at it from behind a handkerchief. You can make it laugh by tickling it. It is in tickling, perhaps, that we find the best evidence of the non-satirical origin of laughter. The psychologists in their works on laughter have written a great deal about tickling, and some of them have even experimented on their children to discover which, in their right order, are the most ticklish parts of the body. The order given by one writer is: "The sole of the foot, the armpit, the neck and part under the chin, the ribs." Darwin even experimented in tickling anthropoid apes, and discovered that they gave out "a reiterated sound, corresponding with our laughter, when they are tickled, especially under the armpits." Several authorities maintain that when dogs are tickled they respond with what is described as "an incipient smile." Others declare that pigs like being tickled, but the author in whose works I have seen a reference to this subject observes: "Never having been on tickling terms with pigs, I have nothing to say about them."

Certainly the pleasure of being tickled is one of the earliest pleasures known to a human being. One of the commonest metaphors used in describing laughter, indeed, is that which speaks of a person's being "tickled to death." This suggests—and I think it is Professor Sully's view—that laughter originated in play rather than in derision. In the baby it is an expression of happiness without a breath of malice in it. And, apart from the evidence of tickling, if laughter be some subtle form of malice, how can we explain the smile with which friends greet each other when they meet and which most people wear when they are being introduced to a stranger? When you are introduced to a man, you smile, not because you have noticed something wrong with his clothes or in his personal appearance, but because you are pleased to meet him, as the saying is, or pretend to be. This may seem to conflict with the theory that angels never laugh, for angels must often experience pleasure. The laughter of human beings, however, seems to me to express an animal rather than a spiritual pleasure. Meredith traced English laughter to its sources in the gastric juices. The laugh has undoubtedly evolved since the days when Pharaoh's daughter tickled the infant Moses, till now we are able to laugh at the wit of Anatole France and the humor of Chekhov. But it is still, at its best, play, even when salted with derision or bitterness.

As with play of all sorts, one of its chief functions is to release us from the hardening formulæ of our daily lives. We cannot help attempting to imprison ourselves and all our opinions and experiences in formulæ. We see our neighbors as formulæ walking. We are turned into formulæ ourselves by our habits. Thus we make a too rigid pattern of life, and deceive ourselves into believing that the world is a mechanical, settled, and law-abiding place in which nearly everybody will behave according to pattern. For instance, the ordinary English child has a formula in accordance with which he thinks that everybody ought to speak more or less like himself. When he hears a foreigner speaking, he is inclined to laugh. He will laugh at what he regards as the mispronunciations of a Scotsman or an Irishman. His laugh is partly derision— derision in defense of the pattern. But I think it is also a playful delight in novelty. Englishmen do not go to hear Sir Harry Lauder in his Scottish songs merely to deride the language of the "braw, bricht, moonlicht nicht." Similarly when they laugh at the mention of a "haggis,"—as Englishmen, being queer creatures, do,—the laughter is not in derision of the Scottish diet so much as a playful escape from the pattern of the English menu.

Laughter at the antics of a drunken man is also due in part to the fact that in not too fatal a way he breaks the expected pattern of life. If an ordinary sober man lets a coin fall on the pavement, his swift stooping down and picking it up does not make us laugh, for this is what we expect him to do. See a drunken man trying to pick up a fallen coin, however. His attempts to preserve his balance at each new bend of the body, his misjudgment of the distance at which the coin lies from his hand, his quite disproportionate air of determination and sobriety, are all a contradiction of common life. He no longer acts with the mechanical regularity which we expect in the behavior of human beings. He has dissolved the human pattern, and we on our part are dissolved in laughter. There are some people who deny that laughter can take drunkenness as one of its themes, but this is because they see drunkenness entirely in terms of its tragedies. They see drunkenness, not as an accident, but as a doom, and, like the saints, are distressed because it is a negation of the perfect world. Ordinary men laugh at a thing, however, not because it is a negation of the perfect world, but because it is a contradiction of everyday life. If everybody were drunk all the time, nobody would see anything to laugh at in Sir Toby Belch.

V

Comedy gives us, indeed, a new and surprising pattern of life—a pattern that is a lampoon on the pattern to which we are accustomed. Mrs. Malaprop breaks the pattern of the ordinary English pronunciation and use of words, and as a result her "allegory on the banks of the Nile" still sets the theater in a roar. Lear in his nonsense verses breaks the pattern of intelligible speech, and we love his nonsense because he enables us to escape for the moment from the iron rule of sense. People do not laugh when a cock crows, but I have heard the gallery laughing uproariously when a man in the audience imitated a cock crowing. This is because, when a cock crows, he is acting in accord with the accepted farmyard pattern, but when a man crows he is breaking the pattern of human behavior. The amusement many people get from talking and performing animals may be explained in the same way. The parrot that uses blasphemous language is not behaving according to the monotonous rules of bird life. The dog that rises on its hind legs and fox-trots across the stage defies the laws laid down by Nature for the behavior of dogs. Lord George Sanger amused thousands of people some years ago by introducing into his circus an oyster that smoked a pipe. This would not have been amusing but for the fact that oysters do not, as a rule, smoke. Nobody would pay a penny to see a human being smoking a pipe. The oyster did not smoke a pipe either, but Lord Sanger was able to make people pretend to themselves that it did, and for one glorious moment the pattern of conventional oysterdom was smashed to pieces.

All the comic writers from Aristophanes to Shakespeare, from Swift to Lewis Carroll, have broken the pattern for us in a comparable way. They have taken us when we were tired of looking at life as though it were a series of demonstrable theories in Euclid, and have torn all those impressive triangles and circles into small pieces, and have dipped them in color and put them into a kaleidoscope, and have invited us to look at the result, in which all the legalism of Euclid has been turned into a chaos of ludicrous and distorted figures. Comedy has no respect even for the hypotenuse of a right-angled triangle. It does not care whether or not two parallel lines ever meet. It does not care whether the radii of a circle are equal. On the whole it prefers to suppose that they are not.

Laughter, then, springs largely from the lawless part of our nature. Hilarity is a kind of heresy—a cheerful defiance of all the laws, including the law of gravity. The planets are not amusing, since they obey fixed laws. Human beings are amusing because they do not. The saint or philosopher who believes that life should be lived according to law may therefore easily be tempted to regard laughter with suspicion. In this, however, I think he would be wrong. We must judge laughter, like other things, by its results. And a reasonable defense of laughter may be founded on the fact that it is not men with a comic sense who are the greatest lawbreakers. Murderers and thieves are not noted as a rule for their hilarity. They are for the most part serious men, who might have remained law-abiding citizens if only they had had a greater capacity for laughing.

It would be going too far to claim that all the laughers are virtuous men and all the non-laughers criminals. At the same time it is probably true that the laughing man, if he is virtuous, will as a result of his laughter be less offensively virtuous, and if he is vicious he will be less offensively vicious. Laughter gives a holiday both to the virtues and to the vices, and takes the imagination on its travels into a country in which the only principle is the principle of comic incongruity. Here man can resign himself to the enjoyment of life as a topsy-turvy wonderland as strange as any that Alice ever visited, and can see his dullest neighbors as a gallery of caricatures. It is a land of happy accidents, of large noses and blown-off hats, where words are misspelt and mispronounced, where men wear spats on their wrists instead of cuffs, the land of paradoxes and bulls and the things that could not happen. Whether it is worth visiting nobody will ever know for certain till the Day of Judgment.

The worst thing that can be said against laughter is that, by putting us in a good humor, it enables us to tolerate ourselves. The best thing that can be said for it is that for the same reason it enables us to tolerate each other.

THE MODERN BIOGRAPHER

By *Andre Maurois*

IS there such a thing as modern biography? Can one name a year in which suddenly the old biography ceased to exist and modern biography came into being? And if so, what is the difference between old and modern biography?

The first question, Is there such a thing as modern biography? can be answered in the affirmative. Read a page of Plutarch or Izaak Walton, of Dr. Johnson, or of a Victorian biographer like Trevelyan or Froude, and read after this a page of Strachey. You will see at once that you have before you two different types of book. You will find the same difference if you read biographers of other countries. Compare, in America, the traditional life of George Washington, of Abraham Lincoln, with the latest lives written. Compare, in Germany, the biographies of the beginning of the nine-teenth century with Ludwig's *Kaiser Wilhelm* or with his *Goethe*. As regards France, the comparison is difficult, because biography with us is a new art, but we seem to be making up for lost opportunities by a period of mass produc-tion, and biographies built after the Stracheyan pattern have been turned out by the dozen in the last three or four years.

If now we come to the second question, Can one name a year in which suddenly the old biography ceased to exist and modern biography came into being? we shall perhaps find an answer in a quotation from the great English novelist, Virginia Woolf. She hazards an assertion that "on or about December, 1910, human character changed." "I am not saying," she writes, "that one went out, as one might into a garden, and there saw that a rose had flowered, or that a hen had laid an

From the *Yale Review*, January 1928; copyright, 1928, by the Yale University Press. Used by special permission.

egg. The change was not sudden and definite like that. But a change there was, nevertheless; . . . let us date it about the year 1910. The first signs of it are recorded in the books of Samuel Butler, in *The Way of All Flesh* in particular; the plays of Bernard Shaw continue to record it. In life one can see the change, if I may use a homely illustration, in the character of one's cook. The Victorian cook lived like a leviathan in the lower depths, formidable, silent, obscure, inscrutable; the Georgian cook is a creature of sunshine and fresh air; in and out of the drawing-room, now to borrow the *Daily Herald*, now to ask advice about a hat. Do you ask for more solemn instances of the power of the human race to change? . . . All human relations have shifted—those between masters and servants, husbands and wives, parents and children. And when human relations change there is at the same time a change in religion, conduct, politics, and literature. Let us agree to place one of these changes about the year 1910."

Making allowance for the conscious exaggerations of a delightful writer, there is a great deal of truth in this paradox. In other countries, the great change took place later, in 1918; but it is, I think, indisputable that the outlook on life of the cultured part of humanity, whether in Europe or in America, has undergone deep transformations in the course of the last decade. Has this change been for better or for worse? This remains to be seen, but the fact cannot be denied by an impartial observer that biography, like the novel—like all forms of literature—has been affected by these changes.

As to the third question, What is the difference between old and modern biography? the differences are of two kinds—difference in motive and difference in method. Let us begin with the motive. Why did the biographers of the old days write? We find an answer in one of them: "Biography sets before us the lives of eminent men that we may imitate their virtues and avoid their vices." The object of Plutarch is to teach morality. The object of Walton is a twofold one—"an honor due to the virtuous dead and the lesson in magnanimity to those who shall succeed them." Walton writes about his friends a few years after their deaths, and his charming lives are nothing but monuments to the memories of those friends.

Sir Sidney Lee, in his *Principles of Biography*, tells us with unconscious humor that biography exists to satisfy a natural instinct in man, the commemorative instinct. This reminds one of the theory of the Doctor in Molière's *Malade Imaginaire:* "Opium facit dormire quia est in eo virtus dormitiva." The creation of instincts makes psychology an easy science. Nevertheless, it is true that most of the old writers of biographies worked, as Sir Sidney says, to keep alive the memories of those who by character and deeds have distinguished themselves from the mass of humanity.

It must not be forgotten that the old biographer had sometimes another motive, which was simply that such lives had been ordered from him by a publisher. Dr. Johnson, for instance, never considered it as a duty towards humanity to write the lives of the British poets. He was asked to do so, and he did so extremely well, because his was a splendid mind, and he could not help giving life and color to everything he wrote.

In the Victorian era, after the death of any great Englishman, his family and his friends chose with care a writer who, they thought, would give suitable praise to the deceased hero. The process was the same in America. "When any distinguished citizen, lawyer or judge, merchant or writer, died," wrote William Roscoe Thayer, "it was taken for granted that his clergyman, if he had one, would write his life, unless his wife, sister, or cousin were preferred." Prudent men, before their death, appointed a biographer just as they appointed an executor of their will. Such choices were sometimes unfortunate. Thus Carlyle found Froude an intimate and dangerous enemy. Byron was hopelessly misunderstood by Moore. The Prince Consort and Cardinal Manning were made ridiculous by two well-meaning biographers. Other choices were happy; for example, the appointment of Monypenny by the trustees of

Lord Beaconsfield; or the appointment of Charles Whibley by the family of Lord John Manners. But in the old Victorian biographies the quality most appreciated by the families of the heroes was respect of the proprieties. The intimate life of a man, his everyday doings, his weaknesses and follies and mistakes, were not to be mentioned. Even if his life had been notoriously scandalous, this should only be vaguely alluded to. "What business," says Tennyson, "has the public to know about Byron's wildnesses? He has given them fine work, and they ought to be satisfied." The author was given all the information available; letters, even private diaries, were generously put at his disposal; but such generosity forced upon him a loyalty which compelled him to be secretive and laudatory. If there was a widow, she kept a careful eye both on the portrait of her deceased husband and on the figure she herself cut in the book before posterity. The results are too well known—"Books so stuffed with virtue," one writer says of them, "that I began to doubt the existence of any virtue."

Of course, such a hard judgment is unfair to the good books of that period. A great deal could be said in favor of the old type of life and letters in three volumes, with notes and appendix. It was an invaluable mass of material, where the modern biographer is very glad to go and dig for precious metal. It was even sometimes fine work of real literary value. Macaulay's life, by Trevelyan, is a very readable book. The custom is to praise Lockhart's life of Scott and Forster's life of Dickens; these are useful books, full of interesting documents; but shall I confess that I do not admire them unreservedly? They are long and badly constructed. On the other hand, Dowden's life of Shelley seems to me perfect.

Even when the Victorian biographer is a good historian and a good writer, we have a grievance against him, which is his attitude of hero-worship. A public man, whether he is an artist or a statesman, always wears a mask. We find in him two characters; one is the man known to the public, or at least the man he would like the public to believe in; the other is the man as he is known to his friends or to himself, if he is sincere. The Victorian biographer always describes a mask, and refuses to look behind it. Read Moore's life of Byron. It is only a mask of Byron. Nobody has ever dared to write about the real Dickens or the real Thackeray. Who has described the real Herbert Spencer, human, rather comical, as we find him in the unconsciously delightful little book, *Home Life with Herbert Spencer*. The tradition was to glide over the real facts if they spoiled the rigid perfection of the mask. Victorian biographers were sculptors of commemorative monuments. Few of them were good sculptors.

We now come to Strachey, who is, I think, by common agreement to be considered as the father and master of modern biography. At once we perceive a difference. Strachey is no hero-worshipper. On the contrary, he is a hero-wrecker, an idol-breaker. Before him the great Victorians were sacred to an English gentleman of letters. General Gordon, great puritan and great soldier, was treated as a sort of national saint. Queen Victoria had Gordon's Bible placed in one of the corridors at Windsor, enclosed in a crystal case. As to the Queen herself, people knew there might be some faint essence of the comic about her, but they preferred not to think about it, and especially not to talk about it.

Then Strachey wrote *Eminent Victorians*. Nobody could complain about the title of the book. The men and women he spoke about were eminent, and they were Victorians. But as soon as one began to read, one perceived that the title was ironic. With great skill, Strachey described these Victorian giants, Cardinal Manning, Thomas Arnold, General Gordon. He did not say a word against them; he never judged; he remained objective; but he portrayed the men as they had been, without hiding anything. He gave us extracts from their letters, from their diaries, and he grouped such extracts in such a cunning way that the intimate life of his unfortunate models was revealed. For instance, he tells us that Cardinal Manning in his diary notes that, having decided to mortify himself, he determined during Lent "to use no pleasant bread except on Sundays and feasts, such as cake and sweetmeat." "But," says Strachey, "a few days later the Cardinal added in the margin 'I do not include plain biscuits.'" No comments from Strachey, but the shaft has gone home.

In Strachey's *Queen Victoria*, you cannot find a single sentence against the Queen, but the quotations and facts collected evoke the image of a fat and resolute little woman, full of pride, accessible to flattery, at the same time touching and ridiculous. The literary method of Strachey is the method of the great humorists. He does not appear himself in his book; he does not judge his model; he walks behind her, imitates her gestures, remains serious, and obtains by such tricks excellent effects of comedy. The fact that he imitates the habits of the Queen, that he underlines like herself all the words of a sentence, that he writes, like her, "Lord M." instead of Lord Melbourne, "Dear Albert" instead of Prince Albert, all these little details create a very natural and very human image. Even the exact quotation of an official document produces an effect of cruel humor. For instance, when he comes to the construction of the Albert Memorial, the ugliest monument in England, Strachey does not say that it is ugly; he simply describes the thing as it is, and gives us the very words of the sculptor: "I have chosen the sitting posture as best conveying the idea of dignity befitting the royal personage. . . . The aim has been, with the individuality of portraiture, to embody rank, character, and enlightenment, and to convey a sense of that responsive intelligence indicating an active, rather than a passive, interest in those pursuits of civilisation illustrated in the surrounding figures, groups, and relieves. . . . To identify the figure with one of the most memorable undertakings of the public life of the Prince—the International Exhibition of 1851—a catalogue of the works collected in that first gathering of the industry of all nations, is placed in the right hand." "The statue was of bronze gilt,"

Strachey continues, "and weighed nearly ten tons. It was rightly supposed that the simple word 'Albert,' cast on the base, would be a sufficient means of identification."

But it would be unfair to see nothing in Strachey but an idol-breaker. He is also a very deep psychologist. As a painter, he has a curious method. He begins by designing a rather crude portrait; then he corrects a line, then another, and he keeps on making it more involved, more confused, but at the same time nearer to life. He often uses expressions like "and yet, and yet," or "There was something—what was it?"— which give the reader the impression that he pursues an indefinable character just as he would do in real life.

Remember the wonderful portrait of the Prince Consort: "Albert, certainly, seemed to be everything that Stockmar could have wished—virtuous, industrious, persevering, intelligent. And yet—why was it?—all was not well with him. He was sick at heart.

"For in spite of everything he had never reached to happiness. His work, for which at last he came to crave with an almost morbid appetite, was a solace and not a cure. . . . The causes of his melancholy were hidden, mysterious, unanalysable perhaps—too deeply rooted in the innermost recesses of his temperament for the eye of reason to apprehend. There were contradictions in his nature, which, to some of those who knew him best, made him seem an inexplicable enigma: he was severe and gentle; he was modest and scornful; he longed for affection and he was cold. He was lonely, not merely with the loneliness of exile but with the loneliness of conscious and unrecognised superiority. He had the pride, at once resigned and over-weening, of a doctrinaire. And yet to say that he was simply a doctrinaire would be a false description; for the pure doctrinaire rejoices always in an internal contentment, and Albert was very far from doing that. There was something that he wanted and that he could never get. What was it? Some absolute, some ineffable sympathy? Some extraordinary, some sublime success? Possibly, it was a mixture of both. To dominate and to be understood! To conquer, by the same triumphant influence, the submission and the appreciation of men—that would be worth while indeed! But, to such imaginations, he saw too clearly how faint were the responses of his actual environment. Who was there who appreciated him, really and truly? Who *could* appreciate him in England? And, if the gentle virtue of an inward excellence availed so little, could he expect more from the hard ways of skill and force? The terrible land of his exile loomed before him a frigid, an impregnable mass. . . . He believed that he was a failure and he began to despair."

One cannot admire too much the skill of the artist and the way in which the description of a mind slowly becomes a monologue of the mind itself. The stream of consciousness, so often alluded to by the modern novelist, is described in the work of Strachey and also in the work of his followers. Nobody, perhaps, has done it better than Harold Nicolson in his *Byron*. Here we follow the moods of the man, just as we would in one of James Joyce's novels—and at the same time every thought attributed to Byron is a thought that Byron really had. Take, for instance, the impressions of Byron when the family of Leigh Hunt invades his house.

"Leigh Hunt was Shelley's fault entirely: Shelley was like that, he let one in for things. One would just mention an idea, and expand it a little, and before one knew what had happened Shelley had shrilled off into another of his enthusiasms. That was the worst of Shelley: he could never see the difference between an idea and a proposal; obviously there was a very great difference. Byron, that hot night at Ravenna when they had sat up together drinking gin and water, had merely suggested that, in certain circumstances, it would be great fun if he and Shelley and Leigh Hunt were all to edit a radical newspaper together from Italy, which could be published by John Hunt in London. Shelley had called it a 'generous proposal': it *wasn't* a proposal, it was only an idea: on second thoughts it was a devilish bad idea.

And there was Shelley writing to him from Pisa saying 'Poor Hunt is delighted by your *noble* offer.' Had Byron ever made an offer? He certainly had never intended to: at least not exactly an offer, only an idea. And then, before he could explain it all away, there was the Hunt family already embarked and well on their way to Italy."

Or, better still, perhaps, take the impressions of Byron at a time when he starts on his Greek adventure. "It would be idle to pretend that Byron set out upon this his last journey with any very spirited enthusiasm. . . . For when it had come to packing up, and destroying old letters, and explaining to Barry what was to be done with the books, and toting up the accounts, and sending the horses down to the harbour, and finding everything at the Casa Saluzzo hourly more disintegrated and uncomfortable, he began, definitely and indignantly, to curse the whole undertaking. It was always like that: people never left one alone; there he was, good-natured and kindly, and they came along and took advantage of him, and extracted promises, and imposed upon him generally. Once again he had been caught in a chain of circumstances: there had been his first visit to Greece, and 'Childe Harold,' and 'The Corsair,' and that silly passage about the 'hereditary bondsmen'; and there had been Hobhouse (damn Hobhouse!), and that egregious ass Trelawny. And as a result here was he, who had never done any harm to anyone, sitting alone in the Casa Saluzzo, with his household gods once again dismantled around him, and his bulldog growling now and then at the distant voice of Trelawny thundering orders to the servants.

"Of all forms of cant, this cant of romanticism was the most insufferable. There was Trelawny, for instance, trying to look like Lara, with his sham eagle eyes, his sham disordered hair, his sham abrupt manners. Why couldn't Trelawny behave quietly and like a man of decent breeding? Surely, if they were committed to this Greek scrape it would be better to take the thing soberly and calmly, instead of all this dust and bustle, of all this cant about Causes, and Liberty, and

Adventure. How he *loathed* adventures! At the mere word he ground his teeth in fury."

In the case of Nicolson, just as in the case of Strachey, there is a curious mixture of irony and tenderness; but such tenderness is rather grim. Even when Strachey pats his heroes on the back, you feel that he is ready to scratch them. To treat a great man as a human being, even if this human being is a lovable one, is to make the great man smaller. The statue is brought down from its pedestal. Yes, it cannot be denied, Strachey and his pupils are idol-breakers.

It seems natural that such a school of biographers should be born in England, because a reaction against the excess of propriety of the Victorians was inevitable. After too much hero-worship, the reaction was even necessary. Strachey, Nicolson, Guedalla, have done in biography what Huxley, Forster, Virginia Woolf, have done in the novel. But though the school was born in England, it was imitated in other countries. In the United States, biographers are now rewriting the lives of most of the illustrious statesmen, and the new lives are more frank, more outspoken, than the old ones. We discover a new Franklin, a new Washington; and as to the men who lend themselves to comic treatment, they are treated without mercy by the new generation. As a good example I may mention the very remarkable life of Brigham Young by Werner.

Is this new type of biography written for the pleasure of destroying heroes? If it were so, it would be a rather despicable art. Humanity has always found a source of consolation in the lives of its great men, and one ought to consider very seriously before one destroys a perhaps useful illusion. It cannot be denied that in some instances the new biographer has overdone it. Strachey himself must be admitted in some instances to be a shade nastier than is really fair. His Disraeli is a courtier without scruples, who dominates through flattery a rather unintelligent old woman. Indeed, Disraeli was apt to pay the Queen hyperbolical compliments; but he also knew how to resist her. On the other hand, the letters of the Queen are not only made of the sentences—of the very amusing sentences—so admirably chosen by Strachey, but also of very wise comments on the political situation and a sort of middle-class wisdom that was not without useful effect upon the fate of the British Empire.

Strachey is so good a psychologist that truth in his hands is never in real danger; but some of his disciples, without imitating his deep insight, have only got hold of his familiar tricks. Instead of choosing, as heroes for biographies, "eminent men, so that we may imitate their virtues," they restrict themselves to individualities which are susceptible of treatment in their favorite mode of irony. The writer treats his hero with an unheard-of familiarity. There is a biography of Longfellow in which the biographer persists in calling the poet Henry. We have regretted in France during the last years the publication of several books where great writers are treated by much lesser writers as rather contemptible schoolmates. They even take the liberty of inventing conversations between well-known men and of putting in their mouths sentences they never pronounced. Some of these books would make us regret the three-volume life and letters which, after all, was an historical and a scholarly work. We sometimes get tired of "the plucking of dead lions by the beard."

But when we judge the modern biographer, we must consider that he represents a reaction, and that a reaction always goes too far. It was necessary to remind the last of the Victorians that a mask is not a man; it is now necessary to remind our contemporaries that a man is never entirely ridiculous, and that his life is very serious for himself.

If some of the writers of the present day have adopted the habit of choosing a hero because they do not quite like him, others, on the contrary, choose him because they are attracted to him and because they think and feel that by writing the lives of great men they may, to a certain extent, express sentiments that they have felt themselves. We all know that art is for the artist an outlet and a mode of self-expression. It is particularly true of the novelist. The novelist, through his hero, gets rid of emotions which, if they could not find such an outlet, would torment him. Samuel Butler when he writes *The Way of All Flesh* builds a hero who is an image of himself. Flaubert, when he was asked who Madame Bovary was, answered, "Madame Bovary, c'est moi."

It may happen that you find in the life of another real man certain similarities of character and idea to your own, which make you think that by writing his life you might explain to yourself some of the difficulties that you have met with. I have—to take an example from my own work—written a life of Shelley. It would, of course, be absurd to say that I find any resemblance between Shelley's life and my own. Shelley was a great poet and I am not; Shelley was the son of an English baronet at the beginning of the nineteenth century, and I am a French commoner of the twentieth. Nevertheless, Shelley was a romantic who, having begun life with certain ideals, attempted to live up to them and found himself confronted by a hard and hostile world. This in a much smaller way had happened to me. I had left school with an idealistic outlook, when I found myself in a practical world of business, where the theories of my adolescence refused to work. It was a very painful experience, so that when I first read a life of Shelley, I felt a sympathy with him, a great desire to know him better, and to understand better what had happened. Going into details, I saw that Shelley was much more human than the beautiful and ineffectual angel depicted by Matthew Arnold. It gave me pleasure to find him human. The superman is not a companion; he is too different from us; we cannot understand him. Happily, he does not exist. Shelley was a great man, but he was not a superman. I did my best to describe him exactly as I had seen him. I did not want to make fun of him. I like and admire him too much for that; but I did not want to conceal any of his weaknesses and errors, because I felt that what made him lovable was that very mixture of greatness and humanity.

In the case of Disraeli, the inducement was the same. Disraeli is again the romantic who attempts to transform ideals into reality. But Shelley died very young and had no time to succeed, whereas Disraeli managed to combine the romantic and the man of action, and died an unrepenting and partly successful romantic. Considered from that point of view, biography becomes an art similar to the art of the novel—not in its treatment but with regard to the spirit in which the work is approached.

Whether they work from the motives of Strachey (reaction) or from the motives that have just been analyzed (self-expression), modern biographers have one thing in common; that is their refusal to paint masks, their desire to get to the real man. Is this a good or a bad thing? Some critics say, Why do away with hero-worship? It is quite true, perhaps, that a hero is at the same time a man, but why say so? Is it not healthier for humanity to keep in view an image of the better type of man, an image which will help us to climb on our own shoulders? Do you not fear that the spectacle of the weaknesses of great men will lead minor men to be easily satisfied with their own conduct? Plutarch was not, perhaps, quite true to life, but he produced Montaigne, and Napoleon.

Yes; but the danger of the old type of biography is that nobody believes in it. We all know that Gladstone was not exactly the man painted by Morley. Would it not be more inspiring to meet real human beings and to treat them as such? This man Byron was not the man Moore makes him out to be; he was full of pride; he was hard on women; he was a strange mixture of his own "Manfred" and a typical English gentleman; but he was a very lovable character just the same. I wonder if make-believe is ever a good policy, and if there is any real greatness outside of perfect truth. In spite of his somewhat brutal sincerity, we must give credit to the modern biographer for his genuine respect of truth.

We shall now try to find out what are the methods of the

new biographer. The essential point about him is that his aim is to build a work of art. When historians accumulated masses of documents without choice or discrimination, the result might be an interesting book, but the works produced were of considerable length, unreadable for the average man, and certainly they were not works of art. The question will be raised, Should a biography be a work of art?

"Art is essentially," Bacon said, "man added to Nature"; that is, facts ordered by a human mind. The novel is constructed; the idea of symmetry, of rhythm, plays an important part in the building of any good novel. But how can symmetry and form be achieved when the author deals with real life? Real life is what it is. We cannot alter it. How shall we give shape to this monster? The author finds himself confronted with long periods in the life of his hero when nothing happens, and then suddenly in the space of a few months events crowd in. Also it may happen that the real life ends where the story begins. Once, in London, an old bookseller said to me, "Well, sir, your life of Shelley—it isn't such a bad book; but I'll give you some advice. Next time, don't make your hero die so young. The public doesn't like it." The sentence sounds absurd, but there is something in it. The real subject of any novel is conflict between man and the universe— what Goethe called the Years of Learning; but the real conclusion of the Years of Learning is reached only in the maturity of man. For Shelley, one does not know what the conclusion might have been had he lived through this maturity.

However, consider the portrait-painter. He also has to deal with a given reality and to build a harmony of colors and lines with this given material. How does he do it? He selects; he leaves out a great many things; he does not add to the face of his model lines that are not there, but he builds by suppression, by concentrating the interest of the onlooker on the important features of the face. This is exactly what the biographer should do. He must not invent anything, but his art is to forget. If he has at his disposal two hundred letters and a long diary, he must know how to exact the few sentences that will convey a general impression.

In any life, there is always a well-hidden harmony; the historian has to discover the mysterious rhythm in that existence. He can give an impression of unity by repeating certain themes, as Wagner does in music. In the biography of Shelley, for instance, there must be a theme of water; water plays a great part in Shelley's life. As a boy he is attracted by it; as a man he spends his life in fragile boats. From the beginning, you feel that he will die by drowning. The writer should give this impression of impending fate. In the life of Disraeli, rain is a poetical element. Implacable, steady rain is a symbol of the universe fighting the romantic. Peacocks also play a curious part in this life. By a careful handling of such themes, the biographer can hope to achieve some sort of musical construction.

Such construction must, of course, coincide with a respect for facts. A strict adherence to historical truth is necessary to the biographer, but after he has collected his facts, he has a right to eliminate some of them.

Now, there are certain rules which practice has proved useful. The first is that one should follow a chronological order. Ancient biographers like Plutarch had no idea of chronology. They started with a recital of facts, and, after they had told us about the death of their hero, they began again with anecdotes and analysis of character. Then came an ethical judgment. This method gave a painful impression of repetition. It was copied from Plutarch by Walton and also by Johnson; they all tell you from the first that their hero was a great man. The Victorian biographer writes "This great poet was born in 1788." This, I think, is wrong. A man is not born a great poet, and he will not interest us if he is shown as a great man from his babyhood. What is interesting is to see the child Byron, the young man at Harrow, at Cambridge, and to discover slowly how he became "Manfred" and "Don Juan."

Of course, this idea of chronological development is new. It comes from the fact that we now believe in the evolution of an individual mind as well as of a race. A biographer like Walton did not feel the need of chronology because he did not believe that a man's nature could change very much. All arts react one upon another. In the last twenty years, Marcel Proust has taught us how to avoid drawing static characters. Some of his heroes are unpleasant at the beginning of the novel and delightful at the end. In the case of other characters, the process is reversed. We want the biographer to be as true to life as the novelist. "My object," says Miss Lowell, "has been to make the reader feel as though he were living with Keats, subject to the same influences that surrounded him, moving in his circle, watching the advent of poems as from day to day they sprang into being." In biography, as in the novel, it is important that the minor characters should be seen from the point of view of the central figure. They should not even be allowed to appear until the very moment when the hero discovers them.

The second rule is to avoid pronouncing moral judgments. The essential difference between art and action is that art builds a world where no real events occur, and where, therefore, man feels that he has no moral decision to make. The characters in *Hamlet* would be painful to meet in real life, because something would have to be done about them, but we accept them on the stage because no moral problem arises for us. If an artist gives the impression that the world he describes is a world where we must act and decide, he may be a great moralist, but he is no more a great artist. A biographer must tell his story in objective and impartial style.

The third rule is to read every word that has ever been written on the subject and to collect all available testimony. What the modern historian wants to describe is not the statue but the man. In official documents, very often he finds nothing but the statue. It may be in the letters or the journal of an unknown woman that he will come across the anecdote that

will suddenly reveal a character. He must hunt for details if
he wants truth. Of course, the question arises, What is truth?
Is there indeed a truth about character? You remember
Walt Whitman's—

When I read the book, the biography famous,
And is this, then (said I), what the author calls a man's life?
And so will some one, when I am dead and gone, write my life?
As if any man really knew aught of my life;
Why, even I myself, I often think, know little or nothing of my real life.

Whitman is partly right. If we think of our own lives, we
realize that some of our most important acts have been accomplished by us without any real motivation. Perhaps we have
said words which meant more than we thought; and a few
months later we found ourselves involved in actions which
did not coincide with our real wishes. This is true of Byron.
Byron never meant to die in Greece, or even to go to Greece.
He had played with the idea because he was bored, because he
thought it would relieve him of the tedium of his Italian life.
Then the moment came when words were turned into acts and
Byron lived up to them.

The writer should be careful not to make the life of his hero
appear too well constructed. A human life is very rarely the
conscious accomplishment of the will. It is that partly, but
you must always leave a certain margin for the action of circumstance. A "tale told by an idiot," says Shakespeare.
There is always something of that madness in the lives of great
men of action. If you leave out the strange atmosphere of fate,
you miss all the real poetry of human life.

Of course, one of the best technical rules to follow in order
to avoid showing the life of the hero as too squarely built is to
allow the reader to see him through the eyes of friends and
enemies who judge him differently. There the biographer can
learn much from the modern novelist. Read a novel like
Forster's *Passage to India;* there you see the English as
they appear to a Hindu, the Hindu as seen by the English,
and the Hindu as seen by himself. In the same way, I have

attempted as well as I could to show Disraeli as seen by Gladstone, and Gladstone as seen by Disraeli. You cannot say that there was one Gladstone; there were as many Gladstones as there were people who knew him, and it is the sum of these portraits which enables the reader to form an idea of the average Gladstone.

There is one more question to deal with, How is one to select the subject of a biography? Sir Sidney Lee says that the theme should be of a certain magnitude. This has been contradicted. Many writers contend that if you could know every thought that crosses the mind of a beggar, you could write a better book than any life of Cæsar. Perhaps; but a great life makes better food for a human soul. Moreover, the life of the beggar leaves very few traces. It may be written by the novelist, not by the biographer, who needs documents, letters, diaries. The man who leaves behind him an historical record is either the great man of thought or the great man of action. In some cases, the theme may be of sufficient magnitude though the man himself is not a great man. This happens when the chosen hero has been the centre of important events. A good example is Mr. Shane Leslie's *George the Fourth*. In such cases, the poetical element might be found in the contrast between the magnitude of the tragedy and the misery of the tragedians.

At the end of his biography of his wife, Alice Freeman Palmer, Mr. Palmer says: "If my portrait of her is correct, invigoration will go forth from it and disheartened souls be cheered." This should apply to any biography worth writing. Such books should help us to bear the difficulties of life. They should help us to understand them. Carlyle said that "a well-written life is almost as rare as a well-spent one." This is true, but "great men, taken up in any way, are profitable company."

SOPHISTICATION

By *L. Wardlaw Miles*

—as like one of these harlotry players as ever I see!
—The Hostess of the Boar's Head.

TWO things youth desires beyond all others: freedom from ridicule, and intensity of sensation. Most men keep something of these desires all their lives, but they come to desire other things as well, and as men grow older fear of ridicule and hunger for sensation gradually grow less intense.

Now when different periods of time are contrasted, some can be distinguished by what may roughly but conveniently be called a spirit of affirmation and others by a spirit of negation.

If there is any truth in the above generalizations it follows that youth in an affirmative period will be more concerned with intensity of sensation, and in a period of negation with a desire to escape ridicule. That the latter is the present situation few observers would deny.

Some years ago something came into fashion which was to exert as far-reaching an effect on popular thought as evolution. The Victorians went in, as we all know, very strongly for seriousness and for simplicity. They explained that life was real; life was earnest—that simple faith was more than Norman blood—that as we grow older we grow simpler. Then after this period in which seriousness and simplicity were cultivated with a conscious intensiveness rarely found in other periods, the thing mentioned came into fashion—and its name was "A Sense of Humor." One doesn't look for exact dates in such matters, but one might guess that the beginning of the popular appeal of a sense of humor starts with Matthew Arnold finding fault with Shelley for failing to possess such a thing. The date of the essay in question was 1888. At any rate in the 80's and 90's and in the first decade of the present century people talked a great deal about this thing—much more than they do today.

A sense of humor is one of those things which different people rate differently in importance, but which no one likes to be accused of lacking. Everybody knows he or she possesses one, and nearly everybody is apt to be a little suspicious of the other fellow's. Everybody likes to recognize the point in a joke at which he is expected to laugh, and everybody likes to reserve his laughter should he consider it unmerited. There are times when one wants the right to say with Queen Victoria: "We are not amused"; there are times when one wants, in answer to the question, "Do you see nothing there?" (*i.e.*, in some pointless joke) to answer (with Queen Gertrude): "Nothing at all; yet all that is I see." Nearly everyone has known the exasperating experience of saying something purposely absurd to which some silly ass immediately calls attention, and either appropriates your joke as his own, or laughs at and not with it, assuming that you had not intended your own absurdity. All of us, even the most insensitive, have suffered excruciating pain from those simple and genial souls who mistake their animal spirits for humor. For instance there is a type of joke in *Punch*, the pawky, pointless, good-natured English joke, which plunges me in gloom and steeps me in bitterness. Fortunately in this case I can always completely recover my cheerfulness by reading Mr. Milne or Mr. Herbert or most of the other contributors. And, finally, in considering this matter there should be noted how a conscious sense of possession enables a person generously to forgive his more obtuse brother. "So and so is the best sort in the world. Pity, of course, he never could see a joke." Or, if it is a lady speaking: "Such a love, but hasn't a *ray*, my dear, not a *ray!*" What a blessed assurance is this which convinces each of us of our own subtle and whimsical point of view—our power to see through the prosaic surface of things into those fascinating incongruities beneath, which are hidden from our simple and sober-sided fellow citizens. Thus, should you, my Reader, find this very poor stuff, do not let that arouse compassion for myself, since I, on the other hand, am prepared to admit all your excellent qualities—excepting just that crowning one you lack.

I said people don't talk about a sense of humor as much as they did. Really smart people don't talk of it at all. You are expected to have one, or rather you are expected to have something yet more precious which includes all its good qualities and adds many more. Somewhat in the same way there was once a time when a dress-suit case (then so called) was a mark of distinction, though no one feels pride in such possession now, that is, no rational adult. (To be accurate, I have known one individual made inordinately proud by such an acquisition, but she was only a little girl aged nine, and therefore does not deserve consideration.) The thing that has—in the best circles, if you know what I mean—superseded the place of humor, possessing all its merits but adding new excellencies, is, of course, Sophistication. At the present hour you don't read that an admired author shows a sense of humor, but you do constantly read that he "shows a deft and daring sophisticated touch." I, for one, read it so constantly that I get heartily bored with its repetition. As with humor, so with its contemporary supplanter, no one cares to be accused of its lack. Perhaps it is because I am really diffident as to my own possession that I am inclined to grumble over its ascription to so many contemporary authors, but really the thing does seem to be cultivated with an enthusiasm for mass production which would appear incompatible with its essential nature.

A sense of humor and a sense of sophistication are two things alike in many ways, and in other ways quite different. The difference might be stated by saying that the former makes you see the fun in a joke and laugh, and that the latter makes you see the fault in a joke, and shows you that it is not worthy of laughter. Obviously that is by no means the whole story, but it is a large part of it. At the heart of humor is surprise, surprise wakened by incongruity and in turn waking laughter. At the heart of sophistication is experience, experience too well acquainted with incongruity to find it mirthful. There are notable exceptions, but they are not sufficient to obliterate the fact that "the sad young men" of the hour are the sophisticated young men, and that is one reason why they are so sad. To feel the humorous is not less to be shocked in an agreeable way than to feel the disgusting is to be shocked in a disagreeable way. That definition of the civilized man which declares him one not easily shocked serves no less for the sophisticated. A further difference in the two things we are considering is apparent when we note that while we can distinguish a thing called "wild humor," and while humor often grows better as it grows wilder, there is no similar thing which we could call wild sophistication. Indeed though *daring*, even oftener than *deft*, is the adjective applied with distressing uniformity to the admired sophisticate, I think his inability to feel either fun or shame is frequently matched by his lack of any spontaneous self-assertion. Of these elegant and unshockable people, it is often their tameness that is shocking to me.

Now I started with the assumption that of youth's two chief desires one was to escape ridicule, and that this was particularly noticeable in an age marked, like our own, by the spirit of negation. If what has been said is true, one can see a reason why young people at the present time are so uniformly and so earnestly determined to prove themselves sophisticated—why for instance we meet the thing as inevitably in any college magazine as we meet suitcases and coonskin coats among a group of traveling collegians. Whether this is a thing good or bad, wise or foolish, temporary or lasting, it is at least undeniably one that is fashionable and usual today.

As with greatness so with sophistication, a modern Malvolio is either born to it, or achieves it, or has it thrust upon him.

It is to the members of the second group that the words of this essay are chiefly addressed. With the naturally sophisticated—or cynical or satirical—those of us who happen to be born under a kindlier planet have no right to quarrel. They are what heredity has made them, and so—however different—are we. Even with those upon whom a disintegrated post-war world has thrust bitter disillusion and paralyzing complexity, we have also perhaps as little right to find fault. But the second group, those who choose this attitude of mind not because it is inherently their own either by natural temperament or by experience, but because it is the proper thing at the moment, the latest, the most correct, thing in intellectual collegiate clothing,—those who would achieve sophistication—to those I speak.

Such may well answer: "Well, what of it? If it suits us—if we like it—isn't that enough?" No, I don't think it is enough, and I am trying to explain why.

First I repeat that I am not chiefly concerned with those wearers to whom the present style is naturally becoming. When such youths are both comfortable and well-fitted there is little more to be said. No, my concern is with two finally eliminated groups: those who like it but to whom it isn't really suitable; those whom it neither pleases nor suits.

The writer boasts no pre-eminent vision or observation. He has, however, had the opportunity to watch young men over a considerable period of time. And his conviction, be it worth much or little, is that a large number of the younger generation who go in for sophistication, cynicism, and satire, are like that large group of people who adopt a particular fashion of dress which in some cases suits their tastes but not their figures, and in some cases suits neither. Some have their natural movements restricted and, however pleased to be stylish, are uncomfortable; some are rendered unpleasing to the sight of any discriminating observer; and many are in both of these unenviable predicaments.

The reasons why a spirit of negation, with its accompaniments of sophistication, cynicism, and satire, is today popular and instinctively chosen as the part of wisdom, and why affirmation, with its simplicity, loyalty, and sympathy, is instinctively repudiated as an old-fashioned, foolish thing, are, of course, manifold and subtle, but a few seem obvious enough. Some applaud and some deplore but all men recognize the dissolving today of all sorts of patterns, whether of manners, conduct, or belief. Such breaking-down of patterns—the reaction to the enthusiasm of the war—the modern discovery of many pious frauds and fraudulent pieties—all these are doubtless causes of the attitude of negation, though it is just as correct to call them results. After all the more significant question is, not how a temper of mind arose, but what we are going to do about it. A few professional historians and philosophers are concerned with the first; everybody—including those who disclaim concern—with the latter. Yet it might be well if a little wider sense of history or philosophy could touch some who suppose that the phase of thought which is last in the sense of latest is necessarily last in the sense of final. Granted that the modern temper of thought is as pessimistic and futilitarian as Mr. Krutch so convincingly interprets it, how can anyone, professional or amateur thinker, dare to assume that it will always remain so. To make such a dogmatic assertion is to throw overboard the previously employed sceptical spirit, and to become the most arrogant of affirmers. The old-style fundamentalist of supernatural orthodoxy finds an odd counterpart in this new-style fundamentalist of rational scepticism; one believes in a physical hell of fire in which the doomed are to be damned, the other in a more tenuous hell of lack of meaning in which the entire universe is damned. There is, one must admit, something which demands respect in both beliefs, at least in such sincere and forcible affirmers as Calvin and Mr. Krutch, but were I the last unbeliever in the world, I should still lift my voice in protest. It is easy for either or both camps to say, "You are damned." It is impossible to prove it.

Now if at this point the writer could mount Mr. Wells' Time Machine and return to fifty years ago, he would doubtless here quote certain popular—that is in 1880 popular—lines from Browning's "Bishop Bloughram." But as these might sound unconvincing in 1930, let him cite instead the dying words of Mr. Wells' own William Clissold. And if even Mr. Wells himself is suspected of a taint of old-fashioned sentimentalism ("cum vix justus sit securus" in this stern day) then let him cite Spandrell's end in Mr. Aldous Huxley's *Point Counterpoint*. I am aware that by the nature of things Mr. Huxley may in turn be regarded tomorrow as an over-kindly and overcredulous observer. Nevertheless today he stands satisfactorily for the hard-boiled. And my point is simply that no one can be too dogmatic in these matters, not even the most sceptical.

Fear, as we are today constantly reminded, lurks ever at the edge of our being, like a hidden savage; at any moment he may appear in the open, hideous, alien, naked, and war-painted, prepared to mutilate and kill us. This enemy has tracked humanity's march through all ages. What distinguishes our own time is a franker acknowledgment and discussion of his unseen presence. An older and more heroic school tried to ignore fear, but we are more sensible if less stoical. Following the tactics of the psycho-analyst we try to lure the enemy into the open and there overcome him. As increasingly with civilization (if that is the name for greater bodily comfort and security) our dangers become less physical, the fear of ridicule concerns us to a greater degree. Perhaps as good a criterion as another of the civilized man would be a sensitiveness to being regarded as uncivilized—and hence absurd—by other civilized men. In the young particularly, but in all people today, one of the greatest fears is that of being laughed at. And sophistication is the trusted weapon of defense against ridicule, the pioneer's Long Tom against the lurking savage.

Of course the true satirist is one who carries his firearms

not only for defense but for offense as well. Whether the fact be contemptible or no (and I for one see nothing contemptible in it) the majority of humans regard such weapons of offense as, on the whole, offensive. The majority of humans do not live to kill though they are prepared to kill in order to live. No sane man ought to deny the perennial worth of the satirist —though unfortunately many sane men do. Bunk is always with us, often in the most respected and unsuspected places. The debunking process, the deflation of solemn men and institutions full of wind not wisdom, this is a matter as salutary as it is amusing. And chiefly we should be grateful to the satirist because he often delivers us from fear—from fear of bad men and institutions, and dares come to mock where cowards remain to pray. It is not my style, but I can admire and applaud it. And seeing the great merits of a type which can unite two such fine things as laughter and courage, I can forgive the satirist many offenses against good taste and charity, and even for his bloodthirstiness when he fights against united piety and stupidity and their foster-child cruelty.

I do object when he tacitly assumes that the satiric spirit natural to himself is natural to all men, when he tacitly claims that those possessing it are necessarily at closer grips with reality than those motivated by altruism and love. The satirist is a specialist and shows all the merits and defects belonging to specialism: enthusiasm for his trade; thorough knowledge, to a certain point, of his material; and a successful technique—all these balanced by ignorance of, or indifference to, the world outside his material; and an innate idée fixé that there is one trade more important than all others, his own.

In such a discussion as the present, one should try to keep in mind, however roughly, some sort of differentiation between a number of words which are sometimes used to mean the same thing but often to mean different ones. Sometimes the qualities they represent are blended in one man; sometimes they can be contrasted by comparing one individual with another. Thus Thomas Henry Huxley, though the father of agnosticism and a realist, was neither cynic nor pessimist. His grandson shares some of his qualities and not others. Mr. Dreiser is not only a pessimist and agnostic but something more positive, a denier,

Der Geist der stets verneint,

and though Mephistopheles' words might be his motto, he is neither diabolist nor cynic. Mr. Mencken is, of course, the satirist, but it is less easy to say in what proportions he exhibits the two different types of satire, that which mocks to mend and that which mocks for mischief and malice. Doubtless he would disclaim the honor—with a wit and vehemence I cannot emulate—but I am suspicious that he shows something of the former as well as the latter. Mr. Shaw certainly mocks to mend, and the self-exposure of his once convincing diabolism is an old story. Mr. Cabell's satire is of the second type, presumably 100% pure in its freedom from the utilitarian and moral. And so with Mr. Nathan who conveniently stands for the cynic. Such differentiations are dull enough, but, however dull and inadequate, they serve here the purpose of attempting to distinguish the spirit of sophistication. Obviously this spirit characterizes some of the above names, applies less to others, and to yet others is quite foreign.

Sophistication rests, as was said, upon experience. Yet no one would be so absurd as to claim it as the invariable result of experience. Saints, stevedores, and scientists are all types of men who get familiar with the world and its good and evil, the rough stuff as well as the fine, yet they are rarely sophisticates. Sophistication, as popularly employed, means one sort of experience—a wide experience of the wrong and evil of the world, combined with a modish tolerance and an amused interest. The real possessor of this spirit can't be shocked and he can't be made ridiculous. And to us unsophisticated unfortunates, who find plenty to shock us and make us absurd, who are neither assured holders of one firm conviction by which we can save the world nor absolute sceptics assured that it can't be saved and isn't worth saving—to us who are merely slightly envious and considerably perplexed members of the great brotherhood of well-meaning duffers—to us there is something exasperating in this smooth self-satisfaction of the sophisticate; it is not only smooth: it is smug, as smug as the smugness of the Unco Guid.

The exponents of this spirit take their place on the Zion of the contemporary elect and are too much at ease there. They exaggerate so fatuously the benefits of a knowledge of evil. Their obsession with sex grows a bore—in a true sense of the words, a beastly bore. They are so apt to refer to unnatural vice as though such knowledge conferred some cachet of esoteric wisdom in all æsthetics and philosophy. They repudiate so stupidly the obvious worth that obtains, when all is said, in certain natural and simple things. (It is not really true that "Providence and Sir Walter Besant have exhausted the obvious," but the contemners of the obvious have really exhausted us.) Their elegance so often combines the morals of a dancing master, the manners of a whore, and a headwaiter's knowledge of the winecard. Surely some appreciation of the conception of life in terms of a dance is not incompatible with the conviction that some of the modern participants are gigolos and some pimps.

And though they call it *decadence*,

(or called it that in the 90's)

It's rotten just the same.

Well, all this may be regarded as ineffectual and blustering protest, but at any rate one cannot deny that the glazed hardness of the sophisticate is one true criterion, though in another direction, of course, his desire for sensitiveness must be admitted. His ideal might be defined as hardening of the heart without hardening of the arteries. "One commandment give I unto you," spoke Zarathustra, and certain modern disciples accept and apply it as though it were the formula of a cure-all patent medicine. It would be as sensible to make a panacea of Be Hot or Be Cold or Be Tender as of that famous Be Hard. It is epigrammatic; it is in many cases arresting and stimulating; but as a universal prescription for health, physical or spiritual, it is silly. Keep Cool too is often an excellent injunction, but to an arctic explorer in danger of freezing it is poor advice. Two large and important groups may, let us admit, doubtless find benefit in the Nietzschean prescription: to the tender-minded religious enthusiasts who see the world only in terms of universal love, to them Be Hard may act as a corrective. And those tough-minded individualists who see existence only as force, to them Be Hard may prove a stimulant. But however large and important these two groups, humanity in general, which is the rest of us, is larger and more important, and we are not altogether either tender or tough. Yet a large part of what is a representative portion of this intermediate class can be found in those contemporary college youths to whom the commandment of the powerful and erratic individualist has become popularized and vulgarized into something less corrective and stimulating: Be Hard-boiled.

"From humility, reverence, and tenderness of heart, Good Lord, deliver us! From all kindliness, and simplicity, save us, O God!" Hear the litany that goes up today in unison from a hundred campuses and a thousand studios to the deity of correct thought and up-to-date youth! Whether more or less musical than a Sabbath of Methodist hymns it is just as monotonous, and it is certainly more comical to hear a thousand individualists praying together that each may be different than to hear a hundred pious souls praying to be united in fellowship.

Let it be repeated that my chief quarrel is not with the genuine hard-bitten realists, but with those who follow them and don't belong in their ranks, those who grow hard at the danger of growing brittle, the

> brittle intellectuals
> Who crack beneath a strain,

and in ten years after graduation have developed nervous breakdowns and nervous dyspepsia, and require very tender care indeed. The flaneur whose philosophy of futilitarian hedonism is native has his real charm. Don Juan in Hell is attractive because he remains a Don Juan though in Hell, and proves that his deviltry will neither bleach nor burn. Mr. Arthur Symonds somewhere makes merry over the anecdote (told in Hutton's life of Scott) of how an English regiment was kept quiet under fire by the reading aloud of "Marmion." What a deliciously absurd test for literary excellence! I am not at all sure it is so absurd, but in any case the thing suggests a practical method of discovering the sincerity of certain disbeliefs. While psychological tests are useful for determining everything else, I submit that to discover whether a man is a real cynic or pessimist, a physical test might be better. The very simple physical tests of pain and danger, grantedly of doubtful efficacy in an inquisition to punish one kind of heresy, might well determine the reality of another kind, of the honest belief in non-belief, so to speak. They would show whether the subject was, so to speak, sincere in his insincerity and solidly confirmed in his irresponsibility. Will the subject still think as poorly of life when immediately threatened with its loss? Will he continue to think as highly of jests when the situation is essentially no joke? The sight of a really great and wicked wit entering the vasty hall of death itself with no loss of his usual ease and epigram has something exhilarating, but when the author of a bottomlessly pessimistic editorial, or a daringly shocking jest, proves to be a gentle lad with big, sensitive eyes, and an embarrassed manner, then you—perhaps illogically—doubt whether personality and philosophy are, as in the other case, altogether consonant. You—it may be unfairly—question whether cancer or shell fire might not render him less indifferent to the value of life, and more indifferent to the worth of flippant wit. Is it overcynical to mistrust whether a good many young diabolists who want to raise the Devil would not be too bashful to dare face him once really raised?

Mr. Cabell and other daring spirits like to remind us that the great Jehovah of the Hebrew Old Testament is no longer a universal ruler but only a small tribal deity. In any case he has done more memorable things than any tribal divinity of whom I have heard. And: "Surely he scorneth the scorners!" is told of him. Whatever one's opinion of the speaker's authority, such an utterance rings with a promise, which, independent of its literal truth or falsity, seems to suggest a blessed hope for humanity. And however incapable of exact exegesis, I, for one, believe the promise bears at least a modicum of eternal truth. I believe that with the rest of humanity, which is so constantly tripped by error and trapped by absurdity, the scorner too is sometimes wrong and sometimes ludicrous. Only a vague and irrational belief, resting on no possible proof, yet I am not ashamed to confess that it gives me great comfort.

It has been the writer's fate to speak at a good many gatherings of youth, where some of my audience were bored and silent, and some bored and more demonstrative. Some were sober and some apparently less so. Like any other man I always protest a little grumblingly when I consent to speak, and yet if honest, I should admit that it is only simple truth to say: "I gladly accept the privilege of this opportunity to address," etc., etc. For it *is* a privilege to speak to youth. Perhaps what I have to say would be of value, could they ever hear. Perhaps this time there will be present one who will listen. . . . That, of course, is doubtful; what, on the other hand, is certain are the ironic cries with which a part of the audience will encourage me: "Is *that* so?" "Mr. Chairman, I propose a song!" "Give him a drink!" "True, brother, true!" "Well, what of it?"

To such accompaniments then, suppose the following delivered:

"My dear boys—dear whether noisy or silent, drunk or sober, sane or mad—I wish I could say what I want to. I wish just this once my faltering lips might be touched with a coal of fire from the altar and my dull brain cleared, that this once the heavy curtains of circumstance and personality would not shut from you what is in my heart. You think that age cannot understand, but it can—a little. A little understanding is what we sometimes receive in payment for our youth.

"Listen: you want two things. The first of them is to be spared ridicule. Age learns to bear ridicule, but it is ignominy, it is death for youth. And you feel how absurd it is to try to believe what isn't true—and later be laughed at for believing. You must be *sure*. And so in sophistication you think to find security; but I tell you this thing too is not sure. The only security is—not sophistication,—the only security, as a wise man has said, is courage.

"The second thing you desire, you desire far more than the first. And this second thing is intensity. More than security you want intensity and sensation. That's what makes you often do such wild mad things in peace. That's what makes you go off to be killed when war comes, and you pour out your blood like water on the ground to the disgust of the pacifists who cannot understand. I understand. I have watched you. You go laughing to death—*but it is no longer sophisticated laughter. . . .*"

Here perhaps the ironic comments of my hearers grow too obvious or the Chairman too restless. Anyway I sit down— and just what I meant to say, and never say, appears before me in distressing clarity—and the Chairman leans over to declare (what he would as inevitably declare had I spoken like Demosthenes, or merely recited irregular French verbs): "*Great* speech!" And soon he is on his feet again: "Our *next* speaker . . ." and so on.

ONE'S GRANDFATHER

By *Meredith Nicholson*

ONE'S relations are not to be paraded in public save in a worthy cause and the caption of these reflections is intentionally misleading—a convenience, a point of departure. What follows is discursive, tangential, the babble of a loquacious guest who changes the subject frequently for fear of losing the attention of the table. I am really thinking of family relationships in general, of orderly and happy households, of the simplicities and sanctities of life. Every well-regulated family should have a grandfather within call, to participate in all ceremonies and festivities and for his consolatory value in hours of adversity. My equipment in the way of grandfathers was complete: there were two of them. If they had created any great stir in the world I should be restrained by every consideration of delicacy from referring to them. It is because they never sought a place in the sun, but walked widely separated paths humbly and in the fear of God that I presume to invoke their spirits.

The older I grow the less I become interested in reports of supermen, in flares of precociousness and genius. It's the average man—an honest average, with no juggling to make a pretty figure for the statistician—that we've got to adjust our ideals to. I throw in this most unoriginal note at this point to reassure those who might suspect that I was about to commit the indiscretion of boasting of my progenitors as extraordinary. On the contrary, my jubilation is rather that they were only average men, who were never inspired to set the world aright but adjusted themselves in good spirit to the state of life into which they were born, and so doing, led happy and contented lives.

Fathers are too close for detached observation; grandfathers are sufficiently remote to be viewed, as one might say, academically. I will go the length of urging the preservation and encouragement of grandfathers as essential to the proper safeguarding of our institutions. Of grandmothers I might say much, but grandfathers have somehow been neglected—their presence tolerated but not encouraged. But the aged are, in a manner of speaking, looking up. Science and the haberdasher are doing better than the poets ever did for the elderly man. No man of spirit who isn't afraid of a red necktie is going to become a lean and slippered pantaloon, slinking into seclusion when there's company in the parlor. The book counters are littered with plausible tracts that relate how old age may be postponed; no items of the daily news are more eagerly read than reports of the birthday celebrations of ancients who sail toward the unknown as serenely as if they expected to cross the pole and sail southward into summer latitudes. This is good, and makes for a cheerfuller world.

It is not, however, my aim to repeat the familiar recommendation of a diet of spinach—that most uninteresting, insipid and depressing product of the vegetable kingdom—or suggest the adoption of any monstrous method of restraint or abstinence to those who covet earthly immortality. My intentions are social, not scientific. There are doctors in my bailiwick who view me with what I interpret as a certain commiserating professional glance when I meet them in the highway. I suspect them of speculating as to the pliability of my arteries, but I pass them with a disdainful lifting of the hand, remembering that both my grandfathers ate fried meat and lived comfortably into the nineties without knowing there was any such thing as blood pressure.

In their sorrowing over the deterioration of moral standards and the general subsidence of civilization in America the prophets of calamity do not neglect the family. We hear nowadays that the home as a social unit is enormously weakened where it is not already tottering, but it is far from my purpose to add the slightest weight to the pressure on the ancient walls. At the holiday season, when the heart kindles under the influence of gracious memories, and chimes are rung, candles lighted and good wishes exchanged among friends and strangers, it is possible to believe that many vestiges remain of what we are fond of calling the good old times. It might even be pointed out that the sentiment we associate with love and loyalty has still in our literature a tangible commercial value. The fundamental virtues may appear to the stern moralist to be much disfigured or obsolete, but wherever they are publicly exhibited they win the heartiest applause. Old stuff, chirrup the critics, when the mother puts the lamp in the window for the thousandth time in the hope that it may catch the eye of her wandering child. Truly enough, it is old stuff, but "safe"—safe because the world refuses to let go of it. There always has been that mother and that prodigal, and just as inevitably the lamp at the window—a pharos that lightens all the world's byways.

It follows that we must be cautious in accepting the conclusions of hasty and prejudiced observers as to human nature which doesn't change as to the fundamentals of right conduct half as fast as the pessimist would have us believe. Man has constantly been played upon by furious disturbances beyond his control, but as often as not he is saved in spite of himself by something inside of him that preserves him from annihilation. He may wander, he may stumble and fall, but Home remains his ultimate destination. The saving forces are not so unevenly matched in their battle with the powers of destruction. Rectitude and the loyalties go right on asserting themselves, planting fortifications which are capable of prolonged and stubborn resistance. And the family does persist and flourish, even when it abandons the front-yard grass and mother's pansy bed for the restricted area of an apartment where the flora is limited to an invalid rubber plant.

Irritating though they become at times, relatives are necessary and, save in regrettable instances where they may in-
considerately land themselves in the penitentiary, they do
confer upon us a measure of dignity and respectability.   I
once heard of a man who was so upset by the constant invasion
of his home by his wife's relatives that he would leave the
table and retire to the parlor to swear.   As he was a deeply
religious person, the unwelcome guests, hearing his mutterings,
attributed his absence to his desire for a few moments of
private devotion.   I introduce this incident to illustrate the
value of a well-established reputation for piety in the family.
A man who can be a hero to his wife's relations may face the
rest of the world fearlessly; the calumniator's tongue is power-
less against him; the purity of his soul would put Galahad to
shame.

Any reorganization of society in such manner as to confide
the newly-born to the care of the State would inevitably destroy the pleasant sentiment that has, for example, grown up
about aunts and uncles.   The State would not only become
in loco parentis, but it would be obliged to provide substitutes
for those benevolent and understanding relatives who so adorn
the best English fiction.   An official uncle in the guise of a
policeman or a species of universal aunt properly uniformed
and badged might serve, though the idea is well calculated to
shock those of us who recall aunts and uncles who appeared
in the households of our youth as veritable angels and rubri-
cated themselves in the book of memory.   The spinster aunt
walks among the stars in regal alpaca; romance clings to her
like a breath of lavender; there is a reason why she weeps softly
as she arrays her nieces in their wedding garments! The aunt
with children fits quite as charmingly into those pictures we
treasure, of households strange enough to touch the youthful
visitor with a sense of adventure and yet having their indubitable relationship with Home.   A very pretty piece could be
written on "The Saintliness of Aunts," and "The Uncle in
Literature" would be an inspiring theme for a thesis. Hamlet's

ill-luck in the matter of uncles, and the dark tradition of the avuncular relationship left by the glowering Gloucester, merely suggest the possibilities of contrast with those genial and benevolent uncles who in classic pages are forever pinching their nephew's ears or tipping them with a sovereign.

My youth was blessed with an uncle who was as delightful as Major Pendennis. He was my earliest hero, superior to any I found in story-books. He wore his hat at a jaunty angle and swung his cane in the manner of one who met the world on something a little better than even terms. He was the kindliest and most generous soul I have known. No friend ever sank so low that he forgot or neglected him. One might have thought that he cultivated improvidence, so marked was his success in maintaining an empty pocket; it was nothing to him whether he had a dollar or not. His dollar was your dollar if he suspected a deficit in your private exchequer. His spacious manner implied the possession of millions, but he entertained no Mulberry Sellers' dream of sudden wealth. Money to him was solely a circulating medium. In his long and laborious life I doubt if he ever possessed at one time a thousand dollars above his liabilities. On an occasion when I was visiting his family his fortunes were low, and I recall the magnificent air with which he announced to my aunt and cousins his purchase of a vast quantity of smoked herring, a product of the salt, estranging sea with which he had previously been unfamiliar, but which, now that he had sampled it at the grocer's, he declared to possess the highest dietary value. He was dark to swarthiness and carried himself with soldierly erectness as became one who had been a captain of infantry in the War between the States. He looked important; he wore an authoritative air. He took me to my first national political convention and passed the difficult doorkeeper merely by exhibiting his calling card, though he wasn't even a member of the party whose deliberations we invaded and his name to the guardian of the wicket meant nothing.

He began life as a printer, having learned the art in his

father's (my maternal grandfather's) newspaper office in a small town in Eastern Indiana. Such honors as he attained at various times in his life (and two presidents bestowed offices of dignity and responsibility upon him out of sheer personal regard rather than as a reward for party service) never obscured for him the fact that he was a printer. And here I must be indulged to note my opinion that justice has never been done to those followers of the art preservative of all the arts who served the rigid apprenticeship of the old times and learned not only the craft but derived no mean education from their pondering of the matter they lifted from the copy hook. Through my family connections with printer's ink I knew great numbers of compositors of the old school. They were most scornful of the ignorance of editors and writers. The fact that I was the nephew of my uncle and the grandson of my grandfather was the happiest of introductions to many of the "prints" I encountered when I began newspaper work.

The picturesqueness of the composing room passed with the invention of mechanical typesetting, which effectually disposed of those noble figures perched on their rickety stools, swaying to the click of the types, with "galluses" dangling, cob pipes in mouth and the most disreputable hats on their heads—by preference old straw hats which attained dignity from their very age. Intemperance was lamentably associated with the craft in those years; and this, coupled with the fact that a compositor could "get cases" for at least a day in any town where there was a printing office, was responsible for the tramp printer, who roved the country earning his way. My uncle's stories of his own pilgrimages immediately after the Civil War would make an enthralling narrative. It was the proudest boast of these peripatetic philosophers that they had "set" Greeley's notoriously puzzling copy on the *New York Tribune*. This was the highest possible achievement, the equivalent of an honorary degree in the craft. Often these men were widely read in the best literature. I knew one who had all Shakespeare at his tongue's end and was cursed with an ambition to play Hamlet. He did in fact appear, whenever occasion offered, as the tortured Dane in scenes from the play at lodge and church entertainments. My uncle told me of the perpetration by another of the fraternity of the most frightful pun I know. The scene was a barrel house in St. Louis much affected by knights of the inky trades. One of a circle of philosophers that had been discussing weighty matters jumped down from a cask and tore his trousers. Gazing ruefully at the rupture he declaimed:

See what a rent the envious Casca made!

But dropping one's uncles, I shall register my opinion that he is a lucky child who enjoys the companionship of a grandfather through those years commonly believed to be impressionable. A grandfather does in a very impressive way make vivid the nearer past; he is an excellent substitute for a university of the broadest curriculum. The grandfather I knew best, from having lived under the same roof with him for many years, thrust back to Revolutionary times. His father, of Welsh origin, was born in Delaware, but was visiting an uncle in the West Indies when the minute men at Concord fired the shot heard round the world. He took ship for home and on the way the vessel was waylaid by a British man-o'-war, and in the fight he was wounded, but recovered and knew arduous service throughout the war. In his old age he received all the honors due one who had fought under Washington, as he sat in the tavern at Troy, Ohio, his last home, or received friends in his own house. Some of the letters he wrote in his last years show him to have wielded a vigorous quill. He signed himself in full—John Wheeler Meredith—a pardonable flourish in one who had served his country well. The revolution seemed only a brief yesterday away as my grandfather visualized it for us children through his recollections of his father.

My grandfather was born in Pennsylvania and at proper age was bound out to a printer and, in the manner of those

non-specializing days, learned the art in all its branches. He
was the editor and publisher of a newspaper at Centerville,
Indiana, when the California gold excitement shook the world.
He became an argonaut, making the passage to the golden
coast by way of the Isthmus, arriving at San Francisco on
New Year's Day, 1850. Employment at his trade was not so
easily found as he had imagined, but while he waited he did
such odd jobs as offered, carrying parcels and the like until
he found work in a printing office at seventy-five dollars a
week. His battered pocket diary contains only meager hints
of his adventures. He did not fail, however, to note his
attendance at church on every Sunday of the year he spent
in San Francisco. He never ventured into the gold-fields but,
thoroughly homesick, returned to his Indiana newspaper.
This whole episode was so unlike my subsequent knowledge
of him that only the journal convinces me that he really entrusted himself to the belly of a ship and sailed the Pacific.
The militant strain manifested in his father must have passed
to another son, Joseph, of whom my grandfather used to
speak with the greatest admiration as a mighty hunter. This
great-uncle was a restless person, who kept a little ahead of
the westward movement of civilization that he might find
game upon which to exercise his prowess with the rifle. Norval,
another of my great-uncles, came less prominently into the
domestic picture. My grandfather, who had a liking for
sonorous phrases, in mentioning this brother never failed to
quote:

> My name is Norval; on the Grampian hills
> My father feeds his flocks. . . .

The profits, if any, from the *Wayne County Whig*, published
in the 'forties, must have been inconsiderable. Those were
the days when household essentials passed as cash in small
communities. Files of the paper covering several years are
preserved, and among the advertisements are frequent and
urgent appeals to delinquent subscribers to replenish the
editor's wood-pile.

When he removed to Indianapolis my grandfather purchased a home and resumed work as a journeyman printer. He had no eye for business; the property he bought was in a neighborhood doomed to deterioration; he put his savings in banks that failed. The collapse of a savings institution in which he had made deposits for his grandchildren was my first demonstration of the transitoriness of riches. No small item of my education was the discussion, round the base-burner in grandfather's house, of hard times, though I hardly knew the meaning of the words used, but realized that expenditures were to be cut and that certain privileges and indulgences dear to youth must be withdrawn. In 'seventy-three and again in 'eighty-four we experienced pinching times, but I have no recollection of any grumbling in our combined households. If one has never known affluence, the cutting off of an allowance of a quarter a week is not an unmitigated calamity.

A man who demanded little of life, this grandfather pursued the even tenor of his way untroubled by large ambitions. In nothing was he more amusing than in his small economies. The cutting of a string was painful to him; the threat of such wanton waste would evoke his protest, and he would take the package himself and patiently untie the knot. In those days when oysters were transported in oblong quart cans, he would take a shovelful of coals to the kitchen steps, soften the solder, and neatly remove the cap. As he had a weakness for oysters, he accumulated in the course of time a great number of these unmutilated receptacles in the vague expectation that one day some use would be found for them.

It is necessary to coin a word properly to describe my grandfather's diligence as a reader; he was the readingest person I have ever known. I can see him now, in the low rocking chair that sufficed for his short compact body, his bald head glowing in the lamplight, his spectacles shining from a careful polishing with the scrap of chamois skin he carried in his pocket. He insisted on keeping at work at his trade long after he was seventy, and he would return with brisk step from the printing house, a basket in which he carried his lunch on one arm and a roll of journals and magazines under the other. While his prior claims would never have been disputed, it pleased him to place such literature as he could not immediately peruse under the red cushion of the rocker—the only sign of selfishness I recall in him. To see a newspaper flung down unfolded was offensive to him; he would painstakingly gather it up and restore it to order. The barn loft was filled with neat bundles of magazines and even of newspapers that covered some episode of recent history that interested him. His unadventurous shy nature delighted in romance. He was an assiduous reader of the *New York Ledger*, a journal so firmly planted in popular affection that it seemed as permanent a national institution as the Constitution itself. He introduced me to Cooper, but William Gilmore Simms was an author he appraised as hardly second to the creator of Leatherstocking. I wonder whether anyone nowadays reads *Castle Dismal, Guy Rivers*, or *The Border Beagles!* Late in life he discovered Felix Gras' *The Reds of the Midi*, a work he immediately wrote high on his list of favorites. He read a chapter in the Bible every night, and in his last years made it his habit to read the sacred writings through continuously, finishing Revelation only to begin all over again with Genesis. He was a walking concordance and could turn instantly to any passage that might be required. A faithful church attendant throughout his life, he kept a record in which he noted the weather, the text, the size of the congregation, with a line as to the quality of the sermon which, with characteristic amiability, he always pronounced good or splendid.

Great spirits trod the earth; kingdoms rose and fell in his day, and man's ingenuity devised many inventions which wrought immeasurable changes, but this kindly, patient, industrious man remained only an attentive spectator, reading the abstract and brief chronicles of his time with the zest with which he devoured a stirring tale.

My paternal grandfather opened vistas wholly alien to

those to which my mother's father introduced me. He, like his father before him, was born in Kentucky, being of that Scotch-Irish strain that spread out from North Carolina and crossed the mountains to assist in the fashioning of new states in the western wilderness. I assume that he departed out of Kentucky for Illinois lured by the promise of cheaper land and afflicted with that restlessness which caused great numbers of pioneers to keep ahead of the crowd. In this case the land was a soldier's grant to my great-grandfather for his participation in St. Clair's defeat.

This grandfather I remember as a stately old gentleman with a crown of fine-spun white hair. He was a farmer, as all his fathers had been (I am the first renegade of the tribe), and he made the black soil of his adopted state pay. He had the inbred fondness of all Kentuckians for a horse. At seventy in attempting to break a colt he fractured a leg, but recovered and enjoyed twenty-one years of comfortable life thereafter with only a slight limp as a reminder of his injury. He was much less communicative than my maternal grandfather, but with a little urging he would talk of the old home in Kentucky and of the pioneer experiences of his father, who had attained the age of ninety-seven. Cities were little to his taste, and when he visited us he spent most of the day in a park near our home, where he amused himself by quizzing me as to the names of the trees. On his farm, after he gave up active work, he was always abroad in fair weather. "Green things growing" never lost their charm for him. I used to be awed by his silence when he would pause abruptly in our walks and gaze meditatively across the fields. I never knew what his thoughts were at these moments, but it pleases me to believe that life-long association with the earth gave him, and probably gives all men of like kinship with the soil, clues to infinity that are denied the rest of us.

As I look back across the years it seems to me that the daily experiences of our household and what I learned, through the family tradition and experience, of history and of social and economic changes were a fair compensation for what I missed in the way of regular schooling. A prowling curious youngster, impartially following torchlight processions of both parties, and attending all public gatherings, I knew my home town thoroughly, saw the mighty put down from their seat and the humble and meek exalted, and was vaguely conscious at least that what I saw and heard was typical of the larger movement of life. The very tameness of these disclosures favors my contention that upon the home rests the main burden of educating the child. Curiosity, an intelligent alert curiosity, is essential to the acquisition of knowledge, and nowhere is this so naturally awakened as in the household. A child is much likelier to be interested in something he hears than in what he is bidden to read; and I doubt whether in all America there is a family that has not some link with history, or some traditions, that are likely to pique the curiosity of the young mind. It is the business of parents to make themselves interesting to their children—to implant in them the idea that the world is a mighty interesting place, and that their chance of happiness is increased in ratio to what they see and hear and absorb.

To be sure, there are perplexities, not to say embarrassments, in following this formula. It is difficult to thrill a child with stories of what used to be when today's events are so exciting. They are likely to think their grandfathers rather foolish to have suffered peril and hardship in the wilderness when by waiting a little they could have accomplished the pioneering adventure so much more comfortably! The son I once conducted to Concord, Saratoga, and Ticonderoga was only mildly thrilled by the contemplation of those scenes of battles long ago. He was impatient to reach Montreal and explore the offerings of the celluloid drama in that metropolis. Wolfe and Montcalm touched him less in storied Quebec than the discovery of a band of enthralling jazziness. And yet, as he has to live in the Twentieth Century, it is possible that he was not so benighted in his preferences. And I enjoyed the band!

The increasing burdens laid upon the public-school teacher, who must communicate knowledge according to a system that is subject to frequent change, and at the same time inspire and discipline a collection of utterly dissimilar youngsters, would be enormously lightened if parents met their responsibilities with intelligence. A decline in courtesy in these free American states is frequently complained of by sensitive persons who resent boorishness, particularly in public servants. It is a dreadful thing indeed to be insulted by an elevator-boy or made the target of contumely by the admiral of a trolley-car. The well-mannered child is its parents' best advertisement.

Once I happened to be in Columbia and visited a cemetery where many of South Carolina's illustrious dead are buried. I found a venerable negro at work on the lot of the Hamptons, and he answered my questions with a charming quaint courtesy. He had followed General Wade Hampton's fortunes through the Civil War, and was still a retainer of the family. This former slave spoke of his own children with a touching pride. The rearing of children was evidently a matter to which he had given serious thought and reduced to a concise formula which he elucidated for my benefit as he leaned on his rake among the dead cavaliers.

Manners come first, he said, then morals, and then learning; but manners, he gravely insisted, should head the list. I left him with a feeling that I had conversed with a gentleman who was also a sound philosopher, and as his words have remained with me for twenty years, I shall allow them to close the argument.

HOME THOUGHTS FROM ABROAD

By *Albert Jay Nock*

I

THE currents of Chance lately washed me up on the shores of a little-visited European country which I soon found to be in some respects perhaps the most interesting in the world, at the moment. I can be more at ease in writing about it if I give it the thin disguise of a pseudonym, so let me call it Amenia. It deserves this name not only because it is a very beautiful land, but also because its inhabitants are so uncommonly amiable and gracious to strangers; I find that they have an international reputation throughout all Europe for this trait. They will take no offense, I am sure, at my masking their country under a fanciful name, for I am merely following an old-fashioned convention which had its root in delicacy, like the convention that governs the British House of Commons, where one member may pretty well say what he likes about another member, provided he do not name him.

What made Amenia so interesting to me, as a visitor fresh from America, can be summed up in a sentence. From our point of view, nearly everything in Amenia is wrong, and yet the country manages to get on remarkably well. By every rule of the game, Amenia ought not to get on at all, but it somehow does. Its politics are frightfully wrong, its economics are wrong, its views of a proper constitution of human society are practically all wrong; yet there the wretched country is, impenitently racking along, quite as if its fundamental theories of collective human life were as sound as ours.

I submit that to a student of civilization this is an interesting state of things, and doubly so at the moment. For example, Amenia is solvent, as I hear few countries are; certainly those I see and read about seem mostly busted. The *publice egestas, privatim opulentia*, which Sallust puts into the mouth of Cato as evidence of a nation's decline, is visible everywhere. I notice in a London paper today the statement that our own national debt now amounts to twenty-two and a quarter billion dollars; also that Britain's national debt is eleven times as much as it was in 1913. My notion is that it would take a bit of scratching to get that amount of money together in either country. Amenia has only a trifle of debt, which worries nobody, and which she could clean up on short notice without overstraining herself. Amenia, moreover, pays as she goes. Amidst the general fiscal dilapidation of the last four years, Amenia has balanced her budget each year. I was told that in the good days when our bankers were dusting money around Europe all so freely, some of them urged a loan on Amenia, but the government said no, much obliged, they thought they would try to squeeze along on their own. Again, business in Amenia is very fair—nothing startling, but probably up to Sam Weller's standard of normality—while in other countries it is apparently slack. Again, Amenia seems to have no unwieldy labor surplus. Everyone able to work has some sort of job which perhaps will not make his everlasting fortune, but which manages to keep him going; and in this respect, too, other countries are not so well off, according to all I hear.

In drawing comparisons between Amenia and other countries, however, I have not the least idea of advertising Amenia as a happy hunting ground for American visitors, and making it out so attractive that everyone will wish to go there. Not at all. On the contrary, I think that for many reasons the average run of our tourists would do better elsewhere; Amenia, I should say, is probably not quite their kind of thing. Still less would I suggest that we ought to copy Amenia's ways and views and ideals. Amenia did not impress me in this stark fashion, either as bait for the vagrant impulse to "go places and do things," or as an institutional model. It impressed me only as an incentive to a study of absolutes. What I saw there turned my mind back on itself, and made me reëxamine a number of matters which we tend to put down as absolute; absolutely Good, absolutely Bad, absolutely True or False, absolutely Right or Wrong. What my conclusions were, or whether I came to any, is of no importance. The only thing I wish to dwell on is the sheer pleasure of being in a situation that moves one strongly to review the *chose jugée*, to reopen questions that mere use-and-wont has led us to regard as definitively closed, and let one's consciousness play over them freely. There are few exercises more exhilarating than this, and Amenia is one of the few spots left in a highly uninteresting world that stimulate one to pursue it.

II

I shall put down my impressions at haphazard as they occur to me, with no special care for arrangement. In the first place, I found that there is a great deal of illiteracy in Amenia; and by the way, I was led to this discovery by the conspicuous and delightful absence of roadside advertising signs. I was told that the Amenians are 50 per cent illiterate; some put it higher. Having no passion for statistics, I did not take the trouble to look up the official figures; it was enough for my purposes to know that most of the people I saw about me were unable to read or write.

In our view, this is of course wrong. It is an absolute of our social faith that illiteracy is Bad. This is one of the very few points, indeed I think the only one, at which Mr. Jefferson succeeded in striking his belief deeply into the American consciousness. He put literacy as a condition of good citizenship, and the people accepted his view; which was in itself, perhaps, an indication that the matter would stand a little sifting. No one now, I imagine, has any doubt that general literacy is a Good-in-Itself—that is to say, an absolute. This belief is a republican heirloom, passed on in complete integrity, and unexamined, from the casket of eighteenth-century political theory to its present place in Columbia's shining crown.

Just so. I noticed, however, that the capital of Amenia is remarkable for its bookstores; it has relatively more and better bookstores, I believe, than any city in the world. In fact, the only commercial exhibits there that strike a stranger's eye are the bookstores and jewelry stores; the rest are unimpressive. Leaving aside all questions of comparative quality, I tried to estimate how many bookstores New York would have in the same ratio, first, to its actual population, and second, to its proportion of literacy; but the figures were so incredibly fantastic that I did not think it worth while even to make a note of them.

These premises seemed to warrant the inference that Amenia has a small but serious reading public; one that owns its books and reads them, and that in general may be thought to regard a book as an instrument of culture rather than as a stopgap for idle time. This inference is borne out by a French authority, who says that Amenia has *une petite élite extrêmement brillante et cultivée*. My mind then went back to the immense masses of garbage shot daily from the press of more literate lands, and I wondered just what the net gain—understand me clearly, the *net* gain—of a general and indiscriminate literacy really is. Our republicanism assumes that there is a net gain, and so indeed there may be, but just what is it? With all our devotion to " research," I do not think that our institutions of learning have ever entertained this question; yet I submit that it is worth attention.

In the eighteenth century, before Western society had been penetrated by the minor commonplaces of republicanism, Bishop Butler—almost a contemporary of Mr. Jefferson—remarked that the great majority of people are far more handy at passing things through their minds than they are at thinking about them; and therefore, considering the kind of thing they usually read, very little of their time is more idly spent than the time spent in reading. This fact is more noticeable now by far than it was in Bishop Butler's day; and when set off against Amenia's condition, it is bound to make one wonder what, precisely, this particular absolute of our republicanism amounts to. What, precisely, would the civilization of Amenia gain by a more general spread of literacy? What, precisely, would ours lose by a shrinkage of literacy to Amenia's level? Does the indiscriminate spread of literacy encounter an unsuspected moral equivalent of Gresham's law, that " bad money drives out good"? Does it encounter a moral equivalent of the law of diminishing returns?

The whole question is rather a pretty one, and as far as I know, our doctrinaire republicanism has hitherto had no better answer for it than the " one plain argument" which Lord Peter applies to the doubts of his brothers, in the *Tale of a Tub;* and this, while in a sense perhaps effective, is hardly satisfactory.

III

One cannot go to and fro among the Amenians for any length of time without perceiving that their theory of business is wrong. Their idea is that supply should follow demand, and that the purchaser should seek the vendor; whereas the Right Idea, as we all know, is that supply should precede demand, and that the vendor should hound and bedevil the purchaser with all kinds of importunities, in order to keep demand going at its maximum speed. Thus the ideal development of a nation's business is a joyous game of what in our youthful days we used to call " outrunning the constable "; and hence, to an American eye, nothing is more unnatural and shocking than the stringency with which Amenia's business is kept down to the level of solid requirement. Hardly anything is done deliberately to increase consumption. The Amenians have only the vaguest and most uncertain notion of " creating a market," or of splitting up purchasing power among a dozen or more competing varieties of what is actually the same thing. Yet, as I said, somehow or other business manages to do very well under these conditions, and it is perhaps equally remarkable that the visiting stranger who comes here quite unaccustomed to these peculiar ideas of business soon finds that he too is doing very well, even though he sees the line pretty sharply drawn between amenities, comforts, and conveniences, on the one hand, and mere gadgets on the other. Perhaps his contentment tends to show that human beings are highly adaptable and very easily corrupted. I argue nothing from it, but offer the fact merely as an object of interesting speculation.

The Amenians have not even learned the art of sophisticating their products. Their excellent staples, such as flour, olive oil, wine, come to you pretty much, one might say, as the Lord made them. Nor have these interesting people learned to sophisticate their workmanship. Amenia reckons its money in écus or *escudos* (pronounced *scoots*), worth at the moment about four cents apiece. You can buy an excellent suit of clothes, custom-made of domestic wool, for five or six hundred scoots, and the workmanship will be as good as the fabric; that suit will stand hard wear, and thrive on it. Shoes, too, that one buys handmade for something like two hundred scoots, show no sign of the familiar devices to "make people shoe-conscious," and thereby increase consumption; and the same may be said for the workmanship put into everything one uses, as far as my observation goes.

These practices seem to spring from the root idea that things should be made to use rather than to sell; a distinction first drawn in literature by Canning, I believe, in the rhymed fable of Hodge's razor. Moreover, the Amenians do not appear to believe that the "pursuit of happiness" contemplated by Mr. Jefferson's great document means only the accumulation and use of purchasable things. Yet, in spite of this handicap, not only does business manage to drag on, but also most of the Amenians whom I saw seemed a great deal happier than under the circumstances they should be.

For example, I spent three weeks at one of Amenia's principal health resorts, which is in a most beautiful mountainous region, with no settlement of any size near by. I never saw a

place where one was thrown more heavily on one's own resources. One could not buy anything more interesting than
postage stamps. One could take delightful walks, and enjoy
the air, birds, trees, and flowers, but there was no golf, tennis,
squash, ping-pong, cinema, radio, or gramophone; the hotel had
only an utterly impracticable billiard table and a decrepit
upright piano of French make, much out of tune. There was
not even the usual job lot of abandoned books lying about the
lobby; not a book on the premises save what one brought for
oneself.

The guests were a good cross-section of Amenian society.
The four learned professions were there, some royal blood and
hereditary high life, some *arriviste* or Brummagem high life,
some industry and trade. The average age of the company ran
unusually young, and on that account I was all the more
curious to see what they would do with themselves. I soon
remarked that no one was at all afraid of being left alone with
his own thoughts; and this, if not absolutely Bad, is seriously
irregular, for if a person is alone and thinking, he is not doing
anything to increase consumption. There was no great " get-
together" movement organized to insure one against the
chance of a moment's solitude. No one seemed in such desperate need of company; on the contrary, the guests kept contentedly each one to himself pretty much all day, except for casual
meetings. There was a very pleasant cordiality all round; if
someone came along, well and good, but if not, well and good.
No one was bored; with nothing whatever to " do," and no
apparatus to help fight off boredom, everybody seemed quite
unreasonably and perversely happy. Again, in the evenings I
remarked how the whole company showed itself capable of
immense enthusiasm over the simplest parlor games, peasant
dances, peasant songs. Royalty, high life, and all grades of
bourgeois rollicked through boisterous and exhausting dances
with bursts of uproarious laughter, and seemed to be having
the best time in the world, up to half-past ten or so, when
all hands went quietly to bed.

St. John's Eve came on while I was there, and the thing to do on St. John's Eve, apparently, is to make brush bonfires of eucalyptus, rosemary, and other aromatic twigs, and leap across them through the flames. It seems a very moderate sort of diversion; I do not know what the significance of it is, nor could anyone tell me. However, everybody went in for it with immense energy and gusto, and got no end of fun out of it, though some of the ladies singed their legs a bit, and only missed setting their skirts afire by the closest kind of shave.

Three weeks of this sort of thing is bound to set one's mind going over the assumption which, though tacit, amounts to an absolute—that happiness is built up of purchasable things. These people were not poor, yet they were not only capable of being happy as lords without a dollar's worth of apparatus to help them, but also they did not appear to care whether they had any apparatus or not. The sum of their activities for three whole weeks did not increase consumption, or assist the development of mass-demand, to the amount of a punched nickel; yet they were quite happy. I could not help recalling the contrasting observation of de Stendhal, on a visit to the United States, where there is such an immense amount of the apparatus of happiness available everywhere, that "the springs of happiness seem to be dried up in this people," and the amazing statement of Edison, eighty years old, when a reporter asked him what human happiness consisted in, "I am not acquainted with anyone who is happy." Perhaps the visitor to Amenia might be a little put to it to say offhand precisely what human happiness does consist in, but the question is forced on him by such incidents as the ones I have just cited.

Indirectly, too, it is forced on him by observation of the instinct for the *ne quid nimis*, the instinct for the level of real requirement, that he sees coming out everywhere. In the matter of transportation, for instance, Amenia's railways are cheap, safe, clean, and good, but that is all one can say, and all one is supposed to say; they do not pretend to lure you into taking them merely for the fun of the thing. The same is true of the motor roads; they are excellent, plenty good enough for anybody who has to use them, but they are not a standing temptation to the canine love of joy-riding. I remember once, when my charming friend Cassandre was standing up stoutly for France, she said there was great hope that the French would remain a civilized people, for they had not yet put down any cement roads; when a nation begins to lay cement roads, she said, it is gone, past any hope of reform or redemption. There would seem to be something in this from the Amenian point of view, which regards a road primarily as a thing of use rather than of pleasure. I took a two-hour walk between four and six o'clock of a beautiful afternoon, on a main road out of one of Amenia's largest towns—her fourth in population, I believe—and in that time I saw only one motor vehicle, a truck.

In three months, during which I covered Amenia pretty thoroughly from end to end, I did not see a single tractor, reaper, or binder. I saw grain being reaped with sickles—only twice did I see scythes in use—and threshed with flails. I saw irrigation carried on in pre-Mosaic fashion by boy power on vertical treading wheels, and by donkey power on horizontal pumps. By all accepted rules, these practices are wrong and bad, yet really—really, now—just how dogmatic may one be about erecting their wrongness into an absolute? They got results—there is no question about that—and as to their effect on the sum of human happiness, it is difficult, very difficult indeed, to assure oneself one way or the other. On the evidence available, I am by no means sure that the net sum of happiness in Amenia would be increased by further mechanization of these processes. It might be; I am simply not sure. On the evidence attested by Edison and de Stendhal, I am not sure that the net sum of happiness in the United States would be reduced by demechanization to the level of Amenia. Again, it might be, but I am not sure; I can only say that I found the question a very powerful solvent of dogmatism, and as such I recommend it.

IV

Amenia's population is most improperly distributed, for two thirds of it is rural. Agriculture is the country's chief industry, and it is carried on mostly by small independent holdings. In urban growth, Amenia is far behind other European countries. One notes with surprise and disapproval that the huge industrial proletarian agglomerations which are perhaps the most conspicuous characteristic of true prosperity —though William Cobbett gruffly called them *hell-holes*—do not exist. Amenia does relatively little in the manufacturing way, and hardly any processing. Almost one might think that the Physiocrats had come to life there, and were spreading their detestable doctrine of the *produit net*. It is here, perhaps, that one sees Amenia's most egregious departure from the Right Way. Surely by this time Amenia should have learned that the chief end of man in his collective capacity is to industrialize himself as completely as possible, remove the land from competition with industry in the labor market in order to force down wages by creating a standing labor surplus, and then go in for a strong policy of economic nationalism; that is to say, a policy of selling everything one can to everybody, and not buying anything from anybody.

Amenia is well off for natural resources, especially in minerals and water power, but there is unanimous testimony that the Amenians are extremely lackadaisical about exploiting them; and if anything can be absolutely Wrong, this is. The Right Way with natural resources is to turn them over wholesale to private enterprise, to be looted as rapidly and thoroughly as possible. All precedents point to this as of the essence of prosperity. Yet it would appear that the Amenians are merely pecking at their minerals, and realizing on only about 8 per cent of their available hydroelectric power. A Scots engineer who has been twenty years in Amenia told me that a couple of foreign prospectors had struck gold there lately, but nobody seemed to be properly worked up about it.

The general sentiment was that the gold would stay put; it would not run away, and there was no occasion to get into a great sweat over digging it out. There seemed to be enough gold around already to go on with, so why not let it lie awhile? This Scotsman told me that the Amenians had always taken this easy attitude towards "development," and hence they still have pretty nearly everything that nature gave them to start with.

This may be put down to lack of enterprise, and properly so in a sense, no doubt; it depends on what one's notion of enterprise is. But there is a little more to it than that, I think. It may be, in part at least, the outcome of a sense of moderation, for the Amenian struck me as being by nature the most consistently temperate person I ever saw. Once led to look for this trait, I kept an eye out for it continually, and saw it exhibited everywhere, whether in small matters or great. To take one instance, rather unimportant in itself, but bearing on a question that has lately been a good deal discussed in the United States, a wine merchant who took me over his property showed me certain casks to which his workpeople were free to resort at any time, for as much as they cared to drink; and he told me that in the whole history of the firm, which ran considerably over a hundred years, there had never been a tipsy person on the premises.

With its colonial resources Amenia follows the same easy policy as with its domestic resources. Though one of the smallest countries of Europe, its colonial holdings are enormous, exceeded only by those of England and France. One is rather surprised by the fact that whereas about fifty-five million of the earth's people speak French, about seventy million speak Amenian; and the Amenian tongue is perhaps the most widely diffused language in the world, except our own. Amenia's colonies are very rich; a really capable and energetic administration, such as the English or French or old Leopold's Belgians or we ourselves know how to furnish, could get simply no end of profit out of them.

Yet Amenia bears the white man's burden very lightly. It gets some return out of its colonies, but nothing like what it might get. A young and progressive Amenian told me sadly that the colonies had for years been "virtually abandoned." Amenian colonial policy does not, in our expressive phrase, crowd the mourners. It seems to be not unlike the policy of "salutary neglect" which farsighted Englishmen advocated in the days of Pitt. It neither exploits the native peoples in an economic way, nor does it essay to moralize either their private convictions and habits or their social customs and practices; it does not tell them what they should eat or drink, or wherewithal they should be clothed. Hence the colonies are contented under Amenian rule, I am told, and are not all the time raising disturbances and insurrections. "The Amenians don't try to civilize their colonies," an Englishman said to me, with a touch of irony in his tone; "consequently they've still got them. We bossed ours around and tried to make them do our way, and so we lost them."

All this again may be put down to mere shiftlessness, but once more I suggest that the innate sense of moderation may account for something; and perhaps the extraordinary spirit of tolerance and courtesy, for which, as I have said, the Amenians are internationally noted, also accounts for something. If one gets a moderate yield out of one's colonies, well, enough is enough, and why jeopardize peace and good feeling by squeezing them? Meanwhile, if the heathen in his blindness bows down to wood and stone, why bother him about it? Why not look the other way and let him bow? If he would rather go naked than wear Amenian textiles, it is bad for business, no doubt, but why force him all at once to accept a strictly cash-registral evaluation of life and its amenities, even though it be orthodox? Why not break the glad news to him a little gently and give it a reasonable time to sink in? If a widow sets out with pomp and ceremony to burn herself alive on her late husband's funeral pyre, why not conclude that there is probably something in it from her point of view, and let it go at that?

V

Amenia's government is a simon-pure military despotism; it governs by general orders. Yet up to date it has been extremely disinterested, able, and efficient; the best and cheapest government, I should say, that is to be found anywhere. Doubtless it will not remain so, for that would be contrary to all human experience with any kind of government, but such is its record at the moment. It went through the motions of submitting itself to a popular mandate the other day, and was approved by a large majority. I do not know how far this election was "on the level," or how sincere the government was minded to be about abiding by it. One's general knowledge of government makes one skeptical; Herbert Spencer cites with approval the generalization that "wherever government is, there is villainy," and it seems to be, on the whole, a sound one. Nevertheless, for all I actually know or have heard, this election may have been honestly undertaken and scrupulously conducted.

I suppose the sight of a military dictatorship should have set me thinking of Spartacus, Masaniello, Jack Cade, Daniel Shays, the Whiskey Boys, and all the other great liberators, until I was ready to turn my back on Amenia in disgust. What it did instead, however, was to set me thinking about some of the absolutes of eighteenth-century political theory, and wondering what basis they have in actual human experience. Representative government; the parliamentary system; universal suffrage; "checks and balances"; a responsible executive— Amenia has thrown all these overboard, and yet is governed well and cheaply. The question is not whether other countries would do well to throw them overboard, but whether the quality of government is as much a matter of systems and institutions as we think it is. Rival systems are now everywhere competing for the world's attention to the color of their several shirts—well, just what is the necessary and inevitable effect of *any* system upon the quality of government?

America had great students of government in its early days;

it is a pity that they are now so much more read about than read. One of them was William Penn. The sight of Amenia's contribution to the great current rivalry of systems brought to my mind this paragraph from the preface which Penn wrote for Pennsylvania's original "frame of government":—

> When all is said, there is hardly any frame of government so ill designed by its first founders that in good hands would not do well enough; and story tells us the best, in ill ones, can do nothing that is great or good. . . . Governments, like clocks, go from the motion men give them; and as governments are made and moved by men, so by them they are ruined too. Wherefore governments rather depend upon men than men upon governments.

Against its background of competing systems, moreover, Amenia's autocracy suggests what is no doubt the most pressing public question of our time, namely: whether eighteenth-century republican doctrine has not put upon the mass-man a burden greater than he can bear. Heretofore the question has not been so much with the mass-man's actual capacity as with the advisability, for purely collateral reasons, of letting him have anything like a free hand in shaping social and political institutions. The rapid spread of republicanism, however, has given us of the present day an uncommonly good chance to appraise the type of social ideal towards which the enfranchised mass-man chooses to move. Therefore, quite aside from all considerations of sincerity, integrity, and good will, the question now is whether the mass-man is able, or will ever be able, to direct the development of society in accordance with his own ultimate best interest. Has he the force of intellect to perceive clearly what that interest is, and the force of character to pursue it steadfastly? Do his present performances encourage the belief that he will ever have them? Has republican doctrine, in short, any basis either in actual experience or in reasonable hope?

We have, too, an uncommonly good chance to observe the kind of leadership which at present succeeds in imposing itself on the mass-man's allegiance, and to remark its conformity to a historical type. At almost every turn of the world's affairs nowadays, one is reminded of the French revolutionist's saying, "I *must* follow the mob, because I lead them." An anonymous book called *An Englishman in Paris* was published in this country about sixty years ago; and let me say in parenthesis that the strongest possible pressure should be put on its publishers to reissue it, for it is in all respects a model of what a volume of memoirs ought to be. The author says he saw two days of the revolution that ousted the July Monarchy, and never again did he open a book purporting to deal with any of the French revolutionary movements of the nineteenth century; it was enough for him to know that they were invariably led by men in want of five or ten thousand a year. The same movements might have taken place under other leaders, no doubt, but if so, those leaders would have been men who were equally in want of five or ten thousand a year. He goes on to give it as his firm belief that if Louis Napoléon had not been as poor as he was, there would have been no Second Empire; that if the Orléans family had not been as rich as they were, there would have been no Third Republic; that if the Second Empire had lasted a year longer, white-hot republican spirits like Gambetta and Émile Ollivier would have been found contentedly holding jobs under it; and he cites the saying of a witty and experienced friend, that "political opinion in France is based on the fact that the louis d'or is worth seven times as much as the three-franc écu."

Finally, aside from the light it throws on the possible unsoundness of republican doctrine and the possibly dubious character of republican mass-leadership, Amenia's condition makes one wonder whether political nationalism has not gone over the margin of diminishing returns. Economic nationalism seems clearly to have done so; may not its political counterpart have done so too? Amenia is small and isolated, and it is possible for a one-man government to maintain political nationalism there at something like reasonable expense. Elsewhere, however, people are uneasy about the rapidly growing cost of Stateism, centralization, and bureaucracy, and well they may be; in the United States, for example, people are extremely uneasy about it, and with reason. Is it not possible that political nationalism, like a business which is economically overgrown, has begun to cost more than it takes in? Or, to cite the comparison attributed to Lincoln, has it become like the tugboat that had a four-foot boiler and a six-foot whistle? When the whistle blew, the boat stopped running. Is political nationalism any longer commercially practicable (if I may so put it) over an area of much more than township size? It is an interesting question and a serious one; one which, from present appearances, the larger and more highly integrated political units will soon be obliged by circumstances to entertain.

VI

Probably Amenia will not long remain as I found it, for there are the beginnings of a lively onset towards "development" and "progress." I heard these words often; they seemed to mean a closer approach to the condition of other nations. Well, improvement is always possible, and the study of other people's ways is always useful. "They measuring themselves by themselves," the Apostle says, "and comparing themselves among themselves, are not wise." One energetic young Amenian assured me that "we shall be a civilized country in ten years."

A visiting stranger may not presume to offer advice to his hosts, but he may perhaps be permitted to observe in a general way that when one is examining other countries one is likely to find that the most valuable testimony they bear to the nature of true civilization is often of a negative kind; and that this is particularly true of civilization's higher and finer concerns. A stranger, too, may without impropriety, I think, venture in all gratitude to express the hope that the "civilized" Amenia of ten years hence will be in all respects as charming and captivating to the cultivated spirit, as interesting and thought-provoking, as the Amenia which I have had the good fortune to visit.

VOCABULARY AND SUCCESS

By *Johnson O'Connor*

W HAT is success? And how is it gained? Whether one thinks of success as financial reward, or as assured social position, or as satisfaction in able work accomplished and recognized, or as a combination of the three and something more, many factors contribute. Most of them elude our understanding and remain intangibly beyond definition. A vital force drives some individuals over every obstacle. With others that great generalization, character, adds strength of a different sort. Neither may ever be restricted to a hard and fast formula; certainly, at the moment, neither can be measured. But other more concrete constituents of success have been isolated and studied in the laboratory. One of these is a large English vocabulary.

An extensive knowledge of the exact meanings of English words accompanies outstanding success in this country more often than any other single characteristic which the Human Engineering Laboratories have been able to isolate and measure.

What is meant by vocabulary? Just what the word signifies. Does the word *enervating* mean *soothing, exciting, distressing, invigorating,* or *weakening?* For most well-educated persons the choice is between *invigorating* and *weakening.* Fifty-two per cent of the college graduates whom we have measured choose *invigorating* as the synonym; only sixteen per cent choose *weakening,* the dictionary definition. Does *stilted* in the phrase, "his stilted manner," mean *irresolute, improper, cordial, stiffly formal,* or *vicious?* A majority of educated persons mark *stiffly formal,* but more than a third mark *irresolute.*

Answers to the meaning of *scurrilous*, in the phrase, "scurrilous rogue," divide themselves more or less evenly between *hurrying, desperate, abusive, frantic*, and *diseased*, with *desperate* the most popular. For *peremptory*, a majority mark *decisive*, but many choose *persuasive, uncertain*, and *angry*. *Pleasant*, the fifth choice, is not as popular. *Linguist* and *glutton* are equally enticing as synonyms for *polyglot*. For *refulgent*, in "a refulgent smile," *repellent* is most intriguing and *very bright* next, with *mischievous, flattering*, and *sour* all following closely in popularity. For *monograph* forty per cent choose *soliloquy* and less than twenty per cent *treatise* and *epitaph* each.

The word *vocabulary*, as used in this article, signifies a knowledge of the dictionary meaning of just such words as *enervating, stilted, scurrilous, peremptory, polyglot, refulgent*, and *monograph*. Not until one attempts to pick an exact synonym does one realize the difficulty. One may like the sound of a word and use it in a picturesque way without being accurate in its meaning.

I

To measure the vocabulary of an individual, the Laboratory uses a list of one hundred and fifty test words. Each is printed in italics in a short phrase and is followed by five choices, all of which fit the phrase but only one of which is a synonym of the test word. The instructions are: "Underline that one of the five choices which is nearest in meaning to the word in italics." The words to be defined were selected by Alexander Inglis of the Graduate School of Education, Harvard University. His intention was to include words which appear once or twice in 100,000 words of printed matter. It is a general reader's vocabulary from which technical terms have been excluded. The test words vary from some that are quite easy, such as

Thrilling experiences—dangerous, exciting, unusual, disgusting, profitable,

to others that are more difficult, such as

Glabrous heads—bald, over-sized, hairy, square, round,

which only twenty-one per cent of college graduates mark correctly. Since one fifth, or twenty per cent, should guess the correct answer, the meaning of *glabrous* is practically unknown. The test measures knowledge of words one recognizes, not necessarily of those one uses. The words one uses accurately are, no doubt, fewer than those one recognizes, but there is probably a relation between the two.

Three hundred high-school freshmen average 76 errors in the list of 150 words. Seven hundred college freshmen average 42 errors. One thousand college graduates from a wide variety of colleges—most of them, however, in the eastern part of the United States—average 27 errors, and vary from the one person in a thousand who achieves a perfect score to the one who knows less than 50 of the 150 items. The college professors whom we have measured average 8 errors; major executives average 7 errors. Major executives score higher in this English vocabulary test than any other selected group with which we have experimented.

By the term "major executives" is meant all individuals who, for five years or longer, have held the position of president or vice president in a business organization. Such a definition includes both successful and unsuccessful executives, provided only that they have survived five years; it includes alike forceful personalities and figure-heads; but it has the great advantage of excluding our personal judgment from the process of selection. Major executives as thus defined average in the top ten per cent of college graduates as a whole.

Although it is impossible to define success rigidly or scientifically, it seems to be true, nevertheless, that a large vocabulary is typical, not exclusively of executives, but of successful individuals. It happens that in the business world successful men and women are designated by this special appellation, "executive." The successful lawyer or doctor is marked by no such name. But if, to the best of one's ability, one selects successful persons in the professions, they also score high in vocabulary.

For one meaning of success the Century dictionary gives "a high degree of worldly prosperity." The measured English vocabulary of an executive correlates with his salary. This does not mean that every high-vocabulary person receives a large salary, but the relation between the two is close enough to show that a large vocabulary is one element, and seemingly an important one.

Furthermore, the executive level which a man or woman reaches is determined to some extent by vocabulary. In many manufacturing organizations the first step in the executive ladder is the leading hand, called sometimes the working foreman. This man is in charge of half a dozen or a dozen others. He works at the bench or at a machine as they do, but is the executive of the group. The next step is the foreman, who may be in charge of as many as a hundred or more individuals. He does no bench work, he is not a producer, but devotes full time to his executive duties, to the keeping of records and to the handling of the personnel. The next step in many large organizations is the department head or superintendent or manager, who ordinarily does not come in direct contact with the workers, but handles them through his foremen. The final step is the major executive or official, the vice president or president of the organization.

These four executive ranks represent four degrees of success, in one sense in which that word is used. One is *advanced* from leading hand to foreman, from foreman to manager, from manager to president. As far as we can determine by measurements, the leading hand and the official have much the same inherent aptitudes. They differ primarily in vocabulary. Typical non-college-graduate shop foremen average, as a group, about as high as college graduates. Department heads score higher, roughly fifteen errors, and major executives the highest of all, averaging only seven errors. Whether the word "executive" refers only to the major group or is used in the broader sense to mean anyone in charge of other workers, it is still true that the executive scores higher than those under him and higher than other persons of similar age and education.

II

An interesting sidelight on the high vocabulary scores of executives is that they were unforeseen. When a scientist expects a result and finally achieves it there is always the feeling that, regardless of the care he has taken, personal bias may have entered. Six or eight years ago the Human Engineering Laboratories tested forty major executives of the Telephone Company who had offered themselves as victims to be experimented upon in a search for executive characteristics. At the same time the Laboratory was also revising the vocabulary test, not with the notion of using it with executives, but with the hope that it might prove of value in education. One day, with no thought of the consequences, I gave it to an executive, and from then on was asked for it regularly because of the interest it aroused. I paid little heed to the results until one day an executive refused to take the test. He had been obliged by lack of money to leave school at fourteen, and had earned his own living since. With no further formal education, he had worked his way to a major position. He had taken the aptitude tests without hesitation, but vocabulary seemed to him so directly the result of schooling that he knew in advance he would fail. His own words were that he had made his way without being found out and he was not willing to give himself away. But in scientific work one cannot test only those who think they will do well, and we finally persuaded him to try the vocabulary test. He made two errors where the average college graduate makes twenty-seven.

Was it luck? Or was it significant of something which we had not recognized? The Laboratory listed the vocabulary scores of one hundred executives and, parallel with them, the scores of one hundred miscellaneous college graduates. The difference between the two arrays was striking. Only nine per cent of the college graduates scored as high as the average major executive.

Why do large vocabularies characterize executives and possibly outstanding men and women in other fields? The final answer seems to be that words are the instruments by means of which men and women grasp the thoughts of others and with which they do much of their own thinking. They are the tools of thought.

Before accepting so far-reaching a conclusion several more obvious explanations must be examined and excluded. The first and most natural supposition is that successful persons acquire words with age and with the experiences of life. Success does not usually occur early. The successful group were necessarily older in both years and experience than the general run of college graduates with whom they were compared; and their large vocabularies might be the inevitable result of age.

To probe this point a study of the growth of vocabulary with age was undertaken. From twelve, the earliest age for which we have a large number of measurements, to twenty-two or twenty-three vocabulary expands steadily and at a uniform rate. Through this school period the score on the vocabulary test of one hundred and fifty items improves five words a year. From twenty-three to fifty vocabulary continues to increase, but changes no more in these twenty-five years than in two school years—not enough to explain the high scores of executives. Normally, vocabulary is acquired early in life, before most men have made appreciable progress toward a responsible position. The large vocabularies of successful individuals come before success rather than after. Age and the experiences of life may contribute new words, but certainly do not explain in full the high vocabulary scores of business executives.

The next thought is that effective schooling may be the source both of a wide vocabulary and of executive success. It is known, from the work which the American Telephone and Telegraph Company has undertaken, that there is a relationship between school success and business success later in life. Although not everyone who leads his class becomes a brilliant executive, and although not everyone who fails in school fails in life, in general school success preludes executive success. Schooling may be the vital factor of which the large vocabularies which we are measuring are but by-products.

To obtain evidence bearing on this point, we measured the vocabularies of twenty men who had left school at the age of fifteen and who had worked their way into major positions. They also averaged only seven errors. Their scores equaled those of the college-graduate executives. In the case of these twenty men it is their vocabularies which are important rather than their formal school education. Their large vocabularies are not the result of schooling and must, we therefore conclude, be significant for some other reason than as a by-product of an educational background.

Is, then, a college background of no importance? Has the non-college man the same chance of becoming an executive as has the college graduate? This fact seemed worth determining. Of the major executives in a large industrial organization, sixty per cent are college graduates, forty per cent non-college. At first glance, college would seem to have done little, for almost half are not college men. But, to be fair to education, there is another angle from which to view this result. Of the college graduates with this same company, more than three quarters are in executive positions, whereas, of the non-college men, well under a tenth are in similar positions. College graduates, in general, average measurably higher in vocabulary than do non-college persons. Furthermore, of the college group a significantly larger percentage are executives.

One would like to conclude without further preamble that the vocabularies of the college group are large because of directed effort and that these purposefully gained vocabularies have contributed to executive success. Non-college executives, then, are those rare individuals who pick up words so easily that their vocabularies are large without effort. But there is one further possibility which must be investigated.

Although the vocabulary test was designed to measure knowledge which must have come through books or by word of mouth, a high score may reveal an underlying aptitude for language. It may be this flair which is the contributing factor in both vocabulary and success later in life.

It should be possible to isolate and measure diathesis apart from knowledge. We have worked on this approach for a number of years, thus far unproductively. For the time being we must leave the conclusion of this part of the research in abeyance and admit that the vocabularies of successful executives may reveal an aptitude.

III

Vocabularies may always be consciously increased regardless of the presence or absence of any gift. A knowledge of the meaning of each word at one's command must have been obtained by word of mouth or through reading, by some educational process.

Furthermore, with groups of individuals of apparently similar aptitudes, the amount of vocabulary added in a given period varies with different educational techniques. At Stevens Institute of Technology the freshman class is divided alphabetically into four sections. Each of these studies freshman English under a different member of the faculty. Four years ago the entire class took the vocabulary test the first week of freshman year. The four sections averaged about the same in vocabulary, and there was no reason to suppose that, selected as they were, one would score higher than another or have more ability. Yet, when remeasured nine months later, two of the sections had improved more than average academic freshmen, one section had improved only half this amount, and the fourth had retrogressed slightly.

The improvement of one section may have been due to the fact that the instructor was interested in the vocabulary test and its implications. The important fact is that differences in vocabulary improvement were caused by differences in teaching techniques—in other words, that an improvement in vocabulary score can be produced by education.

Those boys and girls whom the Laboratory has measured
and urged to better their vocabularies, and then remeasured
at the end of two or three years, have shown more than average improvement. Here again vocabulary is induced independent of aptitude. It is for this reason that the Human
Engineering Laboratories, in helping a youngster to find himself and start in the right direction, use a vocabulary test in
lieu of a general intelligence test.

We come now to the question of whether or not that incre-
ment of vocabulary directly due to educational stimulation
contributes to success. The four sections of the freshman class
at Stevens Institute of Technology to which reference has
been made, which took freshman English with different members of the faculty and improved different amounts in vocabulary, were followed to see the effect of these new vocabularies
on school work the next year. The four sections averaged
nearly the same in school marks freshman year. Sophomore
year the two sections which had enlarged their vocabularies
the previous year showed general gain in all school subjects—
not strikingly, not enough to prove the point once and for
all time, but enough to suggest that a vocabulary acquired
consciously reflects in general school improvement the next
year.

It is always possible that the improvement in school work
was due to inspired teaching, to added incentive, but if this
were true it would seem as if the improvement in school work
should appear immediately freshman year, whereas it did not
appear until sophomore year after the vocabulary had been
acquired. This seems to indicate that it is the additional words
themselves which are the tools used the next year, that words
are important in and for themselves.

IV

Granted that diction is important, and many would agree
without elaborate proof of the point, how, from the standpoint
of the school, can it best be given; and, from that of the in-

dividual, how best achieved? Is it a knowledge of Latin and Greek which lays a sound foundation for a real understanding of words? Or is it constant reading? Or the assiduous perusal of the dictionary? Probably all contribute; as yet we have found no straight and easy road.

In the search for a road to vocabulary we have unearthed several facts which throw light on the learning process. One of these, which, if rightly interpreted, may prove to be of far-reaching importance to education, is that vocabulary advances with an almost unbroken front. The words at the command of an individual are not a miscellany gathered from hither and yon. With a very few exceptions they are all of the words in the dictionary up to those of an order of difficulty at which his vocabulary stops abruptly, and almost no words beyond. In the revised form of the test which is now available for school use, the items are arranged in order of difficulty as determined by actual test results. The first fifteen or twenty words of the test are known to the average high-school freshman or sophomore. The next thirty to forty are on the border line of his knowledge. Some he recognizes, others are vaguely familiar, and others he has not yet encountered. The balance are so far beyond him that he marks correctly no more than the one in five which he guesses by pure chance.

For convenience of scoring, the words are divided into ten groups of constantly increasing difficulty. One who knows the words of Group II, second in difficulty, almost invariably marks correctly every word of Group I. Another youngster who may know the words of, let us say, Group VI rarely fails on a single word in any of the first five easier groups. Similarly, one who fails on twelve of the fifteen words in any one group—that is, marks correctly only the one word in five which he guesses—almost never knows a word in any more difficult group. There are not, as we had expected, stray words in the difficult part which one who fails earlier in the test has stumbled upon and remembered. These unusual words, if previously encountered as they must have been in reading and conversation, are too far beyond the point he has reached to make any lasting impression.

The one exception to this rule is the foreign student who may know difficult words because of their similarity to his own language, but miss much easier ones. Thus the Southern European often marks correctly such difficult words as *cephalic*, *garrulity*, and *piscatorial*, because of knowledge of Italian and French, but fails to know much easier words of Old English origin, such as, for instance, *knack*, *blotch*, and *cope*.

In the region where learning is taking place, the commonest error is the confusion of a word with its exact opposite. Among seventh- and eighth-grade and first-year high-school pupils, nearly a third mark *found guilty* as the correct meaning of *acquitted*. *Upright* is the most popular misconception for the meaning of *reclining;* and, strange as it may seem, *neat* is the commonest misconception of *untidy*. The seventh-grade youngster berated for keeping an untidy room quite often evidently receives the impression that he is too orderly. The failing is not limited to the high-school group. For *incontrovertible* the correct answer *indisputable* is usually marked by college men, but of the remaining four choices *unsound* is by far most popular. In the phrase "You *allay* my fears,"—where the five choices are *justify*, *calm*, *arouse*, *increase*, and *confirm*,—*calm* is usually answered by the educated group, but *arouse* is next most popular. In the phrase "He *retracts* his criticism," *withdraws* is the correct answer and *repeats* is the most common delusion. In "He *vented* his wrath," *poured forth* is correct and *restrained* is the commonest misapprehension.

One need but turn to words of which one is not quite certain to see how difficult it is to distinguish opposites. One evening at dinner with a delightful Dean of education, we fell to discussing this question. He recognized *cathode* and *anode* instantly as electrical terms designating the two poles, but hesitated a moment before saying which was which. *Port* and *starboard* he admitted he had never straightened out and resorted to some such phrase as "Jack left port." *Gee* and *haw* were beyond him.

He surmised that they meant *up* and *down*, but said frankly he did not know the words. When told that they were used in ploughing, he was instantly interested, but did not care at all which was which. He was taking the first step in the learning process, placing them in their correct environment. The fifty-two per cent of college graduates who choose *invigorating* as the meaning of *enervating* are on the verge of knowing the word. The dictum of modern education, never to teach what a thing is not, has perhaps come from a realization of this confusion of opposites. The confusion seems, however, to be a natural step in the learning process.

V

In the study of human beings the factors involved are so numerous and so intertwined with one another that the experimenter, in unraveling the strands, must pause periodically to make certain that he is progressing. What then has been discovered? An exact and extensive vocabulary is an important concomitant of success. So much is known. Furthermore, such a vocabulary can be acquired. It increases as long as an individual remains in school or college, but without conscious effort does not change materially thereafter.

There may be some subtle distinction between a natural vocabulary picked up at home, at meals, and in reading, and one gained by a study of the dictionary. The latter may not be as valuable as the former. But there is nothing to show that it is harmful and the balance of evidence at the moment suggests that such a consciously, even laboriously, achieved vocabulary is an active asset.

OPTIMISM AND PESSIMISM

By *William Lyon Phelps*

I AM often called an optimist, and so I am; but perhaps not in the popular meaning of the word. When a worldly wise man calls a person an optimist, he usually regards him with intellectual contempt, just as the elaborate courtesy toward women in the age of chivalry thinly disguised a cynically sensual attitude. Optimism is associated in many minds either with ignorance of life or mental inferiority; and when certain persons call others optimists, look out for them!

Thus recent definitions of the optimist illustrate the superior attitude of the pessimist: "An optimist is a fool unfamiliar with the facts." "An optimist is one who falls out of a fourth-story window, and as he goes by the third story, he says, 'So far, so good.'" "An optimist is one who at night makes lemonade out of the lemons that have been handed to him all day." "A pessimist is one who lives with an optimist."

Now the familiarly unpleasant back-slapping cheerio person, with a genius for the inopportune, is not necessarily an optimist. He is a nuisance. He was well known and dreaded like a pestilence among the ancient Jews. See the Book of Proverbs, 27:14, "He that blesseth his friend with a loud voice, rising early in the morning, it shall be counted a curse to him," and 25:29, "As he that taketh away a garment in cold weather and as vinegar upon nitre, so is he that singeth songs to an heavy heart."

A man who attempts to console another by making light of his troubles or by pretending that things are otherwise than what they obviously are will not get very far. One might as well pretend in January that it is June. You cannot get rid of obstacles by ignoring them any more than you can solve problems by forgetting them. Nor can you console sufferers by reminding them of the woes of others or by inopportunely emphasizing other things.

Taking this stiff definition, are there then any genuine pessimists? Certainly there are. Thomas Hardy was exactly such a pessimist. He affirmed in his last volume of poems that man would have been happier if he could have remained at the stage of lower animal development, with no power of thought. Alfred Housman, the great lyrical poet, says we could all be happy, if only we did not think. It is when we think that we are overwhelmed with gloom.

The custom of congratulating others on their birthdays is really an acquiescence in optimism. We instinctively (and I believe rightly) regard life as an asset. But Swift believed that the worst thing that had ever happened to him was being born. He therefore, like the honest man he was, kept his birthdays as days of fasting and mourning. He wore black and refused to eat.

For my part I find daily life not always joyous, but always interesting. I have some sad days and nights, but none that are dull. As I advance deeper into the vale of years, I live with constantly increasing gusto and excitement. I am sure it all means something; in the last analysis, I am an optimist because I believe in God. Those who have no faith are quite naturally pessimists and I do not blame them.

If a man slips on an orange peel that some moron has left on the pavement and breaks his leg, you will not help him by saying, "Yesterday a man fell here and broke his *neck*." If a manifold father loses one of his sons by a motor accident, you can't help him by saying, "Cheer up! You've got three sons left."

"Sufficient unto the day is the evil thereof." These terrible words were spoken not by a peevish invalid or by a bankrupt, but by the Light of the World. He always and everywhere recognized the forces of evil and never pretended that life was all sunshine. Religion does not pretend that everything is easy and comfortable, for religion is not meant to fill our minds with illusions but rather with fortitude. Our Lord came into the world to show us how to bear the burden of life cheerfully and bravely; life is not easy, but His yoke is.

A true optimist is one who recognizes the sorrows, worries, drawbacks, misfortunes of life, its injustice and inequalities. But while seeing these things, the optimist believes that no matter how strong error may be, truth in the long run will triumph, even though it may not be our truth.

The optimist believes that in the long run virtue has superior staying power as compared with vice; that goodness will eventually defeat evil; that life means something; that character counts; that men and women are of more consequence than sparrows; in short, that this is God's world and that the moral law is as unshakeable as the law of gravitation.

What, then, is a pessimist? A pessimist is one who believes that the evolutionary process is the tragedy of the universe or, as Mark Twain put it, that life is the worst practical joke ever played on man by destiny. That from one primordial cell should have developed all complex forms of life through the vegetable kingdom, through the lower forms of animal existence up to man, is generally regarded as an advance. The true pessimist regards it as an irremediable disaster, as the worst of all possible mistakes. According to him, it would have been better had the evolutionary march stopped with the lower forms of animal life and never reached self-consciousness.

The fish, for example, is better off than men and women. The fish functions perfectly. He does exactly what he was meant to do, he has not the torture of self-conscious thought, no fear of death, and dies at the appointed time. But man has thoughts and dreams and longings that seem to belong to eternal life and eternal development, whereas in reality he dies like the fish; only with all his dreams and longings unsatisfied and with the constant fear and horror of annihilation in a universe where, no matter how sublime or far-reaching his thoughts, he is, in reality, of no more importance than a fish and must in the end share the same fate.

AN APOLOGY FOR BAD PIANISTS

By *J. B. Priestly*

IGNORING those musical labourers who are paid so much per hour, at cinemas and dance-halls, to make some sort of rhythmical sound, all pianists, I think, may be divided into four classes. There are, first, the great soloists, the masters, Paderewski, Pachmann, and the rest, who would seem to have conquered all difficulties. With them the piano, a dead thing of wires and hammers, becomes a delicately responsive organism; its hammers are extra muscles, and its strings added nerves running and leaping to obey every fleeting impulse; their playing is as saturated with personality as their gait or speech. Not so with the members of the second class, which is, to my mind, a dubious fraternity. They may be called the serious amateurs. Very often they take expensive lessons from some professor, who undertakes to "finish them off." But they never are finished off. The sign and mark of the serious amateur is that he practises assiduously some piece of music, maybe a Chopin study or a Brahms sonata, until he has it by heart; after which he assembles a number of friends (or more often, new acquaintances), squashes their attempts at conversation, and amid a tense silence, begins to play—or, as he would say, "interpret"—his laboured solo. The fourth class consists of odd strummers, vampers and thumpers; young ladies who play waltzes and old ladies who play hymns; cigarette-in-mouth youths with a bang-and-rattle style of performance; all inexorable, tormenting noise-makers, from those who persist in riveting—rather than playing—Rachmaninoff's C sharp minor Prelude to those who buy Sunday newspapers in order that they may pick out with one finger the tune of a comic song.

From *Self-Selected Essays;* published, 1932. by Harper & Brothers. Used by special permission.

All such are enemies of peace and harmony, and as they cannot be ignored in any other place, here they can be quickly dismissed with all the more pleasure.

It remains now to say something of the third class of pianists, which, if it were reduced to such straits, could count me among its members. To write at some length of one's class after perfunctorily dismissing others may seem to savour of egotism, but the truth is, we—I speak fraternally—have been so much maligned and misunderstood up to now, we have endured so many taunts in silence, that we have a right to be heard before we are finally and irrevocably condemned.

It is only on the score of technique, the mere rule of thumb business, that we stand below the serious amateurs; we belong to a higher order of beings and have grander souls; in spirit we come nearer to the great masters. The motives of the serious amateur are not above suspicion. In his assiduous practice, his limited repertoire, his semi-public style of performance, is there not a suggestion of vanity? Is his conscious parade of skill, taken along with his fear of unknown works, the mark of selfless devotion to music, and music alone? I doubt it.

But our motives are certainly above suspicion. Music has no servants more disinterested, for not only do we gather no garlands in her service, but daily, for her sake, we risk making a fool of ourselves, than which there can be no greater test of pure devotion. We, too, are the desperate venturers among pianists; every time that we seat ourselves at the keyboard we are leading a forlorn hope; and, whether we fall by the way or chance to come through unscathed, the only reward we can hope for is a kindly glance from the goddess of harmony.

It is hardly necessary to dwell on the fact that our execution is faulty, that we are humanly liable to make mistakes, seeing that our weaknesses have been for years the butt of musical pedants and small souls. In the dim past we received some sort of instruction, perhaps a few years' lessons, but being bright children with wills of our own we saw no use in labouring at scales and arpeggios, at the tepid compositions of Czerny, when there were balls to throw, stones to kick, and penny dreadfuls to be devoured. An unlocked door or an open window—and we escaped from the wretched drudgery, thus showing early that eager zest of life which still marks our clan.

Now, it is enthusiasm alone that carries us through. Our performance of any "piece of average difficulty" (as the publishers say) is nothing short of a series of miracles. As we peer at the music and urge our fingers to scurry over the keys, horrid gulfs yawn before us, great rocks come crashing down, the thick undergrowth is full of pitfalls and mantraps, but we are not to be deterred. Though we do not know what notes are coming next, or what fingers we shall use, if the music says presto it must be; the spirit of the tune must be set free, however its flesh may be lacerated. So we swing up the dizzy arpeggios as a hunted mountaineer might leap from crag to crag; we come down a run of demi-semi-quavers with the blind confidence of men trying to shoot the rapids of Niagara. Only the stout-hearted and great of soul can undertake these perilous but magnificent ventures.

Unlike the serious amateurs, we do not pick and choose among pieces until we have found one to which we can give the cold glitter of an impeccable rendering. We attend concerts (for, above all, we are the concert-goers and dreamers of dreams, as O'Shaughnessy might have said) and come reeling out, intoxicated with sound; for days we are haunted by a lovely theme or an amazing climax, until we can bear it no longer; we rush off to the music shops to see if it is possible to capture this new lovely thing and keep it for ever; more often than not we return home in triumph, hardly giving ourselves time to flatten out the music before plunging into the opening bars. Nothing that has been arranged for the piano or that can be played in some sort of fashion on the instrument comes amiss if it has once aroused our enthusiasm; symphonies, opera, tone-poems, string-quartets are all welcome. Nay, we often prefer the arrangements of orchestral things, for we do not think of the piano merely as a solo instrument; to us it is the shining ivory and ebony gateway to the land of music. As our fingers wander over the keys our great dream-orchestra wakens to life.

I believe that at the very end, when the depths of our folly and ignorance are fully revealed, when all our false notes have been cast up into one awful total by the recording angel of music, it will be found that we, the bad pianists, have been misjudged among men, that we, too, have loved and laboured for the divine art. When we file into Elysium, forlorn, scared, a shabby little band, and come within sight of Beethoven, whom we have murdered so many times, I believe that a smile will break through the thunder-cloud of his face. "Ach! Come you in, children," he will roar, "bad players, eh? . . . I have heard. . . . Very bad players. . . . But there have been worse among you. . . . The spirit was in you, and you have listened well. . . . Come in. . . . I have composed one hundred and fifty more symphonies and sonatas, and you shall hear them all."

IN PRAISE OF IDLENESS

By *Bertrand Russell*

LIKE most of my generation, I was brought up on the saying "Satan finds some mischief still for idle hands to do." Being a highly virtuous child, I believed all that I was told and acquired a conscience which has kept me working hard down to the present moment. But although my conscience has controlled my *actions*, my *opinions* have undergone a revolution. I think that there is far too much work done in the world, that immense harm is caused by the belief that work is virtuous, and that what needs to be preached in modern industrial countries is quite different from what always has been preached. Every one knows the story of the traveler in Naples who saw twelve beggars lying in the sun (it was before the days of Mussolini), and offered a lira to the laziest of them. Eleven of them jumped up to claim it, so he gave it to the twelfth. This traveler was on the right lines. But in countries which do not enjoy Mediterranean sunshine idleness is more difficult, and a great public propaganda will be required to inaugurate it. I hope that after reading the following pages the leaders of the Y.M.C.A. will start a campaign to induce good young men to do nothing. If so, I shall not have lived in vain.

Before advancing my own arguments for laziness, I must dispose of one which I cannot accept. Whenever a person who already has enough to live on proposes to engage in some everyday kind of job, such as school-teaching or typing, he or she is told that such conduct takes the bread out of other people's mouths, and is, therefore, wicked. If this argument were valid, it would only be necessary for us all to be idle in order

From *Harper's Magazine*, October 1932; copyright, 1932, by Harper & Brothers. Used by special permission.

that we should all have our mouths full of bread. What people who say such things forget is that what a man earns he usually spends, and in spending he gives employment. As long as a man spends his income he puts just as much bread into people's mouths in spending as he takes out of other people's mouths in earning. The real villain, from this point of view, is the man who saves. If he merely puts his savings in a stocking, like the proverbial French peasant, it is obvious that they do not give employment. If he invests his savings the matter is less obvious, and different cases arise.

One of the commonest things to do with savings is to lend them to some government. In view of the fact that the bulk of the expenditure of most civilized governments consists in payments for past wars and preparation for future wars, the man who lends his money to a government is in the same position as the bad men in Shakespeare who hire murderers. The net result of the man's economical habits is to increase the armed forces of the State to which he lends his savings. Obviously it would be better if he spent the money, even if he spent it on drink or gambling.

But, I shall be told, the case is quite different when savings are invested in industrial enterprises. When such enterprises succeed and produce something useful this may be conceded. In these days, however, no one will deny that most enterprises fail. That means that a large amount of human labor, which might have been devoted to producing something which could be enjoyed, was expended on producing machines which, when produced, lay idle and did no good to anyone. The man who invests his savings in a concern that goes bankrupt is, therefore, injuring others as well as himself. If he spent his money, say, in giving parties for his friends, they (we may hope) would get pleasure, and so would all those on whom he spent money, such as the butcher, the baker, and the bootlegger. But if he spends it (let us say) upon laying down rails for surface cars in some place where surface cars turn out to be not wanted, he has diverted a mass of labor into channels where it gives pleasure to no one. Nevertheless, when he becomes poor through the failure of his investment he will be regarded as a victim of undeserved misfortune, whereas the gay spendthrift, who has spent his money philanthropically, will be despised as a fool and a frivolous person.

All this is only preliminary. I want to say, in all seriousness, that a great deal of harm is being done in the modern world by the belief in the virtuousness of *work*, and that the road to happiness and prosperity lies in an organized diminution of work.

First of all: what is work? Work is of two kinds: first, altering the position of matter at or near the earth's surface relatively to other such matter; second, telling other people to do so. The first kind is unpleasant and ill paid; the second is pleasant and highly paid. The second kind is capable of indefinite extension: there are not only those who give orders but those who give advice as to what orders should be given. Usually two opposite kinds of advice are given simultaneously by two different bodies of men; this is called politics. The skill required for this kind of work is not knowledge of the subjects as to which advice is given, but knowledge of the art of persuasive speaking and writing, *i.e.*, of advertising.

Throughout Europe, though not in America, there is a third class of men, more respected than either of the classes of workers. These are men who, through ownership of land, are able to make others pay for the privilege of being allowed to exist and to work. These landowners are idle, and I might, therefore, be expected to praise them. Unfortunately, their idleness is rendered possible only by the industry of others; indeed their desire for comfortable idleness is historically the source of the whole gospel of work. The last thing they have ever wished is that others should follow their example.

From the beginning of civilization until the Industrial Revolution a man could, as a rule, produce by hard work little more than was required for the subsistence of himself and his family, although his wife worked at least as hard and his children added their labor as soon as they were old enough to do so. The small surplus above bare necessaries was not left to those who produced it, but was appropriated by priests and warriors. In times of famine there was no surplus; the warriors and priests, however, still secured as much as at other times, with the result that many of the workers died of hunger. This system persisted in Russia until 1917, and still persists in the East; in England, in spite of the Industrial Revolution, it remained in full force throughout the Napoleonic wars, and until a hundred years ago, when the new class of manufacturers acquired power. In America the system came to an end with the Revolution, except in the South, where it persisted until the Civil War. A system which lasted so long and ended so recently has naturally left a profound impression upon men's thoughts and opinions. Much that we take for granted about the desirability of work is derived from this system and, being pre-industrial, is not adapted to the modern world. Modern technic has made it possible for leisure, within limits, to be not the prerogative of small privileged classes, but a right evenly distributed throughout the community. The morality of work is the morality of slaves, and the modern world has no need of slavery.

It is obvious that, in primitive communities, peasants, left to themselves, would not have parted with the slender surplus upon which the warriors and priests subsisted, but would have either produced less or consumed more. At first sheer force compelled them to produce and part with the surplus. Gradually, however, it was found possible to induce many of them to accept an ethic according to which it was their duty to work hard, although part of their work went to support others in idleness. By this means the amount of compulsion required was lessened, and the expenses were diminished. To this day ninety-nine per cent of British wage-earners would be genuinely shocked if it were proposed that the King should not have a larger income than a working man. The conception of duty, speaking historically, has been a means used by the holders of power to induce others to live for the interests of their masters rather than their own. Of course the holders of power conceal this fact from themselves by managing to believe that their interests are identical with the larger interests of humanity. Sometimes this is true; Athenian slave-owners, for instance, employed part of their leisure in making a permanent contribution to civilization which would have been impossible under a just economic system. Leisure is essential to civilization, and in former times leisure for the few was rendered possible only by the labors of the many. But their labors were valuable, not because work is good, but because leisure is good. And with modern technic it would be possible to distribute leisure justly without injury to civilization.

Modern technic has made it possible to diminish enormously the amount of labor necessary to produce the necessaries of life for every one. This was made obvious during the War. At that time all the men in the armed forces, all the men and women engaged in the production of munitions, all the men and women engaged in spying, war propaganda, or government offices connected with the War were withdrawn from productive occupations. In spite of this, the general level of physical well-being among wage-earners on the side of the allies was higher than before or since. The significance of this fact was concealed by finance: borrowing made it appear as if the future was nourishing the present. But that, of course, would have been impossible; a man cannot eat a loaf of bread that does not yet exist. The War showed conclusively that by the scientific organization of production it is possible to keep modern populations in fair comfort on a small part of the working capacity of the modern world. If at the end of the War the scientific organization which had been created in order to liberate men for fighting and munition work had been preserved, and the hours of work had been cut down to four, all would have been well. Instead of that, the old chaos was restored, those whose work was demanded were made to work long hours, and the rest were left to starve as unemployed.

Why? Because work is a duty, and a man should not receive wages in proportion to what he has produced, but in proportion to his virtue as exemplified by his industry.

This is the morality of the Slave State, applied in circumstances totally unlike those in which it arose. No wonder the result has been disastrous. Let us take an illustration. Suppose that at a given moment a certain number of people are engaged in the manufacture of pins. They make as many pins as the world needs, working (say) eight hours a day. Someone makes an invention by which the same number of men can make twice as many pins as before. But the world does not need twice as many pins: pins are already so cheap that hardly any more will be bought at a lower price. In a sensible world everybody concerned in the manufacture of pins would take to working four hours instead of eight, and everything else would go on as before. But in the actual world this would be thought demoralizing. The men still work eight hours, there are too many pins, some employers go bankrupt, and half the men previously concerned in making pins are thrown out of work. There is, in the end, just as much leisure as on the other plan, but half the men are totally idle while half are still overworked. In this way it is insured that the unavoidable leisure shall cause misery all round instead of being a universal source of happiness. Can anything more insane be imagined?

The idea that the poor should have leisure has always been shocking to the rich. In England in the early nineteenth century fifteen hours was the ordinary day's work for a man; children sometimes did as much, and very commonly did twelve hours a day. When meddlesome busy-bodies suggested that perhaps these hours were rather long, they were told that work kept adults from drink and children from mischief. When I was a child, shortly after urban working men had acquired the vote, certain public holidays were established by law, to the great indignation of the upper classes. I remember hearing an old Duchess say, "What do the poor want with holidays? they ought to *work*." People nowadays are less frank, but the sentiment persists, and is the source of much economic confusion.

II

Let us, for a moment, consider the ethics of work frankly, without superstition. Every human being, of necessity, consumes in the course of his life a certain amount of produce of human labor. Assuming, as we may, that labor is on the whole disagreeable, it is unjust that a man should consume more than he produces. Of course he may provide services rather than commodities, like a medical man, for example; but he should provide something in return for his board and lodging. To this extent, the duty of work must be admitted, but to this extent only.

I shall not develop the fact that in all modern societies outside the U.S.S.R. many people escape even this minimum of work, namely all those who inherit money and all those who marry money. I do not think the fact that these people are allowed to be idle is nearly so harmful as the fact that wage-earners are expected to overwork or starve. If the ordinary wage-earner worked four hours a day there would be enough for everybody, and no unemployment—assuming a certain very moderate amount of sensible organization. This idea shocks the well-to-do, because they are convinced that the poor would not know how to use so much leisure. In America men often work long hours even when they are already well-off; such men, naturally, are indignant at the idea of leisure for wage-earners except as the grim punishment of unemployment, in fact, they dislike leisure even for their sons. Oddly enough, while they wish their sons to work so hard as to have no time to be civilized, they do not mind their wives and daughters having no work at all. The snobbish admiration of uselessness, which, in an aristocratic society, extends to both sexes, is under a plutocracy confined to women; this, however, does not make it any more in agreement with common sense.

The wise use of leisure, it must be conceded, is a product of

civilization and education. A man who has worked long hours
all his life will be bored if he becomes suddenly idle. But without a considerable amount of leisure a man is cut off from
many of the best things. There is no longer any reason why
the bulk of the population should suffer this deprivation; only
a foolish asceticism, usually vicarious, makes us insist on work
in excessive quantities now that the need no longer exists.

In the new creed which controls the government of Russia,
while there is much that is very different from the traditional
teaching of the West, there are some things that are quite unchanged. The attitude of the governing classes, and especially
of those who control educational propaganda, on the subject
of the dignity of labor is almost exactly that which the governing classes of the world have always preached to what were
called the "honest poor." Industry, sobriety, willingness to
work long hours for distant advantages, even submissiveness
to authority, all these reappear; moreover, authority still
represents the will of the Ruler of the Universe, Who, however,
is now called by a new name, Dialectical Materialism.

The victory of the proletariat in Russia has some points in
common with the victory of the feminists in some other countries. For ages men had conceded the superior saintliness of
women and had consoled women for their inferiority by maintaining that saintliness is more desirable than power. At last
the feminists decided that they would have both, since the
pioneers among them believed all that the men had told them
about the desirability of virtue but not what they had told
them about the worthlessness of political power. A similar
thing has happened in Russia as regards manual work. For
ages the rich and their sycophants have written in praise of
"honest toil," have praised the simple life, have professed a
religion which teaches that the poor are much more likely to
go to heaven than the rich, and in general have tried to make
manual workers believe that there is some special nobility
about altering the position of matter in space, just as men
tried to make women believe that they derived some special

nobility from their sexual enslavement. In Russia all this teaching about the excellence of manual work has been taken seriously, with the result that the manual worker is more honored than anyone else. What are, in essence, revivalist appeals are made to secure shock workers for special tasks. Manual work is the ideal which is held before the young, and is the basis of all ethical teaching.

For the present this is all to the good. A large country, full of natural resources, awaits development and has to be developed with very little use of credit. In these circumstances hard work is necessary and is likely to bring a great reward. But what will happen when the point has been reached where everybody could be comfortable without working long hours?

In the West we have various ways of dealing with this problem. We have no attempt at economic justice, so that a large proportion of the total produce goes to a small minority of the population, many of whom do no work at all. Owing to the absence of any central control over production, we produce hosts of things that are not wanted. We keep a large percentage of the working population idle because we can dispense with their labor by making others overwork. When all these methods prove inadequate we have a war: we cause a number of people to manufacture high explosives, and a number of others to explode them, as if we were children who had just discovered fireworks. By a combination of all these devices we manage, though with difficulty, to keep alive the notion that a great deal of manual work must be the lot of the average man.

In Russia, owing to economic justice and central control over production, the problem will have to be differently solved. The rational solution would be as soon as the necessaries and elementary comforts can be provided for all to reduce the hours of labor gradually, allowing a popular vote to decide, at each stage, whether more leisure or more goods were to be preferred. But, having taught the supreme virtue of hard work, it is difficult to see how the authorities can aim at a paradise in which there will be much leisure and little work. It seems more likely that they will find continually fresh schemes by which present leisure is to be sacrificed to future productivity. I read recently of an ingenious scheme put forward by Russian engineers for making the White Sea and the northern coasts of Siberia warm by putting a dam across the Kara Straits. An admirable plan, but liable to postpone proletarian comfort for a generation, while the nobility of toil is being displayed amid the ice-fields and snow-storms of the Arctic Ocean. This sort of thing, if it happens, will be the result of regarding the virtue of hard work as an end in itself, rather than as a means to a state of affairs in which it is no longer needed.

III

The fact is that moving matter about, while a certain amount of it is necessary to our existence, is emphatically not one of the ends of human life. If it were, we should have to consider every navvy superior to Shakespeare. We have been misled in this matter by two causes. One is the necessity of keeping the poor contented, which has led the rich for thousands of years to preach the dignity of labor, while taking care themselves to remain undignified in this respect. The other is the new pleasure in mechanism, which makes us delight in the astonishingly clever changes that we can produce on the earth's surface. Neither of these motives makes any great appeal to the actual worker. If you ask him what he thinks the best part of his life, he is not likely to say, "I enjoy manual work because it makes me feel that I am fulfilling man's noblest task, and because I like to think how much man can transform his planet. It is true that my body demands periods of rest, which I have to fill in as best I may, but I am never so happy as when the morning comes and I can return to the toil from which my contentment springs." I have never heard working men say this sort of thing. They consider work, as it should be considered, as a necessary means to a livelihood, and it is from their leisure hours that they derive whatever happiness they may enjoy.

It will be said that while a little leisure is pleasant, men would not know how to fill their days if they had only four hours' work out of the twenty-four. In so far as this is true in the modern world it is a condemnation of our civilization; it would not have been true at any earlier period. There was formerly a capacity for light-heartedness and play which has been to some extent inhibited by the cult of efficiency. The modern man thinks that everything ought to be done for the sake of something else, and never for its own sake. Serious-minded persons, for example, are continually condemning the habit of going to the cinema, and telling us that it leads the young into crime. But all the work that goes to producing a cinema is respectable, because it is work, and because it brings a money profit. The notion that the desirable activities are those that bring a profit has made everything topsy-turvy. The butcher who provides you with meat and the baker who provides you with bread are praiseworthy because they are making money but when you enjoy the food they have provided you are merely frivolous, unless you eat only to get strength for your work. Broadly speaking, it is held that getting money is good and spending money is bad. Seeing that they are two sides of one transaction, this is absurd; one might as well maintain that keys are good but keyholes are bad. The individual, in our society, works for profit; but the social purpose of his work lies in the consumption of what he produces. It is this divorce between the individual and the social purpose of production that makes it so difficult for men to think clearly in a world in which profit-making is the incentive to industry. We think too much of production and too little of consumption. One result is that we attach too little importance to enjoyment and simple happiness, and that we do not judge production by the pleasure that it gives to the consumer.

When I suggest that working hours should be reduced to

four, I am not meaning to imply that all the remaining time should necessarily be spent in pure frivolity. I mean that four hours' work a day should entitle a man to the necessities and elementary comforts of life, and that the rest of his time should be his to use as he might see fit. It is an essential part of any such social system that education should be carried farther than it usually is at present, and should aim, in part, at providing tastes which would enable a man to use leisure intelligently. I am not thinking mainly of the sort of things that would be considered "high-brow." Peasant dances have died out except in remote rural areas, but the impulses which caused them to be cultivated must still exist in human nature. The pleasures of urban populations have become mainly passive: seeing cinemas, watching football matches, listening to the radio, and so on. This results from the fact that their active energies are fully taken up with work; if they had more leisure they would again enjoy pleasures in which they took an active part.

In the past there was a small leisure class and a large working class. The leisure class enjoyed advantages for which there was no basis in social justice; this necessarily made it oppressive, limited its sympathies, and caused it to invent theories by which to justify its privileges. These facts greatly diminished its excellence, but in spite of this drawback it contributed nearly the whole of what we call civilization. It cultivated the arts and discovered the sciences; it wrote the books, invented the philosophies, and refined social relations. Even the liberation of the oppressed has usually been inaugurated from above. Without the leisure class mankind would never have emerged from barbarism.

The method of a hereditary leisure class without duties was, however, extraordinarily wasteful. None of the members of the class had been taught to be industrious, and the class as a whole was not exceptionally intelligent. It might produce one Darwin, but against him had to be set tens of thousands of country gentlemen who never thought of anything more intelligent than fox-hunting and punishing poachers. At present, the universities are supposed to provide, in a more systematic way, what the leisure class provided accidentally and as a by-product. This is a great improvement, but it has certain drawbacks. University life is so different from life in the world at large that men who live in an academic milieu tend to be unaware of the pre-occupations of ordinary men and women; moreover, their ways of expressing themselves are usually such as to rob their opinions of the influence that they ought to have upon the general public. Another disadvantage is that in universities studies are organized, and the man who thinks of some original line of research is likely to be discouraged. Academic institutions, therefore, useful as they are, are not adequate guardians of the interests of civilization in a world where every one outside their walls is too busy for unutilitarian pursuits.

In a world where no one is compelled to work more than four hours a day every person possessed of scientific curiosity will be able to indulge it, and every painter will be able to paint without starving, however excellent his pictures may be. Young writers will not be obliged to draw attention to themselves by sensational pot-boilers, with a view to acquiring the economic independence needed for monumental works, for which, when the time at last comes, they will have lost the taste and the capacity. Men who in their professional work have become interested in some phase of economics or government will be able to develop their ideas without the academic detachment that makes the work of university economists lacking in reality. Medical men will have time to learn about the progress of medicine. Teachers will not be exasperatedly struggling to teach by routine things which they learned in their youth, which may, in the interval, have been proved to be untrue.

Above all, there will be happiness and joy of life, instead of frayed nerves, weariness, and dyspepsia. The work exacted will be enough to make leisure delightful, but not enough to produce exhaustion. Since men will not be tired in their spare time, they will not demand only such amusements as are passive and vapid. At least one per cent will probably devote the time not spent in professional work to pursuits of some public importance, and, since they will not depend upon these pursuits for their livelihood, their originality will be unhampered, and there will be no need to conform to the standards set by elderly pundits. But it is not only in these exceptional cases that the advantages of leisure will appear. Ordinary men and women, having the opportunity of a happy life, will become more kindly and less persecuting and less inclined to view others with suspicion. The taste for war will die out, partly for this reason, and partly because it will involve long and severe work for all. Good nature is, of all moral qualities, the one that the world needs most, and good nature is the result of ease and security, not of a life of arduous struggle. Modern methods of production have given us the possibility of ease and security for all; we have chosen instead to have overwork for some and starvation for others. Hitherto we have continued to be as energetic as we were before there were machines. In this we have been foolish, but there is no reason to go on being foolish for ever.

THE *NEW* NEW TESTAMENT

By *F. A. Spencer*

ONLY yesterday the science of physics was transformed by the discoveries of Albert Einstein. Conservatives at first found the Einstein theory a bitter pill to swallow. Many will recall that certain die-hards among both scientists and clergy accused this gentle scholar of everything in the book, from subtle hypocrisy and deception to downright immorality. When the new physics is mentioned a few academicians of my acquaintance still mutter in their beards, deplore the degeneracy of the times, and hope that a savior will arise who can explode an hypothesis so inherently vicious.

A somewhat parallel situation has recently developed in New Testament exegesis. Long ago the second-century writer, Papias of Hierapolis, as quoted in Eusebius' *Church History*, said that Matthew wrote his Gospel in Aramaic, that is, the vernacular spoken as far back as five hundred years before Christ, when Hebrew became mainly a literary tongue. This statement has never been able to carry conviction as literal truth, but it may now be regarded as a hint in the right direction. For internal evidence has been brought forth which shows, so far as such demonstration ever can, that our Gospels were not *composed* in Greek, but *translated*, sometimes rather badly, from Aramaic originals based on ultimate sources which date in part from the lifetime of Jesus himself. The corollary of this hypothesis is that, far from being a precipitate of Greek influence, committed to paper at the end of the first or the beginning of the second century, the *original* Gospels were all written before the destruction of Jerusalem in 70 A.D.

This theory, only recently published in fuller form, has been held by Professor Torrey of Yale and has been known to those on the inner circle for about thirty years. During all this time conservatives have been uttering half-choked cries of protest or have occasionally brought out articulate objections. It is not pleasant to confess a major error, and still less so to admit that the whole basis of a lifetime's work is wrong. Yet this is precisely what now confronts conservative New Testament exegetes, who have not only clung to the notion that the Gospels were composed in Greek, but have accepted it as a truism that the Pauline epistles were the first bit of Christian literature ever set down on paper.

Classical philologians, I venture to say, are more reluctant than natural scientists to abandon a cherished hypothesis. In the domain of New Testament criticism there are added doctrinal complications. A fundamentalist, of course, will reject with horror the notion that the Greek which he has so painfully acquired is not the last court of authority on all matters, doctrinal and otherwise. If he lacks the intelligence to master Greek he will probably remain content with the English version which he has been using all along. Even a liberal churchman or exegete, who has a good knowledge of New Testament Greek and a nodding acquaintance with Hebrew, is likely to shy at the thought of admitting that in the old familiar text he has not after all "the very words of God." Such a shaking of the foundations of authority is well-nigh intolerable to one who has devoted a lifetime to preaching and teaching on the basis of a minute interpretation of the Greek text. This minister or teacher may confess that in many spots he must twist the Greek out of its normal sense, he must dodge, paraphrase, emend, or excise in order to obtain any tolerable meaning. He may admit that there are passages in the Gospels where the ethical teaching of Jesus seems curiously lower than the standard generally set. But for the most part he will worry along with the "explanations" which have satisfied generations of scholars.

Every-one doubtless is familiar with the story of the Kentucky preacher brought up on his King James Bible who brushed aside the study of foreign tongues with this classic pronouncement, "The English language was good enough for Jesus and Paul, and it's good enough for me." One hesitates to bring the parallel home too closely, yet in essentials it applies. A prime reason for the opposition to Professor Torrey's thesis is downright ignorance of Aramaic. The study of Greek, not to mention Hebrew or Aramaic, has almost died out as a compulsory feature of the curriculum in our theological seminaries. Only a few men now living possess sufficient acquaintance with Aramaic, the Greek of the Septuagint Bible, and the language of the Gospels to pass judgment on an hypothesis of this kind. But when these invaders come over into the New Testament, conservative Greek scholars cannot help feeling that the whole affair is mutiny. When honest exegetes profess their willingness to collaborate with expert professors of Semitics in a new interpretation of the New Testament they may mean what they say, yet in their heart of hearts they cannot help resenting those bold, bad Orientalists who threaten to break up the meeting.

And yet scholars in the orthodox camp have not been insensible to the difficulties and peculiarities of the Gospel language. The character of New Testament Greek has, in fact, been long disputed, and has been estimated in ways that differ astoundingly. The very oldest view may be designated as the "God's Greek" hypothesis. This is all of a piece with the notion, still presented in certain hinterland seminaries, that one fine day, a few hundred years ago, Yahweh himself sat down and, calling for a stenographer, proceeded to dictate word by word in Greek the Gospels as we know them. Obviously a divine tongue of this sort would not need to conform to any human literary standard.

Toward the beginning of the twentieth century it did seem that a definite mortal norm had been brought to light. A number of non-literary papyri, couched in Hellenistic or Common Greek, were discovered in Egypt. The New Testament, like the translations from Hebrew or Aramaic which we call the Septuagint Bible, was plainly written in Common Greek. New Testament exegetes, therefore, came gradually to hold that a full comparison between the language of the papyri and that of the Gospels would solve almost all difficulties. Workers in this field were able to shed light on single words and phrases, but they could not produce any extensive parallels to the prose of the Septuagint or of the Gospels. And from the very first the wide divergence in the views of those who exploited it most successfully pointed to a fundamental lack in the thesis itself. For the adherents of the "papyri school" appear even yet unable to make up their minds just how natural and easy, or how awkward and uneasy, just how literary and refined, or barbarous and unpolished, they must term the language of the Gospels. Their theory, however interpreted, will not explain all the difficulties at hand, that is to say in summary, the presence of a wide and subtle vocabulary handled with masterful skill, but used to clothe idioms which are demonstrably awkward and un-Greek.

It is a rule of elementary common sense to compare like with like. The only extensive parallel to the prose of the Gospels which can be brought forward is that of the Septuagint, which is admittedly translation Greek. By any standard of composed Greek, the language of the Gospels simply will not fall into any other category than that of translation. This fact the followers of another school were almost on the point of recognizing. About the same time that the papyri were discovered the view developed that the writers of the Gospels, accustomed as they were to speaking Aramaic in the home, blundered at times when they attempted to use Greek as a literary language. Hence they wrote a Jewish-Greek *patois*, or to put the matter a little differently, they thought in Aramaic and wrote in Greek.

The difficulty with this hypothesis is that no parallels to such a jargon can be found anywhere in a literary context, unless one admits such jocose barbarities as the ramblings of the Thracian policeman in Aristophanes' *Thesmophoriazusae*. The speech of this barbarian illustrates precisely what the Greek of the Gospels is not. He gets his vocabulary, case and verb-endings, as well as syntax, hopelessly mixed in the well-known manner of all raw foreigners. But the translators of the Gospels are patently masters of Greek vocabulary. Their diction is distinguished by its uniform excellence and subtlety. It is their *idiom* which is Semitic. And that is exactly what one would expect of a translator striving to render faithfully, word for word in Greek, Aramaic documents which he considered essential to his own and the world's salvation.

Variations of the Jewish-Greek hypothesis have in time past brought several scholars—Wellhausen, Burney, and Montgomery among others—close to the view of which Professor Torrey has the honor to be first champion. A number of research men, dallying with the notion that the Gospels are based on Semitic sources, have pointed to evidences of mistranslation. But the prevailing conception that, based on Semitic documents or not, the Gospels were composed freely in Greek has prevented these corrections from leading to the logical conclusion that the Gospels are in their entirety translations from Hebrew or Aramaic.

II

As a proof at the outset that the translation hypothesis does indeed create a new New Testament, I cite two examples where our Authorized Version, closely following the Greek, makes Jesus quote Scripture which does not exist and, what is worse, advise his representatives to be downright rude in a fashion which no courteous Oriental would dream of following. It should be said in advance of more detailed explanation further on that the Aramaic of the Gospels was written in continuous, unpointed script, only the consonants (not the vowels) being represented. One word, therefore, could easily be mistaken for another and distinctions in gender might slip the attention of the most careful translator.

In John 7.38 Jesus declares, "He that believeth on me, as the scripture hath said, out of his belly shall flow rivers of living water." Now modern translators are likely to soften this down, though they can do nothing to relieve the inherent absurdity of the quotation attributed to Jesus, by rendering "belly" as "heart." But the same Aramaic word means both "middle of a man" and "midst of a city." A slight change of pointing makes the assumed Aramaic original read "midst of her," that is Jerusalem, instead of "midst of him." The reference is to Psalms 46.4–5: "There is a river, the streams whereof shall make glad the city of God . . . God is in the midst of her; she shall not be moved: God shall help her, and that right early." As Professor Torrey translates, the pertinent part of the sentence runs, "Out of the midst of Her shall flow rivers of living water." According to Luke 10.4, Jesus counsels his seventy disciples to "salute no man by the way." Modern exegetes wriggle round the difficulty by saying that Jesus meant only to stress the urgent nature of the mission on which he was sending his disciples. The truth lies elsewhere. Two Aramaic verbs, as even the monolingual can see, are quite hard to distinguish from one another in a continuous script. "Sh'lem l'" means "join oneself to, take as a companion." "Shallem l'" signifies "greet, speak to." The translator of this passage chose the second alternative when he should have read the first. Professor Torrey renders, "enter into fellowship with no one on the road."

Examples such as these, conservative exegetes may "explain," though they cannot refute. Their method is rather to disclaim all knowledge of Aramaic and yet to say that New Testament scholars who *know* no Aramaic must accept the translation hypothesis before it can really be considered sound! Before we go on to define the term Aramaic more closely and to give further examples of how Professor Torrey's demonstration restores sense in crucial passages of the Gospel text, the arguments of the enemy, which constitute the theory's best defense, must be answered. The process incidentally may supply a certain amount of background which the lay reader does not possess.

Those on the other bank maintain that the whole thesis, with its corollary, is psychologically improbable. They proceed first of all on the assumption that the Gospels were produced when the Church had already cut the umbilical cord of Jewish tradition. More than that, some of them astoundingly maintain that there was never such a thing as Jewish Christians. We cannot point to any first-century Christian literature extant in Aramaic originals. Therefore, there was never an early group, set apart from normal Judaism, for which writings of this type could have been designed. Hence, these supposed documents are merely a figment of the imagination. How, they ask, could the Gospels have been composed at an early period, when the Church was not yet conscious of its wider mission and importance, when its horizon was definitely Palestinian, when the divinity of Jesus was not yet fully recognized?

Back of these objections lies an initial point of view so naïve that it ought to have perished in Edward Gibbon's time. There is involved here a totally wrong conception of intellectual and religious life in Palestine during the first century A.D. That the Greek world outside was illiterate those in the enemy trenches would certainly not affirm. It is in fact admitted that the opening centuries of our era were more literate than any other until the modern period of compulsory education. Of this there is solid proof, contemporary letters written on every subject under heaven by men and women of all ranks and professions. In a period somewhat later than the first century the laborers of Britain amused their leisure by scribbling verses from the *Æneid* on the bricks they made.

But when it comes to a judgment of Palestine, the case changes. There was forsooth no Hellenistic, no specifically Greek influence in Palestine during the early part of the first century A.D. and its inhabitants, according to the opposition, must have been a pretty illiterate lot. A certain Irishman knew better than that, as his novel, *The Brook Kerith*, gives evidence. Here, as often, a mere novelist has gone straighter to the truth than professors, who have grown slightly muzzy from being locked too long in their own compartment and who will admit no guesses except their own.

Jesus and his disciples spoke Aramaic. Of this there can be no doubt. Whenever Mark quotes a saying of Jesus *directly*, the language is always Aramaic transliterated into Greek. Yet we are asked to believe that Jesus and his disciples, addressing a public which spoke the same tongue, would create no demand for the preservation in vernacular of their notable words and deeds. About two hundred years before Christ the author of Ecclesiastes, in a quotation known wherever the Bible is read, had declared that book-buying was an endless business and that close study was a weariness to the flesh. This at a period when parts of Ezra existed in the Aramaic original, when Aramaic was the recognized speech of Jews and had been for more than two centuries past.

Nearly six generations previous to the birth of Christ the revolt of the Maccabees, under Judas the Hammer, was brought about and the development of the Pharisees, the "Separatist" group, came to a head because of the pervasive character of pagan influence in Jewish life and thought. And had not Jerusalem for years been a veritable trading-ground of ideas as well as material goods? Her very festivals were a Mecca for philosophers and thinkers as well as for merchants. Egypt, and especially Alexandria, always remained in close touch with Palestine. Yet presumably such "Alexandrian Greek philosophy" as one finds in John's Gospel could not permeate to Palestine before the end of the first century or the beginning of the second! The Church, having remained in a Judaeo-Christian or, not to beg the question, a Palestinian vacuum for nearly a century, emerged at last with a shout and cried: "Lo, here is Greek culture!" A curious vibration of opinion which denies that there were Jewish Christians and yet maintains that the Church during this pre-Gospel period had a specifically Palestinian outlook.

If one examines the Gospels with minute attention, one finds that the point of view is distinctly Palestinian. The writers admit of course that Gentiles must enter into the scheme of salvation. The good news must be preached to the ends of the earth. But this was nothing more than they could discover in the writings of Second Isaiah. At crucial points one expects to find that the vision of the Gospels, written as they presumably were under Greek influence, has expanded to a cosmopolitan range equal to or surpassing that of Paul. But the contrary is true. Jesus commands the Twelve not to go among the Gentiles, but rather to the lost sheep of the house of Israel. They will, he says, not have covered the towns of Israel before the Son of Man arrives. The Jewish children must be fed first. It is unjust to take bread from them and throw it to the (Gentile) dogs. One expects Jesus in his interview with the Greeks in the twelfth chapter of John to outline a wide and tolerant missionary program for the Gentiles. But there is not a word of this—only some lovely verses which sound like a paraphrase of the central doctrine of the Eleusinian Mysteries.

Two things become quite clear when such an examination is made. In the first place, the Gospels take a much narrower view of missionary work than does Paul. Consequently their sources must be earlier in date than the Pauline epistles. Secondly, there is no historical allusion in any of the Gospels which forces us to date it *after* 70 A.D. On the contrary Mark makes a reference, what looks startlingly like a contemporary reference instinct with horror, to Caligula's attempt in 40 A.D. to place his statue as Jupiter Olympius in the Holy of Holies— "But when ye shall see the abomination of desolation, spoken of by Daniel the prophet, standing where it ought not. . . ." Supposed references to the destruction of Jerusalem turn out upon close scrutiny to be literally and without exception repeated from Old Testament prophecies, where it is foretold that foreign armies will surround Jerusalem, that city and Temple will be destroyed, and that two-thirds of the people in the land will be butchered. The activity of that quasi-Nazi party, the Zealots, culminating in a revolt which did eventually bring about the destruction of Jerusalem, began while Jesus was still very young. Reverberations of its plots and propaganda could be heard, and oracles regarding the possible issue when the inevitable clash came would be invoked, long before underground work broke out into open mutiny.

The argument that Jesus would not have been acclaimed as divine during his lifetime will not hold for a moment. In the fifth century B.C. the Greek poet Empedocles said that he was honored as an immortal god, not as a mortal, in his native island of Sicily. Men followed after him by thousands, asking the way to wealth, demanding oracles and cures. Empedocles claimed, moreover, that he could teach his disciples to control the weather and even bring the dead back to life. Lysander, the Spartan general who took Athens at the end of the Peloponnesian War, was deified during his lifetime. So was Alexander the Great. In the East Augustus was hailed as a god before ever Jesus of Nazareth was born. It was the custom of enthusiastic Orientals to deify their rulers and salute their prophets, not a generation after their death, but in their lifetime. Such was and such has remained the custom of the Orient, where a religious movement runs from Dan to Beersheba almost overnight and a new healer quickly obtains recognition. If the audience who saw Jesus work and heard him preach recognized him as divine, literary men would not refrain from canonizing him until after his death. Neither Xenophon nor Plato waited a century before embalming Socrates in prose.

III

The opponents of Dr. Torrey's theory invoke the sacred name of science. To admit such a theory, they contend, lets loose a brood of conjectural emendations in the field of scientific textual criticism. Well, textual criticism is perhaps a science when it dates handwriting or plots the family tree of manuscripts, estimating mutual relationships within the family, and noting variant readings where tribes among the clan disagree. When the subjective element enters—and it does to a certain degree when one attempts to choose between the "better" and the "worse" reading, or to emend, exclude, or in any way trifle with the Greek—then the only verdict must be: "Interesting, if true." Would anyone maintain that New Testament exegetes always agree on crucial points of reading and interpretation?

Then, they say, there is confusion and lack of agreement in the Semitic camp. Lists of Semitisms thus far noted in the Gospels do not at all coincide. Naturally, for the subject is new, cases thus far examined have often been ambiguous or doubtful, and the amount of Aramaic possessed by previous investigators has varied widely. Competent professors of Semitics would hardly disagree about individual Semitic idioms. But to recognize the individual words lying behind a given passage in Greek requires not only constant study of Aramaic but wide familiarity with translation Greek and the Gospel language as well. To these tasks Professor Torrey has given more time than any other man living. The test of his method is whether it solves difficulties without presuming anything unnatural or improbable.

An excellent proving-ground is offered by the Septuagint, a Greek version of the Hebrew Bible which according to tradition was made in the third century B.C. at Alexandria by a rabbinical committee of "seventy" (hence the name Septuagint), but which most probably was done by men from various regions over a period of about four centuries. Our Massoretic text, the one "handed down" by Hebrew scholars from the second century A.D., is of course not so old as that used for the Septuagint and does not always coincide with it. But by comparison of the two, and by careful study of the various translation methods, we can be sure in literally thousands of cases what Hebrew reading was used. In simple narrative or discourse the wording of the original is to a large degree unmistakable, though synonyms afford some range of choice and error. With regard to poetry or prophecy a judgment is much more difficult to form and conjectures will sometimes vary. However, a competent Hebrew scholar can take as a test case some section with which he happens to be rather unfamiliar in both the Greek and the Hebrew texts, such a passage, say, as the twentieth chapter of II Samuel, and, translating a few verses, can hit 72 out of 80 words exactly right and in the precise order of the Hebrew original. The remaining eight will be synonyms. Any mistranslation in the Greek will probably guide him at once to the precise wording of the Hebrew.

I say competent Hebrew scholar, for the dabblings of amateurs here are more likely to afford amusement than information to specialists in the field, who have not only mastered the Semitic tongues but also given careful consideration to the methods of Septuagint translation. The results may be stated as follows. In general the older versions, though in the main sticking close to the Hebrew, are freer than the late ones, which become increasingly rigid and literal. Now the Gospel translators followed the same method as those who made our later Old Testament versions, and competent scholars can identify the resulting phenomena with a great degree of accuracy. In one celebrated case the cleavage between composition and translation is earmarked by the author himself. The preamble to his grandson's version of Ben Sira's Hebrew proverbs, our Ecclesiasticus, resembles in the quality of its Greek the prologue to Luke's Gospel. With the actual beginning of the proverbs Ben Sira's translator lapses into the same stiff medium employed throughout the remainder of Luke.

To be sure, translation from Aramaic into Greek is not so easy to recognize as a similar rendering from Hebrew. The word order of the Aramaic was more flexible and varied, while its idiom was less archaic, obscure, and less markedly poetic than that of the literary language. In the Gospels, moreover, another important guide to translation and mistranslation is lacking, for their originals, unlike the Hebrew, had been very little corrupted by the passage of time. Yet examples taken from both will show that scrupulous fidelity of rendering produced in either case an identical quaintness, an identical union of Common Greek vocabulary with Semitic idiom and word order.

The seventeenth chapter of Judges yields this specimen: "And there was a young man from Bethlehem . . . and he a Levite, and he dwelt there." Luke in his nineteenth chapter renders thus: "And behold a man by name called Zacchæus, and he was a chief publican, and he rich." Both versions in their distribution of the superfluous pronoun exhibit plainly the result of following an original with painstaking literalness. Such instances could be multiplied indefinitely. When scholars approach the subject of translation Greek in the Gospels they do not shy away from the test of the Septuagint, as opponents of the Torrey hypothesis seem to think, but proceed to their task on the basis of detailed research, which has made abundantly clear the main characteristics of translation Greek in the Old Testament.

Lesser adherents of the Greek original school often speak as if we had no literature in Aramaic, while amateurs on the other side frequently let patriotism outrun their knowledge. One should distinguish between Western Aramaic, the dialect spoken throughout Palestine, and Eastern Aramaic, which we now call Syriac. The latter helps to illuminate the former, because it has a very extensive literature, mainly religious. The vocabularies of both are similar; their idioms are identical. Just here a mind of comparison exists in the Syriac versions of the Greek Gospels. These include not only older ones, but also the Peshitta or "Simple" translation made at the beginning of the fifth century A.D. by Rabbula, Bishop of Edessa. The date deserves emphasis, for news stories have recently appeared in which the Peshitta is confused with the *lost* originals of Matthew, Mark, Luke, and John.

Taken as a whole then, Aramaic possesses a far larger body of literature than does classical Hebrew. And during the first century A.D. the literary language was uniform throughout Palestine as well as the Jewish Dispersion. For the benefit of his scattered countrymen Josephus wrote his *Wars of the Jews* originally in Aramaic, and only later furbished it forth in Greek. A circular letter such as that dispatched by Rabbi Gamaliel II shortly after Paul's death could be sent from the Black Sea to Upper Egypt, or from Cilicia through Arabia and Mesopotamia as far as the bounds of India and, if opened anywhere along the line, would seldom lack understanding readers.

IV

There are two broad answers as to why the Aramaic originals of our Gospels have not been handed down to us. Generally speaking, the categories of preservation are permanence of material (or the exceptional saving of a flimsy material like papyrus in the soil and climate of Egypt, so different from those of Palestine) and the universality of interest which the writings in question are able to arouse. Thus, for one example, we have brick tablets from Assyria and Babylonia, but no literature on skin or papyrus. And, on the other hand, an extensive Phœnician literature has perished, seemingly because not enough people cared to preserve it. A fluent journalist, sitting up at night with coffee and cigarettes, could duplicate the bulk, if not the quality, of our Bible in little more than a year. Yet that Bible hands down to us all that is left of more than a thousand years of Jewish literary activity. Whole continents of classical Greek literature have sunk without leaving much more than a ripple on the water, let alone complete translation into another language. We should never believe that they once existed had not industrious compilers and gossips told us so.

In regard to the Aramaic Gospels, they must largely have disappeared when the Romans devastated Palestine and took Jerusalem. Some of them would be carried away by Christian refugees. But, as worn Jewish synagogue rolls were destroyed to prevent contact with profane hands, so cherished copies of the Gospels may have gone into the flames when Christians girded themselves and took staves in hand to set out for the mountains. But, most important of all, the leaders of the Jewish-Christian church, when they met increasing hostility from the Jews, and turned to the Greek-speaking branch, would let their Aramaic Gospels go the way of all manuscripts in which people have lost interest.

The mention of Jewish Christians leads us directly to a consideration of how the Aramaic sources were probably developed, edited, and translated. A flood of popular literature on Messianic themes had evidently been poured out, both in Hebrew and in Aramaic, generations preceding the birth of Jesus. A whole program of epithets and activities was ready at hand when Jesus began his public teaching and was first recognized as *the* Messiah. How soon these epithets would be applied to Jesus, how soon his forerunner would be identified as John the Baptist and his entire program of teaching and healing squared with that of the prophesied Messiah we cannot know. Certainly much of it would be done informally during his lifetime. At any rate, in the face of Messianic literature already let loose before Jesus' birth concerning a vague Messiah to come, in face of the fact that neither before nor since Jesus has the *whole* Messianic program ever been pinned to one Jewish savior, let alone a peasant carpenter, it is inconceivable that there were no early "Jewish Christians," recognizable by religious authorities of the time as a special phenomenon in Judaism, or that a vernacular Messianic literature regarding Jesus which would appeal specially to such a group was not in some degree created before his death. The only answer to those who contend otherwise, and on this ground reject the translation hypothesis, is a popular injunction against folly

couched in three short, sharp words. Nor can one believe
that the rabbis, who defined heresy as a setting up of another
authority in addition to that of God, who refused always to
believe in a preëxistent, a superhuman Messiah, who in fact
ignored apocalyptic literature completely or spoke of it only
to condemn it, would very long regard the Nazarenes as a
mere conventicle within Judaism.

After the death of Jesus, the tragedy of the cross and the
universal belief of Jewish Christians in his resurrection and
second coming would, with an increasing appeal to Old Testament oracles, be superimposed upon the documents concerning
his life and teaching as *these*, floating about orally or written
down in part (and thus doubly diffused), were collected and
edited. Aramaic Mark (it is necessary to distinguish editor
and composer from translator except in the case of Luke)
made a careful abridgment of such scattered documents with
some attempt at chronology and form, apparently around the
year 40 A.D. Shortly afterward Matthew produced a finished
Gospel, using Mark and Mark's sources as well as additional
documents. Luke not only drew from Mark and Matthew
and their first originals (especially the one employed by
Matthew, which scholars have long designated as Q, short for
German *Quelle*, "Source"). Rummaging about in Palestine,
he also discovered other Aramaic writings and the Hebrew
narrative of Jesus' infancy as well. These he collected, edited,
and translated sometime before 60 A.D. with a special eye to
Gentile Christians. About the same period Aramaic John,
doubtless a resident of Jerusalem, produced mainly for Jews
a highly polished narrative, based on Matthew, Mark, their
sources, and other documents.

Among this group the translator of John, who perhaps
made his version outside of Palestine after 70 A.D., makes
most errors, averaging nearly two blunders for each page (of
Professor Torrey's English translation). With about one error
to the page the translator of Mark, who did a rather hasty
piece of work, nearly parallels Luke, who appears to have been

somewhat unfamiliar with specifically Palestinian Hebrew and
Aramaic. Matthew's translator makes the best record, having
a little more than one error to every other page. Such blunders
as arise (they number in all about 250) have to do usually
with single words or letters or a wrong punctuation, and flow
naturally from the character of the rather confusing Aramaic
language as well as the continuous script in which it is written.
They are the sort that any man might make who, although a
master of Aramaic, yet owned Greek as his mother speech.
anyonewhoreadswhatnowfollowsinjustthisformwillhavesome
notionofthedifficultyinherentinascriptwhichbearsnoindication
ofclausesandsentenceswhichcontainstwolettersthatareidentical
andothersthatareambiguousunlessmeticulouslywritten.　　In
Aramaic too there is a basic root which makes it possible for
a given word of three or four letters to be a noun or one of
several nouns, an adjective, adverb, or verb active or passive.
The vowels of course are never indicated. It is much as if,
having written in English the four letters grnd, one should
then proceed to open them up successively into grand, grind,
and ground.

From this last source of blunders, the existence in Aramaic
of an ambiguous root, spring a number of glaring mistrans-
lations. The case I choose illustrates not only the confusion
of active with passive voice, but also yields a version which
is in flat defiance of known Jewish custom regarding divorce.
According to Jewish law a woman could not "put away her
husband." If he was impotent, frigid, or afflicted with a loathsome ailment, if he had a nasty occupation such as tanning,
or kept her from attending funerals and weddings (the woman
in turn who scorched her husband's food could be herself "put
away")—for these among other causes she could sue in the
courts for a divorce, which the husband was then ordered to
give her. Yet Mark 10.12, reading *pāt' rā l' gabrah*, the active,
instead of *p' tīrā l' gabrah*, the passive which is here correct,
renders, "divorcing her husband."

Other errors into which the Greek versions fall give flat

nonsense, which modern renderings soften by paraphrase, dodge by omission, or get around by themselves mistranslating and straining the Greek. According to our text, Mark 7.3 reads: "For the Pharisees and all the Jews, unless they wash their hands *with a fist*, will not eat . . ." Moffatt renders the italic words "up to the wrist"; the American Revised, "diligently" (the revisers anticipate Moffatt and go him one better in their alternative translation, "up to the elbow"); Goodspeed, "in a particular way." The Aramaic read *ligmār*, "at all." The translator into Greek saw *ligmod* (confusion of the identically-written end letters *daleth* and *resh*), which is to say, "with a fist." The point, then, is not that the Pharisees before meals scrub their faces childlike with their fists, but that if they have not washed, they will not eat *at all*.

Failure to recognize a perfectly familiar Semitic idiom, always appearing in the same form, has produced such a Mad Hatter time sequence as one finds in the English version of Luke 23.54: "It was the Preparation Day, and the sabbath was just beginning." The Greek says "was dawning," not "was beginning." How could Saturday morning be dawning when it was still Friday, Preparation? The idiom, correctly rendered as in Professor Torrey's translation, means: "It was now the night between Friday and the dawn of the sabbath." The same criticism applies to such versions as the American Revised rendering of Matthew 28.1: "Now late on the sabbath day, as it began to dawn toward the first day of the week." This should run: "In the night between the close of the sabbath and the dawn of the first day of the week."

Other examples in the same category range from a recommendation of blasphemy to a prediction of universal roasting. In Matthew 5.48 we are exhorted to be "perfect," as is our heavenly father. Here the Greek translator has mistaken an active for a passive. He should have rendered: "Be therefore all-including (in your good will), even as your heavenly Father includes all." The present Greek and English versions do not run with the context and hardly stop short of advising man to seek the prerogatives of God. Luke 8.27 makes a naked man who did not live in a house but the tombs hail *from the town!* Luke thus rendered according to the usage of outlanders; but in Palestinian Aramaic, with which the translator Luke was not intimately acquainted, the word could only mean: "a man from the open country." As Mark 14.68 tells the story, Peter is supposed to deny his Lord thus: "I neither know nor understand what you are saying." What he actually replied to the maid who accused him of having been with the Nazarene was: "I am neither an acquaintance of the man of whom you speak, nor do I know him at all." This is something like a denial, the other certainly is not. The mistranslation involves a wrong rendering of both a pronoun and a verb. Mark 9.49 reads: "For everyone shall be salted with fire." The translator, since Hebrew had been quoted in the context, assumed that citation continued and rendered the Hebrew "hā' ēsh," which does mean "fire," instead of Aramaic "bā' ēsh," participle of a verb signifying "become spoiled." The verse should go thus: "Whatever would spoil, is salted."

Much more serious is the case of those passages where Jesus behaves or speaks in a way not consonant with his usual actions and standard of ethical teaching. Perhaps no part of the Gospels has troubled modern commentators more than the verses which represent Jesus as giving way to bursts of anger. The classic instance of course is John 11.33. There at the tomb of Lazarus Jesus beholds Mary in tears before him and the Jews who have accompanied her also lamenting. His feelings, as toned down by modern translators, are thus described: "he chafed"; "repressing a groan." But the Greek, heaven save the mark, means "snorting in anger" (like a horse). This it means and this alone it can mean by what we thus far know of its lexicography. The Aramaic word at the base usually did signify "anger." Here, however, as in some other exceptional cases it denoted "agitation, deep distress of soul."

If we credit Luke 16.8 ff. in its present form, Jesus actually seems to say that one should take a parasitical attitude toward "rugged individualists," and should use them for all they are worth. I refer, of course, to the famous verses, "And the lord commended the unjust steward, because he had done wisely: for the children of this world are in their generation wiser than the children of light. And I say unto you, Make to yourselves friends of the mammon of unrighteousness; that, when ye fail, they may receive you into everlasting habitations." In Aramaic *ironical questions* are clearly indicated by the context and this is a case in point. The whole, as Professor Torrey translates, should run, "Did the lord of the estate praise his faithless manager, because he had acted shrewdly (for the sons of this world are more sagacious than the sons of light, in the dealings with their fellow men)? and do *I say* to *you*, Gain friends for yourselves with base lucre, so that when it is gone, you may be received into the eternal abodes?" This simple explanation avoids the necessity for emending, pruning, and generally disarranging the Greek of the whole section, as commentators so often have done.

Briefly, then, the translation hypothesis restores dignity and sense to about 250 passages which have long puzzled interpreters. It creates substantially a new New Testament that must be reckoned with by all future editors and translators. And it dates at long last in their proper period the Gospel versions which many historians have felt must be early, contemporary sources. Surveying this new solution of old difficulties, one finds it remarkable that the Gospels should have stood up so superbly under all the misunderstanding, mishandling, and misquotation which they have sustained up till now. They have been superstitiously consulted as proof-texts by saints and sinners of every hue. They have weathered the romancing of novelists and the wrong-headed exegesis of specialists probing with needles or slashing with knives; yet even today they stand out in pristine freshness. Classicists know to their joy that students who have never felt the reality of ancient Greek often come alive when they reach Lucian and the Gospels. Here is something modern and spontaneous.

What we need now to reinforce that feeling is a friendly union of classicists and New Testament exegetes and Orientalists who do not disdain anything either old or new which will throw light on perhaps the most fascinating series of books in all of ancient literature.

THE PRIVATE LIFE OF
SHERLOCK HOLMES

By *Vincent Starrett*

IT is, of course, notorious—we have Watson's word for it—that Mr. Sherlock Holmes "loathed every form of society with his whole Bohemian soul." The word *society* is poorly chosen. What Watson—a careless writer—intended to convey was that *social life* offended the Bohemian soul of his companion; in consequence of which emotion he preferred to spend his time in Baker Street when others might have gone to teas and parties: "buried among his old books," as Watson says, "and alternating from week to week between cocaine and ambition—the drowsiness of the drug and the fierce energy of his own keen nature."

In time, it is true, the doctor weaned him from the drug—to the detriment of romantic interest, whatever the benefit to Holmes—but even then it is seldom that one finds the saturnine detective accepting or turning down an invitation. He simply didn't get them. No doubt there had been plenty of them in his youth; but in the face of his consistent declinations—after an experience or two, perhaps, with bores—he would in time, of course, be let alone. It is, one fancies, almost as great a nuisance to be a detective as to be a doctor: there are always guests with problems to present.

The fact is Watson, too, preferred the silences or the friendly arguments of Baker Street to any attraction London had to offer—a circumstance in which he is at one with his adoring readers. Each man preferred the company of the other, and was glad enough, no doubt, even to see a client leave the doorstep. Even, perhaps, Lestrade or Tobias Gregson. Even, perhaps, Inspector Stanley Hopkins; although for Hopkins Holmes had a considerable admiration, and on a cold night a prescription containing whisky.

To the casual student of the detective's cases it may appear that the rooms in Baker Street were always crowded. His first impression may be that of a bewildered client teetering on the rug; an armchair in which the detective is curled like a Mohammedan, smoking shag; a cane-backed chair or sofa containing Watson; and Mrs. Hudson entering to announce Lestrade—whose footstep is on the stair. In actuality, there were long hours of comradely communion between the occupants. Seldom indeed did anyone stay the night. And some of the happiest memories, surely, of the epic history are those of Holmes and Watson living their simple, private lives. Not Crusoe and his admirable Friday—one had almost said his goat—were more resolutely at home upon their island than Sherlock Holmes and Watson in their living-room. They passed there some of the most felicitous moments of their common life.

Not that they did not, on occasion, venture the Victorian whirl. There is ample record that Holmes, at least, was fond of opera—sufficiently so to hurry to Covent Garden, on a Wagner night, with no hope of arriving before the second act. This was after the successful culmination of the *Red Circle* adventure, and was possibly in the nature of a reward. Similarly, it will be remembered, after some weeks of severe work on the problem presented by Sir Henry Baskerville, the pair went off to hear the De Reszkes in *Les Huguenots*. Holmes had procured a box, and on the way they stopped at Marcini's for a little dinner. "Turning their thoughts into more pleasant channels" was the way in which Holmes described the De Reszke adventure. A musician himself, he would naturally turn to music for rest and surcease, after a desperate morning round with murderers. Not always was his own violin sufficient.

As early in their association as the celebrated *Study in Scar-let* the detective had dragged his companion off to Hallé's concert, after a triumphant morning of detection at Lauriston Gardens. Neruda was to play: "Her attack and her bowing are splendid," commented Sherlock Holmes. "What's that little thing of Chopin's she plays so magnificently?" If he really expected Watson to answer him, the suggestion is clear that the doctor also knew something about music. And lunch-eon, of course, immediately preceded Neruda. Both men, without being gluttons, were fond of eating, and frequently they posted off to some favourite London restaurant. After the hideous comedy of the *Dying Detective* it was to Simpson's they went for sustenance, however; not Marcini's. Possibly it seemed a better place to eat when food in quantity was what was needed. Holmes, it will be recalled, had been at that time fasting for several days.

St. James's Hall was also a favourite sanctuary when it was possible for Holmes to interrupt his sleuthing. "And now, Doctor, we've done our work; it's time we had some play," one hears him cry to Watson, after a brilliant morning of deduction. "A sandwich and a cup of coffee; then off to violin land, where all is sweetness and delicacy and harmony, and there are no red-headed clients to vex us with their conun-drums." The occasion of this pleasant interlude was the inter-mission, as it were, before the "crash" in the fantastic problem of Mr. Jabez Wilson. And all that afternoon, the doctor tells us, "he sat in the stalls, wrapped in the most perfect happiness, gently waving his long thin fingers in time to the music"— listening to Sarasate play the violin.

The picture galleries, too, it must be assumed, were brows-ing-spots attractive to the collaborators. No doubt they served as stop-gaps in the long days of criminal investigation—when it was possible pleasantly to while away an hour while waiting for an appointment. A clue to this diversion is to be found in the early pages of the *Hound*, after the profitable discovery of the bearded man, in Regent Street: "And now, Watson, it only remains for us to find out by wire the identity of the cabman . . . and then we will drop into one of the Bond Street picture-galleries and fill in the time until we are due at the hotel." But the incident was not, we may be sure, an isolated one. The mind turns easily at such times to the familiar groove. Did they, one wonders, care for Mr. Whistler? Or was "The Charge of the Scots Greys" more to their British taste?

It is quite clear, at any rate, that the occasional social exercises of the two were largely cultural. When they went forth from Baker Street, it was upon a trail of evil import or to a place of decent entertainment. Occasionally, to a Turkish bath; and very likely—one suspects—now and again to Madame Tussaud's. On the whole, however, they preferred to stay at home. Away from it, the detective's temper was always uncertain. "Without his scrapbooks, his chemicals, his untidiness, he was an uncomfortable man."

From time to time they travelled on the Continent, not always on the business of a client; and several parts of rural England knew them well. It was on one of these joint vacation jaunts that they chanced upon the ugly business of the *Reigate Squires*—when they were the guests of Colonel Hayter, down in Surrey; and it was presumably a sort of holiday adventure that furnished them the instructive problem of the *Three Students*—a sort of pendant to Holmes's laborious researches into early English charters. Again, it was a vacation trip that took them—in 1897—to the small cottage near Poldhu Bay, at the further extremity of the Cornish peninsula, in which singular and sinister neighbourhood there befell that gruesome experience chronicled by Watson as *The Devil's Foot*. Once, it is certain, they went to Norway; but if aught of criminal interest developed during the visit, it has yet to be reported.

From these vacation trips—interrupted as they invariably were by theft or murder—Holmes always returned to Baker Street refreshed. It was, however, only the thefts and murders that consoled him for the time thus spent away from home.

And it is at home, in Baker Street, that one likes best to think of them—alone and puttering with their secret interests. Little vignettes of perfect happiness, wreathed in tobacco smoke and London fog.

Of course they took in all the daily papers, and read them with a diligence almost incredible. Did not the detective prop his journal against the breakfast sugar bowl? And did not Watson, when he sat down at table, invariably thump his knee against the leg? For Watson, at any rate, there was usually a lecture. . . . After the return from Switzerland—by way of Lhassa—the papers rather disappointed Holmes. With Moriarty dead, London, from the point of view of the criminal expert, he said, had become a singularly uninteresting city. . . . "With that man in the field one's morning paper presented infinite possibilities. Often it was only the smallest trace, Watson, the faintest indication, and yet it was enough to tell me that the great malignant brain was there, as the gentlest tremors of the edges of the web remind one of the foul spider which lurks in the center. Petty thefts, wanton assaults, purposeless outrage—to the man who held the clue all could be worked into one connected whole. To the scientific student of the higher criminal world no capital of Europe offered the advantages which London then possessed. But now——!"

One sees the pile of papers growing in a corner, mounting up toward the gasogene and pipe-rack, till in a fit of energy Holmes scissored them to fragments. That rid the room of papers, for the nonce, but presented the new problem of the clippings: there were probably thousands waiting to be pasted up. And then, another night, another burst of energy, and some hundreds would at length be docketed. Over the years the row of scrapbooks lengthened on the shelf. Cold winter evenings or rainy nights of autumn were likely to be dedicated to the pasting-up; sometimes to indexing what already had been pasted. A never-ending chore. When and if ever the

British Museum shall acquire the scrapbooks of Mr. Sherlock Holmes one hopes to read the volume under "V"—a fascinating miscellany. *The Voyage of the Gloria Scott* is there, and a biography of *Victor Lynch* the forger. Also the case of *Vanderbilt* and the Yeggman—unchronicled by Watson—and somewhat concerning *Vittoria* the circus belle. *Vigour*, the Hammersmith Wonder; and *Vipers*—possibly *Vodka*—and a Draculian paper on *Vampires*. . . .

Holmes obviously had a system of his own. Most scrapbook makers would simply have listed *Lynch* and lizard under the letter "L," letting it go at that. But the detective indexed his clippings to the last adjective and adverb.

The relationship between the collaborators was ideal, after the years had taught them to know each other. About his own share in the partnership Watson had no illusions; but he was not too servile. Some thousands of his readers, he must have known, would happily have traded places with him. His statement as to himself and Sherlock Holmes, candidly prefixed to the adventure of *The Creeping Man*, is admirably lucid and not a little penetrating: "The relations between us," he asserts, "were peculiar. He was a man of habits, narrow and concentrated habits, and I had become one of them. As an institution I was like the violin, the shag tobacco, the old black pipe, the index books, and others perhaps less excusable. When it was a case of active work and a comrade was needed upon whose nerve he could place some reliance, my rôle was obvious. But apart from this I had uses. I was a whetstone for his mind. I stimulated him. He liked to think aloud in my presence. His remarks could hardly be said to be made to me —many of them would have been as appropriately addressed to his bedstead—but none the less, having formed the habit, it had become in some way helpful that I should register and interject. If I irritated him by a certain methodical slowness in my mentality, that irritation served only to make his own flame-like intuitions and impressions flash up the more vividly and swiftly. Such was my humble rôle in our alliance."

During the day, when no active occupation offered, Holmes smoked his pipe and meditated. With a case on hand, he also smoked and meditated. Sometimes—the picture is famous— he would sit for hours "curled up in the recesses of his shabby chair." Sometimes, in search of information, he "sat upon the floor like some strange Buddha, with crossed legs, the huge books all around him, and one open upon his knees." Obviously, the nature of the problem offered for his solution had an important bearing on his habits. Sometimes "a formidable array of bottles and test-tubes, with the pungent cleanly smell of hydrochloric acid" would tell the doctor—hastening in, himself, after a session with his patients—that he had "spent his day in the chemical work which was so dear to him." Sometimes, horizontal upon a couch, wrapped in a purple gown— "a pipe-rack within his reach upon the right, and a pile of crumpled morning papers . . . near at hand"—the doctor would discover him in rapt examination of a hat which was for the moment an intellectual problem.

There is a curious glamour in the most trivial passages between the two, a sense of significance—of impending revelation—perhaps not always justified by the detective's disclosure. It is part of Watson's charm that he sets down everything. One would not have it otherwise. The little triumphs that are no part or parcel of the tale are his habitual prolegomena; they are our glimpses of that private life they lived together, when only the reader's eye might spy them out. . . .

"Sherlock Holmes," one genuinely thrills to hear, "had been bending for a long time over a low-power microscope. Now he straightened himself up and looked round at me in triumph. 'It is glue, Watson,' said he. 'Unquestionably it is glue. Have a look at these scattered objects in the field!' "

Actively engaged upon a malodorous bit of brewing, "his long, thin back curved over a chemical vessel" and his head sunk upon his chest, the detective looked to Watson "like a strange, lank bird, with dull grey plumage and a black topknot." There is no need to illustrate the scene. But this would be, of course, upon a day when Holmes had put on his dressing-gown of grey, instead of the more familiar purple horror. On the whole, the picture that Watson has most vividly conveyed is that of Holmes recumbent—languid yet somehow rigid in his chair, wreathed in the vapours from his favourite pipe. The favourite pipe, of course, being subject always to change; since nothing, as Holmes himself remarked, has more individuality than a pipe, "save perhaps watches and bootlaces." For every mood in Baker Street there was a pipe. One sees him still as Watson saw and described him in that last of all the series of adventures. . . . "Holmes lay with his gaunt figure stretched in his deep chair, his pipe curling forth slow wreaths of acrid tobacco, while his eyelids drooped over his eyes so lazily that he might almost have been asleep were it not that at any halt or questionable passage of my narrative they half lifted, and two grey eyes, as bright and keen as rapiers, transfixed me with their searching glance."

One notes with interest that Holmes's eyes were grey. It is the only record of their colour.

Occasionally, when the day was really fine, the friends walked in the streets, savouring the singular sights and sounds of London. Shop windows were of interest to them both, and passers-by absorbing. "The park"—some park or other—was close at hand, and it is of record that they sometimes strolled there. Watson's account of one such episode is subdued. . . . "The first faint shoots of green were breaking out upon the elms, and the sticky spearheads of the chestnuts were just beginning to burst into their five-fold leaves. For two hours we rambled about together, in silence for the most part, as befits two men who know each other intimately." But this diversion was not customary, since it encroached on office hours. And on the afternoon described they missed a client. "There had been a gentleman asking for them."

"Holmes glanced reproachfully at me," confesses Watson. " 'So much for afternoon walks!' said he."

The afternoons then were spent in running down their cases

—the detective's cases—not often strolling in the park. And for all his love of Baker Street, it may be noted, during the active progress of a case Holmes was quite capable of hiding out. It is an interesting revelation, frequently overlooked, that Watson makes in his account of the adventure called *Black Peter.* . . . "He had at least five small refuges in different parts of London in which he was able to change his personality." The reference is tantalizing and obscure. The rooms of Mycroft Holmes, opposite the Diogenes Club, would certainly be one of them; but it would be satisfying to know the others. At such times—when he was operating in disguise—Holmes sometimes took the name of "Captain Basil," the better to deceive his casual assistants and to deceive and confound his unsuspecting enemies. It may be assumed that in all of his five refuges he stored the materials of deception, as well as quantities of shag tobacco.

Not all of the detective's cases, though, drove him to his retreats or to his armchair. Sometimes for hours—once, certainly, for a whole day—he rambled about the living-room with knotted brows, his head upon his breast, charging and recharging his strongest pipe, and deaf to all of Watson's questionings. These were his bad days, when the trail was faint, and even Watson had failed him as a whetstone.

But it was to the papers that both invariably returned. The everlasting, never-ceasing papers. Edition after edition of them was delivered at the rooms, probably by the stout and puffing Mrs. Hudson, who would have them from the urchin at the door. Not only Holmes but Watson saturated himself with the unending chronicle of news; and they read it—it must be admitted—with a surprisingly reckless acceptance of its accuracy. In America, Holmes would have taken *none* of the papers in. In America, the papers are for the credulous Watsons.

It is at night one likes them best, these curious companions. And preferably with a beating rain outside. If Stanley Hopkins has dropped in from Scotland Yard, no matter; their simple hospitality is as hearty as it is restrained and masculine.

They did not always save the whisky for Stanley Hopkins. Themselves, occasionally, good fellows, they tippled companionably. And usually in the early morning hours, after a trying day with thug or cracksman. Whisky-and-soda and a bit of lemon. And all the credit gone to Scotland Yard. Midnight or very early in the morning—the time of relaxation and revelation, while the "undying flame" leaps on the hearth. Holmes lifts out a glowing cinder with the tongs, lights the long pipe of sprightly disputation. "You see, Watson," he patiently begins, "it was all perfectly obvious from the first. . . ."

In the long evenings, too, Holmes played his fiddle. Doubtless his bowing was not comparable to Neruda's, but it was good enough for Watson. "Sometimes the chords were sonorous and melancholy. Occasionally they were fantastic and cheerful. Clearly they reflected the thoughts which possessed him, but whether the music aided those thoughts, or whether the playing was simply the result of a whim or fancy," was more than Watson could determine. And when some haunting strain had charmed and soothed the doctor—moved him to ask the name of the composer—as like as not it would be something by Sherlock Holmes.

Then, of an evening in the depths of February, one fancies Watson questing another tale. Permission, perhaps, to reveal an untold problem—one of the many hinted and then withheld. The truth, perhaps, about the atrocious conduct of Colonel Upwood, or the peculiar persecution of John Vincent Harden. It is understandable that some reticence must be observed with reference to the sudden death of Cardinal Tosca —an investigation carried out at the personal request of His Holiness, the Pope—and in that delicate matter arranged by Holmes for the reigning family of Holland; but surely the time must be at hand, thinks Watson, for the full disclosure of facts in the Tankerville Club Scandal. That often he spoke of these to Holmes, there can be no doubt at all. Having half-promised his readers that he would some day tell them, his position may well have seemed to him embarrassing.

One sympathizes heartily with Watson. Too long has the world awaited the adventure of the Amateur Mendicant Society—which had a luxurious clubroom in the lower vault of a furniture warehouse—and the little problem of the Grosvenor Square Furniture Van. The case of Wilson, the Notorious Canary-Trainer, too, is a whisper full of fascinating suggestion; and one would give much to read the long-suppressed adventure of the Tired Captain.

Holmes, we may be certain, listened to some urgent argument on evenings when the doctor decided to consider his reading public. Frequently he chided the narrator for his literary shortcomings, pretending that the tales were sad affairs; but when he came to write two of them himself he changed his tune.

One can imagine them in whimsical discussion of the *ifs* of their achievements—the *what ifs*, as it were, conducted *post mortem* upon their cases. As for instance, after the rocket-throwing episode in the amusing case of Irene Adler. It is impossible to read the tale without a bit of wonderment: what if the ingenious rocket had missed fire? Would not the whole planned sequence have gone agley? But Watson, although he may have faltered, never actually blundered. Holmes knew the qualities of his assistant. No case was ever lost by Watson's failure. And his reward—all that he ever asked or cared for—was an approving word or nod from Holmes. Did not he get them both, outside the record? During those nights in Baker Street, perhaps? After the problem had been solved forever—after the reader had put down the book?

How many matters of absorbing interest must then have been revealed! By means most dexterously disingenuous, Holmes managed a glimpse of Godfrey Staunton's telegram; and on the first attempt. Yet he had seven different schemes, he told the doctor, if one had failed. What were the other six?

How many, many questions must also have gone unanswered. Holmes was at times blood-brother to the Sphinx. There is a bit of dialogue that is in nearly all the tales. "You have a clue?" asks Watson eagerly. The answer is immortal. "It is a capital mistake, my dear Watson, to theorize before one has the facts." If one were called upon to find in literature the best inscription for a tombstone, it would be Holmes's cautious apophthegm. Watson should bargain for it on his grave. For Holmes's tombstone—"Elementary!"

But there can be no grave for Sherlock Holmes or Watson. . . . Shall they not always live in Baker Street? Are they not there this instant, as one writes? . . . Outside, the hansoms rattle through the rain, and Moriarty plans his latest devilry. Within, the sea-coal flames upon the hearth, and Holmes and Watson take their well-won ease. . . . So they still live for all that love them well: in a romantic chamber of the heart: in a nostalgic country of the mind: where it is always 1895.

THE GREAT DIARIST

By *Chauncey Brewster Tinker*

I

I REMEMBER to have read somewhere in the pages of Mark Twain the account of a youthful attempt to keep a diary, the result of which was the endless repetition of the simple sentence, "Got up, washed; went to bed." I forget what the anecdote was meant to illustrate—the fact that there was nothing in a boy's life worth recording, or the fact that the diarist's art is a difficult one. In either case, I submit modestly but firmly that Mark Twain was wrong. A true diarist will be interesting about anything and about everything; whether the dog has ruined the carpet or a king been seated on his ancestral throne, the true journalist is never dull. The Creator has dispensed him from boring his audience.

Take, for instance, the three incidents of the day recited above: one gets up, one washes, and one goes to bed, all processes sufficiently common—even washing—to seem useless to the literary artist; yet who would spare them from the pages of Samuel Pepys? "Up and to my office" . . . "Up betimes, and to St. James's" . . . "Lay in bed, it being Lord's Day, all the morning, talking with my wife; then up." I find that I resent the entries in his Diary that lack this familiar beginning, as though something essential had been omitted. As for the companion phrase, consecrated to the close of day, it has in our own time achieved such popularity that it bids fair to be permanently enshrined in the daily speech of men, and cease to be recognized as a quotation: "And so to bed. . . ." Sentiment will ultimately make an epitaph of it, like "Say not good-night," or "Good-bye, proud world."

As for bathing, that may be the most exciting of events, as the poets know: "the cool silver shock of the plunge," whether it be into the "pool's living water" or into the chilly waters of the domestic tub. "One clear, nice, cool squirt of water o'er your bust."

> Up, and to the office . . . where busy till noon, and then my wife being busy in going with her woman to a hot-house to bathe herself, after her long being within doors in the dirt, so that she now pretends to a resolution of being hereafter very clean. How long it will hold I can guess.
>
> 22nd. Lay last night alone, my wife after her bathinge lying alone in another bed. So cold all night.
>
> 25th. Thence home to the office, where dispatched much business; at night, late home, and to clean myself with warm water; my wife will have me, because she do herself, and so to bed.

Verily, nothing that is human is alien to the diarist. For him life contains nothing that is common or dull. Let him tell us what he ate for dinner, or how cold he was in bed, or how a duchess smiled on him, or what is his balance at the bank, or how he has lost his faith in God, or regained it, or been snubbed by a rival, or cursed his enemy in his heart, or cast eyes of desire upon the parlor maid—all is grist to his mill. How near is grandeur to our dust! How easily does this mortal put on immortality!

But immortality is bought at a price, even by the diarist. It is a razor edge, as the Mohammedan tells us, across which the aspirant to Heaven must make his way. And the diarist, like the rest of us, is in perpetual danger of damnation for his sins. He may make much of them in his journals, and even delight us by his own delight in them; but he must not take pride in displaying them. He would do well to set down naught in the hope of admiration or in the fear of derision. Thus, if a genuine diarist records that he was cold in bed, he does so with a childlike simplicity, as a grievance, as a count against his wife, or as a humble, human fact; but the gods forbid him to enjoy the sensation of being clever at his work. As soon as he becomes clever, attending to his style and aspiring to smart phrase and graceful posture, he is a self-conscious artist, a skillful operative. He may, with luck, become Shaw or Mencken, but he will never be a Samuel Pepys. The artist seeks, properly enough, success and applause; but the diarist is not concerned with such matters. He is not permitted to anticipate or even to desire them. When once his record is complete, he may realize, I suppose, in some dim fashion that he has prevailed over oblivion, so that he cannot destroy his work, even though he may, so far as the outward and surface part of him is concerned, be unwilling that any eye save his own should ever see what he has written.

II

This setting down of events and emotions precisely as one has known them, and almost immediately after their occurrence, simply, and because one must—this is the *sine qua non* of a true diarist. But why the compulsion? What is the goad that drives him on?

He must, I imagine (for I am myself no diarist), set down an abstract and brief chronicle of life because he loves it so. He cannot bear to let it all perish without leaving a trace behind. I do not mean that he will record only his delights. Sin, pain, and woe have their place in the great diaries of the world, and must always have, since they are of the very fabric of existence. Indeed, a journal may be almost exclusively a recital of these, so as to become painful or even tragic reading; but throughout it all there must be a conviction on the part of the diarist that, in spite of it all, life was worth having. It would not be easy to discover a diarist who was also a sincere and heartbroken pessimist, one who really felt that life was not worth living. If life be not worth living, obviously a journal is not worth writing.

Consider a diary as unlike that of Pepys as could be found: *La Doulou*, by Alphonse Daudet—*Suffering*, or, as I prefer to render the Provençal word, *Anguish*. It is the intimate and personal account of the daily life of a man suffering from locomotor ataxia. He watches the approach of his enemy day by day and inch by inch, and studies his own physical, nervous, and mental symptoms with the most anxious attention, like a prisoner condemned to the scaffold who watches the moments and days lapsing from him. He knows that he is conquered, but he will not surrender. Like the hero in the old ballad, when he can no longer stand upon his feet, he fights upon his knees; he struggles not so much for himself as for his wife and family, in the hope of concealing from them as long as he can the horrible trap into which he has fallen. Thus *La Doulou* has the intimate, secret note which marks this type of writing; but at no point does Daudet curse life and lie down to die. Black as are the colors of this book, and dire as is its story, there is something invigorating in the account of the victim's prolonged agony, for it is the triumph of a human soul. The book is a vivid contrast to the diary and letters of Obermann, which, even when they have something cheerful to recall, exude a lethal atmosphere which makes the reader, like the author, long to have done, not only with the book, but with the whole futile affair of living.

Perhaps the most recent diary published is that of the Yorkshire parson, the Reverend Benjamin Newton, a typical sporting clergyman of the early nineteenth century, who was interested in everything about him, except perhaps the souls of his flock. Like Pepys, he was acutely susceptible to the charms of the other sex, and listed handsome women in numerical order, according to their beauty of (*a*) face and (*b*) figure. He is perpetually entertaining because of his unfailing vivacity. This is the quality which endears Pepys to his readers:—

I home to set my journall for these four days in order, they being four days of as great content and honour and pleasure to me as ever I hope to live or desire, or think any body else can live. For methinks if a man would but reflect upon this, and think that all these things are ordered by God Almighty to make me contented . . . in my life and matter of mirth, methinks it should make one mightily more satisfied in the world than he is.

Neither syntax nor theology here is beyond criticism, but what vitality it reveals, what sincerity, what contentment! I like to think that the gratitude of young Mr. Pepys was acceptable to his Creator.

So dispatched all my business, having assurance of . . . all hearty love from Sir W. Coventry, and so we staid and saw the King and Queene set out toward Salisbury, and after them the Duke and Duchesse, whose hands I did kiss. And it was the first time I did ever, or did see any body else, kiss her hand, and it was a most fine white and fat hand. But it was pretty to see the young pretty ladies dressed like men, in velvet coats, caps with ribbands and with laced bands, just like men. Only the Duchesse herself it did not become. They gone, we with great content took coach again, and hungry come to Clapham about one o'clock, and Creed there too before us, where a good dinner . . . and so to walk up and down in the gardens, mighty pleasant. By and by comes by promise to me Sir G. Carteret, and viewed the house above and below, and sat and drank there, and I had a little opportunity to kiss and spend some time with the ladies above, his daughter, a buxom lass, and his sister Fissant, a serious lady, and a little daughter of hers that begins to sing prettily. Thence with mighty pleasure, with Sir G. Carteret by coach, with great discourse of kindnesse, with him to my Lord Sandwich, and to me also; and I every day see more good by the alliance. Almost at Deptford I 'light and walked over to Half-way House, and so home, in my way being shown my cozen Patience's house, which seems, at distance, a pretty house. At home met the weekly Bill, where above 1,000 encreased in the Bill, and of them in all about 1,700 of the plague, which hath made the officers this day resolve of sitting at Deptford, which puts me to some consideration what to do. Therefore home to think and consider of every thing about it, and without determining anything, eat a little supper, and to bed, full of the pleasure of these 6 or 7 last days.

All this mighty pleasure in the midst of a plague-stricken city! Terror hangs over the world like an ever-blackening cloud, but the diarist's appetite for existence endures undiminished. And so it remains to the end of the journal, when, with the dread of blindness descending upon him and faced with the necessity of closing his Diary, he can still record:—

Dined at home, and in the afternoon by water to White Hall, calling by the way at Michell's where I have not been many a day till just the other day, and now I met her mother there, and knew her husband to be out of town. And here je did baiser elle, but had not opportunity para hazer some with her as I would have offered if je had had it. And thence had another meeting with the Duke of York, at White Hall, on yesterday's work, and made a good advance: and so, being called by my wife, we to the Park, Mary Batelier and a Dutch gentleman, a friend of hers being with me. Thence to " The World's End," a drinking-house by the Park; and there merry, and so home late.

No trace is here of gloom or apprehension; yet the sentences speed forward to the most pathetic utterances of the great Diary. Even as he prays for mercy in the blindness which he believes to be coming on him, he does not forget his "amours to Deb" and all "other pleasures" which his eyesight now compels him to resign.

III

This very quality in which Pepys excels was well described by another great writer of journals:—

The minds of some men are like a dark cellar—their knowledge lies concealed; while the minds of others are all sunshine and mirror, and reflect all that they read or hear in a lively manner.

These are the words of James Boswell, a man who, quantitatively at least, rivals Pepys as a diarist. Pepys covers but nine years; Boswell, who had no trouble with his visual organs, remained an inveterate journalist to the end, and, no doubt, presented himself at the gate of Heaven notebook in hand. Now Boswell was a vastly less healthy person than Pepys; he suffered through life from a recurrent melancholia which introduces the strangest lights and shadows into his journals; but in his happier hours he had to a very high degree indeed the passion of which I have been speaking. Johnson himself described Boswell's fondness for the metropolis as a "*gust* for London." And there are other powers which Pepys and Boswell share.

Both, for instance, were collectors. Both belong to that hungry set who save things, who gather relics and preserve souvenirs, who love long rows of well-filled shelves and all the paraphernalia of a library. These men leave treasures to posterity.

There is an intimate connection between this mania and the relish of existence which both men display so noticeably. It is because of his gusto that the diarist attempts to preserve some memorial of it, however inadequate. He cannot bear to think that experiences so rich should perish without leaving a rack behind, and he therefore enters into mortal combat with oblivion. The closer his record to the event itself, the more nearly satisfied he will be. Boswell provides many amusing examples of this desire for verisimilitude. Once when he sent his friend Temple as a sort of ambassador to the young lady with whom he was, or thought he was, in love, he provided him with a long series of detailed directions, the most pointed of which is the command, "Takes notes." By taking notes, you see, the ambassador may hope to preserve not only the *ipsis-vima verba* of the interview, but even the very atmosphere and tone of it. The incident will be preserved, as book collectors say, "in the original condition." As long as the scenes of one's past are dear to the heart, so long will a man try to prepare for his future nostalgia by the writing of diaries and the preservation of relics. A true diarist is like a great portrait painter who takes his own likeness. The Diary of Mr. Pepys is, in a way, the greatest *Selbstbildnis* ever painted. "A man loves to review his own mind," said Johnson to Mrs. Thrale; "that is the use of a diary or journal." To whom Lord Trimlestown, who was present, said, "True, Sir. As the ladies love to see themselves in a glass, so a man likes to see himself in his journal."

All the reader's interest in the mirror of a mind arises from a conviction of the writer's truthfulness. Any suspicion of insincerity, any hint that the diarist is looking over his shoulder to see whether he is being admired or marveled at, any betrayal of a hope that it will all one day get into good black print—

this will at once, in some degree, vitiate the reader's pleasure. For the reader of diaries is an eavesdropper. He has his ear to the keyhole, seeking to pry into intimacies. If he suspects that the conversation to which he listens is intended for his ear, and that the speaker wants to be overheard, all the fun ends at once. Neither the *Soliloquies* of Saint Augustine nor the *Confessions* of J. J. Rousseau (different as they are in every way) is a true diary, for both men are too much interested in the reader's response to what has been set down. Miss Burney, too, is aware of her audience, and indulges her love of fine writing—a sin of which Pepys was as ignorant as the babe unborn. She sometimes carries her art to the point at which one begins to wonder how much of the original fact is left. She was an inaccurate person, the sort of woman who dates a letter "Wednesday." How far does her indifference to such detail extend? To the words alone? Or to whole conversations? Are the speeches she writes down like those of the generals in Thucydides?

But there is no carelessness or inaccuracy, or rhetoric, no heightening and coloring, in Pepys or Boswell. Both men were professionally concerned with recording facts: Pepys was engaged in filing records for the Naval Office—lists of battleships, with their tonnage and personnel, their movements and their whereabouts, and thousands upon thousands of similar details of no special interest to posterity. Boswell, as a Scotch lawyer, had to present his cases to the court in written form. Such work begets in a man a sense of fact, and a respect for the moving finger of time. He is not likely to date an important letter "Wednesday."

Much of our pleasure in reading Pepys springs from our conviction of its authenticity. It is this that sweeps us along, page after page, over the names of persons of whom we know nothing. But we do know that they are real, like the persons whom we pass in the street, even though we can tell nothing whatever about them. Some of them are acquainted with Pepys, and we are acquainted with him—that is sufficient.

With a few of them we, too, become better acquainted as we read on, so that, if we persevere, we find our pleasure constantly mounting, since our knowledge of what is going on is gradually clarified. We shall never come to a perfect vision of it all,—even the most painstaking research will never attain to that,—but life as it was three hundred years ago, and Samuel Pepys in his habit as he lived, these we may come to know.

IV

Let us not mistake. Pepys is not great merely because he brings us into contact with the exciting events of his time. True, he lived through the *annus mirabilis* of 1666, and so had intimate personal knowledge of the defeat of the Dutch fleet, the great plague that swept over the city, and the Great Fire which swept over it in a more literal sense. These are important events, as are a thousand others with which Pepys brings us in contact, and so the Diary is an invaluable source book for historians. But this is not the reason that Pepys has the devotion of his readers.

The fact is that the man had the fine art of making his record sparkle with vitality. I cannot analyze that gift. I have never met anybody who could. Most essays on Pepys—and there are many delightful ones—rely for their charm on liberal quotations from the Diary. The more quotations, the more charm. The essayist usually contents himself, as in the present instance, with a characterization of the man, not with a critical analysis of his style. How shall one show the component parts of anything so artless?

Yet Pepys was an artist, and I believe that he knew it. It would be more accurate to say that he came in time to know it. It seems to me preposterous to try to believe that a man who has produced a vast work of genius should be unaware of what he has done. He may very well have been ignorant of its largest relations and of its permanent value to mankind; but that he should have had no intimation of its pictorial and panoramic quality, no realization of the fact that it plumbs the depths of human nature—this is to me beyond belief. I should as soon expect the builder of the pyramids to be unaware of the shape which he had erected.

And I believe, furthermore, that it was this knowledge of what he had done that prevented Pepys from destroying or ordering the destruction of the Diary. He could not do it, nor do I think that another man who had created such a thing (if we may tolerate such an assumption) could bring himself to destroy it. For Pepys it would have been a kind of suicide.

He was aware, of course, that it could be readily decoded,— was not the same code used in his office?—and, indeed, a cipher that cannot be decoded, if such there be, would be simply a form of oblivion. And yet there was a certain protection in it. A cipher does furnish a screen against casual observation; a long diary, like that of Pepys, might hope to survive many years unread. After a lapse of a couple of generations, secrecy was no longer of consequence. This was perhaps, consciously or subconsciously, what Pepys wished. He wanted privacy— protection, that is, from the inquisitiveness and derision of his neighbors; and this the cipher afforded, and would probably continue to afford as long as any of his contemporaries re- mained alive. To most of us posterity hardly matters. The genial soul of Pepys may very well have been content to meet it and entrust his reputation to it. I cannot see why any man should shrink from that. It is one's neighbors and relatives whom one wishes to elude. In the masquerade of life a man does not care to give himself away. It is a world in which we are all making a plucky pretense. One takes conscious pride in "getting away" with one's pose, and none more so than Pepys in public life. But there is solid comfort in making a clean breast of it, whether one is purging the stuffed bosom of the perilous stuff that weights upon the heart or merely setting down the various devices by which he has succeeded in snatch- ing the pleasures of existence as they fly. But it is so hard to get a hearing and to utter all that one would like to say! Con- fessors, I have been told, find some difficulty in persuading their penitents to abridge the tale of their sins. "No excuses, please; no details," they must be always hinting. But the diarist feels no such restraint and hears no such monitor. He may go on forever.

And as for being read by posterity, is there not a certain pleasure in that, even though everything has to come out? It is certainly no worse than dying and meeting the Recording Angel, which is the experience that awaits us all. But, thanks be to God, it is an angel and not our neighbors, our wives, or our professors whom we have to meet. Perhaps it will not be so bad after all. Who knows but there may be a solid satisfaction in it, upon getting a hearing at last? The angel will probably do the best he can for us. It is the way of angels.

Posterity has been friendly to Pepys. Not even an angel, I imagine, could have been more indulgently kind. Where is there an author more beloved by his readers? Boswell is still despised by multitudes, Walpole is disliked, Cowper pitied, and Rousseau distrusted. But Pepys is like Lamb, loved by everybody. I have encountered but one sneer at Pepys, and that was from the pen of a Communist, writing for the *New Masses*, one Michael Gold—

> Samuel Pepys is esteemed by bourgeois readers because he did the things they do, or want to do: he accepted bribes, he dodged his taxes, he was unfaithful . . . to his wife, he beat his servants.

In the new world of Communism there will, I suppose, be none of these dreadful things, for sin and the knowledge of it will have been abolished (by law), and nobody will care whether he is loved by posterity or not.

PILLAGING THE LANGUAGE

By *Frank H. Vizetelly*

I

AMERICAN speech and the English tongue have long been hospitable to the stranger that has knocked at the door; but, when no stranger knocked, their votaries have not hesitated to play the part of buccaneers, appropriating all the foreign terms that they thought would be of use to them in advancing their aims, whether cultural or otherwise; and the practice of piracy continues. So it has come about that we speak the one tongue that is nearer to polyglot than any other now spoken.

A few years after the World War,—before the flapper and her boy friend, the sheik, crashed into our civilization, and before the influx of aëronautical and radiological terms,—the New York *Sun* remarked editorially that the English language had arrived "rather early at a comparative sterility, so far as its own stock was concerned," and "proceeded to adopt the waifs and strays of other tongues." This adoption had been going on silently for centuries before the words quoted were penned, but they remind the writer of a gracious invitation received from the distinguished editor of the sheet then famous for its slogan, "If you see it in the *Sun* it's so," to write an article on the number of words in the tongue that British and Americans speak in common. For reasons that it is unnecessary to dwell on here, the invitation could not be accepted. How very sincere the writer of the editorial referred to was in his belief in the sterility of our word-producing powers is shown by his further comment: "Putting aside Indian,

From the *Atlantic Monthly*, August 1932; copyright, 1932, by The Atlantic Monthly Company. Used by special permission.

Chinese, immigrant's importations, and slang, we are still doomed to receive an alarming influx of new words."

While the World War abruptly checked the work of lexicographical research, this had been progressing steadily, on both sides of the Atlantic, for years before the cataclysm occurred. Terms running into the thousands, which had been overlooked by trained readers of past time, were discovered, and the riches that certain of our sciences contributed were revealed, and these were added to the total, until it became evident to philologists that, together with the terms already recorded in the dictionaries of the day, the sum of words available for use approximated one million.

The coining of words is a perpetual performance, sometimes the result of necessity, often the fruit of ignorance, for those persons who have the fewest words at their command suffer from the temptation to create new forms, and thus necessity becomes the mother of invention. Our love for new terminology, for new uses of old words, or for the revival of words long dead, has been shown by a number of our presidents, from the days of Andrew Jackson to the present time—that is, from "O.K.," claimed to be a misreading of Jackson's ill-formed "O.R." for "Ordered recorded," to the "noble experiment" attributed to President Hoover, not forgetting Warren Harding's "normalcy." To this love we may attribute the novel creations of the manufacturing world. The man who has goods to sell wants a word that will arrest attention, or a slogan that is easily memorized.

This spirit of publicity is still in evidence on the pages of some of our leading periodicals, one of which is known as "the Prince of Weeklies"; another advises us to "Tell it to the World," and another boasts of "All the News that's fit to print." Progressive journalism pays little heed to the slogan today. It is out to score a "beat" off sundry competitors, and thus win the advertiser to the pages under its control.

Commerce has enriched our vocabulary with many useful words and has embellished it with great numbers of arbitrarily formed terms, if two hundred thousand may be so characterized, and the increase continues weekly. Some of the latter class, once familiar, are so well known today that they are remembered without the need of advertising to create demand; others needs must continue to keep in the spotlight or they will be crowded out of sight and pass quickly out of use. We still "have a little *fairy* in our home," side by side with the Sapolio that won fame and fortune for Ward and Gow; but, if the present proprietors of these indispensables to every home still advertise, the range of their advertising seems to be restricted. Inasmuch as trade-mark names are lures for trade,—to create demand as well as to protect the proprietors from unscrupulous competitors,—their purpose is to attract custom and awaken desire or the wish to obtain. To the men who coin them, these names seem the best that they can coin. Sometimes the coinage shows creative genius; often it shows a total lack of it. Once in a great while mental ability of an uncommon kind produces a term that arrests public attention. Such a one is "mulsified"; another is "tabloid." It may safely be said that in coining these terms no attempt was made at wit or beauty, but the desire for suitability or fitness is evident. As a general rule, efforts at word coinage by synthesis result in fantastic formations that often defeat the purposes in view. Of course there are certain notable exceptions, such as "escalator," "Nabisco," "radiotron," and "rayon." In common with "kodak," they are in excellent standing throughout the world. "Rayon," however, is not a protected trade name, but a word that has been admitted to our vocabulary on the same standing as "cotton" and "wool."

II

No one should cavil at the arbitrarily formed term duly registered and otherwise protected, but who shall be blamed for protesting against the registration or protection of a term that has been in common use for two, three, or perhaps for ten years or longer before such registration or protection is applied for and granted? Word piracy is not uncommon, and against such a form of buccaneering one may protest, for it threatens some of the choicest of our vocables, others having already been misappropriated.

Why should a term like "point lace," which has been used for years to designate a lace made by hand and wholly with a needle, be debased to the level of a registered trade-mark used to name certain wheat products? And why should the homestead and burial place of George Washington be desecrated, and become a registered trade-mark name for certain food ingredients? This may be "good business," but, if it be not downright desecration, it is certainly not free from indelicacy.

My dictionary tells me that an enchantress is "a bewitching woman," and to be told that the word designates "a variety of cantaloupe," with its native rotundity, puts one's powers of imagination and realization under a great strain; yet the "enchantress" cantaloupe is a product of a Californian fruit grower. From the same lexicon one may learn that a witch is "a sorceress" as well as "the opposite of a wizard." The latter term, trimmed to "wiz," might have provided a fitter name for a remover of chemical carbon than all of the witches of Salem or elsewhere; yet "witch" is a registered trade-mark name for a decarbonizer.

Picture the Presbyterian or Brownist "Puritans," endeared to us as Pilgrim Fathers, defined as they should be, with the decoration "a trade-mark name for printed shirtings and percales registered in the United States Patent Office."

To one who loves words, there is something incongruous in taking "rosemary," etymologically "the dew of the sea," with its beautiful blue flowerets, its refreshing perfume, and its symbolic significance of "remembrance," and applying it to a grade of wheat flour. And what is there in wheat flour, of whatever grade, that it should be signalized "star," presumably as above all competitors, when we already have sufficient misapplications of the term to confuse the wise?

Some manufacturers concede the common right to the

words they use. Others do not, and insist that registration gives title to the exclusive use of the term registered and that this fact, together with that of registration, must be stated in the dictionaries of the day. It is such insistence, supported by the services of unscrupulous attorneys, that heads ill-advised clients toward the courts to assert the "exclusive rights" to which they have foolishly been led to believe they hold title.

The word "lollypop" will serve to illustrate the way in which the indiscriminate granting, to such persons as apply for them, of registered trade-mark rights to words established in the language affects the rights of the public.

"Lollypop" is a term in general use for a particular kind of sweet, made usually of sugar or treacle, that dissolves easily in the mouth. This has been so for more than a century, and as long ago as 1790 the lollypop was a popular sweetmeat made of sugar and butter. It was flavored variously, with orange, peppermint, lemon, and the like. The word is to be found in Grose's *Dictionary of the Vulgar Tongue*, published in 1790. A maker of lollypops applies for registration of the word as a trade-mark, registers it, and then protests against its being recorded in the dictionaries and retained there without due acknowledgment of his rights, and requests that it be removed. Nothing more brazen concerning a word that has been established in the language for nearly one hundred and fifty years has ever been attempted.

About the year 1920, a company of well-known New York lens manufacturers applied for and obtained trade-name protection for "azurine" and "azurlite." The first of these terms has been a part of the language since Hakluyt made use of it in his *Voyages* (III, 37) in 1600, and means blue, azure, or, according to Littré, pale blue inclining to gray. The patentees of "azurine" used the term for a greenish blue, and compounded their word from "azure" and "marine." "Azurlite" is a gem stone from Arizona, and is formed of "azure" and the suffix "-lite," which ultimately comes from the Greek *lithos*, stone. Although well established in our common tongue, these terms are now registered trade names.

Other idiosyncrasies of the owners of trade names are in evidence when a pharmacal company, for example, manifests its willingness to enjoy the publicity afforded by the pages of a dictionary by supplying a definition of its proprietary term, but repudiates the transaction twenty years later and requests the withdrawal of both letter and word. Such was the case with an antiseptic sold under an acknowledged trade-mark name that was removed from the pages of the dictionary a few years ago.

Among other owners whose agents or representatives originally sought dictionary publicity, and willingly supplied definitive statements and illustrative material to supplement them, were the proprietors of alundum, carborundum, the caterpillar-tractor, celotex, dictophone, neutrodyne, pantasote, and so forth. Later the proprietorate suffered change of heart, or was impelled to protest by counsel unfamiliar with the facts, with the result that removal from the works of reference was sought.

Karel Čapek's Robot is drawn from the Polish word *robota*, "work." In the speech of the Poles, a *robot* is a workman. Čapek's creation is original in that it has introduced a new term to designate a person who works mechanically—without interest in his job. *R.U.R.* stands for "Rossum's Universal Robots." The word was copyrighted by Karel Čapek as the name for an automaton invented to provide cheap labor and take care of all hard toil, and it behooves everyone who makes use of this or like terms to bear in mind that they are protected by the copyright law. Few editors care to include such words in dictionaries until they have burst the bonds of the law by repeated usage, and have become accepted as part of our daily speech.

Sometimes an applicant for proprietary rights combines two words that have been in common use in the language for generations, forms a solid compound, and then applies to the

United States Patent Office for registration and protection. If such protection is granted, the people may be deprived of the use of the normal terminology of the language. Several examples of this practice have already been cited above.

III

Under the trade-mark laws of the United States, a trade-mark cannot be registered if it consists of or contains matter that is not susceptible of exclusive appropriation; as, for instance, personal names and geographical or place names, which are excluded as being held to be common words currently used, and therefore inapplicable for use in designating articles for which trade-marks are desired. Notwithstanding this, "tabasco sauce," cut to "tabasco" by the public, is a trade name, and since 1905 its manufacturers have been granted proprietary trade-name protection. Now, "tabasco sauce" does not describe the article in question, which is properly a pepper sauce that masquerades under the descriptive appellation Tabasco, the name of a state in Mexico since the federation of that country in 1824.

Among would-be trade names we have "celluloid," a word that was in use more than a year before it was introduced into the patent granted in Great Britain to protect the manufacture of soluble cotton or pyroxyline into a solid. The process for producing the substance was invented in the United States, and first patented in April 1871, as a material used for dental plates. The specifications of the first British patent, No. 1025 (1871), do not contain the word "celluloid," but the specifications of Hyatt's patent, No. 3101, issued in 1872, contain the following: "The manufacture of pyroxyline or soluble cotton into a solid (which is herein denominated *celluloid*)." But "celluloid" had obtained currency in the dental profession before that date, for in the *British Journal of Dental Science* for 1871, Volume XIV, we find, "The material is named the *celluloid* base, so called from the material from which it is composed." This shows the term to have been common property by usage for more than a year prior to protection or registration.

As I have said, some manufacturers, seeking the registration of words drawn from the language, concede the common right to such as they use, and waive all but title in a specific form or design. Among the manufacturers who have done this is the American Lock Manufacturing Company, of Chicago, which, in applying for registration of "grip tumbler" as a trade name for its types of locks, made no exclusive claims for the words "grip" and "tumbler" "except as a part of the mark shown by their drawing."

Words like "aërogram," "marconigram," and "radiogram" are proprietary and in restricted use, but the genius of the language seems to prefer "radio," which, regardless of the fact that it is an adjective, is now commonly used as a noun. And "radio" has given us a rich harvest of trade names. Exactly which to select from this store for inclusion in the dictionary is one of the uneasy problems the man at the helm has to solve. The great corporations that support this new science—the public, the broadcasting stations—may seek for terms not yet recorded. Why? Because no term should be included that is not likely to be inquired for by a large body of persons. The problem itself is not solved by mere inclusion.

Formed from the Latin *radius*, "ray," the word "radio" itself is having a varied experience. It has already given us "radiogram" and "radiolog" as compounds of recent formation. Itself it is used generally to designate (1) the science of transmitting matter by wireless telegraphy; (2) the apparatus and paraphernalia required to erect either a transmitting or a receiving point or station; and (3) that which is transmitted or broadcast by these means. But in Philadelphia "radio" is the trade-mark name for a bay rum!

The adoption of "T.N.T." as a trade name for a footbath-wash provokes a smile, for "trinitrotoluene" has held undisputed possession of this symbol for many years. Why permission should be granted to anyone to use "seaplane" as a name for a self-raising wheat flour is perhaps not so much of a puzzle as "sun set," which has been assigned to a similar product. A *self-r*aising wh*eat flour* might not inappropriately be named, by the telescope process, "sereator."

Some years ago the word "opticist," which dates from 1884, found its way into the dictionary as a legitimate word. The optician, unaware of the fact that the term had been given copyright protection, but seeing it in the dictionary, would naturally think it to be a general term, to the use of which he was as much entitled as the rest of mankind. But there have been cases in which opticians who set up the sign "Opticist" over their stores were sued by the man who had been so astute as to protect the word.

"A 1" is commonly known as a term designating "of the first or highest class: used of shipping to denote the condition of a vessel as to hull and equipment. By extension, of the highest class of other things and in any respect; as, an *A 1* musician; an *A number one* cook: read *A one* or *A number one.*" But the term is claimed as a trade-mark for electrical apparatus, machines, and supplies for welding, manufactured by an English corporation established in Bradford without "claim to the exclusive use of the letters *A 1*, or of the letter *A* and the numeral *1.*"

Though star-spangled our "banner," that fact has not prevented the appropriation of this word as a registered trademark name for one of our food products that consists of rolled oats. Some years ago William Beverly Winslow, a noted New York attorney, was interested in a case in which the proprietors of a breakfast food maintained that they had coined the word "shredded." The term was traced through American sources back to 1864; a further search, made in England, revealed that the word was in use as long ago as 1577. It was found in Hammer's *Ancient Ecclesiastical History,* which said, "Others gnawing the small, *shredded* tops of green grass used them for food." "Shredded herbs" and "shredded forage" were in existence in 1656 and 1662, and in the latter year, according to Olearius's *Voyages*, the ordinary forage for horses was "rice mixed with *shredded* straw."

Except for its hybrid form, the term "hydrofoam"—a bit of Greek combined with a bit of Anglo-Saxon—might pass muster as an English word, for we have many others of like formation in the language, but it is a trade name for a shampoo manufactured in St. Paul.

"Tabloid," to which reference has already been made, is one term that has caused its coiners and proprietors—Burroughs, Wellcome and Company of London—much trouble. It is a copyright trade-mark designating the concentrated products made by the company. Naturally the proprietors are jealous of this word, and have endeavored by legal process to restrict its use to their products, but they are merely emulating Mrs. Partington in her famous contest with the Atlantic Ocean. The term has won favor with the press and the public at large, and none but perpetual effort, if that be possible, can restrict its use. The Eskimos of Alaska might as well try to prevent the use of the word "hooch" in bootleg lore because it is a corruption of *hoochinoo*, the fermented drink they manufacture from yeast, flour, molasses, and sugar, which is one of the earliest of home-brews.

A large percentage of the so-called trade terms are telescope words—also sometimes called portmanteau words—or mere misspellings. That it is possible to name products or manufactures without resorting to the vocabulary we share in common with the rest of the English-speaking world has already been proved, so there is no need to grant registered trade-mark protection to such words as "inspiration," used to designate cotton or woolen piece goods; "sparkle," for neckties; "tiller," which smacks of the sea, for canned goods (except that one variety consists of fish); "zenith" for vehicle timepieces, alarm clocks, and watches, and hundreds of other common words that have been used by persons too indolent to employ the mental faculty with which they have been endowed. Our

Patent Office can easily awaken the public conscience to this abuse by refusing registration.

While a "pig'n a blanket" may be as good as an angel on horseback, for aught the writer knows to the contrary, it may strike the epicure as a somewhat woolly name for a meat pie or a meat dumpling, or for some other article of food having a meat "filler" and a casing or cover made from flour or other cereal. The delicacy may be appetizing enough, but its name affords no evidence of it.

In these days of "this freedom," no one will protest against "Polly Prim" as applied to certain types and qualities of ladies' and children's aprons, or against "weldene," as used in metal working for a type of solder; but why anyone should be privileged to pillage the printers' craft and deprive it of its characteristic "quad," in favor of a special type of shingle strip, only the Patent Office can tell, and this especially in view of the fact that the owners do not waive rights to exclusive use.

Against the use of a family name as a trade-mark name by persons who bear it, no legitimate objection can be made, even if such use should prove detrimental to the ambitions of other members of the family that bear it. Particularly is this so in a republic where the bearers of such names as Carnegie, Edison, Ford, Hoe, Singer, and the like, have contributed largely to public welfare.

IV

The work of making dictionaries frequently brings one face to face with problems that make things very interesting. One of these is the problem of inclusion and exclusion of trade names. Around these, political interests may revolve, as they may around the geographical names of foreign countries. So far as the trade names are concerned, there was a time when the owners of these urged dictionary makers to include them in the pages of their books.

The experience is somewhat as follows. The proprietors

advertise their goods widely; writers take the terms and introduce them in their stories or in general literature, and for ten or fifteen years all goes well. Then the owning company reorganizes, appoints new officers, engages new attorneys, and soon after this the dictionary maker receives letters requesting the removal of the terms from the pages of the dictionary, as inclusion infringes the owners' rights, and protesting against such inclusion in peremptory terms. Naturally, to one who knows the circumstances, these proceedings appear as a joke, but there is another side to them. Patented articles or products are protected for a certain period of years; but if, before the expiration of that period, the rights are sold to another company, and that company does the work that the first company may or may not have neglected to do,—goes to the Patent Office and registers its trade-mark,—the new company acquires a fresh lease of life for the name of the property that should, on the expiration of patent rights, belong to the public.

Now let us suppose that all rights in the original company lapse within four, five, or six years, and the registration of the trade-mark is only of recent entry or renewal. The name, which under the lapse of the patent would become public property (for the time in which the original inventor or creator is permitted by law to enjoy exclusively the benefits of his idea has expired), gets an extension of life that in these days of oversight—intentional or otherwise—might be continued in perpetuity for all that may be done to prevent it. This concerns the rights of the people as against the "rights" of the owner—and the Federal Trade Commission.

Men who make dictionaries do not like to omit terminology about which the public is likely to inquire, nor do they care to be threatened with vexatious lawsuits when their good faith is shown by the care that they exercise in the work they do.

THE UNINTENTIONAL CHARM
OF MEN

By *Frances Lester Warner*

SUPPOSE the bachelor son of a family, at home in vacation, is erecting an aërial mast for the radio on top of the house. And suppose that several feminine suggestions are proffered to him from below. Watch him as he goes politely to the edge of the roof and peers down. By virtue of his position up aloft he is free to do as he will. By virtue of filial and fraternal tradition he inclines an attentive ear. He feels anything but charming. Yet there he is, completely expressive, the high-perched male, uncatchable, precarious, his independent situation only emphasized by the harassed inquiry of his gaze.

He is more charming, at such a moment, to observe impersonally than he is to cope with. Cope with him too insistently from your advisory position below-stairs, and you will find that your messages to him will, in wireless parlance, begin to "fade." You can push your supervision of him only just so far. He can always remove himself neatly out of range.

This is one of the most tantalizing of the unpremeditated charms of men: the inaccessibility of their outposts, the facility of their escapes. They are lithe and very agile, and to their expeditions no definite bounds are set.

Suppose, again, an entirely different sort of man. He is not a bachelor, he is not young, and no longer does he have to scale roof-trees of the world in order to perch on high. He is a certain very dignified United States Senator who has offered to amuse his two smallest grandsons, while their mother and grandmother step out to pay a call. The favorite form of entertainment is the running of an electric train on a system of tracks in the sun-room near the relics of the Christmas tree. Around and around the wondrous train has gone, now entitled the Wolverine, now the Federal Express. The Senator has been brakeman, electrician, flagman, ticket-vender, and locomotive-whistle all by turns. He is beginning to be just a trifle tired of working on the railroad and more than a trifle stiff. Consulting his watch, he finds that it is already long past the hour when his wife and daughter promised to come back.

A happy thought strikes him; a ray of hope for occupational change. He remembers that his wife did not take the latch-key with her and will have to ring the doorbell when she comes home.

"What do you say," he inquires of his grandsons, "if we all go very quietly down to the library, so that Nellie won't hear us, and hide under the piano; and when Mother and Grandmother come in, we can jump out and surprise them, each of us making a loud noise?"

"Oh, yes!" rejoins the elder grandson, enchanted. "I will be a big brown bear, and Bobbie will be a little white dog, and, Drandpa, you will be the whistle on the Fedewal Expwess."

Forthwith the three conspirators go stealing like footpads down the stairs. They pull the Paisley shawl off from the end of the piano just enough so that it hangs down like a curtain; and when the doorbell rings, they scramble underneath and hide themselves among the pedals with beating hearts, in the very nick of time.

"Now!" whispers the Senator, as footsteps come along the hall; and out they spring in unison on all fours, big bear growling, little dog barking, locomotive-whistle shrieking loud and long, all making straight for the ladies' feet. And behold, it is not Mother and Grandmamma at all, but two representatives from the League of Women Voters being shown into the library by the maid.

A patriarch and a Senator is never more adorable than at the precise fraction of a split second when he is suddenly ceasing to be the locomotive-whistle on the Federal Express.

And for a third phase of the unintentional, suppose that a brisk Boy Scout, aged ten, has arrived home early on an afternoon, to find the house empty and himself locked out. Awaiting the family's return, he is pacing the quarter-deck, and as time wears away he begins to sing to himself a chant that he composes as he goes along. His voice rises and falls with hammer-like strokes, in the primitive rhythm of a tom-tom heard from the African bush. He has composed also the words that he is chanting, and this is the entire libretto of his song: "Oh, I—Am—So—*Sick* of myself! Oh, I—amso—Sick of myself!" over and over it goes, in a kind of thumping recitatif, *sforzando*, *ponderoso*, like the old Church litany about Whales. He does not dream that anyone is listening, but through your garage window you can watch him as he paces up and down, hands in pockets, stockings in a spiral, singing his grim song.

The very vigor of his sentiments strikes home. Here is charm of the one who walks, no matter how or where, by his individual Wild Lone. Attractiveness is inherent in the thought that any masculine being is uncompanioned on the earth. A man going it alone has always whetted the imagination of the world: witness the solitary horseman of old romantic tales, Thoreau, Dreyfus, the Flying Colonel, Robinson Crusoe, Daniel Boone. And if one of them happens to have strong convictions in that solitude and expresses them, we prick an attentive ear.

Taking these three homely illustrations as a clue, one perceives that a certain portion of men's most tantalizing, most lovable, most unexpected charm may be entirely unintentional; and it is lucky that this is so. The devotion of mothers and wives and employees is largely abetted and explainable by the fact. This does not mean that any devoted woman is consciously upheld in paths of duty by winning masculine traits; but at least they furnish something permanent to fall back on when the man himself is by no means striving to please.

Perhaps the exact shading of meaning here was best brought out by a very fastidious old lady who had successfully brought up four sons. They had been "difficult" boys, but everybody had considered them very promising—everybody but their father, who was sure that they were headed straight for Sing Sing, four abreast. There were many times in that household when the father in high dudgeon went marching out of the house and down the street, his coat-tails flapping with rage at every stride, while the boys celebrated his departure in the top of a tall tree. Yet the boys all turned out thoroughly well, all of them notable in their professions, one of them the endower of a great institution, another the pastor of a great Church. At the time of their parents' Golden Wedding, they all came home with their families and held a gay reception to their friends. In the midst of the festivity, one of the sons happened to remark that he had never seen his mother ruffled or disturbed by any of their oldtime frays. The other sons and their father all agreed. Through the hottest crises of their turbulent family life, they said, she had kept her temper invariably serene.

"How did you ever do it?" some young mothers asked her, later, when they met her at a Home Missionary Meeting one day.

"Well," said she, folding her hands (she looked, by the way, like an exquisite combination miniature portrait of Whistler's Mother and Saint Cecilia at Seventy-Three), "I have never told anybody about it. But since you girls ask me, I will tell you. When things used to get so bad that I simply couldn't stand it another minute, I would go up to my room and lock my door and go to the window and sit down and look out through the Venetian blinds at my husband stamping off down the road and the boys swinging by their feet in the tree. And I would sit quietly for a minute rocking in my little rocking-chair; and then I would say to myself, 'Damn.'"

Any observer watching this lovely lady today with her splendid family about her would never dream that their manly ways had ever goaded her to such a pass—to the terrific profanity of a delicate gentle-woman when she finds herself inexplicably related to strange beings who go stamping out of houses with indignant coat-tails, or who swing by their feet in trees.

But one notices that at the very height of her irritation, when she was trying her very hardest to calm down, she went to the window and looked out at them all through the Venetian blinds. Here is the other side of the shield from the one that Hecuba had in mind when she begged Menelaus not to look at Helen. For different reasons, but with similar psychology, if a woman wants to remain furiously angry with an interesting man, she had better not watch him.

A mere turn of his expression may upset all her logic, as happened once when the President of an industrial firm sent his confidential secretary down to the office of one of the vice-presidents, to get a valuable deed which the Vice-President had been interested to see. The Vice-President did not have it any longer and said that he had left it with the President on the previous afternoon.

"Oh, no, no!" insisted the President when this was reported to him. "Scott has it. I haven't seen it. Search his files."

"I have," said the Secretary. "He and I searched the whole place together to make sure. The deed really isn't there. Please may I just glance through that pile of papers on your desk?"

"No! No! No!" growled the President, guarding the papers with his enormous hand. "I tell you Scott has it. You search him again."

The Secretary obeyed and also searched the office of the second Vice-President for good luck. Then she returned to her chief.

"I wish you would let me look among those papers," she pleaded. "Mr. Scott and Mr. Colby both remember that

Mr. Scott handed it to you at this desk only yesterday afternoon."

"But he didn't," retorted the President irascibly. "He must have made a mistake and left it on your desk, and you must have slipped it among the newspapers that the man has just taken down in the rubbish cart. I'll have all the rubbish in the building searched."

At this, the Confidential Secretary put on her coat and hat and walked out of the building, ostensibly to lunch, but really to a church around the corner where she sometimes paused at noontime to let her emotions sizzle down. On a beautiful stained-glass window was a picture of Moses looking out from Mount Nebo into the Promised Land, at which she always gazed. Moses is the patron saint of all frazzled dispositions, but today even the great Rock-Smiter was of no avail. To work in one office for years without once mislaying a single scrap of paper, and then to be told categorically that you must have put a valuable deed into the newspaper pile! The die was cast. No apology could change her purpose now. Back to her desk she went and wrote out her formal resignation. Just then her buzzer sounded, and by force of habit she rose and went into the office of her chief. But she sailed in with stately mien and icy mood, ruffling her pure cold plume like Tennyson's swan.

"Look," said the President of the firm, and raised one tiny corner of the heap of papers just a fraction of an inch, only barely enough so that she could see the edge of the missing deed folded into a copy of *The Iron Age*. Not another word was said, but the expression of the President as he looked up through his bushy eyebrows was like the expression of a big dog who has just noticed that he has a chicken-feather sticking to his paw.

What arguments and apologies could not have accomplished that solemn glance had done. The swan-secretary dissolved in laughter and went back to work.

It all boils down to this: men of ability on a rampage are disquieting, and impervious to reasoning, and very maddening withal; but after everything is said and done, how entertaining they do look!

This has nothing whatever to do with their looking handsome. Far more appealing than Apollo Belvedere, Don Juan, and Beau Brummel all rolled into one is the state of mind expressed by a certain little red-headed nine-year-old leader of a brigand crew who rushed into the house one day, walked up to the tall mirror, took one look at himself, put his head down in his mother's lap, and cried as if his heart would break. Little by little his mother arrived at the true kernel of his woe. He could not bear it any longer to have red hair. His mother assured him that artists love the color, and that he would like it better when he grew up. Bravely he choked back the sobs, raised his head, took one more look in the glass, and then broke down again. "But I don't like this face either," objected he. It was the lament of a man's man for the beauty that he felt he lacked.

We have a right, I think, to say that this small boy's charm was unintentional. But have we a right to say that Don Juan's is necessarily intentional? We have not. We know only that it looked that way. There is a very interesting intermediate zone where one never can be sure.

Take, for instance, two companion pictures of quite similar young men, both on a vacation, both in the simple act of performing upon a musical instrument, but in very different moods. One of them was the royal herald in a May-time pageant of an artist colony far up in the hills. Near the close of the pageant this herald, his mediæval costume all aglow with color, stood in the sunset and blew his silver trumpet at the castle gate. A twilight breeze fluttered the banner that fell from his long trumpet. The plume of his velvet hat brushed against the branch of an ancient oak. He looked like the spirit of all masterful things arriving and waiting confidently as he stood there, alert, imperative, yet paradoxically wistful, sounding the King's summons at the drawbridge of the baron's tower.

If that young artist with his slender velvet costume and his emblazoned tabard and his silver trumpet raised on high was not aware of his charm, then his looks belied him.

The contrasting scene, the gay climax of the unintentional, was enacted by another young musician who needed to play his clarinet one note lower than a clarinet will go. He had discovered a rare museum manuscript of an early composition for the clarinet, but one note of the haunting melody went down below the instrument's deepest range. He had copied the venerable music, but he did not want to transpose it into a higher key. An extension of the clarinet must be arranged. This happened when his entire family-in-law was enjoying a reunion at the seaside summer home, and around the grounds like a wailing banshee went the clarinetist, asking all members of the tribe if they had perchance a mailing-tube, of just the size to fit on and add an extra length to the slim-bored barrel of the clarinet.

His home-in-law was the kind of rambling homestead in which unexpected commodities like mailing-tubes may always be unearthed at will. Several were discovered, but each of a caliber too large.

"I seem to remember——" ventured one of the party, and vanished up the attic stairs. Full of curiosity, everybody followed. And there, among some rolls of charts and blue prints, a long thin mailing-tube of fitting size was duly found. Balancing himself on the relics of an early rocking-horse under the rafters, the musician attached the entire length of the brown pasteboard mailing tube to the lower end of his glorious instrument, and through that elongated funnel he blew a mournful blast. It sounded like a basso profundo organ-pipe half as big as a church.

Then he chopped off experimental fractions with his knife until he reached the length that added just the desired low note. And thereupon he played over the theme of the old tune, critically, listening sharply to himself as he played, his tall frame astride the rocking-horse, his purposeful eyes intent. When he came to the successful extra added note below, he gazed out at his audience abstractedly over the mailing-tube. Almost certainly, at that moment, he was no longer aware of his own agile and versatile self. As far as his self-consciousness was concerned, he was only a mere pneumatic accessory to his clarinet.

A wind-instrument, whole-heartedly performed upon, is likely to bring out unexpected facial possibilities in an intensely masculine human being as he huffs and he puffs. Suppose one could have seen General Washington playing down the scale on that old flute of his which rests upon the little harpsichord at Mount Vernon. Would he not be transformed, this General Washington, off duty, his face thus attentively blown down to a focus, his personality centered upon precisely the accurate quality of tone? Gilbert Stuart should have sketched him once that way.

Here is one secret of the merry charm that attends any self-forgetful man who performs a highly specialized deed with might and main. By reason of his very unawareness of his appearance, he dramatizes the spirit of the thing he is doing. He becomes a kind of colophon, an emblem of the relationship between the doer and the thing done. There is a decorative value about the action, as symbolic as the composition of an heraldric device, whether the man himself is a dragoon or a duck-hunter, a fisherman in his dory off Gloucester Harbor, or an Arctic explorer in his hood of fur.

And yet the most interesting men do not think of themselves as primarily ornamental and will resist being used for such purposes if they can. Watch them efface themselves from the pageantry of a pretty wedding, drifting out of the picture whenever they find it possible, even at times the necessary groom.

A determined rebellion in this line was staged not long ago by the father of a popular bride. He had been forced to succumb to a large wedding, but on one final detail he took his stand: he would not wear a gardenia in his button-hole.

"You needn't provide a gardenia for my husband," said the bride's mother to the florist, "for he won't wear it."

"Oh, yes, we will," said the florist. "I promise that he will."

"Oh, no, he won't," rejoined the bride's mother, who knew her man.

"I'll have it ready, anyway," said the florist. "He will wear it. You'll see."

And so, on the evening of the wedding, when the wedding march began, the bride's mother glanced back circumspectly to watch the procession coming in. First she looked at her daughter and then at her husband's button-hole. The gardenia was there. Incredulously she watched it advancing in good order up the aisle. After everything was over she touched the petals of the waxy flower in her husband's lapel and murmured, "How did it happen?"

"Well," explained her husband, "that florist fellow waited until I had my first foot out to step into the church, and then he came up to me and pinned the posy on. If he had put a pink petticoat on me at that moment, I'd have worn it in."

For a fascinating study in postures notice a group of men standing insecurely about at a fashionable wedding, and compare them with a group of the same men going to a fire. Men show up at their very best at fires. They silhouette well, for one thing, and they mass well in active groups together. And the scene is complete if, in addition to helmets gleaming, rubber coats dripping, tall boots splashing, there is a small boy also dancing midge-like in the shadows, longing to help the firemen with the hose. It is a picture of the earliest form of eager masculine ambition doing its electrified dervish dance at the sight of great achievement—the spirit of Aspiration in the presence of the Arrived.

Of course a picture like this is ultra-dramatic, its spiritual values mixed up with bulk and blaze and noise. Mere variation in the size-scale is pleasant to the eye. But the most decorative exhibition of energy that I ever saw was the performance of a very slender man, a Canadian fisherman on a coastwise island far to the north. The afterglow was fading on the lighthouse ridge one evening, when over the crest of the dune came rushing a swift group of three, racing merrily; a horse unharnessed all but his halter, a man with the end of the halter in his hand, and a collie dog barking and capering beside them, his lovely plume waving in the air. Along they came, three abreast, sweeping gloriously across the deserted meadow and over the next high dune. There is an old Connecticut proverb, "A hen, a cow, and a woman should never run." Conversely, a dog, a horse, and a man always should.

In energy and unexpectedness and the achieving mood, there is a permanent charm in men's affinity for the maximum. Full-scale ambition seems suitable to them, even in so primitive a matter as their ability to make enormous and terrifying noise. It is a pity that modern signaling devices have done away in such large measure with opportunities for the unmitigated roar of man. The roaring of the old-time skippers of sailing ships was a very famous thing. We miss it nowadays in the universe, for we need it to offset men's capacity for great silence, for the massive depths of the unspoken and the unexplained.

This capacity for silence, this command of pause, is closely allied to the ultimate charm of men, the capacity for loneliness and grandeur in old age.

Grandfathers should always live long enough to dramatize their old age for their grandchildren in lovable and understandable form. Children so favored receive an impression that does not desert them soon. My sister and I never suspected that our own grandfather was growing old until it was decreed that he must not drive his favorite spirited horses any more. The decision went forth and we children all mourned about it, but a safe and elderly animal named Billy Horse was duly found. There is no possible come-down nowadays comparable to that; for there is no such discrepancy between any two makes of motor-cars as there was between that lumbering old bay Billy and the sensitive black horses that our grandfather had loved. At first he did not care to drive at all. But one of the happiest family customs had been the sleigh-rides on which, in snowy weather, he had always taken his grandchildren, one of us each time. We rarely talked much on these rides, for we all had New England in our bones, but our companionship was perfect none the less. It was my sister's turn to go with him one morning after an ice-storm, when icicles were hanging from the elm trees, and all the rose-bushes were made of glass.

Far out of town, just as they reached the foot of a steep hill, they saw a lumber-sledge coming towards them, slewing down from the hilltop, out of control. Quickly our grandfather drew rein to turn Billy, as he would have turned his other horses, into a farm-lane, so as to give the sledge the road. But Billy did not grasp the situation. At best, the process of warping him around was always a good deal like coming about in a square-rigger, a matter for premeditation and much tugging at the yards. In vain our grandfather tried all devices that horses and horsemen know. And finally, just as the big pung was almost upon them, he summoned all the strength in his power-ful frame and bodily hoisted the astonished Billy out of the road.

Not a word was said by anybody, by Billy least of all. When the danger was passed, my sister stole a glance at our grand-father's profile, unmoved as a granite side-hill made of solid rocks, only the least suggestion of a sardonic set to the furrows of his thoughtful face. On and on they went through the fairy-land of frozen country, saying not a word. At length, more than half an hour later, our grandfather deliberately spoke.

"You can't turn Billy Horse *instantly*," said he.

As soon as my sister got home from that ride she told me about our grandfather's remark. We were only little girls, but we were old enough to perceive that there was in our grand-father's long-considered statement something delightfully more than true. Together we ran to the side-window for a last glimpse of him as he vanished up the street. Red sleigh, big buffalo-robe, tucked-in scarf-end, furry cap—silver sleighbells ringing under the crystal elms—O beloved, from the snowy highroads of the world can such things pass away?

I have had a good many memorable pictures of old age since

then: Dr. Lyman Abbott, for instance, white-haired, white-bearded, near the end of his long life, coming across a college campus to springtime vespers, when the pink hawthorn by the library was in full bloom. No girl who attended chapel that vesper time will forget how he opened the great Bible, rested his long thin hands upon it, and thoughtfully read to us his text: "If a man die, shall he live again?"

There is a loneliness and majesty about a man's old age that has in it more than the simple pathos of things that have passed away. There is the nobility of all that dominant action piling up behind him, the cumulative sense of the sheer duration of so many days.

And yet, to those who know them best, to their families and friends, it is evident that the grandest of old men retain their pristine unexpectedness and intractability when putting their projects through. A very aged celebrity made a remark one day that is typical of the not-easily-influenced quality of man in masterful mood. He had asked several high officials to one of his famous dinners and had assured them that they were to enjoy a favorite kind of mammoth pudding that he had invented in old days. When the guests were seating themselves, the venerable epicure turned to his wife and suggested that they reverse the menu and start with the pudding, so that its flavor might be enjoyed at the peak of appetite.

"I'm sorry," said she, grasping at the first excuse she could think of, "but I don't believe the pudding is quite done."

"Never mind," said her lord, sitting back and beaming at her with the effulgence of a more elderly Holbein's Henry the Eighth, "just ring the bell and Sam will fetch it in." I always like my puddings rather *raw*. One cannot be sure that the great man's wife found this moment preëminently charming. Conjugal appreciation has its ups and downs.

There was once a man of versatile tastes who learned that his wife was not enthusiastic about digging clams. Like a good responsible husband, he felt that she should be initiated into the appreciation of all seashore joys; and so he caused her to go clamming with him and dig enough for chowder from the oozing clam-flats of Cape Cod. After a generous supply had been obtained, he invited her to perch with him on their tethered dory and watch the waves. The ocean was very peaceful, and the tide was out. They sat so still that a white seagull alighted on the water near them and went bobbing on the surface like a duck. Finally the lady came out of her brown study and tried to put the upshot of her thinking into words.

"It's an odd thing," she began, "but you modify my tastes in fifty thousand ways and I never modify you in any way at all."

"Oh, yes, you do," rejoined her husband reassuringly. "You modify me as an adverb modifies a verb, or as an adverb modifies another adverb. You modify me like the adverb 'very.'"

Possibly there is a parable here for any woman who aspires to create an artistic and peaceful home-life for any given man. It behooves her to pay rather perceptive and appreciative attention to his entire verbal and adverbial equipment just as it stands. She may be able selectively to enhance it; and she may put the adverb "very" in front of it. But she will probably not be able vitally to change it. For men, in the full tilt of their achievements, are independent about their verbs and unintentional about their adverbs—a fact in which, very largely, resides their charm.

A LITTLE OLD LADY PASSES AWAY

By *John P. Waters*

THE familiar essay, that lavender-scented little old lady of literature, has passed away. Search the magazines for her sparrowy whimseys, and in all but one or two of them you will find, in her stead, crisp articles, blatant exposés, or statistic-laden surveys. Even in the few that admit her pale ghost to their circle of economists, sociologists, and Washington correspondents, her position is decidedly subordinate: a scant column or two near the insurance advertisements at the back of the book. Her mourners—and there still are many—wonder why. There was a time. . . .

There was a time when the familiar essay was important; so important that The Atlantic Monthly Press issued four printings of a book explaining its characteristics and construction; so important that Christopher Morley, the little old lady's favorite American nephew, took time off to anthologize her for admiring high-school teachers and their victims in English I–II, who were often led to believe that all literature, like all Gaul, was divided into three parts: fiction, poetry (pronounced poy'tree), and the familiar essay, with the familiar essay far in the lead as a literary form.

This last, this classifying it as a form, was not always easy to do. Those who tried usually gave Montaigne the credit for originating it and traced its development through Abraham Cowley, Thomas Browne, *Blackwood's Magazine*, Lamb, Hazlitt, and Thackeray. In tone and content, however, the essays of these pioneers little resembled the ones that this generation of readers remembers. Indeed, about all that links them is the common note of personal expression, the feeling that behind

From the *Forum*, July 1933; copyright, 1933, by The Forum Publishing Company, Inc. Used by special permission.

the words is a human being and not an omniscient voice. Yet even in this quality there is a difference between the old and the new.

In the former, though one was aware of personality, one was still conscious of the writer's dignity, of a slight barrier that he raised between himself and his audience. In the latter, this dignity was all too often missing, discarded for buttonholing intimacy, cracker-barrel philosophizing, and Winnie-the-Pooh whimsey.

What brought about this change? Why did so many modern essayists err in carrying familiarity too far? To find the answer, we must consider what the modern form was like at its best, and why it was popular.

At its best, the familiar essay was "a kind of improvisation on a delicate theme, a species of soliloquy; as if a man were to speak aloud the slender and whimsical thoughts that come to his mind when he is alone on a winter evening before a warm fire."

Intimacy, reverie, whimsey—these were the qualities that won it thousands of devoted readers, that made it kindly relief from frowning treatises, ramrod sermons, and all the high and mighty didacticism our fathers were flayed with before its advent. It was warm and human, unconcerned with life's granite problems but fascinated with the trifles, moods, and humors that colored the lives of its readers. It was comfortable literature, muddying no quiet pools with a stirred-up sense of sin, goading no laggard ambition to be something. Instead, it chatted easily and urbanely, graceful successor to the gradually dying art of conversation.

With so much in its favor, what caused its downfall? The answer is: the same qualities that made it popular—intimacy, reverie, whimsey. These qualities elicited so many gurgles of, "How charming! What a delightfully helpless fellow the author must be!" from sisters, wives, and maiden aunts, that literarily inclined gentlemen who had not been gushed over for years immediately concluded that the way to become inundated in gush was to put themselves in print as quaint old fuss-budgets. As a consequence, starveling hacks raced bony clergymen to the mailboxes with manuscripts that would make them "dears" and "darlings" to the petticoated portion of the populace.

They succeeded, of course, for the trick was easy. One had only to empty his mind of all knowledge, all common-sense, all everything, except tender quotations from Horace and Tennyson, and start reacting. Anything was a fit subject, the simpler and more far-fetched the better. For example, Mr. Percival Biggs—a six-foot giant who had played tackle for Yale in the days when football was played with the feet—would suddenly develop all the cute physical attributes of a pansy when confronted by the relatively simple problem of stoking his hot-air furnace. Instead of being a harmless cylinder of sheet-metal, it became "an insatiable scarlet-mawed monster." His modest two tons of winter coal became "sable diamonds" to be "immolated thrice daily." He himself was transformed from a lazy suburbanite to a "quaking panderer to Zoroaster." He wallowed in self-pity.

There were other schools, too. The mellowists, for example, did not want to be darlings. They wanted to be ripe, winey. Young men of twenty, green as quinces, ripened overnight. No Village attic lacked its fireside philosopher with his bowl of russet apples, his October cider, his Sherlock Holmes pipe, and his tin of Craven's Mixture—as unmellow a blend of grass and red-pepper, by the way, as Britain's abominable tobacconists ever foisted upon gullible Anglophiles. Reverie took the place of all other mental functions, and bookish archaisms from Evelyn and Pepys bid fair to drive out all other words from thesaurus and dictionary.

Worst of all, however, were the coy writers, the ones who defied death-by-strangulation with little tinklings called "An' Him Went Home to Him's Muvver." Others of these twitterers delighted in tickling the risqué with the feather end of their pens. Never boorishly, of course. A mild *damn*—in quotation marks—perhaps. Or the impish suggestion that they—pagans that they were—sometimes didn't quite close their shower-curtains all the way. This group was especially dear to schoolmarms from Brookline, Mass., who—during the months that Columbia Summer School was open—made life on the West Side subway utterly unbearable for native-born New Yorkers by staring them into nervous fits in an effort to gather first-hand material for hellish little papers on "The Typical New Yorker—Poor Thing."

At first, of course, these insect pests were few in number, and their buzzings were harmless enough. But when ever-increasing hordes discovered that writing the familiar essay was the ovaltine their egos needed, the end was near. No literature that is peopled exclusively with doddering loons afraid of sewing-machine flywheels, bewildered by the complex mechanics of hot-water faucets, and hero-stricken with such worthies as tympani thumpers, elevator starters, scissor grinders, and street cleaners can survive long.

The final axe fell when the high schools, with well-meaning but pitifully misdirected affection, took to teaching the fragile art to their fuzzy-lipped brats. Where there was one asinine but educated gush-hunter before, there were now whole herds of pubescent illiterates to annoy friends, relatives, and editors with misspelled masterpieces patterned after, or swiped from, the models their texts supplied.

For texts were essential paraphernalia in the tax-supported essay mills. Though the ninth-grade savants brashly disregarded the fact that the only endurable familiar essayist is a person with well-digested learning, impeccable syntax, urbane humor, pleasant sophistication, and indisputable savoir-faire, they were realistic to the extent that they provided inspiration for off-days when their darlings were not quite equal to scintillating out a three-hundred-word tiara for Miss Sophie Spragg to display at the next Parent-Teacher meeting. Consequently, they selected texts that made plagiary as easy as possible by presenting carefully preserved specimens in neatly labelled blocks: "Essays of Type I—Personal Experiences, Confessions, Self-Analyses; Essays of Type II—Reflections on Life, Human Nature, Customs, and Experience; Essays of Type III—Observations and Discoveries in the familiar and the Commonplace; Essays of Type IV—Nature Essays; Essays of Type V—General Observations, Comments, and Opinions of the Author."

Yet helpful as this break-down was, it was only preliminary and padding to the real meat of the book—the Appendix, which listed some two hundred and fifty "suggested titles." These were always added apologetically; for of course out of the adolescents' wide reading, mature wisdom, and glowing personalities would flow so many "topics" that such a list was almost an insult. Still, to be on the safe side, the text-writers always left it there; and it is remarkable how hungrily, and thankfully, the mute inglorious Morleys swallowed its insults and wrote, as per suggestion, on "My Ailments" (No. 27), "On Being Small" (No. 38), "Why the Dessert Course Last?" (No. 67), "Nature's Languages" (No. 174), or—supreme inspiration—"Diddling" (No. 225).

With such near-Beerbohm flowing into it, no form, let alone the most delicate, could retain its sparkle. Worse still, the public's palate became corrupted. Those who did not turn away in disgust either preferred the spurious stuff to the vintage products of the Morleys, Conrads, and McFees or took to regarding all essays and all essayists with stiff-necked contempt. And why not? Weren't they themselves able to bat out essays by the yard? Didn't they know all the tricks the masters used in building up their effects? And what, pray, was so wonderful about Hilaire Belloc? Anybody could do as well; and because anybody could, nobody wanted to.

What else, then, could the little old lady do but die as unobtrusively as possible? The children who had gathered around her hassock to hear her thin little musings had all grown up and gone away—or remained to mock her quaintness with their new-found wisdom. Radio, prohibition, and prosperity were stinging their senses with more peppery fare. A new and dizzyingly complex world had roared across the quiet hearth; and listeners once sure of their philosophies and content to roam in the pleasant meadows of reverie now groped bewilderedly for *facts*, explanations, anything to help them realign their lives before new discoveries, new techniques, drove out all meaning from life itself. Reverie, whimsey, and humor were out; they didn't get you anywhere.

Hence, gradually, the little old lady deserted her familiar haunts and faded away. Occasionally a sentimental editor, remembering her pleasant tea-table chatter, invites her fluttery ghost to visit his prim Caslon pages. There, politely baffled by the loud talk of collectivism and social trends and economic determinism all about her, she sits a while and muses with her old friends. Then she leaves and does not come back for months at a time. One day, perhaps, her pale ghost will not appear at all, and the hard young sociologists can have her pages all to themselves. But I hope not. For all their cocksure *-ologies*, they cannot comfort us the way she did—when she was at her best.

THE SECRET GARDEN

By *Edith Wharton*

I HAVE hesitated for some time before beginning this article, since any attempt to analyze work of one's own doing seems to imply that one regards it as likely to be of lasting interest, and I wish at the outset to repudiate any such assumption. Every artist works, like the Gobelins weavers, on the wrong side of the tapestry, and if now and then he comes around to the right side, and catches what seems a happy glow of color, or a firm sweep of design, he must instantly retreat again, if encouraged yet still uncertain; and once the work is done, and he hopes to contemplate it dispassionately, the result of his toil too often presses on his tired eyes with the nightmare weight of a cinema "close-up."

Nevertheless, no picture of myself would be more than a profile if it failed to give some account of the teeming visions which, ever since my small-childhood, and even at the busiest and most agitated periods of my outward life, have incessantly peopled my inner world. I have decided, therefore, to try to describe, as simply as I can, what seems to have gone to the making of my books; and there is the more reason for doing this because so few writers seem to have watched themselves while they wrote, or, if they did, to have set down their observations. Not a few painters have painted themselves at their easels, but I can think of nothing corresponding to these self-confessions in the world of letters, or at any rate of fiction, except the prefaces of Henry James. These, however, in the main are analyses of the way in which he focused a given subject and of the technical procedure employed, once he had

From *A Backward Glance;* copyright, 1933, by D. Appleton-Century Company. Used by special permission. [First printed in the *Atlantic Monthly*, April 1933, as "Confessions of a Novelist."]

determined his angle of vision. Even that beautiful and deeply moving fragment, the appeal to his genius, the knowledge of which we owe to Mr. Percy Lubbock's vigilance, is an invocation to the goddess and not a detached objective notation of her descent into his soul.

What I mean to try for is the observation of that strange moment when the vaguely adumbrated characters whose adventures one is preparing to record are suddenly *there*, themselves, in the flesh, in possession of one, and in command of one's voice and hand. It is there that the central mystery lies, and perhaps it is as impossible to fix in words as that other mystery of what happens in the brain at the precise moment when one falls over the edge of consciousness into sleep.

As for the rest of my colleagues, especially among English and American novelists, my impression is that the deeper processes of their art do not greatly interest them, or even arrest their attention; their conscious investigations of method seldom seem to go deeper than syntax, and it is immeasurably deeper that the vital interest begins. Therefore I shall try to say something of the growth and unfolding of the plants in my secret garden, from the seed to the shrub-top—for heaven forbid that I should try to magnify my vegetation into trees!

II

When I first began to talk with novelists about the art of fiction I was amazed at the frequently repeated phrase, " I've been hunting about for months for a good subject." Hunting about for a subject! Good heavens! I remember once, when an old friend of the pen made this rather wistful complaint, carelessly rejoining: " Subjects? But they swarm about me like mosquitoes! I'm sick of them: they stifle me. I wish I could get rid of them!" And only years afterward, when I had learned more from both life and letters, did I understand how presumptuous such an answer must have sounded. The truth is that I have never attached much importance to subject, partly because every incident, every situation, about me is perpetually presenting itself to me in the light of story-telling material, and partly from the conviction that the possibilities of a given subject are—whatever a given imagination can make of them. But by the time I had written three or four novels I had learned to keep silence on this point.

The examination of the story-telling process may be divided into two parts: that which concerns the technique of fiction (in the widest sense), and that which tries to investigate what, for want of a simpler term, one must call by the old bardic name of inspiration. On the subject of technique I have found only two novelists explicitly and deeply interested— Henry James and Paul Bourget. I have talked long and frequently with both of them, and profitably also, I hope, though on certain points we always disagreed. I have also, to the best of my ability, analyzed this process, as I understood it, in my book, *The Writing of Fiction;* and therefore I shall deal here, not with any general theory of technique, but simply with the question of how some of my own novels happened to me, how each little volcanic island shot up from the unknown depths, or each coral atoll slowly built itself out of them. But first I will try to capture the elusive moment of the arrival of the characters.

In the birth of fiction, it is sometimes the situation, the "case," which first presents itself to the mind, and sometimes the characters who first appear, asking to be fitted into a situation. I have often speculated on the conditions likely to give the priority to one or the other, but I doubt if fiction can be usefully divided into novels of situation and of character, since a novel, if worth anything at all, is always both at once, in inextricable combination. I can only say that in my own case a situation sometimes occurs to me first, and in others a single figure suddenly walks into my mind. If the situation takes the lead, I leave it lying about, as it were, in a quiet place, and just wait till the characters creep stealthily up and wriggle themselves into it. All I seem to have done is to say, at the outset: "This thing happened—but to whom?" Then I wait, holding my breath, and one by one they appear and take possession of the case. When it befalls in the other way, I may be strolling about casually in my mind, and suddenly a character will start up before me, coming seemingly from nowhere; and again, but more breathlessly, I watch; and presently the character draws nearer, and seems to become aware of me, and to feel the shy but desperate need to unfold his or her tale. I cannot say in which way my subject will probably present itself—though perhaps in short stories the situation, in novels one of the characters, is most likely to appear first.

This, however, is not the most interesting point of the adventure. Compared with what follows it is not interesting at all, though it has, in my case, one odd feature I have not heard of elsewhere—that is, that my characters always appear with their names. Sometimes these names seem to me affected, sometimes almost ridiculous; but I am obliged to own that they are never fundamentally unsuitable. And the proof that they are not, that they really belong to the people, is the difficulty which arises when I try to substitute other names. For many years the attempt always ended fatally; any character I unchristened instantly died on my hands, as if it were some kind of sensitive crustacean, and the name it bore were its shell. Only very gradually, and in very few cases, have I gained enough mastery over them to be able to effect the change, and even now, when I do, I have to resort to *piqûres* and oxygen, and not always successfully.

These names are hardly ever what I call "real names"—that is, the current patronymics one would find in an address book or a telephone directory; and often it is their excessive oddness which makes me try to change them. When in a book by someone else I meet people called by current names I always say to myself, "Ah, those names were tied on afterward"; and I often find that the characters thus labeled are less living than the others. Yet there seems to be no general rule, for, in the case of certain famous novelists whose characters have out-of-the-way names, many are tied on too. Balzac had to hunt the

streets of Paris for names on shop signs; and Thackeray and
Trollope bent their genius to the invention of the most labored
and dreary pleasantries in the pointless attempt to characterize their people in advance. Yet Captain Deuceace and the
Rev. Mr. Quiverful are alive enough, and I can only suppose
that the oddity of the prenamed characters is a peculiarity of
my own mental make-up. But I often wonder how the novelist
whose people arrive without names manages to establish relations with them!

III

A still more spectral element in my creative life is the sudden
appearance of names without characters. Several times, in this
way, a name to which I can attach no known association of
ideas has forced itself upon me in a furtive shadowy way, not
succeeding in making its bearer visible, yet hanging about
obstinately for years in the background of my thoughts. The
Princess Estradina was such a name. I knew nothing of its
origin, and still less of the invisible character to whom it
presumably belonged. Who was she, what were her national-
ity, her history, her claims upon my attention? She must have
been there, lurking and haunting me, for years before she
suddenly walked into *The Custom of the Country*, in high-
colored flesh and blood, cool, dominant, and thoroughly at
home.

Another such character haunts me today. Her name is still
odder—Laura Testvalley. How I should like to change that
name! But it has been attached for some time now to a
strongly outlined material form, the form of a character figuring largely in an adventure I know all about, and have long
wanted to relate. Several times I have tried to give my character another name, since the one she bears, should it ever
appear in print, will be even more troublesome to my readers
than to me; but Miss Testvalley is strong-willed, and even
obstinate, and turns sulky and unmanageable whenever I try
to hint at the advantages of a change; so it is more than likely

that she will one day force her way into my tale burdened with her impossible patronymic.

But this is a mere parenthesis; what I want to try to hint at is the elusive moment when these people who haunt my brain actually begin to speak within me with their own voices. The situating of my tale, and its descriptive and narrative portions, I am conscious of conducting, though often unaware of how the story first came to me, pleading to be told; but when the dialogue begins, then I become merely a recording instrument, and my hand never hesitates because my mind has not to choose, but only to set down what these stupid or intelligent, lethargic or passionate, people say to each other in a language, and with arguments, that appear to be all their own. It is for this reason that I attach such importance to dialogue, and yet regard it as an effect to be so sparingly used. For by dialogue I do not mean the pages of "Yes" and "No," of platitudes and repetitions, of which most actual talk is composed, and which any writer with a photographic mind and a good memory can set down by the yard. The vital dialogue is that exchanged by characters whom their creator has really vitalized, and only the significant passages of their talk should be recorded, in high relief against the narrative, and not uselessly embedded in it.

In my case these moments of high tension, when the creature lives and its creator listens to it, have nothing to do with the "walking away with the subject," the "settling it in their own way," with which some novelists so oddly charge their characters. It is a necessity to me that the note of inevitableness should be sounded at the very opening of my tale, and that my characters should go forward to their ineluctable doom like the "murdered man" in *The Pot of Basil*. From the first I know exactly what is going to happen to every one of them; their fate is settled beyond rescue, and I have but to watch and record. When I read that great geniuses like Dickens and Trollope "killed off" a character, or changed the conclusion of a tale, in response to the request or the criticism of a reader, I am dumbfounded. What then was their own relation to their subject? But to show how mysterious and incalculable the whole business is, one has only to remember that Trollope "went home and killed" Mrs. Proudie because he had overheard some fool at his club complaining that she had lived long enough; and yet that the death scene thus arbitrarily brought about is one of the greatest pages he ever wrote, and places him momentarily on a level with Balzac and Tolstoy!

But these people of mine, whose ultimate destiny I know, walk to it by ways unrevealed to me beforehand. Not only their speech, but what I might call their subsidiary action, seems to be their very own, and I am sometimes startled at the dramatic effect of a word or gesture which would never have occurred to me if I had been pondering over an abstract "situation," as yet uninhabited by its "characters."

I do not think I can get any nearer than this to the source of my story-telling faculty; I can only say that the process, though it takes place in some secret region on the sheer edge of consciousness, is yet always illuminated by the clear light of my critical attention. What happens there is as real and as tangible as my encounters with my friends and neighbors, often more so, though it is entirely different in quality. It produces in me a great emotional excitement, quite unrelated to joy or sorrow caused by real happenings, but as intense, and with as great an appearance of reality; and my two lives, divided between these equally real yet totally unrelated worlds, have gone on thus, side by side, equally absorbing, but wholly isolated from each other, ever since in my infancy I "read stories" aloud to myself out of Washington Irving's *Alhambra*, which I generally held upside down.

IV

After writing *The Valley of Decision*, and my book on Italian villas, I felt that I had said my say about Italy, and the idea of attempting a novel of contemporary life in New York began to fascinate me. Still I hesitated. *The Valley of Decision* was not (in my sense of the term) a novel at all, but only a romantic chronicle, unrolling its episodes like the frescoed legends on the palace walls of its background; my idea of a novel was something very different, something far more compact and centripetal, and I doubted whether I should ever acquire enough constructive power to achieve anything beyond isolated character studies, or the stringing together of picturesque episodes. But my mind was full of my new subject, and, whatever else I was about, I went on, in Tyndall's brooding phrase, trying to "look into it till it became luminous."

Fate had planted me in New York, and it was always my instinct as a story-teller to use the material nearest to hand, and most familiarly my own. Novelists of my generation must have noticed, in recent years, as one of the unforeseen results of "crowd-mentality" and the general habit of standardizing, that the modern critic requires every novelist to treat the same kind of subject, and relegates to insignificance the author who declines to conform. At present the demand is that only the man with the dinner pail shall be deemed worthy of attention, and fiction is classed according to its degree of conformity to this rule.

There could be no greater critical ineptitude than to judge a novel according to *what it ought to have been about*. The bigger the imagination, the more powerful the intellectual equipment, the more different subjects will come within the novelist's reach; and Balzac spread his net over nearly every class and situation in the French social system. As a matter of fact, there are only two essential rules: one, that the novelist should deal only with what is within his reach, literally or figuratively (in most cases the two are synonymous), and the other that the value of a subject depends almost wholly on what the author sees in it, and how deeply he is able to see into it. Almost—but not quite; for there are certain subjects too shallow to yield anything to the most searching gaze. I had always felt this, and now my problem was how to make use of a subject—fashionable New York—which, of all others, seemed most completely to fall within the condemned category. There it was before me, in all its flatness and futility, asking to be dealt with as the theme most available to my hand, since I had been steeped in it from infancy, and should not have to get it up out of notebooks and encyclopædias—and yet!

The problem, of course, was how to extract from such a subject the typical human significance which is the story-teller's excuse for telling one story rather than another. In what aspect could a society of irresponsible pleasure seekers be said to have, on the "old woe of the world," any deeper bearing than the people composing such a society could guess? The answer to my musings was that a frivolous society can acquire dramatic significance only through what its frivolity destroys. Its tragic implication lies in its power of debasing people and ideals. The answer, in short, was my heroine, Lily Bart.

Once I had understood that, the tale rushed on toward its climax. I already had definite ideas as to how any given subject should be viewed, and from what angle approached; my trouble was that the story kept drawing into its web so many subordinate themes that to show their organic connection with the main issue, yet keep them from crowding to the front, was a staggering task for a beginner.

V

The novel was already promised to *Scribner's Magazine*, but no date had been fixed for its delivery, and between my critical dissatisfaction with the work, and the distractions of a busy and hospitable life, full of friends and travel, reading and gardening, I had let the months drift by without really tackling my subject. And then, suddenly, my friend Mr. Burlingame, then the editor of *Scribner's*, came to my rescue by asking me to come to his. It was found that a novel which was to have preceded mine would not be ready in time, and I was asked to replace it. The first chapters of my tale would have to appear almost at once, and it must be completed within four or five months! I have always been a slow worker, and was then a very inexperienced one, and I was to be put to the severest test to which a novelist can be subjected: my novel was to appear in print, and be exposed to public comment, before I had worked it out to its climax. What that climax was to be I had known before I began; nor have I ever understood the mental state of the novelist who starts out without knowing where or how he will end. To me the last page is always latent in the first, but the intervening windings of the way become clear only as I write; and now I was asked to gallop over them before I had even traced them out! I had expected to take at least another year or eighteen months to complete my tale, instead of which I was asked to have it ready within six months, and nothing short of "the hand of God" must be suffered to interrupt my labors, since my first chapters would already be in print!

I hesitated for a day, and then accepted, and buckled down to my task; and I can only say that, of all the friendly turns that Mr. Burlingame ever did me, his exacting this effort was the most helpful. Not only did it give me what I most lacked,— self-confidence,—but it bent me to the discipline of the daily task, that inscrutable "inspiration of the writing table" which Baudelaire, most wayward and nerve-racked of geniuses, proclaimed as insistently as Trollope. When the first chapters began to appear, I had written hardly fifty thousand words; but I kept at it, and finished and delivered my novel at the date appointed.

To be turned from a drifting amateur into a professional was a great advance; but it was as nothing compared to the effect on my imagination of a systematic daily effort. I was really like the servant who went out to find an ass, and came back with a kingdom—the kingdom of mastery over my tools. I remember saying to myself, when the book was done: "I don't yet know how to write a novel; *but I know how to find out how to*."

From that day I went on trying systematically to exercise this faculty of "finding out how to"; but I wrote two or three novels without feeling that I had made much progress. It was not until I wrote *Ethan Frome* that I suddenly felt in full control of my *métier*, as an artisan should be of his tools. I mention this because, when *Ethan Frome* first appeared, I was severely criticized by the reviewers for what was considered the clumsy structure of the tale. I had pondered long on this structure, had felt its peculiar difficulties, and possible awkwardness, but could think of no alternative which would serve as well in the given case; and though I am far from thinking *Ethan Frome* my best novel, and am bored and even exasperated when I am told that it is, I am still sure that its structure is not its weak point.

From that day until now I have always felt that I had my material fairly well in hand, though so often, alas, I am conscious that the strange beings who have commissioned me to tell their story are not satisfied with the portraits I have drawn of them. I think it was Sargent who said that, when a portrait was submitted to the sitter's family, the comment of the latter was always: "There's something wrong about the mouth."

It is the same with my sitters; though they are free to talk and even to behave in their own way, the image of them reflected in my pages is often, I fear, wavering, or at least blurred. "There is something wrong about the mouth"—and the great masters of portraiture, Balzac, Tolstoy, Thackeray, Trollope, have neglected to tell us how they not only "caught the likeness," but carried it on, in all its flesh-and-blood actuality and changefulness, to the very last page.

VI

All novelists who describe (whether from without or within) what is called "society life" are pursued by the idiotic accusation of putting "real people" (that is, persons actually known to the author) into their books. Anyone gifted with the least creative faculty knows how utterly beside the mark such an accusation is. "Real people" transported into a work of the imagination would instantly cease to be real; only those born of the creator's brain can give the least illusion of reality. But it is hopeless to persuade the unimaginative—who make up the bulk of novel readers—that to introduce real people into a novel would be exactly like gumming their snapshots into the vibrating human throng in a Guardi picture. If one did, they would be the only dead and unreal objects in a scene quivering with life. The low order, in fiction, of the genuine *roman à clef* (which is never written by a born novelist) naturally makes any serious writer of fiction indignant at being suspected of such methods. Nothing can be more exasperating to the creative writer than to have a clumsy finger point at one of the beings born in that mysterious other-world of invention, with the arch accusation, "Of course we all recognize your Aunt Eliza!" or to be told (and this has more than once happened to me), "We all thought your heroine must be meant for Mrs. X, *because their hair is exactly the same color.*"

Of what, then, are the mysterious creatures compounded who come to life (sometimes) under the novelist's pen? Well, it would be insincere to deny that there are bits of Aunt Eliza in this one, of Mrs. X in that—though in the case of Mrs. X it is hardly likely that the psychological novelist would use the color of her hair as a mark of identity, and more than probable that the bits of Mrs. X which have actually served him are embedded in some personage where the reader alive only to outward signs would never think of seeking them. The process is, in fact, inexplicable enough to the author, and doubly so to his readers. No "character" can be made out of nothing, still less can it be successfully pieced together out of heterogeneous scraps of the "real," like dismembered statues of which the fragments have been hopelessly mixed up by the restorer.

The process is more like that by which sham Tanagra statuettes used, I am told, to be manufactured for the unsuspecting collector. The experts having discovered that ancient terra cotta acquires, through long burial, a peculiar flavor, were in the habit of testing the genuineness of the piece

by *tasting it;* and the forgers, discovering this, ground fragments of old Tanagras into powder, ran the powder into one
of the old moulds, and fearlessly presented the result as an
antique. Experience, observation, the looks and ways and
words of "real people," all melted and fused in the white heat
of the creative fires—such is the mingled stuff which the novelist pours into the firm mould of his narrative. And yet it
must be owned that this does not wholly solve the problem
either; in reality, it is only a step or two nearer the truth than
the exasperating attributions of the simple-minded. . . .

These attributions are exasperating, no doubt; but they
are less so because of the accidental annoyance that may result
in a given case than because they bring home to the creator,
each time with a fresh shock, the general lack of imaginative
response to his effort. It is discouraging to know that the
books into the making of which so much of one's soul has
entered will be snatched at by readers curious only to discover
which of the heroes and heroines of the "society column" are
to be found in it. But I long ago made up my mind that it is
foolish and illogical to resent even such a puerile form of
criticism. If one has sought the publicity of print, and sold
one's wares in the open market, one has sold to the purchasers
of one's books the right to think what they choose about them;
and the novelist's best safeguard is to try to put out of his
mind the quality of the praise or blame likely to be meted
out to him by reviewers and readers, and to write only for
that dispassionate and ironic critic who dwells within the
breast.

Appendix

BIOGRAPHICAL NOTES

JAMES TRUSLOW ADAMS (page 1) has been for many years a student of American history. In 1921 he won the Pulitzer Prize in History with his *Founding of New England*. His *Hamiltonian Principles* (1928) and *Jeffersonian Principles* (1929) are of especial value to those interested in government. It was his *Epic of America* (1931), however, that made him almost overnight into a best-seller. His *March of Democracy* in two volumes appeared in 1932–1933. His most recent work is *America's Tragedy* (1934), which many critics believe is his best. His one collection of essays, most of which had previous magazine publication, is *Tempo of Modern Life* (1931).

WALTER BARNES (page 16), professor of English in New York University, is a distinguished teacher of English. He has written extensively in his chosen field—especially on the subject of the teaching of English in the elementary and secondary schools. His *New Democracy in the Teaching of English* (1923) attracted national attention.

CHARLES A. BEARD (page 22), for many years professor of political science in Columbia University, is an authority in his chosen field of American government and politics. Among his better known books are *American City Government* (1912), *Economic Interpretation of the Constitution* (1913), *Economic Interpretation of Jeffersonian Democracy* (1915). His *Rise of American Civilization* (written in collaboration with his wife Mary Beard, and published in two volumes in 1927) is undoubtedly his best known work. His volumes of essays are *Whither Mankind* (1928), *Towards Civilization* (1930), *America Faces the Future* (1932), and *A Century of Progress* (1933).

WILLIAM BEEBE (page 39) has been Curator of Ornithology of the New York Zoological Society since 1899. He is particularly well known for his investigations into the living creatures of the deep sea. Besides his many books and monographs on birds, the best known of which are probably *Pheasants—Their Lives and Homes* (1926) and *Pheasant Jungles* (1927), he has written such volumes of nature essays as *Jungle Peace* (1918), *Edge of the Jungle* (1921), and *Jungle Days* (1925). His study of the weird animal life of the Galapagos Islands, in *Galapagos, World's End* (1923), reached a large general reading public.

ROBERT C. BENCHLEY (page 55) was for many years dramatic critic of *Life*. More recently he has been on the staff of the *New Yorker*. For two years he played in the company of the Music Box Revue. Lured to Hollywood, he made a series of short subjects for the films, the most famous of which was his deservedly popular "Treasurer's Report." His volumes of essays, which usually appear first in magazine form, would fill a good-sized shelf. Among his better known collections are *Of All Things* (1921), *Love Conquers All* (1922), *Pluck and Luck* (1925), *The Early Worm* (1927), *Twenty Thousand Leagues under the Sea, or David Copperfield* (1928), *The Treasurer's Report* (1930), and *No Poems, or Around the World Backwards and Sideways* (1932), and his latest, *From Bed to Worse, or Comforting Thoughts about the Bison* (1934).

RALPH BERGENGREN (page 60) has served in various capacities on the staffs of newspapers and magazines of New England. He has written verse, fiction, editorials, reviews, and articles; but his best known writing is in the field of the familiar essay. Among his volumes of collected essays are *The Comforts of Home* (1918), *The Perfect Gentleman* (1919), *The Seven Ages of Man* (1922), and *Gentlemen All and Merry Companions* (1922).

GEORGE BOAS (page 67) has been, for a number of years, professor of philosophy in Johns Hopkins University. He has written extensively in his chosen field of philosophy. Among his better known books are *French Philosophies of the Romantic Period* (1925), *Never Go Back* (1928), *The Major Traditions of European Philosophy* (1928), *Our New Ways of Thinking* (1930), and *Philosophy and Poetry* (1933). His articles will be found in the current magazines— especially *Harper's*.

MARY BORDEN (page 79), born in Chicago, Illinois, is now the wife of Brigadier-General E. L. Speare, of the British Army and lives in England. She contributes articles frequently to the current magazines—especially on aspects of the subject of English-American relations. Among her books are *Three Pilgrims and a Tinker* (1924), *The Romantic Woman* (1925), *Jericho Sands* (1925), *Four O'Clock* (1926), *Flamingo* (1927), *Jehovah's Day* (1928), *The Forbidden Zone* (1929), *A Woman with White Eyes* (1930), and *Sarah Gay* (1931).

ERNEST BOYD (page 89) was born in Dublin, Ireland. After serving on the staff of the *Irish Times*, he entered the English consular service, at one time being stationed in Baltimore, Maryland. He resigned his position and came to New York, where he joined the editorial staff of the New York *Times*. He is now living in New York City, doing free-lance writing. Among his writings are many books on the theater, the best known being *The Contemporary Drama of Ireland*. Other titles are *Ireland's Literary Renaissance* (1922), *Portraits—Real and Imaginary* (1924), *Studies in Ten Literatures* (1925), *Guy de Maupassant—a Biographical Study* (1926). His definitive translations of the works of De Maupassant, published over a period of several years, have been accepted as the standard translations of the great French writer of fiction.

VAN WYCK BROOKS (page 100), after a career first as a teacher of English and then as a publisher, settled down to the life of the writer. He has interested himself especially in literary criticism. Among his best known books are *America's Coming-of-Age* (1915), *Letters and Leadership* (1918), *The Ordeal of Mark Twain* (1920—revised in 1932), *The Pilgrimage of Henry James* (1925), *Emerson and Others* (1927), *The Life of Emerson* (1932), and *Essays in Criticism* (1932). His *Ordeal of Mark Twain* aroused a great deal of discussion, much of which found its way into the current magazines and into a number of books. The most effective refutation of Brooks' position will be found in Bernard De Voto's *Mark Twain's America* (see page 157).

EARNEST ELMO CALKINS (page 104) until his retirement in 1931 headed the great advertising firm of Calkins and Holden of

New York City. He has written and lectured extensively on the art of printing as well as on the subject of his principal interest—advertising. In 1924 he published an autobiography under the title of *Louder, Please* (the significance of which lies in the author's deafness), a book that made a very wide appeal. His most noteworthy collection of essays on timely subjects is *Business the Civilizer* (1927). In 1925 he was awarded the Edward Bok gold medal for distinguished service in advertising.

STUART CHASE (page 120) after serving the United States Government as a special investigator allied himself with the Labor Bureau, of New York City. He contributes articles frequently to the current magazines in which he sets forth the problems and point of view of labor. His best known books are *The Tragedy of Waste* (1925), *Your Money's Worth* (written in collaboration with F. J. Schlink), *Men and Machines* (1929), *Prosperity—Fact or Fiction* (1930), and *The Nemesis of American Business* (1931). *His Mexico—A Study of Two Americas* (written in collaboration with Marian Tyler, his wife, and published in 1932) has been widely read.

GILBERT K. CHESTERTON (page 137), an English writer, is distinguished as a poet, a writer of fiction, and an essayist. He is a student of Chaucer and Dickens and has written authoritative books on both—notably *Dickens* (1906) and *Chaucer* (1932). His greatest fictional creation is the detective Father Brown, who appears in such volumes of detective stories as *The Innocence of Father Brown* (1911), *The Wisdom of Father Brown* (1914), *The Incredulities of Father Brown* (1926), and *The Secrets of Father Brown* (1927). Among his other fictions are *The Man Who Knew Too Much* (1925), *Tales of the Long Bow* (1925), and *The Four Faultless Felons* (1930). His volumes of collected essays are *Generally Speaking* (1928), *The Poet and the Lunatics* (1929), *Come to Think of It* (1930), and *All I Survey* (1932).

ROBERT P. TRISTRAM COFFIN (page 141) after serving a number of years as professor of English in Wells College has now returned to the English faculty of his alma mater, Bowdoin College. He has written many volumes of verse, biography, and essays. *The Book of Crowns and Cottages* (1925) and *An Attic Room* (1929) represent him at his best in the essay. His most recent volume, *Lost Paradise* (1934), is the story of a boyhood on a Maine seacoast farm—the home of the man described in his earlier *Portrait of an American* (1931).

WILBUR L. CROSS (page 146) has had a distinguished career both as an educator and as a statesman. For many years he served as professor of English and dean of the graduate school in Yale University. He founded—and has edited since its founding—the *Yale Review*, one of the foremost quarterlies in the English language. In 1899 he published a book, *The Development of the English Novel*, which is still reckoned a standard work for the period it covers. With his *Life and Times of Lawrence Sterne* (1909, revised edition 1923) and his *History of Henry Fielding* (1918) he established himself as one of the leading authorities on English fiction of the eighteenth century. That he maintains a genuine interest in contemporary literature is evidenced by his *The Modern English Novel* (1929) and *Four Contemporary Novelists* (1930). He is editor-in-chief of the *Yale Shakespeare*. In 1931 he was elected governor of Connecticut and is now serving his second term.

BERNARD A. DE VOTO (page 157) grew up in Utah, his birthplace. After serving in the army during the World War and completing his graduate work at Harvard on his return to the United States, he joined the English faculty of Northwestern University. In 1927 he resigned his position in order to give all his time to writing. His novels are *The Crooked Mile* (1924), *The Chariot of Fire* (1926), *The House of Sun-Goes-Down* (1928), and *We Accept with Pleasure* (1934). His essays, usually of a historical interest, will be found in the current magazines. His *Mark Twain's America* (1932), written as a refutation of Van Wyck Brooks' *Ordeal of Mark Twain* (see page 100), started a literary controversy that has not even yet subsided.

FELIX FRANKFURTER (page 175) has been, since 1914, professor of law in Harvard University. In 1933–1934 he was visiting professor at Oxford University, England. Many times the American Government has called him into its legal service. In 1932 he declined an offer of appointment to the Supreme Court of Massachusetts, preferring to continue his teaching at Harvard. He has written extensively in the field of law. His examination of the case of Sacco and Vanzetti resulted in a book, *The Case of Sacco and Vanzetti* (1927), that has become one of the important documents in that celebrated case. His best known, and most popular, book is *The Public and Its Government* (1930), a collection of papers that had previous magazine publication.

CLAUDE M. FUESS (page 196), honored by Amherst, Columbia, and Dartmouth with their doctor of literature degrees, has achieved fame as an educator in the field of secondary education. Since 1933 he has been headmaster of Phillips Academy at Andover, Massachusetts. He has written many books of local New England interest. It is in the field of biography, however, in which he has become a writer of national significance. In 1927 appeared his *Rufus Choate*. His *Daniel Webster* (1930) is probably his greatest work—certainly his most popular. His biography of Carl Schurz appeared in 1932.

EDGAR J. GOODSPEED (page 216) has been for many years professor of Biblical and Patristic Greek in the University of Chicago. He has written many scholarly works in the field of New Testament Greek. One of his books, *The Story of the New Testament* (1916), has been translated into many languages. But his life work has been the translation of the New Testament into the idiom of present-day English. His *New Testament—an American Translation* appeared in 1923. Since that time it has gone into many editions. In 1925 appeared his *The Making of the English New Testament*. But Dr. Goodspeed's avocation has been writing essays of the familiar type. His best known volumes are *Things Seen and Unseen* (1925) and *Buying Happiness* (1932).

GEORGE ELLERY HALE (page 224) is one of the most famous living astronomers. He was the organizer and director of the great Yerkes Observatory. Later he became the organizer and first director of the Mount Wilson Observatory of the Carnegie Institution of Washington, D. C. Naturally, most of his writings are in his chosen field of astronomy. Among them are *The Study of Stellar Evolution, Ten Years Work of a Mountain Observatory, The New Heavens, The Depths of the Universe, Beyond the Milky Way,* and *Signals from the Stars*. But he finds time to write an occasional article for the current magazines.

ALAN PATRICK HERBERT (page 239) is an English writer of fiction, light verse, and familiar essays. He has been, for a number of years, one of the most valuable members of the staff of *Punch*, the great English humorist magazine. His novel, *The Secret Battle*, is one of the finest fictions that came out of the World War. His most recent success is *Water Gypsies*. His *Old Flame* is a novel in the best tradition of the light fiction. Some of his best light verse will be found in such volumes as *Laughing Ann, She Shanties*, and *Ballads for Broadbrows*. Two volumes of his essays are *The Man about Town* and *Topsy*.

ROBERT HERRICK (page 243), for many years a professor of English in the University of Chicago, is best known for his novels of contemporary American life. Such stories as *The Common Lot* (1904), *Together* (1908), *A Life for a Life* (1910), *The Healer* (1911), *One Woman's Life* (1913), *Clark's Field* (1914), *Waste* (1924), *Chimes* (1926), *The End of Desire* (1931), and *Sometimes* (1933) cover life in America for the first third of the Twentieth Century. His *Master of the Inn* (1908), a long short story or novelette, has become virtually a classic.

WALTER S. HINCHMAN (page 254) taught English for a number of years in the Groton School, a famous private school for boys in Massachusetts. Later he became professor of English in Haverford College. But the lure of work in the field of secondary education was too strong. So he resigned his college position in order to become headmaster of Milton Academy, another famous private school in Massachusetts, where he is located at the present time. He has written and edited many books in the field of American and English literature. His *History of English Literature* is one of the very best one-volume manuals to be had. For many years he conducted a column in the *Forum*, which he signed "The Pedestrian." These contributions to the *Forum* he collected into a volume, *Pedestrian Papers*, in 1928.

ALDOUS LEONARD HUXLEY (page 258) is an English writer. His gift for satire is evident in both his novels and his essays. *Point*

Counter Point is probably his best novel. *Brief Candles* (1930) is a collection of short stories. A recent satiric fiction, *This Brave New World* (1932) attracted much attention both in England and in this country. *On the Margin* (1923), and *Music at Night* (1931) are collections of essays.

JULIAN S. HUXLEY (page 270), a brother of Aldous Huxley, and a grandson of Thomas Huxley, is a noted English biologist. At one time he served as a professor of biology in Rice Institute, Texas. He is now on the faculty of King's College, London. His published volumes include *Essays of a Biologist* (1923), *Essays in Popular Science* (1926), and *What Dare I Think?* (1931).

HOWARD MUMFORD JONES (page 288) is professor of English in the University of Michigan. He has written extensively in the field of English and American literature. His articles in the current magazines show a happy faculty of correcting popular notions that he shows are false.

RONALD A. KNOX (page 302) is Catholic Chaplain at the University of Oxford, England. Among his published volumes of essays are *Essays in Satire* (1928), *On Getting There* (1929), *Caliban in Grub Street* (1930), and *Broadcast Minds* (1933).

JOSEPH WOOD KRUTCH (page 319), after spending several years teaching English, first in Columbia and later in the Brooklyn Polytechnic Institute, became dramatic critic of the *Nation*. His dramatic criticisms and articles, which appear regularly in the *Nation*, are unquestionably the ablest now being written in America. Among his more important books are *Comedy and Conscience After the Restoration* (1924), *The Modern Temper* (1929), *Five Masters* (1930), and *Experience and Art* (1932). His book on Poe— *Edgar Allan Poe—a Study in Genius* (1926) aroused a tremendous amount of controversy upon its publication.

JOHN LANGDON-DAVIES (page 329) is an English writer who lives most of his time in Spain. He has lectured extensively in America. His articles appear from time to time in the current magazines. Among his books are *Dancing Catalans, Inside the Atom,* and *Man and His Universe.*

HAROLD J. LASKI (page 346), an English writer, is professor of political science in the University of London. His articles, usually on subjects in his field of political science, appear frequently in the American magazines. His *Dangers of Obedience* is a collection of essays that show him at his best. Other volumes of his are *A Grammar of Politics* (1925), *Liberty in the Modern State* (1930), and *Democracy in a Crisis* (1933).

"GEOFFREY LAYMAN" (page 360) is an English writer and publicist who prefers to use this pseudonym for his articles that appear in the current magazines of England and America.

STEPHEN LEACOCK (page 380) is by profession a professor of political economy in McGill University, Montreal, Canada; but by avocation he is a humorist both as a lecturer and as a writer. His essays, usually in a light satirical vein, appear in the current magazines. Their popularity is so great that they are invariably gathered up later into a published volume. His *Nonsense Novels*, published years ago (1911), seems well on the road to becoming a classic. Among his more recent volumes are *Short Circuits* (1928), *The Iron Man and the Tin Woman* (1929), *Wet Wit and Dry Humor* (1931), and *Afternoons in Utopia* (1932).

JAMES WEBER LINN (page 383) has the reputation of being one of the most popular and most effective teachers of English composition in the whole country. He has been for many years professor of English in the University of Chicago. He is also on the staff of the Chicago *Daily News* as a special writer. He has written two novels—*The Second Generation* and *The Cameleon*—and a number of textbooks in English.

EDWARD V. LUCAS (page 398) is an English writer and publisher. For a number of years he was on the staff of the *London Globe*, later on that of *Punch*. He is editor of a notable edition of the works of Charles and Mary Lamb. He is now Chairman of the Board of the great English publishing firm of Methuen and Company. His volume of reminiscences—*Reading, Writing, and Remembering* (1932)—is of special value to anyone interested in writing. Among his published volumes are *Encounters and Diversions* (1924), *The*

Joy of Life (1927), *Out of a Clear Sky* (1928), *Turning Things Over* (1929), *Lemon Verbena* (1932), *English Leaves* (1933), and *Postbag Diversions* (1933).

ROBERT LYND (page 402) was born and educated in Ireland. For a number of years he has been on the staff of the *London News Chronicle*. Some of his earlier books deal with Ireland—*Irish and English: Portraits and Impressions* (1908), *Home Life in Ireland* (1909), and *Rambles in Ireland* (1912). His volumes of essays include *Blue Lion* (1923), *Peals of Bells* (1924), *Money-Box* (1925), *Orange Tie* (1926), *It's a Fine World* (1930), and *Cockle Shell* (1933).

ANDRE MAUROIS (page 419) is a distinguished French biographer, who has not only written biographies but has made a study of the theory of biography writing. Among his more famous biographies are *Ariel*, a life of the poet Shelley (1923), *Disraeli* (1927), *Byron* (1930), and *King Edward and His Times* (1933). His theory of biography he explained in a series of lectures delivered at Cambridge University (later brought together in the volume *Aspects of Modern Biography*). Like the other two great modern biographers—Lytton Strachey, the Englishman, and Gamaliel Bradford, the American—he is interested in the very important question of whether biography is to be regarded as a science or an art. One novel of his has been translated into English — *Weigher of Souls* (1931). *A Private Universe* (1932) is his one collection of essays available in English.

L. WARDLAW MILES (page 437) is professor of English in Johns Hopkins University. His essays, which appear in the current magazines from time to time, have been collected into the volume *The Tender Realist and Other Essays* (1910).

MEREDITH NICHOLSON (page 451) is the author of a long list of "best-selling" novels, among which are *The House of the Thousand Candles* (1905), *The Port of Missing Men* (1907), *The Little Brown Jug at Kildare* (1908), *The Lords of High Decision* (1909), and *Otherwise Phyllis* (1913). Among his collections of essays are *The Provincial American* (1913), *The Valley of Democracy* (1918), and *Old Familiar Faces* (1929). Two very famous papers of his are "Should Smith Go to Church?" and "Confessions of a Best Seller," both of which will be found included in the volume *The Provincial American*. Mr. Nicholson is now the American minister to Venezuela.

ALBERT JAY NOCK (page 464) is visiting professor of American history and politics in St. Stephens College (Columbia University). He writes extensively in the current magazines on topics of present-day interest. His principal volumes are *On Doing the Right Thing* (1926), a collection of essays, and several books on a favorite subject of his—François Rabelais, the great French writer of the sixteenth century.

JOHNSON O'CONNOR (page 480) is a psychologist who is greatly interested in what is sometimes called "personnel work." He has been retained at one time or another by many of the great industrial corporations of this country to help them in their relations with their employees. He organized the Human Engineering Laboratory of the General Electric Company. Later he organized a similar laboratory for Stevens Institute of Technology. Since 1931 he has been on the faculty of the Massachusetts Institute of Technology.

WILLIAM LYON PHELPS (page 492) is probably the best known teacher of English in this country. For many years was professor of English at Yale University, known familiarly on the Yale campus as "Billy" Phelps. Upon his retirement from active teaching last June he received from Yale University its highest honorary degree of doctor of literature. For a number of years he has conducted a column in *Scribner's Magazine* known as "As I Like It." The great popularity of this column has resulted in several volumes made up of "As I Like It" material. *Essays on Things*, following a long sequence of volumes of *Essays on Modern Novelists*, *Essays on Modern Dramatists*, *Essays on Books*, etc., appeared in 1930.

J. B. PRIESTLY (page 495) is an English writer who attracted much attention several years ago with two very successful novels— *Good Companions* (1929) and *Angel Pavement* (1931). His play, *Dangerous Corner*, was a stage success in 1932. He is the author of the study of George Meredith in the English Men of Letters series. His *English Novel* appeared in 1927 and his *English Humor* in 1928.

In 1932 he made his own selection of his own essays and published them under the title of *Self-Selected Essays*.

BERTRAND RUSSELL (page 499), third Earl Russell, is a distinguished English writer and publicist. For a number of years he was a lecturer in mathematical philosophy in one of the English universities. His interest in this subject is evident in many of his earlier books—*Philosophy of Mathematics, Introduction to Mathematical Philosophy* (1919), *On Education* (1926), *An Outline of Philosophy* (1927). His *Marriage and Morals*, which appeared in 1929, stirred up a tremendous amount of discussion that has not yet subsided. Other works of his are *Conquest of Happiness* (1930), *Scientific Outlook* (1931), and *Education and the Social Order* (1932).

F. A. SPENCER (page 513) is professor of classics in New York University. His forthcoming book, *Beyond Damascus*, is a biography of Paul.

VINCENT STARRETT (page 534), after several years of newspaper experience, turned to a career as a writer. He has many volumes to his credit—novels, biographies, literary studies, and essays. He has been especially interested in Robert Louis Stevenson. His *Private Life of Sherlock Holmes* (1933) added his name to the growing list of those who have fallen under the spell of Conan Doyle's great creation. (A most remarkable thing is the large number of articles and books that have appeared in the last two or three years having to do with Sherlock Holmes.)

CHAUNCEY BREWSTER TINKER (page 546), a professor of English at Yale University, is a recognized authority on Dr. Samuel Johnson and his biographer James Boswell. He is the author of *Dr. Johnson and Fanny Burney* (1911), *The Salon and English Letters* (1915), *Young Boswell* (1922), and *The Good Estate of Poetry* (1929).

FRANK H. VIZETELLY (page 557), a great lexicographer, has been editor of the Standard Dictionary for many years. He has become greatly interested in the subject of spoken English of the radio and has been retained by a number of the large broadcasting companies as an expert consultant in the matter of pronunciation. He is the author of a long list of books in the field of spoken and written English, the most recent of which are *How to Use English* (1932), *How to Speak English Effectively* (1933), and *Our Color-Box of Speech* (1933). His *Conjunctions—Their Use and Abuse* (1924) and *Prepositions—How to Use Them* (1924) are standard works of reference.

FRANCES LESTER WARNER (page 569) (Mrs. Mayo D. Hersey) is one of America's best known writers of the familiar essay. After teaching English for a number of years in various secondary schools she became assistant professor of English in Mt. Holyoke College, later associate professor of English in Wellesley College. For two years she was assistant to the editor of the *Atlantic Monthly*. Her best known volumes of essays are *Endicott and I* (1919), *Life's Minor Collisions* (written in collaboration with her sister Gertrude Chandler Warner, 1921), *Groups and Couples* (1923), *Surprising the Family* (1926), *The Unintentional Charm of Men* (1928), *To People We Like* (1929), and *Pleasures and Palaces* (with Gertrude Chandler Warner, 1933).

JOHN P. WATERS (page 583) is a "reformed humorist now writing advertising and publicity." He has contributed to *Life, Judge,* and the *Saturday Evening Post.*

MRS. EDITH WHARTON (page 589) is one of America's most distinguished novelists. She has received many honors here and abroad—the Litt. D. degree from Yale University, election as officer of the Legion of Honor of France and as Chevalier of the Order of Leopold of France. Her novel, *The House of Mirth* (1905), has become a classic. Her *Writing of Fiction* (1925) is a valuable volume for anyone interested in creative writing. Her mastery of the short story is evidenced in such volumes as *Crucial Instances* (1901), *The Greater Inclination* (1899), and *Xingu* (1916). Her *Ethan Frome* (1911), a novelette or long short story, is generally regarded as one of the finest fictions in American literature. Her autobiographical volume, *A Backward Glance*, appeared in 1934.

NAMES AND ADDRESSES OF PUBLISHERS REFERRED TO IN THE "VOLUMES OF ESSAYS"

D. Appleton Century Company, 35 West 32nd Street, New York.
Bobbs-Merrill Company, Indianapolis, Indiana.
Albert & Charles Boni, 66 Fifth Avenue, New York.
Columbia University Press, 2960 Broadway, New York.
Covici-Friede, Inc., 386 Fourth Avenue, New York.
Coward-McCann Company, 425 Fourth Avenue, New York.
T. Y. Crowell Company, 393 Fourth Avenue, New York.
Dial Press, 152 West 13th Street, New York.
Dodd, Mead and Company, 4th Avenue & 30th Street, New York.
Doubleday, Doran and Company, Garden City, New York.
E. P. Dutton and Company, 300 Fourth Avenue, New York.
Greenberg, Publisher, 160 Fifth Avenue, New York.
Harper & Brothers, 49 East 33rd Street, New York.
Harrison Smith & Robert Haas, 17 East 49th Street, New York.
Harvard University Press, Cambridge, Massachusetts.
Henry Holt and Company, 1 Park Avenue, New York.
Houghton Mifflin Company, 2 Park Street, Boston, Massachusetts.
Alfred A. Knopf, 730 Fifth Avenue, New York.
J. B. Lippincott Company, Philadelphia, Pennsylvania.
Little, Brown and Company, 34 Beacon Street, Boston, Massachusetts.
Liveright Publishing Corporation, 386 Fourth Avenue, New York.
Longmans, Green and Company, 114 Fifth Avenue, New York.
Robert M. McBride Company, 7 West 16th Street, New York.
The Macmillan Company, 60 Fifth Avenue, New York.
Minton, Balch & Company, 2 West 45th Street, New York.
New Republic, 40 East 49th Street, New York City.
W. W. Norton Company, 70 Fifth Avenue, New York.
Oxford University Press, 114 Fifth Avenue, New York.
Princeton University Press, Princeton, New Jersey.
G. P. Putnam's Sons, 2 West 45th Street, New York.
Charles Scribner's Sons, 5th Avenue & 48th Street, New York.
Sears Publishing Company, 114 East 32nd Street, New York.
Simon & Schuster, 386 Fourth Avenue, New York.
Stanford University Press, Stanford, California.
University of Chicago Press, 5760 Ellis Street, Chicago, Illinois.

University of Minnesota Press, Minneapolis, Minnesota.
University of North Carolina Press, Chapel Hill, North Carolina.
University of Pennsylvania Press, Philadelphia, Pennsylvania.
Vanguard Press, 100 Fifth Avenue, New York.
Viking Press, 18 East 48th Street, New York.
Yale University Press, New Haven, Connecticut.

VOLUMES OF ESSAYS[1]

ADAMS, JAMES TRUSLOW. *Tempo of Modern Life*. Boni, 1931.
ADDAMS, JANE. *Excellent Becomes the Permanent*. Macmillan, 1932.
ALDINGTON, RICHARD. *French Studies and Reviews*. Dial, 1926.
————. *Literary Studies and Reviews*. Dial, 1924.

BABBITT, IRVING. *Democracy and Leadership*. Houghton, 1924.
————. *On Being Creative, and Other Essays*. Houghton, 1932.
BARING, MAURICE. *Lost Lecture; or, The Fruits of Experience*. Knopf, 1932.
BEACH, JOSEPH WARREN. *Outlook for American Prose*. University of Chicago Press, 1926.
BEARD, CHARLES A. *America Faces the Future*. Houghton, 1932.
————. *Century of Progress*. Harper, 1933.
————. *Toward Civilization*. Longmans, 1930.
————. *Whither Mankind: a Panorama of Modern Civilization*. Longmans, 1928.
BELLOC, HILAIRE. *Conversation with a Cat, and Other Essays*. Harper, 1931.
————. *Conversation with an Angel, and Other Essays*. Harper, 1929.
————. *Short Talks with the Dead, and Other Essays*. Harper, 1926.
BENCHLEY, ROBERT. *Early Worm*. Holt, 1925.
————. *From Bed to Worse; or, Comforting Thoughts about the Bison*. Harper, 1934.
————. *No Poems; or, Around the World Backwards and Sideways*. Harper, 1932.
————. *Pluck and Luck*. Holt, 1925.
————. *Treasurer's Report*. Harper, 1930.
————. *Twenty Thousand Leagues under the Seas; or, David Copperfield*. Holt, 1928.
BENNETT, ARNOLD. *Savour of Life: Essays in Gusto*. Doubleday, 1928.
BENSON, A. C. *Rambles and Reflections*. Putnam, 1926.
BLACK, ALEXANDER. *American Husbands and Other Alternatives*. Bobbs, 1925.
BOLITHO, WILLIAM. *Twelve against the Gods; the Story of Adventure*. Simon, 1929.

[1] For a list of volumes of essays published previous to 1925 see *Essays by Present-Day Writers*, edited by R. W. Pence, Macmillan, 1924.

BOYD, ERNEST. *Literary Blasphemies*. Harper, 1927.
———. *Portraits: Real and Imaginary*. Doran, 1924.
———. *Studies from Ten Literatures*. Scribner, 1925.
BOYNTON, PERCY H. *More Contemporary Americans*. University of Chicago Press, 1927.
———. *Some Contemporary Americans*. University of Chicago Press, 1924.
BRADFORD, GAMALIEL. *As God Made Them; Portraits of Some Nineteenth-Century Americans*. Houghton, 1929.
———. *Bare Souls*. Harper, 1924.
———. *Biography and the Human Heart*. Houghton, 1932.
———. *Damaged Souls*. Houghton, 1923.
———. *Daughters of Eve*. Houghton, 1930.
———. *Naturalist of Souls; Studies in Psychography* (New Edition). Houghton, 1926.
———. *Portraits and Personalities*. Houghton, 1933.
———. *Quick and the Dead*. Houghton, 1931.
———. *Saints and Sinners*. Houghton, 1932.
———. *Wives*. Harper, 1925.
BRADLEY, A. C. *Miscellany*. Macmillan, 1929.
BRADLEY, GODFREY F. *The Brontës, and Other Essays*. Oxford, 1932.
BREWSTER, DOROTHY, and BURRELL, ANGUS. *Dead Reckonings in Fiction*. Columbia University Press, 1924.
———. *Modern Fiction*. Columbia University Press, 1934.
BRIGGS, LEBARON R. *Men, Women, and College*. Houghton, 1925.
BROOKS, CHARLES S. *Like Summer's Cloud*. Harcourt, 1925.
BROOKS, VAN WYCK. *Emerson and Others*. Dutton, 1927.
———. *Sketches in Criticism*. Dutton, 1932.
BROWN, CHARLES R. *They Were Giants*. Macmillan, 1934.
BROWN, ROLLO W. *Lonely Americans*. Coward, 1929.
BURT, MAXWELL S. *Other Side*. Scribner, 1928.
BUTLER, NICHOLAS M. *Between Two Worlds*. Scribner, 1934.

CALKINS, EARNEST ELMO. *Business the Civilizer*. Boni, 1927.
CALVERTON, V. F. *The Newer Spirit: A Sociological Criticism of Literature*. Liveright, 1925.
CANBY, HENRY S. *American Estimates*. Harcourt, 1929.
———. *Classic Americans*. Harcourt, 1931.
CARDOZO, BENJAMIN N. *Law and Literature and Other Essays and Addresses*. Harcourt, 1931.
CHASE, MARY ELLEN. *Golden Asse and Other Essays*. Holt, 1929.
CHASE, STUART. *Nemesis of American Business and Other Essays*. Macmillan, 1931.

CHESTERTON, GILBERT F. *Generally Speaking*. Dodd, 1928.
————. *Poet and Lunatics*. Dodd, 1929.
————. *Sidelights on New London and Newer New York and Other Essays*. Dodd, 1932.
CHESTERTON, GILBERT K. *All I Survey*. Dodd, 1933.
————. *All Is Grist*. Dodd, 1932.
————. *Come to Think of It*. Dodd, 1931.
COFFIN, ROBERT P. TRISTRAM. *Attic Room*. Doubleday, 1929.
COHEN, MORRIS R. *Law and the Social Order*. Harcourt, 1933.
COLLINS, NORMA. *Facts of Fiction*. Dutton, 1933.
CONRAD, JOSEPH. *Last Essays*. Doubleday, 1926.
CROSS, WILBUR L. *Four Contemporary Novelists*. Macmillan, 1930.
CROTHERS, SAMUEL M. *Thought Broker*. Houghton, 1928.

DE KRUIF, PAUL H. *Hunger Fighters*. Harcourt, 1928.
————. *Men against Death*. Harcourt, 1932.
————. *Microbe Hunters*. Harcourt, 1926.
DEMILLE, GEORGE E. *Literary Criticism in America: a Preliminary Survey*. Dial, 1931.
DE SELINCOURT, BASIL. *Towards Peace and Other Essays*. Oxford, 1932.
DEWEY, JOHN. *Character and Events*. Holt, 1929.
————. *Philosophy and Civilization*. Minton, 1931.
DOBREE, BONAMY. *Essays in Biography: 1680–1726*. Oxford, 1925.
————. *Lamp and the Lute*. Oxford, 1929.
————. *Variety of Ways*. Oxford, 1932.
DOUGLAS, NORMAN. *Experiments*. McBride, 1925.
DRINKWATER, JOHN. *Muse in Council*. Houghton, 1925.
————. *This Troubled World*. Columbia University Press, 1933.
DURANT, WILLIAM J. *Adventures in Genius*. Simon, 1931.

EASTMAN, MAX. *Literary Mind*. Scribner, 1931.
EDMAN, IRWIN. *Adam, the Baby, and the Man from Mars*. Houghton, 1929.
————. *Contemporary and His Soul*. Viking, 1931.
ELIOT, T. S. *Selected Essays, 1917–1932*. Harcourt, 1932.
————. *Use of Poetry and Use of Criticism*. Harvard University Press, 1933.
ELLIS, HAVELOCK. *More Essays of Love and Virtue*. Doubleday, 1931.
ERSKINE, JOHN. *Delight of Great Books*. Bobbs, 1928.

FIRKINS, OSCAR W. *Selected Essays*. University of Minnesota Press, 1933.
FOERSTER, NORMAN. *American Culture: a Study in Literary Theory from Poe to the Present*. Houghton, 1928.
FOSDICK, HARRY E. *Adventurous Religion and Other Essays*. Harper, 1926.

FRANKFURTER, FELIX. *The Public and Its Government.* Yale University Press, 1930.
FRAZER, SIR JAMES G. *Garnered Sheaves.* Macmillan, 1931.
——. *Gordon's Head.* Macmillan, 1927.

GALES, RICHARD L. *Dwellers in Arcady: Essays in Folk-Lore.* Macmillan, 1931.
GALSWORTHY, JOHN. *Candelabra: Selected Essays and Addresses.* Scribner, 1933.
——. *Castles in Spain and Other Screeds.* Scribner, 1927.
GARROD, HEATHCOTE W. *Poetry and the Criticism of Life.* Harvard University Press, 1931.
——. *Profession of Poetry and Other Lectures.* Oxford, 1929.
GOODSPEED, EDGAR J. *Buying Happiness, 1932.* University of Chicago Press, 1932.
——. *Strange New Gospels.* University of Chicago Press, 1931.
——. *Things Seen and Heard.* University of Chicago Press, 1925.
GRANDGENT, CHARLES H. *Getting a Laugh and Other Essays.* Harvard University Press, 1924.
——. *Prunes and Prisms: with Other Odds and Ends.* Harvard University Press, 1928.
——. *Imitation and Other Essays.* Harvard University Press, 1933.
GUEDALLA, PHILIP. *Bonnet and Shawl.* Putnam, 1928.
——. *Fathers of the Revolution.* Putnam, 1926.
——. *A Gallery.* Putnam, 1924.
——. *Masters and Men.* Putnam, 1923.
——. *Supers and Supermen.* Putnam, 1924.

HALDANE, JOHN B. *Possible Worlds and Other Papers.* Harper, 1928.
——. *Science and Human Life.* Harper, 1933.
HAMILTON, COSMO. *People Worth Talking About.* McBride, 1933.
HAMILTON, EDITH. *The Greek Way.* Norton, 1930.
——. *The Roman Way.* Norton, 1932.
HERBERT, A. P. *Man About Town.* Doubleday, 1928.
——. *Topsy.* Doubleday, 1932.
HERGESHEIMER, JOSEPH. *Swords and Roses.* Knopf, 1929.
HINCHMAN, WALTER. *Pedestrian Papers.* Houghton, 1928.
HODGSON, LEONARD. *Essays in Christian Philosophy.* Longmans, 1930.
HOLLIDAY, ROBERT C. *Literary Lanes and Other Byways.* Doubleday, 1925.
HOWE, M. A. DEWOLFE. *Causes and Their Champions.* Little, 1926.
——. *Classic Shades: Five Leaders of Learning and Their Colleges.* Little, 1928.

HUGHES, GLENN. *Imagism and the Imagists: A Study of Modern Poetry.* Stanford University Press, 1931.

HUXLEY, ALDOUS L. *Along the Road: Notes and Essays of a Tourist.* Doubleday, 1925.

———. *Do What You Will.* Doubleday, 1929.

———. *Music at Night and Other Essays.* Doubleday, 1931.

———. *On the Margin.* Doubleday, 1923.

———. *Proper Studies.* Doubleday, 1928.

HUXLEY, JULIAN S. *Essays in Popular Science.* Knopf, 1927.

———. *Essays of a Biologist.* Knopf, 1923.

———. *What Dare I Think?* Harper, 1931.

INGE, WILLIAM R. *Church in the World.* Longmans, 1927.

———. *Labels and Libels.* Harper, 1929.

———. *Lay Thoughts of a Dean.* Putnam, 1926.

———. *More Lay Thoughts of a Dean.* Putnam, 1932.

JACKS, L. P. *Living Universe.* Harper, 1924.

———. *Realities and Shams.* Harper, 1924.

———. *Responsibility and Culture.* Yale University Press, 1924.

JAFFE, BERNARD. *Crucibles: The Lives and Achievements of the Great Chemists.* Simon, 1930.

KNOX, RONALD A. *Caliban in Grub Street.* Dutton, 1930.

———. *Essays in Satire.* Dutton, 1928.

———. *On Getting There.* Dutton, 1929.

KEYNES, JOHN H. *Essays in Biography.* Harcourt, 1933.

———. *Essays in Persuasion.* Harcourt, 1932.

KRUTCH, JOSEPH W. *Experience and Art.* Smith, 1932.

———. *Five Masters.* Smith, 1930.

LASKI, HAROLD J. *Dangers of Obedience and Other Essays.* Harper, 1930.

———. *Studies in Law and Politics.* Yale University Press, 1932.

LAWRENCE, D. H. *Assorted Articles.* Knopf, 1930.

———. *Studies in Classic American Literature.* Viking, 1923.

LEACOCK, STEPHEN. *Afternoons in Utopia.* Dodd, 1932.

———. *Iron Man and Tin Woman.* Dodd, 1929.

———. *Short Circuits.* Dodd, 1928.

———. *Wet Wit and Dry Humor.* Dodd, 1931.

LESLIE, SHANE. *Studies in Sublime Failure.* Scribner, 1933.

LEWISOHN, LUDWIG. *Cities and Men.* Harper, 1927.

LIDDELL-HART, BASIL HENRY. *Great Captains Unveiled.* Little, 1928.

———. *Reputations Ten Years After.* Little, 1928.

LIPPMANN, WALTER. *Men of Destiny*. Macmillan, 1927.
LOWELL, ABBOTT LAWRENCE. *Conflicts of Principle*. Harvard University Press, 1932.
LOWELL, AMY. *Poetry and Poets*. Houghton, 1930.
LUCAS, E. V. *Lemon and Verbena, and Other Essays*. Lippincott, 1932.
——. *Turning Things Over; Essays and Fantasies*. Dutton, 1929.
——. *Visibility Good: Essays and Excursions*. Lippincott, 1931.
——. *Saunterer's Rewards*. Lippincott, 1934.
LUDWIG, EMIL. *Genius and Character*. Harcourt, 1927.
——. *Nine Etched from Life*. McBride, 1934.
LYND, ROBERT. *Blue Lion and Other Essays*. Doubleday, 1923.
——. *Money-Box*. Appleton, 1926.
——. *Peal of Bells*. Appleton, 1925.

MCFEE, WILLIAM. *Swallowing the Anchor*. Doubleday, 1925.
MACKAIL, WILLIAM. *Classical Studies*. Macmillan, 1925.
——. *Studies of English Poets*. Longmans, 1926.
MACKENNA, ROBERT W. *As Shadows Lengthen*. Dutton, 1933.
MACY, JOHN, Editor. *American Writers on American Literature*. Liveright, 1931.
MANN, THOMAS. *Past Masters and Other Papers*. Knopf, 1933.
MASSON, THOMAS. *Our American Humorists*. Dodd, 1931.
MAUROIS, ANDRE. *Private Universe*. Appleton, 1923.
MEIKLEJOHN, ALEXANDER. *Freedom and the College*. Appleton, 1923.
MENCKEN, H. L. *Selected Prejudices*. Knopf, 1927.
MILES, L. WARDLOW. *Tender Realist and Other Essays*. Holt, 1930.
MILLIKAN, ROBERT A. *Evolution in Science and Religion*. Yale University Press, 1927.
——. *Science and the New Civilization*. Scribner, 1930.
MILNE, A. A. *By Way of Introduction*. Dutton, 1929.
MINNIGERODE, MEADE. *Certain Rich Men*. Putnam, 1927.
——. *Lives and Times; Four Informal American Biographies*. Putnam, 1925.
——. *Some American Ladies; Seven Informal Biographies*. Putnam, 1926.
MONROE, HARRIET. *Poets and Their Art*. Macmillan, 1932.
MORDELL, ALBERT. *Notorious Literary Attacks*. Liveright, 1926.
MORE, PAUL ELMER. *Demon of the Absolute*. Princeton University Press, 1928.
MORLEY, CHRISTOPHER. *Essays*. Doubleday, 1928.
——. *Romany Stain*. Doubleday, 1926.
——. *Internal Revenue*. Doubleday, 1933.

MORLEY, FELIX. *Aspects of the Depression.* University of Chicago Press, 1932.
MUIR, EDWIN. *Latitudes.* Viking, 1924.
——. *Transition; Essays on Contemporary Literature.* Viking, 1926.
MUMFORD, LEWIS. *Brown Decades: a Study of the Arts in America, 1865–1895.* Harcourt, 1931.
MUNSON, GORHAM B. *Destinations: a Canvass of American Literature Since 1900.* Sears, 1928.
MURRY, JOHN MIDDLETON. *Countries of the Mind: Essays in Literary Criticism.* Oxford, 1931.
——. *Things to Come: Essays.* Macmillan, 1928.

NEWTON, A. EDWARD. *Greatest Book in the World and Other Papers.* Little, 1925.
——. *This Book-Collecting Game.* Little, 1928.
——. *End Papers.* Little, 1933.
——. *Derby Day and Other Papers.* Little, 1934.
NOCK, ALBERT JAY. *On Doing the Right Thing and Other Essays.* Harper, 1928.
NOYES, ALBERT. *New Essays and American Impressions.* Holt, 1927.

ORCUTT, WILLIAM D. *In Quest of the Perfect Book.* Little, 1926.
——. *Kingdom of Books.* Little, 1927.
——. *Magic of the Book.* Little, 1930.
OSLER, SIR WILLIAM. *Student Life and Other Essays.* Houghton, 1931.
OVERTON, GRANT. *American Nights Entertainment.* Appleton, 1923.
——. *Authors of the Day: Studies in Contemporary Literature.* Doubleday, 1924.
——. *Women Who Make Our Novels* (New Edition). Dodd, 1928.

PACH, WALTER. *Masters of Modern Art.* Viking, 1924.
PATTEE, FRED L. *Tradition and Jazz.* Appleton, 1925.
PEARSON, EDMUND LESTER. *Queer Books.* Doubleday, 1928.
PERRY, HENRY T. *Comic Spirit in Restoration Drama.* Yale University Press, 1925.
PHELPS, WILLIAM LYON. *Adventures and Confessions.* Scribner, 1926.
——. *As I Like It.* Scribner, 1923.
——. *Essays on Things.* Macmillan, 1930.
——. *Howells, James, Bryant and Other Essays.* Macmillan, 1924.
PRIESTLEY, J. B. *The Balconinny.* Harper, 1930.
——. *English Comic Characters.* Dodd, 1925.
——. *Figures in Modern Literature.* Dodd, 1924.
——. *I for One.* Dodd, 1923.

PRIESTLEY, J. B. *Open House: a Book of Essays.* Harper, 1927.
———. *Self-Selected Essays.* Harper, 1932.
———. *Too Many People and Other Reflections.* Harper, 1928.

QUILLER-COUCH, SIR ARTHUR T. *Charles Dickens, and Other Victorians.*
Putnam, 1925.
———. *Studies in Literature.* First, Second, and Third Series. Three
Volumes. Putnam, 1918–1930.

RALEIGH, SIR WALTER. *On Writing and Writers.* Longmans, 1926.
RASCOE, BURTON. *Titans of Literature, from Homer to the Present.*
Putnam, 1932.
———. *Prometheans: Ancient and Modern.* Putnam, 1933.
READ, HERBERT E. *Sense of Glory: Essays in Criticism.* Harcourt,
1930.
REILLY, JOSEPH J. *Dear Prue's Husband, and Other People.* Macmillan,
1932.
REPPLIER, AGNES. *Times and Tendencies.* Houghton, 1931.
———. *Under Dispute.* Houghton, 1924.
ROOSEVELT, FRANKLIN D. *Government—Not Politics.* Covici, 1932.
———. *Looking Forward.* Day, 1933.
ROSENFELD, PAUL. *By Way of Art.* Coward, 1928.
———. *Men Seen: Twenty-Four Modern Authors.* Dial, 1925.
———. *Port of New York: Essays on Fourteen American Moderns.*
Harcourt, 1924.
RUSSELL, BERTRAND A. *Mystic and Logic.* Norton, 1929.
———. *Sceptical Essays.* Norton, 1928.

SAINTSBURY, GEORGE. *Collected Essays and Papers, 1875–1923.* Four
Volumes. Dutton, 1923–1924.
———. *Prefaces and Essays.* Macmillan, 1933.
SANTAYANA, GEORGE. *Some Turns of Thought in Modern Philosophy.*
Scribner, 1933.
SEDGWICK, HENRY D. *Art of Happiness.* Bobbs, 1933.
SEITZ, DON. *The "Also Rans"; Great Men Who Missed Making the
Presidential Goal.* Crowell, 1928.
———. *Famous American Duels.* Crowell, 1929.
———. *Uncommon Americans: Pencil Portraits of Men and Women
Who Have Broken the Rules.* Bobbs, 1925.
SELDES, GILBERT V. *Seven Lively Arts.* Harper, 1924.
SHARP, DALLAS LORE. *Sanctuary! Sanctuary!* Harper, 1926.
SHEEN, FULTON J. *Moods and Truth.* Appleton, 1932.
———. *Old Errors and New Labels.* Appleton, 1931.

SHEPARD, ODELL. *Harvest of a Quiet Eye: A Book of Digressions*. Houghton, 1927.

——. *Joys of Forgetting: A Book of Bagatelles*. Houghton, 1929.

SHERMAN, STUART. *Critical Woodcuts*. Scribner, 1926.

——. *Emotional Discovery of America and Other Essays*. Farrar, 1932.

——. *Main Stream*. Scribner, 1927.

——. *Points of View*. Scribner, 1924.

SHOTWELL, WALTER G. *Driftwood: Being Papers on Oldtime American Towns and Some Old People*. Longmans, 1927.

SINGER, CHARLES J. *From Magic to Science: Essays on the Scientific Twilight*. Liveright, 1928.

SINGER, EDGAR A. *Fool's Advice*. Holt, 1925.

——. *Modern Thinkers and Present Problems*. Holt, 1923.

SITWELL, EDITH. *English Eccentrics*. Houghton, 1933.

SKINNER, OTIS. *Mad Folk of the Theatre*. Bobbs, 1928.

SLAUGHTER, MOSES S. *Roman Portraits*. Yale University Press, 1925.

SMITH, C. ALPHONSO. *Southern Literary Studies*. University of North Carolina Press, 1927.

SMITH, RUSSELL G. *Fugitive Papers*. Columbia University Press, 1930.

SPINGARN, JOEL B. *Creative Criticism and Other Essays* (New Edition). Harcourt, 1931.

STRACHEY, LYTTON. *Portraits in Miniature and Other Essays*. Harcourt, 1931.

——. *Characters and Commentaries*. Harcourt, 1933.

STRUNSKY, SIMEON. *Rediscovery of Jones: Studies in the Obvious*. Little, 1931.

SWIFT, EDGAR J. *Jungle of the Mind*. Scribner, 1931.

SWINNERTON, FRANK. *Authors and the Book Trade*. Knopf, 1932.

SYMONS, ARTHUR. *Studies in Seven Arts* (New Edition). Dutton, 1925.

TARKINGTON, BOOTH. *Looking Forward and Other Essays*. Doubleday, 1926.

THOMAS, CALVIN. *Scholarship and Other Essays*. Holt, 1924.

THOMPSON, ELBERT N. *Literary Bypaths of the Renaissance*. Yale University Press, 1924.

THOMSON, SIR JOHN ARTHUR. *Riddles of Science*. Liveright, 1932.

THORNDIKE, ASHLEY H. *Outlook for Literature*. Macmillan, 1931.

TINKER, CHAUNCEY B. *Good Estate of Poetry*. Little, 1929.

TOMLINSON, HENRY M. *Out of Soundings*. Harper, 1931.

TOWNSEND, REGINALD T. *This, That, and the Other Thing*. Doubleday, 1919.

TREVELYAN, GEORGE M. *Clio, a Muse, and Other Essays*. Longmans, 1930.

TURNER, FREDERICK J. *Significance of Sections in American History.* Holt, 1932.

UNAMUNO Y JUGO, MIGUEL DE. *Essays and Soliloquies.* Knopf, 1925.
UNTERMEYER, LOUIS. *American Poetry Since 1900.* Holt, 1923.
UTTER, ROBERT. *Pearls and Pepper.* Yale University Press, 1924.

VALERY, PAUL. *Variety.* Harcourt, 1927.
VAN DOREN, CARL. *Many Minds.* Knopf, 1924.
———. *Roving Critic.* Knopf, 1923.
VAN DYKE, HENRY. *Man Behind the Book; Essays in Understanding.* Scribner, 1929.
VAN VECHTEN, CARL. *Excavations: a Book of Advocacies.* Knopf, 1926.
———. *Sacred and Profane Memories.* Knopf, 1932.
VILLARD, OSWALD G. *Prophets, True and False.* Knopf, 1928.

WALKLEY, ARTHUR B. *Still More Prejudice.* Knopf, 1925.
WARD, JAMES. *Essays in Philosophies.* Macmillan, 1927.
WARNER, FRANCES. *Surprising the Family.* Houghton, 1926.
———. *The Unintentional Charm of Men.* Houghton, 1928.
———. *To People We Like.* Houghton, 1929.
WARNER, FRANCES, and WARNER, GERTRUDE. *Pleasures and Palaces.* Houghton, 1933.
WEEKLEY, ERNEST. *Adjectives—and Other Words.* Dutton, 1930.
WEIGALL, ARTHUR E. *Personalities of Antiquity.* Doubleday, 1928.
WEST, REBECCA. *Ending in Earnest: a Literary Log.* Doubleday, 1931.
———. *Strange Necessities.* Doubleday, 1928.
WEYGANDT, CORNELIUS. *Tuesday at Ten.* University of Pennsylvania Press, 1928.
WHIPPLE, THOMAS K. *Spokesmen: Modern Writers and American Life.* Appleton, 1928.
WHITE, WILLIAM A. *Masks in a Pageant.* Macmillan, 1928.
WHITEHEAD, ALFRED N. *Aims of Education and Other Essays.* Macmillan, 1929.
———. *Science and the Modern World.* Macmillan, 1925.
WHITMAN, WILLIAM. *Dog Corner Papers.* Houghton, 1927.
WICKHAM, HARVEY. *The Impuritans.* Dial, 1929.
———. *The Unrealists.* Dial, 1930.
WILLIAMS, CHARLES W. S. *English Poetic Mind.* Oxford, 1932.
———. *Poetry at Present.* Oxford, 1930.
WILLIAMS, ORLO. *Some Great English Novels: Studies in the Art of Fiction.* Macmillan, 1926.
WILLIAMS, STANLEY T. *Studies in Victorian Literature.* Dutton, 1923.

WILLIAMSON, HENRY. *Lone Swallows and Other Essays of the Country Green.* Dutton, 1926.

WILSON, EDMUND. *American Jitters: a Year of the Slump.* Scribner, 1932.

———. *Axel's Castle: a Study in Imaginative Literature of 1870–1930.* Scribner, 1931.

WINTERLICH, JOHN T. *Books and the Man.* Greenberg, 1929.

WOOLF, VIRGINIA. *Common Reader.* Harcourt, 1925.

———. *Second Common Reader.* Harcourt, 1932.

WOOLLCOTT, ALEXANDER. *Enchanted Aisles.* Putnam, 1924.

WRIGHT, RICHARDSON L. *Forgotten Ladies: Nine Portraits from the American Family Album.* Lippincott, 1928.

YEATS, WILLIAM B. *Essays.* Macmillan, 1924.

YOUNG, STARK. *Encaustics.* New Republic, 1926.

———. *Glamour: Essays on the Art of the Theatre.* Scribner, 1925.

ZIMMERN, ALFRED E. *America and Europe and Other Essays.* Oxford, 1929.

———. *Solon and Croesus and Other Greek Essays.* Oxford, 1928.

INDEX

DATE DUE
